# ROMANTICISM

# ROMANTICISM

## Critical Concepts in Literary and Cultural Studies

*Edited by*
*Michael O'Neill and Mark Sandy*

**Volume I**
**Definitions and Romantic Form**

Routledge
Taylor & Francis Group

LONDON AND NEW YORK

First published 2006
by Routledge
2 Park Square, Milton Park, Abingdon, OX14 4RN

Simultaneously published in the USA and Canada
by Routledge
270 Madison Avenue, New York, NY10016

*Routledge is an imprint of the Taylor & Francis Group*

Typeset in 10/12pt Times by Graphicraft Limited, Hong Kong
Printed and bound in Great Britain by MPG Books Ltd, Bodmin, Cornwall

*British Library Cataloguing in Publication Data*
A catalogue record for this book is available from the British Library

*Library of Congress Cataloging in Publication Data*
A catalog record for this book has been requested

ISBN 0-415-24722-5 (Set)
ISBN 0-415-21953-1 (Volume I)

**Publisher's Note**

References within each chapter are as they appear in the original complete work

# CONTENTS

## VOLUME I   DEFINITIONS AND ROMANTIC FORM

CONTENTS

CONTENTS

# VOLUME II   ROMANTICISM AND HISTORY

CONTENTS

CONTENTS

CONTENTS

## VOLUME IV   ROMANTICISM, BELIEF, AND PHILOSOPHY

# CONTENTS

# ACKNOWLEDGEMENTS

We would like to thank the Department of English Studies at the University of Durham, where we both work, for its support. We are indebted to our colleague Dr Sarah Wootton for her advice. Throughout the project, we have been greatly helped by our research assistant, Dr Mary Buckingham, who took chief responsibility for obtaining and copying the articles included in our volumes. Mary has been the embodiment of cheerfulness, efficiency, and intelligence, and we are very grateful to her. We would also like to thank the authors included in the work for many instances of helpfulness, advice, and good humour. The editorial staff at Routledge have been uniformly encouraging and supportive.

*Michael O'Neill and Mark Sandy*

The publishers would like to thank the following for permission to reprint their material:

Palgrave Macmillan for permission to reprint A. C. Bradley, 'Shelley's View of Poetry', in *Oxford Lectures on Poetry*, 1909, London: Macmillan, 1965, pp. 151–74. This was first published in 1909.

Modern Language Association of America for permission to reprint Arthur O. Lovejoy, 'On the Discrimination of Romanticisms', *PMLA*, 39 (1924): 229–53. Reprinted by permission of the Modern Language Association of America from PMLA.

Modern Language Association of America for permission to reprint Morse Peckham, 'Toward a Theory of Romanticism', *PMLA*, 66 (1951): 5–23. Reprinted by permission of the Modern Language Association of America from PMLA.

W. W. Norton and Company for permission to reprint M. H. Abrams, 'English Romanticism: The Spirit of the Age', from *The Correspondent Breeze: Essays on English Romanticism* by M. H. Abrams, foreward by Jack Stillinger, New York: Norton, 1984, pp. 44–75. Copyright © 1984 by M. H.

Abrams and Jack Stillinger. Used by permission of W. W. Norton & Company Ltd. This was first published in 1963.

W. W. Norton and Company for permission to reprint HAROLD BLOOM, 'The Internalization of Quest-Romance' from *Romanticism and Consciousness: Essays in Criticism* by Harold Bloom, editor, New York: Norton, 1970, pp. 3–24. Copyright © 1970 by W. W. Norton & Company, Inc. Used by permission of W. W. Norton & Company, Inc.

Columbia University Press for permission to reprint Northrop Frye, 'The Drunken Boat: The Revolutionary Element in Romanticism', in Northrop Frye (ed.) *Romanticism Reconsidered: Selected Papers from the English Institute*, New York: Columbia University Press, 1963, pp. 1–25. Copyright © 1963 Columbia University Press. Reprinted with permission of publisher.

Geoffrey H. Hartman for permission to reprint Geoffrey H. Hartman, 'Romanticism and Anti-Self-Consciousness', in *Beyond Formalism: Literary Essays 1958–1970*, New Haven: Yale University Press, 1970, pp. 298–310.

McGann, Jerome, 'Rethinking Romanticism', *ELH* 59 (1992): 735–54. © The Johns Hopkins University Press. Reprinted with permission of The Johns Hopkins University Press.

Charles Altieri for permission to reprint Charles Altieri, 'Wordsworth's Poetics of Eloquence: A Challenge to Contemporary Theory', in Kenneth R. Johnston *et al.* (eds.) *Romantic Revolutions: Criticism and Theory*, Bloomington: Indiana University Press, 1990, pp. 371–407.

Oxford University Press for permission to reprint M. H. Abrams, 'Structure and Style in the Greater Romantic Lyric' from Frederick W. Hilles and Harold Bloom (eds.) *From Sensibility to Romanticism; Essays Presented to Frederick A. Pottle*, New York: Oxford University Press, 1965, pp. 527–60. Copyright © 1965 by Oxford University Press, Inc. Used by permission of Oxford University Press, Inc.

Oxford University Press for permission to reprint Stuart Curran, 'Form and Freedom in European Romantic Poetry', from *Poetic Form and British Romanticism*, New York: Oxford University Press, 1986, pp. 204–20. Copyright © 1986 by Oxford University Press, Inc. Used by permission of Oxford University Press, Inc.

Durham University Journal for permission to reprint Michael O'Neill, '"The Mind Which Feeds This Verse": Self- and Other-Awareness in Shelley's Poetry', *Durham University Journal* 85 (1993): 273–92.

Oxford University Press for permission to reprint Jane Stabler, 'Transition in Byron and Wordsworth', *Essays in Criticism*, 50 (2000): 306–28.

'Keats and the Use of Poetry' reprinted by permission of the publisher from *The Music of What Happens*, by Helen Vendler, pp. 115–31, Cambridge,

Mass.: Harvard University Press, Copyright © 1988 by the President and Fellows of Harvard College.

Studies in Romanticism for permission to reprint Susan J. Wolfson, 'What Good is Formalist Criticism? Or: *Forms* and *Storms* and the Critical Register of Romantic Poetry', *Studies in Romanticism* 37 (1998): 77–94.

Keats-Shelley Association of America Inc. for permission to reprint Grant F. Scott, 'Beautiful Ruins: The Elgin Marbles Sonnet in its Historical and Generic Contexts', *Keats-Shelley Journal* 39 (1990): 123–50.

Edinburgh University Press for permission to reprint Mark Sandy, ' "To See as a God Sees": the Potential *Übermensch* in Keats's *Hyperion* Fragments', *Romanticism*, 4 (1998): 212–23. www.eup.ed.ac.uk

The *Wordsworth Circle* for permission to reprint Nicola Trott, 'Wordsworth in the Nursery: the Parodic School of Criticism', *Wordsworth Circle*, 32 (2001): 66–77. With permission of *The Wordsworth Circle*.

## Disclaimer

The publishers have made every effort to contact authors/copyright holders of works reprinted in *Romanticism: Critical Concepts in Literary and Cultural Studies.* This has not been possible in every case, however, and we would welcome correspondence from those individuals/companies who we have been unable to trace.

# Chronological table of reprinted chapters and articles

| Date | Author | Chapter/article | Reference | Vol. | Chap. |
|---|---|---|---|---|---|
| 1909 | A. C. Bradley | Shelley's view of poetry | *Oxford Lectures on Poetry*, London: Macmillan, pp. 151–74. This has been reprinted from the 1965 edition. | I | 1 |
| 1924 | Arthur O. Lovejoy | On the discrimination of Romanticisms | *PMLA* 39: 229–53 | I | 2 |
| 1951 | Morse Peckham | Toward a theory of Romanticism | *PMLA* 66: 5–23 | I | 3 |
| 1963 | Northrop Frye | The drunken boat: the revolutionary element in Romanticism | *Romanticism Reconsidered: Selected Papers from the English Institute*, ed. Northrop Frye, New York: Columbia University Press, pp. 1–25 | I | 6 |
| 1963 | M. H. Abrams | English Romanticism: the spirit of the age | *The Correspondent Breeze: Essays on English Romanticism*, New York: Norton, pp. 44–75. This has been reprinted from the 1984 edition. | I | 4 |
| 1965 | M. H. Abrams | Structure and style in the greater Romantic lyric | Frederick W. Hilles and Harold Bloom (eds.), *From Sensibility to Romanticism: Essays Presented to Frederick A. Pottle*, New York: Oxford University Press, pp. 527–60 | I | 10 |
| 1970 | Harold Bloom | The internalization of Quest-Romance | *Romanticism and Consciousness: Essays in Criticism*, ed. Harold Bloom, New York: Norton, pp. 3–24 | I | 5 |
| 1970 | Geoffrey H. Hartman | Romanticism and anti-self-consciousness | *Beyond Formalism: Literary Essays 1958–1970*, New Haven: Yale University Press, pp. 298–310 | I | 7 |
| 1970 | Paul de Man | Intentional structure of the romantic image | *Romanticism and Consciousness*, ed. Harold Bloom, New York: Norton, pp. 65–77 | III | 49 |
| 1978 | Lawrence Kramer | The return of the gods: Keats to Rilke | *Studies in Romanticism* 17: 483–500 | IV | 57 |
| 1979 | Mary Jacobus | Wordsworth and the language of the dream | *English Literary History* 46: 618–44 | IV | 62 |

**Chronological Table** continued

| Date | Author | Chapter/article | Reference | Vol. | Chap. |
|---|---|---|---|---|---|
| 1980 | Tilottama Rajan | Introduction | *Dark Interpreter: The Discourse of Romanticism*, Ithaca, NY: Cornell University Press, pp. 13–26 | IV | 60 |
| 1982 | Marilyn Butler | Godwin, Burke, and *Caleb Williams* | *Essays in Criticism* 32: 237–57 | II | 19 |
| 1982 | Jerome J. McGann | Romanticism and its ideologies | *Studies in Romanticism* 21: 573–99 | II | 23 |
| 1986 | Stuart Curran | Form and freedom in European Romantic poetry | *Poetic Form and British Romanticism*, New York: Oxford University Press, pp. 204–20 | I | 11 |
| 1986 | William Keach | Cockney couplets: Keats and the politics of style | *Studies in Romanticism* 25: 182–96 | II | 25 |
| 1986 | Marlon B. Ross | Naturalizing gender: women's place in Wordsworth's ideological landscape | *English Literary History* 53: 391–410 | III | 38 |
| 1986 | Paul H. Fry | History, existence, and 'To Autumn' | *Studies in Romanticism* 25: 211–19 | III | 50 |
| 1986 | Karen Swann | *Christabel*: the wandering mother and the enigma of form | *Studies in Romanticism* 23: 533–54 | IV | 61 |
| 1988 | Helen Vendler | Keats and the use of poetry | *The Music of What Happens: Poems, Poets, Critics*, Cambridge, Mass.: Harvard University Press, pp. 115–31 | I | 14 |
| 1988 | Nicholas Roe | 'A sympathy with power': imagining Robespierre | *Wordsworth and Coleridge: The Radical Years*, Oxford: Clarendon Press, pp. 199–233 | II | 24 |
| 1989 | Jonathan Bate | Criticism | *Shakespearean Constitutions: Politics, Theatre, Criticism 1730–1830*, Oxford: Clarendon Press, pp. 144–84 | III | 45 |
| 1990 | Charles Altieri | Wordsworth's poetics of eloquence: a challenge to contemporary theory | *Romantic Revolutions: Criticism and Theory*, ed. Kenneth R. Johnston et al., Bloomington: Indiana University Press, pp. 371–407 | I | 9 |
| 1990 | Grant F. Scott | Beautiful ruins: the Elgin Marbles sonnet in its historical and generic contexts | *Keats-Shelley Journal* 39: 123–50 | I | 16 |
| 1990 | Margaret Homans | Keats reading women, women reading Keats | *Studies in Romanticism* 29: 341–70 | III | 37 |

| Year | Author | Title | Publication | Vol | No |
|---|---|---|---|---|---|
| 1990 | Ross Woodman | Nietzsche, Blake, Keats and Shelley: the making of a metaphorical body | *Studies in Romanticism* 29: 115–49 | IV | 55 |
| 1991 | Morton D. Paley | Apocapolitics: allusion and structure in Shelley's *Mask of Anarchy* | *Huntington Library Quarterly* 54: 91–109 | IV | 52 |
| 1992 | Jerome McGann | Rethinking Romanticism | *English Literary History* 59: 735–54 | I | 8 |
| 1992 | Andrew J. Bennett | 'Hazardous magic': vision and inscription in Keats's "The Eve of St. Agnes" | *Keats-Shelley Journal* 41: 100–21 | III | 47 |
| 1993 | Michael O'Neill | 'The mind which feeds this verse': self- and other-awareness in Shelley's poetry | *Durham University Journal* 85: 273–92 | I | 12 |
| 1993 | Michael C. Gamer | Marketing a masculine romance: Scott, antiquarianism, and the gothic | *Studies in Romanticism* 32: 523–50 | III | 42 |
| 1993 | Timothy Webb | Romantic Hellenism | *The Cambridge Companion to British Romanticism* ed. Stuart Curran, Cambridge: Cambridge University Press, pp. 148–76 | IV | 58 |
| 1995 | Jeffrey N. Cox | Keats, Shelley, and the wealth of imagination | *Studies in Romanticism* 34: 365–400 | II | 21 |
| 1995 | Saree Makdisi | Colonial space and the colonization of time in Scott's *Waverley* | *Studies in Romanticism* 34: 155–87 | II | 27 |
| 1995 | Jonathan Wordsworth | Ann Yearsley to Caroline Norton: women poets of the Romantic period | *The Wordsworth Circle* 26: 114–24 | III | 40 |
| 1995 | John Kerrigan | Revolution, revenge, and romantic tragedy | *Romanticism* 1: 121–40 | III | 44 |
| 1995 | Lucy Newlyn | Coleridge and the anxiety of reception | *Romanticism* 1: 206–38 | III | 48 |
| 1996 | Hugh Roberts | Chaos and evolution: a quantum leap in Shelley's process | *Keats-Shelley Journal* 45: 156–94 | II | 33 |
| 1996 | Jonathan Bate | Living with the weather | *Studies in Romanticism* 35: 431–47 | II | 34 |
| 1996 | Jerome McGann | Mary Robinson and the myth of Sappho | *The Poetics of Sensibility: A Revolution in Literary Style*, Oxford: Clarendon Press, pp. 94–116 | III | 35 |
| 1997 | Judith Pascoe | 'That fluttering, tinselled crew': women poets and Della Cruscanism | *Romantic Theatricality: Gender, Poetry, and Spectatorship*, Ithaca, NY: Cornell University Press, pp. 68–94 | III | 36 |

**Chronological Table continued**

| Date | Author | Chapter/article | Reference | Vol. | Chap. |
|---|---|---|---|---|---|
| 1997 | Pamela Clemit | From *The Fields of Fancy* to *Matilda*: Mary Shelley's changing conception of her novella | *Romanticism* 3: 152–69 | III | 43 |
| 1997 | Robert M. Ryan | 'A sect of dissenters' | *The Romantic Reformation: Religious Politics in English Literature 1789–1824*, Cambridge: Cambridge University Press, pp. 13–42 | IV | 53 |
| 1997 | Paul Hamilton | The new Romanticism: philosophical stand-ins in English romantic discourse | *Textual Practice* 11: 110–31 | IV | 54 |
| 1998 | Susan J. Wolfson | What good is formalist criticism? Or: *Forms* and *Storms* and the critical register of Romantic poetry | *Studies in Romanticism* 37: 77–94 | I | 15 |
| 1998 | Mark Sandy | 'To see as a god sees': the potential *Ubermensch* in Keats's *Hyperion* Fragments | *Romanticism* 4: 212–23 | I | 17 |
| 1998 | Nigel Leask | *Kubla Khan* and orientalism: the road to Xanadu revisited | *Romanticism* 4: 1–21 | II | 26 |
| 1998 | Fiona Robertson | British Romantic Columbiads | *Symbiosis* 2: 1–23 | II | 28 |
| 1998 | Alan Bewell | 'Cholera cured before hand': Coleridge, abjection and the 'dirty business of laudanum' | *Romanticism* 4: 155–73 | II | 32 |
| 1998 | Charles Rosen | The intense inane: religious revival in English, French, and German Romanticism: M. H. Abrams, William Empson | *Romantic Poets, Critics, and Other Madmen*, Cambridge, Mass.: Harvard University Press, pp. 31–50 | IV | 51 |

# PREFACE

Romanticism is a literary movement that defies precise definition. And yet it is indisputable that a major literary and cultural revolution took place in Britain and Europe between 1780 and 1830. Writers such as Wordsworth, Shelley and Keats may not have thought of themselves as Romantics; they may even have been conscious of ideological differences as much as imaginative affinities. But Shelley was not alone in recognising, as he puts it in *A Defence of Poetry*, that 'our own will be a memorable age in intellectual achievement'. It has been clear to subsequent generations that Shelley was right to speak of the 'electric life which burns within [the] words' of his contemporaries. Indeed, to adapt another of Shelley's phrases (from the Preface to *Hellas*), it might well be asserted that 'We are all Romantics',[1] and there is currently no more absorbing subject for literary criticism than the nature of Romanticism's legacy.

The nature of that legacy is implicitly or explicitly at stake in all the articles and chapters which we have included in this four-volume collection. Our purpose has been to make available a range of twentieth- and twenty-first century criticism on many aspects of Romanticism and on many different writers. We have organised the contents of the volume by theme, which allows us to underscore what we see as productive differences of critical perspective. At the same time, we are aware of the mobile overlap between our categories, and we sometimes point up such connections in our volume introductions. These introductions seek to offer exposition rather than evaluation, but the very fact of an essay's inclusion bears witness to our view that the piece warrants serious consideration. Within our thematic clusters, we group the essays in ways that highlight both the unique and the shared. We frequently depart from straightforward chronological arrangement where our sense of developing critical narratives suggests otherwise.

The reader of these volumes will find continuity, variety and debate. Views expressed in our chosen essays include scepticism about the possibility of defining the Romantic; warnings against the power of so-called 'Romantic Ideology'; celebration and critique; essays on canonical authors and texts; demonstrations of the importance of non-canonical or marginal writers; feminist emphases; and approaches that underscore formal, historical, philosophical, and religious perspectives. All the essays contribute to a critical dialogue that is restless, enquiring, delighted, contentious, and exploratory.

All serve as testimony of Romanticism's continuing, complicated, and inspiring presence.

This has been a joint editorial venture in every way. Michael O'Neill took principal responsibility for writing the introductions to Volumes I and II; Mark Sandy took principal responsibility for writing the introductions to Volumes III and IV (though Michael O'Neill took principal responsibility for the section on Jonathan Bate's chapter in the introduction to Volume III and for the sections on Morton D. Paley's article and Robert M. Ryan's chapter in the introduction to Chapter 4).

Michael O'Neill and Mark Sandy
Durham, January 2005

## Note

1 *Percy Bysshe Shelley: The Major Works*, ed. Zachary Leader and Michael O'Neill (Oxford: Oxford University Press, 2003), pp. 700, 701, 549 (where Shelley writes, 'We are all Greeks').

# INTRODUCTION

## Volume I Definitions and Romantic Form

The present set of four volumes includes twentieth- and twenty-first century critical texts that reflect on the multi-faceted nature of Romanticism. The volumes are organised round central thematic concerns. In the first volume, the emphasis is three-fold: on early twentieth-century constructions or critiques of the Romantic; on subsequent explorations offered by a group of eminent American critics; and on criticism that emphasises the formal and generic aspects of Romantic writing. As with the other three volumes, this first volume is preceded by an introduction whose main purpose is to comment on principal features of the arguments put forward in our selected texts.

## Part 1

### *Some twentieth-century constructions and definitions*

We have chosen to begin our selection with an essay on Shelley by **A. C. Bradley**, a critic who is better known for his *Shakespearean Tragedy* (1904), but a figure who can be seen as inaugurating a distinctively twentieth-century view of Romanticism. In his essay on Wordsworth, for example, he ushers in a new way of looking at a poet in danger of being reified as the Sage of Rydal. Insisting on the poet's 'strangeness and his paradoxes', Bradley disputes Matthew Arnold's opinion that Wordsworth averted his eyes from 'the cloud of human destiny'. He defines the 'visionary feeling' of passages from *The Prelude*, such as the Waiting for Horses episode in Book XI, as bound up with 'the intimation of something illimitable, over-arching or breaking into the customary "reality"'.[1] Later critics such as Geoffrey Hartman and Jonathan Wordsworth will build on Bradley's insights.[2]

In the essay included here, Bradley turns his attention to Shelley's view of poetry, especially as expressed in his *A Defence of Poetry*. Along with Wordsworth's Preface to *Lyrical Ballads*, Coleridge's *Biographia Literaria*, Byron's and Keats's letters, and Hazlitt's *The Spirit of the Age*, Shelley's essay, written in response to an attack on poetry by his friend, Thomas Love Peacock, in *The Four Ages of Poetry*, is among the contemporary prose documents central to an understanding of English Romanticism. Bradley points out the hold over Shelley's thought of Platonic notions, and argues that Shelley sees poetry as 'the revelation of those eternal ideas which lie behind the many-coloured, ever-shifting veil that we call reality or life' (22). In describing Shelley's poetic vision in these terms, Bradley says explicitly that he is using 'the language so dear' (22) to the poet, and his critical mode is at once empathetic and judicious. Bradley, that is, recreates the flavour and the tone of Shelley's arguments, and subjects them to intelligent questioning.

He is prepared to use his own metaphors to convey the characteristic nature of Shelley's poetic vision: sometimes in Shelley's compositions, Bradley writes, 'The glowing metal rushes into the mould so vehemently that it overleaps the bounds and fails to find its way into all the little crevices' (27), a description that alludes suggestively to Satan entering Eden and to processes associated with the Industrial Revolution. It is Bradley's attentiveness to detail and patient readiness to analyse difficulties that make him recognisable as an ancestor of later developments in Romantic criticism. So, for example, he looks closely at the assertion by Shelley 'that the poet ought neither to affect a moral aim nor to express his own conceptions of right and wrong' (31). Bradley recognises the importance of this idea and links it to a Romantic emphasis on the workings of imagination. Much subsequent criticism will debate the claims for imagination made by the Romantics, but it is Bradley's strength that he perceived clearly what was at stake for Shelley in making his assertions about the priority of the imaginative over the morally doctrinal, and he concludes by applying the idea to Shelley's own work.

In his essay 'The Long Poem in Wordsworth's Age', Bradley discusses differences between English and German Romanticism, arguing that the superiority of imaginative writer to rational thinkers in England is not echoed in Germany where 'the philosophers . . . were as a body not at all inferior to the poets'.[3] Awareness of Romanticism as a movement that crosses national borders and is extremely hard to define informs much twentieth-century criticism. A major starting-point in this debate is **Arthur O. Lovejoy**'s 'On the Discrimination of Romanticisms', first published in 1924. Lovejoy wittily points out 'the rich ambiguity' of the term, Romanticism, illustrating 'the present uncertainty concerning the nature and *locus* of Romanticism' (38) by the fact that Romanticism has been 'variously conceived to be a passion . . . for talking exclusively about oneself' and for 'losing oneself in an ecstatic contemplation of nature'. He asserts that 'The word "romantic" has come to mean so many things that, by itself, it means nothing' (38). The remedy proposed by Lovejoy for 'this confusion of terminology' (39) is simple and yet far-reaching in its implications: it is that 'we should learn to use the word "Romanticism" in the plural' (40), and recognise that what we are dealing with in the case of movements in Germany, France, and England are a series of unstable and complicated 'thought-complexes, a number of which', Lovejoy adds in case he should be thought to be recommending divisions along national lines, 'may appear in one country' (40).

Lovejoy's arguments have been contested by subsequent critics, notably René Wellek who argued that there was an essence one could conceive of as 'Romantic', offering, as Morse Peckham puts it in his summary of Wellek's argument, 'three criteria of romanticism: imagination for the view of poetry, an organic concept of nature for the view of the world, and symbol and myth for poetic style' (58). But Lovejoy's scepticism is salutary, and brings into play awareness of difference and complexity. He takes issue with the idea that Joseph Warton's poem *The Enthusiast* is 'identical in essence' with Friedrich Schlegel's concept of '*romantische Poesie*' (42). Warton's poem is less the precursor of Schlegelian Romanticism than a celebration of what had been a commonplace in Rabelais, Montaigne, and Pope: 'the superiority of "nature" to "art"' (42). Warton's 'naturalism', in fact, differs wholly from the emphasis in the German Romantic movement on the unavoidability of 'reflection and self-conscious effort' (46); the difference is between 'the assertion of the superiority of "nature" over conscious "art" and that of the superiority of conscious art over mere "nature"' (47). Lovejoy's essay retains its capacity to provoke thought. For example, he observes how polemical attacks on Romanticism for its supposed belief in 'the "natural goodness" of man' (49) ignore the fact that, certainly in Germany, the Romantic centred on 'the inner moral struggle as the distinctive fact in human experience' (50). The fact that Lovejoy selects French and German writers on whom to concentrate does not lessen his essay's relevance to British Romantic-period writing.

**Morse Peckham**, in his article 'Toward a Theory of Romanticism' (1951), seeks to offer, in the face of Lovejoy's scepticism in his 1924 essay, 'a theory of the historical romanticism of ideas and art' (57). He discerns in Lovejoy's classic study *The Great Chain of Being* (1936) 'the foundations for a theory of romanticism' (59) that is at odds with Lovejoy's earlier essay, and he seeks not only to 'reconcile Wellek and Lovejoy' but also 'Lovejoy with himself' (59). Peckham draws attention to a 1941 article by Lovejoy, 'The Meaning of Romanticism for the Historian of Ideas' in which Lovejoy emphasised three main Romantic ideas: 'organicism, dynamism, and diversitarianism' (59). Whereas Lovejoy sees these ideas as appearing separately, Peckham argues that 'they are all related to and derived from a basic or root-metaphor, the organic metaphor of the structure of the universe' (62). Moreover, he interprets Wellek's own criteria for romanticism – organicism, imagination, and symbolism – as also 'derived from' what Peckham calls 'dynamic organicism' (62). This root-metaphor, posited with great clarity and argumentative force by Peckham as the basis for a theory of romanticism, can also embrace a further idea which he regards as crucial to such a theory: namely, the 'idea of the unconscious mind' (63).

Peckham devotes much of his essay to expounding the relation of 'negative romanticism to 'positive romanticism', not to proliferate kinds of romanticism but to show how apparent divergences can be brought under the shelter of an all-embracing theory. For Peckham, the characteristic development of romantic text is tripartite, or as he puts it: 'A man moves from a trust in the universe to a period of doubt and despair of any meaning in the universe, and then to a re-affirmation of faith in cosmic meaning and goodness' (65). Peckham illustrates this triple movement through readings of Wordsworth's *Prelude*, Carlyle's *Sartor Resartus*, and Coleridge's 'The Rime of the Ancient Mariner'. Wordsworth, for example, experienced doubt after the failure of his hopes in the French Revolution, but he 'reorganized all his ideas, with Coleridge's and Dorothy's intellectual and emotional help, and reaffirmed in new terms his faith in the goodness and significance of the universe' (66). In an illuminating aside, the critic explains Wordsworth's loss of creative power as owing to his adoption of 'a kind of revised Toryism, . . . a concept of an organic society without dynamic power' (67). Negative romanticism corresponds to the midway stage of the thesis-antithesis-synthesis model proposed by Peckham. It is the stage reached by Wordsworth in the aftermath of his rejection of Godwin, by Carlyle in his formulation of the Everlasting No, and by the Mariner when he is 'alone on the wide, wide sea' (69). The 'typical symbols' of negative romanticism are figures such as Byron's Childe Harold or his Manfred or his Cain. When they 'begin to get a little more insight into their position', they 'become Don Juans' (69). Within his dance of terms, Peckham squares various circles neatly. Above all, he makes plausible the idea of romanticism as a historical phenomenon driven by a belief in organic change, as a result of which 'We have a universe of emergents' and 'there are no pre-existent patterns' (61).

Our next piece is by **M. H. Abrams**, who in two major studies, *The Mirror and the Lamp* (1953) and *Natural Supernaturalism* (1971), as well as several crucial essays, develops the idea of romanticism as a coherent if complex movement. We have represented Abrams by two of his essays in this first volume (the second essay is printed in the 'Formalism and Genre' section below; see pp. 197–224). Our first essay by Abrams is 'English Romanticism: The Spirit of the Age' (1963, taken from a 1984 collection). Abrams echoes the title of Hazlitt's 1825 collection of searching pen-portraits, and he eloquently endorses Hazlitt's sense that 'the Romantic period was eminently an age obsessed with the fact of violent and inclusive change' (75). He seeks to avoid 'easy and empty generalizations about the *Zeitgeist*' (76), but he shows in considerable detail how the 'revolutionary upheaval' (75) of the period 'affected the scope, subject-matter, themes, values, and even language of a number of Romantic poems' (76). The essay is divided into five sections. In the first section, Abrams evokes 'the spirit of the 1790s' (76), captured in Southey's middle-aged recollection that 'Few persons but those who have lived in it can conceive or comprehend what the memory of the French

Revolution was, nor what a visionary world seemed to open upon those who were just entering it. Old things seemed passing away, and nothing was dreamt of but the regeneration of the human race' (quoted 76). Abrams stresses the presence in the poetry of or about the 1790s of 'apocalyptic expectations, or at least apocalyptic imaginings' (79).[4] In section 2, he dwells on the difference between poets of 'The Age of Sensibility', such as Collins, Gray, and the Wartons, whose enthusiasm for creativity constituted a limited 'literature of revolt' (80), and the altogether more extreme and confident assertion of the poet's role and power in Blake.

The next section considers 'attributes' (82) shared by Blake, Wordsworth, Southey, Coleridge, and Shelley (Abrams carefully relegates Byron and Keats to the margins of his essay). He proposes three shared attributes: that they 'were all centrally political and social poets' (82), 'obsessed', however much the popular caricature of the Romantic poet might suggest otherwise, 'with the realities of their era' (82); that they are not didactic writers but poets who frequently speak (or sing) 'in the persona of the inspired prophet-priest' (83); and that they seek to 'incorporate . . . the stupendous events of the age in the suitably great poetic forms' (83). These generalisations are supported by a wealth of judiciously selected examples. In the fourth section, Abrams offers an arresting complication to his argument. For all the revolutionary fervour of the poets he has been discussing, he contends that, in fact, 'The great Romantic poems were written not in the mood of revolutionary exaltation but in the later mood of revolutionary disappointment or despair' (87). However, these poems continue to use ideas and images from the initial revolutionary phase of Romanticism, even as they switch from hopes of political change to an affirmation of the internalised powers of the imagination. When in *The Prelude*, Book VI, Wordsworth crosses the Alps unaware, he discovers the mind's power, a power to which images associated with 'overt political action' are subordinated (89). When Shelley moves from *Queen Mab* to *Prometheus Unbound*, he moves from a poetry of 'bald literalism' to 'an imaginative form increasingly biblical, symbolic, and mythic' (91). The positive turn given to these changes in Abrams's argument, fully developed in *Natural Supernaturalism*, would be challenged by critics who, in the wake of Jerome McGann's *The Romantic Ideology* (1983), stated that the claims made for the imagination were a form of escapism. In the fifth section Abrams turns his attention to Wordsworth's contributions to *Lyrical Ballads*, and to the presence in them of a poetics, ultimately deriving, so Abrams contends, from Christianity, of 'the oxymoron of the humble-grand, the lofty-mean, the trivial-sublime' (93). Both of Wordsworth's voices – the 'plain style' or the 'elevated voice' (97) – are, then, expressive of what, in the first instance, was a sympathy with revolutionary change, though that sympathy transmutes itself into imaginative and spiritual terms.

Abrams presides over a younger generation of critics who take his general ideas about the Romantic in new directions. **Harold Bloom** is among the most notable of such critics, and in 'The Internalization of Quest-Romance' (1970) he alludes to Abrams's discussion of 'the apocalypse of imagination' in 'English Romanticism: The Spirit of the Age' (see Bloom's essay, 104). Bloom tries to get closer than Abrams does to the workings of the apocalyptic imagination, and he argues that in its internalised remodelling of romance this imagination is more than able to hold its own against rationalisms of many kinds, including and especially Freudian analyses. By 'internalization' Bloom means that 'paradises' are found 'within a renovated man'; the cost of such internalisation he sees as showing itself 'in the arena of self-consciousness' (104). The Romantic poet, on Bloom's reading, struggles imaginatively with the 'shadow of imagination' or 'solipsism'. Such a struggle is at the heart of the authenticity and tough intelligence of the canonical Romantic poets, who compare favourably, in Bloom's view, with those Modernists who think – heads full of 'Eliotic cant' – that they are engaged in a 'supposed revolt against Romanticism' (105).

Bloom agrees with Bradley that Wordsworth's distinction resides in the degree to which his poetry 'shows the power of the mind over outward sense' (108). But 'the power of the mind' is no easy achievement for the Romantics, in Bloom's analysis, since the imagination has always to overcome 'a recalcitrance in the self' (110). This inner struggle is interpreted by Freud as the quarrel between enchantment and the reality principle, but by the Romantics, according to Bloom, as a 'dialectical matter', the possibility of enchantment being resisted both by 'an anxiety principle' and by a 'creative' impulse (111). In Blakean terms, the imagination resists the enchantments of Beulah in favour of the more strenuously creative contentions that constitute Eden. Bloom sees the Romantics as more daring, more tough-minded, and more intransigent in their refusal to accept reductive accounts of human existence than is often allowed. Freud is their intermittent ally and formidable antagonist. If Bloom affirms a faith in the 'Romantic counter-critique of Freud's critique of Romantic love' (112), his essay is full of a sense of Romantic poetry as staging poetic dramas centred on inner struggle. He sees the 'major phase of the Romantic quest', that associated with Blake and Wordsworth, as involving both 'the inward overcoming of the Selfhood's temptation' and 'the outward turning of the triumphant Imagination' (115). The second generation of Romantic poets repeats these movements, but in Keats and Shelley, on Bloom's account, 'the argument of the dream with reality becomes an equivocal one' (118). Written with Bloom's characteristic intensity, the essay manages to demonstrate the visionary intelligence of Romanticism and to see the poetic movement which is its expression as both coherent and self-divided.

Bloom acknowledges the influence of **Northrop Frye**'s criticism at one point in his essay, when he refers to Frye's work on the connection between quest-romance and dream. Frye's criticism offers X-ray-like unearthings of archetypes and mythic patterns. In the essay we have included, 'The

Drunken Boat: The Revolutionary Element in Romanticism' (1963), Frye
claims that what is found in Romanticism 'is the effect of a profound change,
not primarily in belief, but in the spatial projection of reality' (124). It is not
clear that Frye's distinction between 'belief' and 'spatial projection' holds
water, but he is compelling on the fact that the imagery of Romantic poetry
has a new cast. Newtonian astronomy, for Blake, had made of the heavens
'only a set of interlocking geometrical diagrams' (125), and he and other
Romantics find a false God in the skies, a Nobodaddy, Urizen, or Jupiter;
the true God, a version of human beings at their best, is located by the
Romantics in what Frye calls '"within" metaphors' (126). Moreover, Frye
finds that the Romantics lay stress 'on the constructive power of the mind,
where reality is brought into being by experience'; they 'defy external reality' by means of 'a uniformity of tone and mood' (128) that bears witness to
the mind's creative power.

Frye's essay is culturally wide-ranging and full of suggestive examples
taken from the Romantics. He argues, for instance, that 'the Romantic poet
is a part of a total process, engaged with and united to a creative power
greater than his own because it includes his own' (128). This 'greater power'
may be imaged as 'a rushing wind' (128–9), as in Shelley's 'Ode to the West
Wind', and its presence explains 'why so much of the best Romantic poetry
is mythopoeic', a poetry in which the 'human' and 'nonhuman worlds' (130)
are identified. Frye remarks shrewdly on the link between the conviction of
a 'greater power' and the formal implications for Romantic poetry of the
'inherently endless romance form' (130). This ignores the capacity of Romantic poets to write shorter and well-constructed poems, but it usefully
explains the fact and nature of the many longer poems that they wrote. The
essay is also valuable for its explanations of Romantic ambivalence towards
politics and nature. In the case of the latter, nature is good or bad depending on whether it is seen as 'revealing' or 'concealing reality' (133). The
'drunken boat' of the title alludes to Rimbaud's *le bateau ivre*, and serves as
Frye's central image for Romanticism's legacy: 'a fragile container of sensitive and imaginative values threatened by a chaotic and unconscious power
below it' (134). Frye, like Bloom, has little time for 'anti-Romanticism' as
anything other than 'a post-Romantic movement' (135), and Romanticism's
'fragile container' ought, he concludes in a line from Herman Melville, to
prompt 'reverence for the Archetype' (quoted 135).

A major essay shaping mid-to-late twentieth-century attitudes to Romanticism is **Geoffrey H. Hartman**'s 'Romanticism and Anti-Self-Consciousnesss'
(first published 1962). Hartman contends that English Romanticism is
'involved with a problematical self-consciousness', which, Lovejoy's assertions to the contrary, is 'similar to that of the Germans' (137). For the
Romantics, in Hartman's view, consciousness has to lead itself beyond its own
'lesser forms' (138), which include the analytical 'passion that "murders to
dissect"', in Wordsworth's phrase (137), until it achieves a self-transcending

state. This state is named by Blake as 'organized innocence', by Wordsworth in *The Prelude* as 'knowledge not purchased by the loss of power', and by Yeats, a self-described latter-day Romantic, as 'Unity of Being (quoted 137, 139). The Romantics, for Hartman, do not seek simply to set consciousness aside in favour of naive primitivism; such a view is a caricature. Nor do they exalt consciousness. Rather, as he puts it, 'Consciousness is only a middle term, the strait through which everything must pass; and the artist plots to have everything pass through whole, without sacrifice to abstraction' (139).

The Romantics overcome the 'lesser forms' of consciousness by practising a self-consciousness that is vigilant about the dangers of solipsism. The reason why the problem of self-consciousness is so acute for the Romantics, according to Hartman, is historical: it is because they lived in 'a time when art frees itself from its subordination to religion or religiously inspired myth and continues or even replaces them'. The privilege and burden of converting 'self-consciousness into the larger energy of imagination' (140) falls to the poets in the Romantic age. Yet their 'autonomous and individual' art and subjectivity must somehow articulate the capacity to 'transcend or ritually limit' mere individualism. Thus, in *The Prelude*, a poem begun 'in the vortex of self-consciousness', Wordsworth 'knows self-consciousness to be at once necessary and opposed to poetry' (141).

Generally, Hartman's essay restores a strong sense of Romanticism's intellectual and artistic bravery and subtlety. Though he offers a new, dialectical 'triad of Nature, Self-Consciousness, and Imagination', he is able elegantly to suggest the limitations of any attempt to impose schemes on a cultural project, Romanticism, which is inseparable from hazard and danger. The achievements of Romanticism are 'always shadowed by cyclicity', on his reading, and involve endless, romance-like 'trials by horror and by enchantment' (142). Hartman dismisses the idea that Romantic poetry offers an uncomplicated celebration of nature. Keats, for example, 'goes far in respecting illusions without being deluded' (142). He and the other Romantics bequeath a question, at once stimulating and productive of anxiety, to later artists, namely: 'can the modern poet . . . achieve the immediacy of all great verse . . . ?' (143).

Yale Romanticism, especially as expressed through the work of Bloom and Hartman, held sway in academe throughout the 1970s. But evidence of an historicist reaction against its concern with 'internalisation' and 'consciousness' comes in the form of two books, Marilyn Butler's *Romantics, Rebels, and Reactionaries* (1981) and Jerome J. McGann's *The Romantic Ideology* (1983). Butler called for a more extensive awareness of the range of Romantic-period writing; McGann warned against uncritical acceptance of Romanticism's own self-representations. Whereas Lovejoy had thought Romanticism existed multifariously and only in the plural, McGann distinguished between romantic-period writing and Romanticism, seeing the latter as composing a species of false consciousness, an ideology against which it behoved the modern critic to be on his or her guard. Too many modern critics, on McGann's account, were merely reduplicating the tenets of that ideology in their commentaries. Both Butler's and McGann's historicist views are represented in Volume II. We have chosen, however, to take matters a stage further in Volume I (in this respect the book's volumes interleave, organised less on chronological than on a thematic basis), and to include at this point a later essay by **McGann**, entitled 'Rethinking Romanticism' (1992).

In this essay, McGann explains his book, *The Romantic Ideology*, as a reaction against a critical tradition from 1945 to 1980 whose view of Romanticism 'derived from a Kantian/Coleridgean line of thought' (148). As a critic and editor of Byron, McGann was conscious that to 'a theory of romanticism like Wellek's, Byron appears either a problem or an irrelevance'. He presents *The Romantic Ideology* as 'a dialectical critique of Wellek's ideological synthesis' (149), one that exposes the falsely totalising nature of the earlier critic's picture of Romanticism. After all, McGann argues, 'Blake does not take "nature as his view of the world" any more than Byron does, though the antinaturisms of Blake and Byron are also non-congruent with each other'. Yet McGann also argues that he does not wish to promote 'a neo-Lovejoyan skepticism' (150), preferring, instead, post-*Romantic Ideology*, 'a dialectical philology that is not bound by the conceptual forms it studies and generates' (151). He wants us to bear in mind that all versions of literary history are constructed, and he describes how he uses his own anthology, *The New Oxford Book of Verse of the Romantic Period* (title later changed to *The New Oxford Book of Romantic Period Verse*), to illustrate his belief in, as he puts it, 'a necessary fall from the grace of one great Mind [Shelley's phrase] into the local world of the poem, where contradiction . . . holds paramount sway' (156). The essay finishes with a brief dialogue between two speakers, 'Anne Mack', who is critical of McGann's views, and 'Jay Rome', who serves as a surrogate for McGann. Anne Mack points out that McGann's choice of two Tennyson poems, 'The Lady of Shalott' and 'The Palace of Art', to conclude his anthology is itself a construction of a 'historical narrative about romanticism' (161). McGann's (or Jay Rome's) answer is that such a charge is true, but that it discounts the fact that the 'two final poems have an authority of their own. They don't have to mean what I take them to mean' (162). The essay's final position, then, is highly provisional, determined, above all, to maintain a dialogical relationship between critic and text.

Such a relationship is promoted by **Charles Altieri** in our next essay, 'Wordsworth's Poetics of Eloquence: A Challenge to Contemporary Theory' (1990). Altieri argues that Wordsworth's poetry challenges contemporary theory through his use of a 'personal lyric mode' made up of 'rhetorical ideals of high eloquence' (166) and 'a psychology . . . responsive to the demands of his own intellectual culture' (166). The main body of the essay consists of seven sections. In the first section, Altieri explores the way traditional theories of eloquence ensure that we conceive of 'the passions themselves as exemplary' (169). In the second section, he turns to Wordsworth's theories of feeling and poetry, and observes that Wordsworth does not share our concern with 'single coherent meanings for entire works of art' (172). Instead, what matters to him is less meaning than what Altieri calls 'questions of projectible imaginative power' (172). Altieri explores the difference between contemporary, sceptical theories of metaphor and Wordsworth's insistence on the all-important question of eloquence; for him, metaphors serve to bring alive the passion of the speaker. In section 3, the essay considers the question of pleasure, and how for Wordsworth pleasure is central to an intricate psychological explanation of the way imaginative powers are cultivated.

Section 4 considers Wordsworth's poem 'Nutting' and focuses on the poem's exploration of destructive passions. It is, Altieri claims, the very capacity of the poem's eloquence to convey not only destructiveness but also an insight into its motivation that 'forces memory and poetry to the constructive work of the concluding lines' (183). The poem offers an equivalent to a Freudian scene of instruction, so long as we do not think that Freudian analysis has interpretative power over a poem that is already self-aware and 'deliberate' (183). In section 5, Altieri deals with Wordsworth's originality, how, in 'Nutting', he is able to 'exemplify certain powers that help an audience adapt itself to similar numinous forces' (185). Troubled though he is by Wordsworth's subject in the poem, the movement from 'the rape of feminine nature' to the 'making visible of imaginative resources' (185), Altieri continues to ask, in sections 6 and 7, how Wordsworth's eloquence is 'still empowering for us' (185), and he seeks to demonstrate Wordsworth's continuing power by turning to a reading of the poem by Jonathan Arac of which Altieri does not approve. Altieri sees Arac's 'post-structuralist' reading as conjuring up a self-created sense of 'scandal' (187) that slights Wordsworth's own emphasis on the recuperative powers of memory and eloquence, and permits (the image is borrowed from 'Nutting') 'no intruding sky' to over-arch our own 'reduced terms' (189). The essay is fascinating for its historically inflected attempt to allow Romantic poetry its own voice.

## Part 2

### *Formalism and genre*

In this second part of the first volume we include essays that demonstrate a particular interest in formal and generic issues. Our first piece is our second essay by **M. H. Abrams**, 'Structure and Style in the Greater Romantic Lyric' (1965). Here Abrams discusses a Romantic lyric paradigm, deployed by all the major Romantics with the exception of Byron (whose refusal to fit into conceptual schemes will lie at the core of Jerome McGann's reaction against Abrams's critical constructions). Abrams regards what he calls 'the greater Romantic lyric' as 'a remarkable phenomenon in literary history', and characterises the form as displaying a 'repeated out-in-out process, in which mind confronts nature and their interplay constitutes the poem' (198). Typically, the greater Romantic lyric begins with a description of a landscape, moves on to develop a 'varied but integral process of memory, thought, anticipation, and feeling which remains closely intervolved with the outer scene' (197), and then 'rounds upon itself to end where it began, at the outer scene, but with an altered mood and deepened understanding which is the result of the intervening meditation' (197).

The very word 'intervolved' conveys Abrams's sense of the skill with which composers of the greater Romantic lyric manage to blend inner with outer. Examples include Coleridge's 'Frost at Midnight', to which T. S. Eliot's 'In my beginning is my end' and his 'In my end is my beginning' are applicable as formal and emotional principles. Much of Abrams's essay explores the 'poetic antecedent' (202) of the greater Romantic lyric; he finds it in John Denham's 'Cooper's Hill', which in turn reflects the belief of metaphysical poets in 'a symbolic and analogical universe' (204), in 'eighteenth-century local poems' (205), and, in Coleridge's case, in the *Sonnets* (1789) of William Lisle Bowles, in which, as Abrams puts it, 'The local poem has been lyricized' (208). The last two sections of the essay bring out the metaphysical implications of the greater Romantic lyric. The new form reflects the Romantic wish to heal the fissure between inner and outer, to 're-domiciliate man in a world which had become alien to him' (212). The essay's importance lies in the fact that it shows how a centrally Romantic idea found an appropriate lyric form.

**Stuart Curran**'s *Poetic Form and British Romanticism* (1986) demonstrates how consciously and intelligently Romantic poets use poetic form. In the chapter we have included (the last in his book), Curran opens by contending that, in their handling of poetic genres as of much else, the Romantic poets 'never remained still, even when formulating structures encompassing ceaseless mental movement'. Genres may, through the accumulated history of their deployment, exert 'ideological pressure' (226), but major poets can win from them new possibilities. A particular feature of the way the Romantics use genres is that the 'constituents' of a genre 'become self-conscious in their application, which is to say self-reflexive in their very conception' (228). This self-reflexiveness, especially in the work of the second-generation Romantics, allies itself with a scepticism that is paradoxically liberating. Experimentation with genres ties in with the 'ubiquity of deconstructive strategies in British Romantic poetry' (229–30) to result in a politically sophisticated art of exploration.

In the second part of the chapter, Curran widens his critical gaze to make comparisons and, especially, contrasts between British and European

Romanticisms. He begins by noting that all the younger British Romantics, in common with European artists such as Foscolo, Leopardi, Hölderlin, Goethe, Schiller, and Chenier, were interested in classicism. Their Romanticism cannot be defined as a revolt against the classic, even as the forms of their Romanticism differ, depending on particular historical and political circumstances. Curran notes affinities between British experimentation, and that of Hölderlin, Foscolo, Schiller, Hugo, and Musset. But he underscores differences, too, observing that in 'In each case Romanticism is dependent not simply on classicism but on versions of classicism that themselves betray the biases of the nation's scholarship and probably its program of education' (234). If this is true of the ode, it is true, too, of the hymn. Curran offers a series of insights into European Romanticism and its generic innovations, pointing out, for example, how Leopardi's 'terrifying calm' builds on and plays against the 'pastoral conventions he knew by heart' (235). He concludes the chapter by demonstrating the pervasive significance of formal means for British and European Romantics, even when they followed wholly opposite formal strategies, 'deconstructive', on the one hand (his example is Keats's *The Fall of Hyperion*), or, on the other hand, a form 'modelled on the total organization of scientific system' (238) (his example is Goethe's *Faust*, the 'supreme example of *genera mixta* in all of literature' (241)).

With the increasing prestige of historicist criticism in the 1980s and 1990s, questions of form have often been subordinated to issues of ideology. Our next piece is among a number of publications by one of the present editors (**Michael O'Neill**) that seek to redress the balance. In this essay '"The Mind Which Feeds This Verse": Self- and Other-Awareness in Shelley's Poetry' (1993), O'Neill looks at the case of one of the most politically engaged Romantic poets and takes the view that 'The drama of Shelley's career as a poet arises out of his uncomplacent and evolving recognition of the cultural significance of poetry'. It is not that Shelley settles for 'narrowly formalist self-delight'. It is, rather, that his poetic self-consciousness reveals him to be 'a poet, and a poet of crisscrossing perspectives – not a philosopher manqué, not a (heterodox) theologian manqué, not a political theorist manqué' (244). The essay defends itself against the McGannian charge (from McGann's *Romantic Ideology* stage) of 'uncritical absorption in Romanticism's own self-representations' (quoted 246) by arguing that Shelley is himself 'far from uncritical' about his 'representations' (246). The essay contends that Shelley (in common with other Romantic poets) is highly vigilant about the rewards and dangers of acute self-awareness, and that such self-awareness often gives later moralising objections the slip. So, *Prometheus Unbound* 'is a poem that is inexhaustibly profligate in its inventions and yet always aware that creativity may flag, that a voice may be wanting, that hope will always need to create "From its own wreck the thing it contemplates"' (269).

O'Neill's essay is concerned with the inner life of Shelley's poetry. In her essay included here, 'Transition in Byron and Wordsworth' (2000), **Jane Stabler** shows how the life of Wordsworth's and Byron's poetry can be illuminated by examining their use of transition. She gives a valuable overview of the way transition was regarded in the eighteenth century, noting, for example, Hugh Blair's objections to odes in which the poet reveals himself to be 'so abrupt in his transitions ... that we essay in vain to follow him' (quoted 276). The main body of her essay considers the two poets' handling of transition, which becomes a means of considering their poetry's representation of consciousness. Though she finds in Wordsworth a preference for gradual change and in Byron a love of rapid alteration of mood, Stabler does not simplify her oppositions. She comments on the fact that, in *The Borderers* and elsewhere, Wordsworth 'analysed the effects of both gradual and sudden turns of feeling' (279). She comments, moreover, on the fact that Coleridge was disturbed by 'the jarring effect' in such Wordsworthian poems as *Resolution and Independence* 'of a sudden turn to bodily matters of fact' (281).

Stabler weaves together such external evidence of the period's concern with transition with analysis of internal formal effects, as when she attends to the effect of rhyme in Byron's poetry. Analysing three stanzas (198–200) from canto 2 of *Don Juan*, she remarks: 'The mercurial transitions of tone in these stanzas show how reductive it is to think of Byron's *ottava rima* simply as six serious lines undercut by two epigrammatic ones' (288). And she offers the suggestion that Wordsworth's 1820 version of the 'Vaudracour and Julia' episode of *The Prelude* responds to 'Byron's way with transitions' (288) since Wordsworth's own interjected questions have an 'unexpected force' that recalls Byron's practice. Stabler concludes by suggesting that transition 'recalls us to the artificiality of the situation, that what is being read is, however true to life, a work of art' (289), reinforcing the claims for the sophistication of Romantic poetry made by other formalist and generic critics represented here.

**Helen Vendler**, the author of *The Odes of John Keats* (1983), possibly the most satisfying formalist study ever written of a Romantic poet, is concerned in 'Keats and the Use of Poetry' (1988), our next essay, with Keats's answers to the question posed by Heidegger, 'What is the poet for in a destitute time?' (quoted on 293). She takes 'the case of Keats to be an exemplary one of a modern poet seeking to define his own worth', the forerunner in so doing of contemporary poets such as Czeslaw Milosz and Seamus Heaney. Vendler does not deny that Keats was a 'political radical' (294), but she sees his poetic distinction as tied up with his recognition of the inadequacies of his early work in which 'claims for the social functions of poetry ... are asserted merely, not poetically enacted' (295). Keats undergoes a complex process of development, on her account: he argues in 'Sleep and Poetry' for 'the therapeutic function of poetry' (297), a view he never foregoes (it is still 'envisaged' (297) in 'Ode on a Grecian Urn'), but a view which is refined by a later conception of poetry 'as a mediating, oracular, and priestlike art' (297).

In particular, Keats recognises in *Endymion* 'the symbolic nature of art', the fact that 'it must always bear an allegorical or emblematic relation to reality' (298). In his greatest poems, 'Ode to a Nightingale' and 'Ode on a Grecian Urn', Keats 'decides to play, in his own poetry, the role of audience and interpreter of symbols', a move which Vendler sees as 'Keats's most successful aesthetic decision' (300). Keats, on Vendler's account, develops a growing sense that art must occupy its own aesthetic space, that the poet must learn how to pursue 'things to their "symbol-essences"'; otherwise, the poet 'will not be able to communicate with ages later than his own' (301). In 'To Autumn', Keats, argues Vendler, 'chooses nature and culture as the two poles of his symbolic system' (301). He allegorises in the poem 'the making of nature into nurture', the dual fact that 'Art does not mimetically resemble nature, any more than cider mimetically resembles apples', and that 'without apples there would be no cider' (302). Vendler's reading of poetry is stringently and subtly aesthetic, as she claims is Keats whose 'To Autumn' concludes with images of sound serving to elevate the 'aesthetic principle of music' (303). Without symbolic form there is no art. The essay serves as a profound formalist rebuke to those who insist that the 'artist's duty is a historically mimetic one' (303). It closes with readings of poems by Milosz ('The Poor Poet') and Heaney ('Chekhov on Sakhalin') in which the later poets are shown to repeat the journey towards 'the creation of a symbolic and musical form' (307) traced by Keats.

**Susan J. Wolfson** has emerged as among the most theoretically sophisticated of contemporary formalist critics of Romanticism. In her *Formal Charges: The Shaping of Poetry in British Romanticism* (1997), she combines attentive interest in the workings of poems with an awareness that 'Romanticism's poetic forms take shape within complicated literary and cultural contexts'.[5] In the essay we have included, 'What Good is Formalist Criticism? Or; *Forms* and *Storms* and the Critical Register of Romantic Poetry' (1998), Wolfson argues, against the assertions of some deconstructive and historicist critics, that 'some poetic events may amount to a form-sensitive criticism, with social and political implications'. She supports this claim with analyses of the work performed in various Romantic poems by 'the word *form*, especially when formed into a meta-rhyme with *storm*' (308). 'Meta-rhyme' means rhyme that comments on its own status as a poetic event, and in this respect, for all their differences, Wolfson is one with Vendler, Stabler, and O'Neill in wishing to give credit to the Romantics for their high degree of sophisticated self-consciousness.

Where Wolfson is particularly original is in her view that formal self-awareness often serves political and social ends in the poetry of the Romantics. Much of the essay consists of a detailed examination of

Rousseau's encounter with the 'shape all light' in Shelley's *The Triumph of Life*, the aftermath of which includes rhymes involving 'storm' and 'form'. Wolfson acknowledges the perceptiveness of Paul de Man's deconstructive reading of the poem, with its emphasis on 'a critically self-conscious meta-formalism' (312), but she does not agree with de Man's view that the poem shows 'the unreadability of history' (323, fn. 10). Instead, she suggests that Shelley's Rousseau makes us aware of form in order to 'present a critique of the kind of aesthetic formalism that emerges as a reflex of failed political forms' (313). Meta-rhymes involving 'form' in *The Triumph of Life* do not imply 'a transcendence of history, redeeming the deforming, shattering force of temporality', as does the rhyme of 'form' and 'storm' in *Epipsychidion* (ll. 27–8), or in Byron's *Childe Harold's Pilgrimage*, 4. 183 (315). Wolfson sees Keats as sharing Shelley's ability to use poetic form to reflect on the complex relationships between art and history, and refers, in support of her argument, to the work done by 'deform', in the final stanza of *The Eve of St Agnes*, a word that speaks of 'a reaction formation against . . . aesthetic vision' (317). In a similar fashion, Felicia Hemans reveals herself to be 'alert to the social text' associated with the gendered implications of 'the *form/ storm* rhyme field' (321).

Wolfson, wearing her formalism with a difference, is able to mingle emphases drawn from diverse critical theoretical approaches, whilst attending closely to the texts she examines. She is keen to distinguish her 'care for forms' from a belief in 'autonomous formal icons of meaning' (322). In recent years, some younger critics of Romanticism have revealed a comparable readiness to combine formalist exploration of poetic device and structure with insights drawn from other theoretical perspectives. Two essays on Keats illustrate the point. In the first, 'Beautiful Ruins: The Elgin Marbles Sonnet in its Historical and Generic Contexts' (1990), **Grant F. Scott** takes a single sonnet and shows how much can be revealed about its meanings by investigations of a number of contexts, including 'the specific genre of ekphrastic poetry' (327). Scott wishes us to see the poem as implicated in and responding to the debate about the Elgin Marbles, as recorded in the *Annals of the Fine Arts*. Scott brings out the ambivalent nature of response to the Marbles, admired for their sublimity and truth to nature, yet viewed, too, as incomplete and fragmentary, and he argues that Keats's 'On Seeing the Elgin Marbles' 'acts as a kind of mediating force between the two predominant viewpoints'. Ultimately, Scott claims, Keats talks more about the nature of 'aesthetic response' (331) than about the formal characteristics of particular artworks. Scott attends perceptively to the way the poem's formal features – its 'abundance of dactyls' (334), 'pronounced enjambment' and abrupt 'transitions' (334), a feature important to Scott as to Stabler – convey, on Keats's part, 'feelings of his own inadequacy' (335). The poem problematises as much as it celebrates. Scott brings out this mixture of attitudes through a lively fusion of formal and contextual insights. In his words, the poem 'refuses the dawn' associated with pro-Hellenist claims for Greek culture as the cradle of civilisation, and 'ends in uncertain twilight' (338).

In the second, the penultimate essay in Volume I, '"To See as a God Sees": The Potential Übermensch in Keats's *Hyperion* Fragments' (1998), written by **Mark Sandy**, co-editor of the present work, the perceptions of Friedrich Nietzsche are drawn on to re-invigorate our understanding of Keats's 'struggle to discover a self' (349) in his *Hyperion* fragments. Keats, according to Sandy, anticipates Nietzsche's rejection of the metaphysical in favour of the metaphorical and of being in favour of becoming. There is even a Derridean 'borderline' effect (353) in Keats's first *Hyperion* as the poet engages in 'writing – or "auto-graphing" – the nature of his new poetic character, which can only derive credibility from a future that is by no means assured' (253). The revised version of the poem, *The Fall of Hyperion*, 'is literally a re-reading and re-writing of the *Hyperion* fragment' (219), and the project's overall importance and pathos inhere in the blend between the affirmation required by 'self-creation' (356) and the recognition that to aspire, in Zarathustra-like manner, to overcome the self, 'serves only to remind individuals of their contingent, culpable, and mortal nature' (358): a nature which Nietzsche urges us to celebrate.

If imitation, even when mocking, is a form of flattery of a kind, then the many contemporary parodies of Wordsworth's poetry bear witness to the skewed but close attention given to his forms and words by reviewers of the day. We conclude Volume I with an essay by **Nicola Trott** entitled 'Wordsworth in the Nursery: The Parodic School of Criticism' (2001), which explores, among other things, 'the use that the reviews themselves made of parodic devices and techniques' (36). So, Byron, reviewing Wordsworth's *Poems, in Two Volumes*, quotes some lines by Wordsworth and asserts that they are 'an imitation of such minstrelsy as soothed our cries in the cradle, with the shrill ditty of "Hey de diddle, / The cat and the fiddle"' (quoted 366). The idea of 'the infantine Wordsworth' (368) is conveyed, as Trott points out, through parody, and, as she also observes, 'Wordsworth, it might be said, was never allowed to grow up' (371). Francis Jeffrey, in particular, contrives to suggest that 'the new school is *itself* already parodic' (373), the author of *Poems, in Two Volumes*, indeed, being represented as 'an "imitator" – and a *bad* imitator – of his own *Lyrical Ballads* style' (374).

Indeed, the pre-publication parody of Wordsworth's *Peter Bell* by John Hamilton Reynolds had the effect of calling into question Wordsworth's own poetic originality: 'imitation Wordsworth usurped genuine Wordsworth in a text of the same name' (378–9). So prevalent is parody as a reviewing method that Trott suggests that the method 'acquired a formal dimension, achieving a sort of simultaneous transmission of poem and parody in which it is the latter that provides the determining context for Wordsworth's reception' (379). The net result of this is that a particular mode is attributed to Wordsworth and yet that parody of his work becomes 'superfluous' (380).

16

What Trott describes is something close to a nightmare version of close reading in which pre-conceived prejudice replaces genuine attention. Not the least acute of Trott's insights is her remark that parody 'comes of age' (she is quoting Marilyn Gaull) at the same time that 'professional criticism' is getting under way (381). Her essay contains much of interest for a criticism interested in the forms of Romanticism; it also serves, in its attention to reception, as an appropriate bridge between this volume and the second volume, which turns its attention to criticism of a contextual and socio-political kind.

## Notes

1 'Wordsworth', in *Oxford Lectures on Poetry* (1909; London: Macmillan, 1965), pp. 101, 124, 134.
2 See Hartman's *Wordsworth's Poetry 1787–1814* (1964; New Haven: Yale University Press, 1971), and Jonathan Wordsworth's *William Wordsworth: the Borders of Vision* (Oxford: Clarendon, 1982).
3 *Oxford Lectures on Poetry*, p. 179.
4 For a full-length study of the 'apocalyptic' element in Romantic poetry, see Morton D. Paley, *Apocalypse and Millennium in English Romantic Poetry* (Oxford: Clarendon, 1999). This topic is also the subject of Paley's article in Volume IV (see pp. 34–50).
5 Susan J. Wolfson, *Formal Charges: The Shaping of Poetry in British Romanticism* (Stanford, CA: Stanford University Press, 1997), p. 21.

# Part 1

# SOME TWENTIETH-CENTURY CONSTRUCTIONS AND DEFINITIONS

# 1

# SHELLEY'S VIEW
# OF POETRY

*A. C. Bradley*

Source: *Oxford Lectures on Poetry* (1909) London: Macmillan, 1965, pp. 151–74.

The ideas of Wordsworth and of Coleridge about poetry have often been discussed and are familiar. Those of Shelley are much less so, and in his eloquent exposition of them there is a radiance which almost conceals them from many readers. I wish, at the cost of all the radiance, to try to see them and show them rather more distinctly. Even if they had little value for the theory of poetry, they would still have much as material for it, since they allow us to look into a poet's experience in conceiving and composing. And, in addition, they throw light on some of the chief characteristics of Shelley's own poetry.

His poems in their turn form one of the sources from which his ideas on the subject may be gathered. We have also some remarks in his letters and in prose pieces dealing with other topics. We have the prefaces to those of his works which he himself published. And, lastly, there is the *Defence of Poetry*. This essay was written in reply to an attack made on contemporary verse by Shelley's friend Peacock,—not a favourable specimen of Peacock's writing. The *Defence*, we can see, was hurriedly composed, and it remains a fragment, being only the first of three projected parts. It contains a good deal of historical matter, highly interesting, but too extensive to be made use of here. Being polemical, it no doubt exaggerates such of Shelley's views as collided with those of his antagonist. But, besides being the only full expression of these views, it is the most mature, for it was written within eighteen months of his death. It appears to owe very little either to Wordsworth's Prefaces or to Coleridge's *Biographia Literaria*; but there are a few reminiscences of Sidney's *Apology*, which Shelley had read just before he wrote his own *Defence*; and it shows, like much of his mature poetry, how deeply he was influenced by the more imaginative dialogues of Plato.

# 1

Any one familiar with the manner in which Shelley in his verse habitually represents the world could guess at his general view of poetry. The world to him is a melancholy place, a 'dim vast vale of tears, illuminated in flashes by the light of a hidden but glorious power. Nor is this power, as that favourite metaphor would imply, wholly outside the world. It works within it as a soul contending with obstruction and striving to penetrate and transform the whole mass. And though the fulness of its glory is concealed, its nature is known in outline. It is the realised perfection of everything good and beautiful on earth; or, in other words, all such goodness and beauty is its partial manifestation. 'All,' I say: for the splendour of nature, the love of lovers, every affection and virtue, any good action or just law, the wisdom of philosophy, the creations of art, the truths deformed by superstitious religion,—all are equally operations or appearances of the hidden power. It is of the first importance for the understanding of Shelley to realise how strong in him is the sense and conviction of this unity in life: it is one of his Platonic traits. The intellectual Beauty of his *Hymn* is absolutely the same thing as the Liberty of his *Ode*, the 'Great Spirit' of Love that he invokes to bring freedom to Naples, the One which in *Adonaïs* he contrasts with the Many, the Spirit of Nature of *Queen Mab*, and the Vision of *Alastor* and *Epipsychidion*. The skylark of the famous stanzas is free from our sorrows, not because it is below them, but because, as an embodiment of that perfection, it knows the rapture of love without its satiety, and understands death as we cannot. The voice of the mountain, if a whole nation could hear it with the poet's ear, would 'repeal large codes of fraud and woe'; it is the same voice as the reformer's and the martyr's. And in the far-off day when the 'plastic stress' of this power has mastered the last resistance and is all in all, outward nature, which now suffers with man, will be redeemed with him, and man, in becoming politically free, will become also the perfect lover. Evidently, then, poetry, as the world now is, must be one of the voices of this power, or one tone of its voice. To use the language so dear to Shelley, it is the revelation of those eternal ideas which lie behind the many-coloured, ever-shifting veil that we call reality or life. Or rather, it is one such revelation among many.

When we turn to the *Defence of Poetry* we meet substantially the same view. There is indeed a certain change; for Shelley is now philosophising and writing prose, and he wishes not to sing from the mid-sky, but, for a while at least, to argue with his friend on the earth. Hence at first we hear nothing of that perfect power at the heart of things, and poetry is considered as a creation rather than a revelation. But for Shelley, we soon discover, this would be a false antithesis. The poet creates, but this creation is no mere fancy of his; it represents 'those forms which are common to universal nature and existence,' and 'a poem is the very image of life expressed in its eternal truth.' We notice, further, that the more voluntary and conscious work of invention and execution is regarded as quite subordinate in the creative process. In that process the mind, obedient to an influence which it does not understand and cannot control, is driven to produce images of perfection which rather form themselves in it than are formed by it. The greatest stress is laid on this influence or inspiration; and in the end we learn that the origin of the whole process lies in certain exceptional moments when visitations of thought and feeling, elevating and delightful beyond all expression, but always arising unforeseen and departing unbidden, reach the soul; that these are, as it were, the interpenetration of a diviner nature through our own; and that the province of the poet is to arrest these apparitions, to veil them in language, to colour every other form he touches with their evanescent hues, and so to 'redeem from decay the visitations of the divinity in man.'

Even more decided is the emphasis laid on the unity of all the forms in which the 'divinity' or ideal power thus attests its presence. Indeed, throughout a large part of the essay, that 'Poetry' which Shelley is defending is something very much wider than poetry in the usual sense. The enemy he has to meet is the contention that poetry and its influence steadily decline as civilisation advances, and that they are giving place, and ought to give place, to reasoning and the pursuit of utility. His answer is that, on the contrary, imagination has been, is, and always will be, the prime source of everything that has intrinsic value in life. Reasoning, he declares, cannot create, it can only operate upon the products of imagination. Further, he holds that the predominance of mere reasoning and mere utility has become in great part an evil; for while it has accumulated masses of material goods and moral truths, we distribute the goods iniquitously and fail to apply the truths, because, for want of imagination, we have not sympathy in our hearts and do not feel what we know. The 'Poetry' which he defends, therefore, is the whole creative imagination with all its products. And these include not merely literature in verse, but, first, whatever prose writing is allied to that literature; and, next, all the other fine arts; and, finally, all actions, inventions, institutions, and even ideas and moral dispositions, which imagination brings into being in its effort to satisfy the longing for perfection. Painters and musicians are poets. Plato and Bacon, even Herodotus and Livy, were poets, though there is much in their works which is not poetry. So were the men who invented the arts of life, constructed laws for tribes or cities, disclosed, as sages or founders of religion, the excellence of justice and love. And every one, Shelley would say, who, perceiving the beauty of an imagined virtue or deed, translates the image into a fact, is so far a poet. For all these things come from imagination.

Shelley's exposition of this, which is probably the most original part of his theory, is not very clear; but, if I understand his meaning, that which he takes to happen in all these cases might be thus described. The imagination—that is to say, the soul imagining—has before it, or feels within it, something which, answering perfectly to its nature, fills it with delight and with a desire to realise what delights it. This something, for the sake of brevity, we may call an idea, so long as we remember that it need not be distinctly imagined and that it is always accompanied by emotion. The reason why such ideas delight the imagining soul is that they are, in fact, images or forebodings of its own perfection—of itself become perfect—in one aspect or another. These aspects are as various as the elements and forms of its own inner life and outward existence; and so the idea may be that of the perfect harmony of will and feeling (a virtue), or of the perfect union of soul with soul (love), or of the perfect order of certain social relations or forces (a law or institution), or of the perfect adjustment of intellectual elements (a truth); and so on. The formation and expression of any such idea is thus the work of Poetry in the widest sense; while at the same time (as we must add, to complete Shelley's thought) any such idea is a gleam or apparition of the perfect Intellectual Beauty.

I choose this particular title of the hidden power or divinity in order to point out (what the reader is left to observe for himself) that the imaginative idea is always regarded by Shelley as beautiful. It is, for example, desirable for itself and not merely as a means to a further result; and it has the formal characters of beauty. For, as will have been noticed in the instances given, it is always the image of an order, or harmony, or unity in variety, of the elements concerned. Shelley sometimes even speaks of their 'rhythm.' For example, he uses this word in reference to an action; and I quote the passage because, though it occurs at some distance from the exposition of his main view, it illustrates it well. He is saying that the true poetry of Rome, unlike that of Greece, did not fully express itself in poems. 'The true poetry of Rome lived in its institutions: for whatever of beautiful, true and majestic they contained, could have sprung only from the faculty which creates the order in which they consist. The life of Camillus; the death of Regulus; the expectation of the senators, in their god-like state, of the victorious Gauls; the refusal of the Republic to make peace with Hannibal after the battle of Cannæ'—these he describes as 'a rhythm and order in the shows of life,' an order not arranged with a view to utility or outward result, but due to the imagination, which, 'beholding the beauty of this order, created it out of itself according to its own idea.'

## 2

If this, then, is the nature of Poetry in the widest sense, how does the poet, in the special sense, differ from other unusually creative souls? Not essentially in the inspiration and general substance of his poetry, but in the kind of expression he gives to them. In so far as he is a poet, his medium of expression, of course, is not virtue, or action, or law; poetry is one of the arts. And, again, it differs from the rest, because its particular vehicle is language. We have now to see, therefore, what Shelley has to say of the form of poetry, and especially of poetic language.

First, he claims for language the highest place among the vehicles of artistic expression, on the ground that it is the most direct and also the most plastic. It is itself produced by imagination instead of being simply encountered by it, and it has no relation except to imagination; whereas any more material medium has a nature of its own, and relations to other things in the material world, and this nature and these relations intervene between the artist's conception and his expression of it in the medium. It is to the superiority of its vehicle that Shelley attributes the greater fame which poetry has always enjoyed as compared with other arts. He forgets (if I may interpose a word of criticism) that the media of the other arts have, on their side, certain advantages over language, and that these perhaps counterbalance the inferiority which he notices. He would also have found it difficult to show that language, on its physical side, is any more a product of imagination than stone or pigments. And his idea that the medium in the other arts is an obstacle intervening between conception and expression is, to say the least, one-sided. A sculptor, painter, or musician, would probably reply that it is only the qualities of his medium that enable him to express at all; that what he expresses is inseparable from the vehicle of expression; and that he has no conceptions which are not from the beginning sculpturesque, pictorial, or musical. It is true, no doubt, that his medium is an obstacle as well as a medium; but this is also true of language.

But to resume. Language, Shelley goes on to say, receives in poetry a peculiar form. As it represents in its meaning a perfection which is always an order, harmony, or rhythm, so it itself, as so much sound, *is* an order, harmony, or rhythm. It is measured language, which is not the proper vehicle for the mere recital of facts or for mere reasoning. For Shelley, however, this measured language is not of necessity metrical. The order or measure may remain at the stage which it reaches in beautiful prose, like that of Plato, the melody of whose language, Shelley declares, is the most intense it is possible to conceive. It may again advance to metre; and he admits that metrical form is convenient, popular, and preferable, especially in poetry containing much action. But he will not have any new great poet tied down to it. It is not essential, while measure is absolutely so. For it is no mere accident of poetry that its language is measured, nor does a delight in this measure mean little. As sensitiveness to the order of the relations of sounds is always connected with sensitiveness to the order of the relations of thoughts, so also the harmony of the words is scarcely less indispensable than their meaning to the communication of the influence of poetry. 'Hence,' says Shelley, 'the vanity of translation: it were as wise to cast a violet into a crucible that you might discover the formal principle of its colour and odour, as seek to transfuse from one language into another the creations of a poet.'

Strong words to come from the translator of the *Hymn to Mercury* and of Agathon's speech in the *Symposium*![1] And is not all that Shelley says of the difference between measured and unrhythmical language applicable, at least in some degree, to the difference between metrical and merely measured language? Could he really have supposed that metre is no more than a 'convenience,' which contributes nothing of any account to the influence of poetry? But I will not criticise. Let me rather point out how surprising, at first sight, and how significant, is Shelley's insistence on the importance of measure or rhythm. No one could assert more absolutely than he the identity of the general substance of poetry with that of moral life and action, of the other arts, and of the higher kinds of philosophy. And yet it would be difficult to go beyond the emphasis of his statement that the formal element (as he understood it) is indispensable to the effect of poetry.

Shelley, however, nowhere considers this element more at length. He has no discussions, like those of Wordsworth and Coleridge, on diction. He never says, with Keats, that he looks on fine phrases like a lover. We hear of his deep-drawn sigh of satisfaction as he finished reading a passage of Homer, but not of his shouting his delight, as he ramped through the meadows of Spenser, at some marvellous flower. When in his letters he refers to any poem he is reading, he scarcely ever mentions particular lines or expressions; and we have no evidence that, like Coleridge and Keats, he was a curious student of metrical effects or the relations of vowel-sounds. I doubt if all this is wholly accidental. Poetry was to him so essentially an effusion of aspiration, love and worship, that we can imagine his feeling it almost an impiety to break up its unity even for purposes of study, and to give a separate attention to its means of utterance. And what he does say on the subject confirms this impression. In the first place, as we have seen, he lays great stress on inspiration; and his statements, if exaggerated and misleading, must still reflect in some degree his own experience. No poem, he asserts, however inspired it may be, is more than a feeble shadow of the original conception; for when composition begins, inspiration is already on the decline. And so in a letter he speaks of the detail of execution destroying all wild and beautiful visions. Still, inspiration, if diminished by composition, is not wholly dispelled; and he appeals to the greatest poets of his day whether it is not an error to assert that the finest passages of poetry are produced by labour and study. Such toil he would restrict to those parts which connect the inspired passages, and he speaks with contempt of the fifty-six various readings of the first line of the *Orlando Furioso*. He seems to exaggerate on this matter because in the *Defence* his foe is cold reason and calculation. Elsewhere he writes more truly of the original conception as being obscure as well as intense;[2] from which it would seem to follow that the feeble shadow, if darker, is at least more distinct than the original. He forgets, too, what is certainly the fact, that the poet in reshaping and correcting is able to revive in some degree the fire of the first impulse. And we know from himself that his greatest works cost him a severe labour not confined to the execution, while his manuscripts show plenty of various readings, if never so many as fifty-six in one line.

Still, what he says is highly characteristic of his own practice in composition. He allowed the rush of his ideas to have its way, without pausing to complete a troublesome line or to find a word that did not come; and the next day (if ever) he filled up the gaps and smoothed the ragged edges. And the result answers to his theory. Keats was right in telling him that he might be more of an artist. His language, indeed, unlike Wordsworth's or Byron's, is, in his mature work, always that of a poet; we never hear his mere speaking voice; but he is frequently diffuse and obscure, and even in fine passages his constructions are sometimes trailing and amorphous. The glowing metal rushes into the mould so vehemently that it overleaps the bounds and fails to find its way into all the little crevices. But no poetry is more manifestly inspired, and even when it is plainly imperfect it is sometimes so inspired that it is impossible to wish it changed. It has the rapture of the mystic, and that is too rare to lose. Tennyson quaintly said of the hymn *Life of Life*: 'He seems to go up into the air and burst.' It is true: and, if we are to speak of poems as fireworks, I would not compare *Life of Life* with a great set piece of Homer or Shakespeare that illumines the whole sky; but, all the same, there is no more thrilling sight than the heavenward rush of a rocket, and it bursts at a height no other fire can reach.

In addition to his praise of inspiration Shelley has some scattered remarks on another point which show the same spirit. He could not bear in poetic language any approach to artifice, or any sign that the writer had a theory or system of style. He thought Keats's earlier poems faulty in this respect, and there is perhaps a reference to Wordsworth in the following sentence from the Preface to the *Revolt of Islam*: 'Nor have I permitted any system relating to mere words to divert the attention of the reader, from whatever interest I may have succeeded in creating, to my own ingenuity in contriving, —to disgust him according to the rules of criticism. I have simply clothed my thoughts in what appeared to me the most obvious and appropriate language. A person familiar with nature, and with the most celebrated productions of the human mind, can scarcely err in following the instinct, with respect to selection of language, produced by that familiarity.'[3] His own poetic style certainly corresponds with his intention. It cannot give the kind of pleasure afforded by what may be called without disparagement a learned and artful style, such as Virgil's or Milton's; but, like the best writing of Shakespeare and Goethe, it is, with all its individuality, almost entirely free from mannerism and the other vices of self-consciousness, and appears to flow so directly from the thought that one is ashamed to admire it for itself. This is equally so whether the appropriate style is impassioned and highly figurative, or simple and even plain. It is indeed in the latter case that Shelley wins his greatest, because most difficult, triumph. In the dialogue part of *Julian and Maddalo* he has succeeded remarkably in keeping the style quite close to that of familiar though serious conversation, while making it nevertheless unmistakably poetic. And the *Cenci* is an example of a success less complete only because the problem was even harder. The ideal of the style of tragic drama in the nineteenth or twentieth century should surely be, not to reproduce with modifications the style of Shakespeare, but to do what Shakespeare did—to idealise, without deserting, the language of contemporary speech. Shelley in the *Cenci* seems to me to have come nearest to this ideal.

**3**

So much for general exposition. If now we consider more closely what Shelley says of the substance of poetry, a question at once arises. He may seem to think of poetry solely as the direct expression of perfection in some form, and accordingly to imagine its effect as simply joy or delighted aspiration. Much of his own poetry, too, is such an expression; and we understand when we find him saying that Homer embodied the ideal perfection of his age in human character, and unveiled in Achilles, Hector, and Ulysses 'the truth and beauty of friendship, patriotism, and persevering devotion to an object.' But poetry, it is obvious, is not wholly, perhaps not even mainly, of this kind. What is to be said, on Shelley's theory, of his own melancholy lyrics, those 'sweetest songs' that 'tell of saddest thought'? What of satire, of the epic of conflict and war, or of tragic exhibitions of violent and destructive passion? Does not his theory reflect the weakness of his own practice, his tendency to portray a thin and abstract ideal instead of interpreting the concrete detail of nature and life; and ought we not to oppose to it a theory which would consider poetry simply as a representation of fact?

To this last question I should answer No. Shelley's theory, rightly understood, will take in, I think, everything really poetic. And to a considerable extent he himself shows the way to meet these doubts. He did not mean that the *immediate subject* of poetry must be perfection in some form. The poet, he says, can colour with the hues of the ideal everything he touches. If so, he may write of absolutely anything so long as he *can* so colour it, and nothing would be excluded from his province except those things (if any such exist) in which no positive relation to the ideal, however indirect, can be shown or intimated. Thus to take the instance of Shelley's melancholy lyrics, clearly the lament which arises from loss of the ideal, and mourns the evanescence of its visitations or the desolation of its absence, is indirectly an expression *of* the ideal; and so on his theory is the simplest song of unhappy love or the simplest dirge. Further, he himself observes that, though the joy of poetry is often unalloyed, yet the pleasure of the 'highest portions of our being is frequently connected with the pain of the inferior,' that 'the pleasure that is in sorrow is sweeter than the pleasure of pleasure itself,' and that not sorrow only, but 'terror, anguish, despair itself, are often the chosen expressions of an approximation to the highest good.' That, then, which appeals poetically to such painful emotions will again be an indirect portrayal of the ideal; and it is clear, I think, that this was how Shelley in the *Defence* regarded heroic and tragic poetry, whether narrative or dramatic, with its manifestly imperfect characters and its exhibition of conflict and wild passion. He had, it is true, another and an unsatisfactory way of explaining the presence of these things in poetry; and I will refer to this in a moment. But he tells us that the Athenian tragedies represent the highest idealisms (his name for ideals) of passion and of power (not merely of virtue); and that in them we behold ourselves, 'under a thin disguise of circumstance, stripped of all but that ideal perfection and energy which every one feels to be the internal type of all that he loves, admires, and would become.' He writes of Milton's Satan in somewhat the same strain. The Shakespearean tragedy from which he most often quotes is one in which evil holds the stage, *Macbeth*; and he was inclined to think *King Lear*, which certainly is no direct portrait of perfection, the greatest drama in the world. Lastly, in the Preface to his own *Cenci* he truly says that, while the story is fearful and monstrous, 'the poetry which exists in these tempestuous sufferings and crimes,' if duly brought out, 'mitigates the pain of the contemplation of moral deformity': so that he regards Count Cenci himself as a *poetic* character, and therefore as in *some* sense an expression of the ideal. He does not further explain his meaning. Perhaps it was that the perfection which poetry is to exhibit includes, together with those qualities which win our immediate and entire approval or sympathy, others which are capable of becoming the instruments of evil. For these, the energy, power and passion of the soul though they may be perverted, are in themselves elements of perfection; and so, even in their perversion or their combination with moral deformity, they retain their value, they are not simply ugly or horrible, but appeal through emotions predominantly painful to the same love of the ideal which is directly satisfied by pictures of goodness and beauty. Now to these various considerations we shall wish to add others; but if we bear these in mind, I believe we shall find Shelley's theory wide enough, and must hold that the substance of poetry is never mere fact, but is always ideal, though its method of representation is sometimes more direct, sometimes more indirect.

Nevertheless, he does not seem to have made his view quite clear to himself, or to hold to it consistently. We are left with the impression, not merely that he personally preferred the direct method (as he was, of course, entitled to do), but that his use of it shows a certain weakness, and also that even in theory he unconsciously tends to regard it as the primary and proper method, and to admit only by a reluctant after-thought the representation of imperfection. Let me point out some signs of this. He considered his own *Cenci* as a poem inferior in kind to his other main works, even as a sort of accommodation to the public. With all his modesty he knew what to think of the neglected *Prometheus* and *Adonaïs*, but there is no sign that he, any more than the world, was aware that the character of Cenci was a creation without a parallel in our poetry since the seventeenth century. His enthusiasm for some second-rate and third-rate Italian paintings, and his failure to understand Michael Angelo, seem to show the same tendency. He could not enjoy comedy: it seemed to him simply cruel: he did not perceive that to show the absurdity of the imperfect is to glorify the perfect. And, as I mentioned just now, he wavers in his view of the representation of heroic and tragic imperfection. We find in the Preface to *Prometheus Unbound* the strange notion that Prometheus is a more poetic character than Milton's Satan because he is free from Satan's imperfections, which are said to interfere with the interest. And in the *Defence* a similar error appears. Achilles, Hector, Ulysses, though they exhibit ideal virtues, are, he admits, imperfect. Why, then, did Homer make them so? Because, he seems to reply, Homer's contemporaries regarded their vices (*e.g.* revengefulness and deceitfulness) as virtues. Homer accordingly had to conceal in the costume of these vices the unspotted beauty that he himself imagined; and, like Homer, 'few poets of the highest class have chosen to exhibit the beauty of their conceptions in its naked truth and splendour.' Now, this idea, to say nothing of its grotesque improbability in reference to Homer, and its probable baselessness in reference to most other poets, is quite inconsistent with that truer view of heroic and tragic character which was explained just now. It is an example of Shelley's tendency to abstract idealism or spurious Platonism. He is haunted by the fancy that if he could only get at the One, the eternal Idea, in complete aloofness from the Many, from life with all its change, decay, struggle, sorrow and evil, he would have reached the true object of poetry: as if the whole finite world were a mere mistake or illusion, the sheer opposite of the infinite One, and in no way or degree its manifestation. Life, he says—

> Life, like a dome of many-coloured glass,
> Stains the white radiance of eternity;

but the other side, the fact that the many colours *are* the white light broken, he tends to forget, by no means always, but in one, and that not the least inspired, of his moods. This is the source of that thinness and shallowness of which his view of the world and of history is justly accused, a view in which all imperfect being is apt to figure as absolutely gratuitous, and everything and everybody as pure white or pitch black. Hence also his ideals of good, whether as a character or as a mode of life, resting as they do on abstraction from the mass of real existence, tend to lack body and individuality; and indeed, if the existence of the many is a mere calamity, clearly the next best thing to their disappearance is that they should all be exactly alike and have as little character as possible. But we must remember that Shelley's strength and weakness are closely allied, and it may be that the very abstractness of his ideal was a condition of that quivering intensity of aspiration towards it in which his poetry is unequalled. We must not go for this to Homer and Shakespeare and Goethe; and if we go for it to Dante, we shall find, indeed, a mind far vaster than Shelley's, but also that dualism of which we complain in him, and the description of a heaven which, equally with Shelley's regenerated earth, is no place for mere mortality. In any case, as we have seen, the weakness in his poetical practice, though it occasionally appears also as a defect in his poetical theory, forms no necessary part of it.

## 4

I pass to his views on a last point. If the business of poetry is somehow to express ideal perfection, it may seem to follow that the poet should embody in his poems his beliefs about this perfection and the way to approach it, and should thus have a moral purpose and aim to be a teacher. And in regard to Shelley this conclusion seems the more natural because his own poetry allows us to see clearly some of his beliefs about morality and moral progress. Yet alike in his Prefaces and in the *Defence* he takes up most decidedly the position that the poet ought neither to affect a moral aim nor to express his own conceptions of right and wrong. 'Didactic poetry,' he declares 'is my abhorrence: nothing can be equally well expressed in prose that is not tedious and supererogatory in verse.'[4] 'There was little danger,' he tells us in the *Defence*, 'that Homer or any of the eternal poets' should make a mistake in this matter; but 'those in whom the poetical faculty, though great, is less intense, as Euripides, Lucan, Tasso, Spenser, have frequently affected a moral aim, and the effect of their poetry is diminished in exact proportion to the degree in which they compel us to advert to this purpose.' These statements may appeal to us, but are they consistent with Shelley's main views of poetry? To answer this question we must observe what exactly it is that he means to condemn.

Shelley was one of the few persons who can literally be said to *love* their kind. He held most strongly, too, that poetry does benefit men, and benefits them morally. The moral purpose, then, to which he objects cannot well be a poet's general purpose of doing moral as well as other good through his poetry—such a purpose, I mean, as he may cherish when he contemplates his life and his life's work. And, indeed, it seems obvious that nobody with any humanity or any sense can object to that, except through some intellectual confusion. Nor, secondly, does Shelley mean, I think, to condemn even the writing of a particular poem with a view to a particular moral or practical effect; certainly, at least, if this was his meaning he was condemning some of his own poetry. Nor, thirdly, can he be referring to the portrayal of moral ideals; for that he regarded as one of the main functions of poetry, and in the very place where he says that didactic poetry is his abhorrence he also says, by way of contrast, that he has tried to familiarise the minds of his readers with beautiful idealisms of moral excellence. It appears, therefore, that what he is really attacking is the attempt to give, in the strict sense, moral *instruction*, to communicate doctrines, to offer argumentative statements of opinion on right and wrong, and more especially, I think, on controversial questions of the day. An example would be Wordsworth's discourse on education at the end of the *Excursion*, a discourse of which Shelley, we know, had a very low opinion. In short, his enemy is not the purpose of producing a moral effect, it is the appeal made for this purpose to the reasoning intellect. He says to the poet: By all means aim at bettering men; you are a man, and are bound to do so; but you are also a poet, and therefore your proper way of doing so is not by reasoning and preaching. His idea is of a piece with his general championship of imagination, and it is quite consistent with his main view of poetry.[5]

What, then, are the *grounds* of this position? They are not clearly set out, but we can trace several, and they are all solid. Reasoning on moral subjects, moral philosophy, was by no means 'tedious' to Shelley; it seldom is to real poets. He loved it, and (outside his *Defence*) he rated its value very high.[6] But he thought it tedious and out of place in poetry, because it can be equally well expressed in 'unmeasured' language—much better expressed, one may venture to add. You invent an art in order to effect by it a particular purpose which nothing else can effect as well. How foolish, then, to use this art for a purpose better served by something else! I know no answer to this argument, and its application is far wider than that given to it by Shelley. Secondly, Shelley remarks that a poet's own conceptions on moral subjects are usually those of his place and time, while the matter of his poem ought to be eternal, or, as we say, of permanent and universal interest. This, again, seems true, and has a wide application; and it holds good even when the poet, like Shelley himself, is in rebellion against orthodox moral opinion; for his heterodox opinions will equally show the marks of his place and time, and constitute a perishable element in his work. Doubtless no poetry can be without a perishable element; but that poetry has least of it which interprets life least through the medium of systematic and doctrinal ideas. The veil which time and place have hung between Homer or Shakespeare and the general reader of to-day is almost transparent, while even a poetry so intense as that of Dante and Milton is impeded in its passage to him by systems which may be unfamiliar, and, if familiar, may be distasteful.

Lastly—and this is Shelley's central argument—as poetry itself is directly due to imaginative inspiration and not to reasoning, so its true moral effect is produced through imagination and not through doctrine. Imagination is, for Shelley, 'the great instrument of moral good.' The 'secret of morals is love.' It is not 'for want of admirable doctrines that men hate and despise and censure and deceive and subjugate one another': it is for want of love. And love is 'a going out of our own nature, and an identification of ourselves with the beautiful which exists in thought, action or person not our own.' 'A man,' therefore, 'to be greatly good must imagine intensely and comprehensively.' And poetry ministers to moral good, the effect, by acting on its cause, imagination. It strengthens imagination as exercise strengthens a limb, and so it indirectly promotes morality. It also fills the imagination with beautiful impersonations of all that we should wish to be. But moral reasoning does not act upon the cause, it only analyses the effect; and the poet has no right to be content to analyse what he ought indirectly to create. Here, again, in his eagerness, Shelley cuts his antitheses too clean, but the defect is easily made good, and the main argument is sound.

Limits of time will compel me to be guilty of the same fault in adding a consideration which is in the spirit of Shelley's. The chief moral effect claimed for poetry by Shelley is exerted, primarily, by imagination on the emotions; but there is another influence, exerted primarily through imagination on the understanding. Poetry is largely an interpretation of life; and, considering what life is, that must mean a moral interpretation. This, to have poetic value, must satisfy imagination; but we value it also because it gives us knowledge, a wider comprehension, a new insight into ourselves and the world.[7] Now, it may be held—and this view answers to a very general feeling among lovers of poetry now—that the most deep and original moral interpretation is not likely to be that which most shows a moral purpose or is most governed by reflective beliefs and opinions, and that as a rule we learn most from those who do not try to teach us, and whose opinions may even remain unknown to us: so that there is this weighty objection to the appearance of such purpose and opinions, that it tends to defeat its own intention. And the reason that I wish to suggest is this, that always we get most from the *genius* in a man of genius and not from the rest of him. Now, although poets often have unusual powers of reflective thought, the specific genius of a poet does not lie there, but in imagination. Therefore his deepest and most original interpretation is likely to come by the way of imagination. And the specific way of imagination is not to clothe in imagery consciously held ideas; it is to produce half-consciously a matter from which, when produced, the reader may, if he chooses, extract ideas. Poetry (I must exaggerate to be clear), psychologically considered, is not the *expression* of ideas or of a view of life; it is their discovery or creation, or rather both discovery and creation in one. The interpretation contained in *Hamlet* or *King Lear* was not brought ready-made to the old stories. What was brought to them was the huge substance of Shakespeare's imagination, in which all his experience and thought was latent; and this, dwelling and working on the stories with nothing but a dramatic purpose, and kindling into heat and motion, gradually discovered or created in them a meaning and a mass of truth about life, which was brought to birth by the process of composition, but never preceded it in the shape of ideas, and probably never, even after it, took that shape to the poet's mind. And *this* is the interpretation which we find inexhaustibly instructive, because Shakespeare's *genius* is in it. On the other hand, however much from curiosity and personal feeling towards him we may wish to know his opinions and beliefs about morals or religion or his own poems or Queen Elizabeth, we have not really any reason to suppose that their value would prove extraordinary. And so, to apply this generally, the opinions, reasonings and beliefs of poets are seldom of the same quality as their purely imaginative product. Occasionally, as with Goethe, they are not far off it; but sometimes they are intense without being profound, and more eccentric than original; and often they are very sane and sound, but not very different from those of wise men without genius. And therefore poetry is not the place for them. For we want in poetry a moral interpretation, but not the interpretation we have already. As a rule the genuine artist's quarrel with 'morality' in art is not really with morality, it is with a stereotyped or narrow morality; and when he refuses in his art to consider things from what he calls the moral point of view, his reasons are usually wrong, but his instinct is right.

Poetry itself confirms on the whole this contention, though doubtless in these last centuries a great poet's work will usually reveal more of conscious reflection than once it did. Homer and Shakespeare show no moral aim and no system of opinion. Milton was far from justifying the ways of God to men by the argumentation he put into divine and angelic lips; his truer moral insight is in the creations of his genius; for instance, in the character of Satan or the picture of the glorious humanity of Adam and Eve. Goethe himself could never have told the world what he was going to express in the First Part of *Faust*: the poem told *him*, and it is one of the world's greatest. He knew too well what he was going to express in the Second Part, and with all its wisdom and beauty it is scarcely a great poem. Wordsworth's original message was delivered, not when he was a Godwinian semi-atheist, nor when he had subsided upon orthodoxy, but when his imagination, with a few hints from Coleridge, was creating a kind of natural religion; and this religion itself is more profoundly expressed in his descriptions of his experience than in his attempts to formulate it. The moral virtue of Tennyson is in poems like *Ulysses* and parts of *In Memoriam*, where sorrow and the consciousness of a deathless affection or an unquenchable desire for experience forced an utterance; but when in the *Idylls* he tried to found a great poem on explicit ideas about the soul and the ravages wrought in it by lawless passion, he succeeded but partially, because these ideas, however sound, were no product of his genius. And so the moral virtue of Shelley's poetry lay, not in his doctrines about the past and future of man, but in an intuition, which was the substance of his soul, of the unique value of love. In the end, for him, the truest name of that perfection called Intellectual Beauty, Liberty, Spirit of Nature, is Love. Whatever in the world has any worth is an expression of Love. Love sometimes talks. Love talking musically is Poetry.

# Notes

1 Statements equally emphatic on this subject may be found in a passage quoted by Mrs. Shelley in a footnote to Shelley's letter to John Gisborne, Nov. 16, 1819 (Letter XXX, in Mrs. Shelley's edition). Cf. also Letter XXXIII, to Leigh Hunt, Nov. 1819.

2 I cannot find the passage or passages to which I referred in making this statement, and therefore I do not vouch for its accuracy. Cf. from the fragment *Fiordispina*,

> The ardours of a vision which obscure
> The very idol of its portraiture.

3 Cf. from the Preface to the *Cenci*: 'I entirely agree with those modern critics who assert that, in order to move men to true sympathy, we must use the familiar language of men. . . . But it must be the real language of men in general, and not that of any particular class to whose society the writer happens to belong.'

4 Preface to *Prometheus Unbound*.

5 I do not discuss the adequacy of Shelley's position, or assert that he held it quite clearly or consistently. In support of my interpretation of it I may refer to the Preface to the *Cenci*. There he repudiates the idea of making the dramatic exhibition of the story 'subservient to what is vulgarly called a moral purpose,' and, as the context shows, he identifies such a treatment of the story with the 'enforcement' of a 'dogma.'

This passage has a further interest. The dogma which Shelley would not enforce in his tragedy was that 'no person can truly be dishonoured by the act of another, and the fit return to make to the most enormous injuries is kindness and forbearance, and a resolution to convert the injurer from his dark passions by peace and love'; and accordingly he held that 'if Beatrice had thought in this manner she would have been wiser and better.' How inexcusable then is the not uncommon criticism on the *Cenci* that he represents Beatrice as a perfect character and justifies her murder of 'the injurer.'

Shelley's position in the *Defence*, it may be added, is in total disagreement with his youthful doctrine and practice. In 1811 he wrote to Miss Hitchener, 'My opinion is that all poetical beauty ought to be subordinate to the inculcated moral,' and a large part of *Queen Mab* is frankly didactic. Even there, however, he reserved most of the formal instruction for the Notes, perceiving that 'a poem very didactic is . . . very stupid.'

6 'I consider poetry very subordinate to moral and political science,' he says in a letter to Peacock, Jan. 1819.

7 And, I may add, the more it does this, so long as it does it imaginatively, the more does it satisfy imagination, and the greater is its *poetic* value.

# 2

# ON THE DISCRIMINATION
# OF ROMANTICISMS[1]

## *Arthur O. Lovejoy*

Source: *PMLA* 39 (1924), 229–53.

## I

We approach a centenary not, perhaps, wholly undeserving of notice on the part of this learned company. It was apparently in 1824 that those respected citizens of La-Ferté-sous-Jouarre, MM. Dupuis and Cotonet, began an enterprise which was to cause them, as is recorded, "twelve years of suffering," and to end in disillusionment—the enterprise of discovering what Romanticism is, by collecting definitions and characterizations of it given by eminent authorities. I conjecture, therefore, that one of the purposes of the Committee in inviting me to speak on this subject was perhaps to promote a Dupuis and Cotonet Centennial Exhibition, in which the later varieties of definitions of Romanticism, the fruit of a hundred years' industry on the part of literary critics and professors of modern literature, might be at least in part displayed. Certainly there is no lack of material; the contemporary collector of such articles, while paying tribute to the assiduity and the sufferings of those worthy pioneers of a century ago, will chiefly feel an envious sense of the relative simplicity of their task. He will find, also, that the apparent incongruity of the senses in which the term is employed has fairly kept pace with their increase in number; and that the singular potency which the subject has from the first possessed to excite controversy and breed divisions has in no degree diminished with the lapse of years.

For if some Dupuis of to-day were to gather, first, merely a few of the more recent accounts of the origin and age of Romanticism, he would learn from M. Lasserre[2] and many others that Rousseau was the father of it; from Mr. Russell[3] and Mr. Santayana[4] that the honor of paternity might plausibly be claimed by Immanuel Kant; from M. Seillière that its grandparents were Fénelon and Madame Guyon;[5] from Professor Babbitt that its earliest well-identified forebear was Francis Bacon;[6] from Mr. Gosse that it originated in the bosom of the Reverend Joseph Warton;[7] from the late Professor Ker that it had "its beginnings in the seventeenth-century" or a little earlier, in such books as "the *Arcadia* or the *Grand Cyrus*"[8]; from Mr. J. E. G. de Montmorency that it "was born in the eleventh century, and sprang from that sense of aspiration which runs through the Anglo-French, or rather, the Anglo-Norman Renaissance"[9]; from Professor Grierson that St. Paul's "irruption into Greek religious thought and Greek prose" was an essential example of "a romantic movement," though the "first great romantic" was Plato;[10] and from Mr. Charles Whibley that the Odyssey is romantic in its "very texture and essence," but that, with its rival, Romanticism was "born in the Garden of Eden" and that "the Serpent was the first romantic."[11] The inquirer would, at the same time, find that many of these originators of Romanticism—including both the first and last mentioned, whom, indeed, some contemporaries are unable to distinguish—figure on other lists as initiators or representatives of tendencies of precisely the contrary sort.

These differing versions of the age and lineage of Romanticism are matched by a corresponding diversity in the descriptions offered by those of our time who have given special care to the observation of it. For Professor Ker Romanticism was "the fairy way of writing,"[12] and for Mr. Gosse it is inconsistent with "keeping to the facts";[13] but for Mr. F. Y. Eccles[14] (following M. Pellissier) "the romantic system of ideas" is the direct source of "the realistic error," of the tendency to conceive of psychology as "the dry notation of purely physiological phenomena" and consequently to reduce the novel and the drama to the description of "the automaton-like gestures of *la bête humaine*." To Professor Ker, again, "romantic" implied "reminiscence": "the romantic schools have always depended more or less on the past."[15] Similarly Mr. Geoffrey Scott finds "its most typical form" to be "the cult of the extinct."[16] But Professor Schelling tells us that "the classic temper studies the past, the romantic temper neglects it; . . . it leads us forward and creates new precedents."[17] Mr. Paul More defines Romanticism as "the illusion of beholding the infinite within the stream of nature itself, instead of apart from that stream"—in short, as an apotheosis of the cosmic flux;[18] but a special student of German Romanticism cites as typical Romantic utterances Friedrich Schlegel's "alles Sichtbare hat nur die Wahrheit einer Allegorie," and Goethe's "alles Vergängliche ist nur ein Gleichnis."[19] From M. Seillière's most celebrated work it appears that the Romantic mind tends to be affected with an inferiority-complex, "une impression d'incomplétude, de solitude morale, et presque d'angoisse";[20] from other passages of the same writer we learn that Romanticism is the "imperialistic" mood, whether in individuals or nations—a too confident assertion of the will-to-power, arising from "the mystic feeling that one's activities have the advantages of a celestial alliance."[21] The function of the human mind which is to be regarded as peculiarly "romantic" is for some "the heart as opposed to the head,"[22] for others, "the Imagination, as contrasted with Reason and the Sense of Fact"[23]—which I take to be ways of expressing a by no means synonymous pair of psychological antitheses. Typical manifestations of the spiritual essence of Romanticism have been variously conceived to be a passion for moonlight, for red waistcoats, for Gothic churches, for futurist paintings;[24] for talking exclusively about oneself, for hero-worship, for losing oneself in an ecstatic contemplation of nature.

The offspring with which Romanticism is credited are as strangely assorted as its attributes and its ancestors. It is by different historians—sometimes by the same historians—supposed to have begotten the French Revolution and the Oxford Movement; the Return to Rome and the Return to the State of Nature; the philosophy of Hegel, the philosophy of Schopenhauer, and the philosophy of Nietzsche—than which few other three philosophies more nearly exhaust the rich possibilities of philosophic disagreement; the revival of neo-Platonic mysticism in a Coleridge or an Alcott, the Emersonian transcendentalism, and scientific materialism; Wordsworth and Wilde; Newman and Huxley; the Waverley novels, the *Comédie Humaine*, and Les Rougon-Macquart. M. Seillière and Professor Babbitt have been especially active in tracing the progeny of Romanticism in the past century; the extraordinary number and still more extraordinary diversity of the descendants of it discovered by their researches are known to all here, and it therefore suffices to refer to their works for further examples.

All this is a mere hint, a suggestion by means of random samples, of the richness of the collection which might be brought together for our Centennial Exposition. The result is a confusion of terms, and of ideas, beside which that of a hundred years ago—mind-shaking though it was to the honest inquirers of La-Ferté-sous-Jouarre—seems pure lucidity. The word "romantic" has come to mean so many things that, by itself, it means nothing. It has ceased to perform the function of a verbal sign. When a man is asked, as I have had the honor of being asked, to discuss Romanticism, it is impossible to know what ideas or tendencies he is to talk about, when they are supposed to have flourished, or in whom they are supposed to be chiefly exemplified. Perhaps there are some who think the rich ambiguity of the word not regrettable. In 1824, as Victor Hugo then testified, there were those who preferred to leave *à ce mot de romantique un certain vague fantastique et indéfinissable qui en redouble l'horreur*; and it may be that the taste is not extinct. But for one of the philosopher's trade, at least, the situation is embarrassing and exasperating; for philosophers, in spite of a popular belief to the contrary, are persons who suffer from a morbid solicitude to know precisely what they are talking about.

Least of all does it seem possible, while the present uncertainty concerning the nature and *locus* of Romanticism prevails, to take sides in the controversy which still goes on so briskly with respect to its merits, the character of its general influence upon art and life. To do so would be too much like consenting to sit on a jury to try a criminal not yet identified, for a series of apparently incompatible crimes, before a bench of learned judges engaged in accusing one another of being accessories to whatever mischief has been done. It is to be observed, for example, that Messrs. Lasserre, Seillière, Babbitt and More (to mention no others) are agreed in holding that something called Romanticism is the chief cause of the spiritual evils from which the nineteenth century and our own have suffered; but that they represent at least three different opinions as to what these evils are and how they are to be remedied. M. Lasserre, identifying Romanticism with the essential spirit of the French Revolution, finds the chief cause of our woes in that movement's breach with the past, in its discarding of the ancient traditions of European civilization; and he consequently seeks the cure in a return to an older faith and an older political and social order, and in an abandonment of the optimistic fatalism generated by the idea of progress. M. Seillière, however, holds that "the spirit of the Revolution in that in which it is rational, Stoic, Cartesian, classical . . . is justified, enduring, assured of making its way in the world more and more";[25] and that, consequently, the ill name of Romanticism should be applied to the revolutionary movement only where it has deviated from its true course, in "the social mysticism, the communistic socialism of the present time." He therefore intimates that the school of opinion which M. Lasserre ably represents is itself a variety of Romanticism.[26] But it is equally certain that M. Seillière's own philosophy is one of the varieties of Romanticism defined by Mr. Babbitt and Mr. More; while Mr. Babbitt, in turn, has been declared by more than one of the critics of his last brilliant book, and would necessarily be held by M. Seillière, to set forth therein an essentially Romantic philosophy. Thus Professor Herford days of it (justly or otherwise) that its "temper is not that of a 'positivist' of any school, but of a mystic," and that "it is as foreign to Homer and Sophocles, the exemplars of true classicism if any are, as it is to Aristotle."[27]

What, then, can be done to clear up, or to diminish, this confusion of terminology and of thought which has for a century been the scandal of literary history and criticism, and is still, as it would not be difficult to show, copiously productive of historical errors and of dangerously undiscriminating diagnoses of the moral and aesthetic maladies of our age? The one really radical remedy—namely, that we should all cease talking about Romanticism—is, I fear, certain not to be adopted. It would probably be equally futile to attempt to prevail upon scholars and critics to restrict their use of the term to a single and reasonably well-defined sense. Such a proposal would only be the starting-point of a new controversy. Men, and especially philologists, will doubtless go on using words as they like, however much annoyance they may cause philosophers by this unchartered freedom. There are, however, two possible historical inquiries which, if carried out more thoroughly and carefully than has yet been done, would, I think, do much to rectify the present muddle, and would at the same time promote a clearer understanding

39

of the general movement of ideas, the logical and psychological relations between the chief episodes and transitions, in modern thought and taste.

One of these measures would be somewhat analogous to the procedure of contemporary psychopathologists in the treatment of certain types of disorder. It has been found that some mental disturbances can be cured or alleviated by making the patient explicitly aware of the genesis of his troublesome "complex," i.e., by enabling him to reconstruct those processes of association of ideas through which it was formed. The result of such analysis is sometimes a disassociation of a very benign sort. Similarly in the present case, I think, it would be useful to trace the associative processes through which the word "romantic" has attained its present amazing diversity, and consequent uncertainty, of connotation and denotation; in other words, to carry out an adequate semasiological study of the term. For one of the few things certain about Romanticism is that the name of it offers one of the most complicated, fascinating, and instructive of all problems in semantics. It is, in short, a part of the task of the historian of ideas, when he applies himself to the study of the thing or things called Romanticism, to render it, if possible, psychologically intelligible how such manifold and discrepant phenomena have all come to receive one name. Such an analysis would, I am convinced, show us a large mass of purely verbal confusions operative as actual factors in the movement of thought in the past century and a quarter; and it would, by making these confusions explicit, make it easier to avoid them.

But this inquiry would in practice, for the most part, be inseparable from a second, which is the remedy that I wish, on this occasion, especially to recommend. The first step in this second mode of treatment of the disorder is that we should learn to use the word "Romanticism" in the plural. This, of course, is already the practise of the more cautious and observant literary historians, in so far as they recognize that the "Romanticism" of one country may have little in common with that of another, and at all events ought to be defined in distinctive terms. But the discrimination of the Romanticisms which I have in mind is not solely or chiefly a division upon lines of nationality or language. What is needed is that any study of the subject should begin with a recognition of a *prima facie* plurality of Romanticisms, of possibly quite distinct thought-complexes, a number of which may appear in one country. There is no hope of clear thinking on the part of the student of modern literature, if—as, alas! has been repeatedly done by eminent writers —he vaguely hypostatizes the term, and starts with the presumption that "Romanticism" is the heaven-appointed designation of some single real entity, or type of entities, to be found in nature. He must set out from the simple and obvious fact that there are various historic episodes or movements to which different historians of our own or other periods have, for one reason or another, given the name. There is a movement which began in Germany in the seventeen-nineties—the only one which has an indisputable title to be called Romanticism, since it invented the term for its own use. There is another movement which began pretty definitely in England in the seventeen-forties. There is a movement which began in France in 1801. There is another movement which began in France in the second decade of the century, is linked with the German movement, and took over the German name. There is the rich and incongruous collection of ideas to be found in Rousseau. There are numerous other things called Romanticism by various writers whom I cited at the outset. The fact that the same name has been given by different scholars to all of these episodes is no evidence, and scarcely even establishes a presumption, that they are identical in essentials. There may be some least common denominator of them all; but if so, it has never yet been clearly exhibited, and its presence is not to be assumed *a priori*. In any case, each of these so-called Romanticisms was a highly complex and usually an exceedingly unstable intellectual compound; each, in other words, was made up of various unit-ideas linked together, for the most part, not by any indissoluble bonds of logical necessity, but by alogical associative processes, greatly facilitated and partly caused, in the case of the Romanticisms which grew up after the appellation "Romantic" was invented, by the congenital and acquired ambiguities of the word. And when certain of these Romanticisms have in truth significant elements in common, they are not necessarily the same elements in any two cases. Romanticism A may have one characteristic presupposition or impulse, X, which it shares with Romanticism B, another characteristic, Y, which it shares with Romanticism C, to which X is wholly foreign. In the case, moreover, of those movements or schools to which the label was applied in their own time, the contents under the label sometimes changed radically and rapidly. At the end of a decade or two you had the same men and the same party appellation, but profoundly different ideas. As everyone knows, this is precisely what happened in the case of what is called French Romanticism. It may or may not be true that, as M. A. Viatte has recently sought to show,[28] at the beginning of this process of transformation some subtle leaven was already at work which made the final outcome inevitable; the fact remains that in most of its practically significant sympathies and affiliations of a literary, ethical, political, and religious sort, the French "Romanticism" of the eighteen-thirties was the antithesis of that of the beginning of the century.

But the essential of the second remedy is that each of these Romanticisms —after they are first thus roughly discriminated with respect to their representatives or their dates—should be resolved, by a more thorough and discerning analysis than is yet customary, into its elements—into the several ideas and aesthetic susceptibilities of which it is composed. Only after these fundamental thought-factors in it are clearly discriminated and fairly exhaustively enumerated, shall we be in a position to judge of the degree of its affinity with other complexes to which the same name has been applied, to see precisely what tacit preconceptions or controlling motives or explicit contentions were common to any two or more of them, and wherein they manifested distinct and divergent tendencies.

## II

Of the needfulness of such analytic comparison and discrimination of the Romanticisms let me attempt three illustrations.

1. In an interesting lecture before the British Academy a few years since, Mr. Gosse described Joseph Warton's youthful poem, *The Enthusiast*, written in 1740, as the first clear manifestation of "the great romantic movement, such as it has enlarged and dwindled down to our day . . . Here for the first time we find unwaveringly emphasized and repeated what was entirely new in literature, the essence of romantic hysteria. *The Enthusiast* is the earliest expression of complete revolt against the classical attitude which had been sovereign in all European literature for nearly a century. So completely is this expressed by Joseph Warton that it is extremely difficult to realize that he could not have come under the fascination of Rousseau, . . . who was not to write anything characteristic until ten years later."[29] Let us, then, compare the ideas distinctive of this poem with the conception of *romantische Poesie* formulated by Friedrich Schlegel and his fellow-Romanticists in Germany after 1796. The two have plainly certain common elements. Both are forms of revolt against the neo-classical aesthetics; both are partly inspired by an ardent admiration for Shakespeare; both proclaim the creative artist's independence of "rules." It might at first appear, therefore, that these two Romanticisms, in spite of natural differences of phraseology, are identical in essence—are separate outcroppings of the same vein of metal, precious or base, according to your taste.

But a more careful scrutiny shows a contrast between them not less important—indeed, as it seems to me, more important—than their resemblance. The general theme of Joseph Warton's poem (of which, it will be remembered, the sub-title is "The Lover of Nature") is one which had been a commonplace for two centuries: the superiority of "nature" to "art." It is a theme which goes back to Rabelais's contrast of Physis and Antiphysie. It had been the inspiration of some of the most famous passages of Montaigne. Pope's *Essay on Man* had been full of it. The "natural" in contrast with the artificial meant, first of all, that which is not man-made; and within man's life, it was supposed to consist in those expressions of human nature which are most spontaneous, unpremeditated, untouched by reflection or design, and free from the bondage of social convention. "Ce n'est pas raison," cried Montaigne, "que l'art gagne le point d'honneur sur notre grande et puissante mère Nature. Nous avons tant rechargé la beauté et richesse de ses ouvrages par nos inventions, que nous l'avons tout à fait étouffée." There follows the *locus classicus* of primitivism in modern literature, the famous passage on the superiority of wild fruits and savage men over those that have been "bastardized" by art.[30]

Warton, then, presents this ancient theme in various aspects. He prefers to all the beauties of the gardens of Versailles

> Some pine-topt precipice
> Abrupt and shaggy;

he rhetorically inquires:

> Can Kent design like Nature?

He laments

> That luxury and pomp . . .
> Should proudly banish Nature's simple charms.

He inquires why "mistaken man" should deem it nobler

> To dwell in palaces and high-roof'd halls
> Than in God's forests, architect supreme.

All this, if I may be permitted the expression, was old stuff. The principal thing that was original and significant in the poem was that Warton boldly applied the doctrine of the superiority of "nature" over conscious art to the theory of poetry:

> What are the lays of artful Addison,
> Coldly correct, to Shakespeare's warblings wild?

That Nature herself was wild, untamed, was notorious, almost tautological; and it was Shakespeare's supposed "wildness," his non-conformity to the conventional rules, the spontaneous freedom of his imagination and his expression, that proved him Nature's true pupil.

Now this aesthetic inference had not, during the neo-classical period, ordinarily been drawn from the current assumption of the superiority of nature to art. The principle of "following nature" had in aesthetics usually been taken in another, or in more than one other, of the several dozen senses of the sacred word.[31] Yet in other provinces of thought an analogous inference had long since and repeatedly been suggested. From the first the fashion of conceiving of "nature" (in the sense in which it was antithetic to "art") as norm had made for antinomianism, in some degree or other— for a depreciation of restraint, for the ideal of "letting yourself go." There seems to be an idea current that an antinomian temper was, at some time in

the eighteenth century, introduced into aesthetic theory and artistic practise by some Romanticist, and that it thence speedily spread to moral
feeling and social conduct.[32] The historic sequence is precisely the opposite.
It was Montaigne again—not usually classified as a Romanticist—who
wrote:

> J'ai pris bien simplement et crûment ce précepte ancien: "que nous
> ne saurions faillir à suivre Nature" ... Je n'ai pas corrigé, comme
> Socrate, par la force de la raison, mes complexions naturelles, je
> n'ai aucunement troublé, par art, mon inclination; je me laisse aller
> comme je suis venu; je ne combats rien.[33]

It was Pope who asked:

> Can that offend great Nature's God
> Which Nature's self inspires?

and who spoke of

> Wild Nature's vigor working at the root

as the source of the passions in which all the original and vital energies of
men are contained.

Aside from a certain heightening of the emotional tone, then, the chief
novelty of Warton's poem lay in its suggesting the application of these ideas
to a field from which they had been curiously and inconsistently excluded,
in its introduction of antinomianism, of a rather mild sort, into the conception of poetic excellence.[34] But this extension was obviously implicit from
the outset in the logic of that protean "naturalism" which had been the most
characteristic and potent force in modern thought since the late Renaissance; it was bound to be made by somebody sooner or later. Nor was
Warton's the first aesthetic application of the principle; it had already been
applied to an art in the theory and practice of which eighteenth-century
Englishmen were keenly interested—the art of landscape design. The first
great revolt against the neo-classical aesthetics was not in literature at all,
but in gardening; the second, I think, was in architectural taste; and all three
were inspired by the same ideas. Since, the "artful Addison" had observed,
"artificial works receive a greater advantage from their resemblance of
such as are natural," and since Nature is distinguished by her "rough, careless strokes," the layer-out of gardens should aim at "an artificial rudeness
much more charming than that neatness and elegancy usually met with."[35]
This horticultural Romanticism had been preached likewise by Sir William
Temple, Pope, Horace Walpole, Batty Langley, and others, and ostensibly
exemplified in the work of Kent, Brown, and Bridgeman. Warton in the

poem in question describes Kent as at least doing his best to imitate in his gardens the wildness of Nature:

> He, by rules unfettered, boldly scorns
> Formality and method; round and square
> Disdaining, plans irregularly great.

It was no far cry from this to the rejection of the rules in the drama, to a revulsion against the strait-laced regularity and symmetry of the heroic couplet, to a general turning from convention, formality, method, artifice, in all the arts.

There had, however, from the first been a curious duality of meaning in the antithesis of "nature" and "art"—one of the most pregnant of the long succession of confusions of ideas which make up much of the history of human thought. While the "natural" was, on the one hand, conceived as the wild and spontaneous and "irregular," it was also conceived as the simple, the naïf, the unsophisticated. No two words were more fixedly associated in the mind of the sixteenth, seventeenth and early eighteenth centuries than "Nature" and "simple." Consequently the idea of preferring nature to custom and to art usually carried with it the suggestion of a program of simplification, of reform by elimination; in other words, it implied primitivism. The "natural" was a thing you reached by going back and by leaving out. And this association of ideas—already obvious in Montaigne, in Pope, and scores of other extollers of "Nature"—is still conspicuous in Warton's poem. It was the "bards of old" who were "fair Nature's friends." The poet envies

> The first of men, ere yet confined
> In smoky cities.

He yearns to dwell in some

> Isles of innocence from mortal view
> Deeply retired beneath a plantane's shade,
> Where Happiness and Quiet sit enthroned,
> With simple Indian swains.

For one term of the comparison, then, I limit myself, for brevity's sake, to this poem to which Mr. Gosse has assigned so important a place in literary history. There were, of course, even in the writings of the elder Warton, and still more in other phenomena frequently called "Romantic," between the 1740s and the 1790s, further elements which cannot be considered here. There is observable, for example, in what it has become the fashion to classify as the early phases of English Romanticism, the emergence of what may be called gothicism, and the curious fact of its partial and temporary fusion with naturalism. It is one of the interesting problems of the analytic history of ideas to see just how and why naturalism and gothicism became allied in the eighteenth century in England, though little, if at all, in France. But for the present purpose it suffices to take *The Enthusiast* as typical, in one especially important way, of a great deal of the so-called Romanticism before the seventeen-nineties—a Romanticism, namely, which, whatever further characteristics it may have had, was based upon naturalism (in the sense of the word which I have indicated) and was associated with primitivism of some mode or degree.

2. For in this fundamental point this earlier "Romanticism" differed essentially from that of the German aesthetic theorists and poets who chose the term "Romantic poetry" as the most suitable designation for their own literary ideals and program. The latter "Romanticism" is in its very essence a denial of the older naturalistic presuppositions, which Warton's poem had manifested in a special and somewhat novel way. The German movement received its immediate and decisive impetus from Schiller's essay *On Naïve and Sentimental Poetry*; and what it derived from that confused work was the conviction that "harmony with nature," in any sense which implied an opposition to "culture," to "art," to reflection and self-conscious effort, was neither possible nor desirable for the modern man or the modern artist.[36] The *Frühromantiker* learned from Schiller the idea of an art which should look back no more to the primitive than to the classical—the notions of which, incidentally, Schiller had curiously fused—for its models and ideals; which should be the appropriate expression, not of a *natürliche* but of a *künstliche Bildung*; which, so far from desiring simplification, so far from aiming at the sort of harmony in art and life which is to be attained by the method of leaving out, should seek first fullness of content, should have for its program the adequate expression of the entire range of human experience and the entire reach of the human imagination. For man, the artificial, Friedrich Schlegel observed, *is* "natural." "Die Abstraktion ist ein künstlicher Zustand. Dies ist kein Grund gegen sie, denn es ist dem Menschen gewiss natürlich, sich dann und wann auch in künstliche Zustände zu versetzen." And again: "Eine nur im Gegensatz der Kunst und Bildung natürliche Denkart soll es gar nicht geben." To be unsophisticated, to revert to the mental state of "simple Indian swains," was the least of the ambitions of a German Romantic—though, since the unsophisticated is one type of human character, his art was not, at least in theory, indifferent even to that. The Shakespeare whom he admired was no gifted child of nature addicted to "warblings wild." Shakespeare, said A. W. Schlegel, is not "ein blindes wildlaufendes Genie;" he had "a system in his artistic practise and an astonishingly profound and deeply meditated one." The same critic seems to be consciously attacking either Joseph Warton's or Gray's famous lines about Shakespeare when he writes: "Those poets whom it is customary to represent as carefree nurslings of nature, without art and without schooling,

if they produce works of genuine excellence, give evidence of exceptional cultivation (*Kultur*) of their mental powers, of practised art, of ripely pondered and just designs." The greatness of Shakespeare, in the eyes of *these* Romantics, lay in his *Universalität*, his sophisticated insight into human nature and the many-sidedness of his portrayal of character; it was this, as Friedrich Schlegel said, that made him "wie der Mittelpunkt der romantischen Kunst." It may be added that another trait of the Romanticism found by Mr. Gosse in Joseph Warton, namely, the feeling that didactic poetry is not poetic, was also repudiated by early German Romanticism: "How," asked F. Schlegel again, "can it be said that ethics (*die Moral*) belongs merely to philosophy, when the greatest part of poetry relates to the art of living and to the knowledge of human nature?"[37]

The difference, then, I suggest, is more significant, more pregnant, than the likeness between these two Romanticisms. Between the assertion of the superiority of "nature" over conscious "art" and that of the superiority of conscious art over mere "nature"; between a way of thinking of which primitivism is of the essence and one of which the idea of perpetual self-transcendence is of the essence; between a fundamental preference for simplicity—even though a "wild" simplicity—and a fundamental preference for diversity and complexity; between the sort of ingenuous naïveté characteristic of *The Enthusiast* and the sophisticated subtlety of the conception of romantic irony: between these the antithesis is one of the most radical that modern thought and taste have to show. I don't deny anyone's right to call both these things Romanticism, if he likes; but I cannot but observe that the fashion of giving both the same name has led to a good deal of unconscious falsification of the history of ideas. The elements of the one Romanticism tend to be read into the other; the nature and profundity of the oppositions between them tend to be overlooked; and the relative importance of the different changes of preconceptions in modern thought, and of susceptibilities in modern taste, tends to be wrongly estimated. I shall not attempt to cite here what seem to me examples of such historical errors; but the sum of them is, I think, far from negligible.

Between the "Romanticism" which is but a special and belated manifestation of the naturalism that dates from the Renaissance, and the "Romanticism" which began at the end of the eighteenth century in Germany (as well as that which appeared a little later in France) there is another difference not less significant. This is due to the identification of the meaning of "Romantic" in the later movement with "Christian"—and mainly with the medieval implications of the latter term. This was not the central idea in the original notion of "Romantic poetry" as conceived by Friedrich Schlegel. Primarily, as I have elsewhere tried to show,[38] the adjective meant for him and the entire school "das eigentümlich Moderne" in contrast with "das eigentümlich Antike." But it early occurred to him that the historic cause of the supposed radical differentiation of modern from classical art could lie only in the influence of Christianity. He wrote in 1796, before his own conversion to what he had already defined as the "romantic," *i.e.*, modern, point of view:

> So lächerlich und geschmacklos sich dieses Trachten nach dem Reich Gottes in der christlichen Poesie offenbaren möchte; so wird es dem Geschichtsforscher doch eine sehr merkwürdige Erscheinung, wenn er gewahr wird, dass eben dieses Streben, das absolut Vollkommne und Unendliche zu realisiren, eine unter dem unaufhörlichen Wechsel der Zeiten und bei der grössten Verschiedenheit der Völker bleibende Eigenschaft dessen ist, was man mit dem besten Rechte modern nennen darf.[39]

When, after reading Schiller's essay, Schlegel himself became a devotee of those aesthetic ideals which he had previously denounced, he wrote (1797):

> Nachdem die vollendete natürliche Bildung der Alten entschieden gesunken, und ohne Rettung ausgeartet war, ward durch den Verlust der endlichen Realität und die Zerrüttung vollendeter Form ein Streben nach unendlicher Realität veranlasst, welches bald allgemeiner Ton des Zeitalters wurde.[40]

"Romantic" art thus came to mean—for one thing—an art inspired by or expressive of some idea or some ethical temper supposed to be essential in Christianity. "Ursprung und Charakter der ganzen neuern Poesie lässt sich so leicht aus dem Christentume ableiten, dass man die romantische eben so gut die christliche nennen könnte,"[41] said Richter in 1804, repeating what had by that time become a commonplace. But the nature of the essentially Christian, and therefore essentially Romantic, spirit was variously conceived. Upon one characteristic of it there was, indeed, rather general agreement among the German Romanticists: the habit of mind introduced by Christianity was distinguished by a certain insatiability; it aimed at infinite objectives and was incapable of lasting satisfaction with any goods actually reached. It became a favorite platitude to say that the Greeks and Romans set themselves limited ends to attain, were able to attain them, and were thus capable of self-satisfaction and finality; and that modern or "romantic" art differed from this most fundamentally, by reason of its Christian origin, in being, as Schiller had said, a *Kunst des Unendlichen*. "Absolute Abstraktion, Vernichtung des Jetzigen, Apotheose der Zukunft, dieser eigentlich bessern Welt!; dies ist der Kern der Geheisse des Christentums," declared Novalis. In its application to artistic practise this "apotheosis of the future" meant the ideal of endless progress, of "eine progressive Universalpoesie" in the words of Fr. Schlegel's familiar definition; it implied the demand that art shall always go on bringing new provinces of life within its domain and achieving ever fresh and original effects. But anything which was, or was supposed to be, especially characteristic of the Christian *Weltanschauung* tended to become a part of the current connotation of "Romantic", and also a part of the actual ideals of the school. Preoccupation with super-sensible realities and a feeling of the illusoriness of ordinary existence was thus often held to be a distinctive trait of Romantic art, on the ground that Christianity is an otherworldly religion: "in der christlichen Ansicht," said A. W. Schlegel, "die Anschauung des Unendlichen hat das Endliche vernichtet; das Leben ist zur Schattenwelt und zur Nacht geworden."[42] Another recognized characteristic of Christianity, and therefore of the "Romantic," was ethical dualism, a conviction that there are in man's constitution two natures ceaselessly at war. The Greek ideal, in the elder Schlegel's words, was "volkommene Eintracht und Ebenmass aller Kräfte, natürliche Harmonie. Die Neueren hingegen sind zum Bewusstsein der inneren Entzweiung gekommen, welche ein solches Ideal unmöglich macht."[43] Directly related to this, it was perceived, was the "inwardness" of Christianity, its pre-occupation with "the heart" as distinguished from the outward act, its tendency to introspection; and hence, as Mme de Stael and others observed, "modern" or "Romantic" art has discovered, and has for its peculiar province, the inexhaustible realm of the inner life of man:

> Les anciens avaient, pour ainsi dire, une âme corporelle, dont tous les mouvements étaient forts, directs, et conséquents; il n'en est pas de même du cœur humain développé par le christianisme: les modernes ont puisé dans le repentir chrétien l'habitude de se replier continuellement sur eux-mêmes. Mais, pour manifester cette exist-ence tout intérieure, il faut qu'une grande variété dans les faits présente sous toutes les formes les nuances infinies de ce qui se passe dans l'âme.[44]

It is one of the many paradoxes of the history of the word, and of the controversies centering about it, that several eminent literary historians and critics of our time have conceived the moral essence of Romanticism as consisting in a kind of "this-worldliness" and a negation of what one of them has termed "the Christian and classical dualism." Its most deplorable and dangerous error, in the judgment of these critics, is its deficient realiza-tion of the "civil war in the cave" of man's soul, its belief in the "natural goodness" of man. They thus define "Romanticism" in terms precisely opposite to those in which it was often defined by the writers who first called their own ideals Romantic; and this fashion, I can't but think, has done a good deal to obscure the palpable and important historical fact that the one Romanticism which has thus (as I have said) an unequivocal title to the name was—among other and often incongruous things—a rediscovery and revival, for better or worse, of what these critics, at least, regard as

49

characteristically Christian modes of thought and feeling—of a mystical and otherworldly type of religion and a sense of the inner moral struggle as the distinctive fact in human experience—such as had been for a century alien to the dominant tendencies in "polite" literature. The new movement was, almost from the first, a revolt against what was conceived to be paganism in religion and ethics as definitely as against classicism in art. The earliest important formulation of its implications for religious philosophy was Schleiermacher's famous *Reden* (1799) addressed "to the cultivated contemners of religion," a work profoundly—sometimes, indeed, morbidly —dualistic in its ethical temper. Christianity, declares Schleiermacher, is *durch und durch polemisch*; it knows no truce in the warfare of the spiritual with the natural man, it finds no end in the task of inner self-disciplines.[45] And the *Reden*, it must be remembered, were (in the words of a German literary historian) "greeted by the votaries of Romanticism as a gospel."[46]

Now it is not untrue to describe the ethical tendency of the "Romanticism" which had its roots in naturalism—that is, in the assumption of the sole excellence of what in man is native, primitive, "wild," attainable without other struggle than that required for emancipation from social conventions and artificialities—as anti-dualistic and essentially non-moral. This aspect of it can be seen even in the poem of the "blameless Warton," when he describes the life of the state of nature for which he yearns. But as a consequence of the prevalent neglect to discriminate the Romanticisms, the very movement which was the beginning of a deliberate and vigorous insurrection against the naturalistic assumptions that had been potent, and usually dominant, in modern thought for more than three centuries, is actually treated as if it were a continuation of that tendency. Thesis and antithesis have, partly through accidents of language, and partly through a lack of careful observation on the part of historians of literature, been called by the same name, and consequently have frequently been assumed to be the same thing. An ideal of ceaseless striving towards goals too vast or too exacting ever to be wholly attained has been confused with a nostalgia for the untroubled, because unaspiring, indolent, and unselfconscious, life of the man of nature. Thus one of the widest and deepest-reaching lines of cleavage in modern thought has been more or less effectually concealed by a word.

3. This cleavage between naturalistic and anti-naturalistic "Romanticism" crosses national lines; and it manifestly cuts, so to say, directly through the person of one great writer commonly classed among the initiators of the Romantic movement in France. The author of the *Essai sur les révolutions* and of the earlier-written parts of *Atala* may perhaps properly be called a Romantic; the author of the later-written parts of the latter work and of the *Génie du Christianisme* may perhaps properly be called a Romantic; but it is obvious that the word has, in most important respects, not merely different but antithetic senses in these two applications of it to the same person. Chateaubriand before 1799 represented in some sort the culmination of

the naturalistic and primitivistic Romanticism of which Mr. Gosse sees the beginning in Joseph Warton;[47] he had not only felt intensely but had even gratified the yearning to live "with simple Indian swains." That the Chateaubriand of 1801 represents just as clearly a revolt against this entire tendency is sufficiently evident from the repudiation of primitivism in the first preface to *Atala*:

> Je ne suis point, comme M. Rousseau, un enthousiaste des sauvages; . . . je ne crois point que la *pure nature* soit la plus belle chose du monde. Je l'ai toujours trouvée fort laide partout où j'ai eu occasion de la voir . . . Avec ce mot de nature on a tout perdu.[48]

Thus the magic word upon which the whole scheme of ideas of the earlier writing had depended is now plainly characterized as the fruitful source of error and confusion that it was. And in his views about the drama the Chateaubriand of 1801 was opposed *both* to the movement represented by *The Enthusiast* and to the German Romanticism of his own time. Shakespeare was (though mainly, as we have seen, for differing reasons) the idol of both; but Chateaubriand in his *Essai sur la littérature anglaise*[49] writes of Shakespeare in the vein, and partly in the words, of Voltaire and Pope. In point of natural genius, he grants, the English dramatist was without a peer in his own age, and perhaps in any age: "je ne sais si jamais homme a jeté des regards plus profonds sur la nature humaine." But Shakespeare knew almost nothing of the requirements of the drama as an art:

> Il faut se persuader d'abord qu' écrire est un art; que cet art a nécessairement ses genres, et que chaque genre a ses règles. Et qu'on ne dise pas que les genres et les règles sont arbitraires; ils sont nés de la nature même; l'art a seulement séparé ce que la nature a confondu . . . On peut dire que Racine, dans toute l'excellence de son art, est plus naturel que Shakespeare.

Chateaubriand here, to be sure, still finds the standard of art in "nature"; but it is "nature" in the sense of the neo-classical critics, a sense in which it is not opposed, but equivalent, to an art that rigorously conforms to fixed rules. And the "great literary paradox of the partisans of Shakespeare," he observes, is that their arguments imply that "there are *no* rules of the drama," which is equivalent to asserting "that an art is not an art." Voltaire rightly felt that "by banishing all rules and returning to *pure nature*, nothing was easier than to equal the *chefs-d'oeuvre* of the English stage;" and he was well advised in recanting his earlier too enthusiastic utterances about Shakespeare, since he saw that "en relevant les beautés des barbares, il avait séduit des hommes qui, comme lui, ne sauraient séparer l'alliage de l'or." Chateaubriand regrets that "the *Cato* of Addison is no longer played" and that consequently

51

"on ne se délasse au théâtre anglais des monstruosités de Shakespeare que par les horreurs d'Otway." "Comment," he exclaims, "ne pas gémir de vior une nation éclairée, et qui compte parmi ses critiques les Pope et les Addison, de la voir s'extasier sur le portrait de l'apothicaire dans *Roméo et Juliette.* C'est le burlesque le plus hideux et le plus dégoûtant." The entire passage might almost have been written with Warton's poem in mind, so completely and methodically does this later "Romanticist" controvert the aesthetic principles and deride the enthusiams of the English "Romanticist" of 1740. It is worth noting, also, that Chateaubriand at this time thinks almost as ill of Gothic architecture as of Shakespeare and of *la pure nature*:

> Une beauté dans Shakespeare n'excuse pas ses innombrables défauts: un monument gothique peut plaire par son obscurité et la difformité même de ses proportions, mais personne ne songe á bâtir un palais sur son modèle.[50]

We have, then, observed and compared—very far from exhaustively, of course, yet in some of their most fundamental and determinative ideas— three "Romanticisms." In the first and second we have found certain common elements, but still more significant oppositions; in the second and third we have found certain other common elements, but likewise significant oppositions. But between the first and third the common elements are very scanty; such as there are, it could, I think, be shown, are not the same as those subsisting between either the first and second or the second and third; and in their ethical preconceptions and implications and the crucial articles of their literary creeds, the opposition between them is almost absolute.

All three of these historic episodes, it is true, are far more complex than I have time to show. I am attempting only to illustrate the nature of a certain procedure in the study of what is called Romanticism, to suggest its importance, and to present one or two specific results of the use of it. A complete analysis would qualify, without invalidating, these results, in several ways. It would (for one thing) bring out certain important connections between the revolt against the neo-classical aesthetics (common to two of the episodes mentioned) and other aspects of eighteenth-century thought.[51] It would, again, exhibit fully certain *internal* oppositions in at least two of the Romanticisms considered. For example, in German Romanticism between 1797 and 1800 there grew up, and mainly from a single root, *both* an "apotheosis of the future" and a tendency to retrospection—a retrospection directed, not, indeed, towards classical antiquity or towards the primitive, but towards the medieval. A belief in progress and a spirit of reaction were, paradoxically, twin offspring of the same idea, and were nurtured for a time in the same minds. But it is just these internal incongruities which make it most of all evident, as it seems to me, that any attempt at a *general* appraisal even of a single chronologically determinate Romanticism—still more, of

"Romanticism" as a whole—is a fatuity. When a Romanticism has been analyzed into the distinct "strains" or ideas which compose it, the true philosophic affinities and the eventual practical influence in life and art of these several strains will usually be found to be exceedingly diverse and often conflicting. It will, no doubt, remain abstractly possible to raise the question whether the preponderant effect, moral or aesthetic, of one or another large movement which has been called by the name was good or bad. But that ambitious inquiry cannot even be legitimately begun until a prior task of analysis and detailed comparison—of the sort that I have attempted here to indicate—has been accomplished. And when this has been done, I doubt whether the larger question will seem to have much importance or meaning. What will then appear historically significant and philosophically instructive will be the way in which *each* of these distinguishable strains has worked itself out, what its elective affinities for other ideas, and its historic consequences, have shown themselves to be. The categories which it has become customary to use in distinguishing and classifying "movements" in literature or philosophy and in describing the nature of the significant transitions which have taken place in taste and in opinion, are far too rough, crude, undiscriminating—and none of them so hopelessly so as the category "Romantic." It is not any large *complexes* of ideas, such as that term has almost always been employed to designate, but rather certain simpler, diversely combinable, intellectual and emotional components of such complexes, that are the true elemental and dynamic factors in the history of thought and of art; and it is with the genesis, the vicissitudes, the manifold and often dramatic interactions of these, that it is the task of the historian of ideas in literature to become acquainted.

## Notes

1 An address delivered by invitation at the fortieth Annual Meeting of the Modern Language Association of America, December 27, 1923.
2 *Le Romantisme français*, 1919, p. 141 and *passim*.
3 *Jour. of Philosophy*, XIX (1922), 645.
4 *Egotism in German Philosophy*, p. 11–20, 54–64.
5 *Mme Guyon et Fénelon précurseurs de Rousseau*, 1918.
6 "Schiller and Romanticism"; *Mod. Long. Notes*, XXXVII, 267, n. 28.
7 *Proc. Brit. Acad.*, 1915–16, pp. 146–7.
8 *The Art of Poetry*, 1923, pp. 79–80.
9 *Contemporary Review*, April, 1919, p. 473.
10 *Classical and Romantic*, 1923, pp. 32, 31.
11 Editor's Introduction to *Essays in Romantic Literature* by George Wyndham, 1919, p. xxxiii.
12 *The Art of Poetry*, p. 79.
13 *Aspects and Impressions*, 1922, p. 5.
14 *La Liquidation du Romantisme*, 1199, pp. 14 f.
15 *The Art of Poetry*, p. 50.
16 *The Architecture of Humanism*, 1914, p. 39.

17 *P. M. L. A.*, XIII, 222.

18 *The Drift of Romanticism*, 1913, pp. xiii, 247.

19 Marie Joachimi, *Die Weltanschauung der Romantik*, 1905, p. 52.

20 *Le mal romantique*, 1908, p. vii.

21 Cf. R. Gillouin, *Une nouvelle philosophie de l'histoire moderne et française*, 1921, pp. 6 ff; Seillière, *Le péril mystique*, etc. pp. 2–6.

22 Wernaer, *Romanticism and the Romantic School in Germany*, p. 3.

23 Neilson, *Essentials of Poetry*, 1912, ch. III.

24 For the last mentioned, cf. Gosse in *Proc. Brit. Acad.*, 1915–16, p. 151.

25 *Le mal romantique*, p. xli.

26 "Il y a même beaucoup de romantique dans la façon dont le combattent certains traditionalistes imprudents, dont M. Lasserre paraît avoir quelquefois écouté les suggestions dangereuses" (*loc. cit.*).

27 *Essays and Studies by Members of the English Association*, VIII (1923), 113.

28 *Le Catholicisme chez les Romantiques*, 1922.

29 "Two Pioneers of Romanticism," *Proc. Brit. Acad.*, 1915, pp. 146–8.

30 *Essais*, I, 31. There is a certain irony in the fact that the sort of naturalism here expressed by Montaigne was to be the basis of a Shakespeare revival in the eighteenth century. For Shakespeare's own extreme antipathy to the passage is shown by the fact that he wrote two replies to it—a humorous one in *The Tempest*, a serious and profound one in the *The Winter's Tale*.

31 This is not rhetorical exaggeration; at least sixty different senses or applications of the notion of "nature" as norm can be clearly distinguished.

32 So apparently Mr. Gosse: "When the history of the [Romantic] school comes to be written, there will be a piquancy in tracing an antinomianism down from the blameless Warton to the hedonist essays of Oscar Wilde and the frenzied anarchism of the futurists" (*op. cit.*, p. 15).

33 *Essais*, III. 12.

34 The title of the poem and some elements of its thought and feeling—especially its note of religious "enthusiasm" for "Nature" in the sense of the visible universe —are akin to, and probably derivative from, Shaftesbury's *Moralists*. But in Shaftesbury there is no opposition of "nature" to "art" and no antinomian strain, either ethical or aesthetic; "decorum," "order," "balance," and "proportion" are among his favorite words.

35 *Spectator*, No. 144.

36 Cf. the writer's "Schiller and the Genesis of Romanticism," *Mod. Lang. Notes*, XXXV. 1–9, 136–146.

37 Quotations in this paragraph from F. Schlegel are from *Athenaeum*, II, 1, p. 29; III, 1, p. 12; I, 2, p. 68; III, 1, p. 19. Those from A. W. Schlegel have already been cited by Marie Joachimi, *Weltanschauung der Romantik*, pp. 179–183.

38 "The Meaning of Romantic," etc. *Mod. Lang. Notes*, XXXI. 385–396; XXXII. 65–77.

39 Review of Herder's *Humanitätsbriefe*; in Minor, *Fr. Schlegel, 1794–1802*.

40 Vorrede to *Die Griechen und Römer*, in Minor, *op. cit.*, I. 82.

41 *Vorschule der Aesthetik*, I, Programm V, § 23.

42 *Vorlesungen über dramatische Kunst und Literatur*, 1809–11, in *Werke*, 1846, V. 16. Cf. also Novalis's *Hymnen an die Nacht*.

43 *Op. cit.*, V, 17.

44 *De l'Allemagne*, Pt. II, chap. XI.

45 Cf. *Fünfte Rede*: "Nirgends is die Religion so vollkommen idealisiert als in Christentum und durch die ursprüngliche Voraussetzung desselben; und eben damit ist immerwährendes Streiten gegen alles Wirkliche in der Religion als eine

Aufgabe hingestellt, der nie völlig Genüge geleistet werden kann, Eben weil überall das Ungöttliche ist und wirkt, und weil alles Wirkliche zugleich als unheilig erscheint, ist eine unendliche Heiligkeit das Ziel des Christentums. Nie zufrieden mit dem Erlangten, sucht es auch in seinen reinsten Erzeugnissen, auch in seinen heiligsten Gefühlen noch die Spuren des Irreligiösen und der der Einheit des Ganzen entgegengesetzten und von ihm abgewandten Tendenz alles Endlichen."

46 Typical is the review of the book in the *Athenaeum*, II, 299: "Für mich ist das Christentum und die Art wie es eingeleitet und das, was ewig bleiben soll in ihm, gesetzt wird, mit das Grösste im ganzen Werk." Cf. also Schlegel's defense of Fichte against the charge of having "attacked religion": "Wenn das Interesse am Uebersinnlichen das Wesen der Religion ist, so ist seine ganze Lehre Religion in Form der Philosophie." There are, undeniably, also occasional manifestations of a conflicting strain in the *Frühromantiker*, especially in Novalis; but these are not the usual, dominant, innovating and characteristic things in the body of ideas of the school; they are rather vestigial structures, such as are to be found remaining in all new developments.

47 There are, for example, passages in the penultimate section of the *Essai sur les révolutions* which present a close parallel to some in *The Enthusiast*; e.g.: "O homme de la nature, c'est toi seul qui me fais me glorifier d'être homme! Ton coeur ne connalt point la dépendance; tu ne sais ce que c'est que de ramper dans une cour ou de caresser un tigre populaire. Que t'imortent nos arts, notre luxe, nos villes? As-tu besoin de spectacle, tu te rends au temple de la nature, à la religieuse forêt . . . Mais il n'y a donc point de gouvernement, point de liberté? De liberte? si: une délicieuse, une céleste, celle de la nature. Et quelle est-elle, cette liberté? . . . Qu'on vienne passer une nuit avec moi ches les sauvages du Canada, peut-être alors parviendrai-je à donner quelque idée de cette espèce de liberté."

48 On the two strains in *Atala*, cf. Chinard, *L'Exotisme américain dans l'oeuvre de Chateaubriand*, 1918, ch. ix.

49 The section on Shakespeare was published in April, 1801 (*Mélanger politiques et littéraires*, 1854, pp. 390ff.).

50 It is somewhat difficult to reconcile this with the eloquent passage on the Gothic church in the *Génie du Christianisme* (V, Ch. 8); yet even there, while acribing to the Gothic style "une beauté qui lui est particulière," Chateaubriand also refers to its "proportions barbares."

51 With this topic, upon which there is a good deal to be said, the writer is dealing elsewhere.

# 3

# TOWARD A THEORY
# OF ROMANTICISM

## *Morse Peckham*

Source: *PMLA* 66 (1951), 5–23.

Can we hope for a theory of romanticism? The answer, I believe, is, Yes. But before proceeding further, I must make quite clear what it is that I propose to discuss.

First, although the word "romanticism" refers to any number of things, it has two primary referents: (1) a general and permanent characteristic of mind, art, and personality, found in all periods and in all cultures; (2) a specific historical movement in art and ideas which occurred in Europe and America in the late eighteenth and early nineteenth centuries. I am concerned only with the second of these two meanings. There may be a connection between the two, but I doubt it, and at any rate whatever I have to say refers only to historical romanticism.

Second, in this historical sense "romanticism" as a revolution in art and ideas is often considered to be only an expression of a general redirection of European life which included also a political revolution, an industrial revolution, and perhaps several others. There may be a connection between the revolution in ideas and the arts and the more or less contemporary revolutions in other fields of human activities, but for the time being, at any rate, I think it is wise to dissociate the romanticism of ideas and art from these other revolutions. Just as one of our greatest difficulties so far has arisen from assuming an identity between general and historical romanticism, so much of our difficulty in considering the nature of historical romanticism has come from assuming its identity with all of the other more or less contemporary revolutions. Let us first isolate the historical romanticism of ideas and arts before we beg any questions about the nature of history. For example, I think it is at present wiser to consider romanticism as one of the means then available for hindering or helping the early-nineteenth-century movement for political reform than it is to assume that romanticism and the desire for political reform and its partial achievement are the same thing.

With these two distinctions in mind, I repeat, Can we hope for a theory of the historical romanticism of ideas and art? Such a theory must be able to submit successfully to two tests. First, it must show that Wordsworth and Byron, Goethe and Chateaubriand, were all part of a general European literary movement which had its correspondencies in the music, the painting, the architecture, the philosophy, the theology, and the science of the eighteenth and early nineteenth centuries. Second, it must be able to get us inside individual works of literature, art, and thought: that is, to tell us not merely that the works are there, to enable us not merely to classify them, but to deliver up to us a key to individual works so that we can penetrate to the principles of their intellectual and aesthetic being. Can we hope for such a theory? *Dare* we hope for such a theory. To this question I answer, "Yes, we can." I feel that we have it almost within our grasp—that one or two steps more and we shall have mastered this highly perplexing literary problem.

Certainly there is no generally accepted theory of romanticism at the present time. Twenty years ago, and for more than twenty years before that, the problem of romanticism was debated passionately, not least because of the redoubtable but utterly misdirected attacks of Babbitt and More. In his *Romanticism and the Modern Ego* (1943) Jacques Barzun has made a good collection of some of the definitions that have been more or less widely used in the past fifty years: a return to the Middle Ages, a love of the exotic, the revolt from Reason, a vindication of the individual, a liberation of the unconscious, a reaction against scientific method, a revival of pantheism, a revival of idealism, a revival of Catholicism, a rejection of artistic conventions, a return to emotionalism, a return to nature—and so on. The utmost confusion reigns in the whole field. In the past fifteen or twenty years, most scholars have done one of two things. Either they have given up hope for any sense to come out of this tangle and have stoutly denied that there was such a movement, or, less pessimistically, they have continued to use one or more concepts or ideas—theories which they feel to be unsatisfactory yet which they continue to employ because there is nothing better. Most students are convinced that something happened to literature between the death of Pope and the death of Coleridge, but not very many are willing, when you question them sharply, to tell you exactly what happened. The situation is all the more discouraging in that it is generally conceded that romanticism is a central problem in literary history, and that if we have failed to solve that problem, we can scarcely hope to solve any general problems in literary history.

Too many scholars, then, will try either to avoid the term entirely, or failing that strategy—and it always fails—will isolate some idea or literary effect and will say, "This is romanticism." Or such a scholar will use the term with the full knowledge that the reader will recognize the difficulties involved and will charitably permit him to beg the question. He will very rarely begin with a theory of romanticism and seek to place a particular poem or author in relation to that theory or seek to use the theory in unlocking a baffling and complex work, or even a simple one for that matter. He will fit his ideas into whatever notion of romanticism he may have, usually without specifying what it might be, but very rarely, at least in public and in print, will he use a considered theory of romanticism as a starting point for his investigations. It is a discouraging situation, but my purpose is to suggest that it is not so discouraging as it appears.

In the last few years there have been signs that some scholars at least are moving toward a common concept of romanticism. In 1943 Jacques Barzun spoke of romanticism as a biological revolution;[1] and in 1949, he defined it as part of "the great revolution which drew the intellect of Europe . . . from the expectation and desire of fixity into desire and expectation of change."[2] Stallknecht, in his fascinating book on Wordsworth, *Strange Seas of Thought* (1945), spoke of how romanticism established the sentiment of being in England, and then, reversing his statement, suggested that the sentiment of being established romanticism. In his admirable introduction to his edition of *Sartor Resartus* (1937) C. Frederick Harrold—whose death has deprived us of one of the most valuable of contemporary students of Victorian literature—wrote of Carlyle's ideas about organicism and dynamism. And in his and Templeman's excellent anthology of Victorian prose (1938) there is an appendix "illustrative of nineteenth-century conceptions of growth, development, evolution." But the most recent attempt to tackle the problem, the best yet, though I think not entirely satisfactory, has been René Wellek's two articles, "The Concept of Romanticism," published in 1949 in the first two issues of *Comparative Literature*. There he offered three criteria of romanticism: imagination for the view of poetry, an organic concept of nature for the view of the world, and symbol and myth for poetic style.

Wellek does establish to my mind three things in his article: first, that there *was* a European intellectual and artistic movement with certain intellectual and artistic characteristics, a movement properly known as romanticism; second, that the participators in that movement were quite conscious of their historic and revolutionary significance; and third, that the chief reason for the current skepticism in America about a theory of romanticism was the publication in 1924 of Arthur O. Lovejoy's famous article, "On the Discrimination of Romanticisms."[3] In this article Lovejoy pointed out that the term is used in a fearful variety of ways, and that no common concept can include them all. Indeed, the growth of skepticism about any solid conclusions on romanticism does seem to begin—or at least start to become very powerful and eventually dominant—with the publication of that article. Wellek decries what he calls Lovejoy's excessive nominalism and skepticism, and refuses to be satisfied with it. He also puts in the same category of nominalism and skepticism Lovejoy's 1941 article, "The Meaning of Romanticism for the Historian of Ideas."[4] Here Lovejoy offered three criteria of romanticism, or rather the three basic ideas of romanticism, "heterogeneous, logically independent, and sometimes essentially antithetic to one another in their implications." These ideas are organicism, dynamism, and diversitarianism. Now in discussing Lovejoy's 1941 paper Wellek has made, I think, an error. He seems to have confused the nature of the two articles, because, apparently, he has forgotten about the last three chapters of *The Great Chain of Being* (1936).[5]

Lovejoy's great book is a landmark of scholarship, and also for scholarship. It is a book on which some of the most useful scholarship of our times has been based, and it is as useful to the teacher who uses it with intelligence as it is to the scholar. Twenty-five years from now, scholars of literature will look back on the publication of *The Great Chain of Being* as a turning point in the development of literary scholarship; for it has been of astonishing value in opening up to our understanding in quite unexpected ways the literature of the sixteenth, seventeenth, and eighteenth centuries. But so far as I know, almost no use has been made of the last three chapters, especially of the last two, in explaining romanticism and romantic works. It is a curious situation; for these chapters contain the foundations for a theory of romanticism which will do everything that such a theory must be able to do—place works and authors in relation to each other and illuminate individual works of art as they ought to be illuminated.

By ignoring (at least in his two papers) *The Great Chain of Being*, Wellek concluded that the same kind of skepticism was present in both Lovejoy's 1924 and 1941 articles. Actually *The Great Chain of Being* is an answer to Lovejoy's 1924 article. Without emphasizing the fact, Lovejoy *did* in 1933 and 1934, when he delivered the lectures on which the book is based, what in 1924 he said could not be done. To be brief, in 1936 he stated simply that literary romanticism was the manifestation of a change in the way of thinking of European man, that since Plato European man had been thinking according to one system of thought—based on the attempted reconciliation of two profoundly different ideas about the nature of reality, both stemming from Plato—and that in the late eighteenth and early nineteenth centuries occidental thought took an entirely different direction, as did occidental art. Furthermore, he says that the change in the way the mind works was the most profound change in the history of occidental thinking, and by implication it involved a similar profound change in the methods and objects of European art.

# I

What I wish to do in the rest of this paper is, first, to explain what these new ideas of the late eighteenth century involved, to reconcile Wellek and Lovejoy, and Lovejoy with himself, and to show the relevance of certain other ideas about romanticism I have mentioned; and second, to make one addition to the theories of Lovejoy and Wellek, an addition which I hope goes far toward clearing up an essential problem which Lovejoy scarcely faced and with which Wellek is unable to come to terms.

It is scarcely necessary in this journal to outline what *The Great Chain of Being* implied. Yet I should like to reduce the concepts involved to what I think to be their essentials. Briefly the shift in European thought was a shift from conceiving the cosmos as a static mechanism to conceiving it as a dynamic organism: static—in that all the possibilities of reality were realized from the beginning of things or were implicit from the beginning, and that these possibilities were arranged in a complete series, a hierarchy from God down to nothingness—including the literary possibilities from epic to Horatian ode, or lyric; a mechanism—in that the universe is a perfectly running machine, a watch usually. (A machine is the most common metaphor of this metaphysic.) Almost as important as these concepts was that of uniformitarianism, implicit both in staticism and in mechanism, whenever these two are separated, as frequently happens. That is, everything that change produces was to be conceived as a part to fit into the already perfectly running machine; for all things conformed to ideal patterns in the mind of God or in the non-material ground of phenomena.

If, in short, you conceive of the universe as a perfectly ordered machine, you will assume that any imperfections you may notice are really things you do not understand. You will think of everything in the universe as fitting perfectly into that machine. You will think that immutable laws govern the formation of every new part of that machine to ensure that it fits the machine's requirements. And, although with delightful inconsistency—as Pope made his *Essay on Man* the basis of his satires[6]—you will judge the success of any individual thing according to its ability to fit into the workings of the machine, your inconsistency will be concealed, for a time, by the influence of either original sin, if you are an orthodox Christian, or of the corruptions of civilization, if you are a deist or a sentimentalist—not that there is much difference. Your values will be perfection, changelessness, uniformity, rationalism.

Now this mighty static metaphysic which had governed perilously the thoughts of men since the time of Plato, collapsed of its own internal inconsistencies in the late eighteenth century—or collapsed for some people. For most people it still remains the unrealized base for most of their values, intellectual, moral, social, aesthetic, and religious. But to the finer minds of the eighteenth and nineteenth centuries, it was no longer tenable. There are a number of reasons why this should have been so. The principal cause was that all its implications had been worked out; they stood forth in all their naked inconsistency. It became impossible to accept a theodicy based upon it. More and more, thinkers began searching for a new system of explaining the nature of reality and the duties of men.

I shall omit the development of the new idea. The grand outlines have been magnificently sketched by Lovejoy, and the details are steadily being filled in. Rather, I shall present the new idea in its most radical form. Let us begin with the new metaphor. The new metaphor is not a machine; it is an organism. It is a tree, for example; and a tree is a good example, for a study of nineteenth-century literature reveals the continual recurrence of that image. Hence the new thought is organicism. Now the first quality of an organism is that it is not something made, it is something *being* made or growing. We have a philosophy of becoming, not a philosophy of being. Furthermore, the relation of its component parts is not that of the parts of a machine which have been made separately, i.e., separate entities in the mind of the deity, but the relation of leaves to stem to trunk to root to earth. Entities are an organic part of that which produced them. The existence of each part is made possible only by the existence of every other part. Relationships, not entities, are the object of contemplation and study.

Moreover, an organism has the quality of life. It does not develop additively; it grows organically. The universe is alive. It is not something made, a perfect machine; it grows. Therefore change becomes a positive value, not a negative value; change is not man's punishment, it is his opportunity. Anything that continues to grow, or change qualitatively, is not perfect, can, perhaps, never be perfect. Perfection ceases to be a positive value. Imperfection becomes a positive value. Since the universe is changing and growing, there is consequently a positive and radical intrusion of novelty into the world. That is, with the intrusion of each novelty, the fundamental character of the universe itself changes. We have a universe of emergents. If all these things be true, it therefore follows that there are no pre-existent patterns. Every work of art, for instance, creates a new pattern; each one has its own aesthetic law. It may have resemblances even in principle to previous works of art, but fundamentally it is unique. Hence come two derivative ideas. First, diversitarianism, not uniformitarianism, becomes the principle of both creation and criticism. The romantics, for example, have been accused of confusing the genres of poetry. Why shouldn't they? The whole metaphysical foundation of the genres had been abandoned, or for some authors had simply disappeared. The second derivative is the idea of creative originality. True, the idea of originality had existed before, but in a different sense. Now the artist is original because he is the instrument whereby a genuine novelty, an emergent, is introduced into the world, not because he has come with the aid of genius a little closer to previously existent pattern, natural and divine.

In its radical form, dynamic organicism results in the idea that the history of the universe is the history of God creating himself. Evil is at last accounted for, since the history of the universe—God being imperfect to begin with—is the history of God, whether transcendent or immanent, ridding himself, by the evolutionary process, of evil. Of course, from both the old and the new philosophy, God could be omitted. Either can become a materialism.

In a metaphysical nutshell, the older philosophy grounded itself on the principle that nothing can come from nothing. The newer philosophy grounded itself on the principle that something *can* come from nothing, that an excess can come from a deficiency, that nothing succeeds like excess.

## II

I have presented these ideas in a radical form to make them as clear as I can and to bring out in the strongest possible colors the contrast between the old and new methods of thought. Now I should like to apply them to Lovejoy and Wellek. Lovejoy stated that the three new ideas of romantic thought and art were organicism, dynamism, and diversitarianism. He says that they are three separate and inconsistent ideas. I agree that they often appear separately, but I am convinced that they are all related to and derived from a basic or root-metaphor, the organic metaphor of the structure of the universe.[7] Strictly speaking, organicism includes dynamism, for an organism must grow or change qualitatively, but I prefer to use the term "dynamic organicism" in order to emphasize the importance of imperfection and change. Diversitarianism, of course, is in these terms a positive value; for the diversity of things and their uniqueness is the proof of the constant intrusion of novelty in the past, the present, and the future.

Turning to Wellek and his three criteria, I have already included one, organicism; the other two are imagination and symbolism. Wellek means the creative imagination, and a little thought will show that the idea of the creative imagination is derived from dynamic organicism. If the universe is constantly in the process of creating itself, the mind of man, his imaginative power, is radically creative. The artist is that man with the power of bringing new artistic concepts into reality, just as the philosopher brings new ideas into reality. And the greatest man is the philosopher-poet, who supremely gifted simultaneously does both. Furthermore, the artist is the man who creates a symbol of truth. He can think metaphorically, and if the world is an organic structure only a statement with the organic complexity of the work of art can create an adequate symbol of it. And is this not the method of symbolism? In allegory, a symbolic unit preserves its meaning when taken from its context. The Cave of Error *is* the Cave of Error. There is a direct one-to-one relationship between any unit in the world of phenomena and any unit in the world of ideas. But in symbolism, a symbolic unit has power only because of its relationships to everything else in the work of art. Ahab has symbolical value because of the whale, and the whale because of Ahab. In symbolism the interrelationships of the symbolic units involved are equated with the interrelationships of a group of concepts. Let a series of 1, 2, 3, 4, etc., stand for a series of ideas in the mind, and a similar series of a, b, c, d, etc., stand for a series of things in the real world or in the world of the concretizing imagination. Now in allegory, if "a" is a symbolic unit, it stands for "1," "b" for "2," and so on. Thus the Dragon in the *Faerie Queene*, Canto i of Book I, stands for Error, whether the Red Cross Knight is there or not, and the Knight, on one level of interpretation, stands for Holiness, whether the Dragon is there or not. But in symbolism, "a" or "b" or "c" has no direct relation to "1" or "2" or "3". Rather, the interrelationships among the first three have symbolic reference to the interrelationships among the second group of three. Moby Dick has symbolic power only because Ahab is hunting him; in fact, he has symbolic power only because almost everything else in the book has symbolic power as well.

The now current though probably not widely accepted critical principle that a symbolic system is capable of an indefinite number of equally valid interpretations is itself a romantic idea, in the sense that the work of art has no fixed or static meaning but changes with the observer in a relationship between the two which is both dialectical, or dynamic, and organic.

Thus we may conclude that Wellek's three criteria—organicism, imagination, and symbolism—are all three derivable from the basic metaphor or concept of dynamic organicism.

There is yet another profoundly important idea which I have not so far mentioned, the idea of the unconscious mind, which appears in Wordsworth, in Coleridge, in Carlyle, and indeed all over the nineteenth and twentieth centuries. In 1830 in his magnificent essay, "Characteristics," Carlyle says that the two big ideas of the century are dynamism and the unconscious mind. The idea of the unconscious mind goes back to Hartley, to Kant, to Leibniz, and is implicit in Locke. Indeed it goes back to any poet who seriously talks about a muse. But it appears only in full force with the appearance of dynamic organicism. Best known to the English romantics in the mechanistic associationism of Hartley, it became a central part of their thought when they made the mind radically creative. Heretofore the divine had communicated with man either directly through revelation or indirectly through the evidence of his perfect universe. But with God creating himself, with an imperfect but growing universe, with the constant intrusion of novelty into the world, how can there be any apprehension of truth? If reason is inadequate—because it is fixed and because historically it has failed—the truth can only be apprehended intuitively, imaginatively, spontaneously, with the whole personality, from the deep sources of the fountains that are within. The unconscious is really a postulate to the creative imagination, and as such continues today without the divine sanction as part of present-day critical theory. It is that part of the mind through which novelty enters into the personality and hence into the world in the form of art and ideas. We today conceive of the unconscious spatially as inside and beneath; the earlier romantics conceived of it as outside and above. We descend into the imagination; they rose into it. The last method, of course, is the method of transcendentalism.

Furthermore, as I shall shortly show, not only was the unconscious taken over from Locke and Kant and Hartley and converted into something radically creative, it also became an integral part of dynamic organicism because a number of the early romantics proved it, as it were, empirically, by their own personal experience. It became to them proof of the validity of the new way of thinking. Hence also Romantic subjectivism, the artist watching his powers develop and novelty emerging from his unconscious mind.

What then is Romanticism? Whether philosophic, theologic, or aesthetic, it is the revolution in the European mind against thinking in terms of static mechanism and the redirection of the mind to thinking in terms of dynamic organicism. Its values are change, imperfection, growth, diversity, the creative imagination, the unconscious.

### III

Perhaps the result of my remarks so far is to make a much larger group of determined skeptics on the subject of romanticism. The proof of the Martini is in the drinking, and in the rest of what I have to say I hope to show not only that a group of literary works can be related in terms of the ideas I have given but also that particular literary works can be genuinely illuminated by these ideas, can be given richer content, can be more readily understood. And in addition I wish also to advance one more concept, the only one indeed to which I lay any claim of originality, for what I have already said is only an attempt to reconcile various ideas about romanticism which seemed to be fairly close together and to develop them into some consistent whole, on the basis of Lovejoy's statement that the coming of romanticism marked a great turn in the direction of European thought. For instance, Barzun's "desire and expectation of change" is an important part of my proposal; Stallknecht's "sentiment of being," i.e., of a living universe, is right at the heart of it; Harrold's ideas of growth are equally central.[8] Nevertheless, the theory is still incomplete.

Dynamic organicism, manifested in literature in its fully developed form with all its main derivative ideas I have called "radical romanticism." To this term I should now like to add "positive romanticism," as a term useful in describing men and ideas and works of art in which dynamic organicism appears, whether it be incomplete or fully developed. But by itself, "positive romanticism" for the purposes of understanding the romantic movement is not only frequently useless; it is often worse than useless. It is often harmful. If some of my readers have been muttering, "What about Byron?" they are quite right in doing so. Positive romanticism cannot explain Byron; positive romanticism is not enough. To it must be added the term "negative romanticism," and to that I now turn.[9]

It may at first seem that I am here denying my basic aim of reducing the multiplicity of theories of romanticism to a single theory, but this is not really so. Negative romanticism is a necessary complement to positive romanticism, not a parallel or alternative to it, with which it must be reconciled. Briefly, negative romanticism is the expression of the attitudes, the feelings, and the ideas of a man who has left static mechanism but has not yet arrived at a reintegration of his thought and art in terms of dynamic organicism. I am here, of course, using a method of analysis which is now so common that one inhales it with the dust of our libraries, the method of analyzing the works of a man in terms of his personal development. Before we study any artist, we begin by establishing his canon and chronology. We *begin*, that is, by *assuming* that there is a development in his art. I hope I am not being merely tedious in pointing out that this method is in itself a particular application of one of the main ideas derived from dynamic organicism, or positive romanticism—the idea of evolution in the nineteenth-century sense. But to show what I mean by negative romanticism, therefore, and how it fits in with positive romanticism, and to show how the theory works in practice, I shall discuss very briefly three works from the earlier years of the Romantic Movement: *The Ancient Mariner*, *The Prelude*, and *Sartor Resartus*.[10]

Briefly, all three works are about spiritual death and rebirth, or secular conversion. In its baldest form, such an experience amounts to this: A man moves from a trust in the universe to a period of doubt and despair of any meaning in the universe, and then to a re-affirmation of faith in cosmic meaning and goodness, or at least meaning. The transition from the first stage to the second, we may call spiritual death; that from the second to the third, we may call spiritual rebirth.

Let us first consider *The Prelude*. The subtitle, not Wordsworth's, is *The Growth of a Poet's Mind*. After Wordsworth had started *The Recluse*, he found that in order to explain his ideas he must first explain how he came to have them. This decision is in itself a sign of positive romanticism. If you think in static terms, you will, as Pope did in *The Essay on Man*, present the result of a process of thought and experience. But if you find that you cannot explain your ideas except in terms of the process of how you have arrived at them, your mind is working in a different way, according to the principles of development and growth. The central experience which Wordsworth describes is spiritual death and rebirth. He began by having a complete faith in the principles of the French Revolution as the deistic *philosophes* and constitutionalists explained it. Their basic political principle was that we have only to restore to man his originally pure but now corrupt political organization and social contract, and a perfect society will necessarily result. Wordsworth accepted this as he also accepted the sentimentality, most notably and fully expressed by Shaftesbury, which was the eighteenth-century emotional expression of faith in the perfection and goodness of the universe, a sentimentalism which became more strident and absurd as its basic theodicy became increasingly less acceptable. Any man who is defending an idea in which he is emotionally involved, will become more emotional and passionate in its defense as his opponent shows with increasing clarity that the idea is untenable.

The French Revolution, to Wordsworth, failed. It made men worse instead of better, and from the creation of political and intellectual freedom it turned to tyranny, slaughter, and imperialist expansion. He saw that he had been misled by his emotions into too facile an acceptance. It was then that he rejected sentimentalism and brought all values before the bar of reason, so that reason might sit in judgment. But reason also was not enough. The boasted reason of the enlightenment could neither explain the failure of the French Revolution nor provide a means of acceptance. Then occurred his spiritual death. He had invested heavily in emotion and in reason. Each had betrayed him. He was spiritually bankrupt. Where was a means of acceptance? Moving to Racedown, rejoining Dorothy, coming to know Coleridge, and going to live near him at Nether Stowey, he reorganized all his ideas, with Coleridge's and Dorothy's intellectual and emotional help, and reaffirmed in new terms his faith in the goodness and significance of the universe. He stood, he said, "in Nature's presence a sensitive being, a *creative* soul"; that is, his creative power was a "power like one of Nature's." Nature and the creative soul maintain, he believed, an ennobling and enkindling interchange of action. The voice of nature was a living voice. And there are moods when that living voice can be heard, when "We see into the life of things," when we feel "a sense sublime / Of something far more deeply interfused; . . . / A motion and a spirit, that impels / All thinking things, all objects of all thought, / And rolls through all things."

The universe is alive, not dead; living and growing, not a perfect machine; it speaks to us directly through the creative mind and its senses. Its truth cannot be perceived from the "evidences of nature" but only through the unconscious and creative mind. And this is the point of the famous description of the ascent of Mt. Snowdon, in the last book of *The Prelude*. Climbing through the mist, Wordsworth comes to the top of the mountain. Around and below him is a sea of clouds, with the moon shining over all, clear, beautiful, and bright. But through a gap in the clouds comes the roar of the waters in the valleys around the mountains. Thus in the moon he beheld the emblem of a mind "That feeds upon infinity, that broods / Over the dark abyss, intent to hear / Its voices issuing forth to silent light / In one continuous stream." This is his symbol of the unconscious mind, both of man and the universe, ultimately identical, both striving to become as well as to be. He has by a profound experience proved to himself the existence and the trustworthiness and the power of the unconscious mind, of the life of the universe, of the continuous creative activity of the cosmos.

Let me also add that he also, unfortunately I think, retained within his new attitudes a nostalgia for permanence, an ideal of eternal perfection.

Thus early do we have the compromise called Victorian. And this inconsistency was to prove his eventual undoing, to cause his loss of creative
power, comparatively speaking, and to effect his return to a kind of revised
Toryism, to a concept of an organic society without dynamic power. But
that is another story and I cannot go into it here.

Leaving chronological order aside, I turn now to *Sartor Resartus*. The
central chapters of Carlyle's work are "The Everlasting No," "The Center
of Indifference," and "The Everlasting Yea." They obviously present a
pattern of spiritual death and rebirth. Carlyle, speaking of himself under
the guise of Professor Teufelsdröckh, tells us how he lost his religious
belief. "The loss of his religious faith was the loss of everything." "It is all
a grim Desert, this once-fair world of his." "Invisible yet impenetrable
walls divided me from all living; was there in the wide world, any true
bosom I could press trustfully to mine? No, there was none . . . It was a
strange isolation I then lived in. The universe was all void of Life, of
Purpose, of Volition, even of, Hostility; it was one huge dead immeasurable
Steam-engine, rolling on, in its dead indifference, to grind me limb from
limb." "The Universe had pealed its Everlasting No authoritatively through
all the recesses of his being." But in the moment of Baphometic fire-baptism
he stood up and cried out that he would not accept that answer. This was
not yet the moment of rebirth, but it was the first step, the step of defiance
and rebellion.

There follows the Centre of Indifference, of wandering grimly across the
face of Europe, of observing the absurdities and cruelty and wickedness of
mankind; he is a wanderer, a pilgrim without any shrine to go to. And then
one day, surrounded by a beautiful landscape, in the midst of nature and the
tenderness of the natural piety of human beings, came a change. "The heavy
dreams rolled gradually away, and I awoke to a new Heaven and a new
Earth . . . What is nature? Ha! Why do I not name thee GOD? Are not thou
the 'Living Garment of God'? The universe is not dead and demoniacal,
a charnel-house with spectres, but godlike and my Father's." It is alive.
Nature—as he tells us later in the book, in the chapter called "Organic
Filaments"—Nature "is not completed, but ever completing . . . Mankind is
a living movement, in progress faster or slower." Here indeed is a positive
romanticism so complete that it is almost a radical romanticism, though
Carlyle, like Wordsworth, retained an inconsistent static principle in his
thought. Like Wordsworth, his nostalgia for a static principle or static
ground to the evolving universe was to prove his undoing, but that again
is another story.

In *The Ancient Mariner* Coleridge tells us of an experience which is the
same as that given by Wordsworth and Carlyle. The mariner, on his journey
around the world, or through life, violates the faith of his fellow-man by
shooting the albatross, the one thing alive in the world of ice and snow,
always symbols of spiritual coldness and death. His fellow mariners reject

him, marking him with the sign of his own guilt. From the world of ice and snow they come to the world of fire and heat, again symbols of spiritual death, alienation, and suffering. The soul of the mariner is won by Life-in-Death. He alone remains alive while his fellow sailors, silently and with reproachful eyes, die around him. As Carlyle put it, "it was a strange isolation I lived in then." And Carlyle also uses the symbols of ice and fire to describe his condition. Isolation, alienation, and guilt possess the soul of the mariner. He is alone, in a burning and evil universe. "The very deep did rot," and the slimy and evil watersnakes surround his ship. And as he watches them in the moonlight he is suddenly taken with their beauty, and "I blessed them unaware." From the depths of the unconscious rose an impulse of affirmation, of love, of acceptance. The albatross drops from his neck into the sea. The symbol of guilt and alienation and despair vanishes. The universe comes alive. It rains, and the rain is the water of life. The wind blows; the breath of a living universe wafts the ship across the ocean. The air is filled with voices and the sky is filled with living light. The spirit of the land of ice and snow comes to his aid. (As Carlyle put it, even in his most despairful moments there was within him, unconscicusly, a principle of faith and affirmation.) Angels come into the bodies of the dead sailors and work the ship. The whole universe comes to the mariner's aid, and he completes his journey.

And thereafter, though he has been forgiven and reaccepted into man's life by the act of confession, there comes an impulse to tell his story, the creative impulse of the poet rising powerfully from his unconscious mind. Poetry is conceived of as a compulsive but creative act. In a sense Coleridge is more profound than either Wordsworth or Carlyle. He knows that for a romantic, once alienated means always alienated. He cannot join the wedding feast. Edwin Markham put it well:

> He drew a circle that shut me out—
> Heretic, rebel, a thing to flout:
> But Love and I had the wit to win:
> We drew a circle that took him in!

Though a man may create a synthesis that includes the ideas of his fellow men, to those very men he will always be outside the circle of accepted beliefs, even though he blesses all things great and small.

At any rate we see here a highly radical positive romanticism. It is the record of a process; it affirms the unconscious mind and the creative imagination; it affirms the principle of the living universe; it affirms diversitarianism; and it is a fully developed symbolism, an organic symbolism in which the shooting of the albatross is without symbolic power unless it is thought of in terms of the power and the interrelations of the various symbolic units.

These interpretations, to me at least, demonstrate the excellence of Lovejoy's three principles of romanticism—organicism, dynamism, and diversitarianism—to get us inside various works of romantic art and to show us the relationships that tie them together into a single literary movement. And again to me, they show that these ideas are not heterogeneous, independent ideas, but closely associated ideas, all related to a central concept or world-metaphor.

And now to define negative romanticism. I have, of course, taken the term from Carlyle's Everlasting No. As various individuals, according to their natures, and their emotional and intellectual depths, went through the transition from affirming the meaning of the cosmos in terms of static mechanism to affirming it in terms of dynamic organicism, they went through a period of doubt, of despair, of religious and social isolation, of the separation of reason and creative power. It was a period during which they saw neither beauty nor goodness in the universe, nor any significance, nor any rationality, nor indeed any order at all, not even an evil order. This is negative romanticism, the preliminary to positive romanticism, the period of *Sturm und Drang*. As the nineteenth century rolled on, the transition became much easier, for the new ideas were much more widely available. But for the early romantics the new ideas had to be learned through personal and painful experience. The typical symbols of negative romanticism are individuals who are filled with guilt, despair, and cosmic and social alienation. They are often presented, for instance, as having committed some horrible and unmentionable and unmentioned crime in the past. They are often outcasts from men and God, and they are almost always wanderers over the face of the earth. They are Harolds, they are Manfreds, they are Cains. They are heroes of such poems as *Alastor*. But when they begin to a get a little more insight into their position, as they are forced to develop historical consciousness, as they begin to seek the sources for their negation and guilt and alienation, they become Don Juans. That is, in *Don Juan*, Byron sought objectivity by means of satire, and set out to trace in his poem the development of those attitudes that had resulted in himself. As I said earlier, positive romanticism cannot explain Byron, but negative romanticism can. Byron spent his life in the situation of Wordsworth after the rejection of Godwin and before his move to Racedown and Nether Stowey, of the Mariner alone on the wide, wide sea, of Teufelsdröckh subject to the Everlasting No and wandering through the Centre of Indifference.

It is the lack of this concept that involves Wellek's second article and much of Barzun's book, for all their admirable insights, in certain difficulties, in such a foredoomed attempt to find in figures who express negative romanticism and figures who express positive romanticism a common and unifying element.[11] Theirs is the same difficulty as that with which Auden gets involved in *The Enchafed Flood*. It is true that both positive and negative romanticism often cause isolation of the personality, but as Coleridge of these three men alone realized, negative romanticism causes isolation and despair because it offers no cosmic explanations, while positive romanticism offers cosmic explanations which are not shared by the society of which one is a part. To Arnold, "Not a having and a resting, but a growing and a becoming, is the character of perfection as culture conceives it." His ideas isolated him from Barbarians, Philistines, and Populace; they were impressed but they did not follow; for they could not comprehend, so far were his fundamental attitudes separated from theirs. Picasso has in his painting expressed profoundly the results of the freedom that romanticism has given to the creative imagination, but he is detested by most people who have seen his cubist or post-cubist paintings—as well as by a great many who have not. He is at home in the universe, but not in his society.[12]

## IV

My proposal is now complete. This theory does, I firmly believe, what such a theory must do. It gets us inside of various works of art, and it shows the relevance of one work of art to another. Consider Beethoven's Fifth Symphony. It builds to a triumphant close. Unlike the symphonies of Haydn and most of those of Mozart, its last movement, not its first or second, is the most important and the most fully developed, for it is an affirmation which is the result of a tremendous struggle. Between the third and fourth movements is a bridge passage which repeats the rhythm and the harmonies of the opening theme, and the whole work is developed from germinal themes, ideas from which are derived the themes of subsequent movements. It is a symphony developmental and organic in construction. It is the record of a process, of an experience. It is a symbol of the cosmos conceived of as dynamic organism.

The same insights can be extended to painting, to impressionism, for example, with its evocation and record of a particular moment; or to modern architecture, especially to the work of Wright, with his life-long search for an "organic architecture" of houses that are part of their sites, with living rooms and gardens which interpenetrate. But I cannot here offer a full history of the development of modern culture. Rather, I wish to make one final suggestion, to issue a warning to anyone who may be taken enough with these ideas to try to employ them.

Although negative and then positive romanticism developed by reaction out of the static-mechanistic-uniformitarian complex, with its cosmic Toryism, its sentimentalism, and its Deism, they were also superimposed upon it. At any point in nineteenth or twentieth-century culture it is possible to take a cross-section and find all three actively at work. The past one hundred and fifty years or so must be conceived as a dramatic struggle, sometimes directly between positive romanticism and static, mechanistic thought, sometimes three-cornered. It is a struggle between minds and within minds. It is seen today in the profound disparity between what is sometimes called high art and popular art; it is expressed in the typical modern cultural phenomena of the *avant-garde*, which is as modern as Wordsworth and Coleridge. It appeared in the struggle over the "packing" of the supreme court, and the wearisome but still vital quarrels about progressive education. It appears in the antagonism between our relativistic critics and our absolutistic critics. It appears in the theological struggle between the theology of such a man as Charles Raven[13] and the proponents of the "theology of crisis." A very pure positive romanticism is at the heart of Ruth Benedict's *Patterns of Culture*; her ideal of a good society is organic, dynamic, and diversitarian. In short, the history of ideas and the arts in the nineteenth and twentieth centuries is the history of the dramatic struggle among three opposing forces: static mechanism, negative romanticism, and positive romanticism. In this drama, to me the hero is dynamic and diversitarian organicism, and I think Goethe and Beethoven and Coleridge and the other founders of the still vital romantic tradition—a tradition often repudiated by those who are at the very heart of it, and understandably—have still much to say to us, are not mere intellectual and aesthetic curiosities. Nevertheless, I am aware that to many scholars and thinkers, positive romanticism is the villain, responsible for all the ills of our century. The drama may indeed turn out to be a tragedy, but if it does, it is because static mechanism persists in staying alive.[14]

Of course the fact that my attitude towards the continuing and future usefulness of positive romanticism may not after all be justified is not essential to my argument, or even germane to it. I ask only that my readers take under serious consideration, and test in their studies, in their reading, and in their classrooms the theories about romanticism which I have outlined. I trust that many of them will find these ideas useful, even though they withhold final assent.

## Notes

1 *Romanticism and the Modern Ego* (New York, 1943).
2 "Romanticism: Definition of a Period," *Magazine of Art*, XLII (Nov. 1949), 243.
3 *PMLA*, XXXIX, 229–253; republished in his *Essays in the History of Ideas* (Baltimore, 1948).
4 *JHI*, II, 237–278.
5 Wellek's confusion, or apparent confusion, lies in his implication that the "Romanticisms" Lovejoy discussed in 1924 are the same as the "romantic ideas" which in 1941 he called "heterogeneous, logically independent, and sometimes essentially antithetic to one another in their implications." As I read the 1941 article, I interpret the latter as these three: organicism, dynamism, and diversitarianism. (See below, Section II of this paper.) These are not the "Romanticisms" of 1924. (See the first paragraph of Wellek's article, "The Concept of 'Romanticism' in Literary History," *CL*, I, 1.)

71

6 See n. 12, below.

7 I am alarmed at finding myself in disagreement with Lovejoy. Although I think his three ideas are not heterogeneous, but homogeneous or at least derived from a common root-metaphor, the possibility that they really *are* heterogeneous does not deprive them in the least of their value in understanding romanticism, nor does their possible heterogeneity have any effect on my proposal which follows.

8 An extremely interesting parallel, although later in time than the period I am immediately concerned with, is Wiener's demonstration that American pragmatism came out of the union of Mill's diversitarian and dynamic dialectic with Darwin's theory of evolution. See Philip P. Wiener, *Evolution and the Founders of Pragmatism* (Cambridge, U.S., 1949).

9 Wellek, for instance, says that Byron "does not share the romantic conception of imagination," or does so "only fitfully." He quotes *Childe Harold*, Canto III, written and published in 1816, when Byron was temporarily under Wordsworth's influence through Shelley. Byron's romantic view of nature as an organism with which man is unified organically by the imagination is equally fitful and limited to the period of Shelleyan influence. Wellek's suggestion that Byron is a symbolist, depending as it does on Wilson Knight's *The Burning Oracle*, is not very convincing. Knight strikes me as a weak reed to lean upon, and Wellek himself calls Knight "extravagant," certainly an understatement. In short, I think Wellek's three categories of romanticism are useless, or only very rarely useful, when they are applied to Byron. So are Lovejoy's three romantic ideas; for the same reasons, of course. (See Wellek's second article, *CL*, I, 165 and 168.) To be sure, Byron uses symbols; but he uses them compulsively, as everyone else does, not as a conscious principle of literary organization and creation.

10 In what follows I shall offer an interpretation of *The Ancient Mariner* which I worked out some years ago, but which is substantially that developed from different points of view by Stallknecht, Maud Bodkin, and various other critics. I shall also suggest that all three works are about the same subjective experience. Stallknecht, so far as I know, is the only commentator who has pointed out—in his *Strange Seas of Thought*—that *The Prelude* and *The Ancient Mariner* are about the same thing; and so far as I know, no one has suggested that *Sartor Resartus* is concerned with the same subject.

11 See, for example, n. 9, above.

12 This is perhaps the place to insert a word about pre-romanticism, a term which I would wholly abandon. Apparently it arose in the first place from a naive application of Darwinian evolution to literary history. If the great romantics liked nature, any eighteenth-century enjoyment or praise of nature became pre-romantic, in spite of the Horatian tradition of neo-classicism. If the romanticists liked emotion, any praise of emotion in the eighteenth century was pre-romantic, as if any age, including "The Age of Reason," could be without emotional expression. In their youth Wordsworth and Coleridge were sentimentalists; therefore sentimentalism is romantic. And so on. James R. Foster, in his recent *History of the Pre-Romantic Novel in England* (New York: MLA, 1949), has shown that sensibility was the emotional expression of Deism, just as Lovejoy has demonstrated in various books and articles that Deism and Neo-Classicism were parallel. If it seems odd that sentimentalism, "cosmic Toryism," and Deism are all expressions of the same basic attitudes, it must be remembered that the eighteenth century was the period when the mechanistic and static theodicy broke down from its own inconsistencies. Romanticism did not destroy its predecessor. It came into existence to fill a void. As an example of the difficulties eighteenth-century figures experienced in trying to hold their world together, consider the

problem of understanding how Pope's *Essay on Man* could possibly be the foundation for his satires. Yet he was working on both at the same time and apparently thought the *Essay* gave him exactly the foundation and justification for satire that he needed. But if whatever is, is right, why is it wrong that there should be such people and such behavior as Pope satirizes in the *Moral Essays*, the imitated and original satires, and *The Dunciad*? It is the old problem of accounting for evil in a world created by a perfect, omnipotent, and benevolent deity. I would recommend the total abandonment of the term "pre-romantic," and the substitution for it of some term such as "neo-classic disintegration." For instance, to refer to Wellek once more, on the first page of his second article he has this to say: "There was the 'Storm and Stress' movement in the seventies which exactly parallels what today is elsewhere called 'pre-romanticism.'" In a widely used anthology, *The Literature of England*, by G. B. Woods, H. A. Watt, and G. K. Anderson, first published in 1936, the section called "The Approach to Romanticism" includes Thomson, Gray, Collins, Cowper, Burns, and Blake; and in Ernest Bernbaum's *Guide through the Romantic Movement*, another widely known and used work (I refer to the first edition, published in 1930), the "Pre-Romantic Movement" includes the following, among others: Shaftesbury, Winchilsea, Dyer, Thomson, Richardson, Young, Blair, Akenside, Collins, the Wartons, Hartley, Gray, Goldsmith, MacKenzie, Burns, Darwin, Blake, Godwin, and Radcliffe. Some of these are "Storm and Stress"; others are quite plainly not. To lump all of them together, as a great many teachers and writers do, is to obliterate many highly important distinctions. To my mind, for *some* individuals neo-classicism disintegrated; thereupon what I call "negative romanticism," of which Storm and Stress is a very important expression, for *some* individuals ensued. Then *some* individuals, initially a very few, moved into the attitudes which I call "positive romanticism." As it is now used, "pre-romanticism" confuses the first two of these three stages, just as "romanticism" as it is now generally used confuses the second two and often all three.

13 Raven is both biologist and theologian. See his *Science, Religion, and the Future* (Cambridge and N.Y., 1943).

14 The romantic metaphysic does not *necessarily* involve optimism. That is, although the world is growing in a better direction, the sum of evil may still outweigh the sum of good. Nor does it *necessarily* involve progressivism. That is, the development from the simple to the complex may mean development towards the better, or it may mean development towards the worse, or it may simply mean development without either improvement or degeneration. However, in the early part of the nineteenth century and generally since then, it usually implies both optimism and progressivism. There have been exceptions, however, of whom Eduard von Hartmann is one of the most thoroughgoing, both in his pessimism and in his positive romanticism. It must be noted that he has a technique of acceptance in the sense that he discerns cosmic order and meaning, though he doesn't like it.

# 4

# ENGLISH ROMANTICISM: THE SPIRIT OF THE AGE

## M. H. Abrams

Source: *The Correspondent Breeze: Essays on English Romanticism* (New York: Norton, 1984), pp. 44–75. This was first published in 1963.

My title echoes that of William Hazlitt's remarkable book of 1825, which set out to represent what we now call the climate of opinion among the leading men of his time. In his abrupt way Hazlitt did not stay to theorize, plunging into the middle of things with a sketch of Jeremy Bentham. But from these essays emerges plainly his view that the crucial occurrence for his generation had been the French Revolution. In that event and its repercussions, political, intellectual, and imaginative, and in the resulting waves of hope and gloom, revolutionary loyalty and recreancy, he saw both the promise and the failures of his violent and contradictory era.

The span covered by the active life of Hazlitt's subjects—approximately the early 1790s to 1825—coincides with what literary historians now call the Romantic period; and it is Hazlitt's contention that the characteristic poetry of the age took its shape from the form and pressure of revolution and reaction. The whole "Lake school of poetry," he had said seven years earlier, "had its origin in the French revolution, or rather in those sentiments and opinions which produced that revolution."[1] Hazlitt's main exhibit is Wordsworth (the "head" of the school), whose "genius," he declares, "is a pure emanation of the Spirit of the Age." The poetry of Wordsworth in the period of *Lyrical Ballads* is "one of the innovations of the time."

> It partakes of, and is carried along with, the revolutionary movement of our age: the political changes of the day were the model on which he formed and conducted his poetical experiments. His Muse (it cannot be denied, and without this we cannot explain its character at all) is a levelling one.[2]

Neither the concept that the age had an identifying "spirit," nor the view that this spirit was one of revolutionary change, was unique with Hazlitt. Just after the revolution of July 1830, John Stuart Mill wrote a series of essays on *The Spirit of the Age* in which he said that the phrase, denoting "the dominant idea" of the times, went back only some fifty years, and resulted from the all but universal conviction "that the times are pregnant with change"—a condition "of which the first overt manifestation was the breaking out of the French Revolution."[3] Shelley, in *A Philosophical View of Reform* (1819), after reviewing the European outbreaks of liberty against tyranny which culminated in the American and French revolutions, asserted that the related crisis of change in England had been accompanied by a literary renascence, in which the poets displayed "a comprehensive and all-penetrating spirit" that was "less their own spirit than the spirit of their age."[4] Conservative critics, like the radical Shelley, recognized the fact of a great new poetry and associated its genesis with political events. "The revolution in our literature," Francis Jeffrey claimed in 1816, had as one of its primary causes "the agitations of the French revolution, and the discussions as well as the hopes and terrors to which it gave occasion."[5] And De Quincey said (1839) that the almost "miraculous" effect of the "great moral tempest" of the Revolution was evident "in all lands . . . and at the same time." "In Germany or England alike, the poetry was so entirely regenerated, thrown into moulds of thought and of feeling so new, that the poets everywhere felt themselves . . . entering upon the dignity and the sincere thinking of mature manhood."[6]

It seems to me that Hazlitt and his contemporary viewers of the literary scene were, in their general claim, manifestly right: the Romantic period was eminently an age obsessed with the fact of violent and inclusive change, and Romantic poetry cannot be understood, historically, without awareness of the degree to which this preoccupation affected its substance and form. The phenomenon is too obvious to have escaped notice, in monographs devoted to the French Revolution and the English poets, singly and collectively. But when critics and historians turn to the general task of defining the distinctive qualities of "Romanticism," or of the English Romantic movement, they usually ignore its relations to the revolutionary climate of the time. For example, in an anthology of "the 'classic' statements" on Romanticism, especially in England, which came out in 1962, the few essays which give more than passing mention to the French Revolution do so to reduce the particularity of Romantic poems mainly to a distant reflection of an underlying economic reality, and to an unconscious rationalization of the bourgeois illusion of "freedom."[7]

It may be useful, then, to have a new look at the obvious as it appeared, not to post-Marxist historians, but to intelligent observers at the time. I shall try to indicate briefly some of the ways in which the political, intellectual, and emotional circumstances of a period of revolutionary upheaval affected the scope, subject-matter, themes, values, and even language of a number of Romantic poems. I hope to avoid easy and empty generalizations about the *Zeitgeist*, and I do not propose the electrifying proposition that "le romanitisme, c'est la révolution." Romanticism is no one thing. It is many very individual poets, who wrote poems manifesting a greater diversity of qualities, it seems to me, than those of any preceding age. But some prominent qualities a number of these poems share, and certain of these shared qualities form a distinctive complex which may, with a high degree of probability, be related to the events and ideas of the cataclysmic coming-into-being of the world to which we are by now becoming fairly accustomed.

## I The spirit of the 1790s

By force of chronological habit we think of English Romanticism as a nineteenth-century phenomenon, overlooking how many of its distinctive features had been established by the end of the century before. The last decade of the eighteenth century included the complete cycle of the Revolution in France, from what De Quincey called its "gorgeous festival era"[8] to the *coup d'état* of November 10, 1799, when to all but a few stubborn sympathizers it seemed betrayed from without and within, and the portent of Napoleon loomed over Europe. That same decade was the period in which the poets of the first Romantic generation reached their literary maturity and had either completed, or laid out and begun, the greater number of what we now account their major achievements. By the end of the decade Blake was well along with *The Four Zoas*; only *Milton* and *Jerusalem* belong to the nineteenth century. By the end of the year 1800 Wordsworth had already announced the overall design and begun writing the two great undertakings of his poetic career; that is, he had finished most of the first two books and a number of scattered later passages of *The Prelude*, and of *The Recluse* he had written *Home at Grasmere* (which included the extraordinary section he later reprinted as the "Prospectus of the design and scope of the whole poem") as well as the first book of *The Excursion*. Coleridge wrote in the 1790s seven-tenths of all the nondramatic material in his collected poems.

"Few persons but those who have lived in it," Southey reminisced in his Tory middle age, "can conceive or comprehend what the memory of the French Revolution was, nor what a visionary world seemed to open upon those who were just entering it. Old things seemed passing away, and nothing was dreamt of but the regeneration of the human race."[9] The early years of the Revolution, a modern commentator has remarked, were "perhaps the happiest in the memory of civilized man,"[10] and his estimate is justified by the ecstasy described by Wordsworth in *The Prelude*—"bliss was it in that dawn to be alive"—and expressed by many observers of France in its glad dawn. Samuel Romilly exclaimed in May 1792: "It is the most glorious event, and the happiest for mankind, that has ever taken place since human affairs have been recorded." Charles James Fox was less restrained in his evaluation: "How much the greatest event it is that ever happened in the world! and how much the best!"[11] A generation earlier Dr. Johnson had written a concluding passage for Goldsmith's *The Traveller* which summed up prevailing opinion:

> How small, of all that human hearts endure,
> That part which laws or kings can cause or cure!
> Still to ourselves in every place consigned,
> Our own felicity we make or find.

But now it seemed to many social philosophers that the revolution against the king and the old laws would cure everything and establish felicity for everyone, everywhere. In 1791 Volney took time out from his revolutionary activities to publish *Les Ruines, ou méditations sur les révolutions des empires*, in which a supervisory Genius unveils to him the vision of the past, the present, and then the "New Age," which had in fact already begun in the American Revolution and was approaching its realization in France. "Now," cries the author, "may I live! for after this there is nothing which I am not daring enough to hope."[12] Condorcet wrote his *Outlines . . . of the Progress of the Human Mind* as a doomed man hiding from the police of the Reign of Terror, to vindicate his unshaken faith that the Revolution was a breakthrough in man's progress; he ends with the vision of mankind's imminent perfection both in his social condition and in his intellectual and moral powers.[13] The equivalent book in England was Godwin's *Political Justice*, written under impetus of the Revolution in 1791–93, which has its similar anticipation of mankind morally transformed, living in a state of total economic and political equality.[14]

The intoxicating sense that now everything was possible was not confined to systematic philosophers. In 1793, Hazlitt said, schemes for a new society "of virtue and happiness" had been published "in plays, poems, songs, and romances—made their way to the bar, crept into the church . . . got into the hearts of poets and the brains of metaphysicians . . . and turned the heads of almost the whole kingdom."[15] Anyone who has looked into the poems, the sermons, the novels, and the plays of the early 1790s will know that this is not a gross exaggeration. Man regenerate in a world made new; this was the theme of a multitude of writers notable, forgotten, or anonymous. In the Prologue to his highly successful play *The Road to Ruin* (1792), Thomas Holcroft took the occasion to predict that the Revolution in France had set the torrent of freedom spreading,

> To ease, happiness, art, science, wit, and genius to give birth;
> Ay, to fertilize a world, and renovate old earth![16]

"Renovate old earth," "the regeneration of the human race"—the phrases reflect their origin, and indicate a characteristic difference between French and English radicalism. Most French philosophers of perfectibility (and Godwin, their representative in England) were anticlerical skeptics or downright atheists, who claimed that they based their predictions on an inductive science of history and a Lockian science of man. The chief strength and momentum of English radicalism, on the other hand, came from the religious Nonconformists who, as true heirs of their embattled ancestors in the English civil wars, looked upon contemporary politics through the perspective of biblical prophecy. In a sermon on the French Revolution preached in 1791 the Reverend Mark Wilks proclaimed: "Jesus Christ was a Revolutionist; and the Revolution he came to effect was foretold in these words, 'He hath sent me to proclaim liberty to the captives.'"[17] The Unitarians—influential beyond their numbers because they included so large a proportion of scientists, literary men, and powerful pulpit orators—were especially given to projecting on the empirical science of human progress the pattern and detail of biblical prophecies, Messianic, millennial, and apocalyptic. "Hey for the New Jerusalem! The millennium!" Thomas Holcroft cried out, in the intoxication of first reading Paine's *The Rights of Man* (1791);[18] what this notorious atheist uttered lightly was the fervent but considered opinion of a number of his pious contemporaries. Richard Price, in 1785, had viewed the American Revolution as the most important step, next to the introduction of Christianity itself, in the fulfillment of the "old prophecies" of an empire of reason, virtue, and peace, when the wolf will "dwell with the lamb and the leopard with the kid." "May we not see there the dawning of brighter days on earth, and a new creation rising?" In the sermon of 1789 which evoked the hurricane of Burke's *Reflections on the French Revolution*, he sees that event capped by one even greater and more immediately promising: "I am thankful that I have lived to [see] it: and I could almost say, *Lord, now lettest thou thy servant depart in peace, for mine eyes have seen thy salvation.*"[19] By 1793 the increasingly violent course of the Revolution inspired the prophets to turn from Isaiah's relatively mild prelude to the peaceable kingdom and the "new heavens and a new earth" to the classic text of apocalyptic violence, the Book of Revelation. In February of that year Elhanan Winchester's *The Three Woe Trumpets* interpreted the Revolution in France as the precise fulfillment of those prophecies, with the seventh trumpet just about to sound (Revelation 11) to bring on the final cataclysm and announce the Second Advent of Christ, in a Kingdom which should be "the greatest blessing to mankind that ever they enjoyed, or even found an idea of."[20] In 1791 Joseph Priestley, scientist, radical philosopher, and a founder of the Unitarian Society, had written his *Letters* in reply to Burke's *Reflections*, in which he pronounced the American and French revolutions to be the inauguration of the state of universal happiness and peace "distinctly and repeatedly foretold in many prophecies, delivered more than two thousand years ago." Three years later he expanded his views in *The Present State of Europe Compared with Antient Prophecies*. Combining philosophical empiricism with biblical fundamentalism, he related the convulsions of the time to the Messianic prophecies in Isaiah and Daniel, the apocalyptic passages in various books of the New Testament, and especially to the Book of Revelation, as a ground for confronting "the great scene, that seems now to be opening upon us ... with tranquillity, and even with satisfaction," in the persuasion that its "termination will be glorious and happy," in the advent of "the millennium, or the future peaceable and happy state of the world."[21] Wordsworth's Solitary, in *The Excursion*, no doubt reflects an aspect of Wordsworth's own temperament, but the chief model for his earlier career was Joseph Fawcett, famous Unitarian preacher at the Old Jewry, and a poet as well. In Wordsworth's rendering, we find him, in both song and sermon, projecting a dazzling vision of the French Revolution which fuses classical myth with Christian prophecy:

> I beheld
> Glory—beyond all glory ever seen,
> Confusion infinite of heaven and earth,
> Dazzling the soul. Meanwhile, prophetic harps
> In every grove were ringing, "War shall cease."
>     ... I sang Saturnian rule
> Returned,—a progeny of golden years
> Permitted to descend, and bless mankind.
> —With promises the Hebrew Scriptures teem:
>     ... the glowing phrase
> Of ancient inspiration serving me,
> I promised also,—with undaunted trust
> Foretold, and added prayer to prophecy.[22]

The formative age of Romantic poetry was clearly one of apocalyptic expectations, or at least apocalyptic imaginings, which endowed the promise of France with the form and impetus of one of the deepest rooted and most compelling myths in the culture of Christian Europe.

## II The voice of the bard

In a verse-letter of 1800 Blake identified the crucial influences in his spiritual history as a series beginning with Milton and the Old Testament prophets and ending with the American War of Independence and the French Revolution.[23] Since Blake is the only major Romantic old enough to have published poems before the Revolution, his writings provide a convenient indication of the effects of that event and of the intellectual and emotional atmosphere that it generated.

As Northrop Frye has said in his fine book on Blake, his *Poetical Sketches* of 1783 associate him with Collins, Gray, the Wartons, and other writers of what Frye later called "The Age of Sensibility."[24] As early as the 1740s this school had mounted a literary revolution against the acknowledged tradition of Waller-Denham-Pope—a tradition of civilized and urbane verse, controlled by "good sense and judgment," addressed to a closely integrated upper class, in which the triumphs, as Joseph Warton pointed out, were mainly in "the didactic, moral, and satyric kind."[25] Against this tradition, the new poets raised the claim of a more daring, "sublime," and "primitive" poetry, represented in England by Spenser, Shakespeare, Milton, who exhibit the supreme virtues of spontaneity, invention, and an "enthusiastic" and "creative" imagination—by which was signified a poetry of inspired vision, related to divinity, and populated by allegorical and supernatural characters such as do not exist "in nature."[26]

Prominent in this literature of revolt, however, was a timidity, a sense of frustration very different from the assurance of power and of an accomplished and continuing literary renascence expressed by a number of their Romantic successors: Coleridge's unhesitating judgment that Wordsworth's genius measured up to Milton's, and Wordsworth's solemn concurrence in this judgment; Leigh Hunt's opinion that, for all his errors, Wordsworth was "at the head of a new and great age of poetry"; Keats's conviction that "great spirits now on earth are sojourning"; Shelley's confidence that "the literature of England . . . has arisen, as it were, from a new birth."[27] The poets of sensibility, on the contrary, had felt that they and all future writers were fated to be epigones of a tradition of unrecapturable magnificence. So Collins said in his *Ode on the Poetical Character* as, retreating from "Waller's myrtle shades," he tremblingly pursued Milton's "guiding steps":

> In vain . . .
> . . . Heaven and Fancy, kindred powers,
> Have now o'erturned the inspiring bowers,
> Or curtained close such scene from every future view.

And Gray:

> But not to one in this benighted age
>     Is that diviner inspiration given,
> That burns in Shakespeare's or in Milton's page,
>     The pomp and prodigality of Heaven.

So, in 1783, Blake complained to the Muses:

> How have you left the antient love
>     That bards of old enjoy'd in you!

Besides *Poetical Sketches*, Blake's main achievements before the French Revolution were *Songs of Innocence* and *The Book of Thel*, which represent dwellers in an Eden trembling on the verge of experience. Suddenly in 1790 came *The Marriage of Heaven and Hell*, boisterously promulgating "Energy" in opposition to all inherited limits on human possibilities; to point the contemporary relevance, Blake appended a "Song of Liberty," which represents Energy as a revolutionary "son of fire," moving from America to France and crying the advent of an Isaian millennium:

EMPIRE IS NO MORE! AND NOW THE LION & WOLF SHALL CEASE.

In 1791 appeared Blake's *The French Revolution*, in the form of a Miltonic epic. Of the seven books announced, only the first is extant, but this is enough to demonstrate that Blake, like Priestley and other religious radicals of the day, envisioned the Revolution as the portent of apocalypse. After five thousand years "the ancient dawn calls us / To awake," and the Abbé de Sieyès pleads for a peace, freedom, and equality which will effect a regained Eden—"the happy earth sing in its course, / The mild peaceable nations be opened to heav'n, and men walk with their fathers in bliss"; when his plea is ignored, there are rumblings of a gathering Armageddon, and the book ends with the portent of a first resurrection: "And the bottoms of the world were open'd, and the graves of arch-angels unseal'd."

The "Introduction" to *Songs of Experience* (1794) calls on us to attend the voice which will sing all Blake's poems from now on: "Hear the voice of the Bard! / Who Present, Past, & Future, sees," who calls to the lapsèd Soul and enjoins the earth to cease her cycle and turn to the eternal day. This voice is that of the poet-prophets of the Old and New Testaments, now descending to Blake from its specifically British embodiment in that "bard of old," John Milton. In his "minor prophecies," ending in 1795, Blake develops, out of the heroic-scaled but still historical agents of his *French Revolution*, the Giant Forms of his later mythical system. The Bard becomes Los, the "Eternal Prophet" and father of "red Orc," who is the spirit of Energy bursting out in total spiritual, physical, and political revolution; the argument of the song sung by Los, however, remains that announced in *The French Revolution*. As David Erdman has said, *Europe: A Prophecy* (1794) was written at about the time Blake was illustrating Milton's *On the Morning of Christ's Nativity*, and reinterprets that poem for his own times.[28] Orc, here identified with Christ the revolutionary, comes with the blare of the apocalyptic trumpet to vex nature out of her sleep of 1,800 years, in a cataclysmic Second Coming in "the vineyards of red France" which, however, heralds the day when both the earth and its inhabitants will be resurrected in a joyous burst of unbounded and lustful energy.[29]

By the year 1797 Blake launched out into the "strong heroic Verse" of *Vala, or The Four Zoas*, the first of his three full-scale epics, which recounts the total history of "the Universal Man" from the beginning, through "his fall into Division," to a future that explodes into the most spectacular and sustained apocalyptic set-piece since the Book of Revelation; in this holocaust "the evil is all consum'd" and "all things are chang'd, even as in ancient times."[30]

## III  Romantic oracles

No amount of historical explanation can make Blake out to be other than a phoenix among poets; but if we put his work into its historical and intellectual context, and alongside that of his poetic contemporaries of the 1790s, we find at least that he is not a freak without historical causes but that he responded to the common circumstances in ways markedly similar, sometimes even to odd details. But while fellow poets soon left off their tentative efforts to evolve a system of "machinery" by which to come to terms with the epic events of their revolutionary era, Blake carried undauntedly on.

What, then, were the attributes shared by the chief poets of the 1790s, Blake, Wordsworth, Southey, Coleridge?—to whom I shall add Shelley. Byron and Keats also had elements in common with their older contemporaries, but these lie outside the immediate scope of my paper. Shelley, however, though he matured in the cynical era of Napoleon and the English Regency, reiterated remarkably the pattern of his predecessors. By temperament he was more inclusively and extremely radical than anyone but Blake, and his early "principles," as he himself said, had "their origin from the discoveries which preceded and occasioned the revolutions of America and France." That is, he had formed his mind on those writers, from Rousseau through Condorcet, Volney, Paine, and Godwin, whose ideas made up the climate of the 1790s—and also, it should be emphasized, on the King James Bible and *Paradise Lost*.[31]

1. First, these were all centrally political and social poets. It is by a peculiar injustice that Romanticism is often described as a mode of escapism, an evasion of the shocking changes, violence, and ugliness attending the emergence of the modern industrial and political world. The fact is that to a degree without parallel, even among major Victorian poets, these writers were obsessed with the realities of their era. Blake's wife mildly complained that her husband was always in Paradise; but from this vantage point he managed to keep so thoroughly in touch with mundane reality that, as David Erdman has demonstrated, his epics are hardly less steeped in the scenes and events of the day than is that latter-day epic, the *Ulysses* of James Joyce. Wordsworth said that he "had given twelve hours thought to the conditions and prospects of society, for one to poetry";[32] Coleridge, Southey, and Shelley could have made a claim similarly extravagant; all these poets delivered themselves of political and social commentary in the form of prose pamphlets, essays, speeches, editorials, or sermons; and all

exhibit an explicit or submerged concern with the contemporary historical and intellectual situation in the greater part of their verses, narrative, dramatic, and lyric, long and short.

2. What obscures this concern is that in many poems the Romantics do not write direct political and moral commentary but (in Schorer's apt phrase for Blake) "the politics of vision," uttered in the persona of the inspired prophet-priest. Neoclassic poets had invoked the muse as a formality of the poetic ritual, and the school of sensibility had expressed nostalgia for the "diviner inspiration" of Spenser, Shakespeare, and Milton. But when the Romantic poet asserts inspiration and revelation by a power beyond himself—as Blake did repeatedly, or Shelley in his claim that the great poets of his age are "the priests of an unapprehended inspiration, the mirrors of gigantic shadows which futurity casts upon the present"[33]—he means it. And when Wordsworth called himself "a youthful Druid taught . . . Primeval mysteries, a Bard elect . . . a chosen Son," and Coleridge characterized *The Prelude* as "more than historic, that prophetic Lay," "an Orphic song" uttered by a "great Bard,"[34] in an important sense they meant it too, and we must believe that they meant it if we are to read them aright.

The Romantics, then, often spoke confidently as elected members of what Harold Bloom calls "The Visionary Company," the inspired line of singers from the prophets of the Old and New Testaments through Dante, Spenser, and above all Milton. For Milton had an exemplary role in this tradition as the native British (or Druidic) Bard who was a thorough political, social, and religious revolutionary, who claimed inspiration both from a Heavenly Muse and from the Holy Spirit that had supervised the creation and inspired the biblical prophets, and who, after the failure of his millennial expectations from the English Revolution,[35] had kept his singing voice and salvaged his hope for mankind in an epic poem.

3. Following the Miltonic example, the Romantic poet of the 1790s tried to incorporate what he regarded as the stupendous events of the age in the suitably great poetic forms. He wrote, or planned to write, an epic, or (like Milton in *Samson Agonistes*) emulated Aeschylean tragedy, or uttered visions combining the mode of biblical prophecy with the loose Pindaric, the "sublime" or "greater Ode," which by his eighteenth-century predecessors had been accorded a status next to epic, as peculiarly adapted to an enthusiastic and visionary imagination. Whatever the form, the Romantic Bard is one "who present, past, and future sees"; so that in dealing with current affairs his procedure is often panoramic, his stage cosmic, his agents quasi-mythological, and his logic of events apocalyptic. Typically this mode of Romantic vision fuses history, politics, philosophy, and religion into one grand design, by asserting Providence—or some form of natural teleology—to operate in the seeming chaos of human history so as to effect from present evil a greater good; and through the mid-1790s the French Revolution functions as the symptom or early stage of the abrupt culmination of

this design, from which will emerge a new man on a new earth which is a restored paradise.

To support these large generalizations I need to present a few particulars.

Robert Southey, the most matter-of-fact and worldly of these poets, said that his early adoration of Leonidas, hero of Thermopylae, his early study of Epictetus, "and the French Revolution at its height when I was just eighteen—by these my mind was moulded."[36] The first literary result came a year later, in 1793, when during six weeks of his long vacation from Oxford he wrote *Joan of Arc: An Epic Poem*,[37] which along with Blake's *French Revolution* is the first English epic worth historical notice since Glover's *Leonidas*, published in 1737. Southey's Joan has been called a Tom Paine in petticoats; she is also given to trances in which "strange events yet in the womb of Time" are to her "made manifest." In the first published version of 1796, Book IX consists of a sustained vision of the realms of hell and purgatory, populated by the standard villains of the radicals' view of history. To Joan is revealed the Edenic past in the "blest aera of the infant world," and man's fall, through lust for gold and power, to this "theatre of woe"; yet "for the best / Hath he ordained all things, the ALL-WISE!" because man, "Samson-like," shall "burst his fetters" in a violent spasm not quite named the French Revolution,

> and Earth shall once again
> Be Paradise, whilst WISDOM shall secure
> The state of bliss which IGNORANCE betrayed.
> "Oh age of happiness!" the Maid exclaim'd,
> "Roll fast thy current, Time, till that blest age Arrive!"[38]

To the second book of *Joan*, Coleridge (then, like Southey, a Unitarian, and like both Southey and Wordsworth, considering entering the clergy) contributed what he called an "Epic Slice," which he soon patched up into an independent poem, *The Destiny of Nations: A Vision*. The vision, beamed "on the Prophet's purgèd eye," reviews history, echoes the Book of Revelation, and ends in the symbolic appearance of a bright cloud (the American Revolution) and a brighter cloud (the French Revolution) from which emerges "a dazzling form," obviously female, yet identified in Coleridge's note as an Apollo-figure, portending that "soon shall the Morning struggle into Day."[39] With the epomania of the age, Coleridge considered writing an epic of his own, laid out plans which would take twenty years to realize, and let it go at that.[40] His ambition to be the Milton of his day was, in practice, limited to various oracular odes, of which the most interesting for our purpose is *Religious Musings*, his first long poem in blank verse; on this, Coleridge said, "I build all my poetic pretensions."[41] The poem as published bore the title "Religious Musings on Christmas Eve. In the year of Our Lord, 1794," and Coleridge had earlier called it "The Nativity."[42] The year is precisely that of Blake's *Europe: A Prophecy*, and like that poem, *Religious Musings* is clearly a revision for the time being of Milton's *On the Morning of Christ's Nativity*, which had taken the occasion of memorializing Christ's birth to anticipate "the wakefull trump of doom" and the universal earthquake which will announce His Second Coming:

> And then at last our bliss
> Full and perfect is.

There is never any risk of mistaking Coleridge's voice for that of Blake, yet a reading of Coleridge's poem with Blake's in mind reveals how remarkably parallel were the effects of the same historical and literary situation, operating simultaneously on the imagination of the two poets.

Coleridge's opening, "This is the time," echoes "This is the Month," with which Milton begins his Prologue, as Blake's "The deep of winter came" reflects "It was the Winter wild," with which Milton begins the Hymn proper. (Blake's free verse is also at times reminiscent of the movement of Milton's marvelous stanza.) Musing on the significance of the First Advent, Coleridge says, "Behold a VISION gathers in my soul"; the vision provides him, among other things, a survey of human history since "the primeval age" in the form of a brief theodicy, "all the sore ills" of "our mortal life" becoming "the immediate source / Of mightier good." The future must bring "the fated day" of violent revolution by the oppressed masses, but happily "Philosophers and Bards" exist to mold the wild chaos "with plastic might" into the "perfect forms" of their own inspired visions. Coleridge then presents an interpretation of contemporary affairs which, following his Unitarian mentor, Joseph Priestley, he neatly summarizes in his prose Argument as: "The French Revolution. Millennium. Universal Redemption. Conclusion." His procedure is to establish a parallel (developed in elaborate footnotes) between current revolutionary events and the violent prophecies of the Book of Revelation. The machinery of apocalypse is allegorical, with the "Giant Frenzy" given the function of Blake's Orc in "uprooting empires with his whirlwind arm." In due course the "blest future rushes on my view!" in the form of humankind as a "vast family of Love" living in a communist economy. "The mighty Dead" awaken, and

> To Milton's trump
> The high groves of the renovated Earth
> Unbosom their glad echoes,

in the adoring presence of three English interpreters of millennial prophecy, Newton, Hartley, and Priestley, "patriot, and saint, and sage."[43] (In Blake's *Europe*, not Milton but Newton had "siez'd the trump & blow'd the enormous blast"; as in Coleridge's poem, however, he seemingly appears not in his capacity as scientist but as author of a commentary on the Book of Revelation.)

Wordsworth thought the concluding section of *Religious Musings* on "the renovated Earth" to be the best in Coleridge's *Poems* of 1796. On this subject Wordsworth was an expert, for a year prior to the writing of the poem, in 1793, he had concluded his own *Descriptive Sketches* with the prophecy (precisely matching the prophecy he attributed to the Wanderer in his *Excursion*) that the wars consequent on the French Revolution would fulfill the predictions both of the Book of Revelation and of Virgil's fourth eclogue:

> —Tho' Liberty shall soon, indignant, raise
> Red on his hills his beacon's comet blaze . . .
> Yet, yet rejoice, tho' Pride's perverted ire
> Rouze Hell's own aid, and wrap thy hills in fire.
> Lo! from th' innocuous flames, a lovely birth!
> With its own Virtues springs another earth:
> Nature, as in her prime, her virgin reign
> Begins, and Love and Truth compose her train. . . .
> No more . . .
> On his pale horse shall fell Consumption go.

"How is it," Blake was to ask in his conclusion of *The Four Zoas*, "we have walk'd thro' fires & yet are not consum'd? / How is it that all things are chang'd, even as in ancient times?"[44]

Some two decades later Shelley recapitulated and expanded these poetic manifestations of the earlier 1790s. At the age of nineteen he began his first long poem, *Queen Mab*, in the mode of a vision of the woeful past, the ghastly present, and the blissful future, and although the concepts are those of the French and English *philosophes*, and the Spirit of Necessity replaces Providence as the agent of redemption, much of the imagery is imported from biblical millennialism. The prophecy is that "a garden shall arise, in loveliness / Surpassing fabled Eden"; when it eventuates, "all things are recreated," the lion sports "in the sun / Beside the dreadless kid," and man's intellectual and moral nature participates in "the gradual renovation" until he stands "with taintless body and mind" in a "happy earth! reality of Heaven!" the "consummation of all mortal hope!"[45]

If I may just glance over the fence of my assigned topic: in Germany, as in England, a coincidence of historical, religious, and literary circumstances produced a comparable imaginative result. In the early 1790s the young Hölderlin was caught up in the intoxication of the revolutionary promise; he was at the time a student of theology at Tübingen, and immersed in the literary tradition of *Sturm und Drang* libertarianism, Schiller's early poems, and Klopstock's *Messias* and allegoric odes. A number of Hölderlin's odes of that decade (the two *Hymnen an die Freiheit*, the *Hymne an die Menschheit*,

*Der Zeitgeist*) are notably parallel to the English form I have been describing; that is, they are visionary, oracular, panoramic, and see history on the verge of a blessed culmination in which the French Revolution is the crucial event, the Book of Revelation the chief model, and the agencies a combination of Greek divinities, biblical symbols, and abstract personifications of his own devising. In the *Hymne an die Freiheit* of 1792, for example, the rapt poet chants a revelation of man's first pastoral innocence, love, and happiness; this "Paradise" is destroyed by a "curse"; but then in response to a call by the Goddess Liberty, Love "reconciles the long discord" and inaugurates "the new hour of creation" of a free, fraternal, abundantly vital, and radiant century in which "the ancient infamy is cancelled" and "der Erndte grosser Tag beginnt"—"there begins the great day of the harvest."[46]

## IV  The apocalypse of imagination

The visionary poems of the earlier 1790s and Shelley's earlier prophecies show imaginative audacity and invention, but they are not, it must be confessed, very good poems. The great Romantic poems were written not in the mood of revolutionary exaltation but in the later mood of revolutionary disillusionment or despair. Many of the great poems, however, do not break with the formative past, but continue to exhibit, in a transformed but recognizable fashion, the scope, the poetic voice, the design, the ideas, and the imagery developed in the earlier period. This continuity of tradition converts what would otherwise be a literary curiosity into a matter of considerable historical interest, and helps us to identify and interpret some of the strange but characteristic elements in later Romantic enterprises.

Here is one out of many available instances. It will have become apparent even from these brief summaries that certain terms, images, and quasi-mythical agents tend to recur and to assume a specialized reference to revolutionary events and expectations: the earthquake and the volcano, the purging fire, the emerging sun, the dawn of glad day, the awakening earth in springtime, the Dionysian figure of revolutionary destruction and the Apollonian figure of the promise of a bright new order. Prominent among these is a term which functions as one of the principal leitmotifs of Romantic literature. To Europe at the end of the eighteenth century the French Revolution brought what Saint Augustine said Christiantiy had brought to the ancient world: hope. As Coleridge wrote, on first hearing Wordsworth's *Prelude* read aloud, the poet sang of his experience "amid the tremor of a realm aglow,"

> When from the general heart of human kind
> Hope sprang forth like a full-born Deity!

and afterward, "of that dear Hope afflicted and struck down. . . ."[47] This is no ordinary human hope, but a universal, absolute, and novel hope which sprang forth from the revolutionary events sudden and complete, like Minerva. Pervasively in both the verse and prose of the period, "hope," with its associated term "joy" and its opposites "dejection," "despondency," and "despair," are used in a special application, as shorthand for the limitless faith in human and social possibility aroused by the Revolution, and its reflex, the nadir of feeling caused by its seeming failure—as Wordsworth had put it, the "utter loss of hope itself / And things to hope for" (*The Prelude*, 1805 text, XI, 6–7).

It is not irrelevant, I believe, that many seemingly apolitical poems of the later Romantic period turn on the theme of hope and joy and the temptation to abandon all hope and fall into dejection and despair; the recurrent emotional pattern is that of the key books of *The Excursion*, labeled "Despondency" and "Despondency Corrected," which apply specifically to the failure of millennial hope in the Revolution. But I want to apply this observation to one of those passages in *The Prelude* where Wordsworth suddenly breaks through to a prophetic vision of the hidden significance of the literal narrative. In the sixth book Wordsworth describes his first tour of France with Robert Jones in the summer of 1790, the brightest period of the Revolution. The mighty forms of Nature, "seizing a youthful fancy," had already "given a charter to irregular hopes," but now all Europe

> was thrilled with joy,
> France standing on the top of golden hours,
> And human nature seeming born again.

Sharing the universal intoxication, "when joy of one" was "joy for tens of millions," they join in feasting and dance with a "blithe host / Of Travellers" returning from the Federation Festival at Paris, "the great spousals newly solemnised / At their chief city, in the sight of Heaven." In his revisions of the 1805 version of *The Prelude*, Wordsworth inserted at this point a passage in which he sees, with anguished foreboding, the desecration by French troops of the Convent of the Chartreuse (an event which did not take place until two years later, in 1792). The travelers' way then brings them to the Simplon Pass.

Wordsworth's earlier account of this tour in the *Descriptive Sketches*, written mainly in 1791–92, had ended with the prophecy of a new earth emerging from apocalyptic fires, and a return to the golden age. Now, however, he describes a strange access of sadness, a "melancholy slackening." On the Simplon road they had left their guide and climbed ever upward, until a peasant told them that they had missed their way and that the course now lay downwards.

> Loth to believe what we so grieved to hear,
> For still we had hopes that pointed to the clouds,
> We questioned him again, and yet again;

but every reply "ended in this,—*that we had crossed the Alps.*"

> Imagination . . .
> That awful Power rose from the mind's abyss
> Like an unfathered vapour that enwraps,
> At once, some lonely traveller. I was lost;
> Halted without an effort to break through;
> But to my conscious soul I now can say—
> "I recognize thy glory."

Only now, in retrospect, does he recognize that his imagination had penetrated to the emblematic quality of the literal climb, in a revelation proleptic of the experience he was to recount in all the remainder of *The Prelude*. Man's infinite hopes can never be matched by the world as it is and man as he is, for these exhibit a discrepancy no less than that between his "hopes that pointed to the clouds" and the finite height of the Alpine pass. But in the magnitude of the disappointment lies its consolation; for the flash of vision also reveals that infinite longings are inherent in the human spirit, and that the gap between the inordinacy of his hope and the limits of possibility is the measure of man's dignity and greatness:

> Our destiny, our being's heart and home,
> Is with infinitude, and only there;
> With hope it is, hope that can never die,
> Effort, and expectation, and desire,
> And something evermore about to be.

In short, Wordsworth evokes from the unbounded and hence impossible hopes in the French Revolution a central Romantic doctrine, one which reverses the cardinal neoclassic ideal of setting only accessible goals, by converting what had been man's tragic error—the inordinacy of his "pride" that persists in setting infinite aims for finite man—into his specific glory and his triumph. Wordsworth shares the recognition of his fellow Romantics, German and English, of the greatness of man's infinite *Sehnsucht*, his saving insatiability, Blake's "I want! I want!"[48] and Shelley's "the desire of the moth for the star"; but with a characteristic and unique difference, as he goes on at once to reveal:

> Under such banners militant, the soul
> Seeks for no trophies, struggles for no spoils
> That may attest her prowess, blest in thoughts
> That are their own perfection and reward.

The militancy of overt political action has been transformed into the paradox of spiritual quietism: under such militant banners is no march, but a wise passiveness. This truth having been revealed to him, Wordsworth at once goes on to his apocalypse of nature in the Simplon Pass, where the *coincidentia oppositorum* of its physical attributes become the symbols of the biblical Book of Revelation:

> Characters of the great Apocalypse,
> The types and symbols of Eternity,
> Of first, and last, and midst, and without end.[49]

This and its companion passages in *The Prelude* enlighten the orphic darkness of Wordsworth's "Prospectus" to *The Recluse*, drafted as early as 1800, when *The Prelude* had not yet been differentiated from the larger poem. Wordsworth's aim, he there reveals, is still that of the earlier period of millennial hope in revolution, still expressed in a fusion of biblical and classical imagery. Evil is to be redeemed by a regained paradise, or Elysium: "Paradise," he says, "and groves / Elysian, Fortunate Fields . . . why should they be / A history only of departed things?" And the restoration of paradise, as in the Book of Revelation, is still symbolized by a sacred marriage. But the hope has been shifted from the history of mankind to the mind of the single individual, from militant external action to an imaginative act; and the marriage between the Lamb and the New Jerusalem has been converted into a marriage between subject and object, mind and nature, which creates a new world out of the old world of sense:

> For the discerning intellect of Man,
> When wedded to this goodly universe
> In love and holy passion, shall find these
> A simple produce of the common day.
> —I, long before the blissful hour arrives,
> Would chant, in lonely peace, the spousal verse
> Of this great consummation . . .
> And the creation (by no lower name
> Can it be called) which they with blended might
> Accomplish:—this is our high argument.[50]

In the other Romantic visionaries, as in Wordsworth, naive millennialism produced mainly declamation, but the shattered trust in premature political revolution and the need to reconstitute the grounds of hope lay behind the major achievements. And something close to Wordsworth's evolution —the shift to a spiritual and moral revolution which will transform our experience of the old world—is also the argument of a number of the later writings of Blake, Coleridge, Shelley, and, with all his differences, Hölderlin. An example from Shelley must suffice. Most of Shelley's large enterprises after *Queen Mab—The Revolt of Islam, Prometheus Unbound, Hellas*—were inspired by a later recrudescence of the European revolutionary movement. Shelley's view of human motives and possibilities became more and more tragic, and, like Blake after his *French Revolution*, he moved from the bald literalism of *Queen Mab* to an imaginative form increasingly biblical, symbolic, and mythic; but the theme continues to be the ultimate promise of a renovation in human nature and circumstances. In *Prometheus Unbound* this event is symbolized by the reunion of Prometheus and Asia in a joyous ceremony in which all the cosmos participates. But this new world is one which reveals itself to the purged imagination of Man when he has reformed his moral nature at its deep and twisted roots; and the last words of Demogorgon, the inscrutable agent of this apocalypse, describe a revolution of spirit whose sole agencies are the cardinal virtues of endurance, forgiveness, love, and, above all, hope—though a hope that is now hard to distinguish from despair:

> To suffer woes which Hope thinks infinite . . .
> To love, and bear; to hope till Hope creates
> From its own wreck the thing it contemplates . . .
> This is alone Life, Joy, Empire, and Victory!

## V Wordsworth's other voice

"Two voices are there: . . . And, Wordsworth, both are thine." I have as yet said nothing about Wordsworth's *Lyrical Ballads* and related poems, although Hazlitt regarded these as the inauguration of a new poetic era and the close poetic equivalent to the revolutionary politics of the age. Yet the *Ballads* seem in every way antithetical to the poetry I have just described: instead of displaying a panoramic vision of present, past, and future in an elevated oracular voice, these poems undertake to represent realistic "incidents and situations from common life" in ordinary language and to employ "humble and rustic life" as the main source of the simple characters and the model for the plain speech.

Here are some of the reasons Hazlitt gives for his claim that "the political changes of the day were the model on which [Wordsworth] formed and conducted his poetical experiments":

> His Muse (it cannot be denied, and without this we cannot explain its character at all) is a levelling one. It proceeds on a principle of equality, and strives to reduce all things to the same standard. . . .
>
> His popular, inartificial style gets rid (at a blow) of all the trappings of verse, of all the high places of poetry. . . . We begin *de novo*, on a tabula rasa of poetry. . . . The distinctions of rank, birth, wealth, power . . . are not to be found here. . . . The harp of Homer, the trump of Pindar and of Alcaeus, are still.[51]

Making due allowance for his love of extravagance, I think that Hazlitt sets out a very plausible case. He shrewdly recognizes that Wordsworth's criteria are as much social as literary, and that by their egalitarianism they subvert the foundations of a view of poetry inherited from the Renaissance. This view assumed and incorporated a hierarchical structure of social classes. In its strict form, it conceived poetry as an order of well-defined genres, controlled by a theory of decorum whereby the higher poetic kinds represent primarily kings and the aristocracy, the humbler classes (in other than a subsidiary function) are relegated to the lowlier forms, and each poem is expressed in a level of style—high, middle, or low—appropriate, among other things, to the social status of its characters and the dignity of its genre. In England after the sixteenth century, this system had rarely been held with continental rigor, and eighteenth-century critics and poets had carried far the work of breaking down the social distinctions built into a poetic developed for an aristocratic audience. But Wordsworth's practice, buttressed by a strong critical manifesto, carried an existing tendency to an extreme which Hazlitt regarded as a genuine innovation, an achieved revolution against the *ancien régime* in literature. He was, Hazlitt said, "the most original poet now living, and the one whose writings could least be spared: for they have no substitute elsewhere." And Wordsworth had not only leveled, he had transvalued Renaissance and neoclassic aesthetics, by deliberately seeking out the ignominious, the delinquent, and the social outcast as subjects for serious or tragic consideration—not only, Hazlitt noted, "peasants, pedlars, and village-barbers," but also "convicts, female vagrants, gipsies . . . ideot boys and mad mothers."[52] Hence the indignation of Lord Byron, who combined political liberalism with a due regard for aristocratic privilege and traditional poetic decorum:

> "Peddlers," and "Boats," and "Wagons"! Oh! ye shades
> Of Pope and Dryden, are we come to this?

In his Preface to *Lyrical Ballads* Wordsworth justified his undertaking mainly by the ultimate critical sanctions then available, of elemental and permanent "nature" as against the corruptions and necessarily short-lived fashions of "art." But Wordsworth also dealt with the genesis and rationale of *Lyrical Ballads* in several other writings, and in terms broader than purely critical, and these passages clearly relate his poems of humble lives in the plain style to his concept and practice of poetry in the grand oracular style.

In the crucial thirteenth book of *The Prelude* Wordsworth describes how, trained "to meekness" and exalted by "humble faith," he turned from disillusionment with the "sublime / In what the Historian's pen so much delights / To blazon," to "fraternal love" for "the unassuming things that hold / A silent station in this beauteous world," and so to a surrogate for his lost revolutionary hopes:

> The promise of the present time retired
> Into its true proportion; sanguine schemes,
> Ambitious projects, pleased me less; I sought
> For present good in life's familiar face,
> And built thereon my hopes of good to come.

He turned, that is, away from Man as he exists only in the hopes of naive millennialists or the abstractions of the philosophers of perfectibility to "the man whom we behold / With our own eyes"; and especially to the humble and obscure men of the lower and rural classes, "who live / By bodily toil," free from the "artificial lights" of urban upper-class society, and utter the spontaneous overflow of powerful feelings ("Expressing liveliest thoughts in lively words / As native passion dictates"). "Of these, said I, shall be my song." But, he insists, in this new subject he continues to speak "things oracular," for though he is "the humblest," he stands in the great line of the "Poets, even as Prophets, each with each / Connected in a mighty scheme of truth," each of whom possesses "his own peculiar faculty, / Heaven's gift, a sense that fits him to perceive / Objects unseen before." And chief among the prophetic insights granted to Wordsworth is the discovery that Nature has the power to "consecrate" and "to breathe / Grandeur upon the very humblest face / Of human life," as well as upon the works of man, even when these are "mean, have nothing lofty of their own."[53]

We come here to a central paradox among the various ones that lurk in the oracular passages of Wordsworth's major period: the oxymoron of the humble-grand, the lofty-mean, the trivial-sublime—as Hazlitt recognized when he said that Wordsworth's Muse "is distinguished by a proud humility," and that he "elevates the mean" and endeavors "(not in vain) to aggrandise the trivial."[54] The ultimate source of this concept is, I think, obvious, and Wordsworth several times plainly points it out for us. Thus in *The Ruined Cottage* (1797–98) the Pedlar (whose youthful experiences parallel Wordsworth's, as the poet showed by later transferring a number of passages to *The Prelude*) had first studied the Scriptures, and only afterward had come to "*feel* his faith" by discovering the corresponding symbol-system, "the writing," in the great book of nature, where "the least of things / Seemed infinite," so that (as a "chosen son") his own "being thus became / Sublime and comprehensive. . . . Yet was his heart / Lowly"; he also learned to recognize in the simple people of rural life what Wordsworth in a note called "the aristocracy of nature."[55] The ultimate source of Wordsworth's discovery, that is, was the Bible, and especially the New Testament, which is grounded on the radical paradox that "the last shall be first," and dramatizes that fact in the central mystery of God incarnate as a lowly carpenter's son who takes fishermen for his disciples, consorts with beggars, publicans, and fallen women, and dies ignominiously, crucified with thieves. This interfusion of highest and lowest, the divine and the base, as Erich Auerbach has

shown, had from the beginning been a stumbling block to readers habituated to the classical separation of levels of subject-matter and style, and
Robert Lowth in the mid-eighteenth century still found it necessary to insist,
as had Augustine and other theologians almost a millennium and a half
earlier, that the style of the Bible had its special propriety and was genuinely
sublime, and not, as it seemed to a cultivated taste, indecorous, vulgar,
barbarous, grotesque.[56] Wordsworth, it should be recalled, had had a pious
mother, attended a church school at Hawkshead, and was intended for the
clergy. In this aspect his poetic reflects a movement in eighteenth-century
Pietism and envangelicalism which had emphasized, in the theological term,
God's "condescension" or "accommodation" in revealing his immense divinity to the limited human mind through the often trivial events of Scripture,
as well as in sending his son to be born as the lowliest among men. The
archetypal figure, among Wordsworth's many numinous solitaries, is the
humble shepherd magnified in the mist, "glorified" by the setting sun, and
"descried in distant sky,"

> A solitary object and sublime,
> Above all height! like an aerial cross
> Stationed alone upon a spiry rock
> Of the Chartreuse, for worship. Thus was man
> Ennobled outwardly before my sight—

apotheosized, rather, as *figura Christi*, the Good Shepherd himself; for
by such means Wordsworth learned, he says, to see Man "as, more than
anything we know, instinct / With godhead," while yet "acknowledging
dependency sublime."[57]

An important document connecting the religious, political, and aesthetic
elements in his poetic theory is Wordsworth's neglected "Essay, Supplementary to the Preface" of 1815, in which he undertakes to explain at length
why his *Lyrical Ballads* had been met with almost "unremitting hostility"
ever since they appeared. The argument is extraordinarily contorted, even
for Wordsworth's prose; but this, I believe, is the gist of it. "The higher
poetry," especially when it "breathes the spirit of religion," unites "grandeur" and "simplicity," and in consequence is apt to evoke dislike, contempt,
suspicion from the reader.

> For when Christianity, the religion of humility, is founded upon the
> proudest faculty of our nature [imagination], what can be expected
> but contradictions? . . . The commerce between Man and his Maker
> cannot be carried on but by a process where much is represented
> in little, and the Infinite Being accommodates himself to a finite
> capacity. In all this may be perceived the affinity between religion
> and poetry.

94

(In the sentence before the last, Wordsworth defines exactly the theological concept of "accommodation" or "condescension.") Wordsworth then puts himself at the end of a long list of great poets who had been neglected or misunderstood; necessarily so, for original genius consists in doing well "what was never done before," and so introducing "a new element into the intellectual universe"; hence such an author has "the task of *creating* the taste by which he is to be enjoyed." Wordsworth's originality, he says (Hazlitt made essentially the same claim), lies in producing a revolutionary mode of sublimity in poetry. Can it, then,

> be wondered that there is little existing preparation for a poet charged
> with a new mission to extend its kingdom [i.e., of sublimity], and to
> augment and spread its enjoyments?

The "instinctive wisdom" and "heroic" (that is, epic) "passions" of the ancients have united in his heart "with the meditative wisdom of later ages" (that is, of the Christian era) to produce the imaginative mode of "sublimated humanity," and "*there*, the poet must reconcile himself for a season to few and scattered hearers." For he must create the taste by which his innovation is to be enjoyed by stripping from the reader's literary responses their ingrained class-consciousness and social snobbery—what Wordsworth calls "the prejudices of false refinement," "pride," and "vanity"—so as to establish "that dominion over the spirits of readers by which they are to be humbled and humanised, in order that they may be purified and exalted."[58] Having given up the hope of revolutionizing the social and political structure, Wordsworth has discovered that his new calling, his divine "mission," condemning him to a period of inevitable neglect and scorn, is to effect through his poetry an egalitarian revolution of the spirit (what he elsewhere calls "an entire regeneration" of his upper-class readers)[59] so that they may share his revelation of the equivalence of souls, the heroic dimensions of common life, and the grandeur of the ordinary and the trivial in Nature.

In his account of this same discovery in *The Prelude*, Book XIII, Wordsworth says that in his exercise of a special power, unprecedented in literature, "upon the vulgar forms of present things, / The actual world of our familiar days,"

> I remember well
> That in life's every-day appearances
> I seemed about this time to gain clear sight
> Of a new world,

capable of being made visible "to other eyes," which is the product of "a balance, an ennobling interchange," between "the object seen, and eye that sees."[60] This carries us back to the "Prospectus" to *The Recluse*, for it is clear that this "new world" is an aspect of the re-created universe there represented as "a simple produce of the common day," if only we learn to marry our mind to nature "in love and holy passion." And if we put the "Prospectus" back into its original context in the concluding section of *Home at Grasmere*, we find that this document, written precisely at the turn of the century, gathers together the various themes with which we have been dealing: the sense of divine mission and illumination, the conversion of his aspiration for millennial achievements beyond possibility into its spiritual equivalent in a militant quietism, and the replacement of his epic schemes by a new poetic enterprise, to communicate his transforming visions of the common man and the ordinary universe.

In the seclusion of Grasmere vale, Wordsworth has dismissed "all Arcadian dreams, / All golden fancies of the golden Age" that is "to be / Ere time expire," yet finds remaining a "sufficient hope." He proclaims that "yet to me I feel / That an internal brightness is vouchsafed," something that "is shared by none," which impels him, "divinely taught," to speak "of what in man is human or divine." The voice of Reason sanctions the lesson which Nature has stealthily taught him:

> Be mild and cleave to gentle things,
> Thy glory and thy happiness be there.
> Nor fear, though thou confide in me, a want
> Of aspirations that *have* been, of foes
> To wrestle with, and victory to complete,
> Bounds to be leapt, darkness to be explored . . .
> All shall survive—though changed their office.

Therefore he bids "farewell to the Warrior's schemes," as well as to "that other hope, long mine, the hope to fill / The heroic trumpet with the Muse's breath!" But having given up his ambition for a Miltonic epic, he at once finds that his new argument exceeds in its scope the height of Milton's "heaven of heavens" and the depths of Milton's hell, and that it presents its imaginative equivalent of a restored paradise. Hence he will need, he claims—in that union of arrogance with humility which characterizes all poet-prophets who know they are inspired, but by a power for which they are not responsible—a Muse that will outsoar Milton's, just as Milton had claimed that his Muse would outsoar "th' Aonian Mount" of the pagan Homer. "Urania," Wordsworth says,

> I shall need
> Thy guidance, or a greater Muse, if such
> Descend to earth or dwell in highest heaven![61]

Wordsworth, then, in the period beginning about 1797, came to see his destiny to lie in spiritual rather than in overt action and adventure, and to conceive his radical poetic vocation to consist in communicating his unique and paradoxical, hence inevitably misunderstood, revelation of the more-than-heroic grandeur of the humble, the contemned, the ordinary, and the trivial, whether in the plain style of direct ballad-like representation, or in the elevated voice in which he presents himself in his office as recipient of this gift of vision. In either case, the mode in which Wordsworth conceived his mission evolved out of the ambition to participate in the renovation of the world and of man which he had shared with his fellow poets during the period of revolutionary enthusiasm. Both the oracular and the plain poetry, in the last analysis, go back beyond Milton, to that inexhaustible source of radical thought, the Bible—the oracular poetry to the Old Testament prophets and their descendant, the author of the Book of Revelation, and the plain poetry to the story of Christ and to His pronouncements on the exaltation of the lowly and the meek. For the Jesus of the New Testament, as the Reverend Mark Wilks had said in 1791, was indeed "a Revolutionist," though not a political one; and Wordsworth, in his long career as apologist for the Anglican Establishment, never again came so close to the spirit of primitive Christianity as in the latter 1790s, when, according to Coleridge, he had been still "a Republican & at least a *Semi*-atheist."[62]

## Notes

1 *Lectures on the English Poets* (1818), in *The Complete Works of William Hazlitt*, ed. P. P. Howe (London, 1930–34), V, 161.
2 *The Spirit of the Age*, ibid., XI, 86–87.
3 John Stuart Mill, *The Spirit of the Age*, ed. Frederick A. von Hayek (Chicago, 1942), pp. 1–2, 67. In 1812 Thomas Belsham spoke of "the spirit of the times," the "mania of the French Revolution," which "pervaded all ranks of society" (*Memoirs of the Late Reverend Theophilus Lindsey*, 2nd ed., London, 1820, p. 216). See also "Letter on the Spirit of the Age," *Blackwood's Magazine*, 28 (1830), 900–920.
4 *Shelley's Prose*, ed. D. L. Clark (Albuquerque, 1954), pp. 239–40; the passage was later used, almost verbatim, as the conclusion of *A Defence of Poetry*. See also the Preface to *Prometheus Unbound*, ibid., pp. 327–28, and the letter to Charles Ollier, 15 October 1819 (*The Letters of Percy Bysshe Shelley*, ed. F. L. Jones, Oxford, 1964, II, 127). Shelley called the French Revolution "the master theme of the epoch in which we live" (ibid., I, 504).
5 Review of Walter Scott's edition of *The Works of Jonathan Swift*, in *Contributions to the Edinburgh Review* (London, 1844), I, 158–67.
6 "William Wordsworth," in *The Collected Writings of Thomas De Quincey*, ed. David Masson (Edinburgh, 1889–90), II, 273–74.
7 *Romanticism: Points of View*, ed. Robert F. Gleckner and Gerald E. Enscoe (Englewood Cliffs, N.J., 1962).
8 "William Wordsworth," in *Collected Writings*, II, 274.

9 *The Correspondence of Robert Southey with Caroline Bowles*, ed. Edward Dowden (Dublin, 1881), p. 52.

10 M. Ray Adams, *Studies in the Literary Backgrounds of English Radicalism* (Lancaster, Pa., 1947), p. 7.

11 Romilly in Alfred Cobban, ed., *The Debate on the French Revolution, 1789–1800* (London, 1950), p. 354; Fox as cited by Edward Dowden, *The French Revolution and English Literature* (New York, 1897), p. 9. "Era of happiness in the history of the world!" John Thelwall described the Revolution; "Dawn of a real golden age" (Charles Cestre, *John Thelwall*, London, 1906, p. 171.

12 C. F. C. de Volney, *The Ruins*, 5th ed. (London, 1807), pp. 92, 98–113.

13 Marquis de Condorcet, *Outlines of an Historical View of the Progress of the Human Mind* (London, 1795), pp. 261–62, 370–72.

14 William Godwin, *Enquiry Concerning Political Justice*, ed. F. E. L. Priestley (Toronto, 1946); see, for example, II, 463–64, 528–29; III, 180–81.

15 *Complete Works*, VII, 99. Some of this minor revolutionary literature is reviewed in Adams, *Literary Backgrounds of English Radicalism*, and Allene Gregory, *The French Revolution and the English Novel* (New York, 1915).

16 *The Road to Ruin* (London, 1792).

17 *The Origin and Stability of the French Revolution: A Sermon Preached at St. Paul's Chapel, Norwich, July 14, 1791*, p. 5, quoted by Mark Schorer, *William Blake: The Politics of Vision* (New York, 1946), p. 205. For apocalyptic thinking among the Illuminists in France, see A. Viatte, *Les Sources occultes du Romantisme* (Paris, 1928), chap. 6.

18 C. Kegan Paul, *William Godwin: His Friends and Contemporaries* (London, 1876), I, 69.

19 Richard Price, *Observations on the Importance of the American Revolution* (London, 1785), pp. 6–7, 21; *A Discourse on the Love of Our Country* (4 November 1789), in S. MacCoby, ed., *The English Radical Tradition, 1763–1914* (London, 1952), p. 54. The dissenter Nash wrote in reply to Burke's *Reflections*: "As I am a believer in Revelation, I, of course, live in the hope of better things; a millennium . . . a new heaven and a new earth in which dwelleth righteousness . . . a state of equal liberty and equal justice for all men" (*A Letter to the Right Hon. Edmund Burke from a Dissenting Country Attorney*, Birmingham, 1790, quoted by Anthony Lincoln, *Some Political and Social Ideas of English Dissent, 1763–1800*, Cambridge, 1938, p. 3).

20 Elhanan Winchester, *The Three Woe Trumpets*, 1st American ed. (Boston, 1794), pp. 37–38, 71. Winchester also published in 1793 *The Process and Empire of Christ: An Heroic Poem* in blank verse, in which Books VIII–XII deal with the Second Advent, the Millennium, and the apocalyptic "New Creation; or, The Renovation of the Heavens and Earth after the Conflagration."

21 *Letters to the Right Honourable Edmund Burke*, 2nd ed. (Birmingham, 1791), pp. 143–50; *The Present State of Europe Compared with Antient Prophecies*, 4th ed. (London, 1794), pp. 18 ff., 30–32. See also Priestley's *Sermon Preached . . . in Hackney, April 19th, 1793*, and *Observations on the Increase of Infidelity* (1796).

22 *The Excursion*, III, 716–65; see also II, 210–23, On the relation of the Solitary to Joseph Fawcett see Adams, *Literary Backgrounds of English Radicalism*, chap. 7.

23 *The Complete Writings of William Blake*, ed. Geoffrey Keynes (London, 1957), p. 799.

24 *Fearful Symmetry* (Princeton, 1947), pp. 167 ff.; "Towards Defining an Age of Sensibility," in *Eighteenth-Century English Literature: Modern Essays in Criticism*, ed. James L. Clifford (New York, 1959), pp. 311–18.

25 *An Essay on the Genius and Writings of Pope* (1756) (London, 1806), II, 402.

26 See M. H. Abrams, *The Mirror and the Lamp* (New York, 1953), pp. 274–76 and nn.

27 Leigh Hunt, *The Feast of the Poets* (London, 1814), p. 90; John Keats, sonnet *Addressed to the Same* (B. R. Haydon), line 1; *Shelley's Prose*, pp. 239–40.

28 *Blake: Prophet Against Empire* (Princeton, 1954), pp. 246 ff.; and see Frye, *Fearful Symmetry*, p. 262.

29 *Europe: A Prophecy*, Plates 9, 12–15. See also *America: A Prophecy* (1793), Plates 6, 8, 16; *The Song of Los* (1795), Plates 3, 7.

30 *Vala, or the Four Zoas*, I, 5, 21; IX, 827, 845.

31 *Proposals for an Association of Philanthropists* (1812), in *Shelley's Prose*, p. 67. Concerning the early formative influences on Shelley's thought, see K. N. Cameron, *The Young Shelley* (London, 1951). Mary Shelley testified that "in English, the Bible was [Shelley's] constant study," that the sublime poetry of the Old Testament "filled him with delight," and that over an extended period in 1816 and 1817 Shelley read both the Bible and *Paradise Lost* aloud to her (*The Complete Poetical Works of Percy Bysshe Shelley*, ed. Thomas Hutchinson, London, 1934, pp. 551, 156, 536). See also Bennett Weaver, *Toward the Understanding of Shelley* (Ann Arbor, 1932).

32 F. M. Todd, *Politics and the Poet: A Study of Wordsworth* (London, 1957), p. 11. Both of Wordsworth's long poems turn on an extended treatment of the French Revolution—in *The Prelude* as the crisis of his own life as exemplary poet, and in *The Excursion* as the crisis of his generation. See also Carl R. Woodring; *Politics in the Poetry of Coleridge* (Madison, 1961); William Haller, *The Early Life of Robert Southey* (New York, 1917); and Cameron, *The Young Shelley*.

33 E.g., Blake's letter to Thomas Butts, 25 April 1803; Shelley, *A Philosophical View of Reform*, in *Shelley's Prose*, p. 240.

34 MS A, III, 82–93, in William Wordsworth, *The Prelude*, ed. Ernest de Selincourt, 2nd ed., rev. Helen Darbishire (Oxford, 1959), p. 75; Coleridge, *To William Wordsworth*, lines 3, 45, 48.

35 On Milton's millennialism see H. J. C. Grierson, *Milton and Wordsworth* (Cambridge, 1937), pp. 32–36.

36 Quoted by Edward Dowden, *Southey* (New York, 1880), p. 189.

37 Preface to *Joan of Arc* (1837), in *The Poetical Works of Robert Southey* (Boston, 1860), I, 11–12. The next year (1794), with even greater revolutionary élan, Southey dashed off in three mornings the Jacobin *Wat Tyler: A Drama* (ibid., II, 28).

38 *Joan of Arc: An Epic Poem* (Bristol, 1796), Book I, lines 497–99; Book IX, lines 825–27, 837–72. In the MS version of 1793, the references to the French Revolution are explicit; see Book XI, lines 633–749, in Benjamin W. Early, "Southey's *Joan of Arc*: The Unpublished Manuscript, the First Edition, and a Study of the Later Revisions" (Ph.D. thesis, Duke University, 1951). Southey wrote in 1830 that "forty years ago I could partake the hopes of those who expected that political revolutions were to bring about a political millennium" (*Correspondence . . . with Caroline Bowles*, p. 200). By 1797, however, he seems to have been prepared to give back to Christ the task of realizing the dreams of Plato and Milton for total "happiness on earth":

Blessed hopes! awhile
From man withheld, even to the latter days,
When Christ shall come and all things be fulfill'd.

(*Inscription IV. For the Apartment in Chepstow Castle*, in *Poems*, 1797)

39 *The Destiny of Nations*, lines 464, 326–38, 421–58. See Woodring, *Politics in the Poetry of Coleridge*, pp. 169–73.

40 To Joseph Cottle, April 1797, *Collected Letters of Samuel Taylor Coleridge*, ed. E. L. Griggs (Oxford, 1956–71), I, 320–21.

41 Ibid., pp. 197, 205.

42 Ibid., pp. 147, 162 and n.

43 *The Complete Poetical Works of Samuel Taylor Coleridge*, ed. E. H. Coleridge (Oxford, 1912), I, 108–23 and nn. David Hartley had included his interpretation of millennial prophecy in his *Observations on Man*, Part II, Sections IV and V. In lines 126–58 of *Religious Musings* Coleridge, like Blake in his later prophecies, interpreted the fall of man as a splintering of social fraternity into anarchic individuality, and his redemption at the Second Coming as a rejunction of separate selves into a single "Self, that no alien knows!" Cf. the opening of Blake's *The Four Zoas*, I, 9–23.

44 *Descriptive Sketches* (1793 version), lines 774–91; Blake, *The Four Zoas*, IX, 844–45; see also Blake, *America*, VIII, 15. For Wordsworth's opinion of the apocalyptic passage in Coleridge's *Religious Musings* see *Collected Letters of Samuel Taylor Coleridge*, I, 215–16. As late as 1808 the Spanish insurrection against Napoleon revived Wordsworth's millennial hopes: "We trust that Regeneration is at hand; these are works of recovered innocence and wisdom . . . redeunt Saturnia regna" (*The Convention of Cintra*, in *The Prose Works of William Wordsworth*, ed. W. J. B. Owen and Jane W. Smyser, Oxford, 1974, I, 297; see also pp. 227–28).

45 *Queen Mab*, IV, 88–89; VIII, 107 ff.; IX, 1–4.

46 Friedrich Hölderlin, *Sämtliche Werke*, ed. Friedrich Beissner (Stuttgart, 1946– ), I, Pt. I, pp. 139–42. See Geneviève Bianquis, "Hölderlin et la révolution française," *Études Germaniques*, 7 (1952), 105–16; and Maurice Delorme, *Hölderlin et la révolution française* (Monaco, 1959). The relevance of Hölderlin was pointed out to me by my colleague Paul de Man.

47 *To William Wordsworth*, lines 34–38. Cf., for example, *The Prelude* (1805 text), II, 448–66, X, 355–81, 690–728; *The Excursion*, II, 210–23; *The Convention of Cintra*, in *Prose Works of William Wordsworth*, I, 227–28, 319, 339; Shelley, Preface to *The Revolt of Islam*, in *Poetical Works*, pp. 33–34; Hazlitt, *Complete Works*, IV, 119–20, XVII, 196–98, 316, and his *Life of Thomas Holcroft*, ed. Elbridge Colby (London, 1925), II, 92–93.

48 It is an interesting coincidence that Blake's "I want! I want!" (which is illustrated by a man climbing a ladder reaching to the moon) was his retort to a political cartoon by Gillray which caricatured the inordinacy of revolutionary hope by depicting a short ladder pointing futilely toward the moon. See Erdman, *Blake: Prophet Against Empire*, pp. 186–88. The parable, in its political application, was a familiar one; thus Edmund Burke had said (1780): "If we cry, like children, for the moon, like children we must cry on" (*The Works of the Right Honorable Edmund Burke*, London, 1899, II, 357).

49 *The Prelude* (1850 text), VI, 322–640. On the glory of infinite promise aroused by the Revolution see also ibid., XI, 105–23. Wordsworth's later revision of the passage of apocalyptic hope in the *Descriptive Sketches* of 1793 parallels the emblematic significance of the Alpine crossing:

> Lo, from the flames a great and glorious birth;
> As if a new-made heaven were hailing a new earth!
> –All cannot be: the promise is too fair
> For creatures doomed to breathe terrestrial air.

(*The Poetical Works of William Wordsworth*, ed. Ernest de Selincourt and Helen Darbishire, Oxford, 1940–49, I, 89).

50 *Poetical Works*, V, 3–5.

51 *The Spirit of the Age*, in *Complete Works*, XI, 87. Cf. "On the Living Poets," ibid., V, 161–64. Christopher Wordsworth, though his loyalties were the polar opposites of Hazlitt's, also accounted for the theory of *Lyrical Ballads* in political terms: "The clue to his *poetical* theory, in some of its questionable details, may be found in his *political* principles; these had been democratical, and still, though in some degree modified, they were of a republican character" (*Memoirs of William Wordsworth*, Boston, 1851, I, 127).

52 *Complete Works*, XI, 89, V, 162–63. On the novelty of Wordsworth's poems see also ibid., V, 156, and XVII, 117.

53 *The Prelude* (1850 text), XIII, 11–312.

54 *Complete Works*, XI, 87–89.

55 *The Ruined Cottage*, in *Poetical Works*, V, 379 ff., lines 53–59, 145–66, 264–75; and p. 411, note to line 341 of the revised version in *The Excursion*, Book I.

56 Robert Lowth, *Lectures on the Sacred Poetry of the Hebrews* (1953) (London, 1847), pp. 79–84 and passim. On earlier theological discussions of the Christian paradox of *humilitas-sublimitas*, see Erich Auerbach, *Mimesis* (Princeton, 1953), pp. 72–73, 151–55, "Sermo Humilis," *Romanische Forschungen*, 64 (1952), 304–64, and "St. Francis of Assisi in Dante's *Commedia*," in *Scenes from the Drama of European Literature* (New York, 1959), pp. 79–98; see also Joseph Mazzeo, "St. Augustine's Rhetoric of Silence," *Journal of the History of Ideas*, 23 (1962), 183 ff.

57 *The Prelude* (1850 text), VIII, 256–76, 492–94. Cf. Phillippians 2:7–9: Christ took on "the form of a servant" and "humbled himself" even unto "the death of the cross. Wherefore God also hath highly exalted him . . ." See also Matthew 23:11–12 and I Corinthians 1:27–28. On the history of the theological concept of "condescensio," with special reference to the eighteenth century, see Karlfried Gründer, *Figur und Geschichte* (Freiburg / Munich, 1958). Bishop Lowth discusses God's condescension, with respect to the form and figures of the Song of Solomon, in his thirty-first lecture.

58 "Essay, Supplementary to the Preface," in *Prose Works of William Wordsworth*, III, 65–83. Cf. the letter to Joseph Kirkham Miller, 17 December 1831 (*The Letters of William and Dorothy Wordsworth: The Later Years*, Pt. II, ed. Ernest de Selincourt, 2nd ed., rev. Alan G. Hill, Oxford, 1979, pp. 464–65). De Quincey agreed with Wordsworth (and Hazlitt) that the *Lyrical Ballads* were without literary precedent: "I found in these poems . . . an absolute revelation of untrodden worlds . . ." (*Collected Writings*, II, 139).

59 In a letter to Lady Beaumont, 21 May 1807, on the same subject as the "Essay, Supplementary," in *The Letters of William and Dorothy Wordsworth: The Middle Years*, Pt. I, ed. Ernest de Selincourt, 2nd ed., rev. Mary Moorman (Oxford, 1969), p. 150.

60 *The Prelude* (1850 text), XIII, 352–78.

61 *Home at Grasmere* (1800), in *Poetical Works*, V, 334 ff., lines 625–34, 664–750; "Prospectus," lines 25–71.

62 To John Thelwall, 13 May 1796, *Collected Letters*, I, 216.

# 5

# THE INTERNALIZATION OF QUEST-ROMANCE†

*Harold Bloom*

Source: *Romanticism and Consciousness: Essays in Criticism*, ed. Harold Bloom (New York: Norton, 1970), pp. 3–24.

Freud, in an essay written sixty years ago on the relation of the poet to daydreaming, made the surmise that all aesthetic pleasure is forepleasure, an "incitement premium" or narcissistic fantasy. The deepest satisfactions of literature, in this view, come from a release of tensions in the psyche. That Freud had found, as almost always, either part of the truth or at least a way to it, is clear enough, even if a student of Blake or Wordsworth finds, as probably he must, this Freudian view to be partial, reductive, and a kind of mirror image of the imagination's truth. The deepest satisfactions of reading Blake or Wordsworth come from the realization of new ranges of tensions in the mind, but Blake and Wordsworth both believed, in different ways, that the pleasures of poetry were only forepleasures, in the sense that poems, finally, were scaffoldings for a more imaginative vision, and not ends in themselves. I think that what Blake and Wordsworth do for their readers, or can do, is closely related to what Freud does or can do for his, which is to provide both a map of the mind and a profound faith that the map can be put to a saving use. Not that the uses agree, or that the maps quite agree either, but the enterprise is a humanizing one in all three of these discoverers. The humanisms do not agree either; Blake's is apocalyptic, Freud's is naturalistic, and Wordsworth's is—sometimes sublimely, sometimes uneasily— blended of elements that dominate in the other two.

Freud thought that even romance, with its elements of play, probably commenced in some actual experience whose "strong impression on the writer had stirred up a memory of an earlier experience, generally belonging

† First published in *The Yale Review*, Vol. LVIII, No. 4 (Summer, 1969). Copyright © 1969 by Harold Bloom.

to childhood, which then arouses a wish that finds a fulfillment in the work in question, and in which elements of the recent event and the old memory should be discernible." Though this is a brilliant and comprehensive thought, it seems inadequate to the complexity of romance, particularly in the period during which romance as a genre, however displaced, became again the dominant form, which is to say the age of Romanticism. For English-speaking readers, this age may be defined as extending from the childhood of Blake and Wordsworth to the present moment. Convenience dictates that we distinguish the High Romantic period proper, during which the half-dozen major English poets did their work, from the generations that have come after them, but the distinction is difficult to justify critically.

Freud's embryonic theory of romance contains within it the potential for an adequate account of Romanticism, particularly if we interpret his "memory of an earlier experience" to mean also the recall of an earlier insight, or yearning, that may not have been experiential. The immortal longings of the child, rather variously interpreted by Freud, Blake, and Wordsworth, may not be at the roots of romance, historically speaking, since those roots go back to a psychology very different from ours, but they do seem to be at the sources of the mid-eighteenth-century revival of a romance consciousness, out of which nineteenth-century Romanticism largely came.

J. H. Van den Berg, whose introduction to a historical psychology I find crucial to an understanding of Romanticism, thinks that Rousseau "was the first to view the child as a child, and to stop treating the child as an adult." Van den Berg, as a doctor, does not think this was necessarily an advance: "Ever since Rousseau the child has been keeping its distance. This process of the child and adult growing away from each other began in the eighteenth century. It was then that the period of adolescence came into existence." Granting that Van den Berg is broadly correct (he at least attempts to explain an apparent historical modulation in consciousness that few historians of culture care to confront), then we are presented with another in a series of phenomena, clustering around Rousseau and his age, in which the major change from the Enlightenment to Romanticism manifested itself. Some of these are analyzed in this volume, by Barfield, Van den Berg, and Frye in particular, not so much as changes in consciousness, but as changes in figuration. Changes in consciousness are of course very rare and no major synthesizer has come forth as yet, from any discipline, to demonstrate to us whether Romanticism marks a genuine change in consciousness or not. From the Freudian viewpoint, Romanticism is an "illusory therapy" (I take the phrase from Philip Rieff), or what Freud himself specifically termed an "erotic illusion." The dialectics of Romanticism, to the Freudians, are mistaken or inadequate, because the dialectics are sought in Schiller or Heine or in German Romantic philosophy down to Nietzsche, rather than in Blake or the English Romantics after him. Blake and Coleridge do not set intellect and passion against one another, any more than they arrive at the Freudian simplicity of the endless conflict between Eros and Thanatos. Possibly because of the clear associations between Jung and German Romanticism, it has been too easy for Freudian intellectuals to confound Romanticism with various modes of irrationalism. Though much contemporary scholarship attempts to study English and continental Romanticism as a unified phenomenon, it can be argued that the English Romantics tend to lose more than they gain by such study.

Behind continental Romanticism there lay very little in the way of a congenial native tradition of major poets writing in an ancestral mode, particularly when compared to the English Romantic heritage of Spenser, Shakespeare, and Milton. What allies Blake and Wordsworth, Shelley and Keats, is their strong mutual conviction that they are reviving the true English tradition of poetry, which they thought had vanished after the death of Milton, and had reappeared in diminished form, mostly after the death of Pope, in admirable but doomed poets like Chatterton, Cowper, and Collins, victims of circumstance and of the false dawn of Sensibility. It is in this highly individual sense that English Romanticism legitimately can be called, as traditionally it has been, a revival of romance. More than a revival, it is an internalization of romance, particularly of the quest variety, an internalization made for more than therapeutic purposes, because made in the name of a humanizing hope that approaches apocalyptic intensity. The poet takes the patterns of quest-romance and transposes them into his own imaginative life, so that the entire rhythm of the quest is heard again in the movement of the poet himself from poem to poem.

M. H. Abrams, in an essay included in this volume, brilliantly traces these patterns of what he calls "the apocalypse of imagination." As he shows, historically they all stem directly from English reactions to the French Revolution, or to the intellectual currents that had flowed into the Revolution. Psychologically, they stem from the child's vision of a more titanic universe that the English Romantics were so reluctant to abandon. If adolescence was a Romantic or Rousseauistic phenomenon of consciousness, its concomitant was the very secular sense of being twice-born that is first discussed in the fourth chapter of *Emile*, and then beautifully developed by Shelley in his visionary account of Rousseau's second birth, in the concluding movement of *The Triumph of Life*. The pains of psychic maturation become, for Shelley, the potentially saving though usually destructive crisis in which the imagination confronts its choice of either sustaining its own integrity, or yielding to the illusive beauty of nature.

The movement of quest-romance, before its internalization by the High Romantics, was from nature to redeemed nature, the sanction of redemption being the gift of some external spiritual authority, sometimes magical. The Romantic movement is from nature to the imagination's freedom (sometimes a reluctant freedom), and the imagination's freedom is frequently purgatorial, redemptive in direction but destructive of the social self. The high cost of Romantic internalization, that is, of finding paradises within a renovated man, shows itself in the arena of self-consciousness. The quest is to widen consciousness as well as to intensify it, but the quest is shadowed by a spirit that tends to narrow consciousness to an acute preoccupation with self. This shadow of imagination is solipsism, what Shelley calls the Spirit of Solitude or *Alastor*, the avenging daimon who is a baffled residue of the self, determined to be compensated for its loss of natural assurance, for having been awakened from the merely given condition that to Shelley, as to Blake, was but the sleep of death-in-life. Blake calls this spirit of solitude a Spectre, or the genuine Satan, the Thanatos or death instinct in every natural man. One of the essays by Geoffrey H. Hartman in this volume concerns the Romantic search for an anti-self-consciousness, a way out of the morass of inwardness. Modernist poetry in English organized itself, to an excessive extent, as a supposed revolt against Romanticism, in the mistaken hope of escaping this inwardness (though it was unconscious that this was its prime motive).

Modernist poets learned better, as their best work, the last phases of W. B. Yeats and Wallace Stevens, abundantly shows, but criticism until recently was tardy in catching up, and lingering misapprehensions about the Romantics still abide. Thus, Irving Howe, in an otherwise acute essay on literary modernism, says of the Romantic poets that "they do not surrender the wish to discover in the universe a network of spiritual meaning which, however precariously, can enclose their selves." This is simply not true of Blake or Wordsworth or Shelley or Keats, nor is the statement of Marius Bewley's that Howe quotes approvingly, that the Romantics' central desire is "to merge oneself with what is greater than oneself." Indeed, both statements are excellent guides to what the major Romantics regarded as human defeat or a living death, as the despairing surrender of the imagination's autonomy. Since neither Howe nor Bewley is writing as an enemy of the Romantics, it is evident that we still need to clear our minds of Eliotic cant on this subject.

Paul de Man terms this phenomenon the post-Romantic dilemma, observing that every fresh attempt of Modernism to go beyond Romanticism ends in the gradual realization of the Romantics' continued priority. Modern poetry, in English, is the invention of Blake and of Wordsworth, and I do not know of a long poem written in English since which is either as legitimately difficult or as rewardingly profound as *Jerusalem* or *The Prelude*. Nor can I find a modern lyric, however happily ignorant its writer, which develops beyond or surmounts its debt to Wordsworth's great trinity of *Tintern Abbey*, *Resolution and Independence*, and the *Intimations of Immortality* ode. The dreadful paradox of Wordsworth's greatness is that his uncanny originality, still the most astonishing break with tradition in the language, has been so influential that we have lost sight of its audacity and its arbitrariness. In this, Wordsworth strongly resembles Freud, who rightly compared his own intellectual revolution to those of Copernicus and Darwin. Van den Berg quietly sees "Freud, in the desperation of the moment, turning away from the present, where the cause of his patients' illnesses was located, to the past; and thus making them suffer from the past and making our existence akin to their suffering. It was not necessary." Is Van den Berg right? The question is as crucial for Wordsworth and Romanticism as it is for Freud and psychoanalysis. The most searching critique of Romanticism that I know is Van den Berg's critique of Freud, particularly the description of "The Subject and his Landscape" included in this anthology:

> Ultimately the enigma of grief is the libido's inclination toward exterior things. What prompts the libido to leave the inner self? In 1914 Freud asked himself this question—the essential question of his psychology, and the essential question of the psychology of the twentieth century. His answer ended the process of interiorization. It is: the libido leaves the inner self when the inner self has become too full. In order to prevent it from being torn, the I has to aim itself on objects outside the self; ". . . ultimately man must begin to love in order not to get ill." So that is what it is. Objects are of importance only in an extreme urgency. Human beings, too. The grief over their death is the sighing of a too-far distended covering, the groaning of an overfilled inner self.

Wordworth is a crisis-poet, Freud a crisis-analyst; the saving movement in each is backwards into lost time. But what is the movement of loss, in poet and in analyst? Van den Berg's suggestion is that Freud unnecessarily sacrificed the present moment, because he came at the end of a tradition of intellectual error that began with the extreme Cartesian dualism, and that progressively learned to devalue contact between the self and others, the self and the outer world, the self and the body. Wordsworth's prophecy, and Blake's, was overtly against dualism; they came, each said, to heal the division within man, and between man and the world, if never quite between man and man. But Wordsworth, the more influential because more apparently accessible of the two (I myself would argue that he is the more difficult because the more problematic poet), no more overcame a fundamental dualism than Freud did. Essentially this was Blake's complaint against him; it is certainly no basis for us to complain. Wordsworth made his kind of poetry out of an extreme urgency, and out of an overfilled inner self, a Blakean Prolific that nearly choked in an excess of its own delights. This is the Egotistical Sublime of which Keats complained, but Keats knew his debt to Wordsworth, as most poets since do not.

Wordsworth's Copernican revolution in poetry is marked by the evanescence of any subject but subjectivity, the loss of what a poem is "about." If, like the late Yvor Winters, one rejects a poetry that is not "about" something, one has little use for (or understanding of) Wordsworth. But, like Van den Berg on Freud, one can understand and love Wordsworth, and still ask of his radical subjectivity: was it necessary? Without hoping to find an answer, one can explore the question so as to come again to the central problem of Romantic (and post-Romantic) poetry: what, for men without belief and even without credulity, is the spiritual form of romance? How can a poet's (or any man's) life be one of continuous allegory (as Keats thought Shakespeare's must have been) in a reductive universe of death, a separated realm of atomized meanings, each discrete from the next? Though all men are questers, even the least, what is the relevance of quest in a gray world of continuities and homogenized enterprises? Or, in Wordsworth's own terms, which are valid for every major Romantic, what knowledge might yet be purchased except by the loss of power?

Frye, in his theory of myths, explores the analogue between quest-romance and the dream: "Translated into dream terms, the quest-romance is the search of the libido or desiring self for a fulfillment that will deliver it from the anxieties of reality but will still contain that reality." Internalized romance—and *The Prelude* and *Jerusalem* can be taken as the greatest examples of this kind—traces a Promethean and revolutionary quest, and cannot be translated into dream terms, for in it the libido turns inward into the self. Shelley's *Prometheus Unbound* is the most drastic High Romantic version of internalized quest, but there are more drastic versions still in our own age, though they present themselves as parodistic, as in the series of marvelous interior quests by Stevens, that go from *The Comedian As the Letter C* to the climactic *Notes Toward a Supreme Fiction*. The hero of internalized quest is the poet himself, the antagonists of quest are everything in the self that blocks imaginative work, and the fulfillment is never the poem itself, but the poem beyond that is made possible by the apocalypse of imagination. "A timely utterance gave that thought relief" is the Wordsworthian formula for the momentary redemption of the poet's sanity by the poem already written, and might stand as a motto for the history of the modern lyric from Wordsworth to Hart Crane.

The Romantics tended to take Milton's Satan as the archetype of the heroically defeated Promethean quester, a choice in which modern criticism has not followed them. But they had a genuine insight into the affinity between an element in their selves and an element in Milton that he would externalize only in a demonic form. What *is* heroic about Milton's Satan is a real Prometheanism and a thoroughly internalized one; he can steal only his own fire in the poem, since God can appear as fire, again in the poem, only when he directs it against Satan. In Romantic quest the Promethean hero stands finally, quite alone, upon a tower that is only himself, and his stance is all the fire there is. This realization leads neither to nihilism nor to solipsism, though Byron plays with the former and all fear the latter.

The dangers of idealizing the libido are of course constant in the life of the individual, and such idealizations are dreadful for whole societies, but the internalization of quest-romance had to accept these dangers. The creative process is the hero of Romantic poetry, and imaginative inhibitions, of every kind, necessarily must be the antagonists of the poetic quest. The special puzzle of Romanticism is the dialectical role that nature had to take in the revival of the mode of romance. Most simply, Romantic nature poetry, despite a long critical history of misrepresentation, was an anti-nature poetry, even in Wordsworth who sought a reciprocity or even a dialogue with nature, but found it only in flashes. Wordsworthian nature, thanks to Arnold and the critical tradition he fostered, has been misunderstood, though the insights of recent critics have begun to develop a better interpretative tradition, founded on A. C. Bradley's opposition to Arnold's view. Bradley stressed the strong side of Wordsworth's imagination, its Miltonic sublimity, which Arnold evidently never noticed, but which accounts for everything that is major in *The Prelude* and in the central crisis lyrics associated with it. Though Wordsworth came as a healer, and Shelley attacked him, in *Mont Blanc*, for attempting to reconcile man with nature, there is no such reconciliation in Wordsworth's poetry, and the healing function is performed only when the poetry shows the power of the mind over outward sense. The strength of renovation in Wordsworth resides only in the spirit's splendor, in what he beautifully calls "possible sublimity" or "something evermore about to be," the potential of an imagination too fierce to be contained by nature. This is the force that Coleridge sensed and feared in Wordsworth, and is remarkably akin to that strength in Milton that Marvell urbanely says he feared, in his introductory verses to *Paradise Lost*. As Milton curbed his own Promethean-ism, partly by showing its dangers through Satan's version of the heroic quest, so Wordsworth learned to restrain his, partly through making his own quest-romance, in *The Prelude*, an account of learning both the enorm-ous strength of nature, and nature's wise and benevolent reining-in of its own force. In the covenant between Wordsworth and nature, two powers that are totally separate from each other, and potentially destructive of the other, try to meet in a dialectic of love. "Meet" is too hopeful, and "blend" would express Wordsworth's ideal and not his achievement, but the try itself is definitive of Wordsworth's strangeness and continued relevance as a poet.

If Wordsworth, so frequently and absurdly called a pantheist, was not questing for unity with nature, still less were Blake, Shelley, and Keats, or their darker followers in later generations, from Beddoes, Darley, and Wade down to Yeats and Lawrence in our time. Coleridge and Byron, in their very different ways, were oddly closer both to orthodox Christian myth and to pantheism or some form of nature-worship, but even their major poems hardly approximate nature poetry. Romantic or internalized romance, especially in its purest version of the quest form, the poems of symbolic voyaging that move in a continuous tradition from Shelley's *Alastor* to Yeats's *The Wanderings of Oisin*, tends to see the context of nature as a trap for the mature imagination. This point requires much laboring, as the influ-ence of older views of Romanticism is very hard to slough off. Even Northrop

Frye, the leading romance theorist we have had at least since Ruskin, Pater, and Yeats, says that "in Romanticism the main direction of the quest of identity tends increasingly to be downward and inward, toward a hidden basis or ground of identity between man and nature." The directional part of this statement is true, but the stated goal I think is not. Frye still speaks of the Romantics as seeking a final unity between man and his nature, but Blake and Shelley do not accept such a unity as a goal, unless a total transformation of man and nature can precede unity, while Wordsworth's visions of "first and last and midst and without end" preserve the unyielding forms both of nature and of man. Keats's closest approach to an apocalyptic vision comes when he studies Moneta's face, at the climax of *The Fall of Hyperion*, but even that vision is essentially Wordsworthian, seeing as it does a perpetual change that cannot be ended by change, a human countenance made only more solitary in its growing alienation from nature, and a kind of naturalistic entropy that has gone beyond natural contraries, past "the lily and the snow."

Probably only Joyce and Stevens, in later Romantic tradition, can be termed unreconstructed naturalists, or naturalistic humanists. Later Romantics as various as Eliot, Proust, and Shaw all break through uneasy natural contexts, as though sexuality was antithetical to the imagination, while Yeats, the very last of the High Romantics, worked out an elaborate sub-myth of the poet as antithetical quester, very much in the mode of Shelley's poetry. If the goal of Romantic internalization of the quest was a wider consciousness that would be free of the excesses of self-consciousness, a consideration of the rigors of experiential psychology will show, quite rapidly, why nature could not provide an adequate context. The program of Romanticism, and not just in Blake, demands something more than a natural man to carry it through. Enlarged and more numerous senses are necessary, an enormous virtue of Romantic poetry clearly being that it not only demands such expansion but begins to make it possible, or at least attempts to do so.

The internalization of romance brought the concept of nature, and poetic consciousness itself, into a relationship they had never had before the advent of Romanticism in the later eighteenth century. Implicit in all the Romantics, and very explicit in Blake, is a difficult distinction between two modes of energy, organic and creative (Orc and Los in Blake, Prometheus bound and unbound in Shelley, Hyperion and Apollo in Keats, the Child and the Man, though with subtle misgivings, in Wordsworth). For convenience, the first mode can be called Prometheus and the second "the Real Man, the Imagination" (Blake's phrase, in a triumphant letter written when he expected death). Generally, Prometheus is the poet-as-hero in the first stage of his quest, marked by a deep involvement in political, social, and literary revolution, and a direct, even satirical attack on the institutional orthodoxies of European and English society, including historically oriented

Christianity, and the neoclassic literary and intellectual tradition, particularly in its Enlightenment phase. The Real Man, the Imagination, emerges after terrible crises in the major stage of the Romantic quest, which is typified by a relative disengagement from revolutionary activism, and a standing aside from polemic and satire, so as to bring the search within the self and its ambiguities. In the Prometheus stage, the quest is allied to the libido's struggle against repressiveness, and nature is an ally, though always a wounded and sometimes a withdrawn one. In the Real Man, the Imagination stage, nature is the immediate though not the ultimate antagonist. The final enemy to be overcome is a recalcitrance in the self, what Blake calls the Spectre of Urthona, Shelley the unwilling dross that checks the spirit's flight, Wordsworth the sad perplexity or fear that kills or, best of all, the hope that is unwilling to be fed, and Keats, most simply and perhaps most powerfully, the Identity. Coleridge calls the antagonist by a bewildering variety of names since, of all these poets, he is the most hag-ridden by anxieties, and the most humanly vulnerable. Byron and Beddoes do not so much name the antagonist as mock it, so as to cast it out by continuous satire and demonic farce. The best single name for the antagonist is Keats's Identity, but the most traditional is the Selfhood, and so I shall use it here.

Only the Selfhood, for the Romantics as for such Christian visionaries as Eckhart before them, burns in Hell. The Selfhood is not the erotic principle, but precisely that part of the erotic that cannot be released in the dialectic of love, whether between man and man, or man and nature. Here the Romantics, all of them I think, even Keats, part company with Freud's dialectics of human nature. Freud's beautiful sentence on marriage is a formula against which the Romantic Eros can be tested: "A man shall leave father and mother—according to the Biblical precept—and cleave to his wife; then are tenderness and sensuality united." By the canons of internalized romance, that translates: a poet shall leave his Great Original (Milton, for the Romantics) and nature—according to the precept of Poetic Genius—and cleave to his Muse or Imagination; then are the generous and solitary halves united. But, so translated, the formula has ceased to be Freudian and has become High Romantic.

In Freud, part of the ego's own self-love is projected onto an outward object, but part always remains in the ego, and even the projected portion can find its way back again. Somewhere Freud has a splendid sentence that anyone unhappy in love can take to heart: "Object-libido was at first ego-libido and can be again transformed into ego-libido," which is to say that a certain degree of narcissistic mobility is rather a good thing. Somewhere else Freud remarks that all romance is really a form of what he calls "family-romance;" one could as justly say, in his terms, that all romance is necessarily a mode of ego-romance. This may be true, and in its humane gloom it echoes a great line of realists who culminate in Freud, but the popular notion that High Romanticism takes a very different view of love is a sounder insight into the Romantics than most scholarly critics ever achieve (or at least state).

All romance, literary and human, is founded upon enchantment; Freud and the Romantics differ principally in their judgment as to what it is in us that resists enchantment, and what the value of that resistance is. For Freud it is the reality principle, working through the great disenchanter, reason, the scientific attitude, and without it no civilized values are possible. For the Romantics, this is again a dialectical matter, as two principles intertwine in the resistance to enchantment—one "organic," an anxiety principle masquerading as a reality principle and identical to the ego's self-love that never ventures out to others, and the other "creative," which resists enchantment in the name of a higher mode than the sympathetic imagination.

This doubling is clearest in Blake's mythology, where there are two egos, the Spectre of Urthona and Los, who suffer the enchantments, real *and* deceptive, of nature and the female, and who resist, when and where they can, on these very different grounds. But, though less schematically, the same doubling of the ego into passive and active components is present in the other poets wherever they attempt their highest flights and so spurn the earth. The most intense effort of the Romantic quest is made when the Promethean stage of quest is renounced, and the purgatorial crisis that follows moves near to resolution. Romantic purgatory, by an extraordinary displacement of earlier mythology, is found just beyond the earthly paradise, rather than just before it, so that the imagination is tried by nature's best aspect. Instances of the interweaving of purgatory and paradise include nearly everything Blake says about the state of being he calls Beulah, and the whole development of Keats, from *Endymion*, with its den or cave of Quietude, on to the structure of *The Fall of Hyperion*, where the poet enjoys the fruit and drink of paradise just before he has his confrontation with Moneta, whose shrine must be reached by mounting purgatorial stairs.

Nothing in Romantic poetry is more difficult to comprehend, for me anyway, than the process that begins after each poet's renunciation of Prometheus; for the incarnation of the Real Man, the Imagination, is not like psychic maturation in poets before the Romantics. The love that transcends the Selfhood has its analogues in the renunciatory love of many traditions, including some within Christianity, but the creative Eros of the Romantics is not renunciatory though it is self-transcendent. It is, to use Shelley's phrasing, a total going-out from our own natures, total because the force moving out is not only the Promethean libido, but rather a fusion between the libido and the active or imaginative element in the ego; or, simply, desire wholly taken up into the imagination. "Shelley's love poetry," as a phrase, is almost a redundancy, Shelley having written little else, but his specifically erotic poems, a series of great lyrics and the dazzling *Epipsychidion*, have been undervalued because they are so very difficult, the difficulty being the Shelleyan and Romantic vision of love.

Blake distinguished between Beulah and Eden as states of being (Frye's essay, "The Keys to the Gates," included in this anthology, is definitive on this distinction), the first being the realm of family-romance and the second of apocalyptic romance, in which the objects of love altogether lose their object dimension. In family-romance or Beulah, loved ones are not confined to their objective aspect (that would make them denizens of Blake's state of Generation or mere Experience), but they retain it nevertheless. The movement to the reality of Eden is one of re-creation, or better, of knowledge not purchased by the loss of power, and so of power and freedom gained *through* a going-out of our nature, in which that last phrase takes on its full range of meanings. Though Romantic love, particularly in Wordsworth and Shelley, has been compared to what Charles Williams calls the Romantic Theology of Dante, the figure of Beatrice is not an accurate analogue to the various Romantic visions of the beloved, for sublimation is not an element in the movement from Prometheus to Man.

There is no useful analogue to Romantic or imaginative love, but there is a useful contrary in the melancholy wisdom of Freud on natural love, and the contrary has the helpful clarity one always finds in Freud. If Romantic love is the sublime, then Freudian love is the pathetic, and truer of course to the phenomenon insofar as it is merely natural. To Freud, love begins as ego-libido, and necessarily is ever after a history of sorrow, a picaresque chronicle in which the ever-vulnerable ego stumbles from delusion to frustration, to expire at last (if lucky) in the compromising arms of the ugliest of Muses, the reality principle. But the saving dialectic of this picaresque is that it is better thus, as there is no satisfaction in satisfaction anyway, since in the Freudian view all erotic partners are somewhat inadequate replacements for the initial sexual objects, parents. Romantic love, to Freud, is a particularly intense version of the longing for the mother, a love in which the imago is loved, rather than the replacement. And Romantic love, on this account, is anything but a dialectic of transformation, since it is as doomed to overvalue the surrogate as it compulsively overvalues the mother.

Our age begins to abound in late Romantic "completions" of Freud, but the Romantic critiques of him, by Jung and Lawrence in particular, have not touched the strength of his erotic pessimism. There is a subtly defiant attempt to make the imago do the work of the imagination by Stevens, particularly in the very Wordsworthian *The Auroras of Autumn*, and it is beautifully subversive of Freud, but of course it is highly indirect. Yet a direct Romantic counter-critique of Freud's critique of Romantic love emerges from any prolonged, central study of Romantic poetry. For Freud, there is an ironic loss of energy, perhaps even of spirit, with every outward movement of love away from the ego. Only pure self-love has a perfection to it, a stasis without loss, and one remembers again Van den Berg's mordant observation on Freud: "Ultimately the enigma of grief is the libido's inclination toward exterior things." All outward movement, in the Freudian psychodynamics, is a fall that results from "an overfilled inner self," which would sicken within if it did not fall outwards, and downwards, into the world of objects, and of other selves. One longs for Blake to come again and rewrite *The Book of Urizen* as a satire on this cosmogony of love. The poem would not require that much rewriting, for it can now be read as a prophetic satire on Freud, Urizen being a superego certainly overfilled with itself, and sickening into a false creation or creation-fall. If Romantic love can be castigated as "erotic illusion," Freudian love can be judged as "erotic reduction," and the prophets of the reality principle are in danger always of the Urizenic boast:

> I have sought for a joy without pain,
> For a solid without fluctuation
> Why will you die O Eternals?
> Why live in unquenchable burnings?

The answer is the Romantic dialectic of Eros and Imagination, unfair as it is to attribute to the Freudians a censorious repressiveness. But to Blake and the Romantics, all available accounts of right reason, even those which had risen to liberate men, had the disconcerting tendency to turn into censorious moralities. Freud painfully walked a middle way, not unfriendly to the poetic imagination, and moderately friendly to Eros. If his myth of love is so sparse, rather less than a creative Word, it is still open both to analytic modification and to a full acceptance of everything that can come out of the psyche. Yet it is not quite what Philip Rieff claims for it, as it does not erase "the gap between therapeutic rationalism and self-assertive romanticism." That last is only the first stage of the Romantic quest, the one this discussion calls Prometheus. There remains a considerable gap between the subtle perfection to which Freud brought therapeutic rationalism, and the mature Romanticism which is self-transcendent in its major poets.

There is no better way to explore the Real Man, the Imagination, than to study his monuments: *The Four Zoas, Milton*, and *Jerusalem*; *The Prelude* and the *Recluse* fragment; *The Ancient Mariner* and *Christabel*; *Prometheus Unbound, Adonais*, and *The Triumph of Life*; the two *Hyperions*; *Don Juan*; *Death's Jest-Book*; these are the definitive Romantic achievement, the words that were and will be, day and night. What follows is only an epitome, a rapid sketch of the major phase of this erotic quest. The sketch, like any which attempts to trace the visionary company of love, is likely to end in listening to the wind, hoping to hear an instant of a fleeting voice.

The internalization of quest-romance made of the poet-hero a seeker not after nature but after his own mature powers, and so the Romantic poet turned away, not from society to nature, but from nature to what was more integral than nature, within himself. The widened consciousness of the poet did not give him intimations of a former union with nature or the Divine, but rather of his former selfless self. One thinks of Yeats's Blakean declaration: "I'm looking for the face I had / Before the world was made." Different as the major Romantics were in their attitudes towards religion, they were united (except for Coleridge) in *not* striving for unity with anything but what might be called their Tharmas or id component, Tharmas being the Zoa or Giant Form in Blake's mythology who was the unfallen human potential for realizing instinctual desires, and so was the regent of Innocence. Tharmas is a shepherd-figure, his equivalent in Wordsworth being a number of visions of man against the sky, of actual shepherds Wordsworth had seen in his boyhood. This Romantic pastoral vision (its pictorial aspect can be studied in the woodcuts of Blake's Virgil series, and in the work done by Palmer, Calvert, and Richmond while under Blake's influence) is Biblical pastoralism, but not at all of a traditional kind. Blake's Tharmas is inchoate when fallen, as the id or appetite is inchoate, desperately starved and uneasily allied to the Spectre of Urthona, the passive ego he has projected outward to meet an object-world from which he has been severed so unwillingly. Wordsworth's Tharmas, besides being the shepherd image of human divinity, is present in the poet himself as a desperate desire for continuity in the self, a desperation that at its worst sacrifices the living moment, but at its best produces a saving urgency that protects the imagination from the strong enchantments of nature.

In Freud the ego mediates between id and superego, and Freud had no particular interest in further dividing the ego itself. In Romantic psychic mythology, Prometheus rises from the id, and can best be thought of as the force of libido, doomed to undergo a merely cyclic movement from appetite to repression, and then back again; any quest within nature is thus at last irrelevant to the mediating ego, though the quest goes back and forth through it. It is within the ego itself that the quest must turn, to engage the antagonist proper, and to clarify the imaginative component in the ego by its strife of contraries with its dark brother. Frye, writing on Keats, calls the imaginative ego *identity-with* and the selfhood ego *identity-as*, which clarifies Keats's ambiguous use of "identity" in this context. Hartman, writing on Wordsworth, points to the radical Protestant analogue to the Romantic quest: "The terror of discontinuity or separation enters, in fact, as soon as the imagination truly enters. In its restraint of vision, as well as its peculiar nakedness before the moment, this resembles an extreme Protestantism, and Wordsworth seems to quest for 'evidences' in the form of intimations of continuity."

Wordsworth's greatness was in his feeling the terror of discontinuity as acutely as any poet could, yet overcoming this terror nevertheless, by opening himself to vision. With Shelley, the analogue of the search for evidences drops out, and an Orphic strain takes its place, for no other English poet gives so continuous an impression of relying on almost literal inspiration. Where Keats knew the Selfhood as an attractive strength of distinct identity that had to be set aside, and Wordsworth as a continuity he longed for yet learned to resist, and Blake as a temptation to prophetic wrath and withdrawal that had to be withstood, Shelley frequently gives the impression of encountering no enchantment he does not embrace, since every enchantment is an authentic inspiration. Yet this is a false impression, though Yeats sometimes received it, as in his insistence that Shelley, great poet as he certainly was, lacked a Vision of Evil. The contrary view to Yeats is that of C. S. Lewis, who held that Shelley, more than any other "heathen" poet (the word is from Lewis), drove home the truth of Original Sin.

Both views are mistaken. For Shelley, the Selfhood's strong enchantment, stronger even than it is for the other Romantics, is one that would keep him from ever concluding the Prometheus phase of the quest. The Selfhood allies itself with Prometheus against the repressive force Shelley calls Jupiter, his version of Blake's Urizen or Freud's superego. This temptation calls the poet to perpetual revolution, and Shelley, though longing desperately to see the tyrannies of his time overturned, renounces it at the opening of *Prometheus Unbound*, in the Imagination's name. Through his renunciation, he moves to overturn the tyranny of time itself.

There are thus two main elements in the major phase of the Romantic quest, the first being the inward overcoming of the Selfhood's temptation, and the second the outward turning of the triumphant Imagination, free of further internalizations—though "outward" and "inward" become cloven fictions or false conceptual distinctions in this triumph, which must complete a dialectic of love by uniting the Imagination with its bride, who is a transformed ongoing creation of the Imagination rather than a redeemed nature. Blake and Wordsworth had long lives, and each completed his version of this dialectic. Coleridge gave up the quest, and became only an occasional poet, while Byron's quest, even had he lived into middle age, would have become increasingly ironic. Keats died at twenty-five, and Shelley at twenty-nine; despite their fecundity, they did not complete their development, but their death-fragments, *The Fall of Hyperion* and *The Triumph of Life*, prophesy the final phase of the quest in them. Each work breaks off with the Selfhood subdued, and there is profound despair in each, particularly in Shelley's; but there are still hints of what the Imagination's triumph would have been in Keats. In Shelley, the final despair may be total; but the man who had believed so fervently that the good time would come had already given a vision of imaginative completion in the closing Act of *Prometheus Unbound*, and we can go back to it and see what is deliberately lacking in *The Triumph of Life*. What follows is a rapid attempt to trace the major phase of quest in the four poets, taking as texts *Jerusalem* and *The Prelude*, and the *Fall* and *Triumph*, these two last with supplementary reference to crucial earlier erotic poems of Keats and Shelley.

Of Blake's long poems the first, *The Four Zoas*, is essentially a poem of Prometheus, devoting itself to the cyclic strife between the Promethean Orc and the moral censor, Urizen, in which the endless cycle between the two is fully exposed. The poem ends in an apocalypse, the explosive and Promethean *Night the Ninth, Being The Last Judgment*, which in itself is one of Blake's greatest works, yet from which he turned when he renounced the entire poem (by declining to engrave it). But this renunciation was completed not before he attempted to move the entire poem from the Prometheus stage to the Imagination, for Blake's own process of creative maturation came to its climax while he worked on *The Four Zoas.* The entrance into the mature stage of the quest is clearly shown by the two different versions of *Night the Seven*, for the later one introduces the doubling of the ego into Spectre of Urthona and Los, Selfhood or *Identity-As*, and Imagination or *Identity-With*. Though skillfully handled, it was not fully clarified by Blake, even to himself, and so he refused to regard the poem as a definitive vision.

Its place in his canon was filled, more or less, by the double-romance *Milton* and *Jerusalem*. The first is more palpably in a displaced romance mode, involving as it does symbolic journeys downwards to our world by Milton and his emanation or bride of creation, Ololon, who descend from an orthodox Eternity in a mutual search for one another, the characteristic irony being that they could never find one another in a traditional heaven. There is very little in the poem of the Prometheus phase, Blake having already devoted to that a series of prophetic poems, from *America* and *Europe* through *The Book of Urizen* and on to the magnificent if unsatisfactory (to him, not to us) *The Four Zoas.* The two major stages of the mature phase of quest dominate the structure of *Milton.* The struggle with the Selfhood moves from the quarrel between Palamabron (Blake) and Satan (Hayley) in the introductory "Bard's Song" on to Milton's heroic wrestling match with Urizen, and climaxes in the direct confrontation between Milton and Satan on the Felpham shore, in which Milton recognizes Satan as his own Selfhood. The recognition compels Satan to a full epiphany, and a subsequent defeat. Milton then confronts Ololon, the poem ending in an epiphany contrary to Satan's, in what Blake specifically terms a preparation for a going forth to the great harvest and vintage of the nations. But even this could not be Blake's final Word; the quest in *Milton* is primarily Milton's and not Blake's, and the quest's antagonist is still somewhat externalized.

In *Jerusalem*, *The Prelude's* only rival as the finest long poem of the nineteenth century, Blake gives us the most comprehensive single version of the Romantic quest. Here there is an alternation between vision sweeping outwards into the nightmare world of the reality principle, and a wholly inward vision of conflict in Blake's ego between the Spectre and Los. The poet's antagonist is himself, the poem's first part being the most harrowing and tormented account of genius tempted to the madness of self-righteousness, frustrated anger, and solipsistic withdrawal even in the Romantic period. Blake-Los struggles on against this enchantment of despair, until the poem quietly, almost without warning, begins to move into the light of a Last Judgment, of a kind passed by every man upon himself. In the poem's final plates the reconciliation of Los and his emanative portion, Enitharmon, begins, and we approach the completion of quest.

Though Blake, particularly in *Jerusalem*, attempts a continuity based on thematic juxtaposition and simultaneity, rather than on consecutiveness, he is in such sure control of his own procedure that his work is less difficult to summarize than *The Prelude*, a contrast that tends to startle inexperienced readers of Blake and of Wordsworth. *The Prelude* follows a rough naturalistic chronology through Wordsworth's life down to the middle of the journey, where it, like any modern reader, leaves him in a state of preparation for a further greatness that never came. What is there already, besides the invention of the modern lyric, is a long poem so rich and strange it has defied almost all description.

*The Prelude* is an autobiographical romance that frequently seeks expression in the sublime mode, which is an invitation to aesthetic disaster. *The Excursion* is an aesthetic disaster, as Hazlitt, Byron, and many since happily have noted, yet there Wordsworth works within rational limits. *The Prelude* ought to be an outrageous poem, but its peculiar mixture of displaced genre and inappropriate style *works*, because its internalization of quest is the inevitable story for its age. Wordsworth did not have the Promethean temperament, yet he had absolute insight into it, as *The Borderers* already had shown.

In *The Prelude*, the initial quest phase of the poet-as-Prometheus is diffuse but omnipresent. It determines every movement in the growth of the child's consciousness, always seen as a violation of the established natural order, and it achieves great power in Book VI, when the onset of the French Revolution is associated with the poet's own hidden desires to surmount nature, desires that emerge in the great passages clustered around the Simplon Pass. The Promethean quest fails, in one way in the Alps when chastened by nature, and in another with the series of shocks to the poet's moral being when England wars against the Revolution, and the Revolution betrays itself. The more direct Promethean failure, the poet's actual abandonment of Annette Vallon, is presented only indirectly in the 1805 *Prelude*, and drops out completely from the revised, posthumously published *Prelude* of 1850, the version most readers encounter.

In his crisis, Wordsworth learns the supernatural and superhuman strength of his own imagination, and is able to begin a passage to the mature phase of his quest. But his anxiety for continuity is too strong for him, and he yields to its dark enchantment. The Imagination phase of his quest does not witness the surrender of his Selfhood and the subsequent inauguration of a new dialectic of love, purged of the natural heart, as it is in Blake. Yet he wins a provisional triumph over himself, in Book XII of *The Prelude*, and in the closing stanzas of *Resolution and Independence* and the Great Ode. And the final vision of *The Prelude* is not of a redeemed nature, but of a liberated creativity transforming its creation into the beloved:

Prophets of Nature, we to them will speak
A lasting inspiration, sanctified
By reason, blest by faith: what we have loved
Others will love, and we will teach them how;
Instruct them how the mind of man becomes
A thousand times more beautiful than the earth
On which he dwells, above this frame of things . . .

Coleridge, addressed here as the other Prophet of Nature, renounced his own demonic version of the Romantic quest (clearest in the famous triad of *Kubla Khan*, *Christabel*, and *The Ancient Mariner*), his wavering Prometheanism early defeated not so much by his Selfhood as by his Urizenic fear of his own imaginative energy. It was a high price for the release he had achieved in his brief phase of exploring the romance of the marvelous, but the loss itself produced a few poems of unique value, the *Dejection* Ode in particular. The essay on the Greater Romantic Lyric, included in this book, is M. H. Abrams' pioneering and greatly illuminating explanation of how Coleridge preceded Wordsworth in the invention of a new kind of poetry that shows the mind in a dialogue with itself. The motto of this poetry might well be its descendant, Stevens' "The mind is the terriblest force in the world, father, / Because, in chief, it, only, can defend / Against itself. At its mercy, we depend / Upon it." Coleridge emphasizes the mercy, Wordsworth the saving terror of the force. Keats and Shelley began with a passion closer to the Prometheus phase of Blake than of Wordsworth or Coleridge. The fullest development of the Romantic quest, after Blake's mythology and Wordsworth's exemplary refusal of mythology, is in Keats's *Endymion* and Shelley's *Prometheus Unbound.*

In this second generation of Romantic questers the same first phase of Prometheanism appears, as does the second phase of crisis, renounced quest, overcoming of Selfhood, and final movement towards imaginative love, but the relation of the quest to the world of the reality principle has changed. In Blake, the dream with its ambiguities centers in Beulah, the purgatorial lower paradise of sexuality and benevolent nature. In Wordsworth, the dream is rare, and betokens either a prolepsis of the imagination abolishing nature, or else a state the poet calls "visionary dreariness," in which the immediate power of the mind over outward sense is so great that the ordinary forms of nature seem to have withdrawn. But in Keats and Shelley, a polemical Romanticism matures, and the argument of the dream with reality becomes an equivocal one.

Romanticism guessed at a truth our doctors begin to measure; as infants we dream for half the time we are asleep, and as we age we dream less and less. The doctors have not yet told us that utterly dreamless sleep directly prophesies or equals death, but it is a familiar Romantic conceit, and may prove to be true. We are our imaginations, and die with them.

Dreams, to Shelley and Keats, are not wish fulfillments. It is not Keats but Moneta, the passionate and wrong-headed Muse in *The Fall of Hyperion*, who first confounds poets and dreamers as one tribe, and then insists they are totally distinct and even sheer opposites, antipodes. Freud is again a clear-headed guide; the manifest and latent content of the dream can be distinct, even opposite, but in the poem they come together. The younger Romantics do not seek to render life a dream, but to recover the dream for the health of life. What is called real is too often an exhausted phantasmagoria, and the reality principle can too easily be debased into a principle of surrender, an accommodation with death-in-life. We return to the observation of Van den Berg, cited earlier: Rousseau and the Romantics discovered not only the alienation between child and adult, but the second birth of psychic maturation or adolescence. Eliot thought that the poet of *Adonais* and *The Triumph of Life* had never "progressed" beyond the ideas and ideals of adolescence, or at least of what Eliot had believed in *his* own adolescence. Every reader can be left to his own judgment of the relative maturity of *Ash Wednesday* and *The Witch of Atlas*, or *The Cocktail Party* and *The Cenci*, and is free to formulate his own dialectics of progression.

The Promethean quest, in Shelley and in Keats, is from the start uneasy about its equivocal ally, nature, and places a deeper trust in the dream; for at least the dream itself is not reductive, however we reduce it in our dissections. Perhaps the most remarkable element in the preternatural rapidity of maturation in Keats and Shelley is their early renunciation of the Prometheus phase of the quest, or rather, their dialectical complexity in simultaneously presenting the necessity and the inherent limitation of this phase. In *Alastor*, the poem's entire thrust is at one with the Poet-hero's self-destruction; this is the cause of the poem's radical unity, which C. S. Lewis rightly observed as giving a marvelous sense of the poet's being at one with his subject. Yet the poem is also a daimonic shadow in motion; it shows us nature's revenge upon the imagination, and the excessive price of the quest in the poet's alienation from other selves.

On a cosmic scale, this is part of the burden of *Prometheus Unbound*, where the hero, who massively represents the bound prophetic power of all men, rises from his icy crucifixion by refusing to continue the cycles of revolution and repression that form an ironic continuity between himself and Jupiter. Demogorgon, the dialectic of history, rises from the abyss and stops history, thus completing in the macrocosmic shadow what Prometheus, by his renunciation, inaugurates in the microcosm of the individual imagination, or the liberating dream taken up into the self. Shelley's poetry after this does not maintain the celebratory strain of Act IV of his lyrical drama. The way again is down and out, to a purgatorial encounter with the Selfhood, but the Selfhood's temptations, for Shelley, are subtle and wavering, and mask themselves in the forms of the ideal. So fused do the ideal and these masks become that Shelley, in the last lines he wrote, is in despair of any victory, though it is Shelley's Rousseau and not Shelley himself who actually chants:

> . . . thus on the way
> Mask after mask fell from the countenance
> And form of all; and long before the day
>
> Was old, the joy which waked like heaven's glance
> The sleepers in the oblivious valley, died;
> And some grew weary of the ghastly dance,
>
> And fell, as I have fallen, by the wayside—

For Shelley, Rousseau was not a failed poet, but rather the poet whose influence had resulted in an imaginative revolution, and nearly ended time's bondage. So Rousseau speaks here not for himself alone, but for his tradition, and necessarily for Coleridge, Wordsworth, and the Promethean Shelley as well, indeed for poetry itself. Yet rightly or wrongly, the image Shelley leaves with us at his end is not this falling-away from the quest, but the image of the poet forever wakeful amidst the cone of night, illuminating it as the star Lucifer does, fading as the star, becoming more intense as it narrows into the light.

The mazes of romance in *Endymion* are so winding that they suggest the contrary to vision, a labyrinthine nature in which all quest must be forlorn. In this realm, nothing narrows to an intensity, and every passionate impulse widens out to a diffuseness, the fate of Endymion's own search for his goddess. In reaction, Keats chastens his own Prometheanism, and attempts the objective epic in *Hyperion*. Hyperion's self-identity is strong but waning fast, and the fragment of the poem's Book III introduces an Apollo whose self-identity is in the act of being born. The temptation to go on with the poem must have been very great after its magnificent beginnings, but Keats's letters are firm in renouncing it. Keats turns from the enchantments of identity to the romance-fragment, *The Fall of Hyperion*, and engages instead the demon of subjectivity, his own poetic ambitions, as Wordsworth had done before him. Confronted by Moneta, he meets the danger of her challenge not by asserting his own identity, but by finding his true form in the merged identity of the poethood, in the high function and responsibilities of a Wordsworthian humanism. Though the poem breaks off before it attempts the dialectic of love, it has achieved the quest, for the Muse herself has been transformed by the poet's persistence and integrity. We wish for more, necessarily, but only now begin to understand how much we have received, even in this broken monument.

I have scanted the dialectic of love in all of these poets. Romantic love, past its own Promethean adolescence, is not the possessive love of the natural heart, which is the quest of the Freudian Eros, moving always in a tragic rhythm out from and back to the isolated ego. That is the love Blake explicitly rejected:

> Let us agree to give up Love
> And root up the Infernal Grove
> Then shall we return and see
> The worlds of happy Eternity
>
> Throughout all Eternity
> I forgive you you forgive me . . .

The Infernal Grove grows thick with virtues, but these are the selfish virtues of the natural heart. Desire for what one lacks becomes a habit of possession, and the Selfhood's jealousy murders the Real Man, the imagination. All such love is an entropy, and as such Freud understood and accepted it. We become aware of others only as we learn our separation from them, and our ecstasy is a reduction. Is this the human condition, and love only its mitigation?

> To cast off the idiot Questioner who is always questioning,
> But never capable of answering . . .

Whatever else the love that the full Romantic quest aims at may be, it cannot be a therapy. It must make all things new, and then marry what it has made. Less urgently, it seeks to define itself through the analogue of each man's creative potential. But it learns, through its poets, that it cannot define what it is, but only what it will be. The man prophesied by the Romantics is a central man who is always in the process of becoming his own begetter, and though his major poems perhaps have been written, he has not as yet fleshed out his prophecy, nor proved the final form of his love.

# 6

# THE DRUNKEN BOAT:
# THE REVOLUTIONARY ELEMENT
# IN ROMANTICISM

## *Northrop Frye*

Source: *Romanticism Reconsidered: Selected Papers from the English Institute*, ed. Northrop Frye (New York: Columbia University Press, 1963), pp. 1–25.

Any such conception as "Romanticism" is at one or more removes from actual literary experience, in an inner world where ten thousand different things flash upon the inward eye with all the bliss of oversimplification. Some things about it, however, are generally accepted, and we may start with them. First, Romanticism has a historical center of gravity, which falls somewhere around the 1790–1830 period. This gets us at once out of the fallacy of timeless characterization, where we say that Romanticism has certain qualities, not found in the age of Pope, of sympathy with nature or what not, only to have someone produce a poem of Propertius or Kalidasa, or, eventually, Pope himself, and demand to know if the same qualities are not there. Second, Romanticism is not a general historical term like "medieval": it appears to have another center of gravity in the creative arts. We speak most naturally of Romantic literature, painting, and music. We do, it is true, speak of Romantic philosophy, but what seems to us most clearly Romantic in that are such things as the existential ethic of Fichte or the analogical constructs of Schelling; both of them, in different ways, examples of philosophy produced by an essentially literary mind, like the philosophies of Sartre or Maritain in our day. So at least they seemed to Kant, if one may judge from Kant's letter to Fichte suggesting that Fichte abandon philosophy, as a subject too difficult for him, and confine himself to lively popularizations.

Third, even in its application to the creative arts Romanticism is a selective term, more selective even than "Baroque" appears to be becoming. We think of it as including Keats, but not, on the whole, Crabbe; Scott, but not, in general, Jane Austen; Wordsworth, but not, on any account, James Mill.

As generally used, "Romantic" is contrasted with two other terms, "classical" and "realistic." Neither contrast seems satisfactory. We could hardly call Wordsworth's preface to the *Lyrical Ballads* anti-realistic, or ignore the fact that Shelley was a better classical scholar than, say, Dryden, who, according to Samuel Johnson, translated the first book of the *Iliad* without knowing what was in the second. Still, the pairings exist, and we shall have to examine them. And yet, fourth, though selective, Romanticism is not a voluntary category. It does not see Byron as the successor to Pope or Wordsworth as the successor to Milton, which would have been acceptable enough to both poets: it associates Byron and Wordsworth, to their mutual disgust, with each other.

Accepting all this, we must also avoid the two traps in the phrase "history of ideas." First, an idea, as such, is independent of time and can be argued about; an historical event is not and cannot be. If Romanticism is in part an historical event, as it clearly is, then to say with T. E. Hulme: "I object to even the best of the Romantics" is much like saying: "I object to even the best battles of the Napoleonic War." Most general value-judgments on Romanticism as a whole are rationalizations of an agreement or disagreement with some belief of which Romantic poetry is supposed to form the objective correlative.

This latter is the second or Hegelian trap in the history of ideas, which we fall into when we assume that around 1790 or earlier some kind of thesis arose in history and embodied itself in the Romantic movement. Such an assumption leads us to examining all the cultural products we call Romantic as allegories of that thesis. Theses have a way of disagreeing with each other, and if we try to think of Romanticism as some kind of single "idea," all we can do with it is what Lovejoy did: break it down into a number of contradictory ideas with nothing significant in common. In literature, and more particularly poetry, ideas are subordinated to imagery, to a language more "simple, sensuous, and passionate" than the language of philosophy. Hence it may be possible for two poets to be related by common qualities of imagery even when they do not agree on a single thesis in religion, politics, or the theory of art itself.

The history of imagery, unlike the history of ideas, appears to be for the most part a domain where, in the words of a fictional Canadian poetess, "the hand of man hath never trod." Yet we seem inexorably led to it by our own argument, and perhaps the defects in what follows may be in part excused by the novelty of the subject, to me at least. After making every allowance for a prodigious variety of technique and approach, it is still possible to see a consistent framework (I wish the English language had a better equivalent for the French word *cadre*) in the imagery of both medieval and Renaissance poetry. The most remarkable and obvious feature of this framework is the division of being into four levels. The highest level is heaven, the place of the presence of God. Next come the two levels of the order of nature, the human level and the physical level. The order of human nature, or man's proper home, is represented by the story of the Garden of Eden in the Bible and the myth of the Golden Age in Boethius and elsewhere. Man is no longer in it, but the end of all his religious, moral, and social cultivation is to raise him into something resembling it. Physical nature, the world of animals and plants, is the world man is now in, but unlike the animals and plants he is not adjusted to it. He is confronted from birth with a moral dialectic, and must either rise above it to his proper human home or sink below it into the fourth level of sin, death, and hell. This last level is not part of the order of nature, but its existence is what at present corrupts nature. A very similar framework can be found in classical poetry, and the alliance of the two, in what is so often called Christian humanism, accounts for the sense of an antagonism between the Romantic movement and the classical tradition, in spite of its many and remarkable affinities with that tradition.

Such a framework of images, however closely related in practice to belief, is not in itself a belief or an expression of belief: it is in itself simply a way of arranging images and providing for metaphors. At the same time the word "framework" itself is a spatial metaphor, and any framework is likely to be projected in space, even confused or identified with its spatial projection. In Dante Eden is a long way up, on top of the mountain of purgatory; heaven is much further up, and hell is down, at the center of the earth. We may know that such conceptions as heaven and hell do not depend on spatial metaphors of up and down, but a cosmological poet, dealing with them as images, has to put them somewhere. To Dante it was simple enough to put them at the top and bottom of the natural order, because he knew of no alternative to the Ptolemaic picture of the world. To Milton, who did know of an alternative, the problem was more complex, and Milton's heaven and hell are outside the cosmos, in a kind of absolute up and down. After Milton comes Newton, and after Newton ups and downs become hopelessly confused.

What I see first of all in Romanticism is the effect of a profound change, not primarily in belief, but in the spatial projection of reality. This in turn leads to a different localizing of the various levels of that reality. Such a change in the localizing of images is bound to be accompanied by, or even cause, changes in belief and attitude, and changes of this latter sort are exhibited by the Romantic poets. But the change itself is not in belief or attitude, and may be found in, or at least affecting, poets of a great variety of beliefs.

In the earlier framework, the disorder of sin, death, and corruption was restricted to the sublunary world of four elements. Above the moon was all that was left of nature as God had originally planned it before the fall. The planets, with their angel-guided spheres, are images of a divinely sanctioned order of nature which is also the true home of man. Hence there was no poetic incongruity in Dante's locating his Paradiso in the planetary spheres, nor in Milton's associating the music of the spheres with the song of the angels in the *Nativity Ode*, nor in using the same word "heaven" for both the kingdom of God and the sky. A post-Newtonian poet has to think of gravitation and the solar system. Newton, Miss Nicolson has reminded us, demanded the muse, but the appropriate muse was Urania, and Urania had already been requested by Milton to descend to a safer position on earth for the second half of *Paradise Lost.*

Let us turn to Blake's poem *Europe*, engraved in 1794. *Europe* surveys the history of the Western world from the birth of Christ to the beginning of the French Revolution, and in its opening lines parodies the *Nativity Ode.* For Blake all the deities associated with the planets and the starry skies, of whom the chief is Enitharmon, the Queen of Heaven, are projections of a human will to tyranny, rationalized as eternal necessity and order. Christianity, according to this poem, had not abolished but confirmed the natural religion in the classical culture which had deified the star-gods. The doom of tyranny is sealed by the French Revolution, and the angel who blows the last trumpet as the sign of the final awakening of liberty is Isaac Newton. The frontispiece of *Europe* is the famous vision of the sky-god Urizen generally called the Ancient of Days, holding a compass in his left hand, and this picture is closely related to Blake's portrait of Newton, similarly preoccupied with a compass and oblivious of the heavens he is supposed to be studying.

Blake's view, in short, is that the universe of modern astronomy, as revealed in Newton, exhibits only a blind, mechanical, subhuman order, not the personal presence of a deity. Newton himself tended to think of God still as "up there," even to the extent of suggesting that space was the divine sensorium; but *what* was up there, according to Blake, is only a set of interlocking geometrical diagrams, and God, Blake says, is not a mathematical diagram. Newtonism leads to what for Blake are intellectual errors, such as a sense of the superiority of abstractions to actual things and the notion that the real world is a measurable but invisible world of primary qualities. But Blake's main point is that admiring the mechanisms of the sky leads to establishing human life in mechanical patterns too. In other words, Blake's myth of Urizen is a fuller and more sophisticated version of the myth of Frankenstein.

Blake's evil, sinister, or merely complacent sky-gods, Urizen, Nobodaddy, Enitharmon, Satan, remind us of similar beings in other Romantics: Shelley's Jupiter, Byron's Arimanes, the Lord in the Prologue to *Faust.* They in their turn beget later Romantic gods and goddesses, such as Baudelaire's female "froide majesté," Hardy's Immanent Will, or the God of Housman's "The chestnut casts his flambeaux," who is a brute and blackguard because he is a sky-god in control of the weather, and sends his rain on the just and on the unjust. The association of sinister or unconscious mechanism with what we now call outer space is a commonplace of popular literature today which is a Romantic inheritance. Perhaps Orwell's *1984*, a vision of a mechanical

125

tyranny informed by the shadow of a Big Brother who can never die, is the terminal point of a development of imagery that began with Blake's Ancient of Days. Not every poet, naturally, associates mechanism with the movements of the stars as Blake does, or sees it as a human imitation of the wrong kind of divine creativity. But the contrast between the mechanical and the organic is deeply rooted in Romantic thinking, and the tendency is to associate the mechanical with ordinary consciousness, as we see in the account of the associative fancy in Coleridge's *Biographia* or of discursive thought in Shelley's *Defence of Poetry*. This is in striking contrast to the Cartesian tradition, where the mechanical is of course associated with the subconscious. The mechanical being characteristic of ordinary experience, it is found particularly in the world "outside"; the superior or organic world is consequently "inside," and although it is still called superior or higher, the natural metaphorical direction of the inside world is downward, into the profounder depths of consciousness.

If a Romantic poet, therefore, wishes to write of God, he has more difficulty in finding a place to put him than Dante or even Milton had, and on the whole he prefers to do without a place, or finds "within" metaphors more reassuring than "up there" metaphors. When Wordsworth speaks, in *The Prelude* and elsewhere, of feeling the presence of deity through a sense of interpenetration of the human mind and natural powers, one feels that his huge and mighty forms, like the spirits of Yeats, have come to bring him the right metaphors for his poetry. In the second book of *The Excursion* we have a remarkable vision of what has been called the heavenly city of the eighteenth-century philosophers, cast in the form of an ascent up a mountain, where the city is seen at the top. The symbolism, I think, is modeled on the vision of Cleopolis in the first book of *The Faerie Queene*, and its technique is admirably controlled and precise. Yet surely this is not the real Wordsworth. The spirits have brought him the wrong metaphors; metaphors that Spenser used with full imaginative conviction, but which affect only the surface of Wordsworth's mind.

The second level of the older construct was the world of original human nature, now a lost paradise or golden age. It is conceived as a better and more appropriate home for man than his present environment, whether man can regain it or not. But in the older construct this world was ordinarily not thought of as human in origin or conception. Adam awoke in a garden not of his planting, in a fresh-air suburb of the City of God, and when the descendants of Cain began to build cities on earth, they were building to models already existing in both heaven and hell. In the Middle Ages and the Renaissance the agencies which helped to raise man from the physical to the human world were such things as the sacraments of religion, the moral law, and the habit of virtue, none of them strictly human inventions. These were the safe and unquestioned agencies, the genuinely educational media. Whether the human arts of poetry and painting and music were genuinely educational in this sense could be and was disputed or denied; and the poets themselves, when they wrote apologies for poetry, seldom claimed equality with religion or law, beyond pointing out that the earliest major poets were prophets and lawgivers.

For the modern mind there are two poles of mental activity. One may be described as sense, by which I mean the recognition of what is presented by experience: the empirical, observant habit of mind in which, among other things, the inductive sciences begin. In this attitude reality is, first of all, "out there," whatever happens to it afterwards. The other pole is the purely formalizing or constructive aspect of the mind, where reality is something brought into being by the act of construction. It is obvious that in pre-Romantic poetry there is a strong affinity with the attitude that we have called sense. The poet, in all ages and cultures, prefers images to abstractions, the sensational to the conceptual. But the pre-Romantic structure of imagery belonged to a nature which was the work of God; the design in nature was, as Sir Thomas Browne calls it, the art of God; nature is thus an objective structure or system for the poet to follow. The appropriate metaphors of imitation are visual and physical ones, and the creative powers of the poet have models outside him.

It is generally recognized that Rousseau represents, and to some extent made, a revolutionary change in the modern attitude. The primary reason for his impact was, I think, not in his political or educational views as such, but in his assumption that civilization was a purely human artifact, something that man had made, could unmake, could subject to his own criticism, and was at all times entirely responsible for. Above all, it was something for which the only known model was in the human mind. This kind of assumption is so penetrating that it affects those who detest Rousseau, or have never heard of him, equally with the small minority of his admirers. Also, it gets into the mind at once, whereas the fading out of such counter assumptions as the literal and historical nature of the Garden of Eden story is very gradual. The effect of such an assumption is twofold. First, it puts the arts in the center of civilization. The basis of civilization is now the creative power of man; its model is the human vision revealed in the arts. Second, this model, as well as the sources of creative power, are now located in the mind's internal heaven, the external world being seen as a mirror reflecting and making visible what is within. Thus the "outside" world, most of which is "up there," yields importance and priority to the inner world, in fact derives its poetic significance at least from it. "In looking at objects of Nature," says Coleridge in the Notebooks, "I seem rather to be seeking, as it were *asking* for, a symbolical language for something within me that already and forever exists, than observing anything new." This principle extends both to the immediate surrounding world which is the emblem of the music of humanity in Wordsworth and to the starry heavens on which Keats read "Huge cloudy symbols of a high romance."

Hence in Romantic poetry the emphasis is not on what we have called sense, but on the constructive power of the mind, where reality is brought into being by experience. There is a contrast in popular speech between the romantic and the realist, where the word "romantic" implies a sentimentalized or rose-colored view of reality. This vulgar sense of the word may throw some light on the intensity with which the Romantic poets sought to defy external reality by creating a uniformity of tone and mood. The establishing of this uniformity, and the careful excluding of anything that would dispel it, is one of the constant and typical features of the best Romantic poetry, though we may call it a dissociation of sensibility if we happen not to like it. Such a poetic technique is, psychologically, akin to magic, which also aims at bringing spiritual forces into reality through concentration on a certain type of experience. Such words as "charm" or "spell" suggest uniformity of mood as well as a magician's repertoire. Historically and generically, it is akin to romance, with its effort to maintain a self-consistent idealized world without the intrusions of realism or irony.

For these reasons Romanticism is difficult to adapt to the novel, which demands an empirical and observant attitude; its contribution to prose fiction is rather, appropriately enough, a form of romance. In the romance the characters tend to become psychological projections, and the setting a period in a past just remote enough to be re-created rather than empirically studied. We think of Scott as within the Romantic movement; Jane Austen as related to it chiefly by her parodies of the kind of sensibility that tries to live in a self-created world instead of adapting to the one that is there. Marianne in *Sense and Sensibility*, Catherine in *Northanger Abbey*, and of course everybody in *Love and Friendship*, are examples. Crabbe's naturalistic manifesto in the opening of *The Village* expresses an attitude which in itself is not far from Wordsworth's. But Crabbe is a metrical novelist in a way that Wordsworth is not. The soldier in *The Prelude* and the leech-gatherer in *Resolution and Independence* are purely romantic characters in the sense just given of psychological projections: that is, they become temporary or epiphanic myths. We should also notice that the internalizing of reality in Romanticism proper develops a contrast between it and a contemporary realism which descends from the pre-Romantic tradition but acquires a more purely empirical attitude to the external world.

The third level of the older construct was the physical world, theologically fallen, which man is born into but which is not the real world of human nature. Man's primary attitude to external physical nature is thus one of detachment. The kind of temptation represented by Spenser's Bower of Bliss or Milton's Comus is based on the false suggestion that physical nature, with its relatively innocent moral freedom, can be the model for human nature. The resemblances between the poetic techniques used in the Bower of Bliss episode and some of the techniques of the Romantics are superficial: Spenser, unlike the Romantics, is consciously producing a rhetorical set piece, designed to show that the Bower of Bliss is not natural but artificial in the modern sense. Man for pre-Romantic poets is not a child of Nature in the sense that he was originally a primitive. Milton's Adam becomes a noble savage immediately after his fall; but that is not his original nature. In Romanticism the cult of the primitive is a by-product of the internalizing of the creative impulse. The poet has always been supposed to be imitating nature, but if the model of his creative power is in his mind, the nature that he is to imitate is now inside him, even if it is also outside.

The original form of human society also is hidden "within." Keats refers to this hidden society when he says in a letter to Reynolds: "Man should not dispute or assert but whisper results to his neighbour ... and Humanity ... would become a grand democracy of Forest Trees!" Coleridge refers to it in the *Biographia* when he says: "The medium, by which spirits understand each other, is not the surrounding air; but the *freedom* which they possess in common." Whether the Romantic poet is revolutionary or conservative depends on whether he regards this original society as concealed by or as manifested in existing society. If the former, he will think of true society as a primitive structure of nature and reason, and will admire the popular, simple, or even the barbaric more than the sophisticated. If the latter, he will find his true inner society manifested by a sacramental church or by the instinctive manners of an aristocracy. The search for a visible ideal society in history leads to a good deal of admiration for the Middle Ages, which on the Continent was sometimes regarded as the essential feature of Romanticism. The affinity between the more extreme Romantic conservatism and the subversive revolutionary movements of fascism and nazism in our day has been often pointed out. The present significance for us of this fact is that the notion of the inwardness of creative power is inherently revolutionary, just as the pre-Romantic construct was inherently conservative, even for poets as revolutionary as Milton. The self-identifying admiration which so many Romantics expressed for Napoleon has much to do with the association of natural force, creative power, and revolutionary outbreak. As Carlyle says, in an uncharacteristically cautious assessment of Napoleon: "What Napoleon *did* will in the long-run amount to what he did *justly*; what Nature with her laws will sanction."

Further, the Romantic poet is a part of a total process, engaged with and united to a creative power greater than his own because it includes his own. This greater creative power has a relation to him which we may call, adapting a term of Blake's, his vehicular form. The sense of identity with a larger power of creative energy meets us everywhere in Romantic culture, I think even in the crowded excited canvases of Delacroix and the tremendous will-to-power finales of Beethoven. The symbolism of it in literature has been too thoroughly studied in Professor Abrams's *The Mirror and the Lamp* and in Professor Wasserman's *The Subtler Language* for me to add more than a footnote or two at this point. Sometimes the greater power of this vehicular form is a rushing wind, as in Shelley's Ode and in the figure of the "correspondent breeze" studied by Professor Abrams. The image of the Aeolian harp, or lyre—Romantic poets are apt to be sketchy in their orchestration—belongs here. Sometimes it is a boat driven by a breeze or current, or by more efficient magical forces in the *Ancient Mariner*. This image occurs so often in Shelley that it has helped to suggest my title; the introduction to Wordsworth's *Peter Bell* has a flying boat closely associated with the moon. Those poems of Wordsworth in which we feel driven along by a propelling metrical energy, *Peter Bell*, *The Idiot Boy*, *The Waggoner*, and others, seem to me to be among Wordsworth's most central poems. Sometimes the vehicular form is a heightened state of consciousness in which we feel that we are greater than we know, or an intense feeling of communion, as in the sacramental corn-and-wine images of the great Keats odes.

The sense of unity with a greater power is surely one of the reasons why so much of the best Romantic poetry is mythopoeic. The myth is typically the story of the god, whose form and character are human but who is also a sun-god or tree-god or ocean-god. It identifies the human with the nonhuman world, an identification which is also one of the major functions of poetry itself. Coleridge makes it a part of the primary as well as the secondary imagination. "This I call *I*," he says in the Notebooks, "identifying the percipient and the perceived." The "Giant Forms" of Blake's prophecies are states of being and feeling in which we have our own being and feeling; the huge and mighty forms of Wordsworth's *Prelude* have similar affinities; even the dreams of De Quincey seem vehicular in the same sense. It is curious that there seems to be so little mythopoeic theory in Romantic poets, considering that the more expendable critics of the time complained as much about the obscurity of myth as their counterparts of today do now.

One striking feature of the Romantic poets is their resistance to fragmentation: their compulsion, almost, to express themselves in long continuous poems is quite as remarkable as their lyrical gifts. I have remarked elsewhere that the romance, in its most naive and primitive form, is an endless sequence of adventures, terminated only by the author's death or disgust. In Romanticism something of this inherently endless romance form recurs. *Childe Harold* and *Don Juan* are Byron to such an extent that the poems about them can be finished only by Byron's death or boredom with the *persona*. *The Prelude*, and still more the gigantic scheme of which it formed part, has a similar relation to Wordsworth, and something parallel is beginning to show its head at once in Keats's *Sleep and Poetry* and Shelley's *Queen Mab*. We touch here on the problem of the Romantic unfinished poem, which has been studied by Professor Bostetter. My present interest, however, is rather in the feature of unlimited continuity, which seems to me connected with the sense of vehicular energy, of being carried along by a greater force, the quality which outside literature, according to Keats, makes a man's life a continual allegory.

We have found, then, that the metaphorical structure of Romantic poetry tends to move inside and downward instead of outside and upward, hence the creative world is deep within, and so is heaven or the place of the presence of God. Blake's Orc and Shelley's Prometheus are Titans imprisoned underneath experience; the Gardens of Adonis are down in *Endymion*, whereas they are up in *The Faerie Queene* and *Comus*; in *Prometheus Unbound* everything that aids mankind comes from below, associated with volcanoes and fountains. In *The Revolt of Islam* there is a curious collision with an older habit of metaphor when Shelley speaks of

> A power, a thirst, a knowledge . . . below
> All thoughts, like light beyond the atmosphere.

The *Kubla Khan* geography of caves and underground streams haunts all of Shelley's language about creative processes: in *Speculations on Metaphysics*, for instance, he says: "But thought can with difficulty visit the intricate and winding chambers which it inhabits. It is like a river whose rapid and perpetual stream flows outwards. . . . The caverns of the mind are obscure, and shadowy, or pervaded with a lustre, beautifully bright indeed, but shining not beyond their portals."

In pre-Romantic poetry heaven is the order of grace, and grace is normally thought of as descending from above into the soul. In the Romantic construct there is a center where inward and outward manifestations of a common motion and spirit are unified, where the ego is identified as itself because it is also identified with something which is not itself. In Blake this world at the deep center is Jerusalem, the City of God that mankind, or Albion, has sought all through history without success because he has been looking in the wrong direction, outside. Jerusalem is also the garden of Eden where the Holy Word walked among the ancient trees; Eden in the unfallen world would be the same place as England's green and pleasant land where Christ also walked; and England's green and pleasant land is also Atlantis, the sunken island kingdom which we can rediscover by draining the "Sea of Time and Space" off the top of the mind. In *Prometheus Unbound* Atlantis reappears when Prometheus is liberated, and the one great flash of vision which is all that is left to us of Wordsworth's *Recluse* uses the same imagery.

> Paradise, and groves
> Elysian, Fortunate Fields—like those of old
> Sought in the Atlantic Main—why should they be
> A history only of departed things,
> Or a mere fiction of what never was? . . .
> —I, long before the blissful hour arrives,
> Would chant, in lonely peace, the spousal verse
> Of this great consummation.

The Atlantis theme is in many other Romantic myths: in the Glaucus episode of *Endymion* and in De Quincey's *Savannah-la-Mar*, which speaks of "human life still subsisting in submarine asylums sacred from the storms that torment our upper air." The theme of land reclaimed from the ocean plays also a somewhat curious role in Goethe's *Faust*. We find the same imagery in later writers who continue the Romantic tradition, such as D. H. Lawrence in the "Song of a Man Who Has Come Through":

> If only I am keen and hard like the sheer tip of a wedge
> Driven by invisible blows,
> The rock will split, we shall come at the wonder, we shall find
>    the Hesperides.

In *The Pilgrim's Progress* Ignorance is sent to hell from the very gates of heaven. The inference seems to be that only Ignorance knows the precise location of both kingdoms. For knowledge, and still more for imagination, the journey within to the happy island garden or the city of light is a perilous quest, equally likely to terminate in the blasted ruin of Byron's *Darkness* or Beddoes's *Subterranean City*. In many Romantic poems, including Keats's nightingale ode, it is suggested that the final identification of and with reality may be or at least include death. The suggestion that death may lead to the highest knowledge, dropped by Lucifer in Byron's *Cain*, haunts Shelley continually. A famous passage in *Prometheus Unbound* associates the worlds of creation and death in the same inner area, where Zoroaster meets his image in a garden. Just as the sun is the means but not a tolerable object of sight, so the attempt to turn around and see the source of one's vision may be destructive, as the Lady of Shalott found when she turned away from the mirror. Thus the world of the deep interior in Romantic poetry is morally ambivalent, retaining some of the demonic qualities that the corresponding pre-Romantic lowest level had.

This sense that the source of genius is beyond good and evil, that the possession of genius may be a curse, that the only real knowledge given to Adam in Paradise, however disastrous, came to him from the devil—all this is part of the contribution of Byron to modern sensibility, and part of the irrevocable change that he made in it. Of his Lara Byron says:

> He stood a stranger in this breathing world,
> An erring spirit from another hurl'd;
> A thing of dark imaginings, that shaped
> By choice the perils he by chance escaped;
> But 'scaped in vain, for in their memory yet
> His mind would half exult and half regret . . .
> But haughty still and loth himself to blame,
> He call'd on Nature's self to share the shame,

132

And charged all faults upon the fleshly form
She gave to clog the soul, and feast the worm;
Till he at last confounded good and ill,
And half mistook for fate the acts of will.

It would be wrong to regard this as Byronic hokum, for the wording is very precise. Lara looks demonic to a nervous and conforming society, as the dragon does to the tame villatic fowl in Milton. But there is a genuinely demonic quality in him which arises from his being nearer than other men to the unity of subjective and objective worlds. To be in such a place might make a poet more creative; it makes other types of superior beings, including Lara, more destructive.

We said earlier that a Romantic poet's political views would depend partly on whether he saw his inner society as concealed by or as manifested in actual society. A Romantic poet's moral attitude depends on a similar ambivalence in the conception of nature. Nature to Wordsworth is a mother-goddess who teaches the soul serenity and joy, and never betrays the heart that loves her; to the Marquis de Sade nature is the source of all the perverse pleasures that an earlier age had classified as "unnatural." For Wordsworth the reality of Nature is manifested by its reflection of moral values; for De Sade the reality is concealed by that reflection. It is this ambivalent sense (for it is ambivalent, and not simply ambiguous) of appearance as at the same time revealing and concealing reality, as clothes simultaneously reveal and conceal the naked body, that makes *Sartor Resartus* so central a document of the Romantic movement. We spoke of Wordsworth's Nature as a mother-goddess, and her psychological descent from mother-figures is clearly traced in *The Prelude*. The corn-goddess in Keats's *To Autumn*, the parallel figure identified with Ruth in the *Ode to a Nightingale*, the still unravished bride of the Grecian urn, Psyche, even the veiled Melancholy, are all emblems of a revealed Nature. Elusive nymphs or teasing and mocking female figures who refuse to take definite form, like the figure in *Alastor* or Blake's "female will" types; terrible and sinister white goddesses like La Belle Dame sans Merci, or females associated with something forbidden or demonic, like the sister-lovers of Byron and Shelley, belong to the concealed aspect.

For Wordsworth, who still has a good deal of the pre-Romantic sense of nature as an objective order, nature is a landscape nature, and from it, as in Baudelaire's *Correspondances*, mysterious oracles seep into the mind through eye or ear, even a bird with so predictable a song as the cuckoo being an oracular wandering voice. This landscape is a veil dropped over the naked nature of screaming rabbits and gasping stags, the nature red in tooth and claw which haunted a later generation. Even the episode of the dog and the hedgehog in *The Prelude* is told from the point of view of the dog and not of the hedgehog. But the more pessimistic, and perhaps more realistic, conception of nature in which it can be a source of evil or suffering as well as good is the one that gains ascendancy in the later period of Romanticism, and its later period extends to our own day.

The major constructs which our own culture has inherited from its Romantic ancestry are also of the "drunken boat" shape, but represent a later and a different conception of it from the "vehicular form" described above. Here the boat is usually in the position of Noah's ark, a fragile container of sensitive and imaginative values threatened by a chaotic and unconscious power below it. In Schopenhauer, the world as idea rides precariously on top of a "world as will" which engulfs practically the whole of existence in its moral indifference. In Darwin, who readily combines with Schopenhauer, as the later work of Hardy illustrates, consciousness and morality are accidental sports from a ruthlessly competitive evolutionary force. In Freud, who has noted the resemblance of his mythical structure to Schopenhauer's, the conscious ego struggles to keep afloat on a sea of libidinous impulse. In Kierkegaard, all the "higher" impulses of fallen man pitch and roll on the surface of a huge and shapeless "dread." In some versions of this construct the antithesis of the symbol of consciousness and the destructive element in which it is immersed can be overcome or transcended: there is an Atlantis under the sea which becomes an Ararat for the beleaguered boat to rest on.

I give an example from Auden, partly because he is prominently featured in this session of the Institute, and partly to show that the Romantic structures of symbolism are still ours. In Freud, when the conscious mind feels threatened by the subconscious, it tries to repress it, and so develops a neurosis. In Marx, the liberal elements in an ascendant class, when they feel threatened by a revolutionary situation, develop a police state. In both cases the effort is to intensify the antithesis between the two, but this effort is mistaken, and when the barriers are broken down we reach the balanced mind and the classless society respectively. *For the Time Being* develops a religious construct out of Kierkegaard on the analogy of those of Marx and Freud. The liberal or rational elements represented by Herod feel threatened by the revival of superstition in the Incarnation, and try to repress it. Their failure means that the effort to come to terms with a nature outside the mind, the primary effort of reason, has to be abandoned, and this enables the Paradise or divine presence which is locked up inside the human mind to manifest itself after the reason has searched the whole of objective nature in vain to find it. The attitude is that of a relatively orthodox Christianity; the imagery and the structure of symbolism is that of *Prometheus Unbound* and *The Marriage of Heaven and Hell*.

In Romanticism proper a prominent place in sense experience is given to the ear, an excellent receiver of oracles but poor in locating things accurately in space. This latter power, which is primarily visual, is associated with the fancy in Wordsworth's 1815 preface, and given the subordinate position appropriate to fancy. In later poetry, beginning with *symbolisme* in France, when there is a good deal of reaction against earlier Romanticism, more emphasis is thrown on vision. In Rimbaud, though his *Bateau Ivre* has given me my title, the poet is to *se faire voyant*, the *illuminations* are thought of pictorially; even the vowels must be visually colored. Such an emphasis has nothing to do with the pre-Romantic sense of an objective structure in nature: on the contrary, the purpose of it is to intensify the Romantic sense of oracular significance into a kind of autohypnosis. (The association of auto-hypnosis and the visual sense is discussed in Professor Marshall McLuhan's new book, *The Gutenberg Galaxy*.) Such an emphasis leads to a technique of fragmentation. Poe's attack on the long poem is not a Romantic but an anti-Romantic manifesto, as the direction of its influence indicates. The tradition of *symbolisme* is present in imagism, where the primacy of visual values is so strongly stated in theory and so cheerfully ignored in practice, in Pound's emphasis on the spatial juxtaposing of metaphor, in Eliot's insist-ence on the superiority of poets who present the "clear visual images" of Dante. T. E. Hulme's attack on the Romantic tradition is consistent in preferring fancy to imagination and in stressing the objectivity of the nature to be imitated; less so in his primitivism and his use of Bergson. The tech-nique of fragmentation is perhaps intended to reach its limit in Pound's publication of the complete poetical works of Hulme on a single page.

As I have tried to indicate by my reference to Auden, what this anti-Romantic movement did not do was to create a third framework of imagery. Nor did it return to the older construct, though Eliot, by sticking closely to Dante and by deprecating the importance of the prophetic element in art, gives some illusion of doing so. The charge of subjectivity, brought against the Romantics by Arnold and often repeated later, assumes that objectivity is a higher attribute of poetry, but this is itself a Romantic conception, and came into English criticism with Coleridge. Anti-Romanticism, in short, had no resources for becoming anything more than a post-Romantic movement. The first phase of the "reconsideration" of Romanticism discussed by this group is to understand its continuity with modern literature, and this phase is now well developed in the work of Professor Kermode and others. All we need do to complete it is to examine Romanticism by its own standards and canons. We should not look for precision where vagueness is wanted; not extol the virtues of constipation when the Romantics were exuberant; not insist on visual values when the poet listens darkling to a nightingale. Then, perhaps, we may see in Romanticism also the quality that Melville found in Greek architecture:

> Not innovating wilfulness,
> But reverence for the Archetype.

# 7

# ROMANTICISM AND ANTI-SELF-CONSCIOUSNESS

## Geoffrey H. Hartman

Source: *Beyond Formalism: Literary Essays 1958–1970* (New Haven: Yale University Press, 1970), pp. 298–310.

The dejection afflicting John Stuart Mill in his twentieth year was alleviated by two important events. He read Wordsworth, and he discovered for himself a view of life resembling the "anti-self-consciousness theory" of Carlyle. Mill describes this strangely named theory in his *Autobiography*:

> Ask yourself whether you are happy, and you cease to be so. The only chance is to treat, not happiness, but some end external to it as the purpose of life. Let your self-consciousness, your scrutiny, your self-interrogation exhaust themselves on that.[1]

It is not surprising that Wordsworth's poetry should also have served to protect Mill from the morbidity of his intellect. Like many Romantics, Wordsworth had passed through a depression clearly linked to the ravage of self-consciousness and the "strong disease" of self-analysis.[2] Book 11 of the *Prelude*, chapter 5 of Mill's *Autobiography,* Carlyle's *Sartor Resartus*, and other great confessional works of the Romantic period show how crucial these maladies are for the adolescent mind. Endemic, perhaps, to every stage of life, they especially affect the transition from adolescence to maturity; and it is interesting to observe how man's attention has shifted from the fact of death and its rites of passage, to these trials in what Keats called "the Chamber of Maiden-Thought" and, more recently still, to the perils of childhood. We can say, taking a metaphor from Donne, that "streights, and none but streights" are ways to whatever changes the mind must undergo, and that it is the Romantics who first explored the dangerous passageways of maturation.

Two trials or perils of the soul deserve special mention. We learn that every increase in consciousness is accompanied by an increase in

136

self-consciousness, and that analysis can easily become a passion that "murders to dissect."[3] These difficulties of thought in its strength question the ideal of absolute lucidity. The issue is raised of whether there exist what might be called *remedia intellectus*: remedies for the corrosive power of analysis and the fixated self-consciousness.

There is one remedy of great importance which is almost coterminous with art itself in the Romantic period. This remedy differs from certain traditional proposals linked to the religious control of the intellect—the wild, living intellect of man, as Newman calls it in his *Apologia*.[4] A particularly Romantic remedy, it is nonlimiting with respect to the mind. It seeks to draw the antidote to self-consciousness from consciousness itself. A way is to be found not to escape from or limit knowledge, but to convert it into an energy finer than intellectual. It is some such thought which makes Wordsworth in the preface to *Lyrical Ballads* describe poetry as the "breath and finer spirit of all knowledge," able to carry sensation into the midst of the most abstract or remotest objects of science. A more absolute figure for this cure, which is, strictly speaking, less a cure than a paradoxical faith, is given by Kleist: "Paradise is locked . . . yet to return to the state of innocence we must eat once more of the tree of knowledge." It is not by accident that Kleist is quoted by Adrian at a significant point in Mann's *Doktor Faustus*, which is *the* novel about self-consciousness and its relation to art.

This idea of a return, via knowledge, to naïveté—to a second naïveté—is a commonplace among the German Romantics. Yet its presence is perhaps more exciting, because suitably oblique, among the English and French Romantics. A. O. Lovejoy, of course, in his famous essay on the "Discrimination of Romanticisms" (1924), questions the possibility of unifying the various national movements. He rightly points out that the German Romantics insist on an art that rises from the plenitude of consciousness to absorb progressively the most sophisticated as well as the most naïve experience. But his claim that English Romanticism is marked by a more primitivistic "return to nature" is weakened by his use of second-rate poetry and isolated passages. One can show that the practice of the greater English Romantics is involved with a problematical self-consciousness similar to that of the Germans and that, in the main, no primitivism or "sacrifice of intellect" is found. I do not mean to deny the obvious, that there are primitivistic passages in Chateaubriand and even Wordsworth, but the primary tendency should be distinguished from errors and epiphenomena. The desire of the Romantics is perhaps for what Blake calls "organized innocence," but never for a mere return to the state of nature. The German Romantics, however, for a reason mentioned later and because of the contemporaneous philosophical tradition which centered on the relations between consciousness and consciousness of self (Fichte, Schelling, Hegel), gained in some respects a clearer though not more fruitful understanding of the problem. I cannot consider in detail the case of French Romanticism. But Shelley's visionary despair, Keats's understanding of the poetical character, and Blake's doctrine of the contraries reveal that self-consciousness cannot be overcome; and the very desire to overcome it, which poetry and imagination encourage, is part of a vital, dialectical movement of soul-making.

The link between consciousness and self-consciousness, or knowledge and guilt, is already expressed in the story of the expulsion from Eden. Having tasted knowledge, man realizes his nakedness, his sheer separateness of self. I have quoted Kleist's reflection; and Hegel, in his interpretation of the Fall, argues that the way back to Eden is via contraries: the naïvely sensuous mind must pass through separation and selfhood to become spiritually perfect. It is the destiny of consciousness or, as the English Romantics would have said, of imagination, to separate from nature so that it can finally transcend not only nature but also its own lesser forms. Hegel in his *Logic* puts it as follows:

> The first reflection of awakened consciousness in men told them they were naked . . . The hour that man leaves the path of mere natural being marks the difference between him, a self-conscious agent, and the natural world. The spiritual is distinguished from the natural . . . in that it does not continue a mere stream of tendency, but sunders itself to self-realization. But this position of severed life has in its turn to be overcome, and the spirit must, by its own act, achieve concord once more . . . The principle of restoration is found in thought, and thought only: the hand that inflicts the wound is also the hand that heals it.[5]

The last sentence states unequivocally where the remedy lies. Hegel, however, does not honor the fact that the meaning he derives from the Fall was originally in the form of myth. And the attempt to think mythically is itself part of a crucial defense against the self-conscious intellect. Bergson in *The Two Sources of Morality and Religion* sees both myth and religion as products of an intellectual instinct created by nature itself to oppose the analytic intellect, to preserve human spontaneities despite the hesitant and complicated mind.[6] Whether myth-making is still possible, whether the mind can find an unselfconscious medium for itself or maintain something of the interacting unity of self and life, is a central concern of the Romantic poets.

Romantic art as myth-making has been discussed convincingly in recent years, and Friedrich Schlegel's call in "Rede über die Mythologie" (1800) for a modern mythology is well known. The question of the renewal of myth is, nevertheless, a rather special response to the larger perplexities of reflective thought. "The poet," says Wallace Stevens in "Adagia," "represents the mind in the act of defending us against itself." Starting with the Romantics, this act is clearly focused, and poetry begins to be valued in contradistinction to directly analytic or purely conceptual modes of thought. The intelligence is seen as a perverse though necessary specialization of the whole soul of man, and art as a means to resist the intelligence intelligently.

It must be admitted, at the same time, that the Romantics themselves do not give (in their conceptual moments) an adequate definition of the function of art. Their criterion of pleasure or expressive emotion leads to some kind of art for art's sake formula, or to the sentimentalism which Mill still shared and which marks the shift in sensibility from Neoclassic to Romantic. That Mill wept over the memoirs of Marmontel and felt his selfhood lightened by this evidence of his ability to feel, or that Lamartine saw the life of the poet as "tears and love," suggests that the *larmoyant* vein of the later eighteenth century persisted for some time but also helped, when tears or even joy were translated into theory, to falsify the Romantic achievement and make Irving Babbitt's criticism possible.

The art of the Romantics, on the other hand, is often in advance of even their best thoughts. Neither a mere increase in sensibility nor a mere widening of self-knowledge constitutes its purpose. The Romantic poets do not exalt consciousness per se. They have recognized it as a kind of death-in-life, as the product of a division in the self. The mind which acknowledges the existence or past existence of immediate life knows that its present strength is based on a separation from that life. A creative mind desires not mere increase of knowledge, but "knowledge not purchased by the loss of power" (*Prelude*, 5). Life, says Ruskin, is the only wealth; yet childhood, or certain irrevocable moments, confront the poet sharply and give him the sense of having purchased with death the life of the mind. Constructing what Yeats calls an anti-self, or recovering deeply buried experience, the poet seeks a return to "Unity of Being." Consciousness is only a middle term, the strait through which everything must pass; and the artist plots to have everything pass through whole, without sacrifice to abstraction.

One of the themes which best expresses this perilous nature of consciousness and which has haunted literature since the Romantic period is that of the Solitary, or Wandering Jew. He may appear as Cain, Ahasuerus, Ancient Mariner, and even Faust. He also resembles the later (and more static) figures of Tithonus, Gerontion, and *poète maudit*. These solitaries are separated from life in the midst of life, yet cannot die. They are doomed to live a middle or purgatorial existence which is neither life nor death, and as their knowledge increases so does their solitude.[7] It is, ultimately, consciousness that alienates them from life and imposes the burden of a self which religion or death or a return to the state of nature might dissolve. Yet their heroism, or else their doom, is not to obtain this release. Rebels against God, like Cain, and men of God, like Vigny's Moses, are equally denied "le sommeil de la terre" and are shown to suffer the same despair, namely, "the self . . . whose worm dieth not, and whose fire is not quenched" (Kierkegaard), And in Coleridge's Mariner, as in Conrad's Marlow, the figure of the wanderer approaches that of the poet. Both are storytellers who resubmit themselves to temporality and are compelled to repeat their experiences in the purgatorial form of words. Yeats, deeply affected by the theme of the Wandering Jew, records a marvelous comment of Mme. Blavatsky's: "I write, write, write, as the Wandering Jew walks, walks, walks."

The Solitary may also be said to create his own, peculiarly Romantic genre of poetry. In "Tintern Abbey," or "X" Revisited, the poet looks back at a transcended stage and comes to grips with the fact of self-alienation. The retrospective movement may be visionary, as often in Hölderlin; or antiquarian, as in Scott; or deeply oblique, as in lyrical ballad and monologue. In every case, however, there is some confrontation of person with shadow or self with self. The intense lyricism of the Romantics may well be related to this confrontation. For the Romantic "I" emerges nostalgically when certainty and simplicity of self are lost. In a lyric poem it is clearly not the first-person form that moves us (the poem need not be in the first person) but rather the I toward which that I reaches. The very confusion in modern literary theory concerning the fictive I, whether it represents the writer as person or only as persona, may reflect a dialectic inherent in poetry between the relatively self-conscious self and that self within the self which resembles Blake's "emanation" and Shelley's "epipsyche."

It is true, of course, that this dialectic is found in every age and not restricted to the Romantic. The notion of man (as of history) seems to presuppose that of self-consciousness, and art is not the only major reaction to it. Mircea Eliade, following Nietzsche, has recently linked art to religion by interpreting the latter as originating in a periodic and ritually controlled abolition of the burden of self, or rather of this burden in the form of a nascent historical sense. It is not true, according to Eliade, that primitive man has no sense of history; on the contrary, his sense of it is too acute, he cannot tolerate the weight of responsibility accruing through memory and individuation, and only gradually does religious myth, and especially the Judaeo-Christian revelation, teach him to become a more conscious historical being. The question, therefore, is why the Romantic reaction to the problem of self-consciousness should be in the form of an aggrandizement of art, and why the entire issue should now achieve an urgency and explicitness previously lacking.

The answer requires a distinction between religion and art. This distinction can take a purely historical form. There clearly comes a time when art frees itself from its subordination to religion or religiously inspired myth and continues or even replaces them. This time seems to coincide with what is generally called the Romantic period: the latter, at least, is a good *terminus a quo*. Though every age may find its own means to convert self-consciousness into the larger energy of imagination, in the Romantic period it is primarily art on which this crucial function devolves. Thus, for Blake, all religion is a derivation of the Poetic Genius; and Matthew Arnold is already matter-of-fact rather than prophetic about a new age in which the religious passion is preserved chiefly by poetry. If Romantic poetry appears to the orthodox as misplaced religious feeling ("spilt religion"), to the Romantics themselves it redeems religion.[8]

Yet as soon as poetry is separated from imposed religious or communal ends it becomes as problematic as the individual himself. The question of how art is possible, though post-Romantic in its explicitness, has its origin here, for the artist is caught up in a serious paradox. His art is linked to the autonomous and individual; yet that same art, in the absence of an authoritative myth, must bear the entire weight of having to transcend or ritually limit these tendencies. No wonder the problem of the subjective, the isolated, the individual, grows particularly acute. Subjectivity—even solipsism—becomes the subject of poems which qua poetry seek to transmute it.

This paradox seems to inhere in all the seminal works of the Romantic period. "Thus my days are passed / In contradiction," Wordsworth writes sadly at the beginning of *The Prelude*. He cannot decide whether he is fit to be a poet on an epic scale. The great longing is there; the great (objective) theme eludes him. Wordsworth cannot find his theme because he already has it: himself. Yet he knows self-consciousness to be at once necessary and opposed to poetry. It will take him the whole of *The Prelude* to be satisfied *in actu* that he is a poet. His poem, beginning in the vortex of self-consciousness, is carried to epic length in the desire to prove that his former imaginative powers are not dead.

I have already confessed to understanding the *Ancient Mariner* as a poem that depicts the soul after its birth to the sense of separate (and segregated) being. In one of the really magical poems in the language, which, generically, converts self-consciousness into imagination, Coleridge describes the travail of a soul passing from self-consciousness to imagination. The slaying of an innocent creature, the horror of stasis, the weight of conscience or of the vertical eye (the sun), the appearance of the theme of deathlessness, and the terrible repetitive process of penitence whereby the wanderer becomes aware through the spirits above and the creatures below of his focal solitude between both—these point with archetypal force to the burden of selfhood, the straits of solitude, and the compensating plenary imagination that grows inwardly. The poem opens by evoking that rite de passage we call a wedding and which leads to full human communion, but the Mariner's story interposes itself as a reminder of human separateness and of the intellectual love (in Spinoza's sense) made possible by it.

To explore the transition from self-consciousness to imagination and to achieve that transition while exploring it (and so to prove it still possible) is the Romantic purpose I find most crucial. The precariousness of that transition naturally evokes the idea of a journey; and in some later poets, like Rimbaud and Hart Crane, the motif of the journey has actually become a sustained metaphor for the experience of the artist during creation. This journey, of course, does not lead to what is generally called a truth: some final station for the mind. It remains as problematic a crossing as that from death to second life or from exile to redemption. These religious concepts, moreover, are often blended in and remind us that Romantic art has a function analogous to that of religion. The traditional scheme of Eden, Fall, and Redemption merges with the new triad of Nature, Self-Consciousness, and Imagination—the last term in both involving a kind of return to the first.

Yet everything depends on whether it is the right and fruitful return. For the journey beyond self-consciousness is shadowed by cyclicity, by paralysis before the endlessness of introspection, and by the lure of false ultimates. Blake's "Mental Traveller," Browning's "Childe Roland to The Dark Tower Came," and Emily Dickinson's "Our journey had advanced" show these dangers in some of their forms. Nature in its childhood or sensuous radiance (Blake's "Beulah") exerts an especially deceptive lure. The desire to gain truth, finality, or revelation generates a thousand such enchantments. Mind has its blissful islands as well as its mountains, its deeps, and its treacherous crossroads. Depicting these trials by horror and by enchantment, Romanticism is genuinely a rebirth of Romance.

In the years following World War I it became customary to see Classicism and Romanticism as two radically different philosophies of life and to place modernism on the side of the antiromantic. André Malraux defined the classical element in modern art as a "lucid horror of seduction." Today it is clear that Romantic art shared that lucidity. Romanticism at its most profound reveals the depth of the enchantments in which we live. We dream, we wake on the cold hillside, and our sole self pursues the dream once more. In the beginning was the dream, and the task of disenchantment never ends.

The nature poetry of the Romantics is a case in point. Far from being an indulgence in dewy moments, it is the exploration of enchanted ground. The Romantic poets, like the Impressionist painters, refuse to "simplify the ghost" of nature. They begin to look steadfastly at all sensuous experience, penetrating its veils and facing its seductions. Shelley's "Mont Blanc" is not an enthusiastic nature poem but a spirit-drama in which the poet's mind seeks to release itself from an overwhelming impression and to reaffirm its autonomy vis-à-vis nature. Keats also goes far in respecting illusions without being deluded. His starting-point is the dream of nature fostered by Romance; he agrees to this as consciously as we lie down to sleep. But he intends such dreaming "beyond self" to unfold its own progressions and to wake into truth. To this end he passes from a gentler to a severer dream-mode: from the romance of *Endymion* to the more austere *Hyperion*. Yet he is forced to give up the *Hyperion* because Saturn, Apollo, and others behave like quest heroes instead of gods. Having stepped beyond romance into a sublimer mode, Keats finds the quest for self-identity elated rather than effaced. It has merely raised itself to a divine level. He cannot reconcile

Miltonic sublimity with the utterly human pathos that keeps breaking through. The "egotistical sublime" remains.

It was Wordsworth, of course, whose poetry Keats had tried to escape by adhering to a less self-centered kind of sublimity: "Let us have the old Poets, and Robin Hood." Wordsworth had subdued poetry to the theme of nature's role in the growth of the individual mind. The dream of nature, in Wordsworth, does not lead to formal Romance but is an early, developmental step in converting the solipsistic into the sympathetic imagination. It entices the brooding soul out of itself, toward nature first, then toward humanity. Wordsworth knew the weight of self-consciousness:

> It seemed the very garments that I wore
> Preyed on my strength, and stopped the quiet stream
> Of self-forgetfulness.
> > [*Prelude* (1850), 5. 294 ff.]

The wound of self is healed, however, by "unconscious intercourse" with a nature "old as creation." Nature makes the "quiet stream" flow on. Wordsworth evokes a type of consciousness more integrated than ordinary consciousness, though deeply dependent on its early—and continuing—life in rural surroundings.[9]

The Romantic emphasis on unconsciousness and organic form is significant in this light. *Unconsciousness* remains an ambiguous term in the Romantic and Victorian periods, referring to a state distinctly other than consciousness or simply to unselfconsciousness. The characteristic of right performance, says Carlyle in *Characteristics* (1831), is an unconsciousness— "'the healthy know not of their health, but only the sick.'" The term clearly approaches here its alternate meaning of unselfconsciousness, and it is to such statements that Mill must be indebted when he mentions the "anti-self-consciousness theory" of Carlyle. In America, Thoreau perpetuates the ambiguity. He also prescribes unconsciousness for his sophisticated age and uses the word as an equivalent of vision: "the absence of the speaker from his speech." It does seem to me that the personal and expressive theory of poetry, ascribed to the Romantics, and the impersonal theory of poetry, claimed in reaction by the moderns, answer to the same problem and are quietly linked by the ambiguity in *unconsciousness*. Both theories value art as thought recreated into feeling or self-consciousness into a more communal power of vision. Yet can the modern poet, whom Schiller called "sentimental" (reflective) and whom we would describe as alienated, achieve the immediacy of all great verse, whatever its personal or historical dilemma?

This is as crucial a matter today as when Wordsworth and Coleridge wrote *Lyrical Ballads* and Hölderlin pondered the fate of poetry in "Der Rhein." Is visionary poetry a thing of the past, or can it coexist with the modern temper? Is it an archaic revelation, or a universal mode springing from every real contact with nature? "To interest or benefit us," says a Victorian writer, "poetry must be reflective, sentimental, subjective; it must accord with the conscious, analytical spirit of present men."[10] The difficulties surrounding a modern poetry of vision vary with each national literature. In England the loss of "poesy" is attributed by most Romantics to a historical though not irreversible fact—to the preceding century's infidelity to the line of Chaucer, Spenser, Shakespeare, and Milton. "Let us have the old Poets, and Robin Hood," as Keats said. Yet for the German and the French there was no easy return to a tradition deriving its strength from both learned and popular sources. "How much further along we would be," Herder remarks, "if we had used popular beliefs and myths like the British, if our poetry had built upon them as wholeheartedly as Chaucer, Spenser and Shakespeare did."[11] In the absence of this English kind of literary mediation, the gap between medieval romance and the modern spirit seemed too great. Goethe's *Faust* tried to bridge it but, like *Wilhelm Meister*, anticipated a new type of literature which subsumed the philosophical character of the age and merged myth and irony into a "progressive" mode. The future belonged to the analytic spirit, to irony, to prose. The death of poetry had certainly occurred to the Romantics in idea, and Hegel's prediction of it was simply the overt expression of their own despair. Yet against this despair the greater Romantic poets staked their art and often their sanity.

## Notes

1 *Autobiography* (1873), chap. 5. Mill says that he had not heard, at the time, Carlyle's theory. The first meeting between the writers took place in 1831; Mill's depression lasted, approximately, from autumn 1826 to autumn 1828. Mill called self-consciousness "that demon of the men of genius of our time from Wordsworth to Byron, from Goethe to Chateaubriand." See Wayne Shumaker, *English Autobiography* (Berkeley and Los Angeles, 1954), chap. 4.

2 Thought as a disease is an open as well as submerged metaphor among the Romantics. There are many hints in Novalis; Schelling pronounces naked reflection (analysis) to be a spiritual sickness of man (*Schellings Sämtliche Werke*, ed. K. F. Schelling [Stuttgart, 1856–61], 2: 13–14); the metaphor is explicit in Carlyle's *Characteristics* (1831) and commonplace by the time that E. S. Dallas in *The Gay Science* (1866) attributes the "modern disease" to "excessive civilization and overstrained consciousness." The *mal du siecle* is not unrelated to the malady we are describing. Goethe's *Die Leiden des Jungen Werthers* (1774) may be seen as its terminus a quo, and Kierkegaard's *Sickness unto Death* (1849) as its noonday point of clarity.

3 Wordsworth, "The Tables Turned" (1798). For the first peril, see Kierkegaard's *Sickness unto Death*, and Blake: "The Negation is the Spectre, the Reasoning Power in Man; / This is a false Body, an Incrustation over my Immortal / Spirit, a Selfhood which must be put off & annihilated alway" *(Milton*, Bk. 2). This last quotation, like Wordsworth's "A reasoning, self-sufficient thing, / An intellectual All-in-All" ("A Poet's Epitaph"), shows the closeness of the two perils. For the

second, see also Coleridge: "All the products of the mere reflective faculty [viz. the 'understanding' contradistinguished from what Coleridge will call the 'reason'] partook of DEATH" (*Biographia Literaria*, chap. 9): Benjamin Constant's definition of one of the moral maladies of the age as "the fatigue, the lack of strength, the perpetual analysis that saps the spontaneity of every feeling" (draft preface to *Adolphe*); and Hegel's preface to *The Phenomenology of Mind* (1807). Hegel observes that ordinary analysis leads to a hardening of data, and he attributes this to a persistence of the ego, whereas his dialectic is thought to reveal the true fluency of concepts. Carlyle most apodictically said: "Had Adam remained in Paradise, there had been no Anatomy and no Metaphysics" (*Characteristics*, 1831).

4 *Apologia Pro Vita Sua* (1864), chap. 5. In the same chapter Newman calls reason "that universal solvent." Concerning Victorian remedies for "this disease / My Self" (Marianne Moore), see also A. Dwight Culler, *The Imperial Intellect* (New Haven, 1955), pp. 234–37.

5 *The Logic of Hegel*, trans. from the *Encyclopedia of the Sciences* by W. Wallace, 2nd ed. (Oxford, 1904), pp. 54–57. The first sentences given here come from passages in the original later than the remainder of the quotation.

6 *Les Deux Sources de la Morale et de la Religion* (1933), chap. 2. Both religion and "la fonction fabulatrice" are "une reaction défensive de la nature contre le pouvoir dissolvant de l'intelligence." (Cf. Newman calling the intellect "that universal solvent.") As Romanticism shades into modernism, a third peril of over-consciousness comes strongly to the fore—that it leads to a Hamlet-like incapacity for action. Bergson, like Kierkegaard, tries to counter this aspect especially.

7 "I lost the love of heaven above, / I spurned the lust of earth below" (John Clare, "A Vision"). By this double exile and their final madness, two poets as different as Clare and Hölderlin are joined. See Coleridge's intense realization of man's "between-ness," which increases rather than chastens the apocalyptic passion: "O Nature! I would rather not have been—let that which is to come so soon, come now—for what is all the intermediate space, but sense of utter worthlessness? . . . Man is truly and solely an immortal series of conscious mortalities and inherent Disappointments" (*Inquiring Spirit*, ed. K. Coburn [London, 1951], p. 142). But to ask death instead of life of nature is still to ask for finality, for some metal quietus: it is the bitter obverse, also met at the beginning of Goethe's *Faust*, of the quest for absolute truth.

8 I have omitted here the important role played by the French Revolution. The aggrandizement of art is due in no small measure to the fact that poets like Wordsworth and Blake cannot give up one hope raised by the Revolution—that a terrestrial paradise is possible—yet are eventually forced to give up a second hope—that it can be attained by direct political action. The shift from faith in the reformation of man through the prior reformation of society to that in the prior reformation of man through vision and art has often been noted. The failure of the French Revolution anchors the Romantic movement or is the consolidating rather than primary cause. It closes, perhaps until the advent of Communism, the possibility that politics rather than art should be invested with a passion previously subsumed by religion.

9 Mill, Hazlitt, and Arnold came to approximately the same estimate of Wordsworth's poetry. Comparing it to Byron's, they found that the latter had too much fever of self in it to be remedial; they did not want their image cast back at them magnified. Carlyle prefers to compare Goethe and Byron ("Close your Byron, open your Goethe"), yet his point is the same: Goethe retains a

strong simplicity in a tormented and divided age, while Byron seems to him a "spasmodically bellowing self-worshipper."

10 R. M. Milnes, *Palm Leaves* (London, 1844).

11 *Von Ähnlichkeit der mittlern englischen und deutschen Dichtkunst* (1777). Cf. Louis Cazamian on French Romanticism: "Le romantisme n'a donc pas été pour la France, comme pour l'Angleterre, un retour facile et naturel à une tradition nationale, selon la pente du tempérament le plus profond" *Essais en Deux Langues* [Paris, 1938], p. 170).

# 8

# RETHINKING ROMANTICISM

## Jerome McGann

Source: *English Literary History* 59 (1992), 735–54.

## I

Until about ten years ago scholars of romanticism generally accepted Rene Wellek's classic modern definition of their subject: "Imagination for the view of poetry, nature for the view of the world, and symbol and myth for poetic style."[1] This formulation represents, on one hand, a synthesis of an originary romantic tradition of thought, and, on the other, the bounding horizon for much of the work on romanticism done between World War II and the early 1980s.

Today that synthesis has collapsed and debate about theory of romanticism is vigorous—from cultural studies, feminist scholarship, even from various types of revived philological investigations. My own work has been much engaged with these revaluations, not least since the publication of *The Romantic Ideology* in 1983. Because these discussions have (inevitably) influenced my own thinking about romanticism, as well as the more general problem of periodization, I want to return to the subject once again.[2]

Between 1978 and 1983, when I first addressed these issues, I was not concerned with the question of periodization as such. I was more interested in the conceptual representations of romanticism—contemporary representations as well as subsequent scholarly representations. The periodization issue entered my purview obliquely—for example, in relation to the kinds of problems that arise when a clear distinction is not maintained between certain cultural formations (like romanticism, modernism, or postmodernism) and the historical frameworks within which they develop and mutate. So I worked to clarify the distinction between "the romantic period" (that is, a particular historical epoch) and "romanticism" (that is, a set of cultural/ideological formations that came to prominence during the romantic period). The distinction is important not merely because so much of the work of that period is not "romantic," but even more, perhaps, because the period is notable for its many ideological struggles. A romantic ethos achieved dominance through sharp cultural conflict; some of the fiercest engagements were internecine—the civil wars of the romantic movement itself.

Later I shall try to examine these topics more closely. For now let me summarize the argument I began to elaborate in *The Romantic Ideology*. It seemed to me then, and it still seems to me: first, that Wellek's position flattens out the rough terrain of the cultural formation(s) we call romanticism; and second, that Wellek's position fails to map the phenomena comprehensively because it is a specialized theoretical view derived from a Kantian/Coleridgean line of thought. In other words, between approximately 1945 and 1980 the most influential interpreters of English romanticism examined their material with a historically determinate theory of their subject. To recognize the historicality of the theory is to understand more clearly its limits (as well as the powers). The recognition also helps one toward possible reimaginations of romanticism—to think beyond the conceptual framework of Wellek's synthetic theory.

The limits of that interpretive line pressed themselves upon me because I was much occupied with Byron and his works. A Byronic vantage on the issue of romanticism immediately puts in question Wellek's imagination/ nature/symbol tercet. That Byron did not figure importantly in the representations of the romantic period of 1945–80 is not an anomaly, it is a theoretical and ideological fate.

The contrast between the view of romanticism that dominated the period 1945–80 and the nineteenth century's view seemed to me equally startling. Once again Byron loomed as the unevadable locus of the issues. The continental vantage exposes the problems in their most telling form. From Goethe and Pushkin to Baudelaire, Nietzsche, and Lautréamont, Byron seems to stand at the very center of romanticism. The nineteenth-century English view is slightly different. Though Byron remained an important resource for England and the English, he had emerged as a highly problematic figure. From different Victorian points of view Byron's famous "energy" (as it was called) seemed one thing—usually a positive thing—whereas his equally famous critical despair seemed something else altogether—typically, something to be deplored. Nineteenth-century England therefore kept opening and closing its Byron with troubled (ir)regularity.

As Coleridge and Wordsworth gradually came to define the "center" of English romanticism in twentieth-century critical thinking, Byron slipped further from view. Wellek's intervention was a key event because Wellek sought to integrate a European philological view with a correspondent line of English cultural thought. In the romanticism that emerged from this synthesis, Byron's deviance seemed virtually complete. "Imagination" is explicitly *not* Byron's view of the sources of poetry, "nature" is hardly his "view of the world" (Byron is distinctly a cosmopolitan writer), and his style is predominantly rhetorical and conversational rather than symbolic or mythic. No one would, I think, disagree with this general representation of Byron, any more than one would deny that Wellek's formulation corresponds very closely to Wordsworth's and Coleridge's work. Wellek's triad can of course be traced through Byron's work, especially via a study of Byron's peculiarly antithetical ways of engaging nature, imagination, and myth. When this is done, however—for instance, in the guiding work of an Abrams or a Bloom—what one discovers are precisely traces and differences.[3] Observed through a theory of romanticism like Wellek's, Byron appears either a problem or an irrelevance.

The difficulty is at its root a historical one. While Byron does not fit easily into Wellek's criteria for romanticism, he cannot easily be removed from the historical phenomena. In the theoretical (and romantic) line synthesized by Wellek, this Byronic contradiction was negotiated very simply. Although the splendor of Byron's miseries initially seemed an astonishment to many, they came at last to be judged a kind of vulgar theater of romanticism, the debased margin of a complex cultural center: at best perhaps historically interesting, at worst probably factitious. The subject of Byron's late masterpiece *Don Juan* was set aside altogether so far as the question of Byron's romanticism was concerned. For while here one could see, very clearly, a panoramic (dis)play of "romantic irony," Byron's work pursued its ironies in an apparently unsystematic and nontheoretical way. Byron's resistance to theory—famous in its time—troubled the romanticism of his ironic masterpiece. It became a negative cultural sign that his work lacked depth and cultural seriousness. Himself at odds with so much of his age's systematic theorizing—"born for opposition," as he flamboyantly declared—Byron courted marginality and inconsequence from the very center of the romantic fame he had acquired.

(Let me say in parenthesis that the recent "return of the Byronic repressed" does not simply reflect the editorial scholarship that has restored his texts to us during the past fifteen years or so. At least as important has been the emergence of postmodernism, with its Derridean concern for textual play and instability and its Foucauldian pressure to recover salient but neglected historicalities.[4])

Working from the antinomy of Byron, then, *The Romantic Ideology* drew out a dialectical critique of Wellek's ideological synthesis. Once begun, such a move lays bare a whole array of similar deviances concealed within the synthetic structure. For example, if romanticism takes "nature" for its view of the world, then Blake falls out of the synthesis. "Nature" corresponds to a romantic *Weltanschauung* as a scene of fundamental innocence and sympathy; conceptually opposed to the urban and the artificial, romantic nature is the locus of what Wordsworth paradigmatically called "feeling." As an artistic resource it generates a constellation of anti-Enlightenment cultural formations that are critically recollected in phrases like "the meddling intellect," and romantically transformed in phrases like "the philosophic mind." Because Blake also attacked key Enlightenment positions, one may overlook or set aside the manifest differences that separate his view of nature from, say, Wordsworth's or Coleridge's. But the fact is that Blake does not take "nature as his view of the world" any more than Byron does, though the anti-naturisms of Blake and Byron are also noncongruent with each other.

A close investigation of the ideas that particular romantic writers had about imagination, nature, and symbol or myth will disclose a series of similar fundamental differences. I recently tried to illustrate what might be demonstrated along these lines by tracing important distinctions between different romantic ideas of imagination.[5] Memory is so important to the theories of Wordsworth and Coleridge, for instance, that their views deviate radically from Blake's. Imagination is a conscious activity for Coleridge, subject to the will, whereas for Shelley it is a faculty precisely distinguished by its total freedom from willful control. Keats evolved from Wordsworth a sensationalist theory of imagination that stands quite at odds with Shelley's more idealistic views. For that matter, Wordsworth's work is so deeply in debt to associationist theories of imagination that Coleridge himself wrote *Biographia Literaria* in large part to demonstrate the crucial differences that separated his aesthetic ideas from those of his early friend. (In doing so, curiously, he aligned himself closely with the criticisms initially raised by Wordsworth's most famous antagonist, Francis Jeffrey.)

Now it might be objected that this general line of critique against Wellek's synthetic representation of romanticism simply returns us to a neo-Lovejoyan skepticism. Differences are so elaborated and insisted upon that we effectively abandon all hope of theorizing the phenomena. Instead we atomize, discriminating ever more particular forms within an enchafed but finally featureless romantic flood.

To the extent that *The Romantic Ideology* was written as a critical polemic against what I took to be a false consciousness of romanticism, its arguments might be used to bolster such a pyrrhonist approach. My own view, however, is very different, as might perhaps be seen from more recent critical projects. These projects have not been specifically addressed to the question of romanticism or to the problem of its periodization. I have been trying rather to develop a general set of research and teaching protocols for the historical study of literary work, regardless of "period." This more general aim grows from investigations into the changing relations of language and textuality, and particularly the changing relations of language and the textuality of literary or poetical work.[6]

From this perspective, romanticism is inadequately characterized by a synthesis like Wellek's because the synthesis is too abstract and conceptual. The best work to utilize this synthesis has tried to resist that conceptual framework, to preserve the dynamism of the phenomena even as a continual resort is made to terms like imagination, nature, and symbol, with their fateful positivist inertias. Nor can we, nor should we, dispense with those terms, which are primary philological data of the originary historical efforts to forge romantic experiences of the world.

What we have to bear clearly in mind, however, is the heuristic and constructivist character of those terms and the ideas they generate and pursue. "Imagination," especially as it was deployed in romantic discourse, is a radically dialogical term. When Coleridge or Shelley, say, use the term in prescriptive and ideological frameworks, they try to limit the dialogism of the word, to set it within a defined conceptual position. The same is true with regard, let us say, to Wordsworth's or Byron's or Blake's expositions of terms like "imagination" and "nature." So we can speak of different (romantic) "theories" of nature or imagination, and we can separate these different theories from each other. However, to the extent that romanticism is executed not as a prescriptive but as a poetical economy—a dynamic scene of evolving tensions and relationships, as in a family—its primal terms and data cannot lapse into systematic rectitude. Romantic poetry, in short, constructs a theater for the conflicts and interactions of the ideologies of romanticism.

In this sense, to define romanticism with Wellek's tercet of keywords is not wrong so much as it is abstract and preliminary. If our critical point of departure is poetry and art rather than culture and society, we have to begin the study of romanticism at least from a Bakhtinian vantage, as a disputatious scene whose internal tensions re-present the strife of historical differentials and ideological conflict. The period is notable, as I have said, for its various cultural/theoretical controversies, and in particular for the emergence of the manifesto as a distinct literary subgenre. The cultural forms of romanticism are famously volatile and shape-changing because they typically hold their ideas and projects open to transformation—even to the point, as I shall try to show, of their own self-destruction.

A book like *The Romantic Ideology*, it has been argued, implicitly reifies this kind of romantic dynamism as a transcendant aesthetic form or set of procedures. The charge is that *The Romantic Ideology* at times simply replaces Wellek's tripartite structural representation with a dialectical view that is, finally, no less conceptual, for all its appeal to dynamic forms. I have come to think this criticism a just one.[7] I also think it an important criticism, for it exposes a residual investment in a type of interpretive thought that I was explicitly trying to avoid.

As I see it, criticism should be seeking a dialectical philology that is not bound by the conceptual forms it studies and generates.[8] The paradox of such a philology is that its freedom would be secured only when it accepts the historical limits of its own forms of thought. It is not bound by its theoretical forms because it holds itself open to the boundary conditions established by other conceptual forms. This is a theory imagined not as a conceptual structure but as a set of investigative practices—and a set of practices that play themselves out under a horizon of falsifiability.[9]

## II

If we take such an approach to a topic like "the romantic period," then, our object will not be to "define" the period but to sketch its dynamic possibilities. In this frame of reference it helps to remember that "periodization" is itself a critical tool fashioned in historicality as such. Periodization is a possible form of historical thinking that has been realized under specific socio-historical conditions of the European Enlightenment. We do not, after all, *have* to think in such terms. A current world-historical perspective will not sweep off the periodic table "Medieval, Renaissance, Enlightenment, Romanticism, Modernism," but it will certainly execute radical and across-the-board changes and options of meaning.

Modern historical method is a tool for bringing order—I would rather call it "possible order"—to cultural change and cultural difference. We want therefore to bear in mind the historicality of the method in order to hold it open to the full range of its possibilities, which necessarily entail the limits it is perpetually constructing and discovering. When we focus attention on a topic like the romantic period, we may willingly (though perhaps not consciously) suspend our disbelief in the period as such, and hence take our studies in the period for pursuits of an *Urphänomen.* This is, in effect, what we observe in Wellek's approach to romanticism and the romantic period. The problem with Wellek's formulation is not so much that it is a limited view—all views are limited—but that it holds out against the possibilities of its own limitations. It does not invite a "suspension of disbelief *for the moment*" but for good and aye.

At issue here is how we pursue a historical method of literary investigation. Because historical method is strictly a form of comparative studies, its goal is not the recovery of some lost originary cultural whole. The presumption must rather be that the object of study is volatile and dynamic—not merely that it (in this case, "the romantic period") *was* an unstable and conflicted phenomenon, but that it continues to mutate as it is subjected to further study; indeed, that its later changes are the effects of such studies. (This situation explains why the basic form of historical studies is not positivist but radically dialogical.)

Thus the standard dates for the romantic period—let us say, 1798–1824—cannot be read as a mere statement of fact. Scholars of course understand the signifying mechanism involved here. "1798" stands for the coming of *Lyrical Ballads*, and "1824" stands for the death of Byron. But those events merely define the critical materials in terms of a simple historical allegory. Most scholars are also aware that the dates could be shifted—typical shifts at the *terminus a quo* are "1789," "1792," and "1800," while at the *terminus ad quem* the dates "1830," "1832," and "1837" (among others) are common enough. All signify some event that is implicitly being asked to carry important cultural meanings. The "facts" come legend-laden through the forest of history. We have to translate those legends, but we also have to realize what is implicit in *the fact of the legends*: that a historical moment (so-called) can and will be (re)constructed in different ways.

That realization should not be left to fend for itself, as it were. We want to get beyond assenting to "the play of difference," beyond describing instances of that play. A fully developed historical method ought to encourage the exploration of alterities. That goal would entail, however—to borrow a thought from Shelley—*imagining* what we know: constructing and deploying forms that will be equal to the pursuit of differential attention. We shall not advance the knowledge we desire, therefore, by continuing to work almost exclusively within the most traditional generic conventions of academic discourse. These forms, after all, evolved from nineteenth-century historicist philology and hermeneutics. As such, they are structurally committed to holistic accounts of history and integrated, self-consistent acts of interpretation.

Derrida has been a great spur (so to speak) to new kinds of critical in(ter)ventions. (The use of dialectal forms that give momentary exposure to language's differential possibilities is now common.) But the academy's turn in the past twenty-five years towards various philosophies of differential attention has remained largely conceptual. Not many critics or scholars have tried to translate these commitments into equivalent generic forms. The most innovative work here has come from extramural writers. Scholars could learn much from the criticism of contemporary poets like Susan Howe and Charles Bernstein.[10] Howe's exploration of *My Emily Dickinson*, for example, is an astonishingly inventive work of historical scholarship. The book's collage format permits her to deploy and then explore a series of nonlinear historical relations. Pivoting about a close reading of a single poem ("My Life had stood—a Loaded Gun"), the book slowly explores multiple intersections of public event and private life—intersections *in* the past as well as *between* the past and its possible futures.

When academics have tried to escape the limitations of traditional critical forms, response tends to be at best interested and wary, and at worst hostile or indifferent. In Renaissance studies one thinks immediately of Randall McLeod, perhaps the most innovative textual scholar of our time (in any period of work.)[11] In the romantic period I would instance the recent work of Jeffrey Robinson, or Donald Ault's struggles (they recall McLeod's work) to force the physical medium of the text to become a critical tool and form of expression.[12] In my own criticism, especially during the past five years, I have been exploring the resources of dialogue as a mode of scholarly investigation.[13]

One thinks as well of the important *New History of French Literature*, which has made a deliberate effort to surmount the limits of narrativized history by subordinating narrative form to an incipient dialectic licensed by the discontinuous chronicle organization of the materials.[14] The *New*

*History* does not seek a synthetic historical account of French Literature. On one hand the work underscores the limits of historical vision by emphasizing the extreme particularity of various accounts. On the other it tries to induce imaginations of new sets of historical relations between different and competing views of the material.

Implicit here is a general critical idea that has great power: to display the constructed and non-natural status of historical information. Insofar as narrative history aspires to a finished account, its rhetoric tends to represent the past as completed—a complex set of "facts" that require thorough research and fair disclosure. The *New History* is an index of a contrary view: that history is a continuous process, and that the past itself is, like the future, a serious possibility. The *New History* subordinates narrative (closure) to dialectic (engagement).

Its general procedures, however, can sometimes be as well or perhaps even better pursued in other expository modes. Consider the critical possibilities of the anthology form. These first became apparent to me in Yeats's great *Oxford Book of Modern Verse, 1892–1935* (1936). By opening his collection in 1892 with a (re)constructed text of Pater's prose, Yeats announced the arbitrary and polemical character of his work. At that point I began to realize the virtues to be gained by "writing" literary history in the editorial structure of the anthology. Several years later, when I was asked to edit *The New Oxford Book of Verse of the Romantic Period*, I seized the opportunity. Concealed within this project was the chance to give a practical demonstration of certain theoretical ideas about history, on one hand, and literary form on the other.

An anthology of this kind necessarily constructs a literary history, but the historical synthesis is subordinated in the formalities of the collection. The anthology focuses one's attention on local units of order—individual poems and groups of poems. As a consequence, these units tend to splinter the synthetic inertia of the work-as-a-whole into an interactive and dialogical scene. Possibilities of order appear at different scalar levels because the center of the work is not so much a totalized form as a dynamically emergent set of constructible hypotheses of historical relations. Built into the anthology form are what topological mathematicians might call "basins" of contradiction: orderly, expository, and linear arrangements that stand at a perpetual brink of Chaotic transformation.

As I began studying the anthology form more closely, I was struck by one of its dominant modern conventions. Since *Tottel's Miscellany* (1557) literary anthologies—even when they are trying to display some more or less comprehensive historical order—tend to arrange themselves by author. Palgrave's *Golden Treasury* (1861) might seem a great exception to this rule, but it isn't. Although poems by different authors are scattered through each of the anthology's four great books, Palgrave's Introduction makes its author-centered form very clear. The four "Books" of the *Golden Treasury* locate the four great periods of what Palgrave calls "the natural growth and evolution of our Poetry." The periods roughly correspond to the sixteenth, seventeenth, eighteenth, and early nineteenth centuries. For Palgrave, however, each of these four evolutionary phases have unfolded under the sign of a single dominant author "who more or less give[s] each [phase] its distinctive character."[15] Consequently, Palgrave tells us that each of the four books of his anthology "might be called the Books of Shakespeare, Milton, Gray, and Wordsworth" respectively.

Yet even as Palgrave's great anthology connects its romantic-evolutionary account of English literary history to certain epochal figures, it deploys two interesting and antithetical forms of order. First, the anthology is formatted into four abstractly arranged "Books." Each book carries no heading other than "Book First," "Book Second," etc., without historical labels of any kind. Second, no effort in made within each book to foreground a local evolutionary cycle, or—for that matter—to isolate individual authors, not even the epochal authors. Each poem comes forward under a title and the author's name is tagged at the end. Neither are an individual author's works grouped into a subunit within the horizon of a particular "Book." The poems are arranged, so far as one can tell, by random and personal choice—Palgrave says simply that he has avoided "a rigidly chronological sequence" in order to pursue what he calls "the wisdom which comes through pleasure." That idiosyncratic remark underscores the anthology's deep commitment to a principle of subjectivity: "Within each book," Palgrave adds, "the pieces have . . . been arranged in gradations of feeling or subject."

What most strikes one about Palgrave's anthology, therefore, is not its rather (in)famous Arnoldian determination toward "the best original Lyrical pieces and Songs in our language." Rather, it is the book's complex structure. Palgrave puts into play several competing and even antithetical forms of order and attention. While the implicit conflict of these forms does not overthrow the book's ultimately Hegelian organization, it allows the reader recurrent waylayings from Palgrave's imperious instruction in his version of a "great tradition." For Palgrave's own project is built upon internal conflict and self-contradiction. On one hand he tells us that local randomness comes from a poetical desire towards "the wisdom that comes through pleasure." On the other hand he associates the "poetical" experience with total form. "In the arrangement," he says, "the most poetically-effective order has been attempted"—by which he means, explicitly, an evolutionary wholeness that he equates with and calls "the sense of Beauty."

> And it is hoped that the contents of this Anthology will thus be found to present a certain unity, "as episodes," in the noble language of Shelley, "to that great poem which all poets, like the co-operating thoughts of one great mind, have built up since the beginning of the world."

Rereading Palgrave made me understand that the differential order achieved (perhaps not altogether consciously) in his book might be deliberately essayed in my *New Oxford Book of Verse of the Romantic Period*. I have therefore made several important departures from the conventional format of a "New Oxford Book" anthology. The most significant departure involves the collection's general historical horizon. The historical scene is more atomized than it is cumulative or developmental: as it were, thirteen ways of looking at the romantic period (or, in this case, forty-seven ways). Not unlike the *New History of French Literature*, the anthology follows a simple chronicle organization, year by year from 1785 to 1832. Within each year the poems are also arranged by elementary chronological sequence.

As a consequence, different authors appear recurrently rather than as coherent authorial units. Wordsworth and his poetry, for example, continually reemerge in new and perhaps unexpected sets of relations. Narrativizing literary events, by contrast, tends to rationalize such historical intersections under the laws of an expository grammar. Similarly, by making individual poems the base units of a "literary history"—as it were the "words" of its "language"—the *New Oxford Book* anthology cuts across what Palgrave called the "certain unity" of literary history. Tracing a historical course by spots of poetical time (rather than by unfolding expository sequence) entails a necessary fall from the grace of one great Mind into the local world of the poem, where contradiction—the ceaseless dialectic of "opposite and discordant qualities"—holds paramount sway.

The anthology pursues this dialectic in one other important respect. It takes a consciously antithetical point of view on the materials to be included. At the outset of this essay I mentioned the sharp difference between Wellek's synthetic view of romanticism and various earlier views. The anthology reflects that differential in three principal ways. First, it includes a good deal of poetry—some of it, like Crabbe's, among the best writing of the period—that is not romantic. Second, it gives a prominent place to work that was famous in its time but that later fell from sight. Third, it represents two key transitional moments of the romantic period— the decades (roughly speaking) of the 1790s and the 1820s—more completely, and hence more problematically, than is done in narrative literary histories or anthologies of the period.

Synthetic historians tends to view their worlds in great sweeps. The romantic period thus typically comes to us through a gradual "pre-romantic" evolution mapped by now familiar signs (for instance, Gray, Collins, Chatterton, Macpherson, and perhaps Cowper). Nor do I mean at all to disparage such a view. But it *is* only a way of seeing things. One gets a very different vision from a tighter focus. At least as important so far as 1790s writers were concerned, for example, was the immediate impact of Sir William Jones's annotated translations of Persian poetry and the spectacular onset of the Della Cruscan movement. By foregrounding Jones's work and the Della Cruscans the *New Oxford Book of Verse of the Romantic Period* invites some alternative imaginings of our historical evidence and understandings.

Because a sense of historicality is so closely connected to causal models, early or precursive materials have always occupied the attention of critics. So romanticism's relation to the late eighteenth-century, if still inadequately treated, is a scene of deep scholarship compared with what we think about the 1820s. The anthology intervenes by printing a good deal of poetry that once occupied the center of cultural attention in the 1820s. These texts represent a small but serious effort toward a great need: the reconstruction of what was being written and read up to the passage of the first Reform Bill and the publication of Tennyson's 1832 *Poems.*

Situating the romantic period and its literary works firmly within the latter perspective affords some startling views and insights. What do we think we see when we look at the 1820s and its cultural work in England? The years following the restoration of the thrones of Europe—a settlement orchestrated by England—have all but sunk from sight so far as English cultural consciousness is concerned. If remembered at all, they commonly define a dismal point of contrast with the earlier phases of triumphant romanticism. At best we track a series of wounded beasts—the failures or madnesses of Darley, Beddoes, Clare. For the rest, critics simply shut the book of a romanticism that seemed to translate itself into a commercialized nightmare: the new craze for Gift Books and Annuals like *Friendship's Offering, The Keepsake, Foreget-Me-Not.* Literary history averts its gaze from this spectacle—there is scarcely a better word for the scene—because culture cannot easily capitalize its values. It seems an elegant dumpheap of factitious and overpriced trash—poor imitations of the life of the great romantics.[16]

That aversion is a negative sign of a version of literary history—what Benjamin called the victor's version. It is the version that wants to distinguish sharply between documents of cilivization—High Romanticism, so called—and documents of barbarism—the gilded poetry and silver fork novels of the 20s and 30s. But suppose one were to read the literature of the 20s as a critical reflection on its romantic inheritance. Writers like Hemans, Clare, Landon, Beddoes, Stoddart—to name a few representative figures—might tell a story of the death of the beauty that romanticism created. Romantic nature is a cultural account of the biological order of things. The "meaning" it ascribes to this order is perpetual development and growth: in Wordsworth's classic formulation, "something evermore about to be." Such a vision translates "death" back into a phase or moment of a benevolent or splendid process of life.

The period of the 1820s presents a serious problem for (romantic) literary history just because it appears to violate, in historical fact, this deep cultural myth of romanticism. A romantic agony begins when things of beauty do not appear joys forever—when no "abundant recompense" appears to balance the costs of romantic commitments. Keats, Wordsworth's immediate inheritor, reveals and undergoes that agony. Of course he does so completely against his will, as it were. He wants nothing more than the joys of beauty and the realms of gold. What he keeps discovering, however, are pale kings and beautiful, merciless ladies: death that is deathless, true, but terrible for that very reason—death that is hardly endurable, and ranged with a beauty that must die not in a benevolent order of nature but in the gorgeous palaces of art, as *Lamia* shows.

In "The Fall of Hyperion" Keats announces this death in speciously heroic tones: "deathwards progressing / To no death was that visage." "Beyond that" shattered splendor with its pale vision of "the lily and the snow," Keats says simply, "I must not think." Beyond it lies the one story no romantic poet wants to tell: the story of the death of art and culture. But the poets of the 1820s followed Keats (and Byron) to explore this "latest dream" dreamt on the cold hillsides of romanticism. In Tennyson's 1832 book of *Poems*—and perhaps most memorably in works like "The Lady of Shalott" and "The Palace of Art"—this romantic death appears to discover a new mode of expression, a form in which the death of art could itself be laid to rest. And at that point a corner had been turned. A Victorian corner.

## III

I hope I shall not be misunderstood. *The Romantic Ideology* was read and criticized by some as a kind of debunking maneuver because of its antithetical readings of celebrated romantic passages and works.[17] To the extent that such texts had been turned into idols of a romantic cave, it might have appeared that I was trying to write them off the cultural scene. But the move was strictly a dialectical one—ultimately, an effort at a historical reimagining of romanticism through an exposure of its concealed, sometimes even repressed, dialogical discourse. We do not debunk "Tintern Abbey" by sketching its sublimely egotistical projection of a sibling relationship; that relationship, cruel and benevolent at once, is one of the most powerful vehicles for the poem's structure of feelings.

Traditional critics have executed similar "debunkings" of romanticism's celebrated works—most famously, I suppose, of Byron's "Fare Thee Well!" Nor is it entirely mistaken to argue, as Wordsworth and others would do, that Byron's poem to his wife is maudlin doggerel. Byron's poem is no less riven by contradictions than Wordsworth's, only in Byron's case the poem's cruelty is being carried by a deliberate *mask* of benevolence. Its doggerel, so-called, is merely the clearest stylistic signal of the poem's masquerade. Unlike Wordsworth, who pursues a style of sincerity and—in "Tintern Abbey"—comes (forward) to believe in his own benevolence toward his sister, Byron in "Fare Thee Well!" writes a rhetorical and quite *in*sincere poem.

The work is self-conscious and duplicitous just where Wordsworth's poem is honest and unself-conscious. The ultimate (and untranscended) contradiction of Byron's poem is that its own awareness of contradiction does not entail an intellectual or moral *Aufhebung*—either for Byron as poet or for his readers. Byron's poem offers up to view—for those who have eyes to see and ears to hear—a vision of ultimate contradiction. The paradoxical result gives yet another turn to the screw of romantic contradiction: Byron's Faustian discovery that truth is unredemptive. In Manfred's famous lament: "The Tree of Knowledge is not that of Life."[18]

\*　　\*　　\*　　\*

Anne Mack. Beauty as death, truth as insecure. You tell a bleak story.

Jay Rome. Perhaps it seems bleak because we so often take for truth what is actually romantic hypothesis: that poetry, or art, will fill the void left by the previous hypothesis of Enlightenment. Romanticism is the battery of tests that the movement applied to its own ideological positions. Tennyson appears the sign of a new epoch because of the way he responded to the famous challenge put to him by his friend Trench: "Tennyson, we cannot live in art."

Anne Mack. Well, he responded—for example in "The Palace of Art"—by arguing that beauty and deep feeling could not substitute for faith—any more than reason and enlightenment could. The Victorians are obsessed with the question of faith, religious as well as secular. Aesthetically absorbed, lacking either "honest doubt" or religious commitment, the Soul presiding in the Palace of Art is weighed and found wanting. Nonetheless, Tennyson's poem does not repudiate beauty and its palace:

> Yet pull not down my palace towers, that are
> 　So lightly, beautifully built.
> Perchance I may return with others there
> 　When I have purged my guilt.
>
> 　　　　　　　　　　　　　　(293–96)[19]

That final play on the word "guilt" tells it all. The problem lies not in beauty and splendor as such but in the Soul's impurity. This poem stands exactly in the Keatsian tradition we glimpsed earlier—the line that passes into the "lightly, beautifully built" silver and gilded writing of the 1820s. If Tennyson turns a corner on romanticism, it is a backward turning, an effort to recover a purified and "purged" ideal.

Jay Rome. True, but that program of correction transforms romanticism into something entirely new. We see this change clearly, I think, at the end

159

of "The Lady of Shalott" when Lancelot muses over the lady's dead body. The poem is famous as an allegory of the death of romantic imagination. Paradoxically, however, nothing becomes this lady's life like the leaving it. Hers is an active death ("Singing in her song she died"), a deliberate move to terminate her ineffectually angelic life. Never had her social agency been more powerful than at the moment her corpse was carried into the heart of Camelot. "Knight and burgher, lord and dame" are terrified that a glory has passed from the earth. For his part, Lancelot reads the scene more calmly.

> He said, "She has a lovely face;
> God in his mercy lend her grace,
> The Lady of Shalott."

At their simplest—which is not their least important—level, the lines make an explicit plea for a grace beyond the reach of art. The prayer to God stands as an objective sign that this is a religious grace, something available through faith alone, not works. Also important is the logic (as it were) of Lancelot's thought. His prayer comes as if the lady's beauty were in need of God's mercy and grace. Her loveliness therefore suggests as well a kind of "fatal gift," the sign of something problematic lying at the heart of her poetical character.

Anne Mack. And yet Tennyson's poem is not savage or tense like equivalent texts in Keats and Byron, or mordantly devalued like the poetry of Landon or Stoddart.

Jay Rome. The flat tone is unmistakable Tennyson—the sign of poetry affecting an absence of anxiety. The general populace reads the lady's face with fear, but Lancelot, the text's point of departure, remains undisturbed. Tennyson has unburdened his poem of the romantic task of salvation. That task is returned to God. Beauty therefore emerges here as a device for clarifying vision. It makes no gestures toward an equivalent truth we might imagine it to symbolize. The poem is allegorical and decorative from the outset. As a result, the meaning of the poem, like the meaning of the lady's death, becomes, as it were, what you will. The poem is not imagined as a deep source from which we might draw life or faith. Romantic poems are organized in those ways, Tennyson's poem is different. Like the Lady of Shalott herself, it looks outward to its readers, without whom it cannot live or imagine living. It is, in short, a consciously social poem. It is Victorian.

The poem's ornamentality therefore marks its distance from a romantic mode of address, where sincerity and personal feeling are paramount. Flaunting its artifice, Tennyson's poetry wears mortality on its face. Such annunciations of beauty, as Keats and Byron predicted, retreat from imaginations of transcendence. Beauty appears the sign of what is mortal. Gendered female, as in the poetry of Landon, such beauty and artifice come as figures of deceit and betrayal. Tennyson studied Landon and her immediate precursors, Keats and Byron, in order to reimagine those dangerous fatalities of beauty. But Tennyson takes his poetry's decorative forms to an extreme, paradoxically, in order to lower the temperature of the verse. The lady of Shalott's face is "lovely" and that is all. It has not launched a thousand ships or burnt the topless towers of Ilium. The citizens of Camelot are needlessly frightened. The poetry invites the reader to approach the poetry as Lancelot approaches the body of the lady: not struck with fear or wonder, but bearing a blessing that clarifies the situation by restoring its ethical and religious dimensions.

Anne Mack. To me that placid surface is little more than a seductive deception. After all, this is *Lancelot* commenting on her beauty. If the death of this lady does not forecast the destruction of Camelot, that ruin appears in the depthless eyes of her beholder. The word "grace," in Lancelot's young mouth, is a sexist—indeed, a necrophiliac—word. Lancelot ultimately blaphemes with the word since his usage translates it into a purely formal and decorative meaning.

You're seduced by Lancelot and by Tennyson's beguiling surfaces, and you're even making us forget our real subject, the problem of periodization. When I cut through all this talk of Tennyson I find you arguing a position far removed from those dialogical modes of literary history you were celebrating a little while ago.

Jay Rome. Not so far removed. When I was talking about the poetry of the 1820s and the *New Oxford Book of Verse of the Romantic Period*, my thoughts inevitably went to Tennyson. His early work reflects and responds to the writing of the 20s. The last two poems in the *New Oxford Book* will be "The Lady of Shalott" and "The Palace of Art."

Anne Mack. Exactly. You end the collection with an editorial move that constructs a mastering (and worse still, a secret) historical narrative about romanticism. So much for all that talk about a dialogical literary history.

Jay Rome. Where's the secret? I'm talking about it now, and it's explicitly present in the Introduction to the collection. It's not a *secret* simply because it's represented in a non-narrativized form. As I said before, we know how to read the grammar of anthologies.

Anne Mack. Alright, let's call it an oblique rather than a secret history.

Jay Rome. Fine. Tell the truth but tell it slant.

Anne Mack. Secret, oblique, slant—whatever. It's a master narrative, isn't it? You begin and end your collection in a certain way, like Yeats in his *Oxford Book of Modern Verse.* Those beginnings and endings constrain the material to particular historical meanings. When you stop your collection with those two Tennyson poems, you want us to imagine the end of romanticism at that point, don't you? And you organize the anthology so that those two poems will come in with maximum effect in terms of the historical tale you're telling. "Obliquely," and so for maximum effect.

Jay Rome. Yes, that's true. But those two final poems have an authority of their own. They don't have to mean what I take them to mean. I might even change my mind about them. And didn't you just fling your different readings in my face a moment ago? Poems don't have to follow party lines.

Besides, you're discounting the formal inertia of the anthology, which is a collection of materials—in this case, evidence of what took place in the romantic period. The evidence is organized to construct an argument for a certain narrative. But it's not a narrative itself. It's more like a building, or a picture.

Anne Mack. And all sorts of evidence is left out.

Jay Rome. Of course, the book has its limits. What most attracts me to the anthology form—I speak from a literary historical point of view—is the *prima facie* character of those limits. "Heard melodies are sweet but those unheard / Are sweeter still." Isn't that always the case? An anthology is the very emblem of Derrida's "supplement of reading." It solicits revision, supplementation—it solicits your critique.

Anne Mack. The devil can quote scripture to his own purpose.

Jay Rome. Who's the devil here, me or you? At any rate, you're the one playing the devil's advocate. If I'm the devil, it's you who take my part. I like spirits of negation. They're really just angels in dark clothes, aren't they?

Anne Mack. You can't seriously want the negation or disproof of your own views.

Jay Rome. You're wrong, I really will settle for nothing less. Because I can't negate my views myself. I want to see the other side of my world. How did Tennyson put it:

> To follow knowledge like a sinking star,
> Beyond the utmost bounds of human thought.
>
> (31–32)

The second voyage of Ulysses, that's what I want. But I can't go by myself.
So can you take me there? Do you know a way?

## Notes

1 Rene Wellek, "The Concept of Romanticism in Literary Scholarship," in *Concepts of Criticism* (New Haven: Yale Univ. Press, 1963), 161 (originally printed in *Comparative Literature* 1 [1949]: 1–23, 147–72).

2 For good surveys of these events see Jon Klancher, "English Romanticism and Cultural Production," in *The New Historicism*, ed. H. Aram Veeser (London: Routledge, 1989), 77–88; and Marjorie Levinson's two essays in *Rethinking Historicism*, "Introduction," and "Rethinking Historicism: Back to the Future" (Oxford: Basil Blackwell, 1989), 1–17, 18–63. For this essay I have adapted the title of Levinson's collection.

3 See, for example, M. H. Abrams, *Natural Supernaturalism* (New York: W. W. Norton, 1971); and Harold Bloom, *The Visionary Company* (Garden City: Doubleday, 1961).

4 Though the work of various recent critics might be instanced here, I cite particularly Peter W. Graham, *Don Juan and Regency England* (Charlottesville: Univ. Press of Virginia, 1990) and the recent work of Peter Manning (see the essays on Byron collected in his *Reading Romantics. Texts and Contexts* [New York: Oxford Univ. Press, 1990], especially "*Don Juan* and Byron's Imperceptiveness to the English Word," 115–44). Jerome Christensen has been writing superbly on Byron for several years, and his work is being gathered in the soon to be published *Lord Byron's Strength: Romantic Writing and Commercial Society* (Baltimore: Johns Hopkins Univ. Press, 1992). Susan Wolfson's studies of Byron are also important and relevant to the present discussion: see "'Their She Condition': Cross-Dressing and the Politics of Gender in *Don Juan*," *ELH* 54 (1987): 595–617, and "'A Problem Few Dare Imitate': *Sardanapalus* and 'Effeminate Character,'" *ELH* 58 (1991): 867–902. Some of my own recent work on Byron has run along similar lines (for example, "'My Brain in Feminine': Byron and the Poetry of Deception," in *Byron: Augustan and Romantic*, ed. Andrew Rutherford [Basingstoke: Macmillan, 1990], 26–51; "Lord Byron's Twin Opposites of Truth," in *Towards a Literature Knowledge* [Chicago: Univ. of Chicago Press, 1989], 38–64; "Byron and 'The Truth in Masquerade,'" forthcoming in *Romantic Revisions*, ed. Tony Brinkley and Keith Hanley [Cambridge: Cambridge Univ. Press, 1992]. Two key points of departure for recent feminist work in romanticism are *Romanticism and Feminism*, ed. Anne K. Mellor (Bloomington: Indiana Univ. Press, 1988) and Marlon Ross, *The Contours of Masculine Desire* (New York: Oxford Univ. Press, 1989).

5 See my "The *Biographia Literaria* and the Contentions of English Romanticism," in *Coleridge's Biographia Literaria: Text and Meaning*, ed. Frederick Burwick (Columbus: Ohio State Univ. Press, 1989), 233–54.

6 The most recent of these studies is in *The Textual Condition* (Princeton: Princeton Univ. Press, 1991).

7 The first to suggest this critique was Marjorie Levinson, in a series of intense conversations and letter-exchanges shortly after the appearance of *The Romantic Ideology*. Her critique of romantic studies continues, but her earliest lines of inquiry are set down in her essays in *Rethinking Historicism* (note 2). See also Clifford Siskin's *The Historicity of Romantic Discourse* (New York: Oxford Univ. Press, 1988). Most recent to argue along these lines is Frances Ferguson in her critical review "On the Numbers of Romanticisms," *ELH* 58 (1991): 477.

8 This is the demand made by (among others) Michael Fischer in his early critique of *The Romantic Ideology* in *Blake: An Illustrated Quarterly* 18 (1984–85): 152–55.

9 Michael Taussig's approach to anthropology, set forth in a series of essays during the 1980s, offers another discipline's model of what I have in mind. The essays have just been collected as *The Nervous System* (London: Routledge, 1992).

10 See Charles Bernstein's collection of essays *Content's Dream. Essays 1975–1984* (Los Angeles: Sun & Moon Press, 1984); and Susan Howe's *My Emily Dickinson* (Berkeley: North Atlantic Books, 1985).

11 Two of Randall McLeod's published essays: "Unemending Shakespeare's Sonnet 111," *SEL* 21 (1981): 75–96; "Unediting Shak-speare," *Sub-Stance* 33/34 (1982): 26–55. Much of his most innovative work remains in typescript (such as "Information on Information"; "The bucke stoppeth here"; "Or Words to that dEffect").

12 Jeffrey Robinson, *The Current of Romantic Passion* (Madison: Univ. of Wisconsin Press, 1991); Donald Ault, *Narrative Unbound: Re-visioning William Blake's The Four Zoas* (Barrytown: Station Hill Press, 1987).

13 A number of these have been published (often under transparent pseudonyms). The most recent (as well as most comprehensive) is "A Dialogue on DIalogue," published in the electronic journal *Postmodern Culture* 2.1 (September, 1991).

14 *New History of French Literature*, ed. Dennis Hollier (Cambridge: Harvard Univ. Press, 1989).

15 My edition here is *The Golden Treasury*, ed. Francis T. Palgrave, introd. William Tenney Brewster (New York: Macmillan, 1937).

16 One of the few recent critics to give any attention to the period is Virgil Nemoiane in his *The Taming of Romanticism: European Literature and the Age of Biedermeier* (Cambridge: Harvard Univ. Press, 1984).

17 See James M. Kee, "Narrative Time and Participating Consciousness: A Heideggerian Supplement to *The Romantic Ideology*," *Romanticism Past and Present* 9 (Summer 1985): 51–63.

18 For a detailed exegesis of the poem along these lines see my "What Difference do the Circumstances of Publication Make to the Interpretation of a Literary Work," in *Literary Pragmatics*, ed. Roger D. Sell (London: Routledge, 1991), 190–207.

19 All Tennyson citations are from *The Poems of Tennyson* (London: Longman, 1969).

# 9

# WORDSWORTH'S POETICS OF ELOQUENCE: A CHALLENGE TO CONTEMPORARY THEORY

*Charles Altieri*

Source: *Romantic Revolutions: Criticism and Theory*, ed. Kenneth R. Johnston *et al.* (Bloomington: Indiana University Press, 1990), pp. 371–407.

But there is a third, and still higher degree of Eloquence, wherein a greater power is exerted over the human mind; by which we are not only convinced, but are interested, agitated and carried along with the Speaker; our passions are made to rise together with his; we enter into all his emotions; we love, we detest, we resent, according as he inspires us; and we are prompted to resolve, or to act, with vigour and warmth. . . . The high Eloquence . . . is always the offspring of passion. . . . Passion, when in such a degree as to rouse and kindle the mind, without throwing it out of possession of itself, is universally found to exalt the human powers. . . . A man actuated by strong passion, becomes much greater than he is at other times. He is conscious of more strength and force, he utters greater sentiments, conceives higher designs and executes them with a boldness and felicity, of which, on other occasions, he could not think himself capable.
—HUGH BLAIR[1]

Most contemporary criticism would find in Blair's effusions a good deal to demystify and to reinterpret in accord with a model of political or psychological interests that such writing labors to disguise. But suppose we were to take his argument seriously, that is, to see it as the effort to provide a passionate rendering about the effects of passion, which then makes sense only if one provisionally adopts the projected state of mind. Or better, since we must remain critics, what if we tried to understand analytically what might be involved in such a shift in both critical and dramatic attitudes? We might begin to appreciate the challenge which Romantic poetry can present to our prevailing theoretical assumptions.

Certainly there is now a vital interplay between the domains. Theory has taught us to value the ironic stances by which Romantic poets manage to

165

grapple with their own passionate ambitions, and it is now teaching us how to appreciate the complexities of the poetry as the production of an ideological discourse at once maintaining and exposing the seams of prevailing social values. Yet the poetry may pay a substantial price for such currency. In the high-status world of "sophisticated" theoretically informed criticism, the only authority that the poetry wields derives from its miming our dominant concerns. At one pole we honor only the poet's efforts at self-demystification; at the other we manage to respect their political sensitivity by continually exposing the gulf between what they see and what they frame within their own interpretive projects. In both cases the same basic model of historical reasoning prevails: the contemporary scene sets the agenda, then we test the hypotheses in relation to examples drawn from the past. As a consequence we have little access to the Romantics' fascination with Shakespeare, Milton, and the Bible, and we leave the poetry precious little otherness for the tasks of helping us demystify our own interpretive ambitions and of exploring ethical ideals which resist current fashions.[2] Therefore an exercise like the one I propose may at the least give us a fresh look at the literature and at ourselves, and it may even lead us to modify the concepts and purposes governing our critical practices.

As the basis for this experiment I shall try to reconstruct what I think was the basic model of poetry taking shape for Wordsworth during the first decade of the nineteenth century. After experimenting with dramatic ballads, Wordsworth found himself increasingly drawn to a personal lyric mode which combined traditional rhetorical ideals of high eloquence like those defined by Blair with a psychology much more responsive to the demands of his own intellectual culture. That project offers two fundamental contributions to contemporary theory: it establishes a model of poetry as direct, passionate personal utterance which has obvious and significant differences from both the dramatic model basic to New Criticism and the models of textuality governing both deconstruction and New Historicist semiotics, and on that basis it makes claims for the social significance of poetry without having to rely on a cult of irony or the languages of demystification.[3] For the display of passions becomes both an index of powers that the reader can identify with and a projected test of their value in engaging the world beyond the text. From this perspective Romantic irony becomes a means rather than an end—it helps clear the stage of the traps inherent in the culture's received versions of eloquence so that the underlying force of those energies can speak as a counter-eloquence, at once different from prevailing taste and responsive to the deeper principles which once were vital sources of that taste.

# I

I define the ideal of eloquence as that feature of rhetorical performance which exemplifies the power of the passions rendered to situate the speaker so that a mutual process of amplification takes place: what the speaker attributes to the world as worthy of the passion rendered can be tested only to the degree that it moves the audience to identify with it as a potentially transformative force in their lives. This effort to make ideal states concrete and plausible seemed necessary to Cicero, Longinus, and Augustine because they needed a plausible alternative to those versions of rhetoric content to stress the rules that help one achieve practical success. Without that alternative, both rhetoric and rhetorician are bound to the rules of the marketplace, so there is no way to dignify rhetoric or the rhetorician as capable of rivaling philosophy by opening and testing alternative ethical vistas. But if one could make the case for an eloquence which, in Cicero's terms, can make "visible stamped or rather branded on the advocate himself" "the very feelings" that he is trying to elicit for his audience, it becomes possible to surpass mere philosophical abstraction because one then demonstrates the power simultaneously to define, to test, and to promulgate ideas or models of character.[4] In the place of mere argument we are offered a site where the idealized claims of the soul "on fire with passion and inspired by something very like frenzy" become self-authorizing and compel by the mode of speaking which they display as a plausible human action. And in the place of mere efforts to persuade an audience one can imagine the orator literally offering that audience new possible identities in which to participate and through which to test a stance in terms of the modes of power that it can convey.

Educated in accord with principles like Blair's, yet situated in a culture where such principles seemed little more than masks for the real business of gathering wealth and status, Wordsworth would adapt two basic features of this tradition: its semantics in which qualities exemplified in the speaker's projected character are more important than any descriptive criteria for "truth," and its efforts to make that semantics ground an ethical model in which the poet can claim to articulate values which have a more significant claim on society than those bound to practices of getting and spending.[5] For the practical rhetorician the single end of rhetoric is to be persuasive. The theory of eloquence insists instead that a focus on practical rules or on consequences cannot account for the kind of passion which actually transforms individual speakers by leading them to states that practical judgment cannot compass, nor can they deal adequately with the possibility that such performances can modify an audience's values in ways that both rhetor and audience can take responsibility for. While the rules treat the passions simply as instruments for gaining effects, the eloquent orator uses their properties as heuristic instruments. On the one hand passions are passive. We can pretend to passion, but we cannot easily make our selves engage in them. Instead we attribute the arousal of passion to a source outside the self, a source both testing and extending what we can claim to be our psychological powers. This means that however exalted the passions that the orator claims, there must remain shareable links to his audience and clear indicators of the kind of affections which are the building blocks of such passions. Indeed, Blair insists that true eloquence depends on virtuous affections (1:13). Yet the passion cannot simply be equated with those affections. For in its active mode passion achieves transcendental states that depend on the ways in which those affections become visible powers.

Consequently when we are persuaded by an eloquent performance, we cannot account for it by appealing to the criteria that hold for practical arguments. Rather, eloquence challenges that realm of shared predicates and expectations by making visible and purposive an intensity of will and an expansion of consciousness carrying us much closer to our imaginative ideals than we ever reach in our more calculating moments. Thus for Cicero the eloquent expression of passions enables the speaker to "be such a man as he would desire to seem" (*De Oratore*, 1:63), thereby invoking in the place of concern for true description complex social theaters of shame risked and exemplary dignity achieved (for example, 1:85). And for Augustine that social theater easily opens on to a metaphysical one as the grand style becomes a secular analog for the Incarnation because it literally takes the word into the flesh: "If the beauties of eloquence occur, they are caught up by the force of things discussed and not deliberately assumed for the decoration," so the speakers "make their own those things which they could not compose." Finally, Longinus shows how even these transcendental energies retain their social force by positing eloquence as a force creating an alternative community of models and judges which then affords the social context addressed by the most ambitious orators.[6]

We need to return to Blair for the second feature, a distinction that will enable us to shift our focus from these claims about the idealizing role of passionate utterance to more concrete arguments about the kind of force such presences can exert within a world bound to quotidian principles of judgment. For he insists that these idealizing projections be understood as a mode of the sublime, and then he makes an important distinction between a sublime located in our relation to nature and a sublime specific to writing. Where the natural sublime resides in an uncanny or alien force taking control over a responding subject, the writerly sublime locates that power of transport within the exemplary authorial act as it "elevates the mind above itself, and fills it with high conceptions and a noble pride" (Blair, 1:58). Rather than referring to states of affairs which confirm or disconfirm statements, writerly action can rely on principles of purposive self-reference, which in turn make it plausible to claim that eloquent discourse establishes states of passion showing the audience a way beyond their ties to practical motives and empirical results. Thus, as contemporary theorists like Lyotard make clear, the sublime offers a sense of surplus carrying intense negative force: the excess of passion that it invokes simply cannot be justified within prevailing mores, yet its intensity leaves an indelible mark on the desires of its audience. But where contemporaries must be content with this disorienting impulse, classical theorists try to build on that negative force an alternative model of judgment enabling one to see fascination as a principle leading us to attempt provisional identifications with the projected passions. Because the passion suspends the hold of both basic forms of empirical reasoning, truth-functional analysis and the assessment of practical consequences, we must use the passions themselves as exemplary. There we must locate possible surrogates or representatives whose ways of surpassing those empirical pressures must be tested for the powers they might make available for any agent who is moved by them and hence drawn to their possible status as exemplars.

Any other attitude toward the performance of eloquence requires translating what has earned the sublime back into the languages of motives that it may have successfully resisted (a phenomenon we see increasingly at work as young academics attempt their moral diatribes against imaginative projections they show themselves unable to appreciate). And any other approach makes it impossible to use the only norm that makes any sense in relation to such performances—that instead of insisting on their possible truth as description or their manipulation of political interests we ask what kind of powers they confer on those willing to attempt those identifications. Some of these powers are simply self-regarding states. But Cicero and Blair are careful to insist that the specific performative powers can serve as both means and ends. For, as our opening passage indicates, eloquence promises to lead us beyond the condition of passive witnesses so that we test in our own engagement the capacity of those authorial sublimities to serve as mediators giving form to values through the passions that the speaker shows a situation or object can elicit. That is why for Augustine the self-celebratory dimensions of the high style can remain subordinate to the transcendental energies that they mediate, why for Cicero the orator demonstrates the highest possibility of virtue under the true spirit of Roman law (1:135–49), and why for Longinus the individual performer elicits affiliations with the community of heroes whom we all can then imagine inspiring and judging our actions.

## II

To move from Longinus' heroes to Wordsworth's "Advertisement" to *Lyrical Ballads* is to enter a very different social theater for the enacting of eloquent speech:

> The majority of the following poems are to be considered as experiments. They were written chiefly with a view to ascertain how far the language of conversation in the middle and lower classes of society is adapted to the purposes of poetic pleasure. Readers accustomed to the gaudiness and inane phraseology of many

modern writers . . . will perhaps have to struggle with feelings of strangeness and awkwardness: they will look round for poetry, and will be induced to enquire by what species of courtesy these attempts can be permitted to assume that title. It is desireable that such readers, for their own sakes, should not suffer the solitary word Poetry, a word of very disputed meaning, to stand in the way of their gratification; but that, while they are perusing this book, they should ask themselves if it contains a natural delineation of human passions, human characters, and human incidents; and if the answer be favorable to the author's wishes, that they should consent to be pleased in spite of that most dreadful enemy to our pleasures, our own pre-established codes of decision.

(Zall, 10)

The high tradition of eloquence has become the worst enemy of genuine passion, syphoning it off into artifice, leaving the majority of people with no alternative to debased popular media and requiring the poet, perhaps for the first time, to stage himself as experimental artist. Yet eloquence is not the problem. The problem is finding a language which can resist the culture's preestablished codes of decision to restore a sense of the pleasure and the awe which will accompany a full rendering of the passions. Therefore Wordsworth finds himself repeating the basic gesture of every ambitious rhetorical theorist—proposing a version of "natural" eloquence at odds with prevailing cultural expectations yet responsive to its deepest potentials for passionate life. But in Wordsworth this sense of counter-eloquence takes on a far more radical cast than one finds in those theorists, a cast that will dominate the next two centuries by shaping the logic of art as experiment. For now the new eloquence is not merely a matter of training new orators. It will require a new language, a new sense of the social affiliations and struggles that the poet must wage to gain authority for a new rhetoric, and a new sense of the psychic economy that will enable the speaker to demonstrate the value of such struggles.[7]

We are all familiar with Wordsworth's specific claims about the changes in content and in diction required for this new eloquence. These, however, are in my view the least interesting features of his poetic. For his career makes it evident that he would soon realize that Coleridge was essentially right in his criticism of those poems in *Lyrical Ballads* written in the spirit of the Preface's doctrines of the common life. In retrospect one might say that although Wordsworth was there trying to locate within a mimetic version of poetry the appropriate grounds for a "more permanent, and far more philo-sophical language" for nourishing "the essential passions of the heart" than he found in his predecessors (Zall, 41), in fact the strength of the theory and his talents as a poet lay elsewhere—in his capacity to cross that social milieu with modes of expressive eloquence best located in first person expression.

Therefore his poetry gradually modulates from imitating the purported eloquence of others with a privileged relation to nature to working out his own passionate responses to such possibilities and the problems they create for one who cannot wholly share those relationships. Yet the principles governing those modulations were already there in the theory—not in the specific social content but in the accounts he gives of the specific psychological processes governing the life of the passions set free by content. Therefore I want to examine the principles that these theoretical resources made available to him so that we can focus attention on the challenges that they present to contemporary poetics. Then I shall try to support my claims by offering a reading of "Nutting" as a paradigm for this poetics.

The ideal of eloquence is for Wordsworth inseparable from the desire to have his poetry speak this "more permanent, and far more philosophical language." For only such ambition could compose a semantic space allowing "the essential passions of the heart . . . a better soil in which they can attain their maturity" (Zall, 41). Once poetry could no longer cast itself as instructing us in a shared set of cultural ideals, the basic alternatives, then and now, leave poetics torn between a cult of discriminating taste that cannot address poetry's capacity to move us by what seem the simplest and most important of human truths and a model of privileged access to certain "original perceptions" whose inadequacies tempt us to prove our authenticity by cultivating a rigorous sense of inescapable and irreducible ironies severely limiting our range of emotional investments in the passions rendered. So it was, and is, necessary to develop a third possibility: suppose that poetry could earn its philosophical status less for what it overtly claimed than for what it displayed as the life of those passions and the fundamental qualities of the soils which nourished them. Rather than concentrating on making descriptive claims about the world, poetics could stress the abilities of language to isolate and intensify those states which "produce or enlarge" the capacity of the mind to be "excited without the application of gross and violent stimulants" (Zall, 43). Philosophical value then would consist in how the activity of the speaking demonstrates certain powers of sensibility so as to put the audience in a position to participate in the states rendered.

In other words, Wordsworth's concern for eloquent passions brings him close to the semantics of exemplification developed in contemporary terms by Nelson Goodman. If we were, however, simply to adapt Goodman's analyses, we would once again give the authority to contemporary culture (as well as ignoring some of the problems that Goodman raises). And, more important, we would let contemporary semantic models deprive us of the central role that Wordsworth attributes to the passions. So I hope instead to remain within the language of traditional poetic theories.[8] Wordsworth's originality consists then in his forging a version of exemplification which manages to synthesize what otherwise remain competing and incomplete models of literary experience. Take, for example, his fundamental statement of purpose—that "all good poetry is the spontaneous overflow of powerful feelings." There is no more radical distinction between a poetry intended to please and to instruct and one devoted to articulating the exalted states of the speaker. It is no wonder then that Wordsworth is usually characterized as having replaced the prevailing concerns for taste and for moral instruction by an essentially expressivist stance. Wordsworth immediately buttresses his claim about feelings by elaborating the subjective conditions allowing for such eloquence. But if we notice only that move, we blind ourselves to how quickly and how smoothly the passage modulates from the singular sensibility to "our influxes and feelings" and "our thoughts," and then from the expression to be contemplated to the effects which such states have on our capacities for action.

> For all good poetry is the spontaneous overflow of powerful feelings; but though this be true, Poems to which any value can be attached were never produced on any variety of subjects but by a man who, being possessed of more than usual organic sensibility, had also thought long and deeply. For our continual influxes of feeling are modified and directed by our thoughts, which are indeed the representatives of all our past feelings; and, as by contemplating the relation of these general representatives to each other, we discover what is really important to men, so, by the repetition and continuance of this act, our feelings will be connected with important subjects. . . .
>
> (Zall, 42)

Clearly we also must bring to bear the general model provided by response theories. Yet contemporary versions of that theory also tend to oversimplify the basic force of this passage. For ours is a hermeneutic age bound to two formulations of response which are incompatible with Wordsworth's concerns. We maintain a sharp dichotomy between those energies and expressions that are deeply subjective and those whose terms can be shared as attributes of an objective world, and we use that opposition within a set of academic practices deeply committed to worries about whether there are single coherent meanings for entire works of art. Consequently if we are to talk about the vitality of subjective life we feel compelled to insist on radically relativist frameworks for constituting the "meaning" of the text. If Wordsworth had to formulate questions our way he might have agreed. But for him, and indeed for most theorists of eloquence, questions of meaning simply drop out in favor of questions of projectible imaginative power. Whether or not we agree on the overall "meaning" is far less important than how we align ourselves to that source of powers that promises not to give us back ourselves but to enlarge us by inviting participation in what matters precisely because it is foreign to our banal quotidian selves. It is

172

those powers we can point to rather than meanings we can explicate that explain why works matter, show how exemplars can define possible attitudes toward the world beyond the text, and set the frame of common references which deepens our sense of community.

Wordsworthian "exemplification" then offers expressive acts eliciting the audience's participation as a means of positioning themselves in accord with the site released by passionate speech and the modes of self-reflection which that allows. By his *Essay, Supplementary to the Preface* of his 1815 collection of poems Wordsworth is clear enough about that site to insist on its distance from the claims posited by cognitive theories of poetry, a distance enabling him to finesse most of the questions about meaning and reference dominating our theoretical discussions: "The appropriate business of poetry (which, nevertheless, if genuine, is as permanent as pure science), her appropriate employment, her privilege and her *duty*, is to treat of things not as they *are* but as they *appear*; not as they exist in themselves, but as they seem to exist to the *senses* and the *passions*" (Zall, 160).[9] This does not mean that poetry is only an aesthetic object, only verbal play that makes nothing happen because it makes no assertions. Rather, it connects the poles of expression and response through the much bolder claim that poetry entails a different theory of language than is necessary for the asserting of propositions. That model of language must be able to handle what agents produce in speaking or writing and how they create effects by those productions.

The theory of language extending this imaginative perspective relies on three basic properties which simply have no place in the aesthetic epistemologies shaped by mimetic principles. There is a radically different account of metaphor; the differences located by that account license an ideal of poetry as testimony, which then replaces the ideal of rendering testable truths that had been the Enlightenment's highest goal of cultural production; and there results a rich theory of pleasure accounting for how these exemplary powers offered as testimony have concrete social force.

The topic of metaphor offers the starkest example of how this Wordsworthian position can assume values different from those dominating contemporary theory. We have moved from the New Critical idealizations of metaphor as the vehicle for nondiscursive truths to a variety of analytic and post-structural myths positing it as the serpent lurking within the garden projected in empiricist theories of language and truth. Derrida, for example, shows that the very idea of "proper sense" is distorted by the metaphors of property and propriety apparently necessary in order to refer to the ideal of an unequivocal relation between word and world. But then the only positive functions given to metaphor become either textualist versions of play (not terribly far from the neoclassical concerns for ornament that so disgusted Wordsworth) or returns like Ricoeur's to quasi-mystical claims for a special kind of truth which cannot be parsed into straightforward referring expressions. Wordsworth can dismiss both positions by focusing not on the world but on the conditions of engaging that world given definition through the eloquent passions of a speaker: "If the poet's subject be judiciously chosen, it will naturally, and upon fit occasion, lead him to passions the language of which, if selected truly and judiciously, must necessarily be dignified and variegated, and alive with metaphors and figures" (Zall, 47–48). Here metaphor does not displace reference. Rather, it clarifies what is at stake in engaging questions of reference in terms of the possible dispositions that a speech act can sanction. Eloquence is quite frankly the sign of an excess that knows it cannot be satisfied by descriptions but seeks impressions of "certain inherent and indestructible qualities of the human mind" and likewise of "certain powers in the great and permanent objects that act upon it, which are equally inherent and indestructible" (Zall, 44).[10]

But how do we know whether the metaphors are judiciously chosen, and how do we know that in yielding to the metaphor we open ourselves to experience that idealized relation between the mind and its dynamic ground? Why is the metaphor, or the entire project of eloquence, not simply an evasion of the empirical realities or of the ironies that deconstruction shows inescapable when we rely on those realities to make judgments regarding human desires? There is no easy answer. Indeed if one stays within empiricist frameworks, there is no possible answer because we can only speak about knowledge where there are clear lines of reference and assessment. But precisely because his version of eloquence can surrender both the desire for particular truths and its enemy twin, the necessity for infinite dissemination, Wordsworth offers concepts of pleasure and of power which I think prove extremely useful in showing the way to other models for assessing speech acts.

Let us begin with Wordsworth's own claims for the philosophical value of poetic utterance:

> Aristotle . . . has said, that poetry is the most philosophic of all writing; it is so: its object is truth not individual and local but general, and operative; not standing upon external testimony, but carried alive into the heart by passion; truth which is its own testimony, which gives competence and confidence to the tribunal to which it appeals and receives them from the same tribunal.
>
> (Zall, 50)

For those who identify with Enlightenment ideals of philosophical rigor it is difficult not to dismiss such enthusiasm contemptuously. Yet there are three claims here that I think both defensible and suggestive. First it makes sense to speak of "general truth" in this context because the aim is not description but exemplification, not statements about the world but the effort to define labels and models for what might be at stake in a range of those descriptions.

That distinction then clarifies Wordsworth's principle of testimony, of "truth" which is confirmed by the immediate passion it elicits. For since the statement does not refer in the usual way, its claims on the world can only be judged by what it makes visible in the particular structure of passionate attention and expression that it makes visible. Wordsworth speaks of testimony because the only relevant criteria are the degree to which the model or label achieves generality by providing a concrete surrogate actually demonstrating the powers it claims. One might say, for example, that a poem like "Tintern Abbey" can only sanction its claims about memory and nature to the degree that it demonstrates how the passions so fostered give the mind certain ways of acting that can be projected as a way of being in the world. In this sense the poem is testimony to a power that it makes visible.

But then we need as our third principle a model of uptake explaining how audiences can use that testimony. This is where the marvelous dialectic of the tribunal in our passage comes into focus. Where propositions and themes stress what lies objectively in the world, testimony bases the burden of the discourse on the powers it exemplifies and the identifications made possible by that exemplification. And there is no better image for that act of identification than Wordsworth's sense of the powers of the tribunal and a deepening sense of the world which they yield as their theater. As we find our relations to the world modified by the poem, we turn back to it with an increasing sense of how that testimony has general claims on us. Response is the locus of value, but the source of value remains in how the work maintains the capacity to modify our sense of identity.

## III

But now how do we measure the consequences of those identifications or those attributions of confidence? How do we make transitions between the passions created in the moment of reading and the commitments that can or must stem from those moments? One could answer that at this point we go beyond poetics to ethics and politics: poetics shows how testimony might work, ethics and politics provide different values at different times which determine the relative use of different expressions. But while this is a reasonable position, it may too quickly subordinate the powers of poetic eloquence to those more analytic worldly attitudes. Therefore Wordsworth insists on having the projection of eloquent testimony carry its own ethical force. Within the Preface to *Lyrical Ballads* he turns again and again to projections of the "Poet" as an ideal psychological type in order to illustrate the kinds of powers which such testimony offers for our identification (for example, Zall, 44, 47–49, 51). More generally, it seems reasonable to view Wordsworth's entire poetic career as a set of efforts to give ethical force to idealized bearers of certain kinds of passions and habits of mind sanctioning those habits. In *Lyrical Ballads*, the idealized figure is one who can in effect draw out the latent powers of passion contained within certain counter-cultural ways of using common language; in *The Prelude* attention shifts to the capacity of a single mind to align itself to what is potential in the forces shaping it, and in the organization of the 1815 *Poems* Wordsworth composes a lyric poet's *Phenomenology of Mind* which defines a range of dispositions "proceeding from, and governed by, a sublime consciousness of the soul in her own mighty and almost divine powers" (Zall, 149). No lesser dream could be consistent with a view of his literary heritage as "grand storehouses of enthusiastic and meditative Imagination, of poetical, as contradistinguished from human and dramatic Imagination" like "the prophetic and lyrical parts of the Holy Scriptures, and the works of Milton" and Spenser (Zall, 149). For our purposes, however, there must remain a substantial gulf between this Longinian effusiveness and a theory sanctioning Longinian effusiveness. Therefore instead of relying directly on those larger models I shall begin with Wordsworth's claim that "The poet writes under one restriction only, namely, the necessity of giving immediate pleasure to a human being possessed of that information which may be expected of him . . . as a Man" (Zall, 50). For it is in his analysis of pleasure that Wordsworth gives the most concrete psychology we have for dwelling on the ways that passionate testimony defines and makes available psychological and ethical powers.

All the ladders start with the peculiar ontological position pleasure occupies. As Aristotle argued, there is no one thing that we can call pleasure. Rather, pleasure is essentially relational—a matter of how we engage in other phenomena rather than something we can pursue in its own right. This means that it makes no sense to ask whether the pleasure lies in the object or in the responder. Rather, the pleasure arrives woven into the event or performance. One might say that the enlargements it brings are not separable from the rendering, from the "how" that can lead attention to the qualities and intensities of the actual moment as well as to the nature of the tribunal responding to such qualities. Such enlargements then serve almost as a natural or immediate principle of amplification, "a homage paid to the native and naked dignity of man" (Zall, 51), at least so long as one can believe that the pleasures also lead us to deeper possibilities of both our own nature and the world which calls that nature forth.

This belief was easier for Wordsworth than it is for us. For him a basic distinction between the gross stimulants that usually govern popular taste and quieter, and hence more natural, modes of attention sanctioned an entire theology (see especially, Zall, 51).[11] If one's pleasures could be freed from such gross impositions, there is a reasonable chance that they could be aligned with both the potential of one's own nature and the ways in which that nature was adapted to participate in its environment. But in our critical climate such appeals to nature carry little suasion. Although Richard Eldridge makes suggestive use of the idea of human nature, and although the associationist aspects of Wordsworth's theory offer intriguing parallels to the materialist psychology of DeLeuze and to Rorty's effort to define a model of political sympathies free of the idealist principles of judgment that pervade post-Kantian thinking, there is little point to making this level of Wordsworth's theory the basis for academic claims. Yet our distance from his metaphysics ought not blind us to the intricacy of his psychology, especially in passages like the following, which tease out a dynamics of pleasure suggesting concrete grounds for believing that eloquence cultivates ethically significant imaginative powers:

> To this knowledge which all men carry about with them, and to these sympathies in which, without any other discipline than that of our daily life, we are fitted to take delight, the Poet principally directs his attention. . . . And thus the poet, prompted by this feeling of pleasure . . . converses with general nature, with affections akin to those, which, through labour and length of time, the Man of science has raised up in himself, by conversing with those particular parts of nature which are the objects of his studies. The knowledge both of the Poet and the Man of science is pleasure; but the knowledge of the one cleaves to us as a necessary part of our existence, our natural and unalienable inheritance; the other is a personal and individual acquisition, slow to come to us, and by no habitual and direct sympathy connecting us with our fellow beings.
>
> (Zall, 52)

Poetry begins as self-delight—both in terms of the intense states it makes available and in terms of the confidence it builds in the tribunal that through language comes to feel its own attachments to the world growing more varied and more engaging. Thus the amplification that is eloquent passion is also an amplifying of the terms of self-regard available for our reflective lives. Yet because that passion takes testimonial form in language, its very intimacies are also the terms that make it far more social in orientation than the kind of knowledge developed by the sciences, or, as I prefer to see it, than all disciplinary knowledge. In the case of disciplinary knowledge, our pleasure lies in our coming to master a specific set of practices which serve as instruments leading to a deeper grasp of certain aspects of the world. But in the case of the poet's conversations with general nature, our pleasure lies less in the contents of knowledge than in the state of the subject we come to see as coextensive with our experience of the object. The very terms of the pleasure become features of what we then reflect on as fundamental to our humanity—as conditions of attention and as ways of positioning the psyche which we have grounds to think also engage the affective lives of other persons. Beginning from self-love, Wordsworth develops a psychology in which there is considerable sense to the claim that the "Poet binds together by passion and knowledge the vast empire of human society" (Zall, 52). At least the kind of discourse that the poet makes basic for both identity and identification *can* perform that task because the ecstatic sites it composes have no role other than making us aware of the pleasure potential in powers and possible identities we so easily forget we have.

Giving sense to the claim is not the same thing as giving a clear demonstration of its validity. That Wordsworth's psychology of self-delight cannot accomplish. Nor could any theory, I suspect. We need eloquence in this domain because the entire subject of powers generated through imaginative activity is so bound up with self-reflection and with idealization that it simply resists any more analytic stance. We do not come to believe in these powers because some argument is made on their behalf. Rather we are invited to participate in the states they make available. Our measure of power is simply the degree to which the resulting modes of self-reflection engage us in new dimensions of ourselves and our world. That is why the most Wordsworth can do as a theorist is try out various idealized versions of the character of the poet and the processes which his exemplary acts of mind make possible. And that is why in trying to elaborate his theory I can do little more than recall what he sees at stake in those idealizations, then turn to a representative poem as my illustration of his deepest thinking on the subject.

The wisest rhetorical strategy for dealing with idealizations is to work with contrasts: while it may be impossible to persuade others directly of one's claims about values, it often proves to be the case that by clarifying what one opposes, or what happens when the prevailing values are left in place, one opens the way for one's audience to try out the identifications necessary to support one's own position. For Wordsworth the most compelling contrasts are with the psychological problems that he shows seem inescapable under the assumptions about poetry that he had inherited. The sharpest of these in his critical prose occurs in the last of his essays on epitaphs, where he builds from an attack on ornamental diction in so serious and "sincere" a genre to the following far more radical critique:

> If my notions are right, the epitaphs of Pope cannot well be too severely condemned; for not only are they almost wholly destitute of those universal feelings and simple movements of mind which we have called for as indispensable, but they are little better than a tissue of false thoughts, languid and vague expressions, unmeaning antithesis, and laborious attempts at discrimination. Pope's mind had been employed chiefly in observation upon the vices and follies of men. Now, vice and folly are in contradiction with the moral principle which can never be extinguished in the mind; and therefore, wanting the contrast, are irregular, capricious, and inconsistent with themselves. . . . All this argues an obtuse moral sensibility and a consequent want of knowledge, if applied where virtue ought to

be described in the language of affectionate admiration. In the mind of the truly great and good everything that is of importance is at peace with itself; all is stillness, sweetness and stable grandeur. Accordingly the contemplation of virtue is attended with repose. . . . The mind would not be separated from the person who is the object of its thoughts. . . . Whereas when meekness and magnanimity are represented antithetically, the mind is not only carried from the main object, but is compelled to turn to a subject in which quality exists divided from some other as noble, its natural ally: a painful feeling! that checks the course of love, and repels the sweet thoughts that might be settling around the Author's wish to endear us; but for whom, after this interruption, we no longer care. If then a man, whose duty it is to praise departed excellence not without some sense of regret or sadness, to do this or to be silent, should upon all occasions exhibit that mode of connecting thoughts, which is only natural while we are delineating vice under certain relations, we may be assured that the nobler sympathies are not alive in him; that he has no clear insight into the internal constitution of virtue; nor has himself been soothed, cleared, harmonized, by those outward effects which follow everywhere her goings— declaring the presence of the invisible Deity.

(Zall, 120–22)

Ornamental diction is dangerous because it is to style what observation is to the life of values. One achieves mastery, but usually at the cost of failing to understand fully both what one would master and what that other could bring out in the self if one could loosen one's oppressive need for control. Pope's epitaphs then represent the limitations of an entire century committed to the public show of principles of judgment that had become terribly distanced from two significantly related dispositions—the capacity for empathy and the capacity to offer the kind of praise which ultimately exalts both the self and the objects that become available to that self once they are seen in the atmosphere which panegyrics compose. Popean judgment mimes too closely the framework of social negotiation and self-control basic to the culture whose praise it seeks, so that it prevents us from making the empathic leaps that lead us beyond social morality to the grace that is deep virtue at peace with itself. So the poet's task must emulate the task that Kant posed for a philosophy that would escape the same eighteenth-century blinders to idealization, that of making manifest and plausible those powers of spirit which lead beyond the social theater to other, more sublime principles of self-delight and social relatedness.

If we remain with Wordsworth's prose it is fairly easy to outline those powers he thought could perform that task. In the Preface to *Lyrical Ballads*, the central psychological traits he cultivates are those that "carry everywhere relationship and love." At times this means attuning us to the ways in which our associative processes can be aligned to deep patterns of lawfulness; at times it takes more closely textured psychological attention to the "accuracy with which similitude in dissimilitude and dissimilitude in similitude are perceived" because on that "depend our taste and moral feelings" (Zall, 57). What takes overt form in the meter of the poem in fact gets played out on several psychological levels—all "imperceptibly" making "up a complex feeling of delight, which is of the most important use in tempering the painful feeling always found intermingled with the powerful descriptions of the deeper passions" (Zall, 58). By the Preface to the edition of 1815, Wordsworth breaks this pursuit of a balanced psychic economy down into three basic powers of imagination, each adding a dimension of synthetic energies enabling a richer sense of how the internal life extends the order of perception. At the simplest level the imagination has the power to confer properties on objects so that the object reacts "upon the mind which hath performed the process like a new existence." If we then envision this faculty elaborating those properties so that they react on one another we begin to see how the play of similitude and dissimilitude balances us between delight in the mobility of our sensations and a comprehensive sense of how the unities that then emerge betoken a higher conjunction of man and nature (Zall, 149). Finally all this admits of a fully self-reflexive mode: "But the imagination also shapes and creates . . . by innumerable processes; and in none does it more delight than in that of consolidating numbers into unity, and dissolving and separating unity into number,—alternations proceeding from, and governed by, a sublime consciousness of the soul in her own mighty and almost divine powers." The most elemental forces brought to attention in rhythmic eloquence serve also to indicate the most sublime delights of the mind becoming conscious of its own processes.

## IV

To stay on this prosaic level in our discussion of powers, however, leaves us very much in the position of Popean judgment. The true test of our noblest sympathies, of criticism as epitaph and projection for the future, is the ways in which the powers of eloquence take on imaginative force in the poetry. For this test I have chosen to dwell on "Nutting."[12] Here Wordsworth most intensely spells out the stakes in his quarrel with lyric sensibilities formed by Enlightenment values, and here the contrast with representative contemporary criticism makes all too evident the degree to which such struggles for a mode of plausible idealization must continue. Nothing could make those stakes clearer than the very different hero Wordsworth puts forward for our identification: this "Figure quaint, / Tricked out in proud disguise of cast-off weeds" (ll. 8–9) can base its claims on our lyric sensibilities only on passions banished by high culture into the world of low mimetic situations and filiations. In order to give this sensibility a voice, and in order to evade the ironic bitterness about such marginalization, which would only rein-force the old values without coming to terms with the imaginative energies that alienate this hero from his heritage, Wordsworth must locate spiri-tual resources that break sharply with the prevailing hierarchy of psychic functions: he must stretch available conditions of representation so that they concentrate attention on a force that cannot be made to appear except in the process of poetic self-reflection, and he must articulate through that reflection a mode of sublimity capable of restoring the ego's sense of connectedness with the natural sources of its energies. Rather than pursue the reflective pathos of "The Castaway" or the exalted contemplative scope of the voice in "Elegy on a Country-Churchyard," this poem demands our working against generalized sentiments and Horatian ideals for poetry in order to focus on close readings of what the compulsion to narrate reveals about the mind's relation to its scenic context.

Given its setting, the poem should be able to rely on pastoral conventions. But within the speaker's narrative these conventions prove a seductive and dangerous form for representing experience. Traditional pastoral expecta-tions seem to leave the mind a frustrating excess that finds its most ready outlet in adolescent violence:

> I heard the murmur and the murmuring sound,
> In that sweet mood when pleasure loves to pay
> Tribute to ease; and, of its joy secure,
> The heart luxuriates with indifferent things
> Wasting its kindliness on stocks and stones,
> And on the vacant air. Then up I rose
> And dragged to earth both branch and bough, with crash
> And merciless ravage: and the shady nook
> Of hazels, and the green and mossy bower,
> Deformed and sullied, patiently gave up
> Their quiet being: and unless I now
> Confound my present feelings with the past;
> Ere from the mutilated bower I turned
> Exulting, rich beyond the wealth of Kings,
> I felt a sense of pain when I beheld
> The silent trees and saw the intruding sky.
> Then, dearest maiden, move along these shades
> In gentleness of heart; with gentle hand
> Touch—for there is a spirit in the woods.

(ll. 38–56)

Apparently the easy humanism of Romance pastoral which the boy in-vokes cannot sufficiently handle difference, cannot handle the very sense of personal intensity that it elicits. Therefore, as the heart luxuriates, the mind all too readily slips from its sweet mood to a sense that its objects become indifferent and its kindliness wasted. Given the rhetoric available to it, the mind has no other way to express its increasing sense of its distinctive powers but to set itself violently against a nature that becomes merely its object.

Yet this play on difference and indifference soon reveals another power, another greater difference which becomes intelligible only by the poem's power to compose another rhetoric based on the fusing of psychological narrative with the pastoral setting. Here then we find a different version of constitutive subjective energies able to compose a more capacious lyrical theater. Cast out of those conventional attitudes initially producing a coherent emotional scenario, the mind's momentary sense of power dissipates and the hero finds himself transformed into a mere object within a scene whose self-sufficiency makes him utterly expendable. Bower yields to silent trees and intruding sky, leaving the ephebe torn on the dualities of "Kindliness" on which the Enlightenment tradition foundered. From the humanist perspective kindliness refers to the appreciation of a distinctively human potential in the encounter. But this makes nature a little less than kin, reduced to hoping for the subject's kindnesses and hence also a fit victim for his tirades. And in that reduced state violence produces another kindliness, linking him to precisely that capacity for disorder in nature which probably made the effort to cover over the differences seem necessary in the first place. From this perspective, consciousness seems to share not nature's depth but the superficiality of its appearances, as if both domains distanced and distorted some deeper possibility of lawfulness.

The logic is pure Augustine: the secular dream of being more than nature reduces one to being less than one's own nature can be. Adequate response depends on finding a way of reading one's experiences so that the awareness of this acculturated blindness becomes a means of redefining spirit. For Wordsworth, the new means is confessional narrative, and the new goal a state of sublimity earned by the narrative process of working through lack and contradiction. In this more dialectical sense of landscape, poetry cannot be content with describing nature or reflecting on the general truths that nature might illustrate. Rather, poetry must become self-reflexive enough to provoke errors, then test the capacities of the composing voice to spell out new lines of relation between a mind in excess of nature and a force of nature that reveals its powers only through the collapse of kindliness. Once the sky can become an intruding presence, the youth must learn how narrative enables him to take responsibility for both his difference from nature and the divisions from himself which generated so unreasoned and ostensibly spontaneous a destructive act. The result is a new, non-Burkean form of the sublime which gives moral force to the state of self-consciousness it presents as testimony. The rude shock of what one is not—not one with the appearance of nature and not one with the rhetoric that gives man superiority over a yielding nature—forces memory and poetry to the constructive work of the concluding lines. There is a spirit in these woods, but its meaning and force are reserved for those who can learn to read it as the poem does— through a series of negations which clear the way for this particular poetic naming to resist a history of false associations. Then it requires the dialectic of narrative memory to show why there must be a spirit and why it must remain on the margins of human experience, beyond the control of an interpretive violence which most ephebes in the culture never outgrow.

Wordsworth's great achievement here is to have his sublime romance and to moralize it too, while making the conjunction testimony to the powers of passion become eloquent about its enabling conditions. On one level, then, it makes sense to cast these Wordsworthian moments in the frame of Freudian instruction scenes. By casting this spirit in the woods as a sur-rogate father punishing the son for raping his sister-mother and thus com-posing (or imposing) nature as a super-ego figure, "Nutting" overdetermines the poem's resolution just as it had the violent act. Yet Freudian language (or Lacanian twists on that language) will not suffice because this over-determination is quite deliberate. The scene instructs because of its overt properties *as* scene, as a mode of presentation that can undo the received model of interpretive authority and make the specific process of unfolding which the poem enacts necessary to define what spirit can be. Rather than limit Spirit to something we find in the unconscious, we are invited to envision it as the active force to which narrative can testify once it comes to understand how the mind is capable of modes of attention and memory more sensitive and more capacious than the models of man the poem seeks to displace.

## V

If such testimony is to earn its modernity, that is, its resistance to dominant cultural ideals, it must possess two concrete means of extending and testing the powers that Wordsworth's prose attributes to it—it must show how the expansive passion opens us to new grounds of value, and it must give that testimony an immediacy and force which for traditional theorists of eloquence could derive in large part from the invocation of high cultural traditions. The second is the easier to describe because what Wordsworth inaugurated is now close to being a cultural cliché to which we presently seek alternatives. Poetry as testimony need not seek authority from an idealized cultural heritage to the degree that the artifact itself maintains a system of internal relations sufficient to lead the reader to and through the projected powers of spirit. But this vision of poetic means puts an enor-mous burden on poetic ends: what possible ground of values could provide a countercultural force simply on the basis of self-reflexive intricacy and the narrative control of shifting investments? Wordsworth's response is to attempt shifting the terms of valuation so that the priority of civic space yields to the priority of autobiographical measures of value. Such values need not be solipsistic or individualist, but they must gain their authority from the relation they allow a person to maintain toward his or her formative experiences.

Establishing those priorities entails developing a model of the resources, the commitments, and the contradictions basic to poetic activity which could overturn the interwoven ideals of judgment, of nobility, and of eloquence that had taken form under the aegis of both Christian Humanism and Enlightenment rationalism. These frameworks cast the noble self as one whose judgment and will managed to subordinate individual interests and passions to some more general categorical frameworks. Selves inherit traditions and through them develop powers of assessment enabling them to align themselves with those ideas and images which define a life worthy of respect. Under those dispensations the role of judgment and imagination is to subordinate the particular to the generalized model, at least in those domains where there are clear public ideals. But Wordsworth was obsessed by the problem of what authorizes those ideals. For him idealization had to remain connected to formative events and influences in particular lives, so that the idealizing would in effect be inseparable from a condition of remembering and the qualities of the remembering could then be subject to public scrutiny against the backdrop of a common world. The result is what might be called a scenic logic which redefines the dynamics of judgment and thus requires shifting from the Miltonic model of public eloquence to a version of eloquence that could take responsibility for its origins in an essentially domestic imaginative theater.

In this Wordsworthian scenic model for the formation of selves the central terms for value derive from persons' capacities to define their own distinctive relationship to the sources of their most intense powers. Because the formation of selves thus involves the dialectical force of all that the intruding sky symbolizes, this scenic logic has affinities with Idealist thought (as Meyer Abrams's *Natural Supernaturalism* magisterially demonstrates). But in order to accommodate his own empiricist values, Wordsworth develops models of reflection and of judgment that do not lead to Kant's and Hegel's synthetic rational processes, and that thereby do not require any specific teleological or transcendental claims. Judgment becomes what Schlegel called a form of "spiritual sensuality" that must locate its generalizing principles within the scene that it composes. No longer confined by abstract ideas or social norms of taste, Wordsworthian judgment depends on a concrete history of negotiations with an environment. The self is scenic, then, because its investments derive from the scenes that it has been attached to and the traces which those leave in its memory. Scenes are not mere instances passively awaiting the forming influence of the mind. Instead they serve as metonyms for behavioral complexes that spread out over time and into a range of repeated habits and related social practices. Because the self neither creates meanings nor can trust dominant cultural generalizations, its deepest powers and most intimate loyalties are shaped by the history of the adjustments it makes to those environmental forces. And because these adjustments involve the measure of time—of repeated connections to nature and other people as well as a history of rewards and instructive failures—the energies they engage can be much more comprehensive and more immediately compelling and flexible than anything generalized principles can afford. The expansive life of scenic consciousness both elicits and rewards a temperament gradually developing patterns of attention and care binding it to its surrounding community. Thus, Wordsworthian versions of testimony, of expansive passion, and of identification enable us to replace Horatian generalization by an ideal of representativeness based simply on the capacity of a work to exemplify certain powers that help an audience adapt itself to similar numinous forces. Because the spirit in the woods can become the spirit defined by the field of energies the poem's narrative act composes, the narrated recognition scene becomes available for the entire society. There can be a spirit in a personal narrative's self-critical activity that can engage the spirit in the woods and can make its contribution to the community the exemplary modes of reflection that it affords for such engagements. Ultimately that engagement even makes it possible to transform the rape of feminine nature into the making visible of imaginative resources that the poet can hope to share with his maiden interlocutor.

## VI

My own diction here, and my uneasiness about Wordsworth's treatment of women, make all too visible the problem that still remains for this essay— how is Wordsworth's eloquence still empowering for us? Why should we make the imaginative effort necessary to identify with it, and how can we be reasonably certain that in pursuing such identifications we are not repeating the initial efforts of the boy in "Nutting" to engage a changing world under the aegis of outmoded fictions? I have tried to cast the values at stake in general enough terms that their application to contemporary culture is clear. But that generality could be considered part of the problem, since our literary culture is becoming adamantly historicist and "materialist." Consequently the only way I know to bring out the force of Wordsworth's position is to borrow the strategy he used against Pope, that is, to draw contrasts between the powers that he pursues and the attitudes toward eloquence which now dominate what Frank Lentricchia calls "advanced" positions in contemporary literary criticism. For this experiment I have chosen a reading of "Nutting" posed by Jonathan Arac's recent book *Critical Genealogies.*[13] If I can show that readings like Arac's fail to account for the probable depth and the possible uses of the poet's intelligence, then there is at least a beginning for the case that these gestures of sophisticated critical intelligence often mask what remains a reactionary submission to academic fashion and to the banal forms of self-congratulation sustained by Enlightenment mythologies of an heroic demystifying lucidity. Not to challenge such readings is to submit to a critical climate in which there is simply no possible positive role for poetic eloquence, and hence little use for the lyric imagination except as a repository of symptoms or of approved revolutionary emotions.

Arac and I pose almost exactly the same question: for him the issue is how "Nutting" can be said to present "the psycho-sexual construction of literary authority" (49), and for me it is how the poem presents one plausible way of handling perceived crises in the possibility of wielding literary authority under post-Enlightenment intellectual values. But Arac also wants the reading of "Nutting" to illustrate a critical stance capable of combining the close reading techniques developed by various modern formalisms with a historical perspective that both situates texts as determinate actions in the past and shows how they help produce strata of assumptions and values which limit our powers as social agents in the present. Therefore rather than identifying provisionally with such eloquence we must learn to dismantle it by means of "a new kind of history writing" (2). This model, perhaps this new version of eloquence committed to the interpreter's activity, can expose the ways in which Wordsworth is instrumental in developing a model of literary autonomy that was "accompanied both by the exclusion of women from the experience that makes literature possible and by the assumption of universality that fetishistically treats sexual differences as 'indifferent things'":

> Once poetic authority was lost, once the previously existing social demand for poetry had been transformed, once the writer was no longer producing on direct demand by patrons, or even subscribers, but was isolated in the marketplace producing for unknown readers whose taste could not be predicted but might with luck be formed, once, in other words, a certain condition of alienation prevailed, then the possibility of literary autonomy also came into existence. The process of internalization by which Wordsworth not only defended but also formed a new literary human nature—the human nature that makes psychoanalysis possible—cannot be understood apart from such externalities. The example of "Nutting" has suggested, moreover, that this literary possibility came only at the cost of reasserting an inequality between the sexes, a form of domination even more fundamental than those of social class and cultural tradition.
>
> (49)

I agree that Wordsworth's achievement cannot be understood apart from "such externalities." I doubt, however, that we will learn much about those historical forces if we rely as heavily as Arac does on common contemporary understandings of concepts like autonomy and women's interests, or if one allows oneself to translate Wordsworthian language so quickly into the available psychoanalytic analogies. For then our examination of the construction of literary authority proves false both to the history in which the labor took place and to the present possibilities of locating within the poet's engagements with those historical forces a form of authority which has the power to challenge dominant contemporary modes of lyrical sensibility or critical intelligence. These difficulties become most pronounced in Arac's reading precisely at the moment when "Nutting" has the speaker turn on eighteenth-century models of pastoral in order to tease out an alternative source of genius and a corresponding model of attention. Once again Arac and I (and almost everyone else) agree that the moment of crisis in the poem is the turn to "indifferent things." But rather than stay within the poem's projected reasons for that shift in focus, Arac struts his post-structuralist sensibility. He wants to show that this poem is a particularly tense crossing of Wordsworthian themes because it occupies a social position in which it does not "lay claim to the traditional elevation of ode and thereby has more difficulty assimilating epic and tragedy" (39). Forced to a make much ado about a homely act like nutting, Wordsworth finds his language for attributing significance subject to three basic strains: Wordsworth must reject his usual lyrical use of "thing" to transcend differences rather than admit indifference; he finds his dialectical sense of spots of time reduced to a narrative that must be content to reproduce a previous experience, with its own beginning suspended within the mimesis until in the last lines it is rationalized by the address to the maiden; and he must also rely on that address to negotiate the specific terms for confronting indifference, in the process revealing the problematic links between autonomy and a disturbing sense of sexual difference.

In order to create the desired scandal Arac must show that Wordsworth's way of handling the problem of indifference is of a piece with the assertion of authority over the maiden which concludes the poem. Arac begins cogently by noting that the boy's action "restored the otherness of things and rescued the boy from fiction. It was an "act of modernity" because it "stripped away old clothes" and restored us to earth (43). But this allusion to modernity soon opens the floodgates by warranting a turn to "certain resources of psychoanalysis," enabling the critic to expose the narrative as fiction and requiring us to examine the feelings at work. "Clearly" we have a case of screen memories, and we are thus led to discover a "shocking scene":

> For if the feminized landscape is also phallic, as theorists of the pre-
> Oedipal suggest that in that stage we attribute both sexes to the
> mother, then the boy's action could be read as castrating the mother.
> This does not actually define Wordsworth's boyish feelings, only

exposes the degree of linguistic figuration that arose from them in his writing. Representation here is not mimetic but allegorical. . . .

The fantastic act of castrating the mother, moreover is originative. By it the father establishes his dominion over what Lacan called the realm of the symbolic . . . in founding by violence the difference between the sexes. The poet thus put himself in the father's place, made himself truly modern, revenging himself on the frugal dame, usurping the law as his own. . . . Rich beyond the wealth of kings by having textually achieved an impossible desire, the speaker has the power to lay down the law to the "dearest maiden." . . . He and he alone has had the experience, but his modernity becomes her tradition. She must believe on faith alone that there is a spirit in the woods, and not find out for herself.

(45–46)

The move from "could read" to "the poet thus put himself in the father's place" exposes the kind of thinking we confront here. Possibilities become facts; the presence of a feminized landscape seems to warrant treating what is staged as an anxiety-ridden rape as if it were an empowering castration; resources of psychoanalysis are invoked at a point where the poem suggests clear dramatic and historical reasons for its shift in focus (which is not away from fiction but from one rhetorical frame to another); and the distinction between actual feelings linked to historical externalities and figural language is immediately ignored in order to claim that the figural possibilities constitute historically effective realities even though they do not define anyone's feelings. Finally, in so collapsing the poem's imaginative movement into allegorical translation, this critical perspective simply ignores the most important feature of the dramatic turn. What begins in frustration over the indifference of things leads to a course of action which over time establishes the possibility of a different relation to nature, to poetry, and to gender relations. To speak of castrating nature is to ignore its recovering authority by propagating a complex third term—the sense of guilt and the resulting awareness of a genius in the woods which is presented as transforming the basic dichotomies between fictions and representations enforced by the old poetic dictions.

Thus the poem's modernity is less its insistence on an autonomy that resists history than on finding a presentational mode which can function as the intruding sky does—that is, first to show us our lacks, then to suggest another way to dispose our psychic energies. This can be done if one can correlate a source of authority outside the poem, the genius in the woods, with resources of eloquence within the poem that the poet can invoke as alternative modes of engaging the temporality of experience. But for Arac the only genius lies in the resources of contemporary criticism, so he is left only with his oppositions between narrative and fictionality, or mimesis and allegory. For Wordsworth, however, there is the possibility of so disposing memory that it at once recovers possible force in past experience and proposes the kinds of intensities that those experiences can maintain for poetic reflection in the present. In "Nutting" those intensities are evoked to transform what begins as rape into particular modes of attention that the poet can share with women, who are thereby released from the figurative identification with a maternal nature. Memory mediates between indifferent nature and the projected fictions of the pastoral imagination. If its force can be rendered by a poetry concerned to project, not to imitate or to displace, there is no need to force the maiden to believe what the poet offers. Rather, she is asked to replace his violence by an act of touch which can test the possible force of genius proposed by the poem's manipulation of imaginative scenes. This is still a patronizing attitude toward the woman, but it does offer the chance to get beyond the culture's all too well-established categories—poetry offers sites where those with different social positions can try to understand and share the forces which can modify our emotional lives.

Providing such information and staging such tests of possible accommodations is the role of a new, "modern" emphasis on the internal complexity of poetic elements. And understanding that is a prelude to seeing why Arac's reliance on Freud is so reductive a gesture. It in no way responds to the concern of Romantic thinkers to make the concept of autonomy link poetic and personal states. And, more important, it displaces attention from the capacity of this specific poem to develop a psychic economy different from Freud's version of interior life. The subject projected by "Nutting" does not insist on extending the event into other autobiographical contexts, and it does not impose discursive expectations on what must retain the specificity and the otherness of an imaginative scenario. Poetry must be allowed its sense of excess if we are not to castrate it. To impose Freud's concept of the subject in the self-righteous moralizing mode of critical historicism allows ourselves no intruding sky, no pressures defining our own limitations, reduced terms for understanding the problems that both beset and enable contemporary poetry, and only the most embarrassing theaters in which to attempt to replace the genius in the woods with its critical counterparts.

## VII

Any doubts that I have about allowing myself this outburst get resolved whenever I remind myself of the remarks that conclude Arac's discussion: "A new literary history must heed the warning of Walter Benjamin, written just after the outbreak of the Second World War, and acknowledge that our 'cultural treasures' are documents not only of civilization but also of barbarism; to the extent that we revere those treasures we carry on the barbarism" (49). Even though Arac does qualify this assertion by warning us not therefore to lose the "live" elements of past texts, his way of reading defines what he can take those live elements to be. And such construals obviously will not suffice. Therefore one cannot but wonder where the greater barbarism lies—in the blindness lurking in the acts of genius that survive from the past, or in the arrogance that assumes that so transforming that past into our own banalities and so denying the space of idealization that eloquence attempts to construct will improve the political and moral features of contemporary life. And as one wonders, perhaps as one begins to doubt there is any escape from those critical stances, the ancient desire for an exemplary eloquence begins to take on perhaps all too much contemporary currency.[14]

## Notes

1 Hugh Blair, *Lectures on Rhetoric and Belles Lettres*, 1783, ed. Harold Harding (Carbondale: Southern Illinois University Press, 1965), 2:6.
2 I obviously oversimplify, especially with respect to historicist work not as tied to a specific political project and with respect to those like Stanley Cavell, Don Bialostosky, and Richard Eldridge, who are committed to recovering the imaginative force of Wordsworth's poetry in contemporary terms. But the best historical work does not come from the most ambitious theoretical minds, and all three in their different ways may be too quick to allegorize the work in terms of contemporary thinking without letting its own emphases take conceptual form.
3 Several years ago I tried a variant of this argument by defending Wordsworth's claims about the immediacy of poetry against Paul de Man. That essay, "Wordsworth's 'Preface' as Literary Theory," *Criticism* 10 (1976), 122–46, was an effort to reconstruct the concept of event as its model for a Whiteadian sense of immediacy, but I did not find a good practical correlate for those metaphysical claims. Here I return to many of those arguments, but this time I try to avoid naturalizing poetic language in order to deal with it simply as a form of eloquence inviting us to assume whatever imaginative world is necessary to participate provisionally in the relevant passions. I shall argue that the point is not to locate some privileged moment of insight but to explain how we can become the kinds of persons for whom the states presented by the speech acts can matter. This does not resolve the problem of deciding whether that eloquent self is a person or a stage construct. But the question can be finessed by insisting that the fundamental rule of this rhetorical theater is that all reference is proleptic: the conditions claimed within the rhetorical construct have reality to the degree that we can live our own lives in their terms. In order to mark the distinction between empirical and proleptic reference, theorists like Blair had to develop a distinction between a descriptive sublime and a writerly one.
4 All quotations in this paragraph are from Antonius' speech in Cicero's *De Oratore*, ed. E. W. Sutton and H. Rackham (Cambridge: Harvard University Press, 1948), 1:325–39.
5 There is also a third aspect of this tradition which impinges only indirectly on Wordsworth. Under the pressure of their pragmatic and skeptical opponents, the best theorists of eloquence are excrutiatingly conscious of the difficulties involved in maintaining so idealized an image of their own practice, in much the same way that the best Romantics maintain ironies sufficient to acknowledge their sense of the limitations involved in having to idealize what remain intensely personal

positions. As my colleague Alan Fisher shows in an unpublished manuscript, that situation leads humanist thought to its own version of dialogical principles because thinkers like Plato, Cicero, and Valla realize that they must grapple with issues and with psyches too complex to be treated from any one perspective. For the Romantics that sense of limits requires the very different, more slippery and often more sublime endless dialogue with oneself—not because the ideals sought are impossibly riven with infinite ironies, but because the only way to make them plausible is to win them against a background constantly acknowledging the complex tensions one must negotiate and offering qualitative contrasts demonstrating there are powers of mind and emotion capable of such tasks.

The first problem resides in the appeal of pure idealization, which then is haunted by the possibility of having simply ignored or evaded the practical realm that authors tell themselves they have surpassed. On the most concrete level this becomes a matter of the relation of eloquence to the demands of practical rhetorical theory—with every idealizing Crassus complemented by a figure like Antonius who continually points out how much the orator misses because he reads human powers in terms only of his own extraordinary abilities. Other versions of that dichotomy entail a constant tension between the art of rhetoric and the claim to overcome that art by sincere and truthful passion: how can one tell that the passion is not itself only a higher artifice, yet how can one be sure that the intense state, however achieved, does not lead to new conditions of full belief? The only test is the audience's reaction, but that is complicated by the fact that the art of rhetoric is precisely the manipulation of the audience's response so its belief may be evidence that the speaker's passion does not transcend its own theatricality.

Other problems with the audience prove even more perplexing. Every rhetor who dreams of changing the values of his audience must also rely sufficiently on those values to win the hearts of those shaped by them. How new then are the orator's visions? Perhaps they are little more than self-congratulatory versions of the old system. Since most effective rhetoric must stage itself as counter-eloquence to some more debased form, every audience one persuades becomes a possible sign that in fact one is no different from the old order, one only shares its illusions of difference. And given all these inducements to self-congratulatory delusion, the rhetor is the last person who should generalize about rhetoric, since all of his skills may have no end but to cast spells. But who knows that temptation better than the rhetor, who must make that knowledge visible if there is to be any hope of escaping its confines?

6 For Augustine, see *On Christian Doctrine*, trans. W. D. Robertson, Jr. (Indianapolis: Bobbs Merrill, 1958), pp. 150, 168. For Longinus see "On the Sublime," in Hazard Adams, ed., *Critical Theory since Plato* (New York: Harcourt Brace Jovanovich, 1971), sects. 13–14. The sense of passion and momentary identity which we find in both thinkers allows Blair a lovely moment of looking down at the world of the rule-governed and artificial rhetoricians as that of fallen creatures: "The emotion occasioned in the mind by some great or noble object, raises it considerably above its ordinary pitch. A sort of enthusiasm is produced, extremely agreeable while it lasts; but from which the mind is tending every moment to fall down into its ordinary situation. Now, when an author . . . throws in any one decoration that sinks in the least below the capital image, that moment he alters the key; he relaxes the tension of the mind; the strength of the feeling is emasculated; the beautiful may remain, but the sublime is gone" (1:66). Although Wordsworth has his quarrels with the cultivation of taste that is basic to theorists like Blair, his writing on the effects of artifice in epitaphs stresses exactly the same sense that artifice disfigures sincere emotion (compare

Paul M. Zall, ed. *Literary Criticism of William Wordsworth* [Lincoln: University of Nebraska Press, 1966], p. 113).

7 Coleridge attempts a different and (perhaps unfortunately) more influential recasting of traditional eloquence. Also committed to a poetry capable of expressing the passions at their fullest, Coleridge defines that fullness by distinguishing between eloquence, which impels to a particular act, and poetry, which tries to give the character of a universal to a particular. Where the orator treats a thing of business as if it were an affair of imagination, the poet "treats a thing of fancy as if it were a matter of business." On this basis "the continuous state of excitement" that the poet generates comes to depend on an internal set of relations rather than on its continuity with the languages of social intercourse, and we are on our way to modernist poetics and contemporary textualism. See Coleridge's *Lectures 1808–1819: On Literature*, ed. R. H. Foakes (Princeton: Bollingen Press, 1987), 1:115, 471). I cannot argue that Coleridge is wrong, since clearly internal patterns are crucial to any eloquence; I can only ask whether his is the most useful way to conceive the matter.

8 I feel free to indulge in this exercise because I have discussed the value of Goodman's specific ideas elsewhere and tried to work out what I think are the problems that it raises, especially in my *Act and Quality* (Amherst: University of Massachusetts Press, 1981) and my forthcoming *Infinite Incantations of Ourselves: Painterly Abstraction in Modernist American Poetry* (New York: Cambridge University Press, 1989).

9 In simply taking this statement at face value I provide a good example of theoretical argument suppressing the author's interest in teasing out the related field of complex tensions, which he then manipulates in order to earn the authority that the assertion presumes. Thus I am not fair to Wordsworth here, but because I weaken the sense of the agent, not because I distort the argument that he ultimately supports.

10 In proposing this view of metaphor Wordsworth is entirely consistent with classical theorists of eloquence, adding only his characteristic demand that the excess has its sanction in the way we relate to nature (whereas for classical theory the excess is more likely to stem from our engagement with social exemplars). For the stress on sublime writing leads beyond descriptive criteria to a concern for how we understand and engage the most ample stagings of human passions, and figuration is central because it replaces the concern for truth with an interest in making visible the terms of passionate engagement that can extend description into the domain of values. In such passion, Longinus tells us, the figure escapes detection as a figure because it becomes folded into the excess of light created by the sublime state: "For just as all dim lights are extinguished in the blaze of the sun, so do the artifices of rhetoric fade from view when bathed in the pervading splendor of sublimity" (89). Such sentiments are often used now to insist that even sublime passion is theatrical and hence a displacing of any claim on the empirical world. But to invoke that attitude with regard to Longinus, or to Wordsworth, is probably to let oneself fall victim to the half-heartedness that Longinus complains of in his concluding paragraph. In Longinian terms such ironic gestures simply refuse to entertain his overall desire to imagine how passion and the desire for fame can compose selves worthy of competing with the great writers of the past. Augustine would make the same charge on different grounds—that to suspect figures is to confine ourselves to a narrow interpretive framework. It is precisely the force of figures that clarifies the limitations in any simple sign theory of language because that force requires us to supplement description with hermeneutics: "There is a miserable servitude of the spirit in this

habit of taking signs for things, so that one is not able to raise the eye of the mind above things that are corporal and created to drink in eternal light" (84).

11 Perhaps the most interesting feature of that theology is the way Wordsworth insists on extending the thematics of pleasure to all three temporal dimensions— as if pleasure were power in its most concrete material manifestation and, at the same time, as if the amplifications worked by pleasure were the best measure of how other aspects of the psyche might be deployed. Pleasure in the present tense is a simple measure of intensity and of the possible harmonious relations to nature which that intensity could release by spreading "everywhere relationship and love" (Zall, 52). But relying on the present lacks the qualitative measures necessary if we are to avoid getting caught in dramas of repression and violent supplementation like those which Wordsworth attributes to the flattering self-love addicting readers to the poetry of extravagant and absurd diction (Zall, 63–64). Those qualitative measures depend on our testing the working of pleasure over time. Pleasure both forms and tests character. On the one hand the history of our pleasure shapes the patterns of memory and habit governing our dispositions (Zall, 50); on the other it is only by the tensions between our pleasures and the demands of nature within and without that we learn to contour our desires more fully to deeper rhythms within the natural and social orders. When we turn from the past to the future it proves precisely this dynamic which makes it feasible for the poet to hope that eloquence in the imaginary sphere will create intensities and sympathies modifying our desires and attaching our feelings to important subjects (Zall, 42).

12 I have used a somewhat different version of my discussion of this poem and of Jonathan Arac's criticism of it in my "Wordsworth and the Options for Contemporary American Poetry," forthcoming in Gene Ruoff, ed., *The Romantics and Us* (Newark, N.J.: Rutgers University Press, 1989), There is also a version in my *Painterly Abstraction in Modernist American Poetry*.

13 *Critical Genealogies* (New York: Columbia University Press, 1987).

14 Had I the space I would have taken up one more aspect of imaginative power— the concern for how the poet can influence the future by shaping taste—because this version of Arac's fear of barbarism became by the *Essay, Supplementary to the Preface* a constant obsession for Wordsworth, and because I think the terms of his hope both plausible and probably necessary for the culture that I see represented in Arac. In essence Wordsworth posits for eloquent poetry the capacity to engage its readers in a dialectic much like the one we have been tracking in "Nutting" with the capacity of

> divesting the reader of the pride that induces him to dwell upon those points wherein men differ form each other, to the exclusion of those in which all men are alike, or the same; and in making him ashamed of the vanity that renders him insensible of the appropriate excellence which civil arrangements, less unjust than may appear, and Nature illimitable in her bounty, have conferred on men who may stand below him in the scale of society? Finally, does it lie in establishing that dominion over the spirits of readers by which they are to be humbled and humanised, in order that they may be purified and exalted.
>
> (Zall, 183)

Thus poetry can maintain hope in its capacity to affect the future to the degree that its intensities can on the one hand get us to call into question the interpretive languages we use and, on the other, provide testimony of an internal and external effort with the promise of establishing a plausible alternative, for example, to readerly attitudes devoted to the measuring of vices and virtues. I ask the reader to consider the entire passage (Zall 183–85), perhaps in conjunction with the idea of antithetical models of authorial activity developed in Hazard Adams, "Canons: Literary Criteria/Power Criteria," *Critical Inquiry* 14 (1988), 748–64. Although I think Adams needs a more concrete model of how the ideal of antithetical projection is constructed by authors and used by audiences, he is good at reminding us of how ultimately the value in those authorial projections is their ability constantly to challenge the discursive terms we elaborate for those models.

# Part 2

# FORMALISM AND GENRE

# 10

# STRUCTURE AND STYLE IN THE GREATER ROMANTIC LYRIC

## M. H. Abrams

Source: *From Sensibility to Romanticism: Essays Presented to Frederick A. Pottle* (New York: Oxford University Press, 1965), pp. 527–60.

There is no accepted name for the kind of poem I want to talk about, even though it was a distinctive and widely practiced variety of the longer Romantic lyric and includes some of the greatest Romantic achievements in any form. Coleridge's "Eolian Harp," "Frost at Midnight," "Fears in Solitude," and "Dejection: An Ode" exemplify the type, as does Wordsworth's "Tintern Abbey," his "Ode: Intimations of Immortality," and (with a change in initial reference from scene to painting) his "Elegiac Stanzas Suggested by a Picture of Peele Castle in a Storm." Shelley's "Stanzas Written in Dejection" follows the formula exactly, and his "Ode to the West Wind" is a variant on it. Of Keats's odes, that to a Nightingale is the one which approximates the pattern most closely. Only Byron, among the major poets, did not write in this mode at all.

These instances yield a paradigm for the type. Some of the poems are called odes, while the others approach the ode in having lyric magnitude and a serious subject, feelingfully meditated. They present a determinate speaker in a particularized, and usually a localized, outdoor setting, whom we overhear as he carries on, in a fluent vernacular which rises easily to a more formal speech, a sustained colloquy, sometimes with himself or with the outer scene, but more frequently with a silent human auditor, present or absent. The speaker begins with a description of the landscape; an aspect or change of aspect in the landscape evokes a varied but integral process of memory, thought, anticipation, and feeling which remains closely intervolved with the outer scene. In the course of this meditation the lyric speaker achieves an insight, faces up to a tragic loss, comes to a moral decision, or resolves an emotional problem. Often the poem rounds upon itself to end where it began, at the outer scene, but with an altered mood and deepened understanding which is the result of the intervening meditation.

What shall we call this Romantic genre? To label these poems simply nature lyrics is not only inadequate, but radically misleading. We have not yet entirely recovered from the earlier critical stress on Wordsworth's statement that "I have at all times endeavored to look steadily at my subject," to the neglect of his repeated warnings that accurate natural description, though a necessary, is an inadequate condition for poetry. Like Blake and Coleridge, Wordsworth manifested wariness, almost terror, at the threat of the corporeal eye and material object to tyrannize over the mind and imagination, in opposition to that normative experience in which

> The mind is lord and master—outward sense
> The obedient servant of her will.[1]

In the extended lyrics we are considering, the visual report is invariably the occasion for a meditation which turns out to constitute the *raison d'être* of the poem. Romantic writers, though nature poets, were humanists above all, for they dealt with the non-human only insofar as it is the occasion for the activity which defines man: thought, the process of intellection.

"The descriptive-meditative poem" is a possible, but a clumsy term. *Faute de mieux*, I shall call this poetic type "the greater Romantic lyric," intending to suggest, not that it is a higher achievement than other Romantic lyrics, but that it displaced what neo-classical critics had called "the greater ode" —the elevated Pindaric, in distinction to "the lesser ode" modeled chiefly on Horace—as the favored form for the long lyric poem.

The repeated out-in-out process, in which mind confronts nature and their interplay constitutes the poem, is a remarkable phenomenon in literary history. If we don't find it strange, it is because our responses have been dulled by long familiarity with such a procedure not only in the Romantic poets, but in their many successors who played variations on the mode, from Matthew Arnold and Walt Whitman—both "Dover Beach" and "Crossing Brooklyn Ferry," for example, closely follow the pattern of the greater Romantic lyric—to Wallace Stevens and W. H. Auden. But at the beginning of the nineteenth century this procedure in the lyric was part of a new and exciting poetic strategy, no less epidemic than Donne's in his day, or T. S. Eliot's in the period after the first World War. For several decades poets did not often talk about the great issues of life, death, love, joy, dejection, or God without talking at the same time about the landscape. Wordsworth's narrative of Michael emerges from a description of the scene around "the tumultuous brook of Green-head Ghyll," to which in the end it returns:

> and the remains
> Of the unfinished Sheep-fold may be seen
> Beside the boisterous brook of Green-head Ghyll.

Coleridge's great, neglected love-poem, "Recollections of Love," opens with a Quantock scene revisited after eight years have passed, and adverts suddenly to the River Greta at the close:

> But when those meek eyes first did seem
> To tell me, Love within you wrought—
> O Greta, dear domestic stream!
>
> Has not, since then, Love's prompture deep,
> Has not Love's whisper evermore
> Been ceaseless, as thy gentle roar?
> Sole voice, when other voices sleep,
> Dear under-song in clamor's hour.

Keats's first long poem of consequence, though it is his introduction to an *ars poetica*, represents what he saw, then what he thought, while he "stood tiptoe upon a little hill." Shelley treats the theme of permanence in change by describing the mutations of a cloud, defines the pure Idea of joy in a meditation on the flight and song of a skylark, and presents his ultimate concept of the secret and impersonal power behind all process in a description of Mont Blanc and the Vale of Chamouni. Wordsworth's *Prelude* can be viewed as an epic expansion of the mode of "Tintern Abbey," both in overall design and local tactics. It begins with the description of a landscape visited in maturity, evokes the entire life of the poet as a protracted meditation on things past, and presents the growth of the poet's mind as an interaction with the natural milieu by which it is fostered, from which it is tragically alienated, and to which in the resolution it is restored, with a difference attributable to the intervening experiences; the poem ends at the time of its beginning.

What I have called "the greater lyric," then, is only a special instance of a very widespread manner of proceeding in Romantic poetry; but it is of great interest because it was the earliest Romantic formal invention, which at once demonstrated the stability of organization and the capacity to engender successors which define a distinct lyric species. New lyric forms are not as plenty as blackberries, and when one turns up, it is worth critical attention. Suppose, therefore, that we ask some questions about this one: about its genesis, its nearest literary antecedents, and the reasons why this way of proceeding, out of the alternatives in common lyric practice, should have appealed so powerfully to the Romantic sensibility. Inquiry into some probable causes of the structure and style of the greater lyric will take us not only to the evolution of certain descriptive genres in the seventeenth and eighteenth centuries, but also to contemporary developments in philosophy and in theology, and to the spiritual posture in which many poets, as well as philosophers, found themselves at the end of the Enlightenment.

I

COLERIDGE AND WORDSWORTH

In this investigation Coleridge must be our central reference, not only because he had the most to say about these matters in prose, but because it was he, not Wordsworth, who inaugurated the greater Romantic lyric, firmly established its pattern, and wrote the largest number of instances. Wordsworth's first trial in the extended lyric was "Tintern Abbey," which he composed in July 1798. Up to that time his only efforts in the long descriptive and reflective mode were the schoolboy effort, "The Vale of Esthwaite," and the two tour-poems of 1793, "An Evening Walk" and "Descriptive Sketches." The first of these was written in octosyllabic and the latter two in heroic couplets, and all differ in little but merit and the detail of single passages from hundreds of eighteenth-century predecessors.[2] Coleridge, however, as early as 20 August 1795, composed a short first version of "The Eolian Harp," and in 1796—two years before "Tintern Abbey"—expanded it to fifty-six lines which established, in epitome, the ordonnance, materials, and style of the greater lyric.[3] It is in the dramatic mode of intimate talk to an unanswering auditor in easy blank-verse paragraphs. It begins with a description of the peaceful outer scene; this, in parallel with the vagrant sounds evoked from a wind-harp, calls forth a recollection in tranquillity of earlier experiences in the same setting and leads to a sequence of reflections which are suggested by, and also incorporate, perceptual qualities of the scene. The poem closes with a summary reprise of the opening description of "PEACE, and this COT, and THEE, heart-honour'd Maid!"

Between the autumn of 1796 and the spring of 1798 Coleridge composed a number of variations on this lyric type, including "Reflections on Having Left a Place of Retirement," "This Limetree Bower," "Fears in Solitude," and "The Nightingale." To these writings Professor G. M. Harper applied the term which Coleridge himself used for "The Nightingale," "conversation poems"; very aptly, because they are written (though some of them only intermittently) in a blank verse which at its best captures remarkably the qualities of the intimate speaking voice, yet remains capable of adapting without strain to the varying levels of the subject-matter and feeling. And within this period, in February of 1798, Coleridge produced one of the masterpieces of the greater lyric, perfectly modulated and proportioned, but so successful in the quiet way that it hides its art that it has only recently attracted its meed of critical admiration. The poem is "Frost at Midnight," and it follows, but greatly enlarges and subtilizes the pattern of "The Eolian Harp." What seems at first impression to be the free association of its central meditation turns out to have been called forth, qualified, and controlled by the opening description, which evokes the strangeness in the familiar surroundings of the solitary and wakeful speaker: the "secret ministry" of the frost, the "strange and extreme silentness" of "sea, and hill, and wood," the life of the sleeping village "inaudible as dreams," and the film that flutters on the grate "the sole unquiet thing." In consonance with these elements, and directed especially by the rhythm of the seemingly unnoticed breathing of a sleeping infant, the meditative mind disengages itself from the physical locale, moves back in time to the speaker's childhood, still farther back, to his own infancy, then forward to express, in the intonation of a blessing, the hope that his son shall have the life in nature that his father lacked; until, in anticipating the future, it incorporates both the present scene and the results of the remembered past in the enchanting close—

> Whether the eave-drops fall
> Heard only in the trances of the blast,
> Or if the secret ministry of frost
> Shall hang them up in silent icicles,
> Quietly shining to the quiet Moon.

In the original version this concluding sentence trailed off in six more verse-lines, which Coleridge, in order to emphasize the lyric rondure, later excised. Plainly, Coleridge worked out the lyric device of the return-upon-itself—which he used in "Reflections on Having Left a Place of Retirement" and "Fears in Solitude," as well as in "The Eolian Harp" and "Frost at Midnight"—in a deliberate endeavor to transform a segment of experience broken out of time into a sufficient aesthetic whole. "The common end of all *narrative*, nay, of *all*, Poems," he wrote to Joseph Cottle in 1815, "is to convert a *series* into a *Whole*: to make those events, which in real or imagined History move on in a *strait* Line, assume to our Understandings a *circular* motion—the snake with its Tail in its Mouth."[4] From the time of the early Greek philosophers, the circle had been the shape of perfection; and in occult philosophy the *ouroboros*, the tail-eating snake, had become the symbol for eternity and for the divine process of creation, since it is complete, self-sufficient, and endless. For Coleridge the perfect shape for the descriptive-meditative-descriptive poem was precisely the one described and exemplified in T. S. Eliot's "East Coker," which begins: "In my beginning is my end," and ends: "In my end is my beginning"; another modern writer who knew esoteric lore designed *Finnegans Wake* so that the headless sentence which begins the book completes the tailless sentence with which it ends.

Five months after the composition of "Frost at Midnight," Wordsworth set out on a walking tour with his sister. Reposing on a high bank of the River Wye, he remembered this among others of Coleridge's conversation poems—the dramatic mode of address to an unanswering listener in flexible blank verse; the opening description which evolves into a sustained meditation assimilating perceptual, personal, and philosophical elements; the free movement of thought from the present scene to recollection in tranquillity, to prayer-like prediction, and back to the scene; even some of Coleridge's specific concepts and phrases—and in the next four or five days' walk, worked out "Lines Composed a Few Miles above Tintern Abbey" and appended it forthwith to *Lyrical Ballads*, which was already in press.

To claim that it was Coleridge who deflected Wordsworth's poetry into a channel so entirely congenial to him is in no way to derogate Wordsworth's achievement, nor his powers of invention. "Tintern Abbey" has greater dimension and intricacy and a more various verbal orchestration than "Frost at Midnight." In its conclusion Wordsworth managed Coleridge's specialty, the return-upon-itself, with a mastery of involuted reference without match in the poems of its begetter. "Tintern Abbey" also inaugurated the wonderfully functional device Wordsworth later called the "two consciousnesses": a scene is revisited, and the remembered landscape ("the picture of the mind") is superimposed on the picture before the eye; the two landscapes fail to match, and so set a problem ("a sad perplexity") which compels the meditation. Wordsworth played variations on this stratagem in all his later trials in the greater lyric, and in *The Prelude* he expanded it into a persisting double awareness of things as they are and as they were, and so anticipated the structural principle of the most influential masterpiece of our own century, Proust's *À la recherche du temps perdu*.

II

THE LOCAL POEM

What was the closest poetic antecedent of this controlled and shapely lyric genre? It was not the ancient lyric formula, going back to the spring-songs of the troubadors, which set forth an ideal spring scene (the *Natureingang*) and then presented a human experience in harmony or contrast—a formula which survived in Burns's

> Ye flowery banks o' bonie Doon,
> How can ye blume sae fair?
> How can ye chant, ye little birds,
> And I sae fu' o' care?

Nor was it Thomson's *Seasons*, that omnibus of unlocalized description, episodic narration, and general reflection, in which the pious observer moves from Nature to Nature's God with the help of Isaac Newton's *Principia*. And certainly it was not the formal descriptive poem such as Collins's "Ode to Evening," which adapted Pindar's ceremonial panegyric to landscape mainly by the device of transforming descriptive and meditative propositions into a sequence of tableaux and brief allegories—a mode which Keats revitalized in his "Ode to Autumn."[5] The clue to the provenance of the greater Romantic lyric is to be found in the attributes of the opening description. This landscape is not only particularized; it is in most cases precisely localized, in place, and sometimes in time as well. Critics have often remarked on Wordsworth's scrupulosity about specifying the circumstances for his poems, but his fellow-poets were often no less meticulous in giving their greater lyrics an exact locality. We have "The Eolian Harp, Composed at Clevedon, Somersetshire" (the first versions also appended to the title a date, 20 August 1795); "This Lime-Tree Bower My Prison," subtitled: "In the June of 1797 . . . the author's cottage. . . . Composed . . . in the garden-bower"; "Fears in Solitude written April, 1798. . . . The Scene, the Hills near Stowey";[6] "Lines Written a Few Miles above Tintern Abbey . . . July 13, 1798"; "Elegiac Stanzas Suggested by a picture of Peele Castle, in a Storm"; "Stanzas Written in Dejection, Near Naples." Even when its setting is not named in the title, the poem usually has an identifiable local habitation, such as the milieu of Coleridge's cottage at Nether Stowey for "Frost at Midnight," or the view from Coleridge's study at Keswick in "Dejection: An Ode." To his "Ode to the West Wind," Shelley was careful to add the note: "Written in a wood that skirts the Arno, near Florence. . . ."

There existed in the eighteenth century a well-defined and immensely popular poetic type, in which the title named a geographical location, and which combined a description of that scene with the thoughts that the scene suggested. This was known as the "local" or "loco-descriptive" poem; Robert A. Aubin, in his compendious and amusing survey of *Topographical Poetry in XVIII-Century England*, lists almost two thousand instances of the form. "Local poetry," as Dr. Johnson concisely defined it in his life of John Denham, was

> a species of composition . . . of which the fundamental subject
> is some particular landscape, to be poetically described, with the
> addition of such embellishments as may be supplied by historical
> restrospection or incidental meditation.[7]

The evidence, I think, makes it clear that the most characteristic Romantic lyric developed directly out of one of the most stable and widely employed of all the neoclassic kinds.

By general consent Sir John Denham, as Dr. Johnson said, was the "author" of the genre, in that excellent poem, "Cooper's Hill," of which the first version was written in 1642. In it the poet inventories the prospect of the Thames valley visible from the hilltop, with distant London on one side and Windsor Castle on the other. As Earl Wasserman has shown, the poem is a complex construction, in which the topographical elements are selected and managed so as to yield concepts which support a Royalist view-point on the eve of the Civil Wars.[8] But if, like Dr. Johnson, we abstract and classify Denham's incidental meditations, we find that some are historical and political, but that others are broadly sententious, and are achieved by the device of adducing to a natural object a correspondent moral idea. Thus the "aery Mountain" (lines 217–22), forced to endure the onslaught of winds and storms, instances "The common fate of all that's high or great," while the Thames (lines 163–4) hastens "to pay his tribute to the Sea,/Like mortal life to meet Eternity."

This latter procedure is worth dwelling on for a moment, because for many of Denham's successors it displaced history and politics to become the sole meditative component in local poems, and it later evolved into the extended meditation of the Romantic lyric. The *paysage moralisé* was not invented as a rhetorical device by poets, but was grounded on two collateral and pervasive concepts in medieval and Renaissance philosophy. One of these was the doctrine that God has supplemented the Holy Scriptures with the *liber creaturarum*, so that objects of nature, as Sir Thomas Browne said, carry "in Stenography and short Characters, something of Divinity"[9] and show forth the attributes and providence of their Author. The second concept, of independent philosophic origin but often fused with the first, is that the divine Architect has designed the universe analogically, relating the physical, moral, and spiritual realms by an elaborate system of correspondences. A landscape, accordingly, consists of *verba visibilia* which enable pious interpreters such as Shakespeare's Duke in *As You Like It* to find "books in the running brooks,/Sermons in stones, and good in everything."

The metaphysic of a symbolic and analogical universe underlay the figurative tactics of the seventeenth-century metaphysical poets who were John Denham's predecessors and contemporaries. The secular and amatory poems exploited unexpected correspondences mainly as display rhetoric, positing the analogue in order to show the author's wit in supporting an argument and to evoke in the reader the shock of delightful discovery. In their devotional poems, however, the poets put forward their figures as grounded in the divine plan underlying the universe. Thus Henry Vaughan, musing over a waterfall, was enabled by the guidance of its Creator to discover its built-in correspondences with the life and destiny of man:

> What sublime truths and wholesome themes,
> Lodge in thy mystical deep streams!
> Such as dull man can never find
> Unless that spirit lead his mind
> Which first upon thy face did move,
> And hatched all with his quick'ning love.

In 1655, the year in which Vaughan published "The Waterfall," Denham added to his enlarged edition of "Cooper's Hill" the famous pair of couplets on the Thames which link description to concepts by a sustained parallel between the flow of the stream and the ideal conduct of life and art:

204

> O could I flow like thee, and make thy stream
> My great example, as it is my theme!
> Though deep, yet clear, though gentle, yet not dull,
> Strong without rage, without o'erflowing, full.

The metaphysical device and ingenuity are still apparent, but we can see why this became the best-known and most influential passage in the poetry of neoclassicism—a model not only for its versification, but also for some of its most characteristic ideas and rhetorical devices. In these lines the metaphysical wit has been tamed and ordered into the "true wit" which became the eighteenth-century ideal; Denham's "strength" (which Dr. Johnson defined as "much meaning in few words"), so universally admired, has replaced the "strong lines" (the compressed and hyperbolic ingeniousness) of John Donne; while the startling revelation of *discordia concors* between object and idea has been smoothed to a neoclassic decency, moulded to the deft play of antitheses around the caesura, and adapted to the presentation of the cardinal neoclassic norm of a mean between extremes.[10]

In the enormous number of eighteenth-century local poems the organization of "Cooper's Hill" around a controlling political motif was soon reduced mainly to the procedure of setting up parallels between landscape and moral commonplaces. The subtitle of Richard Jago's long "Edge Hill" (1767) neatly defines the double-function: "The Rural Prospect Delineated and Moralized"; while the title of an anonymous poem of 1790 reveals how monstrous this development could be: "An Evening's Reflection on the Universe, in a Walk on the Seashore." The literal belief in a universe of divine types and correspondences, which had originally supported this structural trope, faded,[11] and the coupling of sensuous phenomena with moral statements came to be regarded as a rhetorical device particularly apt to the descriptive poet's double aim of combining instruction with delight. John Dyer's "Grongar's Hill" (1726) was justly esteemed as one of the most deft and agreeable of prospect poems. Mounting the hill, the poet describes the widening prospect with a particularity beyond the call of the moralist's duty. Yet the details of the scene are duly equated with *sententiae*; and when he comes to moralize the river (always, after Denham's passage on the Thames, the favorite item in the topographic inventory), Dyer echoes the great theological concept of a typological universe lightly, as a pleasant conceit:

> And see the rivers how they run . . .
> Wave succeeding wave, they go
> A various journey to the deep,
> Like human life to endless sleep!
> Thus is nature's vesture wrought,
> To instruct our wand'ring thought;
> Thus she dresses green and gay,
> To disperse our cares away.

Thomas Gray's "Ode on a Distant Prospect of Eton College" (1747) provides significant evidence that the local poem evolved into the greater Romantic lyric. It is a hill-poem, and its setting—Windsor heights and the Thames valley—is part of the very prospect which Denham had described. The topographical form, however, has been adapted to the Horatian ode, so that the focus of interest is no longer in the analogical inventory of scenic detail, but in the mental and emotional experience of a specific lyric speaker. The meditation becomes a coherent and dramatic sequence of thought, triggered by what was to become Wordsworth's favorite device of *déja vu*: the scene is a scene revisited, and it evokes in memory the lost self of the speaker's youth.

> I feel the gales that from ye blow
> A momentary bliss bestow,
> As, waving fresh their gladsome wing,
> My weary soul they seem to soothe,
> And, redolent of joy and youth
> To breathe a second spring.

As he watches the heedless schoolboys at their games, the speaker's first impulse is to warn them of the ambuscades which the "ministers of human fate" are even now laying for them: "Ah, tell them they are men!" But a new thought leads to a reversal of intention, for he suddenly realizes that since life's horrors are inescapable, forewarning is a useless cruelty.

We are a long way, however, from the free flow of consciousness, the interweaving of thought, feeling, and perceptual detail, and the easy naturalness of the speaking voice which characterize the Romantic lyric. Gray deliberately rendered both his observations and reflections in the hieratic style of a formal odic *oratio*. The poet's recollection of times past, for example, is managed through an invocation to Father Thames to tell him "Who foremost now delight to cleave/With pliant arm thy glassy wave," and the language throughout is heightened and stylized by the apostrophe, exclamation, rhetorical question, and studied periphrasis which Wordsworth decried in Gray—"more than any other man curiously elaborate in the structure of his . . . poetic diction."[12] Both reminiscence and reflection are depersonalized, and occur mainly as general propositions which are sometimes expressed as *sententiae* ("where ignorance is bliss/'Tis folly to be wise"), and at other times as propositions which, in the standard artifice of the contemporary ode, are converted into the tableau-and-allegory form that Coleridge derogated as Gray's "translations of prose thoughts into poetic language."[13] Gray's poem is structurally inventive, and excellent in its kind, but it remains distinctly a mid-century period piece. We need to look elsewhere for the immediate occasion of Coleridge's invention of the greater Romantic lyric.

206

III

COLERIDGE AND BOWLES

I have quoted Coleridge's derogation of Gray from the first chapter of the *Biographia Literaria*, in which Coleridge reviewed his own early development as a poet. To Gray's style he opposed that of three poems, the only contemporary models he mentioned with approval; and all three, it is important to note, were of a type which combines local description with associated meditation. One was William Crowe's conventional prospect poem, *Lewesdon Hill* (1788) and another was Cowper's *The Task*, which incorporated a number of episodic meditations evoked by the environs of the river Ouse. Both these poems, however, he read later— *The Task*, he says, "many years" later—than a publication which at once seized irresistibly upon his sensibility, William Lisle Bowles's *Sonnets* of 1789. By these poems he was "year after year . . . enthusiastically delighted and inspired," and he worked zealously to win "proselytes" to his poetic divinity by buttonholing strangers and friends alike, and by sending out as gifts more than forty copies of Bowles's volume, which he had himself transcribed.[14]

Coleridge mentioned also Bowles's "Monody Written at Matlock" (1791), which is a long prospect-poem written in blank verse. But most of Bowles's poems of 1789 were obvious adaptations of this local-meditative formula to the sonnet form. As in both the local poems and the Romantic lyric, a number of Bowles's titles specify the place, and even the time: "To the River Wensbeck"; "To the River Itchin Near Winton"; "On Dover Cliffs. July 20, 1787"; "Written at Ostend. July 22, 1787." The whole was "Written," as the title of 1789 points out, "Chiefly on Picturesque Spots, during a Tour," and constitutes a sonnet-sequence uttered by a latter-day wandering *penseroso* who, as the light fades from the literal day, images his life as a metaphoric tour from its bright morning through deepening shadow to enduring night. Within this over-arching equation, the typical single poem begins with a rapid sketch of the external scene—frequently, as in so many of Denham's progeny, a river scene—then moves on to reminiscence and moral reflection. The transition is often managed by a connecting phrase which signalizes the shift from objects to concepts and indicates the nature of the relation between them: "So fares it with the children of the earth"; "ev'n thus on sorrow's breath/A kindred stillness steals"; "Bidding me many a tender thought recall/Of summer days"; "I meditate/On this world's passing pageant."

Bowles wrote in a Preface of 1805, when his poems had already achieved a ninth edition, that his sonnets "describe his personal feelings" during excursions taken to relieve "depression of spirits." They exhibit "occasional reflections which naturally rose in his mind" and were in general suggested by the scenes before them; and wherever such scenes appeared to harmonise with his disposition at the moment, the sentiments were involuntarily prompted.[15]

The local poem has been lyricized. That is, Bowles's sonnets present a determinate speaker, whom we are invited to identify with the author himself, whose responses to the local scene are a spontaneous overflow of feeling and displace the landscape as the center of poetic interest; hence the "occasional reflections" and "sentiments," instead of being a series of impersonal *sententiae* linked to details of the setting by analogy, are mediated by the particular temperament and circumstances of the perceiving mind, and tend to compose a single curve of feelingful meditation. "To the River Itchin, Near Winton"—which so impressed Coleridge that he emulated it in his sonnet "To the River Otter"—will represent Bowles's procedure, including his use of the recollection of an earlier visit to stimulate the meditation:

> Itchin, when I behold thy banks again,
>   Thy crumbling margin, and thy silver breast,
>   On which the self-same tints still seem to rest,
> Why feels my heart the shiv'ring sense of pain?
>   Is it—that many a summer's day has past
> Since, in life's morn, I carol'd on thy side?
> Is it—that oft, since then, my heart has sigh'd,
>   As Youth, and Hope's delusive gleams, flew fast?
> Is it—that those, who circled on thy shore,
> Companions of my youth, now meet no more?
>   Whate'er the cause, upon thy banks I bend
> Sorrowing, yet feel such solace at my heart,
>   As at the meeting of some long-lost friend,
>   From whom, in happier hours, we wept to part.

Why Coleridge should have been moved to idolatry by so slender, if genuine, a talent as that of Bowles has been an enigma of literary history. It is significant, however, that Bowles's *Sonnets* of 1789 had an impact both on Southey and Wordsworth which was also immediate and powerful. As Wordsworth later told Samuel Rogers:

I bought them in a walk through London with my dear brother. . . . I read them as we went along; and to the great annoyance of my brother, I stopped in a niche of London Bridge to finish the pamphlet.[16]

And if we take into account Coleridge's intellectual preoccupations between the ages of seventeen and twenty-five, as well as his growing discontent with current modes of poetry, including his own, we find a sufficiency of reasons to explain the power of Bowles over his sensibility and his practice as a poet. Some of these are literary reasons, pertaining to Bowles's characteristic subjects and style, while others concern the philosophy of mind and its place in nature which, Coleridge believed, was implicit in Bowles's habitual manner of proceeding.

Bowles's sonnets represent the lonely mind in meditation, and their *fin de siècle* mood of weary and self-pitying isolation—what Coleridge called their "lonely feeling"[17]—proved irresistible to a vigorous young newcomer to poetry. Of much greater and more enduring importance, however, as Coleridge emphasized in his *Biographia*, was the revelation to him of the possibility of a style "so tender and yet so manly, so natural and real, and yet so dignified and harmonious, as the sonnets etc. of Mr. Bowles!"[18] Even while he was absorbedly reading and tentatively imitating Bowles, Coleridge himself in his major efforts was primarily the poet "To turgid ode and tumid stanza dear," of Byron's unadmiring comment. In his poetic volume of 1796, as enlarged in 1797, the most ambitious undertakings were the "Religious Musings" and "Ode on the Departing Year." Of this publication Coleridge said in the *Biographia* that though, even then, he clearly saw "the superiority of an austerer and more natural style" than his own obscure and turgid language, he failed to realize his ideal, partly out of "diffidence of my own comparative talent," and "partly owing to a wrong choice of subjects, and the desire of giving a poetic colouring to abstract and metaphysical truths, in which a new world then seemed to open upon me."[19] In the turbulence and crises of the early period of the French Revolution, he had been obsessed with the need to give public voice to his political, religious, and philosophical beliefs, and he had tried to poetize such materials in the fashion current in the 1790s.[20] That is to say, he had adopted a visionary and oracular persona—in accordance, as he said in the Dedication to his "Ode on the Departing Year," with the practice of the ancients, when "the Bard and the Prophet were one and the same character"[21]—and had compounded Biblical prophecy, the hieratic stance of Milton, and the formal rhetoric, allegorical tactics, and calculated disorder of what he called "the sublimer Ode" of Gray and Collins, in the effort to endow his subjects with the requisite elevation, passion, drama, and impact. As Coleridge wrote to Southey in December of 1794, while Bowles's poems were his "morning Companions," helping him, "a thought-bewilder'd Man," to discover his own defects: "I am so habituated to philosophizing, that I cannot divest myself of it even when my own Wretchedness is the subject."

> And I cannot write without a *body* of *thought*—hence my *Poetry* is crowded and sweats beneath a heavy burthen of Ideas and Imagery! It has seldom Ease.[22]

This "Ease" Coleridge had early discovered in Bowles. And as he said in the *Biographia*, the example of Bowles—together with Cowper the first of the living poets who, in the style "more sustained and elevated" than in Percy's collection of popular ballads, "combined natural thoughts with natural diction; the first who reconciled the heart with the head"—rescued him from the unnatural division between intellect and feeling, and consonantly, from his use of "a laborious and florid diction"; but only, as he adds, "gradually."[23] The reason for the delay in making, as he put it, his "practice" conform to his "better judgment" is, I think, plain. Coleridge succeeded in emulating Bowles's ease only after he learned to adopt and commit himself to the lyric persona which demands such a style. That is, in place of philosophical, moral, and historical pronouncements translated into allegoric action by Pindaric artifice and amplified for public delivery in a ceremonious bardic voice, Bowles's sonnets opened out to Coleridge the possibilities in the quite ordinary circumstances of a private person in a specific time and place whose meditation, credibly stimulated by the setting, is grounded in his particular character, follows the various and seemingly random flow of the living consciousness, and is conducted in the intimate yet adaptive voice of the interior monologue. (Bowles's style, as Coleridge said, unites the possibilities both of colloquialism and elevation—it is "natural and real, and yet . . . dignified and harmonious.') It was in "the compositions of my twenty-fourth and twenty-fifth years," Coleridge goes on to say, including "the shorter blank verse poems"—that is, the poems of 1796–97, beginning with "The Eolian Harp," which established the persona, idiom, materials, and ordonnance of the greater Romantic lyric—that he achieved his "present ideal in respect of the general tissue of the style."[24] No doubt the scholars are right who claim some influence on these poems of the relaxed and conversational blank verse of Cowper's *The Task*,[25] in the recurrent passages, within its mock-Miltonic manner, of serious description or meditation. I see no reason, however, to doubt Coleridge's repeated assertion that Bowles's sonnets and blank-verse poems were for him the prior and by far the pre-eminent models.

So much for the speaker and voice of Bowles's sonnets. Now what of their central structural trope, by which, as Coleridge described it in 1796, "moral Sentiments, Affections, or Feelings, are deduced from, and associated with, the scenery of Nature"? Even so early in his career Coleridge was an integral thinker for whom questions of poetic structure were inseparable from general philosophic issues, and he at once went on to interpret this device as the correlate of a mode of perception which unites the mind to its physical environment. Such compositions, he said,

> create a sweet and indissoluble union between the intellectual and the material world. . . . Hence the Sonnets of BOWLES derive their marked superiority over all other Sonnets; hence they domesticate with the heart, and become, as it were, a part of our identity.[26]

This philosophical and psychological interpretation of Bowles's lyric procedure was not only, as Coleridge indicates, a cardinal reason for his early fascination with Bowles, but also the chief clue to his later disenchantment, and it merits attention.

IV
THE COALESCENCE OF SUBJECT AND OBJECT

In the opening chapter of his *Literary Life*, Coleridge introduces Bowles's sonnets not on their own account, but as representing a stage in his total intellectual development—"as introductory to the statement of my principles in Politics, Religion, and Philosophy, and an application of the rules, deduced from philosophical principles, to poetry and criticism."[27] Hence he moves from his account of the shaping influence of Bowyer, Bowles, and Wordsworth into a summary review of the history of philosophy, as preliminary to establishing his own metaphysical and critical premises, of which the culmination was to be the crucial distinction between fancy and imagination.

In the course of his survey of the dominant philosophy of the preceding age, it becomes clear that Coleridge found intolerable two of its main features, common both to philosophers in the school of Descartes and in the school of Locke. The first was its dualism, the absolute separation between mind and the material universe, which replaced a providential, vital, and companionable world by a world of particles in purposeless movement. The second was the method of reasoning underlying this dualism, that pervasive elementarism which takes as its starting point the irreducible element or part and conceives all wholes to be a combination of discrete parts, whether material atoms or mental "ideas."

Even in 1797, while Coleridge was still a Hartleian associationist in philosophy, he had expressed his recoil from elementarist thinking. The fault of "the Experimentalists," who rely only on the "testimony of their senses," is that "they contemplate nothing but *parts*—and all *parts* are necessarily little—and the Universe to them is but a mass of *little things.*" "I can contemplate nothing but parts, & parts are all *little*—!—My mind feels as if it ached to behold & know something *great*—something *one & indivisible.* . . ."[28] And he wrote later in *The Friend* about that particular separation between part and part which divides mind from nature:

> The ground-work, therefore, of all true philosophy is the full apprehension of the difference between . . . that intuition of things which arises when we possess ourselves, as one with the whole . . . and that which presents itself when . . . we think of ourselves as separated beings, and place nature in antithesis to the mind, as object to subject, thing to thought, death to life.[29]

As to Coleridge, so to Wordsworth in 1797–98, "solitary objects . . . beheld/ In disconnection" are "dead and spiritless," and division, breaking down "all grandeur" into successive "littleness," is opposed to man's proper spiritual condition, in which "All things shall live in us and we shall live/ In all things that surround us."[30] Absolute separation, in other words, is death-dealing—in Coleridge's words, it is "the philosophy of Death, and only of a dead nature can it hold good"[31]—so that the separation of mind from nature leads inevitably to the conception of a dead world in which the estranged mind is doomed to lead a life-in-death.

To the Romantic sensibility such a universe could not be endured, and the central enterprise common to many post-Kantian German philosophers and poets, as well as to Coleridge and Wordsworth, was to join together the "subject" and "object" that modern intellection had put asunder, and thus to revivify a dead nature, restore its concreteness, significance, and human values, and re-domiciliate man in a world which had become alien to him. The pervasive sense of estrangement, of a lost and isolated existence in an alien world, is not peculiar to our own age of anxiety, but was a common-place of Romantic philosophy. According to Friedrich Schelling, the most representative philosopher of that age, division from unity was the fall of man consequent upon his eating the fruit of the tree of knowledge in the Enlightenment. The guilt of modern men must be

> ascribed to their own will, which deviated from unity. . . . [This is] a truly Platonic fall of man, the condition in which man believes that the dead, the absolutely manifold and separated world which he conceives, is in fact the true and actual world.[32]

Long before he read Schelling, and while at the height of his enthusiasm for Bowles, Coleridge had included in his visionary "Religious Musings" (1794) an outline of human history in which mankind's highest good had been "to know ourselves/Parts and proportions of one wondrous whole"; the present evil was defined as a fall into an anarchic separation in which each man, "disherited of soul," feels "himself, his own low self the whole"; and man's redemption at the Second Coming was anticipated as a reintegration into his lost unity by a "sacred sympathy" which makes "The whole one Self! Self, that no alien knows! . . . all of all possessing!"[33] And in 1815 Coleridge recalled that the plan of Wordsworth's projected masterpiece, *The Recluse*, as he had understood it, had also been to affirm "a Fall in some sense, as a fact," to be redeemed by a

> Reconciliation from this Enmity with Nature . . . by the substitu-tion of Life, and Intelligence . . . for the Philosophy of mechanism which in every thing that is most worthy of the human Intellect strikes *Death*.[34]

In the *Biographia Literaria*, when Coleridge came to lay down his own metaphysical system, he based it on a premise designed to overcome both the elementarism in method and the dualism in theory of knowledge of his eighteenth-century predecessors, by converting their absolute division between subject and object into a logical "antithesis," in order to make it eligible for resolution by the Romantic dialectic of thesis-antithesis-synthesis. The "primary ground" of his theory of knowledge, he says, is "the coincidence of an object with a subject" or "of the thought with the thing," in a synthesis, or "coalescence," in which the elements lose their separate identities. "In the reconciling, and recurrence of this contradiction exists the process and mystery of production and life."[35] And the process of vital artistic creation reflects the process of this vital creative perception. Unlike the fancy, which can only rearrange the "fixities and definites" of sense-perception without altering their identity, the "synthetic and magical power" of the secondary imagination repeats the primal act of knowing by dissolving the elements of perception "in order to recreate" them, and "reveals itself in the balance or reconciliation of opposite or discordant qualities"—including the reconciliation of intellect with emotion, and of thought with object: "the idea, with the image."[36]

In short, the reintegration of the divided self (of "head and heart") and the simultaneous healing of the breach between the ego and the alien other (of "subject and object") was for Coleridge a profound emotional need which he translated into the grounds both of his theory of knowledge and his theory of art. How pivotal the concept of human-nonhuman reconciliation came to be for Coleridge's aesthetics is apparent in his essay "On Poesy or Art," in which he specifically defined art as "the reconciler of nature and man . . . the power of humanizing nature, of infusing the thoughts and passions of man into every thing which is the object of his contemplation." It is "the union and reconciliation of that which is nature with that which is exclusively human."[37]

\* \* \*

Perhaps now, to return at last to the sonnets of Bowles, we can understand better why those seemingly inconsequential poems made so powerful an impact on Coleridge, in their materials as well as their structure and style. Bowles's primary device by which sentiments and feelings "are deduced from, and associated with, the scenery of Nature" had seemed to Coleridge evidence of a poetry which not only "reconciled the heart with the head," but also united the mind with nature; in the terms available to him in 1796, it created "a sweet and indissoluble union between the intellectual and the material world." Through the next half-decade, however, Coleridge carried on his own experiments in the descriptive and meditative lyric, came to know the early poetry of Wordsworth, had his introduction to German metaphysics, and, in intense and almost fevered speculation, groped his way out of the mechanism and associationism of David Hartley and other English empiricists. Increasingly in the process he became dissatisfied with the constitution of Bowles's poems, and the reasons came sharply into focus in 1802, at about the time he was recasting his verse "Letter to [Asra]" into his highest achievement in the greater Romantic lyric, "Dejection: An Ode." On 10 September he wrote a letter to William Sotheby which shows that his working his way through and beyond Bowles was an integral part of his working his way toward a new poetry, a new criticism, and a new world view. The letter is a preliminary sketch for the *Biographia Literaria*, for like that work it moves from a critique of Bowles through a view of the relation of mind to nature in perception to a theory of poetic production, and culminates in Coleridge's first explicit distinction between the elementaristic fancy and the synthetic imagination.

Bowles had just published a new edition of his sonnets, supplemented by several long poems in blank verse which reverted to a process of scenic inventory and incidental meditation very close to the eighteenth-century local poem. Bowles's second volume, Coleridge begins, "is woefully inferior to its Predecessor."

> There reigns thro' all the blank verse poems such a perpetual trick of *moralizing* every thing—which is very well, occasionally—but never to see or describe any interesting appearance in nature, without connecting it by dim analogies with the moral world, proves faintness of Impression. Nature has her proper interest; & he will know what it is, who believes & feels, that every Thing has a Life of its own, & that we are all *one Life*. A Poet's *Heart & Intellect* should be *combined*, *intimately* combined & *unified*, with the great appearances in Nature—& not merely held in solution & loose mixture with them, in the shape of formal Similes. . . . The truth is—Bowles has indeed the *sensibility* of a poet; but he has not the *Passion* of a great Poet. . . . He has no native Passion, because he is not a Thinker.[38]

Bowles's exaggeration in his later poems of his earlier devices has opened out to Coleridge his inherent failings. Bowles is able to reconcile the heart with the head, but only because of an equality of weakness in the antagonist powers of intellect and passion. And what Coleridge had earlier described as an "indissoluble union between the intellectual and material world" now turns out to be no better than "a loose mixture," in which the separate parts, instead of being "*intimately* combined & *unified*," are merely held together by the rhetorical expedient of "formal Similes." In other words, what to Coleridge, the Hartleian associationist, had in 1796 appeared to be an adequate integration of mind and its milieu reveals itself—when he has learned to think of all higher mental processes in terms of a synthesis of contraries—to be what he later called the "conjunction-disjunctive" of neoclassic unity by a decorum of the parts.

In the letter to Sotheby, Coleridge goes on to draw a parallel distinction between the treatment of nature in Greek mythology and in the Hebrew poets, and ends by assigning the former type to the collocative process of the lower productive faculty, or Fancy. To the Greek poets

> all natural Objects were *dead*—mere hollow Statues—but there was a Godkin or Goddessling *included* in each. . . . At best it is but Fancy, or the aggregating Faculty of the mind—not *Imagination*, or the *modifying*, and co-adunating Faculty. . . . In the Hebrew Poets each Thing has a Life of its own, & yet they are all one Life.

Bowles's poems, it becomes apparent, remain in the mode of the Fancy because they fail to overcome the division between living mind and a dead nature by that act of the coadunating Imagination which fuses the two into "one Life"; for when Bowles joins the parts *a* and *b* they form an aggregate *ab*, instead of "interpenetrating" (in terms of Coleridge's critique of elementarist thinking) to "generate a higher third, including both the former," the product *c*.[39] For the "mystery of genius in the Fine Arts," as Coleridge said in "On Poesy or Art," is

> so to place these images [of nature] . . . as to elicit from, and to super-induce upon, the forms themselves the moral reflexions to which they approximate, to make the external internal, the internal external, to make nature thought, and thought nature.[40]

The shift in Coleridge's theory of descriptive poetry corresponded with a change in his practice of the form; and in the sequence of sonnets and conversation poems that he wrote under Bowles's influence we can observe him in the process of converting the conjunction of parts, in which nature stays on one side and thought on the other, into the Romantic interfusion of subject and object. W. K. Wimsatt has acutely remarked that Coleridge's sonnet "To the River Otter"—though written in express imitation of Bowles's "To the River Itchin," perhaps so early as 1793—has begun to diverge from Bowles's "simple association . . . simply asserted" by involving the thought in the descriptive details so that the design "is latent in the multiform sensuous picture."[41] "The Eolian Harp" (1795–96) set the expanded pattern of the greater lyric, but in it the meditative flight is a short one, while the thought is still at times expressed in the mode of *sententiae* which are joined to the details of the scene by formal similes. We sit

> beside our Cot, our Cot o'ergrown
> With white-flower'd Jasmin, and the broad-leav'd Myrtle,
> (Meet emblems they of Innocence and Love!)
> And watch the Clouds, that late were rich with light,
> Slow-sadd'ning round, and mark the Star of eve
> Serenely brilliant (such should WISDOM be!)
> Shine opposite.

In "Frost at Midnight," however, written two years later, the images in the initial description are already suffused with an unstated significance which, in Coleridge's terms, is merely "elicited" and expanded by the subsequent reflection, which in turn "super-induces" a richer meaning upon the scene to which it reverts. "Fears in Solitude," a few months after that, exemplifies the sustained dialogue between mind and landscape which Coleridge describes in lines 215–20 of the poem: the prospect of sea and fields

> seems like society—
> Conversing with the mind, and giving it
> A livelier impulse and a dance of thought!

And "Dejection: An Ode," on which Coleridge was working in 1802 just as he got Bowles's poems into critical perspective, is a triumph of the "coadunating" imagination, in the very poem which laments the severance of his community with nature and the suspension of his shaping spirit of imagination. In unspoken consonance with the change of the outer scene and of the responsive wind-harp from ominous quiet to violent storm to momentary calm, the poet's mind, momentarily revitalized by a correspondent inner breeze, moves from torpor through violence to calm, by a process in which the properties earlier specified of the landscape—the spring rebirth, the radiated light of moon and stars, the clouds and rain, the voice of the harp—reappear as the metaphors of the evolving meditation on the relation of mind to nature; these culminate in the figure of the one life as an eddy between antitheses:

> To her may all things live, from pole to pole,
> Their life the eddying of her living soul!

On Coleridge's philosophical premises, in this poem nature is made thought and thought nature, both by their sustained interaction and by their seamless metaphoric continuity.

The best Romantic meditations on a landscape, following Coleridge's examples, all manifest a transaction between subject and object in which the thought incorporates and makes explicit what was already implicit in the outer scene. And all the poets testify independently to a fact of

216

consciousness which underlay these poems, and was the experiential source and warrant for the philosophy of cognition as an interfusion of mind and nature. When the Romantic poet confronted a landscape, the distinction between self and not-self tended to dissolve. Coleridge asserted that from childhood he had been accustomed to "unrealize . . . and then by a sort of transfusion and transmission of my consciousness to identify myself with the Object"; also that

> in looking at objects of Nature while I am thinking . . . I seem rather to be seeking, as it were *asking*, a symbolical language for something within me that already and forever exists, than observing any thing new.

So with Wordsworth: "I was often unable to think of external things as having external existence, and I communed with all that I saw as something not apart from, but inherent in, my own immaterial nature." Shelley witnessed to "the state called reverie," when men "feel as if their nature were dissolved into the surrounding universe, or as if the surrounding universe were absorbed into their being. They are conscious of no distinction." Even Byron's Childe Harold claimed that "I live not in myself," but that mountains, waves, and skies become "a part/Of me, and of my soul, as I of them." Keats's experience differs, but only in the conditions that, instead of assimilating the other to the self, the self goes out into the other, and that the boundary of self is "annihilated" when he contemplates, not a broad prospect, but a solid particular endowed with outline, mass, and posture or motion. That type of poet of which "I am a Member . . . has no self" but "is continually [informing] and filling some other Body"—a moving billiard ball, a breaking wave, a human form in arrested motion, a sparrow, an urn, or a nightingale.[42]

V

THE ROMANTIC MEDITATION

The greater Romantic lyric, then, as established by Coleridge, evolved from the descriptive-meditative structure of the eighteenth-century local poem, primarily through the intermediate stage of Bowles's sequence of sonnets. There remains, however, a wide disparity between the Romantic lyric and its predecessors, a disparity in the organization and nature of the meditation proper. In local poetry the order of the thoughts is the sequence in which the natural objects are observed; the poet surveys a prospect, or climbs a hill, or undertakes a tour, or follows the course of a stream, and he introduces memories and ideas intermittently, as the descriptive occasion offers. In Bowles's sonnets, the meditation, while more continuous, is severely limited by the straitness of the form, and consists mainly of the pensive commonplaces of the typical late-century man of feeling. In the fully developed Romantic lyric, on the other hand, the description is structurally subordinate to the meditation, and the meditation is sustained, continuous, and highly serious. Even when the initial impression is of the casual movement of a relaxed mind, retrospect reveals the whole to have been firmly organized around an emotional issue pressing for resolution. And in a number of the greatest lyrics—including Coleridge's "Dejection," Wordsworth's "Intimations," Shelley's "Stanzas Written in Dejection" and "West Wind," Keats's "Nightingale"—the issue is one of a recurrent state often called by the specialized term "dejection." This is not the pleasing melancholy of the eighteenth-century poet of sensibility, nor Bowles's muted self-pity, but a profound sadness, sometimes bordering on the anguish of terror or despair, at the sense of loss, dereliction, isolation, or inner death, which is presented as inherent in the conditions of the speaker's existence.

In the English literary tradition these Romantic meditations had their closest analogue in the devotional poems of the seventeenth century. In his study *The Poetry of Meditation* Professor Louis Martz has emphasized the importance, for the religious poets we usually class as "metaphysical," of the numerous and immensely popular devotional handbooks which undertook to discipline the casual flow of ordinary consciousness by setting down a detailed regimen for evoking, sustaining, and ordering a process of meditation toward resolution. A standard sub-department was the "meditation on the creatures" (that is, on the created world) in order, as the title of Robert Bellarmine's influential treatise of 1615 put it, to achieve *The Ascent of the Mind to God by a Ladder of Things Created*. The recommended procedure, as this became stabilized at the turn of the century, tended to fall into three major divisions. The first involved what Loyola called the "composition of place, seeing the spot"; that is, envisioning in vivid detail the person, object, or scene which initiates the meditation. The second, the meditation proper, was the analysis of the relevance to our salvation of this scene, interpreted analogically; it often included a turn inward to a close examination of conscience. The last specified the results of this meditation for our affections and will, and either included, or concluded with, a "colloquy"—usually a prayer, or discourse with God, although as St. Francis de Sales advises, "while we are forming our affections and resolutions," we do well to address our colloquy also "to ourselves, to our own hearts . . . and even to insensible creatures."[43]

Few seventeenth-century meditative poems accord exactly with the formulas of the Catholic or Anglican devotional manuals, but many of them unmistakably profited from that disciplining of fluid thought into an organized pattern which was a central enterprise in the spiritual life of the age. And those poetic meditations on the creatures which envision a natural scene or object, go on, in sorrow, anguish, or dejection, to explore the significance for the speaker of the spiritual signs built into the object by

God, and close in reconciliation and the hope of rebirth, are closer to the best Romantic lyrics in meditative content, mood, and ordonnance than any poem by Bowles or his eighteenth-century predecessors. Good instances of the type are Vaughan's "The Waterfall," "Regeneration," "Vanity of Spirit," and "I walkt the other day (to spend my hour,)/Into a field"—an hour being a standard time set aside for formal meditation. "Regeneration," for example, begins with a walk through a spring landscape which stands in sharp contrast to the sterile winter of the poet's spirit, finds its resolution in a sudden storm of wind which, as *spiritus*, is the material equivalent both of the breath of God and the spirit of man, and ends in a short colloquy which is a prayer for a spiritual dying-into-life:

> Here musing long, I heard
> A rushing wind
> Which still increas'd, but whence it stirr'd
> No where I could not find. . . .
> Lord, then said I, on me one breath,
> And let me die before my death!

The two key figures of the outer and inner seasons and of the correspondent, regenerative wind later served as the radical metaphors in a number of Romantic poems, including Coleridge's "Dejection" and Shelley's "Ode to the West Wind."[44]

Or consider the meditation on a creature which—at least in his later life—was Coleridge's favorite poem by one of his favorite lyrists, George Herbert's "The Flower."[45] Reflecting upon the annual death and rebirth of the plant, the poet draws a complex analogy with his own soul in its cycles of depression and joy, spiritual drouth and rain, death and spring-like revival, alienation from God and reconcilement; in the concluding colloquy he also (as Coleridge and Shelley were to do) incorporates into the analogy the sterility and revival of his poetic powers:

> And now in age I bud again,
> After so many deaths I live and write;
> I once more smell the dew and rain,
> And relish versing. Oh, my only light,
> It cannot be
> That I am he
> On whom thy tempests fell all night.[46]

Herbert is describing the state of inner torpor through alienation from God known in theology as accidie, dejection, spiritual dryness, interior desolation; this condition was often analogized to circumstances of the seasons and weather, and was a matter of frequent consideration in the devotional manuals. As St. Francis de Sales wrote, in his section "Of Spiritual Dryness and Sterility":

> Sometimes you will find yourself so deprived and destitute of all devout feelings of devotion that your soul will seem to be a fruitless, barren desert, in which there is no . . . water of grace to refresh her, on account of the dryness that seems to threaten her with a total and absolute desolation. . . . At the same time, to cast her into despair, the enemy mocks her by a thousand suggestions of despondency and says: "Ah! poor wretch, where is thy God? . . . Who can ever restore to thee the joy of His holy grace?"[47]

Coleridge, during the several years just preceding "Dejection: An Ode," described in his letters a recurrent state of apathy and of the paralysis of imagination in terms which seem to echo such discussions of spiritual dryness: "My Imagination is tired, down, flat and powerless. . . . As if the *organs* of Life had been dried up; as if only simple BEING remained, blind and stagnant!" "I have been . . . undergoing a process of intellectual *exsiccation*. . . . The Poet is dead in me"[48]

The Romantic meditations, then, though secular meditations, often turn on crises—alienation, dejection, the loss of a "celestial light" or "glory" in experiencing the created world—which are closely akin to the spiritual crises of the earlier religious poets. And at times the Romantic lyric becomes overtly theological in expression. Some of them include not only colloquies with a human auditor, real or imagined, and with what De Sales called "insensible creatures," but also with God or with a Spirit of Nature, in the mode of a formal prayer ("Reflections on Having Left a Place of Retirement," "Ode to the West Wind"), or else of a terminal benediction. Thus Coleridge's "Frost at Midnight" falls into the ritual language of a blessing ("Therefore all seasons shall be sweet to thee")—a tactic which Wordsworth at once picked up in "Tintern Abbey" ("and this prayer I make. . . . Therefore let the moon/Shine on thee in thy solitary walk") and which Coleridge himself repeated in *Dejection* ("Visit her, gentle Sleep! with wings of healing. . . . To her may all things live, from pole to pole").

We must not drive the parallel too hard. There is little external evidence of the direct influence of the metaphysical poem upon the greater Romantic lyric; the similarity between them may well be the result of a common tradition of meditations on the creatures—a tradition which continued in the eighteenth century in so prodigiously popular a work as James Hervey's *Meditations and Contemplations* (1746–47).[49] And there is a very conspicuous and significant difference between the Romantic lyric and the seventeenth-century meditation on created nature—a difference in the description which initiates and directs the process of mind. The "composition of place" was not a specific locality, nor did it need to be present

220

to the eyes of the speaker, but was a typical scene or object, usually called up, as St. Ignatius and other preceptors said, before "the eyes of the imagination,"[50] in order to set off and guide the thought by means of correspondences whose interpretation was firmly controlled by an inherited typology. The landscape set forth in Vaughan's "Regeneration," for example, is not a particular geographical location, nor even a literal setting, but the allegorical landscape common to the genre of spiritual pilgrimages, from the *Divine Comedy* to *Pilgrim's Progress.* And Herbert's flower is not a specified plant, described by the poet with his eye on the object, but a generic one; it is simply the class of all perennials, in which God has inscribed the invariable signatures of his providential plan. In the Romantic poem, on the other hand, the speaker merely happens upon a natural scene which is present, particular, and almost always precisely located; and though Coleridge occasionally alludes to it still as "that eternal language, which thy God utters,"[51] the primary meanings educed from the scene are not governed by a public symbolism, but have been brought to it by the private mind which perceives it. But we know already that these attributes also had a seventeenth-century origin, in a poet who inherited the metaphysical tradition yet went on, as Dryden and many of his successors commented,[52] to alter it in such a way as to establish the typical meter, rhetoric, and formal devices of neoclassic poetry. The crucial event in the development of the most distinctive of the Romantic lyric forms occurred when John Denham climbed Cooper's Hill and undertook to describe, in balanced couplets, the landscape before his eyes, and to embellish the description with incidental reminiscence and meditation.

## Notes

1 *The Prelude* (1850), XII, 222–3. Even Keats, though he sometimes longed for a life of sensations rather than of thought, objected to the poems of John Clare that too often "the Description overlaid and stifled that which ought to be the prevailing Idea." (Letter to John Clare from John Taylor, 27 September 1820, quoted by Edmund Blunden, *Keats' Publisher* [London, 1936], p. 80).

2 *Descriptive Sketches* (1793) drew from a contemporary reviewer the cry: "More descriptive poetry! Have we not yet enough? . . . Yes; more, and yet more: so it is decreed." *The Monthly Review*, 2d series, XII (1793), 216–17; cited by Robert A. Aubin, *Topographical Poetry in XVIII-Century England* (New York, 1936), p. 255; see also pp. 217–19.

3 Perhaps that is the reason for Coleridge's later judgment that "The Eolian Harp" was "the most perfect poem I ever wrote." (Quoted by J. D. Campbell, ed., *The Poetical Works of S. T. Coleridge*, London, 1893, p. 578). The first version of the poem and a manuscript version of 1797 (Coleridge then entitled it "Effusion") are reproduced in *The Complete Poetical Works*, ed. E. H. Coleridge (2 vols.; Oxford, 1912), II, 1021–3. For an account of the revisions of the poem, see H. J. W. Milley, "Some Notes on Coleridge's 'Eolian Harp,'" *Modern Philology*, XXXVI (1938–39), 359–75.

4 *Collected Letters*, ed. Earl Leslie Griggs (Oxford, 1956–), IV, 545.

5 Keats used a different figure for the poetic return. In a letter of Dec. 1818–Jan. 1819, he transcribed "Ever let the Fancy roam" and "Bards of Passion and of Mirth," in which the last lines are variants of the opening lines, and said: "These are specimens of a sort of rondeau which I think I shall become partial to" (*The Letters*, ed. H. E. Rollins, 2 vols., Cambridge, Mass., 1958, II, 21–6). In the next few months he exemplified the rondeau form in "The Eve of St. Agnes" and "La Belle Dame sans Merci," as well as in the descriptive-meditative lyric, "Ode to a Nightingale."

6 So titled in the Dowden MS. in the Morgan Library; see Carl R. Woodring, *Politics in the Poetry of Coleridge* (Madison, Wisconsin, 1961), p. 255, note 16.

7 *The Works of Samuel Johnson*, ed. Arthur Murphy (12 vols.; London, 1824), IX, 77.

8 *The Subtler Language* (Baltimore, 1959), Chap. III.

9 *Works*, ed. Geoffrey Keynes (6 vols.; London, 1928), I, 17.

10 The opening eight lines of "Cooper's Hill," despite some approximation to neo-classic neatness and dispatch, are much closer to Donne's couplets, in the cramped syntax of their run-on lines, which deploy a tortuous analogical argument to demonstrate a paradox that inverts and explodes a mythological cliché:

> Sure there are Poets which did never dream
> Upon *Parnassus*, nor did taste the stream
> Of *Helicon*, we therefore may suppose
> Those made no Poets, but the Poets those.
> And as Courts make not Kings, but Kings the Court,
> So where the Muses and their train resort,
> *Parnassus* stands; if I can be to thee
> A Poet, thou Parnassus are to me.

Compare the opening of Andrew Marvell's "Upon the Hill and Grove at Billborow" (probably written in the early 1650s) for the jolting movement, the doughty hyperbole, and witty shock-tactics of the thoroughly metaphysical management of a local hill-poem.

11 See Earl R. Wasserman, "Nature Moralized: The Divine Analogy in the Eighteenth Century," *ELH*, XX (1953), 39–76. For commentators on the local poem, the chief structural problem was how to establish easy, just, yet varied connections between its two components, the *visibilia* and the *moralia*. Joseph Warton's observation is typical, that "it is one of the greatest and most pleasing arts of descriptive poetry, to introduce moral sentences and instructions in an oblique and indirect manner." *An Essay on the Genius and Writings of Pope*, 1756 (London, 1806), I, 29.

12 Preface to *Lyrical Ballads, The Poetical Works of William Wordsworth*, ed. E. de Selincourt (5 vols.; Oxford, 1949), II, 391.

13 *Biographia Literaria*, ed. J. Shawcross (2 vols.; Oxford, 1907), I, 13.

14 Ibid. pp. 8–16.

15 *The Poetical Works of William Lisle Bowles*, ed. George Gilfillan (2 vols.; Edinburgh, 1855), I, 1.

16 *Recollections of the Table-Talk of Samuel Rogers* (New York, 1856), p. 258, note. For Bowles's effect on Southey see William Haller, *The Early Life of Robert Southey* (New York, 1917), pp. 73–6. As late as 1806–20, in *The River Duddon*, Wordsworth adopted Bowles's design of a tour represented in a sequence of local-meditative sonnets.

17 Coleridge, Introduction to his "Sheet of Sonnets" of 1796, *The Complete Poetical Works*, II, 1139. As early as November of 1797, however, Coleridge as "Nehemiah Higginbottom" parodied "the spirit of *doleful egotism*" in the sonnet. See *Biographia Literaria*, I, 17, and David Erdman, "Coleridge as Nehemiah Higginbottom," *Modern Language Notes*, LXXIII (1958), 569–80.

18 *Biographia Literaria*, I, 10.

19 Ibid. pp. 2–3, and pp. 203–4, note. Coleridge's claim that he had recognized the defects of the "swell and glitter" of his elevated style, even as he employed it, is borne out by his Preface to the Poems of 1797, *Complete Poetical Works*, II, 1145.

20 See M. H. Abrams, "English Romanticism: The Spirit of the Age," in *Romanticism Reconsidered*, ed. Northrop Frye (New York, 1963), pp. 37–72.

21 *Complete Poetical Works*, II, 1113–14; see also p. 1145.

22 11 December 1794, *Collected Letters*, I, 133–7.

23 *Biographia Literaria*, I, 10, 15–16.

24 Ibid. p. 16.

25 See, for example, Humphry House, *Coleridge* (London, 1953), Chap. III; George Whalley, "Coleridge's Debt to Charles Lamb," *Essays and Studies* (1958), pp. 68–85; and Max F. Schulz, *The Poetic Voices of Coleridge* (Detroit, 1963), Chap. 5. A comment of Lamb to Coleridge in December 1796 substantiates Coleridge's own statements about the relative importance for him of Bowles and Cowper: "Burns was the god of my idolatry, as Bowles of yours. I am jealous of your fraternising with Bowles, when I think you relish him more than Burns or my old favourite, Cowper." *The Works of Charles and Mary Lamb*, ed. E. V. Lucas (7 vols.; London, 1903–5), VI, 73.

26 Introduction to the "Sheet of Sonnets" of 1796, *Complete Poetical Works*, II, 1139.

27 *Biographia Literaria*, I, 1.

28 *Collected Letters*, I, 354, 349. See also ibid. IV, 574–5, and *The Notebooks of Samuel Taylor Coleridge* (New York, 1957), II, note 2151.

29 *The Friend* (3 vols.; London, 1818), III, 261–2.

30 *The Ruined Cottage*, addendum to MS. B (1797–98), *The Poetical Works*, V, 402.

31 *Theory of Life*, ed. Seth B. Watson (London, 1848), p. 63.

32 Schelling, *Sämmtliche Werke* (Stuttgart and Augsburg, 1857), Pt. I, Vol. VII, 81–2.

33 "Religious Musings," ll. 126–58, *Complete Poetical Works*, I, 113–15.

34 To Wordsworth, 30 May 1815, *Collected Letters*, IV, 574–5.

35 *Biographia Literaria*, I, 174–85.

36 Ibid. I, 202; II, 12. See *The Friend*, III, 263–4, on the "one principle which alone reconciles the man with himself, with other [men] and with the world."

37 In *Biographia Literaria*, II, 253–5. Though "On Poesy or Art" takes its departure from Schelling's "On the Relation of the Plastic Arts to Nature," the quoted statements are Coleridge's own.

38 10 September 1802, *Collected Letters*, II, 864.

39 *Theory of Life*, p. 63.

40 In *Biographia Literaria*, II, 258.

41 "The Structure of Romantic Nature Imagery," in *The Verbal Icon* (New York, 1958), pp. 106–10.

42 Coleridge, *Collected Letters*, IV, 974–5, and *The Notebooks*, II, 2546; Wordsworth, *Poetical Works*, IV, 463; *Shelley's Prose*, ed. David Lee Clark (Albuquerque, 1954), p. 174; Byron, *Childe Harold*, III, lxxii, lxxv; Keats, *The Letters*, I, 387.

43 *Introduction to the Devout Life*, translated by John K. Ryan (Garden City, N. Y., 1955), p. 88.
44 See M. H. Abrams, "The Correspondent Breeze: A Romantic Metaphor," in *English Romantic Poets: Modern Essays in Criticism* (New York, 1960), pp. 37–54.
45 Coleridge's comments on Herbert are gathered in *Coleridge on the Seventeenth Century*, ed. Roberta Florence Brinkley (Duke University Press, 1955), pp. 533–40.
46 Coleridge wrote his later poem of aridity in a spring landscape, "Work Without Hope" (1825), expressly "in the manner of G. HERBERT." See *Complete Poetical Works*, II, 1110–11.
47 *Introduction to the Devout Life*, pp. 256–7; on "spiritual desolation," see also Loyola's *Spiritual Exercises*, ed. Orby Shipley (London, 1870), pp. 139–40.
48 *Collected Letters*, I, 470; II, 713–14; also I, 643.
49 In the *Meditations and Contemplations* (7th ed., 2 vols.; London, 1750), II, xv–xvii, Hervey describes his aim to "exhibit a Prospect of still *Life*, and grand *Operation*" in order "to *open* the *Door* of Meditation," and show how we may "*gather up* the unstable, fluctuating *Train* of Fancy; and collect her fickle Powers into a consistent, regular, and useful Habit of Thinking."
50 See Louis L. Martz, *The Poetry of Meditation* (New Haven, 1954), pp. 27–8.
51 "Frost at Midnight," ll. 58–62; cf. "This Lime-Tree Bower," ll. 39–43, and "Fears in Solitude," ll. 22–4. In Coleridge's "Hymn before Sunrise" (1802), unlike his greater lyrics, the meditation moves from the creatures to the Creator by a hereditary symbolism as old as Psalm 19: "The heavens declare the glory of God; and the firmament sheweth his handywork."
52 Dr. Johnson listed Denham among the metaphysical poets, then added, in the great commonplace of neoclassical literary history, that he "and Waller sought another way to fame, by improving the harmony of our numbers." (*The Life of Cowley, Works*, IX, 23.)

# 11

# FORM AND FREEDOM IN EUROPEAN ROMANTIC POETRY

## Stuart Curran

Source: *Poetic Form and British Romanticism* (New York: Oxford University Press, 1986), pp. 204–20.

> Natur und Kunst, sie scheinen sich zu fliehen
> Und haben sich, eh man es denkt, gefunden;
> Der Widerwille ist auch mir verschwunden,
> Und beide scheinen gleich mich anzuziehen.
> Es gilt wohl nur ein redliches Bemühen!
> Und wenn wir erst in abgemessnen Stunden
> Mit Geist und Fleiss uns an die Kunst gebunden,
> Mag frei Natur im Herzen wieder glühen.
>
> So ists mit aller Bildung auch beschaffen.
> Vergebens werden ungebundne Geister
> Nach der Vollendung reiner Höhe streben.
> Wer Grosses will, muss sich zusammenraffen.
> In der Beschränkung zeigt sich erst der Meister,
> Und das Gesetz nur kann uns Freiheit geben.
>
> > Johann Wolfgang von Goethe,
> > "Natur und Kunst"[1]

## I

The composite orders of Wordsworth, Byron, and Shelley are the most daring and sophisticated formal experiments in British Romantic poetry. The poets' knowledge of their literary heritage is brilliantly tempered to a determined conceptual purpose, and yet their individual ideologies, if clearly associated in a shared concern with the values of process and progress that dominate their culture, are as distinctive in constitution as they are in purpose. The generic inclusiveness of *The Prelude*, *Don Juan*, and *Prometheus Unbound* is of such complexity that each poem becomes the locus for an

225

encompassing world view, and thus it is natural for us as readers, generally speaking, to refer the entire canon of the authors to these supreme
embodiments of their genius. So enveloping a synoptic form, we are wont to
say, must constitute the poet's largest and ultimate vision of life. The critical
instincts by which we enforce an ideological centering of such intensity are
not only natural, but they also accord with our own experience, moral no
less than aesthetic.

Nevertheless, they are implicitly reductive. We have only to look at the
wanderers elsewhere in Wordsworth who cannot discover meaning or solace
—his Female Vagrant, his burned-out old soldiers, the intellectually dessicated
Solitary of *The Excursion*—to temper any simple sense of Wordsworth's
faith in his progressive imaginative liberation. Providing the obverse of
or necessary balance to Byron's fluid comic vision are the four historical
tragedies he wrote contemporaneously with *Don Juan*, all centering on heroes
ground down by cultural fixities each vainly tries to escape. And there
can be observed in Shelley's writing another way of construing a universal
democratic paradigm that inhibits any urge to read the final act of his lyrical
drama sentimentally, the republic of despair enacted in *The Triumph of Life*.
What is most to be celebrated in these poets, and their fellow artists of the
Romantic movement as well, is not an encompassing ideological vision, but
that they never remained still, even when formulating structures encompassing ceaseless mental movement. And the preceding chapters as a whole suggest
an even more cautionary injunction against too facile an equation of art and
life among these poets. If poetic forms embody a logic that constrains the
intellect to its dictates and if genres necessarily presuppose that certain values
will be honored over others, even with composite orders—perhaps most
especially with composite orders—such interwoven generic constraints, though
they may well enable creativity, exert a continual ideological pressure on
imaginative vision. That is not to say that a genre constitutes an ideological
absolute. The history of literary genres within the Romantic period suggests
that, whatever the metal from which an artistic superstructure is formed,
even an alloy of intricate molecular complexity, it is always malleable. Bend
it as the poet wills, however, the metal does not change.

And yet, the continuing implication of this discussion, whether involving
sonnets or epics, is that the ideological pressure of a genre can, at least
in the hands of a major artist, be liberating. Classical pastoral offered
Wordsworth a model for a democratic sufficiency of such balanced clarity
that it took him a decade to plumb its implications. An entire generation in
Blake's life as a poet issued from his endeavor to grapple with the logical
possibilities inherent in the epic as it was left by Milton to his successors.
The shift in cultural values that transpired during the Enlightenment
allowed the entire period to reconceive, from a necessary distance, the ethos
of the English Renaissance. In these instances, and many more suggested
by the foregoing pages, recovery stimulated a process of reformation, of

reimagining the past; and that in turn, at least from the midpoint of the eighteenth century to the political realignment that took place between 1827 and 1832, equally prompted the reimagining of the present, which, by the perverse logic of history, had in the Enlightenment lost much of its past and all of its mythology. The received traditions of literature, particularly as channeled through the centuries by their generic momentum, could compensate where other cultural embodiments had been emptied of palpable meaning. Against the failure of myth, the factionalism and proliferation of religious sects, the dissolution of iconographical knowledge, their resilient conceptual syntax kept its integrity and was thus able to counter and assimilate the demythologizing rationalism whose stream forged a new and dangerously rapid tributary in the eighteenth century.

The result was not so much a universally understood program—though there are assuredly contentious manifestos among Romantic poets—as the necessary adjustment of European culture to fundamentally altered circumstances. The peculiar isolation of Britain from the continent coincided, fortuitously it would appear in retrospect, with the pressure of Enlightenment rationalism to create the charged arena of Romanticism in which a skeptical epistemology closed with, and transformed, its literary heritage within a single generation. The Renaissance hierarchy of genres was tested, inverted, then reconstituted through those inverted values. To place that transformation within a sharper ideological and cultural framework, where the literary inheritance had been conceived upon an aristocratic model, resolutely tempered to sacramental purposes, and generally secured against openended philosophical speculations, the shift of underlying cultural values necessarily subjected it to a democratic ethos, a progressive secularization, and the skeptical assumptions of Berkeley and Hume. Byron may disagree profoundly with Wordsworth's sense of the decorum appropriate to such an inversion, asserting the worldly voice of Pope and Gay against a reincarnation of "namby-pamby" Phillips, but he participates in the same process; and, indeed, his entire poetic career, viewed in a glance, is one extended inversion of the traditional genres in order to reconstitute them according to an aristocratic notion of the democratic, secular, and skeptical. As Byron's example suggests, the inherent logic of such a thorough transformation tends to force a genre to pivot on its axis. In such a process of turning inside out, it is no wonder that paradox invests the entire process. Not the least of its results is that the more resistant to altered circumstances are the conventions of a genre, the more likely they are not to be discarded but rather forced into new alliances flaunting their shifted values. Of all the major Romantic poets Byron might be counted the least likely to write a religious quest romance, which, without our overstraining the logic, is probably why he did so. Yet also, as even such a reverse of expectations as this attests, the transformation of generic convention resolves itself in a continual process of testing. The consequences are major and, as the previous pages continually

227

exemplify, they are twofold. Because the constituents of a genre cannot be simply appropriated without question, they become self-conscious in their application, which is to say self-reflexive in their very conception. Moreover, this process of testing also necessarily forces them into organic relationship with the overall artistic purpose, as Coleridge so perceptively argued from his own experience.

We have ourselves inherited a common metaphor for representing at least one element of this studied inversion, which is the mode by which light, enlightenment, is seen to be transmitted by the means of art. There are, on the one hand, mirrors and, on the other hand, lamps; and these two means of representation, which are not in fact means at all but simply metaphorical tropes, imply a rude dichotomy between simple mimesis and a self-conscious creativity. In the rough, this metaphorical extrapolation from the tangled maze of the history of consciousness helps to separate its strands. The accepted function of literature did perceptively shift ground in the eighteenth century, partly because the potential readership and the number of publications both vastly expanded, contributing to and being reinforced by the attendant alteration in cultural values we have been remarking. But to conceive that shift as also involving the spurning of tradition or a disregard for the generic underpinnings of that tradition is to be seduced by the apparent logic implicit in simplistic metaphor. In our own time that logic has become something of a historical assumption, and, unquestionably, there were some few souls in the nineteenth century who also pursued it. It is, however, significant that at least in England those who grasped for such an understanding did so while standing in the perplexing trough of genius that separated a definable Romantic period from what would come to be discerned as the early manifestations of Victorian art. John Stuart Mill's "What is Poetry?" of 1833 and John Keble's lectures from the Oxford Chair of Poetry from 1832 to 1841, published in 1844 as *De poeticae vi medica*, redefine poetry as the mere expression of lyrical emotion, an art of spontaneous overflow empowered by an aesthetic clearly derived from what were mistakenly conceived by the writers to be Wordsworth's notions of his art. That the chief beneficiary of this aesthetic in Great Britain, the short-lived Spasmodic School, bowed in and then out with less effect than the inhabitant of the previous generational trough sixty years earlier, the Della-Cruscan school (of which, it might be said, its lamp was the Spasmodics' mirror), should give us both pause and historical perspective. But, at least with Mill, the cultural ramification has been wrongly construed from the first, for the driving question of his essay is actually the nature of fiction, and it had far more importance for conceiving the ground rules of the Victorian novel as a repository of cultural stresses than for influencing in any lasting way its poetry. As an assessment of Romanticism, it participates in the fantasy by which Browning was to clear ground for his genius, defining the previous two generations as centers of lyric verse and ignoring their notable achievements in narrative poetry. The arguments by which Mill and Keble safely encompassed, and distorted, the poetry of the previous half-century are as transparently indicative of the insecurity of their decade as Shelley's celebration of his culture in the *Defence of Poetry*, separated by a mere dozen years from Mill's essay, is also inimitably of its time. Since, however, Mill and Keble provide the most substantial evidence adduced to promulgate the myth of a generic breakdown in British poetry, they have assumed an importance beyond their intellectual means and a centrality that masks their fearful belatedness.[2]

Yet, to give due credit to the sources of a distorting misapprehension, it is surely possible that the generation that followed the Younger Romantics mistook the remarkable freedom with which they learned to manipulate traditional genres, not the least from the example of Wordsworth and Coleridge themselves, for a total liberation from them. Though attempts to distinguish the two generations of British Romanticism generally founder because of the signal contributions of the older poets to the poetic ferment of the Regency, the patterns discernible from the evidence of the preceding chapters suggest that what may have been tentative generic experiments in the first generation quickly established firm principles for the artistry of the second. Yet against what in retrospective logic might be anticipated— and, perhaps because the logic seems so obvious, it has now been fairly embalmed in customary literary history—the enlarging skepticism of the Younger Romantics paradoxically coincides with an increasing preoccupation with generic possibility. A moment's contemplation should explode the seeming paradox and comprehend why inherited traditions would prove so imperative to a school of poetry that is self-professedly engaged in social and psychological liberation.

Where the Younger Romantics inherit the democratic, secular, and skeptical ethos of their predecessors, an ethos invested in a revitalization of generic traditions, they implicitly assume a notion of genre as both a mode of apprehension and a repository of conflicting values, exemplified in Wordsworth's resurrecting the paradigms of classical pastoral against Renaissance Christian allegory or eighteenth-century aristocratic mannerism. Through all these cultural manifestations, they recognize, the conventions remain and the metal bends to necessity. So from Ephesus to Haija Sophia to St. Peter's, Byron pursues his religious quest. So Keats, in *Hyperion*, juxtaposes the Miltonic fall into knowledge with its equivalent in classical myth. So Shelley, in *Prometheus Unbound*, intrudes a vision of the crucified Christ before the eyes of his hero martyred by Jupiter. As certainly as a conceptual syntax embodies an ideological syntax, it resists any single system of belief; and especially where such systems are brought into confrontation, the syntax allows the contemplation of essential mysteries of human experience through multivalent contexts and a liberating artistic perspective. What we learn from the ubiquity of deconstructive strategies in

British Romantic poetry is that the generic perspective, if the poet is clever enough, can be profoundly exploratory. The art that results is therefore likely to have no purpose beyond that of exploration.

Needless to say, it is a defensible political posture. In an age of reaction, and with a European conflict that seemingly disallowed every alternative to a British compromise that had in those stresses barely held together—that had indeed through those stresses proved that the compromise was more a matter of conventional rhetoric than of law—not to serve, but to stand and wait openly, is perhaps the only comprehensible stance for those who can neither revert to the past nor do more than hope for the future. From our comfortable distance it is easy either to accord faith in a remythologized prospect as though it were a program uniting the culture, or to puncture those seemingly inflated hopes as if unaware that they were, as Shelley said of *Prometheus Unbound*, only saving "idealisms of moral excellence." One extreme of critical perspective inevitably produces its alternative, yet neither ultimately is true to the conditions of the culture.[3] What is profoundly true is that literary traditions, particularly those associated with generic tradition, allowed a neutral, yet critical and self-integrating, stance for poets who stood ineffectually outside it.

What we learn from the concentrated generic transformations of British Romanticism is a simple truth that can be expressed without resort to theoretical jargon or reductive abstractions, which is that art continually recreates life as well as further extensions of art. In one sense or another every poem of substance in the Romantic period reveals the pattern. Form is a refuge from the systems of belief forced, and understandably so, by a culture in siege and at war. It is a link with the past as a conceptual repository, its contents not construed as involving (though it was, of course, the case) even more constricting belief systems, but rather liberating imaginative structures that reaffirm the commitments all of us have to what transcends the necessary limitations of any cultural epoch. Shelley's remark in *A Defence of Poetry* that the poetry of Dante and Milton is essentially distinct from their religious beliefs is characteristic of how we may imagine they were read as well by a great many less candid admirers: "The distorted notions of invisible things which Dante and his rival Milton have idealized, are merely the mask and mantle in which these great poets walk through eternity enveloped and disguised. . . . The Divina Commedia and Paradise Lost have conferred upon modern mythology a systematic form" (pp. 498–499). A different time—indeed, a later time trying to contain the fearful energy released by Humean skepticism—might revert to the repository of traditional Christian paradigms for moral comfort or philosophical distance, as Arnold does in his claims for literary touchstones. But the British Romantics look to genre for a much more radical purpose, to supply a geometry for art that is, or can be made to be, itself both morally neutral and a driving force.

## II

But does that then mean that an isolated Britain, however distinguished the literary productions of its Romanticism, is to occupy a no-man's-land, sharing an identifying term with continental literatures from which it would be better to differentiate it? By no means. And yet the very question suggests that the relationship between British and continental Romanticisms is complex and requires a continual adjustment of cultural perspective if it is to be viewed without distortion. First of all, we have to recognize that Romanticism, conceived as a European phenomenon, lasted well over a century, yet at the same time occurred in national phases. Thus Goethe was already being enthusiastically celebrated as a genius before any of the Italian or French Romantics were born and stood as sage and septuagenarian when the great commotion of French Romanticism began with the *Méditations Poétiques* of Lamartine in 1820. Just four years after that milestone, with the death of Byron, the flowering of British Romanticism had abruptly ceased; but the central figure of the French movement, Victor Hugo, did not die until 1885, leaving, true to his nature as a cultural monument, two epic poems to be published after his death. The anomalies interwoven within such dates could be multiplied considerably but would only underscore the extent to which, even when we identify Romanticism as pan-European, it is keyed to the discrete exigencies of national cultures.[4] And yet the effort to discuss it in a transnational setting inevitably encourages a discourse about what is shared in, rather than what separates, these national Romanticisms, with the result that vital distinctions easily become blurred.

If we attempt to define the movement by contrast, we are bound to renew the polemical debate over classicism and Romanticism, but even that debate is culturally determined, surfacing in Germany in the 1790s, where it occupied something less than a decade of spirited polemics, reerupting in Italy in the 1810s, slightly tinging the British cultural scene at the same time, and then being suddenly resuscitated in France during the 1820s and 30s. The latter, almost comic, gesture of belatedness should alert us to the fact that the dispute between classic and romantic, so vague though noisy in its polemics and so incongruously reconceived within every stirring of national literatures, is a component of Romanticism itself, the surest mark of the self-consciousness by which the movement, in country after country, came to understand its power and to galvanize its momentum. Moreover, on close inspection it is almost impossible to mark a dividing line and identify anticlassical Romantics, at least among the intellectual and artistic giants of the period. In Italy one must rule out Foscolo, who so celebrated his birth on a Greek island that, even without his translation of *The Iliad*, claim might be made for him as Greece's Romantic poet, as well as Leopardi, who prided himself on his ability to read classical Greek poetry with the stylistic discernment of a native-speaker. In Germany we must exclude Hölderlin, who not only reinvented the Greek pantheon but earnestly tried to believe in it, and the arch neo-Hellenists Goethe and Schiller, who defended classicism in the preliminary debate; but also, if we regard Friedrich Schlegel as their chief antagonist, we are faced with the irreducible fact that he was a learned antiquarian, wrote a history of classical poetry, and was by appointment a professor of Sanskrit. The Younger British Romantics all resuscitate classical myth, and it might even be said that Byron gave his life for the sake of a myth he had assiduously deconstructed. It is true that the study of Greek rather gave way to Roman martial arts under Napoleon's empire, but if the posthumous publication of Chenier's bucolics in 1819 offered the French Romantics their point of departure, Hugo's odes a central voice, and Sainte-Beuve's celebration of classical models in the 1840s and 50s a new impetus, the French debate appears to have continued at least into the 1870s when Rimbaud introduced modernism at the age of seventeen. And yet it is entirely symptomatic of this century of debate that the first indication of Rimbaud's prodigious genius was a Latin prize poem written at the age of fourteen.

Even when we locate the classic-romantic debate within Romanticism itself, however, it does not escape the inevitable cultural determinism. Broadly speaking, we might wish to see it in T. S. Eliot's terms, as a confrontation of a tradition and the individual talent, and often that was how the argument ran. But whose tradition and in relation to what talent? Foscolo's conception of himself as neo-Hellenist empowers his writing and, indeed, even mythologizes it in a poetry of endless exile: his Greece is irrecoverable, but incarnate in him. In a sense, that frees Foscolo from other components of literary tradition that any Italian poet must inherit, the quattrocento, and behind it, the heritage of Latin literature. And yet, for Foscolo's countrymen it would appear a specious freedom for a dispirited, partitioned, and repeatedly occupied country—if that term is even applicable—to throw off what gave it identity, continuity, and dignity.

If we cross the Alps, the entire argument shifts. Classical order becomes profoundly antinationalistic, at least as the Schlegels or Madame de Staël represent it. The romantic signifies the northern, the rugged poetry of the heroic past: the pine tree, not the palm, as Heine would succinctly mark the distinction. In generic terms Romanticism is the romance, Germany's indigenous mode, competing with the Homeric and Virgilian epic for literary primacy. Toward the west the issues are more academic and perhaps subtler. The neo-Hellenism of the British Romantics is, as we have continually remarked, an easy inheritance, one already assimilated in the Renaissance, but revived, along with the formidable classical scholarship spearheaded by Richard Porson, as a respectable cloak for skeptical, non-Christian thought. The very late classical revival of France had first to contend with the legacy of the Empire's Roman trappings and then with the academic canon of French literature. Sainte-Beuve's new classicism coincided exactly with the recovery of the French Renaissance, particularly Ronsard.[5] Yet, as the debate raged, it is apparent that both elements became crucial to the liberation the Romantic faction wanted. If classicism is seen as a lapidary, unchanging, and aristocratic order, then it is an aspect of rationalism, or benevolent despotism, or Aquinean Catholicism. But if it resides in the mythmaking of Hesiod, the dynamic energy of Homer, or the erotic spontaneity of Theocritus on the one hand, and on the other the plain honesty of Horace, the brooding double vision of Virgil, or the lyric virtuosity of Catullus, it represents an ancient freedom from the constraints of modern culture. The other side of the European defense of classicism, in other words, is Romanticism.

As British Romanticism constitutes a renaissance of the Renaissance, both a recovery of its earlier literature and of that earlier literary recovery itself, we can reliably transfer the applicability of this entire complex, with due allowance for what the past meant in each national literature and the extent to which it had been obscured, to the whole of western European Romanticism. And if we add to that recognition a balanced awareness that what writers do and what they propound are often distinct, we are also able to extend the significance of traditional forms that we have observed in British Romanticism to the poetic ferment on the continent. There is clearly a link binding British experimentation with genre to Hölderlin's attempts to forge a new free verse form in German from Greek iambs and hexameters and Schiller's recovery of the grand style, to Foscolo's *Odes and Sonnets* of 1803 and his driving Pindaric ode, *Dei Sepolchri*, of 1806, and to the splendid incongruity by which French Romanticism trumpeted its originality in Lamartine's elegies, Hugo's odes, and Musset's epyllions.[6] Yet if we concentrate attention just on the reappropriation and central positioning of the ode in all three cultures, we must acknowledge that what binds these revivals are radically different notions of the form. It is not the same kind in any of them, and even where there are certain correspondences, they are apt to strike us as anomalous rather than as generically constitutive. For instance, the early odes of Coleridge—"Ode to the Departing Year," "France: An Ode"—do share the public themes and hortatory inflations of Hugo's odes of a generation later. Yet, their poetical models are as different as their politics. Coleridge's poems derive their impetus from the political odes— particularly the Whig progress piece—of the British eighteenth century, whereas Hugo's are conditioned by the alexandrine encomium and by seventeenth-century French stage conventions. A new form of the ode will arise among the second group of French Romantics to compete with the grand rhetoric and dramatic postures of Hugo, but it will derive from reclaiming Ronsard, whose odes have nothing in common with Pindar's, to the French literary canon, The Pindaric odes of Hölderlin, Schiller, and Foscolo do stem from a single source but are similarly filtered through very different national understandings of classical form, the former two reconceiving Winkelmann's marble, the latter a Mediterranean passion. The characteristic odes of the later British Romantics, on the other hand, derive their power, as we have noted, from the choral odes of Greek tragedy, converting the oppositional structure of strophe and antistrophe into dialectical rhythms demanding a synthesis that usually the poet is unable or unwilling to effect. In each case Romanticism is dependent not simply on classicism but on versions of classicism that themselves betray the biases of the nation's scholarship and probably its program of education. Even more is this the case with the hymn. We can compare, but it is probably more fruitful to contrast, Novalis's *Hymnen an die Nacht*, Manzoni's *Inni Sacri*, Shelley's "Hymn to Intellectual Beauty," and the hymnic meditations of Lamartine. The religious climate of each culture is so distinct, so enveloped by centuries of national development, and so infused with contemporary European politics that only the fact of the kind itself allows common ground.

The complexity of these formal problems seems far removed from what might appear normative a century before, and therein lies an expansion of the singular paradox observed earlier in the relationship of British Romanticism and the Enlightenment. To survey European literature around 1750 is to discover common ground, something approaching an observed and universal canon over which reigns the flexible Voltaire. It was that because— at least in Britain, France, and Germany—it was so small a cultivated tract. Though neither Italy nor Spain ever lost its principal heritage, in the other three countries Romanticism coincides as a movement with reclaiming the wilderness beyond—which is to say, particularly medieval literature, and in England and France the sixteenth century as centered in Spenser and the Pléiade. The explosion of lyrical forms in Romanticism is exactly the reverse of poetic anarchy; rather, it testifies to the revelation of literary possibility from the past against which the dull sameness of heroic couplets and of bifurcated alexandrines suggested undeserved, long-endured, and wholly unnecessary poverty. Yet at least in the initial stages of this recovery, it is for obvious reasons intensely nationalistic, though connected to a further common ground in the resurgence of classical scholarship. Everywhere in European literature the observed canons were revealed as inadequate to encompass the burden not just, as a strictly historical overview might have it, of startling new material and creative conditions, but of a revived heritage. And after the first wave, national recovery, came its sharing through translation.

Another feature of that early Enlightenment landscape was the codification of generic rules by French arbiters of taste: Boileau, Rapin, Le Bossu *et al.* But again, the British experience is written large when one crosses to the recovery of continental literatures. There were no rules to encompass the verse of the Troubadors and Minnesingern, or the *Niebelungenlied*, or the succession of Italian Orlando poems, or the ballad. Not only had neoclassical categories constricted literature to a small number of approved texts and an implicit hierarchy of genres, but it had through its exclusivity reduced generic possibility itself. The gradual critical enlargement of the number of stipulated genres we observe in England during the eighteenth century occurs throughout Europe as the history of literature was at last understood and for the very first time written. The hegemony of rules could not survive such a test. For a history of national literature is perforce diachronic and evolutionary, even when, as was the case with Bishop Percy and Thomas Warton, it is obsessed with prehistoric sources. To such a history critical arbiters of another culture and an opposite ideology—representing, as it were, a synchronic poetics—were irrelevant. It is not, then, to choose a single case, that the numerous attempts to write a new epic in England and France threw the prescriptions of Le Bossu to the wind. History had done so in the revival of romance throughout Europe. The dialectical relationship between the two perspectives on narrative offered intellectual and artistic challenge, and it was accepted on all sides, first in England and then, with a life force that is truly astonishing, throughout nineteenth-century France, culminating in the posthumous publication of Victor Hugo's unfinished theosophical epics, *La Fin de Satan* and *Dieu*.[7]

To underscore the extent to which European Romanticism grounded itself in an Enlightenment program whose dynamics reached far into the nineteenth century, however, is not to deny major shifts in sensibility and concomitant generic developments in literature. The pastoral, for instance, does not disappear but becomes so transfigured and, so to speak, natural-ized that it takes a second glance to recognize how deeply it embues the exotic landscapes of Hugo's *Orientales*. On the continent, indeed, Words-worthian naturalism is less discernible than Churchill's or Crabbe's austere antipastoral, which only accords with a generation of warfare on Europe's pastoral plains. French Romanticism truly finds its first voice, echoing across the gulf of history, in Chenier's *Bucoliques*, written in prison before his execution under the Terror and first published in 1819. His repre-sentation of the lambs of eighteenth-century aristocracy being led to their slaughter is, arguably, the farthest-reaching of modern antipastorals, inas-much as its inversions mark the doom of an entire culture as well as its unfortunate author. Yet something of its like also emerges in the terrifying calm of Leopardi's "Canto notturno di un pastore errante dell'Asia"—"Night Song of a Wandering Shepherd of Asia." Leopardi's youth was spent in studying the classics, and his career began with translation of the bucolic poetry of Moschus. In the "Canto notturno" he systematically inverts the pastoral conventions he knew by heart: alienation intrudes where we expect fellowship; the nomad's illimitable desert blurs into an infinite sky instead of the *hortus conclusus* of the pastoral bower; the menace of midnight replaces the otium of noon; and even Virgil's melancholy shadows—his reiterated "umbrae"—are exaggerated into an "Abisso orrido, immenso"— the horrid, immense abyss into which all of value disappears. This haunting song of despair, however, issues in a compassion that is exactly commensurate with the assurance of its metrics and the refinement of its style, reproducing the balance between the beauty that sustains and the entropy that threatens in the First *Idyll* of Theocritus and the First *Eclogue* of Virgil. As great pastoral subsumes the antipastoral, insisting on the vulnerability of its enclosed circle, in the "Canto notturno" the circle is expanded to cosmic dimensions and the vulnerability is proportionately infinite.

One notable feature of the European Romantic landscape, self-evident in even the most cursory of surveys, is its remarkable exfoliation of verse forms, both in new patterns of rhyme and meter and revivals of older models. Despite the occasional experiments in prose poetry (such as Aloysius Bertrand's exercises in hortatory medieval exoticism, *Gaspard de la Nuit*) or gestures toward *vers libres* (Hölderlin's neo-Hellenist odes), it is almost impossible to think of unrhymed French and German verse during this period. Indeed, rather than concentrate on Bertrand's self-conscious experimentation, we should recognize its actual context, which is the tyranny—and astonishing resilience—of the alexandrine couplet or quatrain in nineteenth-century French verse. As late as the dazzling surrealism of Rimbaud's "Bateau Ivre" of 1873, its preeminence is taken for granted, so much so that Hugo created an uproar, and eventually his reputation as the national arbiter of poetic taste, by daring to shift the position of its caesura. Rhyme is scarcely the only constituent of poetic form, but especially in reference to German poetry, the mere examples of Eichendorff and Heine, who polished an already glistening marble, should keep the theoretical pronouncements of the Jena school about liberating poetry from its constraints in necessary perspective.[8] So, in fact, might the actual achievements of Friedrich Novalis, all too briefly its major poetic genius. For, though his *Hymns to the Night*, with their combination of breathless, rhapsodic prose and chiselled hymnody, vaunt their freedom from classical restraint, they do so from within the framework of Gothic lyricism provided Novalis by medieval German mystical poetry and the Christian meditative tradition. In Italy, significantly, the formal terms are wholly different. To unrhyme Italian verse seems to have been a cultural effort going back at least to Dante; so the relative delicacy of a Leopardi in this respect, and his concern for refined syllabic symmetries, have their indigenous cultural underpinnings that mirror these other constants.

It is true that rhyme and meter can be freely reconstituted for the circumstances of the moment and therefore have no necessary connection with the long tradition of European poetry, with generic expectation, or with the example of precursors. Yet, if we look specifically at the kinds of continuities in form examined in the early chapters, we discover not only their presence but even more importantly their revival and dissemination across national boundaries. The sonnet in England, as we have traced its path, has a truly resilient formal continuity. It had a potent prehistory for Italian poets as well, much less so for the French (who recovered the form before resuscitating its French history), and virtually none for the Germans. Yet, given that disparity, what we can immediately observe as a constant of comparative Romanticism, without quibble or cultural adjustment, is the ubiquity of sonnets on the sonnet, a self-reflexive subgenre containing multitudes. The epigraph to this chapter, Goethe's sonnet "Natur und Kunst," is a studied import, proclaiming Goethe's adherence to a pan-European literary tradition and, in effect, Germany's union with it: "Und das Gesetz nur kann uns Freiheit geben": only that law will give German poetry its freedom. Wordsworth's independent view in "Nuns fret not at their Convent's narrow room," the prefatory sonnet to his 1807 collection, is exactly congruent, even to the adoption of the same imagery of confinement: "In truth, the prison, unto which we doom / Ourselves, no prison is." In the perspective of Goethe's sonnet, Wordsworth's resolute return to the nature of the Petrarchan and Miltonic sonnet forms in his 1807 volumes, to ground their dynamics in the psychology of perception, takes on added resonance. Wordsworth's use of the form as a metaphor for the self's reaching out to center space and time, to effect a unity between the mundane and supernal, is not only uncannily what it enacts, but, as with Goethe's sonnet, a statement about the nature of art itself. His comparison of the sonnet to an orbicular construction, the cosmos of a drop of dew, nicely invokes the geometric shape that, in Marshall Brown's view, haunts German Romanticism, particularly among the Jena school.[9] Though not so systematically self-reflexive as Wordsworth, Foscolo appears to have something of the same ends in mind in the sonnets he published in 1803, where the form becomes a bridge that reunites the isolated voice with human and mythic continuities from which it has been exiled. In England during the Regency, as we have seen, Leigh Hunt took up the quiet intensities with which Wordsworth had invested the form and domesticated it to his suburban circle, and Keats and Shelley in turn stretched its newly discovered elasticity to see just how much of the sublime could be held and intensified within its constraints. But Wordsworth's most striking influence is unexpected, for Sainte-Beuve also seems to have drawn from his sonnets possibilities for the domestication of the poetic voice. His introduction of the sonnet into French Romanticism had far-reaching consequences.[10] Nerval converted its polarities into an enclosed tabernacle enshrining symbolic mystery. Baudelaire similarly found in the sonnet what he called a "Pythagorean beauty" and through his long career continually elaborated its "constraining form" to reach a "more intense idea" of inherent correspondences.[11] And, deliberately following in their wake, finally Mallarmé compacted the sonnet into the oxymoronic *tombeau* of an art sustaining its vitality within an impenetrable labyrinth. Indeed, with French symbolism the sonnet is converted from the Miltonic reaching out toward cultural ideals into the embodiment of an art without relationship to anything else but its own dynamics. In an art that exists for its own sake, form is essential.

Yet that very fact should underscore why form was so inescapable a necessity for Romantic subjectivity, a ground for either commitment or disengagement, but always a ground for self-mirroring and self-creation. And simple logic would suggest the necessity within such a dialectical field of a complementary mirroring and recreation of the predicated other as well. Hence the crucial importance of Coleridge's definition of "organic form" as art's "self-witnessing and self-effected sphere of agency." What Coleridge's term presents, and what Romanticism as a whole wanted to embrace, was the challenge of definition from the inside out, in life as in art. Sonnets are not written according to Petrarchan rules but according to the inherent dynamics and geometery of the form (to which Petrarch's own understanding is of course a guide), and that in essence is the most universal urge of generic development throughout Western literature. The sonnet's prominence throughout Romanticism and its remarkable candor in artistic self-reflexiveness make it a simple index to the nature of poetic form in culture after culture. Its history in the nineteenth century, with the necessary adjustments made for formal continuities and experiments, is replicated in the ode, the elegy, the ballad, the romance, the epic, and in every shade between.

Yet, its history also traces a growing disengagement, an involution into formal self-witnessing as a refuge from bourgeois culture, that could not have been intended by the Enlightenment renaissance, even if it was, by the strange quirks of history, its principal inheritance for modernism. The customary division of nineteenth-century French poetry between Romanticism and Symbolism, though notoriously hard to place, testifies to a general awareness that Romanticism, though forced to wait out the Napoleonic Wars, did not embrace its disengagement with pleasure or with pride. Indeed, generally speaking, it turned to art as a resource of forms of intellectual power, as a means to reconceive and expand a European conceptual syntax too restrictive to accommodate the new historical forces represented by the French Revolution. For Romanticism form became a guarantor of intellectual freedom, at once a framework for psychological exploration and a means, through reimagining the past, to enlarge future possibilities. Although the past chapters have indicated numerous ways in which this was accomplished, here at the end we might contemplate two opposite strategies—the one deconstructive and the other modelled on the total organization of scientific system—which, in their sum, demonstrate how imperative formal means were to the Romantic enterprise and how intellectually liberating was the result.

*The Fall of Hyperion*, composed at the end of Keats's tragically foreshortened career and resonant with the knowledge of what impends, bears witness through its strategies of ideological displacement to an intellectual bravery that will neither succumb to convention nor pretend to its irrelevance. The poem represents Keats's reassimilation and testing of the values tentatively asserted in the fragmentary trial of *Hyperion* a year and a half before. Yet this second fragment, even if it is far more intense in its multiple confrontations, never even approaches the point of forcing the cosmological impasse upon which the original poem faltered. The shift of generic models is the key. For the supposedly objective truths of epic tradition Keats substitutes the mode insinuated upon the genre by Dante, the dream vision, which forestalls distance and accentuates the ways in which truths are perceived and ordered within the mind.

But the genre is adopted only to be insistently questioned even as it organizes the poem. The first episode within its fiction is the poet's dream of a deserted Eden, our most primordial of cultural myths and memories, which, simply because it is so unavailing of satisfaction, gives way to a second and antithetical dream. There the poet comes upon dispossessed collosi, who, with their strange mythic distance, embody our exclusion from the paradise at the infancy of our cultural and psychological development— or our primal alienation. After a struggle to attain an equilibrium, figured as a matter of life or death (and perhaps, after all, that is exactly what it is), the poet looks deeply within the inarticulate eyes of Moneta and is afforded his third vision, which appears to be the culminating one. For a month, immobile, he contemplates the similarly immobile and inarticulate Titans, lost like them in an extended daydream in the twilight of the gods. Yet, whatever internal recognitions might have been elicited by that reverie are never articulated: they constitute a marked resemblance to the deep eyes of Moneta into which the poet stares and upon which he is reflected. As an oracle Moneta has nothing whatsoever to tell; she only parts the curtains on a scene, where, though we assume it to be a *tableau vivante*, nothing occurs through the month-long vigilance. Yet she does speak before unveiling this enigmatic vision, and then it is to question the understanding and pronouncements of "dreamers weak," which, if we have managed to keep our bearings in this conceptual labyrinth, is to question the very dream in which she appears. As it starts to assimilate the cosmic myth of the earlier poem, *The Fall of Hyperion* breaks off, having intimated a majesty and a portent of meaning that it will not allow us to delimit. Relatively short as it is, it offers an accumulation of visions, not just those described but also those far interwoven in the vortex of their succession, all displacing meaning into a further interior, transferring symbolic import to that distance which is never reached. The effect is exactly, yet symmetrically, opposite to the breaking-point of the original experiment, *Hyperion*, where Apollo is left forever in the process of coming convulsively to a knowledge neither he nor we will ever comprehend.

The state in which *The Fall of Hyperion* suspends its discourse, if such a term applies where there is no reality principle in evidence, is either a plenum of too many visions compacted or a vacuum in which all are mutually canceling, a visionary intensity or a visionless emptiness. In either case it is a state that questions the value of its own enterprise as sharply as Moneta —or as formatively as does its own preliminary premise: "Fanatics have dreams." The proem frames the dream vision by questioning its value, and the dreams accumulate without answer. They all begin from the inception of Cartesian mental process: "Methought I stood where trees of every clime. . . ." The enclosed and self-referential mind contemplates the paradise of its own elaboration—its desperate, never-satisfied need—and can assert but one sole assurance, that it thinks, or that in doing so, it once forced a poem to be conceived: "Methought." The term, removed from the present moment by its tense no less than its archaism, by its nature implies self-questioning, and in its purity introduces us to visions that elaborate that self-questioning beyond the point where any answer is ascertainable. Is there then no truth in these embedded enigmas, no assurance that impels us forward? The very recognition of the reader's momentum ironically enforces what is the one solemn certainty that we can ever know from *The Fall of Hyperion*, which is at least a more comforting truth than is to be gleaned from the similarly involuted fragment of a dream vision with which Shelley ended his career. In "The Triumph of Life" Shelley looks metaphor directly in its face and recognizes that there may be nothing else. Keats's vision pursues the larger conflation of values, the conceptual syntax that is genre, affirming that there is in human history a legacy of dream visions, all of which testify to a genuine desire for universal truth, and which are, by the nature of art, composed of and recognized by conventions that are utterly arbitrary. That they have no intrinsic meaning Keats is at pains to demonstrate, but that they allow him to structure a poem that represents the deeper and deeper search for ultimate certainties is a value to be exemplified, even self-reflexively celebrated. "There is a budding morrow in midnight" he claimed on behalf of the blind bardic visionary who impelled Western literature on its course through endless traces of imaginative conception. Having characteristically represented an oxymoron at the very inception of generic traditions, Keats pursues his fascination with the Phoenix that forever survives its own consuming in this complicated visionary experience in which he juxtaposes multiple planes of reality, all of which are traditionally sanctioned and all of which, even as they deny what they affirm, leave untouched the shrine of affirmation they can never reach. That shrine is the embodiment of human desire that systems of belief may ultimately codify but that visions empower and genres organize. The seemingly arbitrary structures that compose the genres of literature are the means by which a poet realizes what in another context Keats called the negative capability of art. Genres allow an imaginative creation to be compounded of "uncertainties, Mysteries, doubts" (*Letters*, I, 193) and even, in the extreme case of *The Fall of Hyperion*, to embody a charged fullness empty of defined meaning, only and profoundly capable.

At the opposite pole from this fragment of dissipating visions lies the most extensive composite order of European Romanticism, Goethe's *Faust*, almost a lifelong undertaking, only finished within the year of the poet's death. Whether or not its multitude of scenes, composed over so many years, all quite fit together, it is the supreme example of *genera mixta* in all of literature, the consummate *Gesammtkunstwerk*. As the defense of the mixed genre invariably rested, Tasso states it clearly, on the poet's duty to create a heterocosm of God's universe in all its varied majesty and contradiction, so Goethe, though he hedged somewhat on the vexed question of God, pursues a like aim. He does so, first, through deliberately embodying and reconciling the debate between Romantic and classical ideals in the elaborate parallels he draws between Christian and Hellenistic structures of thought and art in the two parts of *Faust* and, second, through the most ambitious reclamation of genres that exists in literature. It is sufficiently ambitious that *Faust* should attempt to revitalize every mode of drama practiced on Western stages, from its double prologue to the opera libretto conceived for one scene of Part II. (Goethe went so far as to inquire of Meyerbeer whether he had time to volunteer his services and furnish the required music.) Even more striking, however, is the panoply of verse forms and of their attendant decorums with which he invests the work: though, as it were, the figured bass of *Faust* is provided by the heroic couplet conventional to the German stage, one scene is written in the stately alexandrine of French neoclassical tragedy, and an entire act recreates Greek tragic decorum. These form a backdrop to interpolated verse forms of almost every variety imaginable: from the antique balladry of "The King of Thule" to the homely *Knittelvers* of folk tradition to the breathless lyrical effusion in dimeter of "Gretchen am Spinnrade"—and even, with startling appropriateness, to one scene being composed in prose to render the moment of Faust's total demoralization in Part I. It is not simply a multitude of genres and forms that are thus assimilated, but with them the concerns of every major religion of the West from primitive cult worship to ethical culture, the range of human sciences, and the vision of Europe's greatest poets as well: Euripides in Act Three of Part II, Dante in the final scene, even in the Euphorion episode the touching tribute to Byron.

The result goes beyond anything contemplated in Wordsworth's term composite order. Rather, Goethe aspires, in Angus Fletcher's phrase, to a "transcendental form," reaching for the infinity of human potentiality that was the subject of his art for sixty years. For Goethe the human lot is a continual striving to become—"immer streben"—against all odds and through every conceivable form. Goethe's attempt to rear a Gothic cathedral from the page, *Faust* in the multiple perfections of its parts incarnates the "Alles Vergängliche" of its final chorus, that "something ever more about to be" that Wordsworth characterized as human destiny and that a later time would come to see as a credo of Romanticism. Goethe poured his life, his art, and an encyclopedic learning into that capacious mold in the faith that it might contain even what he might only imagine and everything he could hope to know. And every block in its construction is a form retrieved, rethought, transformed. In this, as it is the grandest, it is also the exemplary conception of European Romanticism.

# Notes

1 Goethe's sonnet translates literally as follows: "Nature and Art—they appear to diverge, but before one even considers it turn out to be the same. For me their contention has disappeared; both seem to attract me equally. Only honest exertion has real value! And if, first having set time aside, we have bound ourselves in spirit and purpose to our art, then Nature will once again be able to stir the heart. So all things under formation are constituted. In vain will liberated spirits strive for a fulfillment of pure heights. Who desires great things must make great effort. Through restriction one proves oneself a master, and only law can give us freedom."

2 With all respect for the value of M. H. Abrams's *The Mirror and the Lamp: Romantic Theory and the Critical Tradition* (New York: Oxford University Press, 1953), its argument that Romanticism participated in a proto-Crocean expressionism, so strongly based on this evidence, has had a widespread and deleterious influence, especially as the putative evidence was gathered into a college handbook under the title of *Romantic Criticism: 1800–1850*, edited by R. A. Foakes (London: Edwin Arnold, 1968). Needless to assert, the evidence supporting the present argument is pointedly to the contrary and implies the need to rewire (or re-fuse) this as yet blazing Romantic lamp.

3 I refer to the scholarly controversy over "the Romantic ideology," a term that furnishes the title for Jerome McGann's refreshing critique of an earlier generation's willingness to raise to ideological certainties what are culturally determined and tentative celebrations of the imaginative propensities of an embattled humanity (*The Romantic Ideology* [Chicago: University of Chicago Press, 1983]). Such an antithetical statement, however, tends to reinforce a dialectic founded on erroneous assumptions, for, as McGann argues, there never existed an independent entity to be construed by this term.

4 Aside from numerous indigenous historical determinants, the way each culture defined its literary canon profoundly influenced its Romanticism. On this aspect one should consult Ernst Robert Curtius' magisterial and cautionary account, "Modern Canon Formation," in *European Literature and the Latin Middle Ages* (1948), tr. Willard B. Trask (New York: Harper and Row, 1953), pp. 264–272.

5 See Margaret Gilman, *The Idea of Poetry in France from Houdar de la Motte to Baudelaire* (Cambridge: Harvard University Press, 1958), pp. 178–189, and Ruth E. Mulhauser, *Sainte-Beuve and Greco-Roman Antiquity* (Cleveland: Press of Case Western Reserve University, 1969).

6 Though Gilman (*The Idea of Poetry in France*, p. 162) argues that "Hugo with the ode, Lamartine with the elegy, Vigny with the 'poëme,' had created great poetry, because they had applied their talents to genres of which the French language offered either no examples or inadequate ones," at least with Hugo generic choices are also profoundly ideological. Laurence M. Porter rightly remarks that "Hugo's theoretical statements in his prefaces to the *Odes* clearly show that he associated the Ode form with the Ancien Régime. Progressively as he evolves from monarchical views towards liberalism, he experiences the ode as inadequate for his poetic vision"—*The Renaissance of the Lyric in French Romanticism: Elegy, "Poëme" and Ode* (Lexington, Kentucky: French Forum, 1978), p. 86.

7 For this history, with a chronological bibliography appended, consult Herbert J. Hunt, *The Epic in Nineteenth-Century France; a study in heroic and humanitarian poetry from* Les martyrs *to* Les siècles morts (Oxford: Blackwell, 1941).

8 The Jena circle of the 1790s, including Novalis, Wackenroder, and preeminently Friedrich Schlegel, from which we derive an Idealist Romantic poetics, represented their aesthetic of liberated poetry in the short-lived periodicals, *Atheneum* and *Lyceum*. Since contemporaneously Goethe and Schiller were developing their notions of a new classicism, it is perhaps natural for later historians to see in the *Atheneumsfragmente* the foundations of a Romantic aesthetics. But a meticulous historicism must paint a more complicated picture. Insofar as these figures were known outside Germany, they were represented by Madame de Staël's *De l'Allemagne* of 1810 in a suggestive but necessarily superficial fashion. Though her account spurred the classic-romantic debate, the ideas of the Jena circle were virtually ignored by Italian culture, generally disavowed by British empiricism and skepticism, and rather splendidly distorted the minute they crossed the borders into the France of the Bourbon Restoration. We might even infer that Schlegel's circle had a comparatively minor influence on the actual achievements of German Romanticism, since for all its energetic spirit of creative innovation, its pronouncements came a quarter of a century after Goethe's own fame was established, and he and Schiller dominated the European view of German Romanticism. Against those titanic presences the effusion of brilliant but gnomic ideas either in short-lived periodicals, through an extensive but unpublished correspondence, or in untranslated philosophical lectures could not compete on a European stage—nor, for that matter, among the general reading public of the German-speaking states. In order to avoid a serious distortion of the record in the interest of theoretical paradigms, the experimentation of the Schlegel circle needs to be grounded in this large pan-European perspective, rather than Romanticism be cut to the proportions of the circle—an enthusiastic avant-garde of a kind that the ensuing century would see recreated repeatedly in Paris. Even so, even at its most radically innovative, this circle was obsessed with the nature and uses of artistic form, and Schlegel himself, in his prescription for criticism, firmly acknowledged that "The determination of the genre and structure, of the general proportions and the limitations of a work of art is ... one of the preparatory labors of actual critical evaluation." See Hans Eichner, "Friedrich Schlegel's Theory of Literary Criticism," in *Romanticism Today*, a collection of diverse essays without stipulated editor (Bonn-Bad Godesburg: Inter Nationes, 1973), p. 24.

9 *The Shape of German Romanticism* (Ithaca: Cornell University Press, 1979).

10 John Porter Houston, *The Demonic Imagination: Style and Theme in French Romantic Poetry* (Baton Rouge: Louisiana State University Press, 1969), pp. 51–53.

11 See Baudelaire, *Correspondance générale*, ed. Jacques Crepet (Paris: L. Conard, 1947–1953), III, 39.

# 12

# 'THE MIND WHICH FEEDS THIS VERSE': SELF- AND OTHER-AWARENESS IN SHELLEY'S POETRY

## Michael O'Neill

Source: *Durham University Journal* 85 (1993), 273–92.

## 1

Why are Shelley's poems often about writing poetry, even as they are about many other things than writing poetry? The present essay argues that this reflexiveness reveals Shelley to be, in a high and embattled sense of the word, a poet, and a poet of crisscrossing perspectives — not a philosopher manqué, not a (heterodox) theologian manqué, not a political theorist manqué. To be a poet involves, for Shelley, an impassioned but complicated trust in the imagination and its products. If, in addition, it involves a sophisticated 'belief in the autonomy of art', such belief is in contact with doubt.[1] Faced by the question 'What is the value of poetry?', *A Defence of Poetry* retorts that poetry is the source of value. Yet close to the heart of the 'crisscrossing perspectives' explored by Shelley are questions about the worth of poetry. The 'belief' and 'autonomy' just mentioned are the reverse of untried; nor are they indicative of facile anti-rationalism or narrowly formalist self-delight. It is more the case that Shelley is alert to the creative, yet at times potentially deconstructive, nature of the medium through which his concerns — often related to philosophy, religion, and politics — shape themselves. Poetry, he writes in *A Defence of Poetry*, 'transmutes all that it touches, and every form moving within the radiance of its presence is changed by wondrous sympathy to an incarnation of the spirit which it breathes';[2] this process of 'change' and 're-incarnation' is frequently both mode and subject in Shelley's poetry.

The drama of Shelley's career as a poet arises out of his uncomplacent and evolving recognition of the cultural significance of poetry. Even as late as 1819 some depreciation of poetry is evident: 'I consider Poetry very sub-ordinate to moral & political science'.[3] But when that comment's addressee (Thomas Love Peacock) insisted wittily in *The Four Ages of Poetry* (1820) on poetry's subordination to other intellectual pursuits, Shelley was needled into sorting out his view of the relative merits of analytical thinkers and poets:

> The exertions of Locke, Hume, Gibbon, Voltaire, Rousseau, and their disciples, in favour of oppressed and deluded humanity, are entitled to the gratitude of mankind. Yet it is easy to calculate the degree of moral and intellectual improvement which the world would have exhibited, had they never lived. [ ... ] But it exceeds all imagination to conceive what would have been the moral condition of the world if neither Dante, Petrarch, Boccaccio, Chaucer, Shakespeare, Calderon, Lord Bacon, nor Milton, had ever existed [ ... ]; and if the poetry of the religion of the antient world had been extinguished together with its belief.
>
> (*PP*, p. 502)

Here the voice that is great in Romanticism rises up. Shelley's defence of poetry dexterously entwines the utilitarian (poetry is important because it appeals to the imagination) and the aesthetically autonomous (poetry is at once superior to and the awakening force which makes possible 'analyti-cal reasoning' (*A Defence of Poetry*, *PP*, p. 502)). The author of *A Defence of Poetry* has travelled a long way from the youthful would-be agitator of February 1812, whose head was full of 'downright proposals for instituting assoc {i} ations for bettering the condition of human kind' (*Letters*, I, 255). By 1821 Shelley was not a political quietist, but he had arrived at the posi-tion that beneficial changes in opinion or institution involve the exercise of sympathy and imagination. To the degree that poets can both work on the imagination of their readers and offer paradigms of meaning and value, they 'are the unacknowledged legislators of the World' (*PP*, p. 508). The initial form of Shelley's sentence, a year or so before it was recycled in *A Defence of Poetry*, was 'Poets and philosophers are the unacknowledged legislators of the world'.[4] However, in the later work philosophy is seen as subordinate to or subsumed within poetry. Apparent philosophers such as Plato and Lord Bacon are praised for being essentially poets (*PP*, pp. 484–85). It is because Shakespeare, Dante, and Milton are great poets that they are also 'philosophers of the very loftiest power' (*PP*, p. 485). If, then, philosophy takes on an honourable but secondary role in *A Defence of Poetry*, religion is viewed by the same work as a codification of the intuitions and insights of poets, at best a 'partial apprehension of the agencies of the invisible world' (*PP*, p. 482); it is 'the *poetry* of the religion of the antient world' (emphasis added) which is of enduring significance, not its 'belief'.

Conceivably, the foregoing account of Shelleyan poetics might be found guilty by some of 'uncritical absorption in Romanticism's own self-representations'.[5] Yet, as indicated above, Shelley's absorption in his own representations is far from uncritical. The privileged position given by Shelley to poetry consciously places on it as well an immense burden. 'A shadow tracks thy flight of fire' (l. 3) says the First Spirit in 'The Two Spirits — An Allegory', and the self-descriptive dimension of the line is applicable to the anxieties inseparable from Shelley's affirmations about poetry. *A Defence of Poetry* celebrates poetry as a 'vitally metaphorical' power which 'marks the before unapprehended relations of things, and perpetuates their apprehension', but laments the restraints imposed by what Shelley calls the 'limitedness of the poetical faculty itself' (*PP*, pp. 482, 504).[6] And yet anxiety does not simply undermine affirmation; rather, the two impulses coexist in a state of productive interaction. 'These words are inefficient and metaphorical — Most words so — No help', Shelley jotted against a sentence in 'On Love' (*PP*, p. 474n.2). His greatest poetry, however, thrives on the 'metaphorical' nature of language, the fact that it is involved in a perpetual process of substitution and approximation. 'What thou art we know not; / What is most like thee?' (ll. 31–32): the famous lines from 'To a Sky-Lark' articulate a creatively enabling formula, one that brings out the close alliance between self- and other-awareness in Shelley's poetry. The pressure exerted by awareness that he is writing poetry often accompanies the impression conveyed through his language of awareness of otherness. The sonnet 'Upon the wandering winds', the first poem in the Scrope Davies Notebook, explores and embodies in the intricate syntax of its single sentence the relations between otherness (including the linguistic 'grace' achieved by other poets) and consciousness (including the awareness of writing poetry); the poet describes how his 'thoughts have swept' (l. 10) upon and over their objects

> until they have resigned
> — Like lutes enforced by the divinest thrall
> Of some sweet lady's voice — that which my mind
> (Did not superior grace in others shown
> Forbid such pride) would dream were all its own.
>
> (l. 10–14)[7]

The writing is responsive to negotiations between self- and other-awareness; the 'they' of line 10 might be 'thoughts' or their objects ('wandering winds' (l. 1), 'waves of Ocean' (l. 2) and so on); 'resigned' means 'released' or 'given back' in the view of the Longman editors,[8] but it also hints at the 're-signing', the reshaping of identity through language, which takes place in a poem. The poet is tempted to dream that the product of his mind's creative interaction with otherness is 'all its [his mind's] own'; and yet the awareness of 'superior grace in others shown' half-forbids him from doing so: 'half-forbids' because the last line's verbal organization plays against its

sense; we end with the dreamed state, not with the self-censoring prohibi-
tion. However, that recognition of 'superior grace in others' saves the poem
from solipsism. The phrase will admit of the construction placed on it above,
according to which the 'grace' is that achieved by other poets (such as
Byron). At the same time, it trawls its net more widely and deeply, inviting
the reader to consider the variety of ways in which the 'grace' of 'others'
might rebuke the poet caught up in the process of poetic composition.

The fact that Shelley can view language as both imagination's medium and
a form of otherness, embodying the assumptions of a culture with which he
was frequently at odds, suggests how fluid and mutually interrogating the
categories of self- and other-awareness are in his work.[9] Coleridge's notion
of *'outness'* — 'Language & all *symbols* give *outness* to Thoughts / & this the
philosophical essence & purpose of Language /'[10] — supposes a greater bin-
ary stability in the relationship between inside and outside, 'Thoughts' and
'Language', than exists for a poet who can write 'speech created thought'
(*Prometheus Unbound*, II. iv. 72), yet who can also assert that 'the most
glorious poetry that has ever been communicated to the world is probably a
feeble shadow of the original conception of the poet' (*A Defence of Poetry*,
*PP*, p. 504). Similarly, Shelley's sense of self and other is often subject to
deconstruction and redefinition. 'On Life' speaks with longing of 'the state
called reverie' which makes those who experience it 'feel as if their nature
were dissolved into the surrounding universe, or as if the surrounding universe were absorbed into their being. They are conscious of no distinction'
(*PP*, p. 477). In this case the writing's grammar, employing subjects who
feel (even if they feel they are no longer subjects), implies that dissolution of
boundaries between self and other is elusive, even un(re)capturable. Shelley
is often at his best when he is working in this area in which boundaries are
under assault, yet still in play, as in the following passage from *Epipsychidion*:

> The glory of her being, issuing thence,
> Stains the dead, blank, cold air with a warm shade
> Of unentangled intermixture, made
> By Love, of light and motion: one intense
> Diffusion, one serene Omnipresence,
> Whose flowing outlines mingle in their flowing,
> Around her cheeks and utmost fingers glowing
> With the unintermitted blood, which there
> Quivers, (as in a fleece of snow-like air
> The crimson pulse of living morning quiver,)
> Continuously prolonged, and ending never,
> Till they are lost, and in that Beauty furled
> Which penetrates and clasps and fills the world;
> Scarce visible from extreme loveliness.
>
> (ll. 91–104)

In a way that is typical of Shelley's most distinguished poetry, the writing here sets going multiple frictions. The sense that words are inadequate to capture 'The glory of her being' collides with an exhilarated intricacy that implies words can glimpse what it is that they wish to apprehend. Again, the impulse to absorb the particular (itself a category that the writing interrogates as well as ratifies) within some absolute ('that Beauty') provokes an instant swerve that establishes the absolute as at best provisional. Shelley returns a few lines later to the individual presence sparking off and defeating his poetry ('See where *she* stands!' (l. 112, emphasis added)); such an act of attention is made to seem at once impossible and necessary. Pervading the passage is a tussle between self-awareness and other-awareness, the two energies briefly coalescing in 'Scarce visible from extreme loveliness', a line which describes the impact of the poem's figurative activity and the effect of 'The glory of her being'. The passage may seem to be vulnerable to a feminist critique that saw in it only the (undesirable) workings of male desire; but Shelley does not simply objectify, or reify the otherness of, the 'she' addressed here. Traces of a latter-day Petrarchism are certainly apparent in the passage. Yet the composure of the gazing subject is ecstatically disrupted; by foregrounding the very difficulty of 'seeing', the passage — like the poem — displays a continual, if subliminal, awareness of the dangers, as well as the imperatives, of idealizing desire.

## 2

I propose now to establish a rough-and-ready taxonomy of kinds of poetic self-awareness by looking at three passages, one each from Byron, Keats, and Wallace Stevens. The passage from Byron is the famous cancelled stanza, printed as a headpiece to *Don Juan* in the 1832–33 edition of Byron's poetry; the stanza seems to me better read as one of the great Romantic short lyrics:

> I would to Heaven that I were so much Clay —
> As I am blood — bone — marrow, passion — feeling —
> Because at least the past were past away —
> And for the future — (but I write this reeling
> Having got drunk exceedingly to day
> So that I seem to stand upon the ceiling)
> I say — the future is a serious matter —
> And so — for Godsake — Hock and Soda water.[11]

The pivot of these lines is 'but I write this reeling'. The High Romantic self with its yearnings, passion, and angst is sent sprawling as the rhyme of 'feeling' with 'reeling' tricksily sticks its foot out. It is less that the highflown is deflated by the authentic than that one form of representation gives way to another. 'Don't suppose I'm a boringly inky scribbler', the lines say, and yet the ex-Regency roué is also a self-conscious poet. If the very force of Byron's opening puts consciousness under pressure (he is already longing to be immune to sensation, to be 'so much Clay'), what scuppers a particular flight of consciousness is a moment of heightened self-consciousness. In turn, self-consciousness sees itself in 'this', the words formulating themselves before the reader, taking on a life that is independent of the poet even as he admits or boasts that he is composing. Byron's achievement is to persuade his reader that the poem knows that the creating self is at the mercy of the protean energies — linguistic and experiential — which it seeks to control. Which is to say that the Byronic self is always creatively provisional, much as Shelley's awareness in *Prometheus Unbound* that 'a voice / Is wanting' (II. iv. 115–16) stimulates the poet's imaginings in the act of suggesting their ultimate inadequacy.

The cancelled stanza quoted above has the desperate exuberance — or should that be exuberant despair? — typical of Byronic self-awareness in *Don Juan*. 'I write this reeling' sends a charge through surrounding lines; like many moments in Romantic poetry it discovers that the poet can only be himself by virtue of rhetorical illusion. 'Words are things' Byron says in the third canto of *Don Juan* (stanza 88); but 'things', such as Byron's pick-me-up — 'Hock and Soda water' — are words. The poet's comic dismay at the complicated dualisms of experience — 'And so — for Godsake' — takes its part in the order that the stanza shapes out of chaos, as it glances wryly at the seemingly heartfelt prayer at the start: 'I would to Heaven'. This feeling of order emerging out of the haphazard contingencies of composition extends to minute details, and explains the half-parodic 'rightness' achieved by the chime of 'And *so*' with '*So*da water'. The stanza's amused sense of its own existence is at once irreverent and poised, alert to the claims of the non-poetic and drawing them into its verbal orbit.

It is, for all its nonchalance, a moment of poetic self-definition. So is my second example, which is drawn from the end of the opening of Keats's *The Fall of Hyperion* when, brooding on his capacities as a poet and the nature of the poem about to get under way, Keats writes:

> Whether the dream now purposed to rehearse
> Be poet's or fanatic's will be known
> When this warm scribe my hand is in the grave.[12]

These lines exemplify self-awareness involved in trial, imaginative ordeal. They go out of their way to avoid the personal, employing a passive construction in 'will be known'; but that 'warm scribe my hand' extends itself with startling intimacy. The reader can almost shake it, or take the pulse of its wrist, and yet its reality is chillingly virtual. The phrasing does justice to the paradoxes that Keats is grappling with. The hand though warm now

249

will have its productions tested when it is cold, when the life that now gives its warmth to, will have been absorbed by, a work whose theme is the desire to die into the life of an achieved poem. The warm scribe will record the deathly cold experienced by Keats as he seeks to advance towards poetic self-discovery: 'the cold / Grew stifling, suffocating, at the heart' (I, 129–30). As a 'scribe' the hand both mediates between 'dream' and 'script', and serves as the instrument by which the former dwindles into, while it is realized by, the latter.[13] The effect is liminal, placing poet and reader on the threshold of ordeal and crisis; yet the lines are an absolute achievement; they compel the reader's attention and so generate the very relationship which they fear will not come into being.

My third example, Wallace Stevens's 'Tea at the Palaz of Hoon', illustrates self-awareness as fictive play, and has a super-agile inwardness about its own procedures:

> Not less because in purple I descended
> The western day through what you called
> The loneliest air, not less was I myself.
>
> What was the ointment sprinkled on my beard?
> What were the hymns that buzzed beside my ears?
> What was the sea whose tide swept through me there?
>
> Out of my mind the golden ointment rained,
> And my ears made the blowing hymns they heard.
> I was myself the compass of that sea:
>
> I was the world in which I walked, and what I saw
> Or heard or felt came not but from myself;
> And there I found myself more truly and more strange.[14]

The writing ensures that the reader will be prompted to allegorize this as a poem about writing poetry and the self constituted in the act of writing poetry. And yet to do so, as though in doing so one had plucked out the heart of its mystery, feels reductive. What is distinctive about the poem is the way its teasing, sumptuous music plays round themes of difference and identity, self and otherness, fiction and reality, metaphor and referentiality. The sceptical reader, or a sceptical aspect of the poet, is allowed a coolly mocked voice in 'through what you called / The loneliest air', where the *de haut en bas* inflection of 'what you called' suggests that to call the air 'loneliest' is to misconceive the predicament of the 'I'. The mock-liturgical question and answer routine of the next two stanzas allows Hoon his resplendent affirmations. But, as Harold Bloom observes, Hoon 'is *not* a solipsist, because the "there" of his world is an arena in which he is at work finding himself'.[15] Though 'I was the world in which I walked' collapses any distinction between self and world, the 'self/world' newly composed is still a 'there', a new place in which 'I found myself more truly and more strange'. 'There' liberates the poem from the cell of self-concern, and can be seen as language, that common possession which the poet has just, before the reader's very eyes, used with verve and originality.

Shelley has his own versions of all three of these, intermittently inter-locking, kinds of poetic self-awareness. *The Witch of Atlas*, his most Byronic piece, shows the skill with which he can manage the performative side of self-awareness. And just as Byron defines his purposes in *Don Juan* by mocking 'A drowsy frowzy poem, call'd the "Excursion," / Writ in a manner which is my aversion' (III. st. 94), so Shelley's introductory stanzas to *The Witch of Atlas* raise a smile at the expense of Wordsworth, a poet solemn enough to inform 'us he was nineteen years / Considering and retouching Peter Bell' (ll. 25–26). Shelley continues with the wit and good humour which give his deftly inventive poem an assurance that includes but transcends satire or polemic and at times overlaps with understated poignancy:

> V
>
> My Witch indeed is not so sweet a creature
>   As Ruth or Lucy, whom his graceful praise
> Clothes for our grandsons — but she matches Peter
>   Though he took nineteen years, and she three days
> In dressing. Light the vest of flowing metre
>   She wears; he, proud as dandy with his stays,
> Has hung upon his wiry limbs a dress
> Like King Lear's 'looped and windowed raggedness.'
>
> VI
>
> If you strip Peter, you will see a fellow
>   Scorched by Hell's hyperequatorial climate
> Into a kind of a sulphureous yellow,
>   A lean mark hardly fit to fling a rhyme at;
> In shape a Scaramouch, in hue Othello.
>   If you unveil my Witch, no Priest or Primate
> Can shrive you of that sin, if sin there be
> In love, when it becomes idolatry.
>
>                               (ll. 33–48)

Byron's satiric verse may have provided Shelley with a model and a stimulus, but the performative aspect of these lines generates a particularized blend of tones, which can be related to the writing's sublimation of what it also partly confesses: its genesis in Shelley's feelings of literary failure and critical persecution. Earlier in the introductory stanzas he has referred with chastened acceptance of regret to 'a winged Vision . . . /Whose date should have been longer than a day', but which is now 'dead' (ll. 17–18, 23): probably alluding to the fate of *The Revolt of Islam*, also preceded by stanzas dedicated to his wife, Mary Shelley. The intimacy of address in the stanzas introducing *The Witch of Atlas* is balanced by the poet's awareness of his wife's coolness towards the poem proper, a balance which acts as asynecdoche of the poem's poised yet ambivalent attitude towards the possibility of a receptive audience. 'Poise yet ambivalence' describes the tone of the stanzas just quoted; in the last three lines, Shelley is at once confidently teasing and almost privately withdrawn, as if in imagining the reader shifting from 'love' to 'idolatry' — which, in context, suggests complete immersion in the poem's figurative inventions — the poet recapitulates a movement of aesthetic response he knows well. Similarly, his satirical glances at Wordsworth are tempered with the 'graceful praise' he ascribes to Wordsworth at his greatest (for Shelley, the lyric poet of works such as 'Ruth' or the Lucy poems). His criticism of the older poet may seem to rest on firm ideological foundations; 'Scorched by Hell's hyperequatorial climate' uses its comic bravura to be scorchingly critical of Wordsworth's readiness to accept notions of damnation. But the positive alternative Shelley has to offer aestheticizes notions of 'sin'; this is a poem which flaunts its use of a discourse that has no truck with the moralistic, and bases its appeal on its twin status as an imaginative performance by the poet and imaginative experience for the reader. The concluding lines warn the reader not to be so crass as to wish to extract an explicitly paraphrasable meaning; and yet they suggest the lure of the 'idolatry' which is the reward of the aesthetic experience about to begin.

Otherness in *The Witch of Atlas* lies the other side of the *ottava rima*'s virtuosities. If the poem is a mirror-world 'which makes beautiful that which is distorted' (*A Defence of Poetry*, *PP*, p. 485), it is conscious that its beauty-making fictions distort the distortions of the real, which are, the poet comments in a wittily mock-grandiose line, 'Not to be mirrored in a holy song' (l. 538). Such a recognition could be said to occupy the space between stanzas LXII and LXIII; the final couplet of LXII describes the Witch's response to human wrong: '"This," said the wizard maiden, "is the strife / Which stirs the liquid surface of man's life."' But the first line of LXIII adds, 'And little did the sight disturb her soul' (ll. 543–45). At this moment the Witch intimates an aesthetic freedom bought at the price of aloofness from human sorrow; the controlled pathos of the writing concedes that this intimation of the limits of the aesthetic has been made possible by a poem that comes close to relishing aesthetic autonomy.

For an example in Shelley's poetry of self-awareness as ordeal, albeit ordeal triumphantly surmounted, one might go to the end of *Adonais*:

55

The breath whose might I have invoked in song
Descends on me; my spirit's bark is driven,
Far from the shore, far from the trembling throng
Whose sails were never to the tempest given;
The massy earth and sphered skies are riven!
I am borne darkly, fearfully, afar:
Whilst burning through the inmost veil of Heaven,
The soul of Adonais, like a star,
Beacons from the abode where the Eternal are.

(ll. 487–95)

Like Keats's *Hyperion*, *Adonais* does not open with an invocation to the muse for inspiration. Both poems begin in a state of almost suspended animation, 'Far sunken from the healthy breath of morn' (*Hyperion*, I, 2). In *Adonais*, as Angela Leighton observes, 'Shelley places the inspiratory formula at the end of the poem';[16] indeed, in this final stanza, inspiration is not invoked, but majestically claimed, by the poet; and its descent is the most incandescent moment in Shelley, precisely because it is so self-questioning about its status as a rhetorical 'moment'. Shelley's dismissal of those 'Whose sails were never to the tempest given' echoes Dante's warning at the start of the *Paradiso*, Canto II:

> O voi, che siete in piccioletta barca,
> > desiderosi d'ascoltar, seguiti
> > retro al mio legno che cantando varca,
>
> tornate a riveder li vostri liti:
> > non vi mettete in pelago; chè forse,
> > perdendo me, rimarreste smarriti.
>
> (O ye who in your little skiff, longing to hear, have followed on my keel that singeth on its way, turn to revisit your own shores; commit you not to the open sea; for perchance, losing me, ye would be left astray.)[17]

As subsequent lines show, Dante does allow 'Voi altri pochi' ('Ye other few', l. 10) who have hungered for 'pan degli angeli' ('bread of angels', l. 11) to follow him. His own course is itself charted with mathematical precision as he ascends through the various levels of Heaven; yet Canto II's moment of self-consciousness is complex because it shows Dante, himself piloted first by Virgil (in the *Inferno* and the *Purgatorio*) and then by Beatrice, reversing roles and serving as the fit reader's guide.[18] But if Dante's self-awareness is complex because his poem knows where it is going, Shelley's self-awareness is complex because his poem does not know where it is going. A voyage

— launched in a way that makes rapture and fear virtually inseparable — is about to begin. It is, among other things, a voyage that leads the reader to ask, with Peter Sacks, whether Shelley has 'somehow burst beyond the elegy as a genre'.[19] Arguably, elegy is a genre that, in fulfilling itself, seeks to undo itself, to hold open the prospect of 'fresh woods, and pastures new'. So Milton's 'uncouth swain' has sung grief out of his system by the close of *Lycidas*, and is ready for new ventures. Yet Shelley's Orphic intensity does not permit of a cathartic diminuendo after crisis; instead, it conducts to an imaginative *ne plus ultra* that is at the same time haunted by the idea of a beyond into which the poet's spirit-bark will be forever driven. When Shelley names 'The breath whose might I have invoked in song', probably referring to the 'breath of Autumn's being' addressed in the first line of 'Ode to the West Wind', he embraces the condition of being a poet which, for Milton in *Lycidas*, is fraught with terrors. These terrors are evoked in the lines lamenting the Muse's inability to save 'her enchanting son' from being sent on another kind of voyage 'Down the swift Hebrus to the Lesbian shore'.[20] Milton can leave these terrors behind, even if they do not feel as though they have ever been finally allayed. Shelley represents inspiration, with its underlying current of disturbance, as the goal of his poem, even if the breath that descends on him will take him on a dangerous journey. The danger courted and enacted in the last stanza is that the poet seems to be on the verge of ignoring his earlier advice to any 'Fond wretch' (l. 416) — such as the poet himself — who might still be tempted to mourn for Adonais. Such a person is advised to

> Clasp with thy panting soul the pendulous Earth;
> As from a centre, dart thy spirit's light
> Beyond all worlds, until its spacious might
> Satiate the void circumference: then shrink
> Even to a point within our day and night;
> And keep thy heart light lest it make thee sink
> When hope has kindled hope, and lured thee to the brink.
>
> (ll. 417–23)

Imagery of centre and circumference is crucial to the affirmations set out a few months earlier in *A Defence of Poetry*, where 'Poetry' is described as 'at once the centre and circumference of knowledge' (*PP*, p. 503). In the lines above, however, the same imagery serves to shade in the imagination's potential limitations as well as its possibilities. The addressee is advised to assert his spirit's power over the material; but the writing is alive with cross-fertilizing suggestions. There is an element of scorn for matter's pretensions, space's 'void circumference' being presented as easily conquerable by the spirit's 'spacious might'. Yet this scorn blends with pleasure at the thought of the 'pendulous Earth' being clasped by the 'panting soul'; 'pendulous' briefly reasserts the Earth's otherness, its existence as an object in space. Nor can the buoyant inflections wholly quell awareness of the vastness of the 'void' emptiness of space. '*As from* a centre' (emphasis added) does not say that the 'spirit's light' is a centre; rather it hints at the rewards which will flow from a risk-taking, nonchalant readiness to see one's spirit as a centre. The curious mix of lightheartedness and near-anguish in the writing stems from Shelley's recognition that the spirit as a centre and matter as the spirit's circumference are no more than ingenious tropes, imaginative constructions. The risk Shelley takes — surmounted, in this stanza, by the writing's awareness of risk — is spelled out in the admonition to 'keep thy heart light lest it make thee sink/When hope has kindled hope, and lured thee to the brink'. Keeping the heart light involves discarding unnecessary expectations that reality will match desire; the power of these concluding lines lies in the way they resist, and experience, the lure of some potentially destructive 'brink' where hope and vertigo are indistinguishable.

The last stanza can be said deliberately to lure itself to, if not over, this brink. Its drive is to assert that reality does match desire, that there is indeed an 'abode where the Eternal are', which this poem has not only sighted but reached. In a special sense the poem does occupy — by virtue of its literary merit — the very 'abode' it describes. This awareness of its own greatness is among the most fascinating aspects of *Adonais*; there are few poems which communicate such an awareness so incontrovertibly to the reader. A split second after you have finished the poem you know that you have read one of the very greatest poems in the language, and what is more you know that the poem — in no boastful spirit, merely in a spirit of certainty — knows this too. However, the last line's 'abode' of absolute essence is the abode of silence, and spells death to the characteristic mode of Shelley's verse: its ever-shifting, existential commitment to redefinition, to becoming. The summoned breath at the end of *Adonais* is sweeping the poet beyond the realms where poetry can operate. He 'is borne darkly, fearfully, afar', where the adverbs destabilize, by adumbrating the hazards of, the surrounding mood of sublime exaltation. However, in the midst of the drive beyond poetry is a counter-movement; transformation is deferred even as it is embraced. True, the stanza draws reality into itself and splits it open, the line 'The massy earth and sphered skies are riven!' intensifying yet confronting the earlier deference to otherness in the account of the 'pendulous Earth'; 'massy', 'sphered' and 'riven' concede and dispatch physicality with remarkably literal force, despite the fact that the line is ultimately metaphorical, a way of describing the trajectory of aspiration. But *Adonais* is not over even when it is over. Beckoning, yet only from within the 'inmost veil of Heaven', the soul of Adonais is at once tantalizingly close and impossibly far. Its unreachableness is the guarantee of poetry.

There is, in fact, in Shelley a dislike of reaching conclusions. Conclusions, however optimistic, define, limit, intimate mortality; hence the appeal for the poet of endings on the verge of redefining, at times undermining, the poems of which they are part. Even the question at the end of 'Ode to the West Wind', 'O Wind, / If Winter comes, can Spring be far behind?' (ll. 69–70), threatens to undercut its status as unquestionably rhetorical. The decision to finish with a question came relatively late in the poem's composition; a draft of the ending concludes with the line, 'When Winter comes Spring lags not far behind'.[21] Question may more eagerly enact the longing to trumpet prophecy than statement; however, it opens itself — at an intermediate rather than final stage of the reading process — to deconstructive rewriting: 'If Spring arrives can Autumn be far off?' If the cylical analogy is accepted 'Spring' will merely be part, rather than the desired end, of a necessarily sinking as well as rising process, itself a sobering reflection; if the partial reading of the cyclical analogy encouraged by the poem is accepted, that is, the reading that pushes the cycle on two stages only (through 'Winter' to 'Spring'), then there is no reason why the cycle might not abruptly conclude with the arrival of 'Winter'. The recalcitrant otherness of history is conceded by the very utterance that seems intent on abolishing such otherness. If the poem survives its own self-deconstruction, it does so by miming the presence of a fierce, driving will intent on affirmation in the face of various forms of resistance. The poem uses its awareness of its status as writing — we have just heard the poet speaking with great power of 'the incantation of this verse' (l. 65) — to promote a double awareness on the reader's part: awareness of the poem's revolutionary longings twines with awareness of the fact that these longings are conveyed through a vulnerable analogy between the historical/experiential and seasonal cycles.[22]

There can be no doubt that the fineness of 'Ode to the West Wind' derives in large part from its promotion of this double awareness. In a comparable manner, 'Ode to Liberty' benefits from the eloquent account in its final stanza of the failing of inspiration when

> My song, its pinions disarrayed of might,
> Drooped; o'er it closed the echoes far away
> Of the great voice which did its flight sustain,
> As waves which lately paved his watery way
> Hiss round a drowner's head in their tempestuous play.
>
> (ll. 281–85)

The poem has sustained a rhapsodic tone, its formal intricacy placed at the service of libertarian ideals. Yet if the ending clarifies the reader's sense of the poem as the medium for an extended flight of inspiration, it also offers an inward poetry in touch with its own energies and entropies. The reader witnesses the fading coal of inspiration fan itself into transitory brightness before a final extinction, beautifully imaged in the last simile, where the poem is consumed by that which nourished it. The clustering swarm of similes (ll. 278–80) preceding the lines just quoted points up the figurativeness on which poetry depends; since the similes all emphasize ephemerality and precariousness, they suggest, too, the ephemeral precariousness of poetic structures. The 'great voice' is but a fiction, or so the lines lay bare; we glimpse again the self-imposed burden of the Shelleyan poem, whose only access to truth is by way of the inspiration it can briefly lay claim to in the act of utterance. In the case of 'Ode to Liberty' the result is to convert what might otherwise be merely a museum-piece into a poem that is affectingly alive.

Shelley has his own version of Stevens's fascination with the fictive, as the conclusion of this essay will show; the passage (from *The Triumph of Life*) discussed there will illustrate the sombre shadings such fictive self-awareness can take on in Shelley. In some ways, poetic self-awareness in Shelley is more intriguing than in Stevens because less programmatic; certainly, it is always bound up with awareness of otherness, since the dialectic between self and world is essential to the utopian transformations which Shelley's poetry often imagines. And yet Shelleyan self-awareness is continually on the verge of arresting dissolutions and self-undoings. At the end of *Alastor*, after the death of the Poet, the poem's Narrator asserts that the Poet's 'divinest lineaments, / Worn by the senseless wind, shall live alone / In the frail pauses of this simple strain' (ll. 704–6). Even this 'frail' affirmation undercuts itself, as it provides a ghostly and somewhat Gothic reprise of the opening, in which the Narrator presents himself as 'a long-forgotten lyre / Suspended in the solitary dome / Of some mysterious and deserted fane' (ll. 42–44) awaiting inspiration. The image, there, of an Aeolian lyre is made grotesquely physical as the Poet's dead 'lineaments' serve as a lyre on which the present 'strain' plays.[23] Shelley's underscoring of the fact that we are reading a poem brings to the surface latent conflicts concerning poetry's scope and limits, and instigates an immediate instability of tone. A few lines later, the Narrator turns on 'Art and eloquence' (l. 710), and their offers of elegiac comfort, doing so in a blank verse that is both artful and eloquent. Much of the poem's final blend of aloof composure and deeply troubled irresolution arises out of the conflict of feelings it has just staged about its own status. In a probing discussion of the conclusion, Vincent Newey asserts that the poem finally attains 'wisdom' by way of 'a commitment to creative acts as a means of surviving' apprehended disharmonies.[24] This recuperative humanism is attractive and salutary. Yet the capacity of *Alastor*'s acutely reflexive narrative for self-examination concerning the worth of 'creative acts' must also weigh heavily with the reader; whether the 'creative' is synonomous with misprision the poem leaves unresolved. Poetry, the poem discovers or fears, approaches adequacy only by virtue of a sense of its own tragic inadequacy. The same is true of the 'Vision and Love' (l. 366) invoked and pursued by the Poet. At the close of *Alastor* reality for the Narrator is a 'world' bereft of the light bestowed by 'some surpassing Spirit' (ll. 715, 714). Otherness there is in abundance at the poem's close, but it is an otherness

257

depicted as impassive, unresponsive, 'Nature's vast frame, the web of human things, / Birth and the grave, that are not as they were' (ll. 719–20). 'Nature's vast frame' and 'human things' are, as Vincent Newey suggests, in opposition,[25] and yet their opposition is appositional; both 'are not as they were' because they have both been enmeshed in the perspective-questioning but possibly futile figurations of the poem.

In 'Hymn to Intellectual Beauty', Shelley's self-awareness about poetry and its relation to otherness is less evidently troubled than in *Alastor*; yet subliminal anxieties haunt and energize the poem. The expression of such anxieties is most daringly original in the extraordinary shifts of direction in stanza 3. Here the poet dismisses as 'Frail spells' (l. 29) orthodox attempts to explain ultimate reality. Then he launches into his own 'frail spell', invoking 'Thy light alone' (l. 32). Intellectual Beauty's light emerges in subsequent similes (ll. 32–35) as flickering, transient, and fragile — and yet it is all this poet has to guide him; and the only place he can speak of it is a poem. Shelley's later self-description in *Adonais* as 'a Power / Girt round with weakness' (ll. 281–82) could be applied to the poetic self-awareness at work here. This is not imply that there is any notable 'weakness' in the quality of Shelley's poetry. Rather, the phrase from *Adonais* serves to gloss the way that in the 'Hymn' invocation of presence recognizes its inextricability from a language driven by desire and need. A stanza later in the 'Hymn' Shelley pushes this recognition to a dizzying extreme when he addresses 'Thou — that to human thought art nourishment, / Like darkness to a dying flame!' (ll. 44–45); the simile confronts the possibility, the fear, that the 'Thou' may be an absence rather than a presence. Indeed, throughout this poem, the writing is an unselfregarding whisker away from the view propounded by Wallace Stevens that 'The final belief is to believe in a fiction, which you know to be a fiction, there being nothing else. The exquisite truth is to know that it is a fiction and that you believe in it willingly'.[26] The poet who at the end of *The Sensitive-Plant* offers an extremely immodest assertion in the form of a 'modest creed' (Conclusion, l. 13) we might find pleasant to consider, or who in mid-course in *Adonais* revises a previous stanza's doubt to assert that the dead Keats 'is not dead, he doth not sleep' (l. 343), has little to learn from Stevens about the creative possibilities of a fictive scepticism. Yet the sceptic in Shelley does keep faith with the chance that there is possibly a true state of things whose light exceeds, to paraphrase the close of *The Sensitive-Plant*, the might of our organs.

3

'Tis to create, and in creating live
A being more intense, that we endow
With form our fancy, gaining as we give
The life we image, even as I do now.[27]

Byron's famous declaration in *Childe Harold*, III, stanza 6 distinguishes between and brings together 'the life we image' and the life lived outside poetry. Shelley's self-dramatizing is, perhaps, less histrionic than Byron's, but no less tangled. '*Self*, that burr that will stick to one. I can't get it off yet' (*Letters*, II, 109): this mock-lament follows a mock-modest suggestion that his correspondent, Leigh Hunt, 'judge whether it is best to throw [*Julian and Maddalo*] into the fire, or to publish it' (*Letters*, II, 108). The relationship between the two statements points up how tricky the connection between the empirical ego and the authorial self can be in Shelley's case. Shelley the man is here seeking to advance his authorial ambitions by persuading his close friend who is also an influential literary editor to publish a poem; at the same time he can be credited with awareness of this motive, and indicates his sensitivity to the promptings of self-interest. A further complication is added by the fact that the poem in question both involves an element of self-portraiture and is remarkably objective. It is a poem whose relevance to Shelley's life is disguised and hinted at in his letter to Hunt, who must have wondered what was implied by his friend's stylistic theorizing: 'in some degree a painting from nature' (*Letters*, II, 108). The delicate web woven from conflicting impulses in this letter makes for a self-divided text, one whose register is a far cry from the august intonations with which 'the principle of Self' is sent packing in *A Defence of Poetry*: 'Poetry, and the principle of Self, of which money is the visible incarnation, are the God and the Mammon of the world.' (*PP*, p. 503.) But '*self*, that burr that will stick to one' could supply the sub-textual epigraph to the opening of *Letter to Maria Gisborne*:

> The spider spreads her webs, whether she be
> In poet's tower, cellar, or barn, or tree;
> The silkworm in the dark green mulberry leaves
> His winding sheet and cradle ever weaves;
> So I, a thing whom moralists call worm,
> Sit spinning still round this decaying form,
> From the fine threads of rare and subtle thought —
> No net of words in garish colours wrought
> To catch the idle buzzers of the day —
> But a soft cell, where when that fades away,
> Memory may clothe in wings my living name
> And feed it with the asphodels of fame,
> Which in those hearts which must remember me
> Grow, making love an immortality.
>
> (ll. 1–14)

The spider is an emblem used by Swift in *The Battle of the Books* for the modern writer who arrogantly 'spins and spits wholly from himself, and scorns to own any obligation or assistance from without'.[28] But in the above lines the relationship of the image of the spider to the subsequent image of the silkworm is by no means one of contrast. Both insects serve as emblems of the poet, and the passage suggests fascinating indecision on Shelley's part about his role as writer, veering as it does between a recognition of the need to adapt to circumstance in the manner of the spider (here Shelley departs from Swift's use of the spider image) and the desire to embark, silkworm-like, only on poetic ventures which will ensure his 'immortality'. It would therefore be partly incorrect, even if possibly Shelley's conscious intention, to read the spider spreading her webs as a first shot at an image for the writer, discarded by the poet in favour of the silkworm which produces a chrysalis. True, the spider might seem the more likely to produce the 'net of words . . . / To catch the idle buzzers of the day', a kind of production explicitly rejected by Shelley. Yet the spider's capacity to respond to chance, to weave a web, whatever the surroundings, so long as there is something for the self-spun threads to attach themselves to, is valued by the jaunty opening. The improvisatory wit, lightness of touch and catching up of apparently accidental particulars in the main body of the poem show that the silkworm also needs a smack of the spider; otherness needs to be located and responded to as well as transmuted.[29] In the first fourteen lines, then, there is something of a sonnet's capacity for inner debate; moreover, the gap between what the passage wishes (to be gathered up into 'immortality') and what it is doing is intriguing. Though Shelley is writing for posterity, to ensure his 'living name' long after his 'decaying form' has perished, the lines make the reader aware of the 'fine threads of rare and subtle thought' they are 'spinning still'; every reading of the passage rehearses the attempt of the poet to turn his thoughts into that forever deferred, and yet inhabitable, 'soft cell' which will ensure his 'immortality'. In other words, the poem's awareness of itself as a performance positions it wittily and affectingly at a point where the empirical self writing poetry is turning into the poet subsumed within his creation.

Such a point is often explored by Shelley's poetry; too deftly self-aware for biographical readings to seem more than ploddingly literal-minded, the poems are themselves intrigued by the links and gaps between man and poet. No amount of spadework about Shelley's and Mary's marital problems is going, I think, to uncover the decisive clue to understanding the Maniac's monologue (ll. 300–510) in *Julian and Maddalo.* This, the pivotal section of the poem, is the more securely protected from the tabloid school of literary criticism because it draws much of its energy from the awareness that as experience passes into words it becomes an experience of a different kind. A similar awareness is evident in Shelley's description, in a letter to his publisher, of *Epipsychidion* as 'a production of a portion of me already dead; and in this sense the advertisement is no fiction'

(*Letters*, II, 262–63). According to the advertisement the author had died, and much of *Epipsychidion*'s self-awareness focuses on the way that the poet's empirical self is transformed into a self inseparable from the life of the poem he has created: 'I am not thine; I am a part of *thee*' (l. 52) has as its explicit addressee Emilia Viviani, but it might also be directed at the poem itself.

In turn, the Maniac can be read as a surrogate of a reluctantly and obliquely confessional poet whose central theme is less the precise nature of his distress than his inability either to confront, or to avoid wishing to broach, this distress. The Maniac's declarations hover between oral and written testimony; the plot demands that he speaks (so that Julian and Maddalo can overhear him); yet another plot unfolded by the poem (its investigation of the nature of writing) requires his words to be interpreted as written. Hence we are told that he 'spoke — sometimes as one who wrote and thought / His words might move some heart that heeded not / If sent to distant lands' (ll. 286–88). Later, the hesitation in 'as one who wrote' momentarily vanishes when the Maniac speaks of 'this sad writing' (l. 340), where the deictic involves the auditors in the act of creating, since it is Julian who we suppose writes the poem we are reading. Even when Julian implies that the Maniac has not been speaking in 'measure', the difference between his 'high' 'language' and what might be 'called poetry' is less striking than the similarity (ll. 541–42). Arguably, the dual status of the Maniac's utterance — made up at once of 'sad writing' and 'secret groans' (l. 341) — thematizes and provides a correlative for Shelley's relation to his own poem; at the very least the poetry blends suggestions that what the Maniac says is wrung from him involuntarily with the notion that he is aware of himself as a shaper of language, as a poet or failed poet. The monologue's conclusion dazzlingly highlights the resulting contradictions:

> I do but hide
> Under these words like embers, every spark
> Of that which has consumed me — quick and dark
> The grave is yawning . . . as its roof shall cover
> My limbs with dust and worms under and over
> So let Oblivion hide this grief . . . the air
> Closes upon my accents, as despair
> Upon my heart — let death upon despair!
> (ll. 503–10)

This hiding is a revealing — of the need to hide. The writing voices a fear of communication and a sense that sparks of revelation are waiting to flare up, until they are doused by the final rime riche. Or, to change the image, by heaping 'despair' upon 'despair' the writing can roll back the tombstone against the tomb of repressed experience which has been threatening a dangerous resurrrection. The 'death' the Maniac desires is partly the death of the desire to write, paradoxically communicated through writing. Something has come to birth, too, if not the birth of tragedy, then a glimpse of the birth of a tragic poetry astride the grave of its own self-suppression. In response to what he has heard the Maniac say, Maddalo develops links between suffering and nurturing in one of Shelley's most quoted comments about poetry: 'He said: "Most wretched men / Are cradled into poetry by wrong, / They learn in suffering what they teach in song"' (ll. 544–46). Such men would seem antitheses of the Shelleyan conception of poets as 'the happiest and best minds' (*PP*, p. 504) in *A Defence of Poetry*; but the dramatic form of *Julian and Maddalo* allows Shelley to explore opposed viewpoints. Indeed, in these lines Maddalo's implicit sense of poetry's value, communicated through the surprising if ironized tenderness of 'cradled' and the suggestion that poets both 'learn' and 'teach', offsets the 'intense apprehension of the nothingness of human life' (*PP*, p. 113) ascribed to him by the poem's Preface. Moreover, *A Defence of Poetry* is often most persuasively read if due allowance is made for the anxieties against which it is defending. Poetry for Maddalo has its origins in some initial 'wrong'; 'song' requires 'suffering'. This dependence, however, bequeaths a residual unease about what is learned through suffering (and therefore taught in song); *Julian and Maddalo* is close at this point to the position that what matters in poetry is intensity rather than significance. If the poem benefits as an imaginative composition from opening itself to the otherness represented by Maddalo, which is simultaneously a way of giving voice to a side of Shelley himself, its narrative framework only just defends Shelley/Julian from being overwhelmed by the darker vision of poetry projected in different forms by the Maniac and Maddalo.

One can set against Maddalo's words seemingly less troubled accounts in Shelley of the poet and poetry. And yet the operative word is 'seemingly'. Close to the centre of Shelley's originality in his dealings with poetry is his recognition of the reifying function played in cultures and institutions by 'the misuse of words and signs, the instruments of [the mind's] own creation' ('On Life', *PP*, p. 477). The fight against tyranny is always a fight against 'the misuse of words and signs'. This acknowledgement of the role of 'signs' gives Shelley's writing its capacity to reach 'outward toward engagement as well as inward toward reflexivity';[30] more than that, it makes reflexivity the means of investigating what is entailed by 'engagement'. The poet is aware that meaning involves construction, and that some meanings may be preferable to others; yet he is also increasingly conscious that he does not write in a cultural, generic or historical vacuum. Not everything concerning the workings or consequences of poetic language can be subjugated to 'the determination of the will' (*A Defence of Poetry*, *PP*, p. 503). After all, perplexingly, we take aesthetic pleasure in 'tragic fiction' (*A Defence of Poetry*, *PP*, p. 501). A poet may be 'hidden / In the light of thought, / Singing hymns

262

unbidden, / Till the world is wrought / To sympathy with hopes and fears it heeded not' ('To a Sky-Lark', ll. 36–40); but, in a spirit of conscious wish-fulfilment, the lyric movement simplifies the influence of poets on readers and in doing so allows for the impossibility of knowing how 'the world' will respond. And though the poet might wish to subsume his identity within the propagation by his work of 'beautiful idealisms of moral excellence' (*PP*, p. 135), he finds himself asserting in the same volume (*Prometheus Unbound . . . with Other Poems*, 1820) that 'Our sweetest songs are those that tell of saddest thought' ('To a Sky-Lark', l. 90): such as the thought of unattainable perfection, which impels 'To a Sky-Lark'. The narrator of *The Mask of Anarchy* is inspired by 'a voice' 'To walk in the visions of Poesy' (ll. 2, 4); however, when he seeks to answer his question 'What art thou Freedom?' (l. 209), he describes the flight of tyrants which would result from 'slaves' (l. 209) finding their voice in terms that link tyranny not only to the unconscious but also to writing: 'tyrants would flee / Like a dream's dim imagery' (ll. 211–12). Tyranny is, then, as already suggested, a kind of bad poetry, a set of falsifying tropes, 'dim imagery', which will be replaced in a free society by 'Science, Poetry, and Thought' (l. 254). By emphasizing the fact that signs can easily be misused, or that they may possess intrinsic or extrinsic indeterminacy, Shelley's affirmations take on their character-istically brave perilousness. *The Mask of Anarchy*'s attempted intervention in post-Peterloo British history is itself decidedly ambivalent; the signs it employs promote non-violence but remind both the governing class and those governed of the, as yet unleashed, power possessed by the latter: 'Ye are many — they are few' (l. 372).

*Prometheus Unbound* enlists 'rapt Poesy' (III. iii. 55) in its account of forces tending to the spiritual betterment of human beings. But coping with the intricate challenges thrown up by the specific historical moment of Romanticism was, Shelley recognized, a burden as much as a privilege. At the back of all the affirmations lies the existential vulnerability which emerges in these words: 'I / Have suffered what I wrote, or viler pain! — / And so my words were seeds of misery — / Even as the deeds of others' (ll. 278–81). So says Rousseau in *The Triumph of Life*, abject confession twisting itself into boast and accusation as he speaks. Here remoteness from classical ideals is deplored, acquiesced in, and, in a savagely ironic way, celebrated. The lines are in touch with what in his Dedication to Leigh Hunt at the head of *The Cenci* Shelley calls 'sad reality' (*PP*, p. 237), with the fact that though poetry may project ideal worlds it is often sparked into being by realities that are far from ideal. Or else the ideal may be contradicted by a reality that will not yield to the blandishments of poetry: a major theme of *Epipsychidion*, which seeks to conjure into being an apprehension of union between self and other, but finally comes up against dualisms that are inseparable from language itself and possibly, the poem finally realizes in its closing (and artfully staged) 'collapse',[31] from existence and identity:

The winged words on which my soul would pierce
Into the height of love's rare Universe,
Are chains of lead around its flight of fire. —
I pant, I sink, I tremble, I expire!

(ll. 588–91)

Here the poetry's sense of its own inadequacy provokes a bravura show of self-deconstruction; and yet this sense keeps in play the chance that 'love's rare Universe' is other than the web of tropes which have sought to define the particular 'Universe' of the poem. The disintegration but partial redemption of the poem's hopes is marked by the fourfold use of the first person in line 591. Perhaps the self cannot be one with the desired other. Yet, in the act of dramatizing this poem's expiration, Shelley sustains the possibility that, despite the failing of the self, the ideal still survives, albeit in a form unattainable through words.

# 4

The co-existence of celebration and anxiety operative in Shelleyan self- and other-awareness gives life to, and can be studied at work in, 'Lines written among the Euganean Hills'. The visionary epiphany (ll. 285–319), when the poet shakes off his initial despondency, uncovers at its conclusion the creative process:

And the Alps, whose snows are spread
High between the clouds and sun;
And of living things each one;
And my spirit which so long
Darkened this swift stream of song, —
Interpenetrated lie
By the glory of the sky:
Be it love, light, harmony,
Odour, or the soul of all
Which from heaven like dew doth fall,
Or the mind which feeds this verse
Peopling the lone universe.

(ll. 308–19)

The last few lines reinforce the conviction that all the things the poet has lyrically catalogued are 'Interpenetrated' 'By the glory of the sky'. Yet they keep an open mind about the reason for this interpenetration, and about the identity of this 'glory'. The final 'Or' speculatively asserts the responsibility of the 'mind which feeds this verse' for the glimpse of universal harmony; in making this assertion it reaps the benefit of surprise which Shelley's long sentence makes possible and indicates a tonal modification. The quasi-transcendent assurance evident in 'the soul of all / Which from heaven like dew doth fall' is replaced by, even as it ambiguously persists into, the disquieted affirmation of the subsequent lines.

My reason for calling this affirmation 'disquieted' will, I hope, emerge shortly. 'The mind which feeds this verse' advances on and is inclusive of 'my spirit which so long / Darkened this swift stream of song'. Those earlier lines imply the influence of 'my spirit' on 'this swift stream of song', and the relative autonomy of the 'stream of song', temporarily 'darkened'. The later lines bring together 'mind' and 'verse'. The result is a moment of self-recognition that is also, in context, a moment of self-escape; it is not 'my mind', but — less personally — 'the mind'. One reason for this is, in Wasserman's words, 'the ambiguity of [Shelley's] conception of selfhood and the attendant ambiguity of inspiration'.[32] But the lines involve the reader in an experience rather than a philosophical conundrum, and a key part of the experience is the way 'the mind' enigmatically shrugs off the self-concern just voiced in the reference to 'my spirit which so long / Darkened this swift stream of song'. At the same time, the strongly physical verb, 'feeds', serves paradoxically to point up the poem's withdrawal from a physical universe into a world of imaginative peopling. And here in the collocation of 'peopling' and 'lone', the two words disconcertingly at right angles to one another, the reader can detect signs of the disquiet mentioned above.

'Peopling', and its cognate forms, is a complex word in Romantic poetry. In Byron, especially, it often betokens a creativity born out of its own despair, as when Harold is said, in Canto III, to 'watch the stars, / Till he had peopled them with beings bright / As their own beams' (st. 14). Typically of Byron the downside of this peopling, the discontent which fuels it, immediately shows itself: 'Could he have kept his spirit to that flight / He had been happy'. But, of course, he cannot. Again, in Canto IV, read by Shelley just before he began composition of 'Lines written among the Euganean Hills' (see *Letters*, II, 471), Byron asserts, 'The beings of the mind are not of clay' (st. 5); the emotions we derive from art are seen by Byron as 'replenishing the void' (st. 5), and 'this worn feeling', he goes on, 'peoples many a page; / And, may be, that which grows beneath mine eye' (st. 6). It is as if, in *Childe Harold*, poetic 'peopling' grows out of disillusionment, or inability to cope, with 'people' and 'unpeoples' ordinary reality. Shelley probably wished to hold Byronic existential despair at bay, even as he admired the creative genius evident in *Childe Harold* IV. The tribute to Byron (ll. 167–205) in 'Lines written among the Euganean Hills' is chequered by hinted ambivalences of this kind.[33] But the poem is haunted by Shelley's own version of Byron's latent fear that 'The beings of the mind' achieve their vitality at the expense of the reality they stand in for and over against.[34]

In the passage under discussion from 'Lines written among the Euganean Hills', the universe which was evoked in all its richness and variety in preceding lines has now, surprisingly, become 'lone' (l. 319): discovered as an absence, as if the moment of self-awareness about imaginative 'peopling' had triggered off an almost idealist abolition of sights and sounds. And yet the moment of poetic self-awareness can be read as restoring to the universe an 'aloneness' which at once demands and resists imaginative peopling. In this regard, self- and other-awareness fuse in the final couplet, as the writing holds together the source and product of inspiration, and looks out at the 'lone universe' peopled by the mind which is feeding this verse.

The chances of rhyme induce a dual understanding of 'verse' and its etymologically associated partner 'universe'. Rhyme suggests the words are the same and are other. Both words derive from the Latin verb, 'vertere', 'to turn'. Shelley foreshadows the kind of linguistic self-awareness revealed by Seamus Heaney in the second of his 'Glanmore Sonnets', which concludes: 'Vowels ploughed into other, opened ground, / Each verse returning like the plough turned round'.[35] Heaney's formulation allows for otherness and for the role played by 'vowels' in giving access to this otherness. Heaney does not simplify or sentimentalize this role; he leaves the reader, not with a claim that the poem has established unmediated contact with the real, but with an enactment of what the reader is experiencing in the process of reading, 'Each verse returning like the plough turned round'. The line, or verse, itself returns as the reader turns across the line-ending, even as the word 'verse' recovers a sense, by way of the final simile, of the use of the Latin word, 'versus', to mean 'turn of plough, furrow' (see under 'verse', *Concise Oxford Dictionary*, 7th edn.).

Yet, for all its quietly absorbed sophistication, Heaney's vision has a more earth-bound rootedness than Shelley's. In Shelley's lines, 'verse' creates, or recreates, 'the . . . universe', and composes a 'universe' of its own. As *A Defence of Poetry* will put it, poetry 'creates for us a being within our being. It makes us the inhabitants of a world to which the familiar world is a chaos' (*PP*, p. 505). However, in *A Defence of Poetry*, as in the poem, there is a fundamental hesitation, which the start of the passage (from *A Defence of Poetry*) reveals: 'whether it [poetry] spreads its own figured curtain or withdraws life's dark veil from before the scene of things, it equally creates for us a being within our being' (*PP*, p. 505). Shelley leaves this fascinatingly and unsettlingly in the air; but if 'verse' spreads its own figured curtain, its relation to any universe other than that created through language is uncertain. For all its poise and polish the poem's language has stumbled on a crisis of representation, one which it is able to turn to its poetic advantage. Through the word 'lone', the universe is made to share in that state of aloneness which from the beginning of the poem has characterized the poet. Indeed, a few lines later Shelley refers to 'The frail bark of this lone being' (l. 331). The poem dramatizes the attempt made by the isolated poetic consciousness to establish connections with contemporary history, apparently deprived of direction after the post-Napoleonic political arrange-ments which have left cities such as Venice 'Stooping to the slave of slaves' (l. 123). By its close the poem has worked its way through to a note of provisional optimism, imagining a 'healing Paradise' (l. 355) which is no more and no less real than a poem, since it will, in part, be sustained by 'The inspired soul' and 'its own deep melodies' (ll. 364, 365). Each 'inspired soul' in this way becomes a legislator of the fictive utopia which 'Lines written among the Euganean Hills' ends up proposing.

## 5

The allusion just made to the concluding phrase in *A Defence of Poetry* takes this essay back to its point of departure; one way of recapitulating and extending the argument so far is to enquire whether poetry's forms of legis-lating for 'the World' involve the creation of a separate, poetic 'universe' which is in danger of slighting the claims of otherness. An answer is that the poetry itself experiences and enacts, often with great intelligence and speed of movement, swerves and near-contradictions of feeling and thought in relation to this issue. Such an assertion is borne out by two poems which draw resonance from key words in the 'Lines written among the Euganean Hills' passage discussed in the previous section. In 'Mont Blanc', the word 'lone' does much to sensitize the reader to the fact the poem is more than a rehearsal of epistemological commonplaces. It is the 'mountains lone' (l. 8) in the first section that bring into the poem one of its most haunting and bewildering notes: that is, a sense that outside human discourse there is a world indifferent to the human (a sense which, in turn, empowers a liber-tarian overthrow of 'Large codes of fraud and woe' (l. 81)). And yet this world can only be known through discourse, through language; indeed, the 'mountains lone', seemingly so physical, merely perform a walk-on part in a simile which is seeking to clarify, but managing only — in an enriching way — to complicate, an argument about the relationship between 'The everlasting universe of things' (l. 1) and 'the mind' (l. 2).[36]

Again, it is the 'loud, lone sound no other sound can tame' (l. 31), made by the River Arve as it pours through its Ravine, that catalyses the poet's 'trance sublime and strange' (l. 35) in which what goes on 'In the still cave of the witch Poesy' (l. 44) emerges explicitly as a central subject of the poem. The poem makes this recognition excitedly and with a fine glancingness, as though it had other matters to attend to, matters which are the concern of sections III and IV when the political and ideological implications of the poet's experience are dwelt on. In section III the poet projects onto the moun-tain the anti-Christian 'voice' (l. 80) which he wrings out of the desolate Alpine landscape; in section IV Shelley describes a cycle of interconnected destruction and creativity, beginning with the 'city of death' (l. 105) made by the glaciers and concluding with the consequent 'majestic River, / The breath and blood of distant lands' (ll. 123–24). Yet this 'River' emerges from the very Coleridgean 'secret chasms in tumult welling' (l. 122); and the echoes of 'Kubla Khan',[37] a poem much concerned with poetic creation, bring Shelley round in section V to confront the poem's ultimate subject and origin, 'the human mind's imaginings' (l. 143). These 'imaginings', invoked by the poem's final question, have just displayed themselves at work in the great lines:

> In the calm darkness of the moonless nights,
> In the lone glare of day, the snows descend
> Upon that Mountain; none beholds them there,
> Nor when the flakes burn in the sinking sun,
> Or the star-beams dart through them: —
>
> (ll. 130–34)

The nights may be 'moonless' and the snows descending on the mountain may be beyond human perception, 'none beholds them there'. But absence, again suggested by 'lone' (in 'the lone glare of day'), licenses the poet's imaginings, which cunningly exemplify themselves in the conjuring up of a silent ballet of snow-flakes and star-beams. The final question ('And what wert thou, and earth, and stars, and sea, / If to the human mind's imaginings / Silence and solitude were vacancy?' (ll. 142–44)) is poised between celebration of the poem's 'imaginings' and awareness that if one can imagine in a way that bestows meaning, one can also do so in a way that allows meaning to topple back into the 'vacancy' which is its perpetual shadow. The fact that meaning and meaninglessness alike are constructions of 'the human mind's imaginings' is the most compelling implication here, and is signalled by 'And' where one might expect 'But' in the antepenultimate line.

Shelley's poetic self-awareness, then, has an imaginative life that is unpredictable and cannot be reduced to aesthetic theorizing in verse. If the use of 'lone' serves as catalyst and symptom of this life in 'Mont Blanc', 'feeds', another word important in the 'Lines written among the Euganean Hills' passage, serves a similar purpose in the famous lyric scripted for the Fourth Spirit in *Prometheus Unbound*. These lines are likely to have been composed about the same time (late 1818) as the passage from 'Lines written among the Euganean Hills' which has been discussed:

> On a Poet's lips I slept
> Dreaming like a love-adept
> In the sound his breathing kept;
> Nor seeks nor finds he mortal blisses
> But feeds on the aerial kisses
> Of shapes that haunt thought's wildernesses.
> He will watch from dawn to gloom

> The lake-reflected sun illume
> The yellow bees i' the ivy-bloom,
> Nor heed nor see, what things they be;
> But from these create he can
> Forms more real than living man,
> Nurslings of immortality! —

(I, 737–49)

*Prometheus Unbound* concerns itself with a multiplicity of subjects; rarely, however, does it take its finger off its own pulse, as these lines make apparent. The 'Poet' here has a bafflingly intricate relation to otherness, or what might be called the 'real world': the world of 'mortal blisses', 'lake-reflected sun', and 'yellow bees'. Against these things, and yet in conjunction with them, the poet sets 'Forms more real than living man'. The writing, it should be pointed out, eats its cake and has it as well, evoking the meditative intensity with which the poet watches the natural world even as it disclaims any interest in 'what things they be'. It is as if Shelley had known he would be chastised for his 'weak grasp upon the actual',[38] and writes a lyric that catches itself in the act of imparting a patterned resonance to the natural in such a way that the natural seems to arrange itself into metaphors for a poem. The writing evokes loss and recompense; the poet finds sustenance in, 'feeds on' 'aerial kisses / Of shapes that haunt thought's wildernesses'. For a second, this feeding sounds distinctly anorexic, starved of sensation; and yet it is delightfully attentive to the interplay of 'shapes', shapes that are at once the product of imaginings and their object. Those 'wildernesses' interiorize an unknowable landscape, an unknowableness which will serve as the poem's best defence against the endlessly narcissistic self-reflection by which it is tempted. Shelley's dealings with the referential in his lyrical drama are caught up in his attempt to create a vast, pervasively relational network of echoes, a poetic embodiment of the claim made that 'Language is a perpetual Orphic song, / Which rules with Daedal harmony a throng / Of thoughts and forms, which else senseless and shapeless were' (IV, 415–17). As a result, *Prometheus Unbound* is much more like a symbolist poem than a decodable allegory; it is a poem that is inexhaustibly profligate in its inventions and yet always aware that creativity may flag, that a voice may be wanting, that hope will always need to create 'From its own wreck the thing it contemplates' (IV, 574). The poem proposes a figuratively pursued, glimpsed and unstable utopia created in the likeness of its hopes and desires; in the process, 'the pains and pleasures of [Shelley's] species' 'become his own', as *A Defence of Poetry* will argue is the duty and power of the imaginative person (*PP*, pp. 487–88). The lyrical drama's way of enacting this duty and power brings out the necessary but potentially tricky interplay between 'a going out' (*PP*, p. 487) and making 'his own' implicit in the passage from *A Defence of Poetry*.

*Prometheus Unbound*'s ending, at once elated and sombre, is shadowed by the fear that recreating hope can easily twist back into its own wreck. The aspiration towards otherness may involve idealizing or solipsistic projection. The desiring self may be merely a bundle of internalized illusions. Indeed, the elusive otherness to itself of the questing mind is a recurrent theme in Shelley's poetry and prose. In the fragment 'Difficulty of Analyzing the Human Mind' he writes:

> But thought can with difficulty visit the intricate and winding cham-
> bers which it inhabits. It is like a river whose rapid and perpetual
> stream flows outwards; — like one in dread who speeds through
> the recesses of some haunted pile, and dares not look behind. The
> caverns of the mind are obscure, and shadowy; or pervaded with
> a lustre, beautifully bright indeed, but shining not beyond their
> portals. If it were possible to be where we have been, vitally and
> indeed — if, at the moment of our presence there, we could define
> the results of our experience, — if the passage from sensation
> to reflection — from a state of passive perception to voluntary
> contemplation, were not so dizzying and so tumultuous, this attempt
> would be less difficult.[39]

The 'dizzying' presence-cum-absence of 'thought' is eloquently rendered by 'the intricate and winding' syntax and the controlled pacing, rapidly flow-ing yet abruptly self-monitoring, of this passage. 'Thought' cannot 'visit' the place it 'inhabits'; its movement is 'outwards'; it seems impossible for us 'to be where we have been'. The result is a passage that owes its fineness to its sense of the 'difficult' nature of self-examination and therefore of other-awareness, complicated as that is by the perplexing movement between 'passive perception' and 'voluntary contemplation'. At the end of his career Shelley re-examines these difficulties, in addition to the allied theme of the workings and betrayals of desire, in the fragment *The Triumph of Life*. In Rousseau's encounter with the 'shape all light' (l. 352), Shelley re-runs the central event, almost the primal scene, of his poetic career: an encounter with an other who is, and may be only, the creation of desire. This 'shape all light' is virtually an incarnation of ambivalence. A beautiful, mesmerizing muse figure, she both represents and presides over a poetry of duplicitous doublings; nothing is one thing only. Her feet move to 'a sweet tune' (l. 382), yet the 'measure' (l. 377) to which they move does not so much uncover 'the before unapprended relations of things' (*A Defence of Poetry*, *PP*, p. 482) as blot 'The thoughts of him who gazed on them' (l. 384). Yet nothing is one thing only. The shape's 'measure', a word suggestive of the composition of poetry, is itself dictated by, and gives form to, the 'ceaseless song / Of leaves and winds and waves and birds and bees / And falling drops' (ll. 375–77). This poetry of the natural world is, in turn, a notion created by another in the 'ceaseless' series of figurations which make up *The Triumph of Life*. A further twist is supplied by the fact that the shape's momentary obliteration of Rousseau's sense of otherness gives way to lines in which she herself comes to represent the yearned-for and seemingly unattainable other. This is the passage promised earlier as showing Shelley's anticipation of Stevensian fictiveness and the sombreness this awareness of fictiveness, of the invention involved in poetic creation, can take on in Shelley. It is, for me, as affecting a passage as Shelley ever wrote:

> So knew I in that light's severe excess
> The presence of that shape which on the stream
> Moved, as I moved along the wilderness,
>
> More dimly than a day appearing dream,
> The ghost of a forgotten form of sleep,
> A light from Heaven whose half extinguished beam
>
> Through the sick day in which we wake to weep
> Glimmers, forever sought, forever lost. —
> So did that shape its obscure tenour keep
>
> Beside my path, as silent as a ghost;
>
> (ll. 424–33)

The workings of Shelley's language issue in an inwardly sympathetic account, rather than a tough-minded critique, of Rousseau's idealizing. And yet the lines, like the poem, benefit from the complicated positionings of poet, character, and reader set in motion by the fragment's involuted narrative structure. The reader is aware of a state being intensely studied by a poet continually refining and modifying hints and suggestions. The very use of the word 'shape' for the desired other implies both Rousseau's shaping, or misshaping, consciousness and an elusiveness, which might, just might, guarantee an almost spectral otherness. Though there is 'presence' here, its 'tenour' is hauntingly 'obscure' rather than potently 'unseen' in the manner of the West Wind ('Ode to the West Wind', l. 2). At once linked to the subjectivity of 'dream' and claiming an objective status ('A light from Heaven'), the 'shape all light' — inspiration and possible nemesis of the idealist poet — is, above all, 'forever sought, forever lost'. Just as the shape previously 'moved in a measure new / Yet sweet' (ll. 377–78), so the poem's *terza rima* will keep moving past premature closure, growing ever more labyrinthine with every attempt to answer the questions which recur throughout. Perplexity sustains otherness. The poem honours and subverts the generic and visionary legacy of Dante's *Commedia* and Petrarch's *Trionfi*; its two main figures, the Poet and Rousseau, are at once like and unlike one another, as well as doubles of and other than the poem's author; and, centrally, the poem dwells on haunting links and hiatuses between the private realm of feeling and the public sphere of history. History may be represented through and as nightmare; but the momentum with which the 'Vision' is 'rolled' (l. 40) on the Poet's brain testifies to the force exerted in the poem by 'the world and its mysterious doom' (l. 244). Indeed, for all its freight of disillusion, *The Triumph of Life*, like many of Shelley's poems, draws creative nourishment from sustaining the finest of relations between awareness of itself as a verbal fiction and sensitivity to otherness.

# Notes

1 Earl J. Schulze, *Shelley's Theory of Poetry: A Reappraisal* (The Hague and Paris: Mouton, 1966), p. 13.

2 Quoted from *Shelley's Poetry and Prose*, ed. Donald H. Reiman and Sharon B. Powers, Norton Critical Edition (New York and London: Norton, 1977), p. 505. Unless indicated otherwise, all quotations from Shelley's poetry and prose are taken from this edition, hereafter cited as *PP*. In *A Defence of Poetry* Shelley uses the word 'poetry' in carefully defined ways, employing it in 'a general sense' (according to which all those who 'imagine and express' an 'indestructible order' are poets) and in 'a more restricted sense' (referring to 'arrangements of language, and especially metrical language'), *PP*, pp. 480, 482, 483. Much of *A Defence* uses the word in the 'more restricted sense', but the relationship between this sense and the 'general sense' is always operative. My own emphasis in discussing Shelley's view of poetry as set forth in *A Defence* is placed on his use of 'poetry' in the 'more restricted sense', though I seek to keep in mind the close relation between this sense and the 'general sense'.

3 *The Letters of Percy Bysshe Shelley*, ed. Frederick L. Jones, 2 vols (Oxford: Clarendon Press, 1964), II, 71; this edition is hereafter cited as *Letters*.

4 *The Complete Works of Percy Bysshe Shelley*, ed. Roger Ingpen and Walter E. Peck, 10 vols (London: Ernest Benn, 1926–30), VII, 20; this edition is hereafter cited as Julian.

5 Jerome J. McGann, *The Romantic Ideology: A Critical Investigation* (Chicago and London: University of Chicago Press, 1983), p. I.

6 Here I am in accord with, and owe a debt to, William Keach, who describes 'Shelley's style' as 'the work of an artist whose sense of the unique and unrealized potential in language was held in unstable suspension with his sense of its resistances and limitations', *Shelley's Style* (New York and London: Methuen, 1984), p. xvi.

7 Quoted from *The Poems of Shelley, volume I, 1804–1817*, ed. Geoffrey Matthews and Kelvin Everest (London and New York: Longman, 1989).

8 *The Poems of Shelley*, p. 521.

9 See Richard Cronin's discussion in *Shelley's Poetic Thoughts* (London and Basingstoke: Macmillan, 1981) of Shelley's efforts to 'achieve an awareness of the conservative force of language and engage in a self-conscious struggle against it' (p. 8). See also Jerrold E. Hogle's subtly formulated view that 'Language must be the alter ego of the imagination because discourse is so inclined to depend upon an other', *Shelley's Process* (New York and Oxford: Oxford University Press, 1988), p. 13. My own use of 'otherness' in relation to Shelley sees 'otherness' as a state posited by awareness that the 'self' is not identical with reality; it lays stress on the interdependence of 'self' and 'other'; it privileges the often intricate

process by which 'otherness' is discovered, but recognizes (and claims that Shelley recognizes) the narcissistic or reifying dangers inherent in the creation of an 'Other'.

10 Notebook entry for April 1803 [?], quoted from *Samuel Taylor Coleridge*, ed. H. J. Jackson, Oxford Authors (Oxford and New York: Oxford University Press, 1985), p. 543.

11 Quoted from *Don Juan*, vol. V (1986) of *Lord Byron: The Complete Poetical Works*, ed. Jerome J. McGann (Oxford: Clarendon Press, 1980–91). All quotations from *Don Juan* are taken from this edition.

12 Canto I, lines 16–18. The poem is quoted from *The Poems of John Keats*, ed. Jack Stillinger (London: Heinemann, 1978). All quotations from Keats's poetry are taken from this edition.

13 For a discussion of 'the implicated status of the artist' in Blake and Shelley germane to my account of *The Fall of Hyperion*, see Lucy Newlyn, *'Paradise Lost' and the Romantic Reader* (Oxford: Clarendon Press, 1993), pp. 216–18; the quoted phrase is on p. 217.

14 Quoted from *The Collected Poems of Wallace Stevens* (London: Faber, 1955; fourth impression, 1971).

15 Harold Bloom, *Wallace Stevens: The Poems of Our Climate* (Ithaca and London: Cornell University Press, 1980; first published in 1977), p. 65.

16 Angela Leighton, *Shelley and the Sublime: An Interpretation of the Major Poems* (Cambridge: Cambridge University Press, 1984), p. 148.

17 Lines 1–6; Italian text and English translation quoted from vol. III of the Temple Classics version of the *Commedia*, 3 vols (London: Dent, 1904; first published in 1900). Shelley's echoing of these lines from Dante in the last stanza of *Adonais* is pointed out in *PP*, p. 406 n.9. Alan M. Weinberg discusses the stanza's relation with Dante's Canto in *Shelley's Italian Experience* (Basingstoke and London: Macmillan, 1991), pp. 197–99.

18 *Paradise*, vol. III of Dante Alighieri, *The Divine Comedy*, trans. with intro. Mark Musa (Harmondsworth: Penguin, 1986), pp. 22–23.

19 Peter Sacks, 'Last Clouds: A Reading of "Adonais"', *Studies in Romanticism*, 23 (1984), p. 399.

20 *Lycidas*, lines 193, 186, 59 and 63, in *Milton: Poetical Works*, ed. Douglas Bush (London and Oxford: Oxford University Press, 1969).

21 Draft line (in Bod. MS. Shelley adds. e. 6) is quoted from Judith Chernaik, *The Lyrics of Shelley* (Cleveland and London: Press of Case Western Reserve University, 1972), p. 205.

22 For a discussion focusing on similar issues, see Ronald Tetreault, *The Poetry of Life: Shelley and Literary Form* (Toronto, Buffalo, and London: University of Toronto Press, 1987), esp. pp. 219–20. Of the ending Tetreault writes: 'Readers who can detach themselves from the poem's rhetoric might easily pose the counter-question: if Autumn comes, can Winter be far behind?' (p. 220).

23 Earl R. Wasserman brings the two passages together, and argues that the Narrator's 'later management of the same image reveals that for man to be but a passive lyre totally submissive to the forces of nature is actually to be a corpse, senseless, motionless, soulless, and gradually eroded by nature's forces', *Shelley: A Critical Reading* (Baltimore and London: Johns Hopkins University Press, 1971), p. 38.

24 'Shelley's "Dream of Youth": *Alastor*, "Selving" and the Psychic Realm', in *Essays and Studies 1992: Percy Bysshe Shelley: Bicentenary Studies*, ed. Kelvin Everest for the English Association (Cambridge: D. S. Brewer, 1992), p. 22. See also Vincent Newey's essay in the present volume.

25 'Shelley's "Dream of Youth"', p. 22.
26 Wallace Stevens, *Opus Posthumous*, ed. with intro. Samuel French Morse (New York: Vintage Books, 1982; first published in 1957), p. 163.
27 Quoted, as are subsequent passages from the poem, from *Childe Harold's Pilgrimage*, vol. II (1980) of *Lord Byron: The Complete Poetical Works*, ed. Jerome J. McGann. For a fuller analysis of this stanza, see my essay, '"A Being More Intense": Byron and Romantic Self-Consciousness', *The Wordsworth Circle*, 22 (1991), p. 170.
28 Jonathan Swift, *A Tale of a Tub and Other Stories*, intro. Lewis Melville, Everyman's Library (London: Dent; New York: Dutton, 1968 rpt. of 1909 edn.), p. 154.
29 James M. Hall argues that 'although Shelley takes the silkworm's existence as a metaphor for his own, much of the poem is written by the spider', 'The Spider and the Silkworm: Shelley's "Letter to Maria Gisborne"', *Keats-Shelley Memorial Bulletin*, 20 (1969), pp. 1–10 (p. 3).
30 Terence Allan Hoagwood, *Skepticism and Ideology: Shelley's Political Prose and its Philosophical Context from Bacon to Marx* (Iowa City: University of Iowa Press, 1988), p. xix.
31 The term 'collapse' is borrowed from D. J. Hughes; see his 'Coherence and Collapse in Shelley, with Particular Reference to *Epipsychidion*', *Journal of English Literary History*, 28 (1961), pp. 260–83.
32 *Shelley: A Critical Reading*, p. 200.
33 See Donald H. Reiman, 'Structure, Symbol, and Theme in "Lines written among the Euganean Hills"', *PP*, pp. 579–96, esp. pp. 588–90; see also my *Percy Bysshe Shelley: A Literary Life* (Basingstoke and London: Macmillan, 1989), p. 77.
34 For a reading of Shelley's passage as educating Byron 'in the redemptive functions of his own creative imagination', see Charles E. Robinson, *Shelley and Byron: The Snake and Eagle Wreathed in Fight* (Baltimore and London: Johns Hopkins University Press, 1976), p. 108.
35 Poem is quoted from Seamus Heaney, *Field Work* (London and Boston: Faber, 1979).
36 See the discussion of the opening section in my *The Human Mind's Imaginings: Conflict and Achievement in Shelley's Poetry* (Oxford: Clarendon Press, 1989), pp. 40–41.
37 Charles Robinson, following Desmond King-Hele, compares 'Kubla Khan', lines 17, 26–28, with 'Mont Blanc', lines 120–25, *Shelley and Byron*, p. 37. Shelley did not receive his copy of Coleridge's 1816 *Christabel* volume (containing 'Kubla Khan') until late August 1816. Robinson speculates that Shelley knew of the poem via Byron who may have 'recited portions of *Kubla Khan* (whether from memory, from a MS transcription of the poem, or from the May edition *of Christabel, Kubla Khan*, and *The Pains of Sleep* received by Byron before August)', *Shelley and Byron*, p. 37.
38 F. R. Leavis, *Revaluation: Tradition and Development in English Poetry* (Harmondsworth: Penguin, 1972; first published in 1936), p. 194.
39 Julian, VII, 64.

# 13

# TRANSITION IN BYRON AND WORDSWORTH

## *Jane Stabler*

Source: *Essays in Criticism* 50 (2000), 306–28.

How we judge the pace of change in poetry hinges upon complex aesthetic and moral effects. For Byron's last Byronic hero, Lady Adeline Amundeville, the ability to act 'all and every part / By turns' calls into doubt 'how much of Adeline was *real*' (XVI. 97, 96).[1] Byron's textual *mobilité*, especially (but not exclusively) in his *ottava rima* verse, was received as an assault 'Against the creed and morals of the land' (IV. 5).[2] Less scandalously, but no less significantly, William Wordsworth – one of Byron's greatest detractors – also faced accusations of poetic deviance. Chapter XXII of Coleridge's *Biographia Literaria* (1817) charges Wordsworth's style with 'INCONSTANCY'.[3] 'Inconstancy' may imply some of Coleridge's resentment about Wordsworth's apparent betrayal of their friendship, but he explains that he means by it 'the sudden and unprepared transitions from lines and sentences of peculiar felicity . . . to a style, not only unimpassioned, but undistinguished', adding that 'There is something unpleasant in the being thus obliged to alternate states of feeling so dissimilar' (ii. 121–2). Coleridge was constitutionally averse to sudden change both in literature and life. On his way to Malta in 1804 he assured the Wordsworths that his ill health was exacerbated by 'the abrupt & violent Transitions from Grasmere and dear you' (shortly after telling Southey that his discomfort was due to 'a wretched Steak' being 'too abrupt a Transition' from his usual meals).[4]

Disputes about the timing and delivery of poetic transitions had continued throughout the eighteenth century. Pope's notes to his *Iliad* (1715–20) invoke Longinus to defend unexpected transitions as marking the 'Impetuosity and Hurry of Passion'.[5] The commentary in Cowper's *Odyssey and Iliad* (1791) similarly reassures the reader that 'the abruptness of the transition follows the original',[6] but Cowper's care with transition was not enough to deflect all criticism and we need only turn to *Biographia Literaria* to find

Coleridge saying that the chief defect of *The Task* is 'that throughout the poem the connections are frequently awkward, and the transitions abrupt and arbitrary' – a criticism consistent with Coleridge's objections to Wordsworth's style and subject matter later in *Biographia* (i. 195).

The epigram and sonnet have their own turns built in; arguments about the propriety of transition focused primarily on such forms as the epic or ode. The fine line between what was emotionally justified by the material and what showed want of authorial consideration for the reader had been exemplified in Congreve's 'discourse on the pindarique ode' (1706), where he characterised some recent lyrics as 'a Bundle of rambling incoherent Thoughts, express'd in a like parcel of irregular Stanzas which also consist of such another complication of disproportion'd, uncertain and perplex'd verses and Rhimes'.[7] To claim that these followed Pindar was mistaken, 'For tho' his Digressions are frequent, and his Transitions sudden, yet there is ever some secret connexion which tho' not always appearing to the Eye, never fails to communicate itself to the Understanding of the Reader'.[8]

Although his *Dictionary* glossed transition as both gradual change and a more abrupt experience of removal ('removal; passage; change; passage in writing or conversation from one subject to another'), Samuel Johnson complained in *The Rambler* in 1751 that contemporary poets were using the 'accidental peculiarity' of ancient writers to free lyric poetry from all laws, 'to neglect the niceties of transition, to start into remote digressions, and to wander without restraint from one scene of imagery to another'. For him, this pandered to a weakness in the uncultivated reader whose attention is 'more successfully excited by sudden sallies and unexpected exclamations, than by . . . more artful and placid beauties'.[9] In 1762, however, Goldsmith's revision of Newbery's *The Art of Poetry on a New Plan* celebrated the unbounded liberty allowed in the ode: 'Fired . . . with his subject', the lyric poet 'disdains grammatical niceties, and common modes of speech, and often soars above rule . . . This freedom . . . consists chiefly in sudden transitions, bold digressions, and lofty excursions'.[10] Nevertheless Goldsmith, too, looked for an underlying coherence where the poet is 'led naturally to his subject again, and like a bee, having collected the essence of many different flowers, returns home and unites them all in one uniform pleasing sweet' (ii. 41). The ode 'should not have that sort of turn which is peculiar to the epigram' (ii. 42).

Revisiting the question of proper transition in 1783, Hugh Blair reported that 'licentiousness of writing without order, method, or connection, has infected the Ode more than any other species of Poetry'.[11] 'The Poet', he complained, 'is out of sight, in a moment. He gets up into the clouds; becomes so abrupt in his transitions; so eccentric and irregular in his motions . . . that we essay in vain to follow him . . . The transitions from thought to thought may be light and delicate, such as are prompted by a lively fancy; but still they should be such as preserve the connection of ideas, and show the Author to be one who thinks, and not one who raves' (ii. 356). Blair was particularly concerned about how the sublime could be sustained or concluded, since 'the mind is tending every moment to fall down into its ordinary situation': as soon as a poet 'alters the key; he relaxes the tension of the mind; the strength of the feeling is emasculated; the Beautiful may remain, but the Sublime is gone' (i. 66).[12] He perceived one of the greatest threats to sublimity to be the incursion of particularity, insisting that if in sublime compositions 'any trivial or improper circumstances are mingled, the whole is degraded' (i. 70). The prevailing acceptance of this view led to Cowper's apology for the detail of his translations of Homer: 'It is difficult to kill a sheep with dignity in a modern language', he says in his Preface, 'Difficult also, without sinking below the level of poetry, to harness mules to a waggon, particularizing every article of their furniture, straps, rings, staples, and even the tying of knots that kept all together. HOMER, who writes always to the eye, with all his sublimity and grandeur, has the minuteness of a Flemish painter' (vii. xvi). With Byron's *ottava rima* poems, critical uneasiness about bathetic plunges from lyrical abstraction to minute detail was to reach a crisis.

The link between transition in a work of art and connection of thought had been strengthened by mid-eighteenth century theories about the association of ideas.[13] For Hume, the words 'transition' and 'association' are almost interchangeable. In a 'just composition . . . the passions make an easy transition from one object to another . . . But were the poet to make a total digression from his subject . . . the imagination, feeling a breach in the transition, would enter coldly into the new scene'.[14] Hume argued that if the reader is not carefully prepared, eccentric digression will sever the sympathetic connection between a work of art and its audience (although the popularity of *The Life and Opinions of Tristram Shandy* suggests that contemporary taste could warm to such oddity in fiction).

Critical debates about Shakespeare's moves between comic and tragic modes added a further layer to discussions about the effects of unexpected transition. At one moment Johnson could celebrate Shakespeare's freedom from 'a due gradation of preparatory incidents', but at another lament that the dramatist 'no sooner begins to move, than he counteracts himself; and terrour and pity, as they are rising in the mind, are checked and blasted by sudden frigidity'.[15] (This idea of Shakespearean 'counteraction' anticipates Coleridge's meditations on the fulcrum motion of the creative mind, and the idea of checking and blasting is taken up by many of Byron's critics.)[16] The rage for literature of sensibility in the later eighteenth century precipitated a division between critical taste and the appetite of the common reader. Robert Dodsley's *A Collection of Poems by Various Hands* (1748; 1765) was accused by Coleridge of exhibiting 'Pseudo-poesy . . . which bursts on the unprepared reader in sundry odes and apostrophes',[17] but as Byron observed in 1814, Dodsley's anthology 'had great success in it's day & lasted several years'.[18] Dodsley's correspondence, moreover, suggests that he took particular care to smooth over the movement from passage to passage in any odes he published. Discussing corrections to Shenstone's 'Rural Elegance. An Ode to the late Duchess of Somerset', he was evidently concerned that 'The Transpositions [should] mend the connexion'.[19] By contrast with 'the startling *hysteric*' in Dodsley's collection and in contemporary magazine verse generally, *Biographia Literaria* presents *Lyrical Ballads* as working more smoothly on the sympathy of the reader through a 'faithful adherence to the truth of nature'.[20] The advertisement to *Lyrical Ballads* of 1798, however, had courted unexpectedness, and many of Wordsworth's poetic contributions to it use sudden turns or transitions both as a formal device and as a dramatic register of feeling in human encounters. Figures such as the Female Vagrant or the weeping man in 'The Last of the Flock', or the genius in 'Lines left upon a Seat in a Yew-tree' frequently 'turn aside', 'turn away', or turn the tables on their interlocutors, creating those sudden blasts of unexpected tragedy or comedy which so unsettled Johnson when reading Shakespeare.

Wordsworth's 'Old Man Travelling' interweaves two sorts of transition. The bending figure of the old man, the way he moves with thought, the tempering of long patience, his continuous leading on by nature are all plotted in blank verse of 'one expression' which suits the gentle gradation of 'animal tranquillity and decay' in the poem's subtitle.[21] The sudden interruption of direct speech, in lines not part of the poem's earliest draft, jolts us abruptly into a world of mischance and untimely death:

> – I asked him whither he was bound, and what
> The object of his journey; he replied
> 'Sir! I am going many miles to take
> A last leave of my son, a mariner,
> Who from a sea-fight has been brought to Falmouth
> And there is dying in an hospital'.

Edward Young's *Night Thoughts* (1742–5) may have recognised death as a 'soft Transition' (III. 440), but although Wordsworth skilfully creates a pace which leads us to accept the old man's death as happening by degrees and therefore easefully, the old man's own words startle the reader out of any such complacency.[22] His phrase for bidding farewell modifies the terminal abruptness of 'last' with a more lingering 'leave', but 'leave' is all the more poignant for holding the sense of what you leave behind, what remains after you when you die. Coleridge agonised over the same sense of loss when he suggested that although the death of the young 'seems more of a *transition*', the death of the aged has a more mournful effect.[23] Even so, Wordsworth seems to have felt that this sudden shift owed too much to the contemporary 'thirst after outrageous stimulation' (p. 249), and in 1800 –

when the speech became indirect – the son's explicit 'dying' was softened to 'lying' (though the revisions of 1802 and 1805 revert to 'dying'). In his 1815 collection, however, Wordsworth discarded the particularity of the last six lines altogether and returned to his original, more distant view of the old man as a type (in Sir Joshua Reynolds's sense) from which 'accident' has been eliminated.[24] The question of which version of the poem is to be preferred has remained critically open: Jonathan Wordsworth, John Jones and Mary Jacobus favour the old man as wordless symbol; Geoffrey Hartman, John Bayley, Susan Wolfson and, most recently, Seamus Perry prefer to retain the interplay of figure and speech.[25]

'Old Man Travelling' compresses a drama of unfolding pain. The first edition of *Lyrical Ballads* appeared in the same year as Joanna Baillie's *A Series of Plays*. In her 'Introductory Discourse', she illuminates the link between transition, transgression and association by focusing on tragedy's ability to explore the 'particular turn of a man's mind': 'what form of story, what mode of rehearsed speech will communicate to us those feelings, whose irregular bursts, abrupt transitions, sudden pauses, and half-uttered suggestions, scorn all harmony of measured verse, all method and order of relation?'[26] Here Baillie follows such eighteenth century critics as Oliver Goldsmith and Nathan Drake by insisting that irregularity is passion's characteristic mode and indeed demands a new form of theatre to accommodate it. But if Baillie's dramatic studies in passion tend towards novel pathological diagnoses, her prefatory essay also makes the more conservative link between the discontinuous and the morally dangerous so far as to remind us of Johnson's axiomatic 'All change is of itself an evil, which ought not to be hazarded but for evident advantage'.[27]

Wordsworth's own experiments with drama anticipate the concern articulated in the Preface to *Lyrical Ballads* (1800) that rapidly changing events risked being too stimulating. His 1797 Preface to *The Borderers* suggests that good actions are 'silent and regularly progressive' whereas vice is more often apparent in sudden breakings out and 'fantastic obliquities'.[28] Wordsworth's earlier ideas about how a character might change seem to have evolved in dialogue with Coleridge, whose notebook exclaims in 1799: 'It is not true that men always go gradually from good to evil or evil to good. Sometimes a flash of lightning will turn the magnetic Poles'.[29] Wordsworth, however, analysed the effects of both gradual and sudden turns of feeling, and he was keen to explore how a radical 'perversion of the understanding' was bound up with his experience of the French Revolution: 'in the trials to which life subjects us, sin and crime are apt to start from their very opposite qualities, so there are no limits to the hardening of the heart' (p. 813). This catastrophe forms the basis for the character of Rivers (later called Oswald) who has doubts about the very possibility of moral 'transition'. After the temptation scene in the 1842 version of the play, in which he seeks to persuade his victim to commit murder, Oswald sneers, 'He talks of a transition in his Soul, / And dreams that he is happy' (III. 1165). The bitter outbursts of Rivers / Oswald leave their imprint on the susceptible mind of Mortimer/Marmaduke, and reveal Wordsworth's fascination with the tension that exists between an instant of 'transitory' action ('a step, a blow, / The motion of a muscle – this way or that') and its prolonged aftermath of 'permanent, obscure and dark' reaction (III. 1540–3).

As its title indicates, 'Lines written a few miles above Tintern Abbey, on revisiting the banks of the Wye during a tour, July 13, 1798' deals with an aftermath in an appropriately changeful form. Wordsworth's 1800 note tells us that although he has not 'ventured to call this Poem an Ode ... it was written with a hope that in the transitions, and the impassioned music of the versification, would be found the principal requisites of that species of composition' (p. 296). One of Wordsworth's characteristic modes of transition in 'Tintern Abbey' is the placing of his own lyrical outbursts against the more gradual transitions of 'the life of things'. His urgent identification of landmarks in the first section of the poem lengthens into a recognition that each feature is continuous with something else: the 'hedge-rows, hardly hedge-rows' are traced back to 'little lines / Of sportive wood run wild' as the poet begins to merge spots of time into the growth of his mind.[30] Two forms of change are thus kept in continual play, and immediate sensations 'Felt in the blood' give way to a state where 'the motion of our human blood' is 'Almost suspended' (ll. 28, 44–5). The slow pace of this underlying transformative process heightens the emotive force of such sharp rhetorical turns as 'If this / Be but a vain belief'. Rhythms of seasonal and tidal ebb and flow are set against reminders of loss and betrayal:

> How oft, in spirit, have I turned to thee
> O sylvan Wye! Thou wanderer through the woods,
> How often has my spirit turned to thee!
>
> (ll. 56–8)

The lines contrast two kinds of motion: the constant 'wandering' progression of the river, and the flux of human contingency. When Wordsworth 'turns' to things or people in his poems, it is often because they are no longer there. In Coleridge's poems the opposite happens: either a transition in metre (as discussed in the preface to 'Christabel') or a change of subject (as in the eighth stanza of 'Dejection: An Ode': 'I turn from it and listen to the wind') signals the emergence of some fearful presence ('I have been always preyed on by some Dread', the January 1805 notebook records).[31] With Wordsworth, comparable moments of transition are usually recognitions of absence, as in the 1820 version of his sonnet 'Surprised by Joy' ('I turned to share the transport – Oh! with whom / But thee deep buried in the silent tomb', ll. 2–3)[32] or his 'Written after the death of Charles Lamb' ('But turn we – rather, let my spirit turn / With thine, O silent and invisible friend', ll. 107–8). These turns reach out for connection across the void, and the poet's struggle to confront the moment of absence may be traced in his revisions to 'Surprised by Joy' where 'I wished to share the transport' became 'I turned to share the transport', and later 'I turn to share the transport'.[33] The turn to Dorothy in 'Tintern Abbey' occurs under the shadow of a parting from her, and the poem's courageous sifting out of what is changed from what 'still' abides is inflected by the dread of removal which affects all human relationships.

This dread materialised in a different form in the estrangement between Wordsworth and Coleridge of 1810, and in Coleridge's need to itemise the defects of Wordsworth's style in *Biographia Literaria*. Chief amongst defects was 'matter-of-factness'. Coleridge praises 'the exquisite description of the Sea Loch' in 'The Blind Highland Boy' ('That rough or smooth is full of change / And stirring in its bed'), but he recoils from the description of the Leech-gatherer as 'stirring thus about his feet / The waters of the pond'. Coleridgean aesthetics can encompass things being disturbed on a large scale, but not the jarring effect of a sudden turn to bodily matters of fact. This concern for poetry's unity of effect follows Blair's dislike of the 'painful shock' of a sudden poetic descent from the sublime.[34]

Another set of terms for Coleridge's sense of Wordsworth's defects – 'abrupt', 'medley', 'incongruity' and 'disharmony' – may have been influenced by the critical ferment aroused by Byron's poetry from 1812 onwards. While Wordsworth was revealing through revisions his own worries about moments of dislocation in his verse, Byron openly flouted his readership's wish not to be interrupted. Just after he published Cantos I and II of *Don Juan* in July 1819, John Murray showed a copy to Francis Cohen (later Palgrave, father of the compiler of *The Golden Treasury*). Cohen wrote back,

> Like Shakespeare he shows that his soul can soar well into the seventh heaven, & that when he returns into this body he can be as merry as if sublimity ne'er was known . . . Nothing can be better calculated to display the labours of a great poet, than a composition admitting of a ready transition from fun & frisking to sublimity & pathos, but . . . we are never drenched & scorched at the same instant whilst standing in one spot.[35]

Byron's response was to deflate Cohen's intimations of sublimity with an incongruous catalogue of bodily sensations:

> I will answer your friend . . . who objects to the quick succession of fun and gravity . . . Ask him these questions about 'scorching and drenching'. – Did he never play at Cricket or walk a mile in hot weather? – did he never spill a dish of tea over his testicles in

281

handing the cup to his charmer to the great shame of his nankeen breeches? – did he never swim in the sea at Noonday with the Sun in his eyes and on his head – which all the foam of ocean could not cool? . . . did he never inject for a Gonorrhea? – or make water through an ulcerated Urethra? – was he ever in a Turkish bath – . . .[36]

Murray backed down in this instance, but he could not prevent the hostility of Tory reviewers towards Byron's poetry and was himself shocked by later cantos of the poem. Even liberals like Hazlitt struggled with Byron's sudden transitions, accusing him of producing a poem 'as disturbed, as confused, as disjointed' as a dream, assembling 'a mass of discordant things' in versification 'as perverse and capricious as the method or the sentiments'.[37] These criticisms, directed at Canto IV of *Childe Harold's Pilgrimage* (1818), make it clear that Byron was notorious for mixture, heterogeneity and sudden transition well before he embarked on *Don Juan*. Reviewing the same canto, the *Literary Gazette* noticed that 'the transitions are so quickly performed . . . from Venice to Rome, from Rome to Greece . . . from Mr. Hobhouse to politics, and back again to Lord Byron; that our head is absolutely bewildered by the want of connexion'.[38] As early as 1814 the *Quarterly* had discerned 'abrupt and perplexing transitions' in *The Giaour*, accentuated by Byron's tendency to disturb the mood of his verse narratives with flippant notes which 'interrupt completely', as the *Scots Magazine* complained, the expected 'tone of deep solemnity which reigns unbroken through the poetry'.[39]

Byron's facility for transition partly comes from his choice of verse form. Rhyme reminds the reader of an earlier sound which is modified in the process. Rhyme was thought to be 'unfavourable' to the sublime by such eighteenth century critics as Hugh Blair and Daniel Webb, and in the early nineteenth century this prejudice became even more pronounced. In 1827 William Crowe ruled that the 'quick return of rhyme destroys the gravity and dignity of verse'.[40] Such critical deprecation was bound up with continuing debate about Pope.[41] Byron's vigorous defence of Pope and the art of rhyme against Bowles and the Lake School helps to explain the hostility Wordsworth expressed in a letter to John Scott in April 1816: 'Let me only say one word upon Lord B. The man is insane; and will probably end his career in a mad-house'.[42] In June 1817, Wordsworth was more explicit about the reasons for his resentment. He refers his correspondent to the stanza on solitude ('midst the crowd, the hum, the shock of men' in *Childe Harold's Pilgrimage*, Canto II) and argues that 'the sentiment by being expressed in an *antithetical* manner, is taken out of the Region of high and imaginative feeling, to be place[d] in that of point and epigram'. 'To illustrate my meaning and for no other purpose', Wordsworth adds, 'I refer to my own Lines on the Wye, where you will find the same sentiment not formally put, as it is here, but ejaculated as it were [fortuit]ously in the musical succession [of preconceiv]ed feeling' (p. 385).

Wordsworth's use of the phrase 'musical succession of preconceived feeling' in relation to 'Tintern Abbey' recalls his description of morally good actions in the Preface to *The Borderers*, as 'regularly successive'. His preference for an even texture suggests that he accepted the more traditional concept of harmonic unity in poetry advocated by conservative critics like Johnson or John Opie, for whom the proper working of poetry was 'successive and cumulative'.[43] Byron, on the other hand, advocated the virtues of rhyme over blank verse and the more intricately regulated harmony of Pope over the 'variazioni' of the Lakers.[44]

Later in June 1817 Wordsworth was still claiming not to have looked at Byron's most recent publication, *Manfred* (published on 16 June 1817) or at *Childe Harold* Canto III (published in November 1816), where, Wordsworth added darkly, 'I am told he has been poaching on my Manor' (p. 394). His sensitivity about style was probably heightened by awareness of the imminent critical onslaught from Coleridge, and the phrase may imply a resentment that Byron had also been trespassing on his manner. In *Biographia Literaria*, Chapter XVIII, Coleridge's detailed analysis of Wordsworthian defects is preceded by a condemnation of 'compulsory juxta-position' as a 'species of *wit*'. This faculty, according to Coleridge, is 'incompatible with the steady fervour of a mind' working with the modifying powers of poetic genius. Coleridge's demand for sustained and unifying acts of imagination extends also to criticism, where he would have the critic 'faithfully distinguishing what is characteristic from what is accidental', and insists that critics and poets should prepare the reader for intellectual or musical developments to follow.[45] It is at this point that Coleridge criticises Wordsworth for '*accidentality*', and for his interweaving 'minute matters of fact' with poetry 'of the loftiest style' (ii. 126, 134). Coleridge's experience of what he terms 'a sort of damp and interruption' follows on from years of objection to Byron's bathetic inclusion of prosaic detail.[46] Epitomising this was Hazlitt's complaint that after a sublime description of a storm at sea with 'lightning and hurricane' in *Don Juan* Byron descended to 'the interior of the cabin and the contents of wash-hand basins'.[47] Coleridge's criticism of Wordsworth, hinting that the reader has been let down by the poet, whose consistency of style has been disrupted to ill effect, parallels the critical furore around Byron. Being dumped by the poet destroys the sympathetic contract assumed to exist between readers and writers of sensibility and brings into question the veracity of lyric feeling itself.

Coleridge's account in *Biographia Literaria* of an 'eddying instead of a progression of feeling' in Wordsworth's poetry also connects with Wordsworth's own doubts about Byron (ii. 136). It seems likely that a mixture of defensiveness about Coleridge's criticism, and a desire to counter Byron's success, led Wordsworth to reorganize his poems in 1820 to demonstrate 'a musical succession of preconceived feeling'. The emergence of Byron as an audible counter-voice in late Wordsworth suggests a reversal of the literary influence hitherto only seen to flow from the older poet to the younger.

In Canto III of *Childe Harold's Pilgrimage* (often considered to be Byron's most Wordsworthian work), Byron recreates Wordsworth's practice of interweaving two modes of temporal transition. In the stanzas on the Field of Waterloo Byron stands where his cousin was killed in action and juxtaposes the seasonal revival of the landscape in spring with the 'ghastly gap' of lost life. The poet then turns to all those bereaved by the Napoleonic wars:

> They mourn, but smile at length; and smiling, mourn:
> The tree will wither long before it fall;
> The hull drives on, though mast and sail be torn;
> The roof-tree sinks, but moulders on the hall
> In massy hoariness; the ruined wall
> Stands when its wind-worn battlements are gone;
> The bars survive the captive they enthral;
> The day drags through though storms keep out the sun;
> And thus the heart will break, yet brokenly live on.
>
> (III. 280–8)

In these lines and those which follow, Byron measures violent change against that which is gradual – a contrast repeatedly explored by Wordsworth in *The Excursion* (which Byron owned, but sold together with his two-volume copy of *Lyrical Ballads* before leaving England in April 1816).[48] In Book VI of *The Excursion*, for example, Wordsworth summons a succession of characters who have undergone 'the transition of that bitter hour' (VI. 133), but then have to live with it:

> Of what ensued
> Within the heart no outward sign appeared
> Till a betraying sickliness was seen
> To tinge his cheek; and through his frame it crept
> With slow mutation unconcealable.
>
> (VI. 154–8)

For all the younger poet's jokes about 'drowsy' poetry, it was Wordsworth who provided Byron with the poetic knowledge of people living with (not dying of) broken hearts. Both poets depict human suffering as a form of decay which sets in early: a single cataclysmic shock leads to a long series of almost imperceptible adjustments. From his image of the withering heart, 'Shewing no visible sign, for such things are untold' (III. 297), Byron makes a transition to one of his most famously morbid stanzas, beginning 'There is a very life in our despair' (III. 298). This recommencement echoes Wordsworth's 'Michael':

> There is a comfort in the strength of love;
> 'Twill make a thing endurable, which else
> Would break the heart.
>
> (ll. 457–9)

Byron's Waterloo meditation uses the movement of Wordsworthian elegy to address disaster on a European scale, without losing touch with the individual.

According to Michael O'Neill, transition is 'often a problem for Wordsworth' but it 'animates Byron's writing'.[49] Both poets, however, use transition to explore the difference between rapid succession in verse and the actual experience of life, in which the passage of time can be neither stopped nor modified. 'But let me change this theme, which grows too sad', Byron remarks (*Don Juan*, IV. 74), much as Wordsworth's Wanderer has said 'enough to sorrow you have given' (*The Excursion*, I. 932). In each case, the poet proceeds in the knowledge that transition is both an aesthetic and ethical necessity.

Wordsworth condemned what he saw as the 'damnable tendency' of *Don Juan* nevertheless. He wrote to Crabb Robinson 'that *Don Juan* will do more harm to the English character, than anything of our time', and urged his friend to set William Gifford on to it: 'What avails it to hunt down Shelley, whom few read, and leave Byron untouched?' (p. 579). Wordsworth's desire to loosen Byron's hold on the reading public seems to have influenced his decision, in autumn 1819, to publish the River Duddon sonnet sequence and, more surprisingly, 'Vaudracour and Julia'. These poems had been bound up with 'Peter Bell', 'The Waggoner' and 'The Thanksgiving Ode' to make a third volume for the two-volume *Poems* of 1815. Writing of this third volume in April 1820 Wordsworth claimed that 'In more than one passage their publication will evince my wish to uphold the cause of Christianity' (p. 594).

The River's function in the Duddon sequence is 'to heal and to restore, / To soothe and cleanse, not madden and pollute!' (Sonnet VIII, p. 10). The sonnets which in effect flow into one poem, together with the topographical description of the English Lakes, exalt calm of mind and a 'Form' that 'remains'. The whole volume is preoccupied with the moral issue of continuity, 'a new habit of pleasure . . . arising out of the perception of the fine gradations by which in nature one thing passes away into another' (pp. 278–9). Wordsworth celebrates the 'intermixture' of iron ore in the scree 'like the compound hues of a dove's neck' (p. 225); the way colours 'play into each other over the surface of the mountains' (p. 227); the 'insensible gradations' of snow lying on the fells (p. 228). His objection to plantations and new buildings in the Lake District is that they represent 'an introduction of discordant objects, disturbing that peaceful harmony of form and colour

which had been through a long lapse of ages most happily preserved'
(p. 278). Such observations show Wordsworth's increasing dependence
on the Burkean category of the beautiful and the Burkean ideal of stable,
slowly evolving government. Wordsworth repeatedly presents such states
as 'Gently [sinking]' into the quiet tomb (p. 163), or gradually ascending the 'hazy ridges' of mountains towards heaven with 'drooping old
men' (p. 195), and heavenly radiance itself 'Blended in absolute serenity'
(p. 207). Although not the sole impetus for the volume, this concept of
gradual transition imaged in both nature and in devout human life stands
as Wordsworth's counter to the irresponsibility, as he saw it, of Byronic
juxta-position and antithesis.

The Duddon has its human counterpart in Wordsworth's prose account
of the Revd Robert Walker, who embodied a 'silent and regularly progressive' pattern of virtue. It is surprising that his memoir, appended to
the Duddon sonnets, should be followed by 'Vaudracour and Julia'.
Wordsworth's narrative from the as yet unpublished *Prelude* touches (albeit
obliquely) on the closely guarded secret of Wordsworth's love affair in
revolutionary France. His motive in publishing 'Vaudracour and Julia'
in 1820 may have been to offer a corrective love story in response to the first
two cantos of *Don Juan*.[50]

The ways in which Wordsworth's and Byron's two Julias deal with sexual
transgression are obvious enough. Twice, in the first cantos of *Don Juan*,
Byron glances at the speed with which erotic urgency can break through
social restraint. His Julia holds out for less than a stanza:

> A little still she strove, and much repented,
> And whispering 'I will ne'er consent' – consented
>
> (I. 117)

Byron shows greater tenderness for Haidee, Juan's second lover, but her rite
of passage into sexual experience is similarly rapid. She has heard of

> hell and Purgatory – but forgot
> Just in the very crisis she should not.
>
> (II. 193)

Wordsworth makes much heavier weather of the situation:

> So passed the time, till, whether through effect
> Of some unguarded moment that dissolved
> Virtuous restraint – ah, speak it, think it not!
> Deem rather that the fervent Youth, who saw
> So many bars between his present state
> And the dear haven where he wished to be

> In honourable wedlock with his Love,
> Was inwardly prepared to turn aside
> From law and custom, and entrust his cause
> To nature for a happy end of all.
>
> (pp. 73–4)

Wordsworth directs the reader to 'bear with their transgression when I add / That Julia, wanting yet the name of wife, / Carried about her for a secret grief / The promise of a mother' (p. 74). Wordsworth's steady blank verse rhythm is more appropriate to prolonged suffering than to a single act. The 'unguarded moment' is presented as a continuous state and Vaudracour's being 'inwardly prepared to turn aside' makes his transgression seem less sudden and more a process of 'secret grief'. Byron is far less apologetic about erotic fulfilment. The first instalment of *Don Juan* in 1819 ends with Juan promptly forgetting Julia when he falls for Haidee. Their first kiss, with 'pulse a blaze' under the night sky, leads on to the scandalous picture of them as 'quite antique, / Half naked, loving, natural, and Greek' (II. 194):

> The Lady watch'd her lover – and that hour
>     Of Love's and Night's, and Ocean's solitude,
> O'erflow'd her soul with their united power;
>     Amidst the barren sand and rocks so rude
> She and her wave-worn love had made their bower,
>     Where nought upon their passion could intrude,
> And all the stars that crowded the blue space
> Saw nothing happier than her glowing face.
>
> Alas! the love of women! it is known
>     To be a lovely and a fearful thing;
> For all of theirs upon that die is thrown,
>     And if 'tis lost, life hath no more to bring
> To them but mockeries of the past alone,
>     And their revenge is as the tiger's spring,
> Deadly, and quick, and crushing; yet, as real
> Torture is theirs, what they inflict they feel.
>
> They are right; for man, to man so oft unjust,
>     Is always so to women; one sole bond
> Awaits them, treachery is all their trust;
>     Taught to conceal, their bursting hearts despond
> Over their idol, till some wealthier lust
>     Buys them in marriage – and what rests beyond?
> A thankless husband, next a faithless lover,
> Then dressing, nursing, praying, and all's over.
>
> (II. 198–200)

The mercurial transitions of tone in these stanzas show how reductive it is to think of Byron's *ottava rima* simply as six serious lines undercut by two epigrammatic ones. The slow time of Haidee's vigil will be set against Juan's future fickleness in forgetting her as well as Julia. The curious quick life-survey so often offered in Byron's verse this time adopts a female perspective. We are moved from the rapture of the infant as it 'drains the breast' (II. 196), to the point when – for the woman – 'all's over'. The decisive gamble of one instant and its lifelong effect – 'And if 'tis lost, life hath no more to bring' – rattles two time-scales together like the dice of Byron's image. It is up to the reader whether or not to let such reflections contaminate the image of Haidee's happiness which is set both against the sky and against the odds of the next stanza.

In the 'Vaudracour and Julia' section of the 1805 *Prelude*, Wordsworth had been reluctant to describe any instants of erotic delight at all: 'I pass the raptures of the pair; – such theme / Hath by a hundred poets been set forth'.[51] In 1820, however, he added this passage about the lovers' first reunion:

> – Through all her courts
> The vacant City slept; the busy winds,
> That keep no certain intervals of rest,
> Mov'd not; meanwhile the galaxy display'd
> Her fires, that like mysterious pulses beat
> Aloft; – momentous but uneasy bliss!
> To their full hearts the universe seemed hung
> On that brief meeting's slender filament!
>
> (pp. 75–6)

This gathers up some of the key moments of Juan's and Haidee's love-making – the 'wind so low', the 'twilight glow', the beating hearts, there being no other 'life beneath the sky' and, most notably, the way that the poet appears to suspend time in line with human wishes while indicating that such intervals are an illusion (II. 185, 188). It may be that Wordsworth was prompted to add this after reading *Don Juan*, converted to the view that rapture ought to be part of the narrative, but not a rapture expressed by Byronic antithesis.

Another addition to the 1820 'Vaudracour and Julia' episode strengthens the possibility that Wordsworth was responding (if subliminally) to Byron's way with transitions. Vaudracour accidentally kills an assailant and is sent to prison. In 1805 the narrative had followed Julia through the hopes and fears of the next three weeks, but in 1820 we get a much more sudden development:

Have you beheld a tuft of winged seed
That, from the dandelion's naked stalk
Mounted aloft, is suffered not to use
Its natural gifts for purposes of rest,
Driven by the autumnal whirlwind to and fro
Through the wide element? or have you marked
The heavier substance of a leaf-clad bough,
Within the vortex of a foaming flood,
Tormented? by such aid you may conceive
The perturbation of each mind; – ah no!
Desperate the Maid, – the Youth is stained with blood!
But as the troubled seed and tortured bough
Is man, subjected to despotic sway.

(pp. 77–8)

Although weighed down by an extended Miltonic simile, the unexpected force of Wordsworth's interrogations suggests Byron's influence. Byron often turns to his readers with tangential questions: 'Did'st ever see a Gondola?' we are asked in *Beppo* (l. 145); 'Grim reader! did you ever see a ghost?' comes later in *Don Juan* (XV. 95). Indeed, in 'Vaudracour and Julia' as revised after 1820, Wordsworth's role as narrator becomes (for him) exceptionally obtrusive. In the 1850 *Prelude* Wordsworth advertises the fact that something has been removed from Book IX. Interrupting himself with parentheses and dashes, Wordsworth teases the reader with how he 'might' begin a tale, before claiming that he will not 'turn / To loiter wilfully', and leaves it untold (IX. 557, 561–2). Inextricably linked with Wordsworth's own personal history, this narrative coquetry is the closest Wordsworth gets to experimenting with a Byronic voice. His transition recalls us to the artificiality of the situation, that what is being read is, however true to life, a work of art. However – like all abrupt transitions, then and now – it runs the risk of alienating the reader it wishes to seduce.

## Notes

1 All quotations from Byron's poetry refer to Lord Byron, *The Complete Poetical Works*, ed. Jerome J. McGann, 7 vols. (Oxford, 1980–93).
2 'Mobilité' is Byron's word. See his note to XVI. 97.
3 Samuel Taylor Coleridge, *Biographia Literaria or Biographical Sketches of My Literary Life and Opinions*, ed. James Engell and W. Jackson Bate, 2 vols. (Princeton, 1983), ii. 121.
4 *Collected Letters of Samuel Taylor Coleridge*, ed. Earl Leslie Griggs, 6 vols. (Oxford, 1956–71), ii. 1116, 1111.
5 *The Iliad of Homer*, ed. Maynard Mack, 2 vols. (1967), ii. 212.
6 *The Life and Works of William Cowper*, ed. Robert Southey, 8 vols. (1854), vii. 291.

7 *A Pindarique Ode, Humbly offered to the Queen to which is prefix'd a discourse on the pindarique ode* (1706), p. i.

8 The appeal to a 'secret connexion' was also made by Abraham Cowley whose talk of 'Invisible Connexions' was picked up by Coleridge. See Paul Magnuson, *Coleridge and Wordsworth: A Lyrical Dialogue* (Princeton, 1988), p. 17. See also H. J. Jackson, 'Coleridge's Lessons in Transition: The "Logic" of the "Wildest Odes"', in eds. Thomas Pfau and Robert F. Gleckner, *Lessons of Romanticism: A Critical Companion* (Durham, NC, 1998), pp. 213–24.

9 Samuel Johnson, *The Rambler*, ed. W. J. Bate and Albrecht B. Strauss, 3 vols. (New Haven, 1969), iii, 77. 'To proceed from one truth to another, and connect distant propositions by regular consequences, is the great prerogative of man. Independent and unconnected sentiments flashing upon the mind in quick succession, may, for a time, delight by their novelty, but they disappear from systematical reasoning, as single notes from harmony, as glances of lightening from the radiance of the sun' (iii. 78).

10 *The Art of Poetry on a New Plan, illustrated with a great variety of examples from the best English Poets*, 2 vols. (1762), ii. 40.

11 *Lectures on Rhetoric and Belles Lettres*, 2 vols. (1783), ii. 356.

12 For further discussion of sudden transition in poetry, see praise of 'beautiful disorder' in *The Beauties of Poetry Display'd*, 2 vols. (1757), i. p. xxxii. Johnson's campaign against the offences of 'lax and lawless versification' is saluted in Robert Potter, *An Inquiry into some passages in Dr. Johnson's Lives of the Poets: particularly his observations of Lyric Poetry, and the Odes of Gray* (1783), p. 11; see also Robert Potter, *The Art of Criticism as Exemplified in Dr Johnson's Lives of the most eminent English Poets* (1789). For a later defence of 'abruptness of transition, and a peculiar warmth of impetuosity and diction', see Nathan Drake, *Literary Hours or Sketches Critical and Narrative* (1798), p. 278.

13 The philosophical and scientific contexts are discussed in Richard Terry, 'Transitions and Digressions in the Eighteenth-Century Long Poem', *SEL*, 32 (1992), 495–510. For discussion of the links and connections of Sensibility, see David Fairer, 'Sentimental Translation in Mackenzie and Sterne', *E in C*, XLIX, 2, (1999), 132–51.

14 *An Inquiry Concerning the Human Understanding*, note to Section III, 'Of the Association of Ideas'; quoted in Martin Kallich, 'The Associationist Criticism of Francis Hutcheson and David Hume', *Studies in Philology*, 43 (1946), 644–67, 663.

15 *Johnson on Shakespeare*, i. 67, 74.

16 For discussion of continuities and differences between Wordsworth and Shakespeare in *Biographia Literaria*, see Seamus Perry, *Coleridge and the Uses of Division* (Oxford, 1999), pp. 246–74.

17 *Biographia Literaria*, ii. 85.

18 *Byron's Letters and Journals*, ed. Leslie A. Marchand, 13 vols. (1982–94), iv. 164.

19 *The Correspondence of Robert Dodsley 1733–1764*, ed. James E. Tierney (Cambridge, 1988), p. 335.

20 *Biographia Literaria*, ii. 5.

21 *Wordsworth and Coleridge, Lyrical Ballads*, ed. R. L. Brett and A. R. Jones (1963; repr. 1971), pp. 106–7.

22 Edward Young, *Night Thoughts*, ed. Stephen Cornford (Cambridge, 1989). See also VI. 48: 'Nor dreadful our *Transition*; tho' the Mind . . . Is prone to paint it dreadful'.

23 *Letters*, i. 317.

24 Sir Joshua Reynolds, *The Discourses on Art*, ed. Robert R. Wark (New Haven, 1975), p. 61. Throughout Discourse IV Reynolds warns the artist about the dangers of 'minuteness', 'minute peculiarities' and 'particularities' (pp. 58, 60).

25 See Jonathan Wordsworth, *The Borders of Vision* (Oxford, 1982), pp. 10–13; Mary Jacobus, *Tradition and Experiment in Wordsworth's Lyrical Ballads 1798* (Oxford, 1976; repr. 1979), pp. 179–81; John Bayley, 'The Order of Battle at Trafalgar', in *The Order of Battle at Trafalgar and Other Essays* (1987), pp. 16–18; Susan Wolfson, *The Questioning Presence: Wordsworth, Keats and the Interrogative Mode in Romantic Poetry* (Cornell, 1986), p. 43; Geoffrey H. Hartman, *The Unremarkable Wordsworth* (1987), p. 37; Seamus Perry, *Coleridge and the Uses of Division*, p. 279. Hartman suggests that the speech of the old man recreates the 'ingenious final turn' of a Greek epigram.

26 Joanna Baillie, *A Series of Plays: in which it is attempted to delineate the stronger passions of the mind* (1798), p. 31.

27 *The Beauties of Johnson* (1781), p. 37.

28 William Wordsworth, *The Borderers*, ed. Robert Osborn (Ithaca, 1982), pp. 63, 65.

29 *The Notebooks of Samuel Taylor Coleridge*, ed. Kathleen Coburn and Merton Christensen, Bollingen Series 50, 4 vols. (1957–90), i. 432, f. 53.

30 For a different reading of the hedgerows as fiction opposed to vision within the 'infra shape' of the poem, see Thomas McFarland, *William Wordsworth: Intensity and Achievement* (Oxford, 1992), pp. 34–56.

31 *Notebooks*, ii. 2398.

32 Wordsworth, *Poetical Works*, ed. Ernest de Selincourt (Oxford, 1936; repr. 1985). Alison Chapman reads this recognition of absence as an epiphany in 'Uncanny Epiphanies in the Nineteenth-Century Sonnet Tradition', in Wim Tigges, (ed.), *Moments of Moment: Aspects of the Literary Epiphany*, Studies in Literature, 25 (1999), pp. 115–35.

33 William Wordsworth, *Shorter Poems 1807–1820*, ed. Carl H. Ketcham (Ithaca, 1989), p. 112.

34 Blair, *Lectures*, i. 72.

35 MS John Murray Archive, first published in Peter Cochran, 'Francis Cohen, *Don Juan*, and Casti', *Romanticism*, 4/1 (1998), 120–4: 123.

36 *Byron's Letters and Journals*, vi. 207.

37 *Byron: The Critical Heritage*, ed. Andrew Rutherford (New York, 1970), pp. 131, 136, 134.

38 *The Romantics Reviewed*, Part B: *Byron and Regency Society Poets*, ed. Donald H. Reiman, 5 vols. (New York, 1972), iv. 1399.

39 Ibid. v. 2012, 2149.

40 *A Treatise on English Versification* (1827), p. 164.

41 See James Chandler, 'The Pope Controversy: Romantic Poetics and the English Canon', *Critical Inquiry*, 10/3 (1984), pp. 481–509.

42 *The Letters of William and Dorothy Wordsworth*, ed. Ernest de Selincourt, 2nd edn., *The Middle Years, 1812–1820*, rev. Mary Moorman and Alan G. Hill (Oxford, 1970), p. 304.

43 John Opie, *Lectures on Painting Delivered at the Royal Academy of Arts* (1809), p. 62.

44 Lord Byron, *The Complete Miscellaneous Prose*, ed. Andrew Nicholson (Oxford, 1991), p. 116.

45 *Biographia Literaria*, ii. 87–8, 107, 122.

46 Ibid. ii. 122.

47 *The Complete Works of William Hazlitt*, ed. P. P. Howe, 21 vols. (1930–34), xi. 75.
48 See the Sale Catalogue of 1816 in *The Complete Miscellaneous Prose*, pp. 244, 242.
49 Michael O'Neill, *Romanticism and the Self-Conscious Poem* (Oxford, 1997), p. 98.
50 For an argument that both narratives were responding to Rousseau's Julie, see Nicola J. Watson, 'Novel Eloisas: Revolutionary and Counter-Revolutionary Narratives in Helen Maria Williams, Wordsworth and Byron', *The Wordsworth Circle*, 23/1 (1991), pp. 18–23.
51 William Wordsworth, *The Prelude 1799, 1805, 1850*, ed. Jonathan Wordsworth, M. H. Abrams and Stephen Gill (New York, 1979), ix. 635–6.

# 14

# KEATS AND
# THE USE OF POETRY

### *Helen Vendler*

Source: *The Music of What Happens: Poems, Poets, Critics* (Cambridge, Mass: Harvard University Press, 1988), pp. 115–31.

Heidegger asked, "What is the poet for in a destitute time?" I want to depart from Heidegger's premises, though not from his question: What can we say is the use of poetry? Heidegger's premises are those of nineteenth-century nostalgia, a nostalgia for the presence of God in the universe. He writes as one deprived of theological reassurance, seeing emptiness about him, and longing for presence. He suggests that the poet exists to restore presence, to testify to its possibility — or at least, like Hölderlin, to testify to felt absence.

These are premises of a particular moment — the moment of Götter-dämmerung. But Heidegger's plangent lament offers only one response to that moment; readers will remember Nietzsche's far more athletic and exulting response to the same moment, and some will recall Wallace Stevens's remark in "Two or Three Ideas":

> To see the gods dispelled in mid-air and dissolve like clouds is one of the great human experiences. It is not as if they had gone over the horizon to disappear for a time; nor as if they had been over-come by other gods of greater power and profounder knowledge. It is simply that they came to nothing . . . It was their annihilation, not ours, and yet it left us feeling that in a measure, we too had been annihilated . . . At the same time, no man ever muttered a petition in his heart for the restoration of those unreal shapes. There was in every man the increasingly human self, which instead of remaining the observer, the non-participant, the delinquent, became constantly more and more all there was or so it seemed; and whether it was so or merely seemed so still left it for him to resolve life and the world in his own terms.

Perhaps we can consider a response like Heidegger's as one dictated not by the facts of the case but by a certain temperament in Heidegger himself. Another temperament, other premises. And in the confidence that the use of the poet, in human terms, remains constant even through the vicissitudes of cultural change, I want to take up the ideas on the social function of poetry expressed by John Keats. Other poets could serve as well, but I choose Keats as a poet I know well whose original position on the question included the lament voiced by Heidegger (see the "Ode to Psyche") but whose final position is one of more sophistication and more buoyancy.

Keats, a resolute nonbeliever and political radical, came into a post-Enlightenment world, it is true, but it was still a world which felt some of those pangs of loss later expressed by Heidegger. Keats too felt a religious nostalgia, and it entered into many of his own meditations on the function of the poet; but he did not confine himself within that framework. I take the case of Keats to be an exemplary one of a modern poet seeking to define his own worth; Keats seems to me to have thought more deeply about the use of poetry than any subsequent poet. And although Keats will be my example, I want to close by bringing the topic into the present day, by quoting two contemporary poets who have reflected profoundly and long on it, the Polish poet Czeslaw Milosz and the Irish poet Seamus Heaney — both of them compelled by their history to inquire into their own social function. But I will begin with Keats as a modern posttheological poet, a forerunner to others contemplating the question of the use of secular poetry.

Keats had hoped, originally, that literary creation could confer therapeutic benefits on its audience. Admirable as the desire is that art could "beguile" Dido from her grief, or "rob from aged Lear his bitter teen" ("Imitation of Spenser"), this concept of art bars it from participation in human grief. Keats later brought this idea of art to its apogee in the "Ode to a Nightingale," where the poet-speaker hopes that the purely musical art of bird notes will enable him to fly away from the world of the dying young, the palsied old, fading Beauty, and faithless Love. We must distinguish Keats's "escapism" (as it has sometimes been called) from an escapism that does not promise a therapeutic result, such as comforting Dido or Lear or Ruth in grief, "charming the mind from the trammels of pain" ("On Receiving a Curious Shell").

Other ends of art early proposed by Keats include the civilizing psychological one of "attuning . . . the soul to tenderness" ("To Lord Byron") and the educative one of expanding the soul, as, by vicarious experience, it strays in Spenser's halls and flies "with daring Milton through the fields of air" ("Written on the Day That Mr. Leigh Hunt Left Prison") — a view of art given its classical Keatsian expression in the sonnet on Chapman's Homer. Keats's concept of the *utile* here is far from the usual didactic one, which emphasizes social responsibility and moral action. To become tender, to expand one's sense of imaginative possibility, are early recommendations consistent with Keats's later program of converting the blank intelligence into a human "soul"; the difference we notice here is the absence of that "world of pains and troubles" which will become the chief schooling agent of the heart in the letter on soul-making.

Keats, in his early poetry, enumerates four social functions of poetry: a historical thematic one, as epic poetry recorded history of an exalted sort, written by "bards, that erst sublimely told heroic deeds"; a representational (if allegorical) one, as Shakespeare gave, in his dramatic poetry, an incarnation of the passions; a didactic one, as in Spenser's "hymn in praise of spotless Chastity" ("Ode to Apollo"); and a linguistically preservative one, which can "revive" for our day an archaic language, "the dying tones of minstrelsy" ("Specimen of an Induction to a Poem"). And yet, Keats perhaps sensed that these functions — historical, allegorically representational, didactic, and linguistically preservative — were not to be his own: these claims for the social functions of poetry are, in his early work, asserted merely, not poetically enacted. A fair example of the feebleness of the early work comes in Keats's epistle to his brother George, where, after describing the living joys of the bard, Keats writes of "posterity's award," the function of the poet's work after he has died, as society makes use of his verse:

> The patriot shall feel
> My stern alarum, and unsheathe his steel . . .
> The sage will mingle with each moral theme
> My happy thoughts sententious; . . .
> Lays have I left of such a dear delight
> That maids will sing them on their bridal night.
> . . . To sweet rest
> Shall the dear babe, upon its mother's breast,
> Be lulled with songs of mine.

These uses of poetry are strictly ancillary; presumably the hero would still be heroic, the sage wise, the maids bridally delighted, and the baby sleepy, even without the help of the poet. In this conception, poetry is chiefly an intensifying accompaniment to life.

Keats's earliest notions of the power of art were concerned chiefly with the theme the poem may embody. The poet's pastoral tale will distract the grieving; his patriotic and moral sentiments will inspire hero and sage; and his love poems will wake an answering echo in the breast of the young. Poems exist to charm the fair daughters of the earth with love tales, and to warm earth's sons with patriotic sententious ideas.

It is to be expected that a poet of Keats's honesty would soon perceive that the embodying of a thematic and didactic intent was not his own sole motive in composing verse. He eventually admitted that in venturing on "the stream of rhyme" he himself sailed "scarce knowing my intent," but rather exploring "the sweets of song: / The grand, the sweet, the terse, the free, the fine; . . . / Spenserian vowels that elope with ease . . . / Miltonian storms, and more, Miltonian tenderness; . . . / The sonnet . . . / The ode . . . / The epigram . . . / The epic" ("To Charles Cowden Clarke"). This avowal of the aesthetic motives of creation, this picture of the artist investigating his medium — its vocal range, its prosodic inventions, its emotional tonalities, and its formal genres — sorts uneasily with Keats's former emphasis on the thematic social service of poetry.

While the emphasis on social service always brings in, for Keats, the relief of pain, the emphasis in descriptions of art itself, in early Keats, dwells always on the pleasure principle, so that even woe must be, in literature, "pleasing woe" ("To Lord Byron"), and poetry must make "pleasing music, and not wild uproar" ("How Many Bards"), full of glorious tones and delicious endings ("On Leaving Some Friends"). In these early poems, Keats expresses the characteristic view of the youthful poet, to whom the aesthetic can be found only in the beautiful.

Keats's first attempt to reconcile his philosophical emphasis on social service and his instinctive commitment to those aesthetic interests proper to composition appears in "I stood tiptoe," where he proposes an ingenious reconciliation by suggesting that form allegorically represents content:

> In the calm grandeur of a sober line,
> We see the waving of the mountain pine;
> And when a tale is beautifully staid,
> We feel the safety of a hawthorn glade.

The myths of the gods are said, in "I stood tiptoe," to be formally allegorical renditions of man's life in nature: a poet seeing a flower bending over a pool invents the myth of Narcissus. This is a promising solution for Keats: that form, being an allegory for content, bears not a mimetic but an algebraic relation to life. But in "I stood tiptoe," this solution is conceptualized rather than formally enacted.

In his next manifesto, "Sleep and Poetry," Keats makes an advance on the thematic level, realizing that his former advocacy of a consoling thematic happiness to cure human sorrow cannot survive as a poetic program. Rather, he says, he must "pass the realm of Flora and old Pan" for a "nobler life" where he may encounter "the agonies, the strife / Of human hearts." With the thematic admission of tragic material, formal notions of power and strength can at last enter into Keats's aesthetic and fortify his former aesthetic values — beauty and mildness — with a new sculptural majesty:

A drainless shower
Of light is Poesy; 'tis the supreme of power;
'Tis might half-slumbering on its own right arm.

Nonetheless, Keats is still critical of a poetry that "feeds upon the burrs, / And thorns of life," arguing rather for the therapeutic function of poetry, "that it should be a friend / To soothe the cares, and lift the thoughts of man" — an end still envisaged in the later "Ode on a Grecian Urn." The poet is simply to "tell the most heart-easing things"; and the poetry of earth ranges only from the grasshopper's delight to the cricket's song "in warmth increasing ever."

A far sterner idea of poetry arises when Keats hopes that something will draw his "brain / Into a delphic labyrinth" ("On Receiving a Laurel Crown"). As soon as he admits thought, prophecy, and labyrinthine mystery into the realm of poetry, Keats becomes frightened at the interpretive responsibilities that lie before him, objectified for him in the example of the Elgin marbles. He cries out that he is too weak for such godlike hardship, that these "glories of the brain / Bring round the heart an undescribable feud."

But Keats obeys the Delphic imperative and writes his first tragic poem, a sonnet on the death of Leander, forcing his art to describe his worst personal specter, the image of a dying youth whom nothing can save. Keats's chief tragic adjective, "desolate," appears for the first time at this period (in his sonnet on the sea), to reappear in the "Hymn to Pan," the passage in "Endymion" on the Cave of Quietude, and the "Ode on a Grecian Urn." Henceforth, Keats can conceive of poetry as a mediating, oracular, and priestlike art, one which, by representation of the desolate in formal terms, can interpret the mysteries of existence to others.

The long romance "Endymion" marks Keats's first success in finding poetic embodiments for the principles he had so far been able merely to assert. The tale of Endymion is not socially mimetic; rather, it is allegorical of human experiences; however, it is still a "pleasing tale," a pastoral, not a tragedy. Even so, Keats admits in "Endymion" two tragic principles that he will later elaborate: that in contrast to warm and moving nature, art must seem cold and carved or inscribed (a marble altar garlanded with a tress of flowers, the inscribed cloak of Glaucus); and that the action demanded of their devotees by Apollo and Pan is a sacrifice of the fruits of the earth. Art is admitted for the first time to be effortful: Pan is implored to be

the unimaginable lodge
For solitary thinkings; such as dodge
Conception to the very bourne of heaven,
Then leave the naked brain.

These daring and difficult solitary thinkings and new concepts will become, says Keats, "the leaven, / That spreading in this dull and clodded earth / Gives it a touch ethereal — a new birth."

In one sense, this passage represents the end of Keats's theoretical thinking about the nature and social value of poetry. But he could not yet describe how solitary original thinkings become a leaven to resurrect society. The poem "Endymion," as it journeys between the transcendent Cynthia and the Indian maid, may be seen as a journeying to and fro between the two elements of solitude and society, as Keats looks for a place where he can stand. He would like to avert his gaze from the misery of solitude, where those solitary thinkings take place, but he summons up the courage to confront the necessities of his own writing. Eventually, he arrives at two embodying symbols. The first is the cloak of Glaucus, "o'erwrought with symbols by . . . ambitious magic," wherein everything in the world is symbolized, not directly or mimetically, but in emblems and in miniaturizations. Gazed at, however, these printed reductions swell into mimetic reality:

> The gulfing whale was like a dot in the spell.
> Yet look upon it, and 'twould size and swell
> To its huge self, and the minutest fish
> Would pass the very hardest gazer's wish,
> And show his little eye's anatomy.

Keats faces up, here, to the symbolic nature of art. Art cannot, he sees, be directly mimetic; it must always bear an allegorical or emblematic relation to reality. Also, art is not a picture (he is speaking here of his own art of writing), but a hieroglyph much smaller than its original. However, by the cooperation of the gazer (and only by that cooperation), the hieroglyph "swells into reality." Without "the very hardest gazer's wish," the little fish could not manifest himself.

In this way, as later in the "Ode on a Grecian Urn," Keats declares that art requires a social cooperation between the encoder-artist and the solitary decoder-beholder. (Keats thought of the transaction between the artwork and its audience in private, not communal, terms.) The prescriptions written on the scroll carried by Glaucus announce Keats's new program for poetic immortality: the poet must "explore all forms and substances / Straight homeward to their symbol-essences"; he must "pursue this task of joy and grief," and enshrine all dead lovers. In the allegory that follows, all dead lovers are resurrected by having pieces of Glaucus's scroll sprinkled on them by Endymion. Endymion goes "onward . . . upon his high employ, / Showering those powerful fragments on the dead."

This allegory suggests that one of the social functions of poetry is to revive the erotic past of the race so that it lives again. But in the fourth book of "Endymion," as Keats admits to the poem the human maiden Phoebe and her companion Sorrow, the poem begins to refuse its own erotic idealizations and resurrections. At the allegorical center of Book IV, the narrator of "Endymion" finds at last his second major symbol of art, the solitary and desolate Cave of Quietude, a "dark Paradise" where "silence dreariest is most articulate; . . . / Where those eyes are the brightest far that keep / Their lids shut longest in a dreamless sleep." This is the place of deepest content, even though "a grievous feud" is said to have led Endymion to the Cave of Quietude.

Keats thought that this discovery of the tragic, hieroglyphic, and solitary center of art meant that he must bid farewell to creative imagination, to "cloudy phantasms . . . / And air of vision, and the monstrous swell / Of visionary seas":

> No, never more
> Shall airy voices cheat me to the shore
> Of tangled wonder, breathless and aghast.

This farewell to "airy" imagination displays the choice that Keats at first felt compelled to make in deciding on a tragic and human art. He could not yet see a relation between the airy voices of visionary shores and human truth; and he felt obliged to choose truth. "I deem," says the narrator of Endymion, "Truth the best music." Endymion," uneasily balancing the visionary, the symbolic, and the truthful, had nonetheless brought Keats to his view of art as necessarily related, though in symbolic terms, to human reality; as necessarily hieroglyphic; as the locus of social cooperation by which the symbol regained mimetic force; and as a social resurrective power.

Shortly afterward, in a sudden leap of insight, Keats came upon his final symbol for the social function of art, a symbol not to find its ultimate elaboration, however, until he was able to write the ode "To Autumn." In the sonnet "When I have fears that I may cease to be," Keats summons up a rich gestalt:

> When I have fears that I may cease to be,
> Before my pen has glean'd my teeming brain,
> Before high-pilèd books, in charact'ry,
> Hold like rich garners the full-ripen'd grain . . .

The poet's "teeming brain" is the field gleaned by his pen; the produce of his brain, "full-ripened grain," is then stored in the hieroglyphic charactery of books, which are like rich garners. Organic nature, after its transmutation into charactery (like that of Glaucus's magic symbols) becomes edible grain. By means of this gestalt, Keats asserts that the material sublime, the teeming fields of earth, can enter the brain and be hieroglyphically processed into print. Keats's aim is now to see the whole world with godlike range and power, with the seeing of Diana, "Queen of Earth, and Heaven, and Hell" ("To Homer"), or that of Minos, the judge of all things ("On Visiting the Tomb of Burns").

Still, Keats has not yet enacted very far his convictions about the social function of art. The audience has been suggested as the consumer of the gleaned wheat that the poet had processed into grain; and the audience has been mentioned as the necessary cooperator in the reading of Glaucus's symbols, and as the resurrected beneficiaries of Glaucus's distributed scroll fragments. Now, in his greatest performative invention, Keats decides to play, in his own poetry, the role of audience and interpreter of symbols, not (as he so far had tended to do) the role of artist. This seems to me Keats's most successful aesthetic decision, one that distances him from his own investments (therapeutic and pleasurable alike) in creating. By playing the audience, he approaches his own art as one of its auditors, who may well want to know of what use this art will be to him.

In the odes on Indolence and to Psyche, Keats had played the role of the creating artist; but in the "Ode to a Nightingale" and the "Ode on a Grecian Urn" he is respectively the listener to music and the beholder of sculpture. Each of these odes inquires what the recipient of art stands to receive from art. Keats here represents the audience for art as a single individual, rather than as a collective social group such as his Greek worshippers on the urn. In the absence of ideational content ("Nightingale"), no social collective audience can be postulated; and a modern beholder does not belong to the society that produced the urn. Keats seems to suggest that the social audience is, in the case of art, an aggregate of individual recipients, since the aesthetic experience is primarily a personal one; but what the individual receives, society, as a multiplication of individuals, also receives, as we conclude from the enumeration of listeners to the nightingale through the ages.

In the two "aesthetic odes" proper to the senses of hearing and sight, Keats begins to enact the theories of the social function of art that he had previously only asserted. As the listener to the nightingale, Keats enters a realm of wordless, nonconceptual, and nonrepresentational song. He leaves behind the human pageant of sorrow and the griefs of consciousness; he forsakes the conceptual faculty, the perplexing and retarding brain. He offers himself up to beauty in the form of Sensation, as he becomes a blind ear, ravished by the consolations of sweet sounds articulated together by the composer-singer, the nightingale.

In the "Ode on a Grecian Urn," by contrast, Keats as audience opens his eyes to representational (if allegorical) art and readmits his brain, with all its perplexities and interrogations, to aesthetic experience. In this fiction, one function of art is still, as in the case of the "Ode to a Nightingale," to offer a delight of an aesthetic and sensuous sort — this time a delight to the eye rather than to the ear. But no longer does art, with consolatory intent, ravish its audience away from the human scene; instead, it draws its audience into its truthful representational and representative pictures carved in stone. The fiction of artistic creation as a spontaneous outpouring to an invisible audience — the fiction of the "Ode to a Nightingale" — is jettisoned in favor of admitting the laborious nature of art, as sculpted artifice. And Keats, in the "Ode on a Grecian Urn," establishes the fact that appreciation need not be coincident with creation; he is appreciating the urn now, even though it was sculpted centuries ago. The freshness and perpetuity of art are insisted on, as is its social service to many generations, each of which brings its woe to the urn, each of which finds itself solaced by the urn, a friend to man. The social function of art, Keats discovers here, is to remind its audience, by means of recognizable representative figures, of emotions and events common to all human life — here, lust, love, and sacrifice — which bind generations each to each.

The Elgin marbles, recently installed in England, were Keats's example of his aesthetic ideal — an art that exerts a powerful aesthetic effect even though created long ago, even though the audience cannot ascribe historical or legendary names to the figures represented. This ode declares that art need not be historically based in order to be humanly meaningful; that art, although representationally mimetic, is not directly or historically mimetic; that art works in a symbolic or allegorical order, like that of Glaucus's cloak. It is wrong, therefore, to demand of an artist that he treat directly — autobiographically, journalistically, or historically — of events; his means are radically other than reportage. In fact, unless he pursues things to their "symbol-essences" he will not be able to communicate with ages later than his own.

Finally, in the ode "To Autumn," Keats finds his most comprehensive and adequate symbol for the social value of art. He does this by playing, in this ode, two roles at once. Once again, as in the "Ode on Indolence" and the "Ode to Psyche," he will play the role of the artist, the dreamer indolent in reverie on the bedded grass or the gardener Fancy engaged in touching the fruits of the earth into life. But he will also play the role of audience, of the one who seeks abroad to behold the creative goddess and sings hymns to her activity and her music.

In "To Autumn," in his final understanding of the social function of art, Keats chooses nature and culture as the two poles of his symbolic system. He sees the work of the artist as the transformation of nature into culture, the transmutation of the teeming fields into garnered grain (the gleaning of the natural into books, as his earlier sonnet had described it). Since civilization itself arose from man's dominion over nature, the processing of nature by agriculture became the symbol in Greece of the most sacred mysteries. The vegetation goddess Demeter, with her sheaf of corn and her poppies, was honored in the Eleusinian rituals. And the two symbolic harvests, bread and wine, food and drink, remain transmuted even to this day in the Christian Eucharist.

301

Keats's autumn ode takes as its allegory for art the making of nature into nurture. The artist, with reaping hook, gleaning basket, and cider press, denudes nature, we may say, but creates food. We cannot, so to speak, drink apples or eat wheat; we can only consume processed nature, apple juice and grain. Since the artist is his own teeming field, art, in this allegory, is a process of self-immolation. As life is processed into art by the gleaning pen or threshing flail, the artist's own life substance disappears, and where wheat was, only a stubble-plain can be seen; but over the plain there rises a song. Song is produced by the steady rhythm of nature transmuted by self-sacrifice into culture. Art does not mimetically resemble nature, any more than cider mimetically resembles apples. But without apples there would be no cider; without life there would be no hieroglyphs of life. In this way, Keats insists again on the radically nonmimetic nature of art but yet argues for its intelligible relation to life in its representative symbolic order, and for its constitutive power in that order.

Keats is the audience for the artist-goddess's sacrifice of herself into food, as she passes from careless girl through ample maternity and into her own death vigil; when all the corn has been threshed, and all the apples pressed, she disappears; nature has become culture. As her beneficiary, Keats is full of an overflowing gratitude — for her generous omnipresence ("whoever seeks abroad / May find thee") and for her elegiac harmonies ("thou hast thy music too"). Her rhythms permeate the whole world until all visual, tactile, and kinetic presence is transubstantiated into Apollonian music for the ear.

We can now put Keats's view over against Heidegger's. Heidegger looks at the world and sees an absence; Keats looks at the world and sees, through the apparition of postharvest absence, a vision of past natural plenty — apples, nuts, grapevines, gourds, honey, and grain. For Keats, the task of the poet is to remember and recreate the immeasurable plenitude of the world and to process it, by the pen, into something which draws from the sensual world but does not resemble it mimetically. The artist must find a charactery, or symbolic order, by which to turn presence into intellectual grain and cider, food and drink. The reaper's hook, the threshing flail, and the cider press are images of the mind at work, processing nature. The work of the mind in aesthetic production is not interrogative or proposition-making (as Keats had thought in the "Ode on a Grecian Urn"), but rather "stationing" — composing symbolic items in a symbolic arrangement until that order bears an algebraic or indicative relation to the order of reality. Only in this way is a vision of reality made intelligible to other minds.

It is not by being a sage or a physician (two roles that appealed to Keats) that the artist produces his result in other minds; it is by his creation of symbolic equivalences arranged in a meaningful gestalt. Once the mind of the audience sees this vision of reality, this shadow of a magnitude, it

302

shares its intelligibility, can "consume" it. The haphazard and unreadable texture of life becomes the interpreted and the stationed. We, as audience, may indeed find ourselves enlightened, solaced, or cured by art; but it cannot be the artist's chief *aim* to enlighten or solace or cure us; he must rather aim to transmute the natural into the hieroglyphic aesthetic, making his music part of a choral harmony contributed to by all his fellow artists. If his art is not music, it has not yet done its work of transubstantiation but is still inert direct mimesis.

By putting the "airy voices" of his choir of creatures (and the "barred clouds") at the end of his ode, Keats places the imaginative (the quality he had thought he might have to forfeit in his quest for reality and truth) in a harmonious relation to the natural. He thus displays the aesthetic principle of music as paramount over even the algebraic or symbolic principle of allegorical representation. Music resembles apples even less than cider does; and yet it is the music of autumn, which arises cotemporally with its trans-mutations and because of them, on which Keats insists as he closes his ode.

I believe that every poet of substance passes through a course of realiza-tions very like those of Keats. Judging from their juvenilia, artists all begin with an exquisite, almost painful, response to the beautiful, and an equal revulsion against the ugly. In their youth, they often equate the tragic and the deformed with the ugly, and attempt therefore to create an idyllic counterspace. This space is usually not a social one; at most it is occupied only by a narcissistically conceived other, the beloved. As soon as the social scene intrudes into the young artist's poetry — either in the form of history (mythological or actual) or in the form of current political or domestic struggle — the poem is forced into the world of human tragedy. This exem-plary process leads to a new aesthetic, in which the dissonant, the mutable, and the ugly must find a place. Usually, a poet writes *about* such disagree-able subjects before he can write *within* them. Later, if the poet can do the requisite work of internalization and symbolizing, there comes the discovery of a virtual order, powerfully organized, through which the complex vision of tragic reality can express itself. The move into the symbolic order always angers those for whom the artist's duty is a historically mimetic one, and for whom the clarity of propaganda is preferable to the ambivalence of human response to the human world. "Art," Yeats said, "is but a vision of reality." In using the concessive "but" and the symbolic word "vision," Yeats argues for the algebraic or allegorical relation between art and reality. One who cannot recognize that algebraic relation, and bring it, by his own gaze, back into "swelling reality," is incompetent to read art.

Those poets who encounter particularly acute political stress, like Czeslaw Milosz and Seamus Heaney, are always urged to be more socially specific in their poetry than poets can be. Poets resist this pressure by offering their own meditations on the social function of the artist faced with the huge and varied questions of the world, and by enacting an aesthetic which embraces social reality in an algebraic way. Imagination, as Stevens says, presses back against the pressure of reality. I want to quote two poems, one by Millosz, one by Heaney, which reaffirm the necessarily symbolic nature of the artist's work and yet repeat and enact its equally necessary connection with social reality.

Milosz's poem, "The Poor Poet," was written in Warsaw in 1944, during the last horrors of the war. It recapitulates the passage that we have seen in the young poet from an aesthetic of joy to an aesthetic of tragedy; it is modernist in its hatred of the mutually tormenting relation between the arranged symbolic order of art and the random tragic scene of life; and it sees the creating of the symbolic order as a form of revenge against the horrors of life. The poet as a man is deformed by the deformations he witnesses; and for all the beauty he creates he cannot himself be beautiful but must share the deformities of the world:

*The Poor Poet*

The first movement is singing,
A free voice, filling mountains and valleys.
The first movement is joy,
But it is taken away.

And now that the years have transformed my blood
And thousands of planetary systems have been born and died in
  my flesh,
I sit, a sly and angry poet
With malevolently squinted eyes,
And, weighing a pen in my hand,
I plot revenge.

I poise the pen and it puts forth twigs and leaves, it is covered
  with blossoms.

And the scent of that tree is impudent, for there, on the real
  earth,
Such trees do not grow, and like an insult
To suffering humanity is the scent of that tree.

Some take refuge in despair, which is sweet
Like strong tobacco, like a glass of vodka drunk in the hour of
  annihilation.
Others have the hope of fools, rosy as erotic dreams.

Still others find peace in the idolatry of country,
Which can last for a long time,
Although little longer than the nineteenth century lasts.

304

But to me a cynical hope is given,
For since I opened my eyes I have seen only the glow of fires,
    massacres,
Only injustice, humiliation, and the laughable shame of
    braggarts.
To me is given the hope of revenge on others and on myself.
For I was he who knew
And took from it no profit for myself.

(Selected Poems, 53–54)

Formally, this poem places its one moment of adult "beauty" in one line, recounting the blossoming of the pen and alluding to Aaron's rod. This brief Keatsian moment (with its promise of fruit to come, following the blossoms), is encapsulated, like a kernel, within Milosz's two mentions of revenge: "I plot revenge . . . To me is given the hope of revenge." It is also encapsulated within tragedy ("Joy . . . is taken away") and the common responses to tragedy, whether despair, hope, or idolatry. The poet's "cynical hope" is the penalty for his creation of poetry, and his revenge is directed not only against others but against himself for daring to "insult" suffering humanity with the perfection of form. Milosz's Manichaean spirit poses the problem of content and form in its most violent aspect, as the serenity of form (even here, in the concentric form of this lyric) tortures the anguish of content ("fires, massacres, . . . injustice, humiliation . . . shame"). There can be, according to Milosz, no political poetry that does not aim at the aesthetic equilibrium of form. Art, in its social function, thus enacts for us the paradox of our orderly symbolic capacity as it exists within the disorder it symbolizes.

A poem by Seamus Heaney about Chekhov traces again the young writer's passage from sensuous pleasure to social obligation. The recognition of social obligation by the writer must pass, the poem suggests, not into social activism but rather into symbolic representation. In the poem, as in fact, Chekhov decides to leave his attractive life in Moscow to go to see the penal colony on the faraway island of Sakhalin, off the east coast of Russia below Japan. Though Chekhov is a doctor, he does not go to Sakhalin to minister to the convicts, but rather to observe, and to write a book. He even forces himself to stay to watch a flogging in order to see the full reality of life in the colony. And then he has to find the right tone to write about what he has seen — not tract, not thesis. Once he has admitted the colony to his consciousness, he will never be able to exorcise it; he will carry a second convict-self within him. The parallels with Northern Ireland need no describing; the poet composing this poem has left Northern Ireland and lives in the Republic, but he writes about the reality he has left behind, and he must find a symbolic way to enact its truth.

Chekhov's biographer recounts that, as he departed for Sakhalin, the friends who came to see him off at the railway station gave him a bottle of cognac to drink when he should have arrived (by rail and boat and troika) at Sakhalin, thousands of miles away. The cognac is Chekhov's last taste of uncomplicated sensual joy; henceforth he will be a symbolic convict.

### Chekhov on Sakhalin

So, he would pay his "debt to medicine."
But first he drank cognac by the ocean
With his back to all he travelled north to face.
His head was swimming free as the troikas

Of Tyumin, he looked down from the rail
Of his thirty years and saw a mile
Into himself as if he were clear water:
Lake Baikhal from the deckrail of the steamer.

That far north, Siberia was south.
Should it have been an ulcer in the mouth,
The cognac that the Moscow literati
Packed off with him to a penal colony —

Him, born, you may say, under the counter?
At least that meant he knew its worth. No cantor
In full throat by the iconostasis
Got holier joy than he got from that glass

That shone and warmed like diamonds warming
On some pert young cleavage in a salon,
Inviolable and affronting.
He felt the glass go cold in the midnight sun.

When he staggered up and smashed it on the stones
It rang as clearly as the convict's chains
That haunted him. In the months to come
It rang on like the burden of his freedom

To try for the right tone — not tract, not thesis —
And walk away from floggings. He who thought to squeeze
His slave's blood out and waken the free man
Shadowed a convict guide through Sakhalin.

*Station Island*, 18–19

Heaney's poem implies that the way to write about the condition of the poet in twentieth-century Ireland is to write about a nineteenth-century Russian incident. The indirection proper to art is reflected thematically here in the repudiation of religious tract and political thesis alike: Chekhov's book is detached, descriptive, the book of a novelist, not an evangelist or a social reformer. Heaney's formal refusal to mention any audience for Chekhov's eventual book enacts the one condition for socially effective art — that it be directed, not to the transformation of its putative audience, but to the transformation of the artist's own self. By acknowledging his own past as the grandson of a serf and the son of a grocer, Chekhov can enter the chains of the convict and write powerfully about them. At the same time, he drinks with full relish and intoxication the brandy of his Moscow self, before he turns to "all he travelled north to face." The self-transformation of Keats's goddess of the corn acknowledged a similar death in the self as the condition of an art that could nourish others.

In separate ways, Milosz and Heaney have retraced the steps toward an analysis of art that we have seen in Keats. It is important to each of them to assert that poetry does perform a social function; it is equally important to them to remove it from a direct and journalistic mimesis. The poet indeed witnesses, constructs, and records; but the creation of a symbolic and musical form is the imperative, in the end, which he must serve if his witness is to be believed.

# 15

# WHAT GOOD IS FORMALIST CRITICISM? OR: *FORMS* AND *STORMS* AND THE CRITICAL REGISTER OF ROMANTIC POETRY

*Susan J. Wolfson*

Source: *Studies in Romanticism* 37 (1998), 77–94.

The question of my title matters mightily for romantic-era studies—in no small part because canonical "romanticism" has been cited for a formalism that is naively idealistic, or even worse, ideologically reactionary.[1] Yet these accounts often miss the complex reports of ideology in poetic form, or of how form, in poetic practice, in epistemology, and in social understanding, reads ideology. This essay examines such intricacy with a focus on passages from poems often cited in two challenging phases of recent criticism: deconstruction, with its interest in form-dissolving theories of language; and the subsequent new-historicism, with its interest in how literary form resolves social contradictions at the (false) level of aesthetic experience. While both schools have identified important avenues of romantic imagination, they have tended to withhold credit from the critical work of form itself: the way some poetic events may amount to a form-sensitive criticism, with social and political implications. One critical trace, or alert register of this work, I shall demonstrate, is the word *form*, especially when formed into a meta-rhyme with *storm*.

In the second book of *The Prelude*, Wordsworth recalls his receptivity to a primary poetry of earth, its disembodied sounds not yet, or never to be, submitted to human art:

> I would walk alone
> In storm and tempest, or in star-light nights
> Beneath the quiet Heavens; and, at that time,

> Have felt whate'er there is of power in sound
> To breathe an elevated mood, by form
> Or image unprofaned: and I would stand
> Beneath some rock, listening to sounds that are
> The ghostly language of the ancient earth,
> Or make their dim abode in distant winds.
>
> $(1805\ 2.321–29)^2$

Even as a romance of prelinguistic sounds—of language that is of the earth rather than of culture—is in the air, it is expressed in a medium that is inescapably, patently antithetical. Poetic form and the material form of writing, Wordsworth is too aware, involve the very profanity of form and image that this remembered sensation transcends. His sense of this contradiction is reflected in a potential rhyme that revision will amplify—the echo of *storm* (322) in the poetically self-reflexive end-word *form* (325)—yet in tandem with a muting enjambment (one of many in these lines): "form / Or image." In this ambivalence about the semantics of this rhyme, Wordsworth puts into play a poetic form that is discernible, but also discernibly faint, only dimly formative, subject to storms. We can see why Geoffrey Hartman cited this passage in his essay for *Deconstruction & Criticism* as emblematic of the tensed "relation between textuality and referentiality" that he saw as the hallmark of Wordsworth's style: "The poet's words are always antiphonal to the phoné of a prior experience" ("voice or sound before a local shape or human source can be ascribed") and so "precariously extended" over an abyss of natural passion. The result is a poetry "formally . . . hesitant, disjunctive," at best a "stumblingly progressive form."[3]

I want to linger over the formal attenuation Hartman sums only as a general conceptual category, because I'm struck by the meta-formalist cast of Wordsworth's revisions. Not only does he make *form* an end-rhyme with *storm*—a visible variant of form in his blank-verse field—but he also inverts the order so that *form* becomes the first, base word. His drafts show a persistent negotiation with how to manage this rhyme:[4]

> {Rising from mood by visible form . . .
>                   by visible form}
> To breathe an elevated mood, by form
>     That elevated visible form

[all words are subsequently canceled except "visible form"]

> By image unprofaned: or when I stood
>         As night grew darker with the          coming storm

He then started again with:

> Have felt whatee'r there is of power in sound
> To breathe an elevated mood, by form
> Or Image unprofaned; & I would stand
> If the night blackened with a coming storm

The passage eventually took this shape:

> for I would walk alone
> Under the quiet stars, and at that time
> Have felt whate'er there is of power in sound
> To breathe an elevated, by form
> Or Image unprofaned: and I would stand,
> If the night blackened with a coming storm,
> Beneath some rock, listening to notes that are
> The ghostly language of the ancient earth,
> Or make their dim abode in distant winds.
>
> (*1850* 2.303–11)

This is still a very ear-y eeriness. No wonder that in an earlier essay Hartman cited this passage to show how Wordsworth "often singles out the ear as an 'organ of vision,'" a dialectic of the senses projected to "counteract the tyranny of the eye."[5]

As a general sounding of Wordsworth's visionary politics and poetics, this is apt; yet the poetry here shows different alliances and lines of action. Wordsworth seems to solicit both ear and eye with his verse form, using their cooperation to counteract the visionary narrative. In revising, he was working out a paradox, how to represent in visible form energies and sounds unprofaned by form, visually or phonically. He decided to draw out from a latency in his verse not just a rare end-rhyme but a semantically potent meta-rhyme of *form* with *storm*. At the same time, his hesitation about the effect still retains that muting enjambment, "form / Or image." As much as the tenor of the verse, the rhyme for both eye and ear makes a semantic point about the difference, and then the eventual relation, between a poet's form and the notes (ghostly languages) wrought by a storm of natural agency. The rhyme does not undo the reverence for an energy, a music, a language uncontained by artifice. But in foregrounding the dependency of such imagination on expression in form, the rhyme reports a formal intelligence: profanities of form are the condition of human language and its poetry, even when the call is to imagine a contrary condition.

The record of this memory might have remained an insular moment of aesthetic biography, did not *The Prelude* embed it in a history in which the tension of storm and form, and the potential of forms to convey storms, keep returning to Wordsworth in different sites of experience. London first dazzles him with its "quick dance / Of colors, light, and forms" (*1850* 7.154–

55), but soon he is overwhelmed by its chaotic social text, shot through with the "forms and pressures of the time" (288)—an allusion to Hamlet's remark on what the aesthetic ought to manage in a controlled show (3.2.27). In this grotesque parody of aesthetic power operating in tyrannical independence of any human agency, the uncontainable life of the city becomes a "perpetual whirl" (725) of

> sundry Forms
> Commingled. Shapes which meet me in the way
> That we must tread.
> *(1850* 7.317–19)

One shape, a blaspheming woman, produces a crisis of conception that finds its best expression in a semantic rupture of form. With this sight, the "race of Man," seemed split

> In twain, yet leaving the same outward Form.
> Distress of mind ensued. . . .
> *(1850* 7.390–92)

In the sight line of these assaults, we see why this poet would conclude Book 7 by celebrating the "Virtue [in] the forms / Perennial of the ancient hills" (756–77)—natural forms that authorize poetic form as a positive power of articulation against the whirl of forms that distress the mind. At the same time, these latest *forms* bear a history as end-rhymes of poetic form, linking, almost as an extended *rime riche*, the sundry *Forms* (of London) and the distressing *Form* (of woman). Such repetition draws an extended meta-formal meditation on how social and historical forces shape poetic imagination. This effect is amplified, moreover, by the larger narrative of *The Prelude*, which involves memories of nature as a generator of storms as well as "forms / Perennial" (or shows storms to be one of these forms). Form and storm are a merely wishful antithesis.

What the plot of *The Prelude* advances on the level of these formalist intuitions is a critique of formalist contentments. It is telling that Shelley's most formally dynamic poem, *Mont Blanc*, can only half propose the subversive rhyme of *forms* and *storms*:[6]

> Mont Blanc appears,—still, snowy, and serene—
> Its subject mountains their unearthly forms
> Pile around it, ice and rock . . .
> A desert peopled by the storms alone.
> (61–63, 67)[7]

Although *storms* is given a personifying place in a nonhuman blankness, the human work of poetry does not give it more than a faint, almost still,

311

internal rhyme with *forms*, themselves the unearthly subjects of something (Mont Blanc) beyond the capacity of human poetry to represent. Condensed and made almost claustrophobically self-reflexive, such signing is what Paul de Man reads in Shelley's version of autobiography, *The Triumph of Life*. In "Shelley Disfigured," another essay in *Deconstruction & Criticism* [39–73] ), he tracks a critically self-conscious meta-formalism: a radically sensuous formalism whose deepest work, he says, is to expose form as blank figure, and whose deepest power is thus to tell a story of disfiguration and forgetting, of relations, past, passing and to come, repeatedly effaced and erased.

The passage that draws his attention presents the "grim Feature" named "Rousseau" describing (and seeming to re-live) his past enchantment by a nepenthe-bearing "shape all light":

> And her feet ever to the ceaseless song
>
>> Of leaves and winds and waves and birds and bees
>> And falling drops moved in a measure new
>> Yet sweet, as on the summer evening breeze . . .
>>
>> (375–78)

Here is a figure, de Man proposes, of language reduced to a bare form of repeated articulations, prior to any signifying function: "'measure' separates from the phenomenal aspects of signification as a specular *representation*, stressing instead the literal and material aspects of language"; and "since measure is any principle of linguistic organization, not only as rhyme and meter but as any syntactical or grammatical scansion, one can read 'feet' not just as the poetic meter that is so conspicuously evident in the terza rima of the poem, but as any principle of signification" (59–60).[8] This is a shrewd analysis and shrewd about the implications, the "subsequent undoing and erasure of the figure" (61). Yet de Man's larger designation of the "dramatic action of the narrative" as the action of the poetic form "disrupt[ing] the symmetry of cognition as representation" notably elides both the location of this effect in a particular actor named "Rousseau" and the formalism with which Shelley identifies him.

What might it mean for Shelley, in 1822, to have Rousseau bear a vision that "bur[ies] the poetic and philosophical light" in this way? To cast him in a poet's dream as a theorist of linguistic decadence and a romancer of language as sensuous form? The "particular seduction" of the linguistic figure, de Man urges, is that "it creates an illusion of meaning," a process enacted by "the shape [that] is a figure," whose undoing and erasure reveal it "to be the figure for the figurality of all signification."[9] Rousseau is no arbitrary vehicle for this lesson, however; he is an epochal figure of ideals betrayed by material history, of Enlightenment turned to Terror and then to aggressive triumph-building Empire, of hopes perhaps forever doomed in terms of political possibility. In this specificity, his reverie of the "shape all light" formulates a sensuous desire that cannot help but reflect, by only half-erased exclusions, the historical disappointment and fragmentation that haunt about its shape. The crisis of representation that he figures into *The Triumph* is simultaneously a crisis of historical narrative and political (self)reflection.[10]

To represent "Rousseau" reflecting on language or, more precisely, on poetic form, in this way in 1822 is to present a critique of the kind of aesthetic formalism that emerges as a reflex of failed political forms. On the dream-stage of *The Triumph*, "Rousseau" speaks as one disillusioned with the possibility of social and political reform, and thus too willing, too prone, to undoing form as figure and force of representation and too prone to lapse into a counterformalism of mere sensualism. We cannot know what the ultimate political report of Shelley's fragment would have been, or what further reflections of form it would have elaborated. Yet it is clear that he was working his formal tropes and textures into a visible tension with what Rousseau romances: the erasure of form as figure, its dissolution into the "literal and material aspects of language." This romance is always staged with irony. Thus "Rousseau" comes on stage in a sweep of history, which Shelley casts as a "form" in rhyming antithesis with the forces of oblitera-tion. His herald is the vehicle of an extended simile describing the "young Moon" shadowed by its own history. Just as this moonphase bears

> The ghost of her dead Mother, whose dim form
> Bends in the dark ether from her infant's chair,
>
> So came a chariot on the silent storm
> Of its own rushing splendour, and a shape
> So sate within as one whom years deform.
>
> (84–88)

Shelley audibly presses dim *form* and silent *storm* through his terza rima into the reverse of *deform*, a course that evokes the encounter with historical process.

Over and against the structure of forgetting and erasing that "Rousseau" configures to de Man, Shelley recalls these same rhymes when he has "Rousseau" recall his plunge into the triumph. "Rousseau" first feels himself moving "along the wilderness" as a trace of history, "the ghost of a forgotten form of sleep" (426–28). Yet if *form* seems "forgotten," it is actually forming its repetition, which emerges as an event of rhyme when "Rousseau" declares his refusal to remain in forgetfulness ("its" in 465) as

> the phantom of that early form
> Which moved upon its motion—but among

313

The thickest billows of the living storm
I plunged, and bared my bosom to the clime
Of that cold light, whose airs too soon deform.—

(464–68)

Even as "that early form"—the phantom trace of the "shape all light"—
seems about to be lost in the "living storm" of life whose forces "deform," the
repetition of the earlier *form* / *storm* / *deform* rhyme not only links this form
to Rousseau's present despair, but also extends this memory by form to the
dreaming poet who wakes to write these rhymes.[11] The "living storm" is
the metaphor, and the evocation, of historical process, the tumult of events
that beset and deform the phantoms of the imagination. It is thus not surprising to discover that Shelley was quite deliberate about having *form* echo
through the rest of Rousseau's telling of this storm. Sensing "the air / . . .
peopled with dim forms" (482–83)—the last phrase echoing the personified
"dim form" in the chariot (84)—Rousseau, says he "became aware // Of
whence those forms proceeded"; Shelley started to write *phan* then chose
*forms* (51ʳ). Rousseau notes how "From every form [Shelley revised from
*countenance* (51ᵛ)] the beauty slowly waned" (516–19), those falling "soonest,
from whose forms [revised from *limbs* (52ᵛ)] most shadows past" (542).
Shelley persistently rewrites to make *form* an actor in his forms, and stresses
its agency with anagramatic links to *from*. For Rousseau's report that "Mask
after mask fell from the countenance / And form of all" (536–37), Shelley even
alliterates the verbal form of 537 (originally "form of every pilgrim" [52ᵛ]) into
this dramatic fall, so that "form of all" can evoke a phantom "form of *fall*."[12]

This career of rhymes, in which *storm* is the crux by which *form* finds
its antonym *deform*, shows Shelley's effort to move beyond the idealizing
oppositions of *form* and *storm* on which he had spun the romance of *Epipsychidion* the year before. Its ideal, hailed as a "radiant form of Woman"
(22), is an abstraction of Form whose value is precisely its antithesis to the
historical contingencies summed in the counterpoint rhyme, *Storm*:

Thou living Form
Among the Dead! Thou Star above the Storm!

(27–28)

The antithesis is intensified when the poet repeats this rhyme to describe
not only her, but also, implicitly, his own labors of imagination. Her spirit
beckons him in words

Of antique verse and high romance—in form,
Sound, colour—in whatever checks that Storm
Which with the shattered present chokes the past.

(210–12)

314

Here, the romance of form, both as spiritual ideal and as ideal poetry, is a transcendence of history, redeeming the deforming, shattering force of temporality. There is a similar saving grace even in Byron's seemingly opposite courtship at the end of *Childe Harold's Pilgrimage*:

> Thou glorious mirror, where the Almighty's form
> Glasses itself in tempests; in all time,
> Calm or convulsed—in breeze, or gale, or storm . . .
>
>                    (4.183)[13]

Although divine form may take the image of storm, rather than check it, as in *Epipsychidion*, Byron contains this as only one of its syntaxes, preserving an idea of Almighty form above the tempest and its world of time. Its mirroring "Ocean" (179 ff.) knows no history, and so is saved from the cultural elegy of an earlier stanza, punctuated by a funereal chime of *storm*, a skeleton *form*, and ashes yet *warm*:

> Rome—Rome imperial, bows her to the storm,
> In the same dust and blackness, and we pass
> The skeleton of her Titanic form,
> Wrecks of another world, whose ashes still are warm.
>
>                    (4.46)

These rhymes play with a difference, not only linking imperial forms to a history of deformation, but also betraying elegiac consciousness as the deep source of ahistorical counter-idealizing.

Shelley's idealism is, similarly, almost habitually checked by the way its forms are shown to emerge from history rather than in transcendence of it. In the lines of *Epipsychidion* where *form* is not the shaper of rhyme, worldly forms betray: "half bewildered by new forms" (252), the poet pursues his veiled Divinity, unable to "find one form resembling hers" (254) among "many mortal forms" (267), and seeking relief from various worldly miseries allegorized in the plural counterpart "storms" (308, 352). By the time he is conceiving *The Triumph of Life*, it is clear that Shelley is reading such idealism of form critically in order to explore its ambiguous affiliations in the historical and temporal processes summed as "storm." And in this meditation, his epipsyche is no female divinity, but the ghost of worldly Rousseau, whose work in the poem is to expose the epochal despair whose symptom is a (futile) suspension of referentiality.

The rhymes of *storm* and *form* with which Shelley involves imagination and history gain a more aesthetically sensitive stage from Keats, a favored target of the critique that charges finely wrought forms such as his with disguising and dissolving social and ideological contradictions.[14] This romance surely called on Keats's imagination (and not in his alone), but he is not uncritically responsive. Though he might have contained *storm* with *form*, using the meta-rhyme to serve a harmonizing aesthetic ideology, he doesn't. Instead, he critically tenses the rhyme in sites of counter-expectation, two highly wrought forms: a Spenserian stanza itself closing an ornate romance, and the couplet of a Shakespearean sonnet. It is no slight context that the composition of both is informed and shaped by the material turmoils in Keats's life in 1818–1819: the loss of one brother to death and the emigration of the other to America, hostile reviews, anxieties over his financial situation and health. No wonder that in both texts Keats confronts his reader with the contingency of poetic form amidst the antagonisms and turmoil of historical existence.

The Spenserian stanza is the one with which he ends *The Eve of St. Agnes*:

> And they are gone: ay, ages long ago
> These lovers fled away into the storm.
> That night the Baron dreamt of many a woe,
> And all his warrior-guests, with shade and form
> Of witch, and demon, and large coffin-worm,
> Were long be-nightmar'd. Angela the old
> Died palsy-twitch'd, with meagre face deform;
> The Beadsman, after thousand aves told,
> For aye unsought for slept among his ashes cold.[15]

We know that Keats revised to get a chord of *storm*, *form* and *worm* to culminate in *deform*, a compositional perseverance noteworthy not only for its semantic momentum but also for its unpleasant effect, the disgusting "Change of Sentiment" about which his publishers' advisor, Richard Woodhouse complained.[16] Keats's use of *deform* as an adjective, moreover, is sufficiently rare, peculiar, and striking as to seem a deliberate revision of a dark enough Miltonic ally—the "dreadful and deform" shape of Death in *Paradise Lost* (2.706), or the vision of the world of death Adam receives from Michael in Book II:

> Sight so deform what heart of Rock could long
> Dry-ey'd behold? *Adam* could not, but wept,
> Though not of Woman born; compassion quell'd
> His best of man, and gave him up to tears
> A space.
>
> (494–98)[17]

Keats's "palsy-twitch'd, with meagre face deform" sounds like a grotesque excess designed to contain what Adam cannot, namely, compassion that blurs the forms of gender—the "best of man" quelled, even without a biological explanation. While Keats insisted that he wrote *The Eve* "for men"

and not "ladies" (*KL* 2.162–63), the *form*, *worm*, and *deform* left in the wake
of the lovers' flight into the *storm* seems, by these Miltonic lights, a reaction
formation against what aesthetic vision, Adam's or Keats's, may evoke from
men, in the space of epic or of romance.

These mazes and betrayals by form write figures quite different from the
way in 1818 Keats played the rhyme field in his description of Glaucus'
cloak (verse Shelley admired):

> Every ocean-form
> Was woven in with black distinctness. Storm,
> And calm, and whispering, and hideous roar,
> Quicksand, and whirlpool, and deserted shore,
> Were emblemed in the woof, with every shape
> That skims, or dives, or sleeps, 'twixt cape and cape.
>
> (*Endymion* 3.199–204)

Here, form and storm are balanced and reconciled in the weavings of art.
A similar aesthetics appears in Byron's containment of the erotic threat
of Gulbeyaz's rage: "the deep passions flashing through her form / Made
her a beautiful embodied storm" (*Don Juan* 5.135).[18] Even *Childe Harold's
Pilgrimage* III, published in 1816, just after the fall of Napoleon, was not so
dark as the end of *The Eve of St. Agnes*. In the wake of this catastrophic era
of war, Byron opted for an idealizing dualism:

> And when, at length, the mind shall be all free
> From what it hates in this degraded form,
> Reft of its carnal life, save what shall be
> Existent happier in the fly and worm,—
> When elements to elements conform,
> And dust is as it should be, shall I not
> Feel all I see, less dazzling, but more warm?
> The bodiless thought? the spirit of each spot?
> Of which, even now, I share at times the immortal lot?
>
> (3.74)

In this hope for the mind's freedom, Byron uses rhymings of *form* to deny
the human linkages on which Keats's rhymes insist. He manages this
idealist opposition even amidst the scathing satire of *The Vision of Judgment*
(written in 1821). Making his claim for the recently deceased George III,
The Prince of Air exhorts the company at Heaven's gate:

> When this old, blind, mad, helpless, weak, poor worm
> Began in youth's first bloom and flush to reign,
> The world and he both wore a different form,

> And much of earth and all the watery plain
>> Of ocean call'd him king; through many a storm
> His isles had floated on the abyss of time;
> For the rough virtues chose them for their clime.
>> (XLII)

The weak worm, a metaphor that snidely conflates the corpse with its imminent inheritor, is contained as a cartoon set in opposition to a still persistent Childe-Harolding idealism of a "different form" able to weather and rise above the "storm" of historical existence.

Worlds away from Byron's worldly satires, Keats's romance casts a colder eye on this idealism and stresses opposite affiliations of form. Involving the storms of the world with bad dreams, death, and the agony of a dying female body, he closes *The Eve of St. Agnes* in a deliberately revisionary and critical mode, purchased against all the consolations Regency readers expect of aesthetic form. In thus refusing "music's golden tongue" (20) and its finer tone of imagination, his stanza does what Jerome McGann says the 1820 volume does not, its poems "issued not to provoke but to allay conflict . . . not [to] open an explicit ideological attack upon the book's audience . . . but to dissolve social and political conflicts in the mediations of art and beauty."[19] McGann pursues this line in reading another poem published in 1820, "A Dream, After Reading Dante's episode of Paulo and Francesca," where swooning pathos, he suggests, signifies political impotence. But "impotence"—impotence in the conflict between romantic love and political fate—is not the only way to measure what Keats is doing with the forms of his sonnet.

As in *The Eve of St. Agnes*, the romance of form as mediation and resolution is contested by the play of form itself. The question is nearly inevitable, given the political heat Keats tapped into: not only were the lovers a political subject in Dante's day, but their romance had also been recently repoliticized by hostile Tory reviews of Hunt's *The Story of Rimini*, a context Keats tweaks by publishing this sonnet in 1820 in Hunt's journal *The Indicator*.[20] He shapes the "Dream" as a satire on dreaming the world away: a poet reads of the famous lovers with such rapture that the material world seems (but only seems) bereft of power, as the dreamer informs and fills, indeed, imagines himself into and usurps Paolo, a young man himself doomed by reading a romance:

> As Hermes once took to his feathers light,
>> When lulled Argus, baffled, swoon'd and slept,
> So on a Delphic reed, my idle spright
>> So play'd, so charm'd, so conquer'd, so bereft
> The dragon-world of all its hundred eyes;
>> And, seeing it asleep, so fled away—

318

> Not unto Ida with its snow-cold skies,
>   Nor unto Tempe, where Jove griev'd a day,
> But to that second circle of sad hell,
>   Where 'mid the gust, the world-wind, and the flaw
> Of rain and hailstones, lovers need not tell
>   Their sorrows. Pale were the sweet lips I saw,
> Pale were the lips I kiss'd, and fair the form
> I floated with about that melancholy storm.[21]

Although the worldly antagonists are already charmed into fictions (Argus, a dragon), this is no simple flight into imagination. The allusion to Ovid's tale also tracks through an intermediary text, in which disciplinary eyes are wakeful, multiple, and intent to drive lovers into the storms of human history: the Cherubim deputized to eject Adam and Eve from Eden, their shapes "Spangl'd with eyes more numerous than those / Of *Argus*, and more wakeful than to drowse, / Charm'd with *Arcadian* Pipe, the Pastoral Reed / of *Hermes*" (*Paradise Lost* 10.130–33). The shape of Keats's imagination whirls through this portent of radical grief, the fair *form* of imagination ultimately absorbed into the melancholy *storm*.

Is this still a soft landing? With a tacit formal allusion to Shakespeare's terse sonnet closures, Keats's couplet deploys a semantically charged enjambment: a desired fair form possessed by the poet even amidst a storm. The poem's dreamiest syntax, the alliterative rhythm of "fair the form / I floated with," seems even to soften the "melancholy storm." But *storm* is the last word, signing the fate of the dream and the subversion of its would-be aesthetic containments. It is apt that more than a few readers, including McGann, see an implied coda to *The Eve of St. Agnes*. The fair form of the poet's desire is absorbed into and dominated by another force in his imagination, the storm that frustrates desire and gives the rhyme. In Keats's imagination, too, is the mother of all storms, *King Lear*. Reading Hazlitt's summary statement on the play, "the greatest strength of genius is shewn in describing the strongest passions," Keats scribbled in the margins: "If we compare the passions to different tons and hogsheads of wine in a vast cellar—thus it is—the poet by one cup should know the scope of any particular wine without getting intoxicated—this is the highest exertion of Power, and the next step is to paint from memory of gone self storms."[22] The highest and particular power of imagination, Keats is convinced, is a capacity to know through the forms of another's imagination, and then to summon one's own history, which he stunningly images as the "memory of gone self storms," to complete the impression.

The worldly knowing of the sonnet's "melancholy storm" is appreciated even by McGann, who nicely disputes the editorial tradition of emending *The Indicator*'s reading, *world-wind*, to the letter's *whirlwind*, where it echoes Keats's description of the infernal scene's "whirling atmosphere" (*KL* 2.91).[23]

"Whirling" also echoes Henry Cary's translation of *Inferno*, which Keats read with care and admiration (writing one draft of the sonnet on a blank leaf at the end of the volume): "The stormy blast of hell / With restless fury drives the spirits on / Whirl'd round and dash'd amain with sore annoy."[24] McGann takes *world-wind* to be a conscious revision of both the letter-draft and Cary: the lovers "suffer not in the misery of their sinful love, but in the cruel assaults of an indifferent and hostile world"—"not in a 'whirlwind' but in a 'world-wind' . . . in the storm of a 'world' antagonistic to everything which [they] represent." I think Keats is even punning Cary's *Whirl'd* into his innovative compound *world-wind*, thus sounding the ironic return of "the dragon *world*" (5)—which his poet imagines, in a mock romance, that his dream has "charm'd" and "conquer'd"—in a vengeful echo, the "world-wind" at the very heart of his dream. As McGann rightly argues, this world is not just the one that punished Dante's lovers; it was also Keats's own in 1819, anguished by his love for Fanny Brawne amidst a frustrated literary career and his inability to achieve the financial security that would qualify him for marriage.

Yet notwithstanding his respect for *world-wind*, McGann presses his case against the sonnet's "Romantic Ideology": its melancholy tone "asserts that the conflicts between the World and Romantic Love cannot be resolved in the terms defined by the poem" (the poet's privileged capacity for sympathy with the lovers); "poetry's power to see these contradictions carries with it the fate of ineffectuality" (42). But at least as much as McGann, Keats understood what motivates the allied fantasies of a world bereft of power and of a poet empowered to fly away and luxuriate in sympathy with the lovers' melancholy impotence. And in a way that slips McGann's account, he undercuts this fantasy even as he indulges it. To the political danger already embedded in 1819–20 in his very sympathy with the lovers, Keats adds the dark work of poetic form in the motives of imagination. These motives are clear enough in the letter that includes this poem, where he describes his "dream" and its poetic rendering as reflexes of a contradictory worldly reality.

He had just been fuming to George and Georgiana over a practical joke played on Tom (recently deceased): in a "cruel deception" of literary trans-vestism, a friend (Charles Wells) had sent him some love letters signed "Amena Bellefila." Tom fell for the ruse and was humiliated when it was exposed. Still burning at this "diabolical scheme," Keats means "to be prudently vengeful," and it is from this fantasy that his letter moves into his infernal dream:

> I will harm him all I possibly can—I have no doubt I shall be able to do so—Let us leave him to his misery alone except when we can throw in a little more—The fifth canto of Dante pleases me more and more—it is that one in which he meets with Paulo and Franc<h>esca—I had passed many days in rather a low state of

mind and in the midst of them I dreamt of being in that region of Hell. The dream was one of the most delightful enjoyments I ever had in my life—I floated about the whirling atmosphere as it is described with a beautiful figure to whose lips mine were joined a[s] it seem'd for an age—and in the midst of all this cold and darkness I was warm.

(KL 2.90–91)

Keats turns to Dante's hell as if it were a positive liberation both from the "low state of mind" possessing him in April 1819 and from his hellish anger over Tom's suffering—that is, the hell of his own life in the world, tormented by Wells' diabolical cruelty and his own low moods. The seeming counterworld of Dante's region of Hell—delightful, warm, erotically animated, even on the verge of inspiring a rhyme scheme that would move from *harm* to *warm*—is more deeply an oppositional desire, emerging from and shaped by the pressures of historical existence, but never in isolation from these, even as the romance of Paolo and Francesca never could be.

Like Keats, Hemans is quite alert to the social text that subtends the gendering of the *form / storm* rhyme field. In one rare instance, a female-troped nature makes the two equivalent:

> Awful is nature in her savage forms,
> Her solemn voice commanding in its might,
> And mystery then was in the rush of storms.
>
> (*Modern Greece* LXIII)

Yet in material human fate, Hemans casts female "form" most frequently as a sign of vulnerability to historical and political circumstances, which she sums in the antithetical rhyme of "storm," as if a product of a universal nature. Thus the political prisoner Arabella Stuart hopes to return to her husband "no faded form, / No bosom chill'd and blighted by the storm" (*Arabella Stuart* 41–42). Learning of an imminent Austrian invasion, the Switzer's Wife collapses:

> Back on the linden-stem she lean'd her form,
> And her lip trembled, as it strove to speak,
> Like a frail harp-string, shaken by the storm.
>
> (*The Switzer's Wife* 62–64)

The Queen of Prussia finds repose only after death, when her image is "A sculptur'd woman's form, / Lovely in perfect rest reclined, / As one beyond the storm" (*The Queen of Prussia* 8–10). In *Woman on the Field of Battle* Hemans chimes this rhyme in its opening stanza to advertise a contradiction to the cultural ideal of "Woman" and a world always at war:

> Gentle and lovely form,
>> What didst thou hear,
> When the fierce battle-storm
> Bore down the spear?
>
> (1–4)

She repeats the rhyme to focus the cultural contradiction of Joan of Arc, another woman on the field of battle. At the dauphin's coronation, a success secured by Joan's victories, a witness exclaims, "That slight form! / Was that the leader thro' the battle storm?" (*Joan of Arc, in Rheims 29–30*). The intertext of this rhyme underscores the vulnerability of Hemans' most famous martyr:

> Yet beautiful and bright he stood,
>> As born to rule the storm;
> A creature of heroic blood,
>> A proud, though child-like form.
>
> (*Casabianca 5–8*)

The beautiful and bright ideal rules the storm only in the syntax of a simile; young Casabianca's imminent death in the Battle of the Nile is already forecast by his transformation into a form in the storm, in which "child" survives only as part of another simile.

"There are many ways to transcend formalism, but the worst is not to study forms," proposed Geoffrey Hartman in 1966, in an essay with the self-consciously contradictory title, "Beyond Formalism."[25] His point is still valid. A care for forms need not romance autonomous formal icons of meaning; it can attend to the several kinds of meanings that poetic form, both as a signifying performance and in its particular events, can enact in relation to ethical, historical, and social inquiry. To read the forms in this way is not to be hoodwinked by fairy fancy but to engage what is most material in aesthetic practice, a critical project for which romantic poetry is an illuminating site as well as an important stage of reflection.

## Notes

1 For my fuller treatment of this question, see *Formal Charges: The Shaping of Poetry in British Romanticism* (Stanford: Stanford UP, 1997).

2 Quotations of the 1805 text follow *The Thirteen-Book "Prelude"*, ed. Mark L. Reed, 2 vols. (Ithaca: Cornell UP, 1991). Quotations of the 1850 text follow *The Fourteen-Book "Prelude,"* ed. W. J. B. Owen (Ithaca: Cornell UP, 1985).

3 Hartman, "Words, Wish, Worth: Wordsworth," *Deconstruction & Criticism* (New York: Seabury P, 1979) 193–94. To Richard Onorato, the listener who half creates this ghostly language displays nostalgia for a kind of Kristevan maternal: "a projection into Nature of a preconscious sense of a lost relationship, of the

dialogue that the infant had with the mother's heart"; *The Character of the Poet: Wordsworth in "The Prelude"* (Princeton: Princeton UP, 1971) 113.

4 Owen, *Fourteen-Book Prelude* 448–90 (Ms D. Book II: 18–19).

5 Hartman, "A Touching Compulsion" (1977); rpt. *The Unremarkable Wordsworth* (Minneapolis: U of Minnesota P, 1987) 23–24.

6 The best discussion of these poetics and the consequences for poetic form, particularly the interplay of rhyme and blank verse, is in William Keach's *Shelley's Style* (London and New York: Methuen, 1984) 194–200.

7 Quotations follow *Shelley's Poetry and Prose*, ed. Donald H. Reiman and Sharon B. Powers (New York: Norton, 1977). Reference to ms. texts follow *The Triumph of Life, The Bodleian Shelley Manuscripts, A Facsimile Edition, with Full Transcriptions and Scholarly Apparatus*, vol. 1, ed. Donald H. Reiman (New York: Garland P, 1986).

8 I would even add that the chime of *feet* and *sweet* (which Shelley revised to achieve [42$^r$]) serves this materiality by forming as well as reporting the quivering of language into the measure of repeated articulations—a material tenor amplified by repetition: "And still her feet, no less than the sweet tune / To which they moved, seemed as they moved, to blot / The thoughts of him who gazed on them" (382–84).

9 "Shelley Disfigured" 60, 61–62; de Man argues that the way Rousseau is "read and disfigured in *The Triumph of Life*" shows a resistance to an "historicism" that generates only "recuperative and nihilistic allegories." Such resistance "turns out to be historically more reliable than the products of historical archeology," because it "warns us that nothing, whether deed, word, thought or text, even happens in relation, positive or negative, to anything that precedes, follows or exists elsewhere" (69).

10 The impact of Rousseau's devolution from Revolutionary ideological monument-making to anti-Jacobin iconoclasm on Shelley's representation in *The Triumph* is succinctly treated by Orrin Wang, "Disfiguring Monuments: History in Paul de Man's 'Shelley Disfigured' and Percy Bysshe Shelley's 'The Triumph of Life,'" *ELH* 58 (1991), esp. 642–45; Wang also queries de Man's case for the unreadability of history. For a full treatment of Rousseau in *The Triumph*, see Edward Duffy, *Rousseau in England: The Context for Shelley's Critique of the Enlightenment* (Berkeley: U of California P, 1979) 106–51. De Man does not elide the importance of Rousseau to Shelley, early or late; yet it is not as Shelley's cultural mirror but as his own theoretical mirror that "Rousseau" matters to him in "Shelley Disfigured": he is the stager of "disfiguration" and those "repetitive erasures by which language performs the erasure of its own positions" (65). Thus de Man opens his Preface to *Allegories of Reading* (New Haven: Yale UP, 1979), which, he says, "started out as a historical study and ended up as a theory of reading. I began to read Rousseau seriously in preparation for a historical reflection on romanticism and found myself unable to progress beyond local difficulties of interpretation. In trying to cope with this, I had to shift from historical definition to the problematics of reading" (ix).

11 47$^v$ shows a revision from "fairest shape" to "early form" in order to set up this rhyme; in *Shelley's "The Triumph of Life": A Critical Study, Based on a Text Newly Edited from the Bodleian Manuscript* (1965; New York: Octagon, 1979), Reiman shows how this repeated, rhyme contributes to the structure of analogy between these two moments (94). Referring to Reiman, William Keach argues that the rhymes "reinforce complexly infolded parallels between the narrator's initial vision of Life's chariot and Rousseau's recollected experience," casting "these two phases of the poem [as] partial re-enactments of each other" (*Shelley's Style* 192).

12 The best study of these effects is Garrett Stewart's *Reading Voices: Literature and the Phonotext* (Berkeley: U of California P, 1990).

13 Quotations here and after are from Lord Byron, *Selected Poems*, ed. Susan J. Wolfson Peter J. Manning (London: Penguin, 1996).

14 For my fuller discussion of Keats's career in formalism, see *Formal Charges*. The chief voices of this critique are Jerome McGann's influential essay, "Keats and the Historical, Method in Literary Criticism" (1979); rpt. *The Beauty of Inflections: Literary Investigations in Historical Method & Theory* (1985; Oxford: Clarendon P, 1988), and Marjorie Levinson, *Keats's Life of Allegory: The Origins of a Style* (London: Basil Blackwell, 1988).

15 Quotation from John Keats, *Lamia, Isabella, and The Eve of St. Agnes and Other Poems* (London: Taylor and Hessey, 1820).

16 For the ms. revisions, see the notes in *The Poems of John Keats*, ed. Jack Stillinger (Cambridge: Harvard UP, 1978) 317–18. Woodhouse's letter is in *The Letters of John Keats, 1814–1821*, ed. Hyder E. Rollins, 2 vols. (Cambridge: Harvard UP, 1958) 2.162–63. Quotations from Keats's letters hereafter appear parenthetically in the text, with the abbreviation *KL*.

17 Quotation from *John Milton, Complete Poems and Major Prose*, ed. Merritt Y. Hughes (New York: Odyssey, 1957).

18 Quotation from vol. 5 of *The Complete Poetical Works*, ed. Jerome J. McGann (Oxford: Clarendon, 1986).

19 McGann, "Historical Method" 53. In a complication of McGann's bracing argument, another historicist critic, Daniel Watkins, sees this storm as deeply implicated in the "social and historical contexts" in which the poem's action is set: "the storm into which Madeline and Porphyro move might be viewed as a sign of the ongoing difficulties and struggles of a rapidly changing world. Stated bluntly, the storm is the object correlative of history itself"; *Keats's Poetry and the Politics of the imagination* (Rutherford, NJ: Fairleigh Dickinson UP, 1989): 82–83.

20 The most virulent attack on *Rimini* (with its sights set on Keats) was "On the Cockney School of Poetry, No. 1," *Blackwood's Edinburgh Magazine* 2 (October 1817): 38–41.

21 Quotation from *John Keats*, ed. Elizabeth Cook (Oxford: Oxford UP, 1990), whose base text is that of *The Indicator* (28 June 1820): 304.

22 Keats's marginalia and the relevant sentences from Hazlitt's *Characters of Shakespear's Plays* (1817) are in *The Poetical Works and Other Writings of John Keats*, ed. H. Buxton Forman, rev. Maurice Buxton Forman, 8 vols. (New York: Charles Scribner's Sons, 1939) 5.286.

23 McGann, "Historical Method" 37–42. Richard Monckton Milnes' *Literary Remains* (1848) privileged the letter-text, which prevailed until McGann's worthy case for *The Indicator* text, which at least Elizabeth Cook's edition now follows, with credit to McGann.

24 Cary's *The Vision; of Hell, Purgatory, and Paradise, of Dante Alighieri* was published in 1814; the relevant lines (*Hell* 5.32–34) are given by Miriam Allott in *The Poems of Keats* (New York: Norton, 1972) 500. It is worth noting that Dante's terza rima—"La bufera infernal, che mai non resta, / mena li spirti con la sua rapina: / voltando e percotendo li molesta" (5.31–33; roughly: "The hellish storm, which never ceases / and drives the spirits with its fury: / Whirling and smiting it torments them")—works a formalist pun, with *voltando* coming at the *volta* or turn of the line; Italian quoted from John Sinclair, *Dante's Inferno: Italian text with English Translation and Comment* (1939; New York: Oxford UP, 1980) 74. The "whirl" of both Cary and Keats's letter-draft further sifts Dante's

Inferno through the outer environs of Milton's phantasmagoric hell, where "a frozen continent / Lies dark and wild, beat with perpetual storms / Of whirlwind and dire hail" (*Paradise Lost* 2.587–89), with Keats making formal capital out of the singular "storm."

25 Hartman, "Beyond Formalism" (1966), in *Beyond Formalism: Literary Essays 1958–1970* (New Haven: Yale UP, 1970) 56.

# BEAUTIFUL RUINS:
# THE ELGIN MARBLES SONNET
# IN ITS HISTORICAL AND
# GENERIC CONTEXTS

*Grant F. Scott*

Source: *Keats-Shelley Journal* 39 (1990), 123–50.

> Still it survives
> Ruin'd, but in its ruin beautiful.
>
> From *Greece: A Poem* by William Haygarth

> The more I study them the more do I feel my own insignificance. God grant
> I may rival them yet—
>
> From Haydon's *Diary*, 9 September 1808

If it has not quickly glossed or refused discussion outright, much of the scarce criticism which surrounds "On Seeing the Elgin Marbles" has understood the sonnet either in terms of Keats's developing aesthetic sensibility (Bate, Bush, Gittings, Hurst, Murray), or as an isolated, rather pained confession of personal inadequacy.[1] Most of the impetus for examining the poem at all has come from its enigmatic closing lines. Various attempts have been made to elucidate the final series of images and to reconstruct them in the framework the rest of the sonnet provides: hence, they have been interpreted variously as constituting "a magnificent conclusion"; as a list of "associations" inscrutable because "linked only in the speaker's mind"; as a sunset, referring back to the earlier allusion to winds and sunrise and thus completing the imagistic pattern in the poem; and even as Keats's veiled reference to the *Mentor*, which was conveying a case of the marbles to England when it sank off the Greek isle of Cytheria in 1804.[2] Recently, William Crisman has argued that the poet's voice might be better understood as dramatic, rather than personal, and that the work as a whole should be seen as more nearly resembling a dramatic monologue than a biographical utterance. In this view, the poet means to distance himself from the speaker, thereby creating an ironic voice in the poem that anticipates those he will later invent in the great odes.

While these critics offer interesting and provocative arguments, they nevertheless separate the sonnet from both its historical context and its original fraternity with other poems on sculpture and painting in the *Annals of the Fine Arts*.[3] The poem has always been analyzed in isolation or in terms of Keats's oeuvre; never, to my knowledge, has it been seen in direct relation to the cultural debate spawned by the arrival of the Elgin Marbles, or the aesthetic skirmishes that ensued as the British government deliberated over whether to purchase and install them in the national museum for permanent exhibition. Further, the sonnet has neither been considered *vis-à-vis* the specific genre of ekphrastic poetry to which it properly belongs, nor has it been compared with a number of popular poems on statues and friezes circulating in the prominent newspapers and journals at the time. If we view the sonnet as in some sense just as much a response to the contemporary enthusiasm over the marbles, as to the marbles *per se*, we gain a more significant insight into the poem's originality and depth. Moreover, by situating the work within its generic boundaries, as well as within its special place in the *Annals*, we are able to see how Keats reshapes the traditional form, fashioning it like a sculptor so that it breathes new life. In the end, Keats's sonnet becomes as fully a response to the genre as to the *objets d'art* before him, and as successfully a *tour de force* in this respect as it seems a failure if seen conventionally as an awkward, embarrassed confession in the face of grandeur. By invoking this kind of intertextuality, we must remember that the poet places enormous stress on his reader's familiarity with the genre's characteristic tropes, its peculiar logic and language. Counterbalanced against its precursors and contemporaries, "On Seeing the Elgin Marbles" achieves a particular meaning it could never reveal on its own or in the more or less limited context of Keats's other writings.

When the Elgin Marbles began arriving in England in 1801, they were greeted with an indifference and lack of fanfare that seems surprising to us today. They collected quietly on Lord Elgin's doorstep in Piccadilly, whence they were ushered into a "dirty pent-house," as Haydon dubbed it, there to await the return of Lord Elgin from imprisonment abroad, and the turning tide of national taste.[4] When the marbles were first exhibited privately in June of 1807, they met with a response that was anything but laudatory. Joseph Farington, better known now for his diary than for his water-colors, recorded the impressions of a number of his colleagues and friends. A fellow painter, Ozias Humphry, "had been to Lord Elgin's & seen the marbles brought from Greece & seemed to be disappointed. He said there certainly was something great and of a high stile of Sculpture, but the whole was 'a Mass of ruins.'"[5] No less dispiriting was Sir George Beaumont's recommendation "that the mutilated fragments brought from Athens by Lord Elgin should be *restored* as at present, they excite rather disgust than pleasure in the minds of people in general, to see parts of limbs, & bodys, stumps of arms, etc.—" (v, 72) or Nolleken's admission that he could "not find anything fine among them" at present, but after "they are all arranged . . . and the broken parts united we shall see more of them" (IV, 145). Farington himself, although he felt that the marbles were of the "highest quality of Art" (v, 31), nevertheless left the exhibit early complaining that the shed was too cold. Perhaps the most famous snub of the period (from perhaps its most famous snob) came from Lord Byron, who in *English Bards and Scotch Reviewers* (1809), called the marbles "Phidian freaks, / Mis-shapen monuments, and maimed antiques,"[6] a comment which sardonically encapsulated the view, evident in the other remarks, that their worn condition greatly diminished their value.

It was undoubtedly this kind of reaction, combined with their banishment to such drab digs, which led Benjamin Haydon to lament in his diary: "I came home from the Elgin Marbles melancholy. I almost wish the French had them; we do not deserve such productions. There they lie, covered with dust and dripping with damp."[7] Indeed, it was to be sixteen years before they were safely established in the British Museum, and this only after a considerable amount of debate and personal rivalry. It seems that they had arrived before their time, or before their brand of aesthetic beauty could be properly appreciated. When the marbles were finally exhibited, as Jacob Rothenberg has noted, the occasion represented a new era in British taste: the acceptance of the marbles "changed the social function of rare antiques from decorative to educational, and from private to public purposes."[8] Their ascendance also encouraged a move away from neoclassical connoisseurship and the restoration of artifacts, and towards "a new respect for the sanctity and inviolability of originals" (445), and for ruins and fragments generally.[9]

As the Select Committee of the House of Commons pondered the value of the Elgin Marbles in February and March of 1816, it soon became evident that the sessions were emerging as far more than a simple juridical formality. Some of the most influential painters and sculptors of the age— men like Benjamin West, Thomas Lawrence, and John Flaxman—had been assembled to give their opinions respecting the merit and value of the marbles and to ascertain whether or not they stood up to the finest class of existing sculpture. What developed out of the hearings was a growing consensus, despite the stubbornness of Richard Payne Knight and one or two others (who insisted that their mutilated state impaired the value of the artifacts), that the marbles were the finest things of their kind ever discovered. They were again and again compared to the Apollo Belvedere (as well as the Farnese Hercules and the Laocoon) and found to be of greater genius and virtuosity.[10]

The argument that consistently arose concerned the collection's "truth to nature." While the Belvedere statue was unarguably magnificent, it was nevertheless a representative of "ideal beauty"; hence it portrayed a god whose skin was smooth and flawless, launching his arrow at the Python with no more effort than it took to lift up an arm, or put one foot in front of the other. Winckelmann captured this *sangfroid* perfectly in his description of the work: "Roam over the realms of incorporeal grace, invoke angelic nature to conceive his perfection; here sick decay, and human flaws dwell not, blood palpitates not here: an empyrean mind, like a flood of light, pours through the whole and marks the outline."[11]

The Theseus or Hercules—which represented the grand centerpiece of the Elgin collection—provided a stark contrast. Here was a naturalistic rendering of muscles and veins, of limbs that responded to movement and strain in a way consonant with the laws of physics found in the actual world. As Haydon noticed, there was a perfect symmetry of arrangement, a balance of action and reaction that could only have been observed from life. His initial sight of the marbles struck him with the force of a revelation:

> The first thing I fixed my eyes on was a wrist of a figure in one of the female groups, in which were visible, though in a feminine form, the radius and ulna. I was astonished, for I had never seen them hinted at in any female wrist in the antique. I darted my eye to the elbow, and saw the outer condyle visibly affecting the shape as in nature. I saw that the arm was in repose and the soft parts in relaxation. That combination of nature and idea which I had felt was so much wanting for in high art was here displayed to midday conviction. My heart beat![12]

One of the observations that often characterized Haydon's descriptions of the marbles was the contrast they offered between surface and depth: "In the Elgin Marbles it is the effect of parts beneath the skin acting above it" (II, 12). He admired the hints of internal movement or bone structure, the suggestion of muscles in the process of protruding or "darting out" from the skin, and felt that these details represented not only the apotheosis of realism, but "the consequence of the soul impelling the body" (I, 233). This reverence for internal effects seems best to epitomize the view that ultimately prevailed in the House debates and eventually won over the marbles for public display and emulation; for it posited an interest in depth dramatically at odds with the persisting Regency norms of "Ideal Beauty" and external polish. Against the eighteenth-century standard of excellence embodied in Payne Knight and personified in the restored Townley Marbles, the new ideal offered a respect for authenticity and iconography that emphasized the marbles as valuable and inspiring in their own right.[13] Reinforced by the Italian sculptor Canova's visit to see the collection and his subsequent letter to Lord Elgin urging strongly against any restoration, the attitude of aesthetic *laissez-faire* gained a rather speedy acceptance in the debates and at last toppled Knight and his cronies.

That the impaired condition of the marbles at all stood in the way of their perceived grandeur and sublimity can scarcely be determined by the testimonies of the witnesses. Indeed, except for the evidence given by Knight, one would be hard pressed to recognize their battered condition. Leafing through the commentary the hearings generated, commentary Keats must certainly have read in the first editions of the *Annals*, one is overwhelmed by the staggering quantity of praise they elicited. It must be seen as due in some part to Haydon's vociferous campaigning that the fragmented nature of the marbles was almost entirely overlooked.[14] A letter sent to *The Champion* not long after the marbles were placed on display and signed "Philo Phidias" aptly summarizes the prevailing climate of enthusiasm and acceptance: the author calls the marbles "matchless works," "exalted in sentiment," "specimens whose peculiar and transcendent quality consists in the total absence of all *manner* whatsoever," and concludes enthusiastically: "Thrice happy he who shall begin his career in art with the exclusive study of these peerless relics; whose mind, unpolluted by the gross and vulgar gusts of later schools, shall unfold its maiden germs to the genial and fructifying beams of their spotless effulgence."[15]

With such a battery of definitive judgments surrounding the marbles, it is easy to see how a young poet, especially one who had never actually seen them, might be intimidated. A key aspect of the commentary thus becomes its undeniable authority. Despite the fact that the praise was somewhat unself-conscious and prone to fashionable academy clichés and superlatives, the majority of it was nonetheless powerfully assertive, and no less so coming from the greatest artists of the time. The weight of this testimony, particularly to an aspiring poet, must have seemed both impressive and somewhat daunting. Prompted by his own curiosity and the infectious enthusiasm of his new friend Haydon, Keats would have read a great deal about the marbles before he went to see them, so that the combination of their idealized magnitude with his own creative imagination must have produced a keen anticipation as well as a mounting sense of anxiety. What could they possibly be like, these Grecian artifacts? How great were they? Could their achievement ever be matched or even excelled? Were their beams really "genial and fructifying" or somewhat less fertile? Presumably these were some of the questions that lingered in his mind as Keats went to see the marbles in March of 1817.

If we pause for a moment to reflect upon the evidence that collected around the marbles, we notice something quite interesting. For one thing, a pronounced split exists between the comments that praise the marbles in spite of their condition and those sponsored by Knight (as well as by the Farington set) that disparage them because of their condition. The one side sees only genius, the other only ruin. That this dialectic transcends any aesthetic boundaries we might draw between neoclassicism and romanticism is made abundantly clear by the opinions offered by the two anonymous gentlemen at the British Museum (see note 12). And this polarity continues into the House debates. The testimonies given by the witnesses, as we have seen, by and large stress the marbles' perfection, elegance, purity, and grandeur of form—qualities we would not ordinarily associate with deteriorated fragments but might link to a nostalgic recreation of ancient Greece. These observations, along with others that echoed them in *The Champion* and *Examiner*, bespeak an organic wholeness or harmony that sharply contradicts our own immediate impression of the stones and suggests that the observers were seeing what they wished to see, or artifacts that they had already restored in their minds. As one reviewer of the collection, stressing the importance of such compensation, advised: "If disappointment clouds the first visit, it vanishes at the second, and by a more constant examination of those divine models, a purity of taste and accuracy of judgment grows up in the mind of the student, till at last—not his fancy, but—his judgment supplies the deficiencies, and repairs the damages of accident and time" (*House of Commons Report*, p. 544).

At the same time, the view of Humphreys or Beaumont or Byron, which argues that we are "disgusted" by the statues because they convey to the eye nothing more than a jumbled "Mass of ruins," is similarly extreme. Some part of us either suspends our experience of ruin and focuses on the patches of virtuosity which still remain, or imaginatively reconstructs the missing fragments (not, however, without retaining a sense of their incompleteness). Our experience, however, rarely seems to conform to one or the other of these reactions, but to partake of both at once, or each in rapid alternation. In so far as the mind perceives both positions, our impression may finally be ambivalent, content to dwell "in uncertainties, Mysteries, doubts."[16]

In this sense, Keats's "On Seeing the Elgin Marbles" acts as a kind of mediating force between the two predominant viewpoints, for it entertains both positions simultaneously: the marbles are "wonders" at the same time that they constitute a "shadow of a magnitude." Keats's own testimony goes some of the way towards reconciling the two positions by offering a specific experience of ambivalence rarely noted in the literature of response. In so doing, as we shall see, the poet provides us with a far greater insight into the mechanism of aesthetic perception than into the artworks themselves. His sonnet finally exists as an exploration of aesthetic response, rather than as an exercise in formal art criticism.

Another element of the commentary that gathered around the Elgin Marbles, no doubt contributing to Keats's anxiety, concerned their purpose as national treasures. One of the primary reasons given for purchasing the marbles was their agreed-upon function as objects of emulation for British artists, particularly for young, hopeful poets, painters, and sculptors. The objects were meant not only to enrich the country's collection of artworks and to educate the public, but more importantly to inspire great art amongst Britain's talented youth. The closing statement of the Select Committee, which Keats would have noticed in the *Annals*, offers the marbles as models and places emphasis on their kinetic spirit:

> Caught by the novelty, attracted by the beauty, and enamoured of the perfection of those newly-discovered treasures . . . [they will] imbibe the genuine spirit of ancient excellence and transfuse it into their own compositions. This, and this only, is the true and genuine method of properly studying the Elgin Marbles.[17]

The same sentiment expressed here and in the *House of Commons Report*, is repeated nearly verbatim in the *Gentleman's Magazine* of 1816. By implication the exhibition of the Elgin Marbles parallels the discovery of "the noblest remains of Antiquity" that ignited the Italian Renaissance:

> Much indeed may be reasonably hoped and expected from the general observation and admiration of such distinguished examples. The end of the fifteenth and beginning of the sixteenth centuries, enlightened by the discovery of several of the noblest remains of Antiquity, produced in Italy an abundant harvest of the most eminent men, who made gigantic advances in the path of Art, as Painters, Sculptors, and Architects. Caught by the novelty, attracted by the beauty, and enamoured of the perfection of those newly-discovered treasures, they imbibed the genuine spirit of antient excellence, and transfused it into their own compositions.[18]

Felicia Hemans echoes this optimism towards the end of her poem *Modern Greece* (1816), when she wonders "who can tell how pure, how bright a flame, / Caught from these models, may illume the west? / What British Angelo may rise to fame, / On the free isle what beams of art may rest?"[19]

The belief that the marbles would somehow transmit their genius to the youth of England had for its foundation a theory of mimetic response exemplified in original Greek ekphrastic poetry—composed largely of epigrams—which established the idea that the work was so closely approximated to nature that it produced an illusion of "breathing" life. As Jean Hagstrum has observed: "In the *Greek Anthology* painters and sculptors are praised for having perpetuated a deception: the reality of their work is such that it becomes confused with nature itself. Calves low at the cow of Myron, and one creature dies vainly sucking the bronze udder."[20] The magical life of the work promoted a correspondent warmth and vitality in the viewer, who was moved passionately by the resemblance of the sculpture to the real world. Of the popular modern poets, William Hayley in his

*Essay on Sculpture* (1800) best illustrates the response a statue might ideally elicit. "In contemplating the Farnesian Hercules," he writes in a note, "I believe many spectators feel an involuntary mechanical impulse to muscular exertion, " and then adds by way of moral exemplum, "The daily contemplation of very fine sculpture, that expressed, with the utmost powers of art, great elevation of mind, would probably have a strong and happy influence on mental character."[21] Such reflection is backed up by as eminent an artist and theoretician as Sir Joshua Reynolds, who, in his tenth discourse on sculpture, wonders rhetorically: "What artist ever looked at the Torso without feeling a warmth of enthusiasm, as from the highest efforts of poetry?"[22]

It was of course with this kind of aesthetic contagion that the members of the Royal Academy hoped the marbles would infect their students—but what they did not see was the delicate balance in this response between rapt and somehow static astonishment and motivating ardor. Characteristic of many of the passages from Hayley and the epigrams he collects is their tendency to turn the spectator into a statue, as he gazes dumbstruck and paralyzed upon the living stone. In these descriptions it is the marble that "breathes," not the viewer.[23] The danger hinted at in Hayley's descriptions— which not only subordinate the spectator to the work of art, but also place enormous importance on the word "imbibe" without fully understanding its connotations of intoxication—also undermines the hopes of the House committee. How the awestruck viewer would convert so much perceived grandeur into his own aesthetic creations without being overwhelmed himself was a question no one ventured to answer; neither did they attempt to explain how the process of "transfusion" would take place. All they knew was that it was not direct imitation of the marbles that would create a national renaissance, but a mysterious assimilation of the spirit of their forms.

One of the things Keats worried about both in his earlier poems ("Sleep and Poetry" and "I Stood Tiptoe" particularly) and in the Elgin Marbles sonnet was precisely this kind of dubious osmosis. Instead of "instructing the talent" or "expanding the heart," as John Scott had said, Keats was more concerned that the marbles would reduce him to passivity and indolence, and not the kind of preparatory, generative indolence he speaks of in his letters either. That he did eventually "imbibe" some of their spirit is clear, as Ian Jack has shown, from his later writings, especially "Ode on a Grecian Urn," and "Hyperion." But in the sonnets that result directly from his visit to the British Museum he is paralyzed by the marbles and oppressed by their spirit. The possibility of inertia in the face of sublimity, which the Greek epigrams so glibly suggest, here finds its direct and terrifying embodiment. The only solace he can manage derives from the statues' fragmented condition, and this is so closely allied with his own mortality that it serves little good.

Even though the marbles do not actually appear in the poem until line 11 ("these wonders"), their spirit nevertheless haunts the opening lines. The speaker's inabilities are conceived in terms of the material properties of the artifacts themselves: "mortality / *Weighs heavily*" on him, "And each imagined *pinnacle* and *steep* / Of godlike *hard*ship" tells him he must die. It is no accident, if we are thinking along these lines, that Keats decides on the word "hardship" instead of the more abstract term "difficulty" in the original manuscript.[24] Further, the sick eagle in the next line presents an image of frozen potential that suggests a statue. Compared with the inspiriting portrait of "Stout Cortez," whose "eagle eyes" stare in wonder at the Pacific in Keats's first great sonnet ("On First Looking Into Chapman's Homer," line 11), the technique of "stationing" here invests the solitary eagle with a painful enervation. The bird can only look at the sky despondently, without the energy or capacity to soar. The negations continue in the next lines (6–8), which make a "gentle luxury" out of "not" being able to do something—in this case the inability to keep cloudy winds "Fresh for the opening of the morning's eye." The awkwardness of the word "undescribable" a line later only deepens this feeling of inadequacy and contributes further to our sense of the poem's inertia.

The correspondence between sonnet and marbles is illustrated in other ways besides the diction, indicating that Keats has perhaps imbibed rather too much of the medium of the objects he surveys. Throughout, we notice an abundance of dactyls: the first and last lines conclude with two such examples ("mortality," "magnitude") which bracket a host of words ("heavily," "pinnacle," "luxury," "opening," "dim-conceived," "billowy") that help contribute to the weak or falling rhythm of the sonnet. A pronounced enjambment, moreover, breaks up the rhythm of the line and dramatizes the poem's ruggedness, its rough-cut apprentice quality. We find ourselves constantly pausing at the wrong times in the verse, unable to gain a sturdy foothold, unable to make the harmonious and comforting connections the rhyme would normally invite. Our eye, no sooner at ease with "pinnacle and steep," is forced rapidly to adjust itself in order to accommodate the phrase to a preposition: "pinnacle and steep / Of godlike hardship." Similarly, our first impulse in seeing "rude" at the end of line 12, is to read it as a noun, balancing "Grecian grandeur" and possibly suggesting the poet himself ("rude" in the sense of untutored, unskilled); however, the next line demonstrates that it is actually an adjective that modifies the activity of old Time.

A thematics of dislocation manifests itself not only in the violence of the enjambment, but also in the abruptness and ambivalence of the transitions. The speaker summons "Yet" to reverse the somber mood of the opening lines, but lays such heavy stress on it that the word cannot help but seem forced. Even as the other transitions, "Such" (line 9) and "So" (line 11), appear in Crisman's term "deliberative" if not overly methodical, they nevertheless "work to subvert [their] own . . . clarity." Thus, it remains difficult to determine how many conditions are qualified by "Yet" (line 6), just as "it is all but impossible" to define the referent for "Such dim-conceived glories" in line 9.[25]

The jagged syntax and ambiguous transitions prefigure the sonnet's conclusion and denote a structural weakness the poet tries vainly to overcome in the terse assurance of the masculine rhymes. As it approaches its climax, the poem appears to waste away, ending in a series of half-articulated images, "a billowy main— / A sun—a shadow of a magnitude" (lines 13–14), which seem comprehensible, as Crisman says, only as dim associations in the mind of the speaker himself. Like the curious mortality of the marbles, which "mingle Grecian grandeur with the rude / Wasting of old time" (lines 12–13), the sonnet—a moment's monument of Keats's own sculpting—crumbles and is at last held up by a scaffolding of makeshift dashes. As such, the poem seeks to attain the "shape," in Murray Krieger's words, of the marbles themselves.[26] By the end of the sonnet we realize that the speaker has assimilated the statues' weight as well as their fragmentation, without being sufficiently apprised of their living, "breathing" form.

What I want to emphasize above all here is Keats's reaction to the boundless and patriotic enthusiasm that typified comments on the marbles. Instead of having the prescribed effect of inspiration—the effect so beautifully, if frenetically, illustrated by Haydon in his revelation before the Lapitha (II, 479)—the marbles depress the poet and drive him towards feelings of his own inadequacy. As Martin Aske suggests in a broader study of Keats and Hellenism: "Antiquity might be found to press its claims too importunately, to the extent that it becomes a compulsive presence which the poet finally has to exorcize from his imagination."[27] Whether he has to "exorcize" this presence or properly "imbibe" it is a moot point; the fact remains that his encounter with the artifacts has left him indolent and weak. In so far as it exists in a contemporary aesthetic milieu characterized by intense optimism, the poem criticizes and ultimately rejects the prevailing response. Keats neither idealizes the experience nor makes it conform to the dominant reaction of uplifting power and felt divinity. As such, the sonnet also serves as a patient rebuke to Haydon's fanaticism, subtly chastening his friend's ardor with its own guarded pessimism.

Haydon's impassioned response upon first reading the sonnet indicates that Keats's purpose was lost on him:

> *I* know not a finer image than the comparison of a Poet unable to express his high feelings to a sick eagle looking at the Sky!—when he must have remembered his former towerings amid the blaze of dazzling Sun beams, in the pure expanse of glittering clouds!—now & then passing Angels on heavenly errands, lying at the will of the wind, with moveless wings; or pitching downward with a fiery rush, eager & intent on the objects of their seeking—You filled me with fury for an hour, and with admiration for ever.
>
> (*Letters of John Keats*, I, 122)

Apparently it was not clear to Haydon that the marbles had reduced Keats to silence—"I cannot speak / Definitively on these mighty things" (lines 1–2) he writes in the companion piece "To Haydon with a Sonnet"—bequeathing him a "dizzy pain" ("On Seeing the Elgin Marbles," line 11) rather than a divine spark. Although his friend's embellishment of the sonnet's ideas is full of energy and enthusiasm, it nevertheless remains hopelessly inaccurate as explication. The poet's "towerings" are not "former" at all; in fact, they have not yet been initiated. As for all the blazing, dazzling, glittering, pitching, and rushing, Haydon might have done better to notice how incapable of movement the poem actually is, how painfully static are its images. Haydon's reaction only recapitulates in miniature all his previous experiences with the marbles themselves and demonstrates how far his enthusiasm could outweigh his judgment when it came to matters of artistic and literary criticism. As such, the reply must certainly have puzzled Keats, for the sonnets are anything but inspirational; on the contrary, they are painful, enigmatic, ambivalent. Even on the surface they conform to neither of the two predominant schools of thought about the sculptures and bespeak a mind tormented by self-doubt and paralyzed by the achievements of the past.

Haydon's response is inappropriate in more ways than this, however. After misreading the poem as the embodiment of precisely that kind of "transfusion" the House committee and the magazine writers prophesied, he then overlooks the work's place in the genre of ekphrastic poetry. As it happened, this genre was undergoing a minor revival of sorts with the appearance not only of Elgin's marbles, but of the Townley, Aegina, and Phigaleian collections as well. As Larrabee and others have noted, the later eighteenth and early nineteenth centuries saw a renewed interest in Hellenism infuse the arts. A number of important scholarly books on Greece and sculpture appeared during this time—among them Fuseli's translation of Winckelmann's *Gedanken über die Nachahmung der griechischen Werke in der Mahlerei und Bildhauerunst (Reflections on the Painting and Sculpture of the Greeks* [1766]), G. E. Lessing's *Laokoon* (1766), and William Hamilton's *Account of the Discoveries at Pompeii* (1777)—along with several relevant collections of poems, including William Haygarth's *Greece, A Poem* (1814), Felicia Heman's *Modern Greece* (1816), and of course Cantos I and II of *Childe Harold's Pilgrimage.*[28]

A clue that the remains of antiquity were becoming a fashionable topic among the cognoscenti was the decision by both Oxford and Cambridge universities to sponsor a competition for the best poems written on sculpture or on ancient Greece. Begun in 1805, the event produced a work each year that was read publicly and later published in a contemporary journal. Among the most popular prize poems were Samuel Richards's "The Temple of Theseus" (1815), Alexander Macdonnell's "The Horses of Lysippus" (1816), and the young Thomas Macaulay's "Pompeii" (1819). Undoubtedly the most famous of these was Henry Milman's "Belvedere Apollo" recited at Oxford in 1812 and published several times subsequently (once in the *Annals of the Fine Arts* for 1820), along with Samuel Rogers's "To the Fragment of a Statue of Hercules" (1802). Although Milman's poem is of less interest to us here because the Apollo was well-preserved and hence did not lend itself to thoughts concerning the medium's susceptibility to time, it is worth taking a closer look at Rogers' poem if only to see how he uses a number of the genre's important formulae and tropes.

> And dost thou still, thou mass of breathing stone,
> (Thy giant limbs to night and chaos hurl'd),
> Still sit as on the fragment of a world;
> Surviving all, majestic and alone?
> What though the Spirits of the North, that swept
> Rome from the earth, when in her pomp she slept,
> Smote thee with fury, and thy headless trunk
> Deep in the dust 'mid tower and temple sunk;
> Soon to subdue mankind 't was thine to rise,
> Still, still unquell'd thy glorious energies!
> Aspiring minds, with thee conversing, caught
> Bright revelations of the Good they sought;
> By thee that long-lost spell in secret given,
> To draw down Gods, and lift the soul to Heaven![29]

Where we anticipate a more conscious examination of form and mortality, we only meet with the opposite, with the same tropes Milman will use a few years later. Here we find all the themes Keats tried so hard to suppress in his own sonnet: the marble's "breathing" nature, in fact a spontaneous energy that practically propels the statue all by itself from beneath piles of ruin; the torso's fragmented but indomitable spirit; its inspirational afflatus; its divine "spell," which lends it that air of self-creation; and its paradoxical immortality.

The construction of a narrative line or a temporal framework for a work that exists *in vacuo* is also a technique apparent in Rogers's treatment of the Hercules torso and one frequently resorted to in ekphrastic poetry generally. The trope involves supplying a background mythology for the figure, in effect creating a chronological and biographical continuum so that the statue appears less nakedly alone and out of place. In this sense the description remains peripheral to the work at hand, avoiding any direct confrontation with what presents itself. For the bald immediacy of the statue, poets substitute mythology and anecdote, seeking solace in anything ancillary to the object—in recognizable names, places, and events. These descriptions represent the poetic equivalent of docents, or of those carefully worded museum plaques that neighbor the statue like gossips and presume to explain it. They place the work in time, hoping to counteract that imperious and haughty self-sufficiency that is so characteristic of statues and that Shelley in "Ozymandias," had to render into words so as to rebuke. Too, they strive to replace immediate spatial presence with temporal sequence; as Lessing writes in *Laokoon* "The rule is this, that succession in time is the province of the poet, co-existence in space that of the artist."[30]

"Surviving all," Rogers's torso relays the same message that emerges from Shelley's "Ozymandias," though we would hardly expect it. While Shelley emphasizes the evanescence of the King's pride and power, he makes it clear at the same time that the "sculptor well those passions read / Which yet survive, stamped on these lifeless things" (*Complete Works*, II, 62). Although sovereignty is effectively undercut towards the end of this sonnet, the immortality of the sculptor's work is never in doubt, in spite of the "trunk-less" legs and "shattered" visage. Along with the poems by Milman and Rogers, then, "Ozymandias" reveals the conventional belief in the art-work's tenacity, its ability to transcend time and project genius even through ruin.

Keats's sonnet questions this theme of endurance in the marbles and points rather to the fragility of their medium, their tenuous form. The motif of "rising" on which Rogers places so much emphasis (and which he sets against "sinking" and the contrasting poetic force of "drawing down" divine power, a trope he lifts from the end of Dryden's "Alexander's Feast") finds its more sober counterpart in the pattern of thwarted upward move-ment in Keats's poem.[31] His eagle can only look at the sky weakly, unable to decipher "that long-lost spell in secret given," like the poet unable to unlock the riddle of inspiration caught in the still stone. Keats's sonnet problem-atizes the process of inspiration, of aesthetic osmosis that both Milman's and Rogers's poems take for granted (and Shelley's ignores). And in so doing, it offers a cogent criticism of the dominant belief in a fluid transferral of genius. Further, "On Seeing the Elgin Marbles" questions the conventional association of Grecian statues with brightness and lucidity, and questions also the ubiquitous contemporary equation of Periclean Greece with the "dawn" of culture. Both Rogers and Milman ally their statues with light, and both argue implicitly that such light emanates from a divine source. Keats, on the other hand, not only believes it "a gentle luxury" (line 6) that he need not witness the sunrise, but also ends his poem indirectly associating both the marbles and his perception of them with a sunset. Where the two contemporary works bask in a lambent glow, Keats's poem refuses the dawn and ends in uncertain twilight.

The same refusal to come to terms with the medium that Rogers, Shelley, and the majority of the witnesses in the House commentary share can also be found in "The Elgin Marbles," a poem that appeared anonymously in the *Gentleman's Magazine*:

Are these the fragments of the glorious prime
  Of that great Empire, mistress of the world,
  Who, Queen of Nations high in air unfurl'd
Her standard, and outstretch'd her arm sublime?—
Yes! and they mock all-devouring Time;
  For oft, in anger, at yon fane he hurl'd
His iron rod, but prostrate at the shrine
  Of the Great Goddess harmlessly it fell,
  Till he, struck motionless, as with a spell,
Gazed wildly and proclaim'd the power divine.
Phidias! thou hast immortalized thy name
  In these thy handy-works, and they will tell
Loud as ten thousand thunderings thy fame
  Wherever truth and beauty deign to dwell.[32]

Even though it is their spirit that supposedly partakes of immortality, we cannot fail to see an obvious contradiction between the author's designation of the works as "fragments" and their perceived inviolability to Time's "iron rod." In reality, the statues appear to personify "all-devouring Time," rather than mock it. With the other poems, this sonnet constitutes a willful misprision of the artifacts that immediately present themselves. The poem suspends any direct perception of the marbles by first restoring them in the "fane" and then situating Time's allegorical attempt to attack them firmly in the past ("For oft, in anger at yon fane he *hurl'd* / His iron rod"). Time tries to overthrow the original statues in the Parthenon, not the extant fragments.

For the author to praise the stones, therefore, he must not only repress their fragmentation, but recreate them *in situ*; he must imaginatively make them whole so that they conform to his audience's conceptions of neo-classical "truth and beauty." Only then can they be safely eulogized. We notice also that it is unclear in the description whether Time falls prostrate before the shrine or the marbles; the metonymic substitution of shrine for marbles further conceals the fact of their impaired state and facilitates (and makes unambiguous) the author's praise. At work in the response is a species of artistic compensation that locates the immortality of the marbles nostalgically in the past and links virtuosity with completeness.

Restoring the marbles enables the poet to invoke the conventional generic response. "Time" becomes a foil for the poet/observer and replicates the now familiar reaction of rapture in the face of absolute mimetic power, as he is "struck motionless" by the spell of divinity the marbles cast. The author not only avoids description of the marbles or direct confrontation with their corroded forms, but also creates an allegorical narrative to replace and affirm his own reaction and to fill the space of instantaneous impression left by the artifacts themselves. This device is then followed by a recourse to Phidias and a proclamation of the collection's fame.

Barry Cornwall's contribution to this genre reveals a slightly different instance of misprision. Written in 1817, "On the Statue of Theseus in the Elgin Collection of Marbles," appeared in the *Gentleman's Magazine* (n.s. I, 157) the following year:

> —Aye, this is he—
>           A proud and mighty spirit:—how fine his form
> Gigantic!—moulded like the race that strove
> To take Jove's heaven by storm, and drive him from
> Olympus.—There he sits—a demigod—
> Stern as when he of yore forsook the maid,
> Who, doating, sav'd him from the Cretan toil,
> Where he had slain the Minotaur—Alas!
> Fond Ariadne!—her did he desert,
> And (heartless) left her on the Naxos' shore                    10
> To languish. . . . Look!—'twas he who dar'd to roam
> The world infernal, and on Pluto's queen
> (Ceres' long-sought Proserpina) to lay
> His hand: thence was he prison'd in the vaults
> Beneath, till freed by Hercules. . . . Methinks
> His mighty Sire, in anger when he saw
> How dark his course and impious, must have stay'd
> (So carv'd to nature is that Phidian stone)
> The flow of life, and with his trident-touch
> Have *struck him into marble*.                                        20

                                                                        (p. 157)

On one level Cornwall's breathless and dramatic retelling of the Theseus myth serves as substitute for the mute statue before him. Although he alludes to the conventionally praised verisimilitude of the sculpture in line 18, his remarks on this score are parenthetical and finally over-shadowed by the larger purpose of the poem—that of expressing the poet's own Romantic sentiment and feeling sympathy. The emotion is expended on the mythical figures and the tale, the signified, not on the artifact, the signifier, that sits in front of him. The descriptive ejaculations and colloquial exclamations of astonishment and wonder emphasize the immediacy of the response and point rather to the poet's acute sensibility than to the artwork's intrinsic greatness. Whereas the dashes in Keats's sonnet function symbolically and serve to mirror the fragmented marbles and to indicate an exhaustion of inspiration—the poet's inability to continue creating similes—the punctuation in Cornwall's poem signifies awe, implying a spontaneity of composition as well as an exuberance of emotion. Sublimity is expressed by the level of enthusiasm Cornwall works up, rather than by any analysis or appreciation of formal features ("Aye, this is he" and "There he sits," the poet says flatly). The greatness of the sculpture for Cornwall thus comes metaphorically, by association with the myth.

But if we look at the poem from another point of view, through another generic lens, as it were, we notice something quite different. The emphasis in the myth Cornwall retells falls on forsaken love, on Theseus' desertion of Ariadne. As such, the poet invokes emotion through a conventional trope borrowed from the novels and poems of sensibility. In this light, the beginning makes more sense. Rather than being a gratuitous opener, "—Aye, this is he—" reverberates with the connotations of an accusing witness. Cornwall identifies the criminal and proceeds to give a character analysis, as the accused sits stern and defiant on the stand; instead of a flat declarative, then, "There he sits" (line 5) resonates with disdain, and with an implicit moral condemnation. The poet throws in another moral charge, "heartless" (line 10), further to remind us of the genre in which he is really working, and at the end makes Hercules punish the recusant by striking him into marble. The wild exclamations can now be read as fully appropriate to the genre: they are cries from the courtroom instead of the museum. Cornwall replaces an aesthetic response with a moral one and makes his experience of the marbles conform to any we might have by reading Fanny Burney or Hannah More. By manipulating the ekphrastic form to the genre in which he works the more adeptly, Cornwall is able to substitute a tale of crime and retribution for a more philosophical aesthetic meditation.

Cornwall's response to the marbles, his generic sleight-of-hand, constitutes yet another attempt to replace the disarmingly battered immediacy of the works with something more complete and palatable. The poet, in addition, puts greater emphasis on the self-consciously subjective nature of his response than do Milman, Rogers, or the anonymous author of "The Elgin Marbles" discussed above. What becomes important for Cornwall, as it had been for Henry Mackenzie in *The Man of Feeling*, is the rather precise and detailed documentation of the heart's reaction to different stimuli, in this case to the various facts concerning Theseus' betrayal of Ariadne. In directing the eye inward towards the heart instead of outward, Cornwall follows a pattern of aesthetic response that characterizes a number of the poems on painting and sculpture that appear in the *Annals of the Fine Arts*.[33]

In his own sonnet Keats also uses the artworks as points of departure but combines the personal response they elicit with a keen awareness of the ambiguity of their forms. The marbles' grandeur is inextricably linked not only with the decay of time, but with the speaker's own "dizzy pain" (line 11). As Crisman reminds us, the antecedent of "That" in line 12 is not the marbles ("these wonders") but indeed the confusion brought on by their presence and the debate they precipitate in his heart. The sonnet denies any firm separation between perceiver and perceived, just as its logic resists any view of the objects that would not subordinate them as parts of the conscious gaze of the observer. From the moment the speaker sees them they are assimilated into his own thoughts, provoking his choice of imagery and diction as well as his feelings of impotency. In this respect, it becomes important that the letter "t" of the word "time" in line 13 remains uncapitalized, for it conceals a quiet pun.[34] Embedded in this traditional rendering of "devouring Time" is a suggestion of the wasting of the poet's own precious time, which has been the painful subject of the octave, as well as a persistent leitmotif of his letters.[35]

The meaning and order of images at the end of the sonnet has presented critics with a thorny hermeneutical problem. Most are divided over whether to see the final series of tableaux as a progression that completes the imagery established earlier, or as an isolated and complex metaphor, describing the poet's state. According to Fitzgerald, Keats suggests a temporal sequence—echoing the trope we have seen employed in Rogers and Cornwall—by providing a narrative line (not this time for the artifacts, but for his fading awareness of them), by invoking the process of a sunset:

> The evening implied in the sestet of "On Seeing the Elgin Marbles" has the similar effect of converting the debilitating experience of inadequacy . . . into a "dizzy pain" that is the sublime experience of "a shadow of a magnitude" as the sun sets in the sea. . . . [T]he basic progression of the sonnet towards evening and aftermath links it with the other Petrarchan sonnets. . . .[36]

Grecian grandeur gives way to the wasting of old time just as the sun, seen first through a wave and then as reflected on the sea, becomes a shadow of its former brightness when it sets. The entire sonnet, in fact, traces the arc of a single day, from dawn to dusk. (Although we might note that there is no middle, no noon; the poem concerns itself solely with beginnings and endings.)

The other prevailing view conceives the final lines spatially, as E. B. Murray does in his paraphrase:

> These wonders [i.e., the Marbles] bring round [his] heart a most dizzy pain which mingles Grecian grandeur with the rude wasting of old time *as* the sun mingles with the waves of the sea *so that* it [the sun] appears as the mere shadow of the magnitude it really is when one looks at it directly.[37]

The concluding image, then, is static, offers an extended metaphor of the poet's dizzy pain, and does not involve the temporal progression a sunset would imply. Murray's concern is with optics, with the reflected nature of the sun's light and how this parallels the fading grandeur of the marbles. The culminating tableau thus is important not because it fulfills a larger pattern or sequence of imagery in the poem, but because it helps clarify the elements that are combining to explain the poet's psychological condition.

Both these interpretations are useful, though in the end only partial. If we take a closer look, it becomes clear that the sonnet accommodates each of these readings by suggesting a temporal progression at the same time that it undermines logical transition and teleology. Keats creates the illusion of sequence in the poem's concluding list, leaving the exact relations between the items, between the parts of speech, between tenor and vehicle purposefully ambiguous and finally indeterminate. Each image—sun, billowy main, shadow of a magnitude—maintains its own spatial integrity while ostensibly qualifying the poet's perception. What would appear to explain his "dizzy pain" by clarifying ever more precisely what mingles with Grecian grandeur only obscures the pain further. And by the end of the poem, we are at sea, having been led by the list into a metaphorical typhoon and lulled by its progression into a false sense of grammatical order.

In disrupting syntactical relations and breaking down the poetic line, Keats not only confuses time and space but enacts the marbles' process of decay in language, within the sonnet's own system of metaphors and images. The poem's structure simply disintegrates in the last lines, reminding us, at least in form, of the conclusion of "After Dark Vapors," which Keats wrote a few weeks earlier.[38] There is perhaps no greater tribute to the success of the poet's ekphrastic experiment than the ostensibly irreconcilable criticism the sonnet has provoked. These responses almost exactly reproduce the historical reactions to the marbles themselves. One view, represented by Jack and Jones, sees only ruin ("disappointing," "dismally thin"); one, in Hewlett and Haydon, only genius ("a magnificent conclusion"); and the most prominent view, upheld by Murray, Fitzgerald, and Crisman, seeks to repair the damaged sonnet by completing its fragmented system of images. That the poem remains in its own way as much a fragment as the statues, can only explain why Murray feels it necessary to provide logical connectives (*as*, *so that*) in order to "restore" the work, as if it were indeed one of the busts in Elgin's collection. His impulse to paraphrase, and by so doing, reconstruct the sonnet, is really no different in kind from Payne Knight's or Farington's; it is the pre-Romantic urge to modify and complete the broken, instead of recognizing and coming to terms with it. Each of the critics who attempts to make the poem conform to a pattern, who gives it an autotelic integrity, in the end supplies the sonnet with a framework it only half concedes.

"On Seeing the Elgin Marbles" manages to use the emotional response of its counterparts in the *Annals of the Fine Arts*, yet remain faithful to the prescriptions of the ekphrastic genre. In order to achieve this, Keats must dissolve the traditional barriers between subject and object and interweave his own giddy perception, his disorientation, with the attenuated forms of the marbles. In the end, perceiver and perceived are fused into one final portrait—"a shadow of a magnitude." Both poet and marbles converge in a metaphor that succinctly characterizes their respective conditions—the one of youthful potential, of rising talent, the other of waning grandeur, of decaying genius. Instead of substituting a temporal narrative for the spatial immediacy of the forms, as his predecessors and contemporaries tend to do, Keats creates an alternate continuum composed of a shifting and unstable phenomenology of personal associations, sensations, and memories. The poet's response to the artifacts is profoundly private, and at times even inscrutable. The final lines of the poem, as we have seen, present a series of mysterious still-lifes, frozen images as fragmentary in nature as the battered marbles. These associations in some sense represent the poet's raw materials, the core of images, possibilities, combinations that exist prior to their precise formulation on the page. We are given a rough draft in these snapshots, a shorthand account of the experience without the semantic bulwark of transitions and modifiers.

In a number of important ways, then, the sonnet offers a complex revaluation of contemporary aesthetic response to the Elgin Marbles; it not only questions the process of artistic inspiration, but tempers the current enthusiasm over the proposed function of the statuary. Moreover, it points out that the broken nature of their medium cannot be overlooked in any appreciation of their greatness. Perhaps more importantly, the sonnet emerges as a meditation on the mortality of aesthetic form and stands in direct opposition to the Renaissance and Shakespearian themes of the sonnet as outlasting time, as the supreme immortal monument. Even as he is launching his own career, Keats worries about the tenuous nature of Fame, worries that the decay so evident in the forms before him will inevitably permeate the medium he has chosen. Most importantly, if ekphrasis at its best, at its most cunning, as Krieger maintains, is the attempt not merely to describe, but to transfer artwork into poetry, to render the painting, statue, or frieze in the medium of words, then Keats has brought it off flawlessly in this sonnet.[39] One need only look to modern criticism of the work for confirmation of his success. Ekphrasis as mimesis, then, or as simile, on the model of George Kurman, governs Keats's first venture into the genre.[40]

## Notes

1 For example, John Jones in *Keats's Dream of Truth* (London: Chatto and Windus, 1969) calls the pair of sonnets which come out of the Elgin Marbles visit "enthusiastic but dismally thin" (p. 162); Ian Jack in *Keats and the Mirror of Art* (Oxford: Clarendon Press, 1967) labels them "disappointing" (p. 35); and Douglas Bush in *John Keats* (New York: Macmillan, 1966) dismisses them as "half-inarticulate" (p. 39).
2 Dorothy Hewlett, *A Life of John Keats* (London: Hutchinson, 1970), p. 62; William Crisman, "Keats's Elgin Marbles Sonnet," *Studies in Romanticism*, 26 (1987), 51; William Fitzgerald, "Keats's Sonnets and the Challenge of Winter," *Studies in Romanticism*, 26 (1987), 65; and Benjamin Griffith, "Keats's 'On Seeing the Elgin Marbles,'" *Explicator*, 31 (1973), 76.

3 For a brief but illuminating analysis of "Ode on a Grecian Urn" in this context, see section vii of Jerome McGann's "Keats and the Historical Method in Literary Criticism," *Modern Language Notes*, 94 (1979), 988–1032; reprinted in *The Beauty of Inflections* (Oxford: Clarendon Press, 1985), pp. 15–65.

4 For a complete history of the Elgin Marbles in England, see William St Clair, *Lord Elgin and the Marbles* (London: Oxford University Press, 1967).

5 *The Farington Diary*, ed. James Grieg (London: Hutchinson & Co., 1925), v, 46. All citations are taken from this edition.

6 *Lord Byron: The Complete Poetical Works*, ed. Jerome J. McGann (Oxford: Clarendon, 1980), I: lines 1029–30.

7 *The Diary of Benjamin Robert Haydon*, ed. Willard B. Pope (Cambridge: Harvard University Press, 1960), 1, 439 (13 May 1815). All subsequent references are to this edition.

8 Jacob Rothenberg, *"Descensus ad Terram": The Aquisition and Reception of the Elgin Marbles* (New York: Garland Publishing, 1977), p. 7.

9 See Thomas McFarland on the diasparactive in *Romanticism and the Forms of Ruin* (Princeton, New Jersey: Princeton University Press, 1981); references to the Elgin Marbles appear on pages 25 and 279.

10 That there were rumors circulating at the time which suggested the Apollo to be a copy from a bronze statue only served to enhance the value of the Elgin Marbles, whose authenticity was beyond doubt.

11 J. J. Winckelmann, "Beschreibung des Torso im Belvedere zu Rom" (trans. Henry Fuseli, 1765).

12 Haydon's anatomical revelation found its plebeian but no less poignant counterparts in two popular anecdotes of the time. One concerned a terse *tête-a-tête* between two members of the public: upon hearing one man's assessment, "How broken they are, a'ant they?," the other replied, "Yes, but how *like* life." The other related the story of a riding master who took his pupils to see the metopes: "See, gentlemen, look at the riders all round the room, see how they sit; see with what ease and elegance they ride; I never saw such men in my life; they have no saddles, no stirrups, they must have leapt upon their horses in a grand style. You will do well to study the position of these noble fellows; stay here this morning instead of riding with me, and I am sure you will seat yourself better tomorrow" (John Thomas Smith, *Nollekens and his Times* (London: Colburn, 1829) 1, 289).

13 It is significant that Knight was the only witness called by the House committee who responded to the question concerning the collection's monetary value. Whereas most of the artists and sculptors refused to speculate on their commercial worth (on being posed this question, for instance, Charles Rossi replied indignantly "never"), Knight greeted this part of the inquiry with scarcely concealed glee, drawing up a meticulous ledger of prices and comparing the items wherever he could with the known values of the Townley and Lansdowne marbles. His descriptions of the articles in Elgin's collection are everywhere marked by a predilection for noting surface detail, always to the detriment of the artifact: "Fourteen metopes, of various degrees of merit, all corroded, and mostly much mutilated"; "A white marble soros complete and entire, but coarse"; "Nine broken marble urns"; "Recumbent statue of Hercules, as on the coins of Croto, with little of the surface remaining": *Report from the Select Committee of the House of Commons on the Earl of Elgin's Collection of Sculptured Marbles* (London: 1816), p. 96.

14 John Flaxman, one of the chief witnesses and perhaps the finest sculptor in England at the time, stated that the marbles were "as perfect nature as it is possible to put into the compass of the marble in which they are executed, and

that of the most elegant kind" (*House of Commons Report*, p. 71), a view seconded by Sir Thomas Lawrence who thought they portrayed "great truth and imitation of nature" and considered them "as united with grand form" (p. 91). In comparison with the Apollo Belvedere, he observed, "there is in them an union of fine composition, and very grand form, with a more true and natural expression of the effect of action upon the human frame than there is in the Apollo" (p. 90). J. B. S. Morritt argued that they represented "the purest specimens of the finest age of Greece" (p. 132); Benjamin West, "His health not permitting him to attend the committee," nevertheless submitted a letter in which he praised their "grand and simple style of composition" (p. 150) and pronounced "the equestrian groupes" in the frieze to be "without example . . . [they do] not appear to be efforts of the human hand, but those of some magic power, which brought the marble into life" (p. 151). Unqualified praise of this variety spilled over into the journals and newspapers of the day as well. The author of an essay in the *Quarterly Review* observed: "They certainly excel . . . all the statues in the world" (14 [1816], 529). John Scott, then editor of *The Champion*, deemed the objects the greatest works of sculpture he had yet seen, even in their impaired state, and recapitulated the opinions of the experts in the House debates: "The ruins and scanty remnants of ancient Greece, are more perfect in beauty, more fresh in the fragrance of elegance, more living and life-giving, than all the preserved and prized stock of what genius has since effected": "The Elgin Marbles," in *The Champion*, 155 (24 December 1815), 390.

15 *The Champion*, 156 (30 April 1816), 102.

16 *The Letters of John Keats*, ed. Hyder E. Rollins (Cambridge: Harvard University Press, 1958), I, 193.

17 *Annals of the Fine Arts* (1817), I, 354. This expression of high hope was probably borrowed from Benjamin West's letter to Lord Elgin in 1810 published as an appendix to a memorandum detailing the Earl's travels in Greece. In it, West relayed his thanks to Elgin for "bringing these treasures of the first and best age of sculpture and architecture into London . . . [and founding] a new Athens for the emulation and example of the British student," *Memorandum on the Subject of the Earl of Elgin's Pursuits in Greece* (London: 1810), p. 167. He went on "to indulge a hope, that . . . sculpture may soon be raised in England to rival the ablest productions of the best times of Greece."

18 *Gentleman's Magazine*, 89 (1816), 326.

19 Felicia Hemans, *Modern Greece* (Oxford: Baxter, 1816), p. 22.

20 Jean H. Hagstrum, *The Sister Arts: The Tradition of Literary Pictorialism and English Poetry from Dryden to Gray* (Chicago: University of Chicago Press, 1958), p. 24.

21 William Hayley, *An Essay on Sculpture* (London: Cadell and Davies, 1800), p. 293. This poem is important because it contains both a compilation of translated Greek epigrams on statues and a series of responses to sculpture that correspond directly with the British Academy's notions, as demonstrated in the House debates. Hayley's descriptions anticipate some of the very same language the committee was to use in illustrating the proposed aesthetic function of the marbles: for instance, when looking on the work of Phidias, he argues that "the rapt mind, to Heaven itself convey'd, / *Imbibes* celestial form by Fancy's aid, / And gives adoring mortals to survey / Features that indicate Almighty sway" (p. 52, italics mine). Later, as the poet turns the general eye towards Glycon's Hercules, he imagines the spectator who will "glow with vigor's flame, / And feel the god reanimate his frame" (p. 77). The mimetic response ennobles the viewer, creating in him some of the same characteristics as the god.

22 Sir Joshua Reynolds, *Fifteen Discourses* (London: J. M. Dent, 1928), p. 159. For a slightly different view, see William Hazlitt's essays "The Elgin Marbles" and "Notes of a Journey through France and Italy" (in *The Collected Works*, IX, ed. A. R. Waller and Arnold Glover [London: J. M. Dent, 1903], where he reacts against Reynolds but proffers some of the very same ideas: "If ever there were models of the Fine Arts fitted to give an impulse to living genius, these are they" (IX, 168).

23 See Shelley's "On Leonardo's Picture of Medusa" for a frightening instance of this process: "Yet it is less the horror than the grace / Which turns the gazer's spirit into stone, / Whereon the lineaments of that dead face / Are graven, till the characters be grown / Into itself, and thought no more can trace" cited from *The Complete Works*, ed. Roger Ingpen and Walter E. Peck (New York: Gordian Press, 1965), III, 298.

24 *The Poems of John Keats*, ed. Jack Stillinger (Cambridge: Harvard University Press, 1978), p. 93: lines 1–4.

25 "Keats's Elgin Marbles Sonnet," *Studies in Romanticism*, 26 (1987), 51–52.

26 See Krieger's "*Ekphrasis* and the Still Movement of Poetry; or, *Laokoon* Revisited," in *The Poet as Critic*, ed. Frederick McDowell (Evanston: Northwestern University Press, 1967).

27 Martin Aske, *Keats and Hellenism* (Cambridge: Cambridge University Press, 1985). p. 2.

28 For a list of relevant publications see Timothy Webb's *English Romantic Hellenism*, 1700–1824 (Manchester: Manchester University Press, 1982) and also Stephen A. Larrabee, *English Bards and Grecian Marbles* (New York: Columbia University Press, 1943).

29 Samuel Rogers, *Poems* (London: Cadell and Davies, 1816), pp. 138–139.

30 Gotthold Lessing, *Laokoon*, trans. Ellen Frothingham (New York: Noonday Press, 1957), p. 109. For a disastrous example of narrative substitution, see Jacob Sadoleti's exhaustive play-by-play in his poem on the Laocoon reprinted by both Hayley and Lessing (p. 209).

31 The predominant metaphor in the *House of Commons Report* is one of height: the marbles consistently prove "the highest achievements of the past," whose workmanship is "higher than that of the Apollo Belvedere," etc. Dugald Stewart had also noted "the bias of the mind to connect together the ideas of antiquity, and of elevated place": *Philosophical Essays* (Edinburgh: 1818), p. 595.

32 *Gentleman's Magazine*, n.s. I (1818), 65. Though published anonymously, this poem sounds suspiciously like Haydon. Note the irrepressible optimism, the characteristic prediction of the marbles' fame, and the echo of Keats in "ten thousand thunderings."

33 Among them, "A Sonnet to Mr. Haydon on a Study from Nature" remains the most effusive, recounting the author's experience in front of "The Judgment of Soloman" and "Christ's Entry into Jerusalem" (both of which are outside the poem, relegated to footnotes). Like Cornwall's poem, it escapes the genuine ekphrastic form by resorting to the requirements of another genre, in this case the elegiac lament.

34 When it was submitted to *The Champion* and *The Examiner*, the editors presumably capitalized "time," thinking Keats meant the traditional personified figure; only the *Annals* left the "t" in its original state, publishing the poem exactly as it appeared in the draft.

35 In the months following the composition of this sonnet Keats is bedeviled by doubts about his own abilities in his chosen endeavor. A number of times, as he is alone at Margate attempting to write *Endymion*, he questions his own stamina

and wonders if his time might be better spent. In a letter of this period to Hunt, Keats describes his reservations in alternating waves of confidence and despair:

> I vow that I have been down in the Mouth lately at this Work. These last two day[s] however I have felt more confident—I have asked myself so often why I should be a Poet more than other Men,—seeing how great a thing it is,—how great things are to be gained by it—What a thing to be in the Mouth of Fame—that at last the Idea has grown so monstrously beyond my seeming Power of attainment that the other day I nearly consented with myself to drop into a Phaeton—yet 't is a disgrace to fail even in a huge attempt, and at this moment I drive the thought from me.

(Letters, I, 139)

The letter ends with a series of half-jocular allusions to suicide and a request for Hunt to tell Shelley about the "stran(ge) stories of the death of Poets—some have died before they were conceived" (140).

36 "Keats's Sonnets and the Challenge of Winter," *Studies in Romanticism*, 26 (1987), 65.

37 "Ambivalent Mortality in the Elgin Marbles Sonnet," *Keats-Shelley Journal*, 34 (1971), 26.

38 On 31 January 1817, to be precise. This poem, however, fulfills the promise of its organic imagery and ends with the poet's death, which comes as little surprise after the previous allusions to autumn, evening, and the sand slipping through an hourglass. Keats's comments on the form of the genre in "To Charles Cowden Clarke" also seem relevant here—"the sonnet swelling loudly / Up to its climax and then dying proudly" (lines 60–61)—as do his remarks to Taylor about "the rise, the progress, the setting of imagery" which should "like the sun come natural . . . to him—shine over him and set soberly although in magnificence leaving him in the Luxury of twilight" (*Letters*, I, 238).

39 See Krieger: "The ekphrastic dimension of literature reveals itself wherever the poem takes on the 'still' elements of plastic form which we normally attribute to the spatial arts," and "The poet must convert the transparency of his verbal medium into the physical solidity of the medium of the spatial arts"—*The Poet as Critic*, p. 6.

40 George Kurman, "Ecphrasis in Epic Poetry," *Comparative Literature*, 26 (1974), 4.

# 17

# 'TO SEE AS A GOD SEES': THE POTENTIAL *ÜBERMENSCH* IN KEATS'S *HYPERION* FRAGMENTS

*Mark Sandy*

Source: *Romanticism* 4 (1998), 212–23.

But cannot I create . . .

(John Keats)

[W]e want to be the poets of our lives . . .

(Friedrich Nietzsche)[1]

Many important historical, cultural and generic differences separate the writings of Keats and Nietzsche, but these have not deterred scholars from establishing parallels between them. Even critics without explicit theoretical agendas, for instance John Jones and Morris Dickstein, have traced significant similarities between the texts of Keats and Nietzsche.[2] Theoretical accounts have gone beyond thematic parallels, and the work of Paul de Man, Tilottama Rajan, and Kathleen Wheeler has drawn upon Nietzschean philosophy as a source for critical practices and an appropriate vocabulary.[3] The *Hyperion* poems have been the subject of much critical debate, often read in conjunction with one another to explore Keats's revisions and align the Apollo of *Hyperion* with the poet-figure of *The Fall*. Yet among these only a handful of commentators explore the poems through a Nietzschean critical lens, or by drawing parallels with Nietzsche's work.[4] This is curious considering that at the heart of the *Hyperion* fragments lies the Keatsian and Nietzschean theme of human suffering, mutability and tragedy. Nietzsche's fictionalising of the self and world can be used to measure Keats's own struggle with the nature of self. In turn, Keats's struggle to discover a self can be read as a precursor to the concerns of Nietzschean philosophy.

349

Both Keatsian and Nietzschean treatments of the self emphasise its potential for multiplicity, rejecting the Enlightenment's understanding of the subject as singular and autonomous.[5] Nietzsche's attack on Enlightenment philosophy, exemplified by Kant's transcendental system, sought to end the duality of soul (or mind) and body, and intellect and desire. In *The Will to Power*,[6] he presents the self as a fiction open to numerous re-inventions:

> The subject: this is the term for our belief in a unity underlying all the different impulses of the highest feeling of reality: we understand this belief as the *effect* of one cause – we believe so firmly our belief that for its sake we imagine 'truth', 'reality', 'substantiality' in general. – The subject is the fiction that many similar states in us are the effect of one substratum; but it is we who first created the 'similarity' of these states.
>
> (*WP*, III, 485, pp. 268–9)

By questioning the autonomy and unity of the subject Nietzsche frees the self from the shackles of a metaphysical and supersensible realm of Reason, so that it can embark upon the process of 'becoming'. Nietzsche reduces the Enlightenment 'will to truth' to only one of many fictions used to interpret self and world. Such a reduction heralds a self freed from the divided and fixed metaphysical world of being, a self aware of itself as a cluster of many processes involved in the act of 'becoming'. Self and the universe are not to be constructed, or interpreted, through the single fiction of Reason, rather, invented and re-invented by an endless creation of competing fictions. This process of 'becoming' is centred around the paradoxical task of partly discovering and partly inventing the self's nature. Consequently, *Übermensch* (taken here to mean 'Overman') is not simply an attainable state or mode of existence, but is dependent upon individual attitudes to the notion of the self and its relation to the phenomenal world. Such attitudes involve, according to Nietzsche, a recognition that metaphysical and totalising explanations are only further fictions used for interpreting the experiential and phenomenal world. Metaphysicians, on the other hand, assert their perspective to be actual: 'Because we have to be stable in our beliefs if we are to prosper, we have made the 'real' world a world not of change and becoming, but one of being' (*WP*, III, 507, p. 276). Effectively, the language of metaphysics originated from a metaphorical – or fictional – interpretation of reality, but because this interpretation has become so commonplace and essential to daily human life, its fictional nature is forgotten: '[W]ithout granting as true the fictions of logic, without measuring reality against the purely invented world of the unconditional and self-identical, without a continued falsification of the world by means of numbers, mankind could not live'.[7]

For Nietzsche, the endless process of 'becoming' opposes the Enlightenment interpretation of reality as 'being' and the logocentric metaphysical language used to construct such a view. To 'become' involves a re-discovery of the creative potentiality of language through a metaphorical mode, in which '[m]an is no longer an artist, he has become a work of art' (*BT*, p. 18). Without the restrictions of a metaphysical system an individual self is free to invent, re-invent, and revise itself rather like a script, as suggested by the title of Nietzsche's unconventional autobiography, *Ecce Homo*.[8] In Nietzsche's eyes, the metaphorical mode must be continually re-invented, or it risks being established as another fixed interpretation of the self and world, another metaphysical 'falsification'. This conflict between metaphysical and metaphorical modes of language, in Nietzschean philosophy, is reflected by a struggle between the Apollonian illusory dream and the Dionysian tragic affirmation of reality (*BT*, pp. 75–7), between the preachings of a priest and the fictions of a poet. They find their ultimate expression in the formulation of '*Dionysos versus the Crucified*' (*EH*, p. 134).

Keats's own concern with the antithesis between poet and philosopher – '[w]hat shocks the virtuous philosopher delights the camelion poet'[9] – anticipates Nietzsche's formulation. In *Lamia* the rainbow's magic and mystery are destroyed by the 'touch of cold philosophy', an equivalent to Nietzsche's metaphysical mode, which places it amongst the 'dull catalogue of common things' (II, 230–233). What Keats opposes is Enlightenment philosophy which, governed by Reason, seeks to identify, label and catalogue all phenomena, producing a world that is accounted for in every detail: 'Philosophy will clip an Angel's wings,/ Conquer all mysteries by rule and line,/ Empty the haunted air, and gnoméd mine –/ Unweave a rainbow' (II, 234–7).

Keats's definition of poetic identity shares with Nietzsche's view an awareness of the self's fictional status and its potential for constant invention and revision. These processes of self-revision and invention are similar to those involved in the composition of a literary work, so the act of writing a self becomes both literal and metaphorical. To free a self from the prison house of metaphysical language may involve loss of a sense of self. Nietzsche advances this loss of self as a pre-requisite to self-discovery and self-invention, asserting '[t]hat one becomes what one is presupposes that one does not have the remotest idea *what* one is' (*EH*, p. 64). Equally, Keats's own formulation of 'Negative Capability' emphasises the importance of undergoing this significant loss of self before its rediscovery is ever possible: '[T]he poetical Character . . . has no self – it is everything and nothing – it enjoys light and shade: it lives in gusto, be it foul or fair, high or low . . . It has as much delight in conceiving an Iago as an Imogen' (*KL*, p. 157). Keats's understanding of poetic identity shares Nietzsche's concept of an endless process of self-revision, freeing the self to occupy the extremities of 'everything and nothing', 'light and shade' and 'foul and fair'. In a manner similar to Nietzsche's attack on the unity of the subject, Keats perceives a direct connection between the creative processes of writing and the creation of a self unable to assert itself as a metaphysical category because of its

351

awareness of its fictional status: 'If then he [the poet] has no self, and if I am a Poet, where is the Wonder that I should say I would ... write no more? ... It is a wretched thing to confess; but is a very fact that not one word I ever utter can be taken for granted as an opinion growing out of my identical nature – how can it, when I have no nature?' (*KL*, pp. 157–8).

Keats's October 1818 letter to Richard Woodhouse is pervaded by uncertainty about the validity of personal opinions. The Keatsian self is forever in potential, wavering between 'everything and nothing', verging on self-discovery and self-invention through writing, enacting its own irretrievable loss. According to Keats and Nietzsche, it is exactly this loss of identity which frees the self from the constraints of a metaphysical system, leading to a recognition of the self's awareness of its own multiple natures. Both Keats and Nietzsche favour a self conceived of as an endlessly revisable – and revising – script.

Struggle between the Olympian and Titanic factions is central to an understanding of Keats's *Hyperion* fragments. This conflict allows Keats further to explore his anxieties about identity and finds a Nietzschean counterpart in the warring of metaphorical and metaphysical modes of language. Like fiery aspirant Apollos, Keats and Nietzsche rise from the ruins of a fading metaphysical order, prophesying a new metaphorical era to replace the old scheme. Emphasis on self-invention as a revisionary process means that construction of a new identity must be rooted in what previously existed. This paradox is played out in Keats's *Hyperion*, where the ardent promotion of revolution results not in Titanic downfall but points to a revolutionary change occurring at some future time.

What prevents narrative and revolutionary fruition in Keats's fragment is a profound crisis of self-identity, enacted both by Saturn, who must define a new identity without the power of kingship (I, 125–6; 129), and the aspiring Apollo, who must define a new ruling identity. Lifeless silence governs the fallen Saturn 'quiet as a stone' in the 'shady sadness of a vale' (I, 4;1), intimating the death of his Titanic voice and his inability to hold sway in the universe. If Saturn is incapable of 'god-like exercise' (I, 107), the metaphysical fiction of a 'strong identity' or 'real self' (I, 114) – once the guarantee of his universal power – is no longer meaningful in a changing cosmos. Paradoxically, Keats's description of the negations of sound, resonance, and life evoke their presence through the depiction of their absence. The text abounds with fresh outgrowths of meaning at the exact narrative point where all else is supposedly silenced and barren. Saturn is never robbed entirely of his capacity for 'godlike exercise' (I, 107). He remains frozen as 'natural sculpture' (I, 85), but contemplates a new fiction for interpreting the self and world: '"But cannot I create?/ Cannot I form? Cannot I fashion forth?/ Another world, another universe ..."' (I, 141–3).

Silencing the Titanic voice is therefore intimated but never achieved. Clearly, *Hyperion*'s cultural transition, represented by the transference of power from Titan to Olympian, cannot occur simply as a sharp break with Titanic reign. Apollo must fashion his own identity, voice, and order, in the light of past Titanic experience, much as Keats must forge his poetic character through a revision of the gigantic literary legacy of Dante, Shakespeare, Spenser, Milton and Wordsworth. The revisionary figure of Apollo (or the poet Keats) reanimates a past cultural and poetical legacy with his own lifeforce – or rather imaginative powers – so that he can confront his own self-negation and 'fashion forth' (I, 142) a new cultural and literary identity for himself. Keats's description of Saturn's lifeless condition does not seal him within a sarcophagus of silence, but reanimates the fallen Titan so that a new poetical voice – whether Olympian or Keatsian – can be liberated.

Apollo's predicament parallels Saturn's past and present dilemma: he must fashion, or create, a new identity if his 'unpractis'd hands' (I, 62) are ever to command the universe. Apollo's deification falters on the text's margins, caught between identity and non-identity, between a metaphysical system of certainty and the uncertainty of a metaphorical mode and, ultimately, between life and death. Such a failed transformation, like Saturn's faltering decline on the 'margin-sand' (I, 15), shows the poem's ability to blur distinctive states of being and modes of consciousness, providing a sense that the whole process of self-construction through fictions – vital to the Negatively-Capable poet – has been disclosed by narrative suspension. *Hyperion*'s abrupt ending forces life and literature to spill over into one another, so that these failed self-transformations force a disclosure about the author's and reader's own inventive efforts to fashion self-identities.

No matter how the lesson of Thea's tragic 'eyes eterne' (I, 117) is interpreted, Apollo's transformation and reign (if it were included within the boundaries of the text) would only create a 'strong identity' and incarcerate Apollo within a metaphysical scheme. The superiority of Apollo's reign over Saturn's depends upon its strategic delay to a point in time and space outside the text, to avoid fixing his identity in the poem's narrative: 'At length/ Apollo shriek'd; – and lo! from all his limbs/ Celestial . . .' (III, 134–5).

Apollo occupies a threshold between mortal man and immortal deity, a deferral indicating a crisis on the margin – or what Derrida terms the 'borderline' – of the text.[10] The Derridean 'borderline' marks a cross-over point between, or interface with, the life and work of an author, forcing a merging of life and literature. *Hyperion*'s textual margin does not provide an explanation of the poem's allegorical meaning; instead, it reveals the text's autotelic structure. The once living, now deceased Keats, is engaged in writing – or 'auto-graphing' – the nature of his new poetic character, which can only derive credibility from a future that is by no means assured.[11] Only Keats's own autograph offers the chance to attain this credibility as, in Derridean terms, he becomes the 'bearer of the name' John Keats (*EOO*, p. 44); a signature eternally returned to by readers of Keats and diversely interpreted – and endlessly constructed – by them through a succession of readings and re-readings, writings and re-writings. The credibility of Keats's poetical character rests with readers' eternal affirmation of his aesthetic revolution through this act of countersigning – or re-constructing – the Keatsian signature.[12] To countersign requires a reader to stamp Keats's autograph with their own personal seal and so ensure the continuation of the 'name' of the deceased John Keats. Consequently, there are no limits on readers' reconstructions of the signature, for as Derrida writes, '[w]hat returns to the name never returns to the living' (*EOO*, p. 44). The conflict between Olympian and Titan, in Nietzsche's words, represents a transitory stage between the 'old shattered law tables', or the 'name' of the deceased poet, and the 'new law tables – half written', which are the partly completed processes of the reader's countersignatures to the author's autograph.[13]

Transformation of Apollo falters in the indistinct textual twilight of the 'borderline', caught between mortality and immortality, linguistic certainty and uncertainty, and identity and non-identity, all of which indicate a return to the prefiguring event of Saturn's crisis on the threshold of the 'margin-sand'. This blurring of two apparent opposites, at the extreme edges of the text, sets a precedent for similarities between Saturn's 'Will to Knowledge' and Apollo's 'Will to Power'; in fact, Saturn's 'Will to Knowledge' could be the product of a corrupted 'Will to Power'. Similarly, the poem's power relations, worked out through the pattern of ascent and descent, are merged in a literal twilight when Hyperion battles to prevent both his own fall from power and Apollo's deification: 'And all along a dismal rack of clouds,/ Upon the boundaries of day and night,/ He stretch'd himself in grief and radiance faint' (I, 302–4).

*Hyperion* is preoccupied with aesthetic self-creation and self-discovery, promising the birth of a new voice and identity through a revolutionary overthrow of the Titans by the Olympians, but the poem never fully realises these events. *Hyperion* does not subscribe to Oceanus's understanding of 'progress', which professes to be 'eternal law', preferring to explore self-creation as process rather than as a means to a particular universal stage; or as Saturn would have it, a specific state of being. *Hyperion*'s focus is on the process of a self writing itself a future fictional identity that has little guarantee of ever existing. Nietzsche, like Keats, places emphasis on this process of self-construction, rather than ascribing to the process a particular end or final state: '[M]an is a bridge and not a goal; counting himself happy for his noontides and evenings, as a way to new dawns . . .' (*Z*, p. 215). Generically, *Hyperion* may take the form of an Eighteenth-Century progress poem,[14] but its Nietzschean understanding of Olympian dawn, as inevitable outcome rather than intended *telos*, belies its apparent enlightenment origins. The Enlightenment myth of human progress is reversed through a negative interpretation of change. Consequently, Apollo's dawn is delayed to avoid Hyperion's overshadowing, 'like the bulk/ Of Memnon's image at the set of sun' (II, 373–4). Titanic decline remains the centrepiece of *Hyperion*, teaching a 'sorrow more beautiful than Beauty's self' (I, 36).

Suffering must be actively embraced by Apollo if he is ever to achieve deification through an act of self-creation: 'But that the creator may exist, that itself requires suffering and much transformation . . . For the creator himself to be the child new-born he must also be willing to be the mother and endure the mother's pain' (*Z*, p. 111). Death is a necessary precondition to self-construction in *Hyperion*, because it is precisely the negation of life and the onset of Titanic decline that will permit the 'new born' voices of Apollo and Keats to speak. Paradoxically, Apollo must die into immortality, as the once living Keats must surrender – through the act of writing – to the death-in-life of the suspended *Hyperion* text, if his immortal voice as author is to be heard by the reader from beyond the grave. Zarathustra, prophet of the noontide, acts as a signpost to the *Übermensch* and a constructed mask from behind which Nietzsche can teach his anti-metaphysical philosophy (even after the event of his own death).[15] He performs a similar function to Apollo, who is prophet of a new dawn and of Keats's unique poetic identity and power soon to be born – or buried in the grave.

Yet Keats was to discard the Olympian mask of 'far-flown Apollo' (I, 204) in *The Fall of Hyperion*, and to experiment more directly with the processes of self-invention. The replacement of 'far-flown Apollo' with a human poet-figure, and the rite of suffering undertaken by the poet in ascending the 'immortal steps' (*The Fall*, I, 117), emphasise how crucial the dark wisdom of the Titans is to *The Fall of Hyperion*. Keats's inclusion of a poet-figure makes *The Fall*'s action more directly relevant to the issue of self-creation. Nonetheless, the poem's events are further distanced by the use of a Dantean dream framework as a narrative device.[16] A retrospective account of the clash between the Olympic and Titanic factions enables a shift of focus from the displacement of one culture, power and identity by another – the subject of the first *Hyperion* fragment – to a greater emphasis on the affirmation of suffering.

'To see as a God sees' (*The Fall*, I, 305) is the aspiration of the poet-figure, who must forge his own unique literary identity by accepting both the fictionality of his own self-identity and the inevitability of mortal suffering and death. Once again poetic self-identity and self-knowledge is to be partly constructed and partly disclosed: a process worked out for the author through the actual writing of text and for the reader through the construction – or reading – of that writing. The implicit relation between reading and writing in *Hyperion* presents the reader as a perpetual countersigner to the poetic fragment – when confronted with the absence of the deceased author who is indefinitely incapable of signing – a role more explicitly explored in *The Fall*: 'Whether the dream now purposed to rehearse/ Be poet's or fanatic's will be known/ When this warm scribe, my hand, is in the grave (*The Fall*, I, 16–19).

Keats establishes a complex relation between the action of writing and reading, as *The Fall* is literally a re-reading and re-writing of the *Hyperion* fragment – a text itself preoccupied with the revision of a literary and cultural tradition – whilst the worth of Keats's own revisionary work as written word rests with readers' individual interpretations of the text. This process involves the potential re-reading of the author's literary identity (or 'name') and re-writing of the reader's self-identity – literature both reads and writes the author and reader as much as it is written or read by them. The double truth of 'dying into life' is written on and read from Moneta's face by the author and reader. The human poet-figure, like his forerunner Apollo, must prove his ability to interpret a lesson from a face that is 'deathwards pro-gressing/ To no death' (I, 261–2). Moneta's visage reveals an active embrace of suffering and so fully grasps the double truth of 'dying into life', unifying the states of life and death. Moneta attains the death-in-life condition sought by the poet-figure (who like Keats desires to be immortalised and so speak from the grave), by Apollo (whose deification requires a dying out of mortal life into immortality), and not least, the faithful countersigning reader (who wishes to reanimate the lifeless poet, Keats). To grasp this essential double truth beyond and over the text of the *Hyperion* fragments is, as Nietzsche writes of Zarathustra, 'to have one foot *beyond* life' (*EH*, p. 42) and to relish both great joy and suffering, existence and self-annihilation. New dawns of self-discovery and self-creation are only possible if the death of a former self-identity is a relished prospect, or even a more literal death embraced. Saturn in the recast fragment accepts, rather than struggles against his demise, affirming the 'high tragedy' through a repetition of 'moan' and the simple words: 'There shall be death' (I, 424).

The lesson in Moneta's face may re-emphasise the 'borderline' indistinction between life and death – in which there is 'constant change . . . progressing to no death' (I, 260; 61) – signposting the way towards the process of 'becoming' without ever affirming its fruition, preferring instead to defer the moment of consummation and its responsibility to the reader. *The Fall* enacts the same suspension of process. Though the *Hyperion* fragments are capable of pointing to the process of aesthetic self-recovery and hint at the double truths such a process requires, neither fragment is able to 'fashion forth' an *Übermensch* from the figure of Apollo, Saturn, or the poet-figure. Instead, the poetic fragments disclose and suspend the autotelic process involved in the self forging its own fictional identity. The responsibility for aesthetic self-loss and recovery is, like the worth of Keats's poetic identity, decisively deferred to the readers who, having traced the 'large foot-marks' of the Titans along the 'margin-sand' (*Hyperion*, I, 15) to the 'borderline' of the fragments, must with Apollo make their choices about the nature of the aesthetic revolution they will countersign.

Elsewhere in his writings Keats expresses a fictional account of the self, which foregrounds the importance of suffering and (in spite of its use of a metaphysical vocabulary of 'Intelligence', 'Mind' and 'World'), prefigures Nietzsche's own favouring of physical desires and sensations over the abstractions of the human intellect. Keats's notion of 'spirit-creation' addresses the question of creating an identity, or soul, through experiencing a 'World of Pains': '[I]ntelligences are atoms of perception – they know and they see and they are pure, in short they are God – how then are Souls to be made? . . . How, but by the medium of a world like this?' (*KL*, p. 250). Keats's '"Vale of Soul-making"' recognised the 'highest terms for man', investing individuals with the immortal potentiality to attain their true identity, prefiguring Nietzsche's advocacy of a return to bodily sensations and his belief that humanity could 'overcome' itself through self-creation: 'Could you *conceive* a god? – But may the will to truth mean this to you: that everything shall be transformed into the humanly-conceivable, the humanly-evident, the humanly-palpable! You should follow your senses to the end!' (*Z*, p. 110).

Both the Nietzschean and Keatsian formulation of a fictionalised self placed emphasis on physical sensation, feeling and desire in reaction to the Kantian metaphysical tradition which reduced the self to a series of rational mental categories. Keats, in anticipation of the Nietzschean union of intellect and desire in the 'Will', maintained the inextricable nature of thought and sensation, asserting '[n]othing ever becomes real till it is experienced' (*KL*, p. 230): 'axioms in philosophy are not axioms until they are proved upon our pulses. We read fine things but never feel them to the full until we have gone the same steps as the author' (*KL*, p. 93).

Such an aesthetic act of self-creation requires an affirmation of the whole of life, its joys and sorrows'; a view which finds ultimate expression in the Nietzschean 'great Yes to life' and literature (*EH*, p. 42). After all, for Nietzsche, the 'existence of the world is *justified* only as an aesthetic phenomenon' (*BT*, p. 8). To 'prove upon our pulses' is to go beyond reading of Titanic loss and Olympian aspiration, or the prophecies of Zarathustra; it is, effectively, to *live* a life and constantly create an identity through 'becoming'. For this reason Apollo must 'die into life' and be willing to accept Titanic suffering by pursuing the 'large footmarks' (*Hyperion*, I, 15) and the poet-figure must, like Apollo, embrace life and death by ascending the stairs with 'iced foot' (*The Fall*, I, 132). Yet if the double truth contained in the self-identity crises of the *Hyperion* fragments is to be grasped the reader must follow these 'same steps'. This responsibility, attributed to the reader by Keats, is echoed by Nietzsche's prescription for grasping the truth of Zarathustra: 'To understand anything at all of my Zarathustra one has to possess a qualification similar to that which I possess – to have one foot *beyond* life' (*EH*, p. 42).

Self-overcoming may involve the grasping of certain double truths but, ironically, although they seem to exist beyond or above literature, or even life, their value does not rest with unlocking the secret of transcendence to the 'becoming' *Übermensch*; rather, with an active engagement in, and affirmation of, human experience and existence. 'To see as a god sees', as Apollo, Saturn and the poet-figure know all too well, involves exercising the divine gift of self-creation and an affirmation of human suffering and tragedy. Inevitably, the god-like aspiration of self-overcoming serves only to remind individuals of their contingent, culpable, and mortal nature for, as Nietzsche urges, the *Übermensch* must joyously embrace the tragic circumstances of our human condition.

Signposts to the process of self-overcoming and self-creation are littered everywhere amongst the ruins of the *Hyperion* fragments; waiting to be read in and written on the tragic faces of the Titans, or the death-in-life visage of the priestess Moneta, or even the hidden countenance of Mnemosyne. The lessons written and read in these faces, as in the failed transformations of Apollo and the human poet-figure, apparently promote an overcoming of life and literary text, through a recognition of the fictive nature of self-identity, and a seizing upon vital double truths about existence.

Neither *Hyperion* fragment is prescriptive about the lessons that are written or read into them for – like Zarathustra's instructions to his disciples – their ultimate authority and meaning rests not with Keats, or Nietzsche, but with their readers' countersignatures. Keats and Nietzsche ensure, through a process of infinite deferral, that the responsibility for reconstructing their texts is firmly placed with the reader. Self-overcoming is not an 'ideal' imposed upon the readers of Keats's *Hyperion* fragments for them to admire, but an 'ideal' that they must fashion into their own.[17] Only then can a reader truly countersign Keats's aesthetic revolution, and proclaim a great Nietzschean 'yes to life' and literature.

## Notes

1 *The Poems of John Keats*, ed. by Jack Stillinger (London: Heinemann, 1979), I, p. 141. All quotations from this edition, hereafter the *Hyperion* fragments are referred to as *Hyperion* and *The Fall*. Friedrich Nietzsche, *The Gay Science*, trans. by Walter Kaufmann (New York: Vintage, 1974), p. 299.

2 Jones reads *Hyperion* in conjunction with Nietzsche's 'system of spirit creation'. See *John Keats's Dream of Truth* (London: Chatto & Windus, 1969), pp. 85–90, hereafter *KDT*. Dickstein reads the Odes as a Nietzschean affirmation of life's tragedy. See *Keats and His Poetry: A Study in Development* (Chicago: Chicago UP, 1971), p. 227; pp. 230–1.

3 Paul De Man's examination of figural language in Nietzsche's *The Birth of Tragedy* has influenced his own concept of a defacing 'I'. See *Allegories of Reading: Figural Language in Rousseau, Nietzsche, Rilke, and Proust* (New Haven: Yale University Press, 1979), pp. 79–131; 'Autobiography as Defacement', in *The Rhetoric of Romanticism* (New York: Columbia University Press, 1984), pp. 93–123; 67–81. See Friedrich Nietzsche, *The Birth of Tragedy: Out of the Spirit of Music*, ed. by Michael Tanner and trans. by Shaun Whiteside (Harmondsworth: Penguin, 1993), pp. 3–12, hereafter *BT*. Rajan argues that Nietzsche offers a

vocabulary for interpreting Romantic poetry; see *Dark Interpreter: The Discourse of Romanticism* (New York: Cornell, 1980), pp. 26–9. Wheeler acknowledges Nietzsche's importance for Romantic studies. See *Romanticism, Pragmatism, and Deconstruction* (Oxford: Blackwell, 1993), p. 15.

4 Ross Woodman's reading recognises the connection. See 'Nietzsche, Blake, Keats and Shelley: The Making of a Metaphorical body', *Studies in Romanticism*, 29 (1990), pp. 115–49.

5 I follow Stanley Corngold's distinction between the subject and the self. The 'subject' is equated with ego, constituting the psychological site of self-reflexivity. In contrast, the 'authentic "Self"' formulates its experiences of the world as self-knowledge. It is this metaphysical fiction of the subject's 'authentic "Self"' that Nietzsche revalues. See *The Fate of the Self: German Writers and French Theory* (New York: Columbia University Press, 1986), p. 4; pp. 96–128.

6 Friedrich Nietzsche, *The Will To Power*, trans. by Walter Kaufmann and R. J. Hollingdale (New York: Vintage Press, 1968). All quotations from this edition, hereafter *WP*.

7 Friedrich Nietzsche, *Beyond Good and Evil: Prelude To A Philosophy of the Future*, trans. by R. J. Hollingdale (Harmondsworth: Penguin, 1990), p. 35.

8 Friedrich Nietzsche, *Ecce Homo: How One Becomes What One Is*, trans. by R. J. Hollingdale (Harmondsworth: Penguin, 1979), p. 64, hereafter *EH*.

9 *The Letters of John Keats*, ed. by Robert Gittings (Oxford: Oxford University Press, 1970), p. 157, hereafter *KL*.

10 Jacques Derrida, *The Ear of the Other: Otobiography, Transference, Translation*, trans. by Peggy Kamuf (New York: Shocken, 1985), p. 15. All quotations from this edition, hereafter *EOO*.

11 I am indebted to Rubin Berezdivin's discussion of autotelic structures. See 'Nietzsche: Drawing (an) affecting Nietzsche: with Derrida', in *Derrida and Deconstruction*, ed. by Hugh J. Silverman (London: Routledge, 1989), pp. 95–102.

12 The term 'aesthetic' seems to draw a line between literature's imaginary worlds and actual life. Yet the 'aesthetic' of Keats and Nietzsche is not a contemplative sphere, opposed to ordinary living, precisely because it embraces the tragedy of human life. Paul Hamilton, '"A Shadow of Magnitude": The Dialectic of Romantic Aesthetics', in *Beyond Romanticism: New Approaches to Texts and Contexts 1780–1832*, ed. by Stephen Copley and John Whale (London: Routledge, 1992), pp. 11–31; Patricia Waugh, *Practising Postmodernism Reading Modernism* (London: Arnold, 1992), pp. 17–24.

13 Friedrich Nietzsche, *Thus Spoke Zarathustra: A Book For Everyone and No One*, trans. by R. J. Hollingsdale (Harmondsworth: Penguin, 1969), p. 216. All quotations from this edition, hereafter *Z*.

14 Alan J. Bewell and Marjorie Levinson describe *Hyperion*'s form as belonging to this Enlightenment genre. See Alan J. Bewell, 'The Political Implications of Keats's Classicist Aesthetics', in *Studies in Romanticism*, 25 (1986), pp. 220–2; *Keats's Life of Allegory: The Origins of a Style* (Oxford: Blackwell, 1988), p. 196, hereafter *KLA*. Michael O'Neill objects to this 'progressive' reading. See '"When this warm scribe my hand": Writing and History in "Hyperion" and "The Fall of Hyperion"', in *Keats and History*, ed. by Nicholas Roe (Cambridge: Cambridge University Press, 1995), pp. 145–64.

15 Like Nietzsche's Zarathustra the 'masks', or numerous faces, which appear in Keats's *Hyperion* fragments do not conceal the complexities of existence, but enigmatically problematise them. Neither Keats nor Nietzsche use the 'mask' as a deceptive device to veil the nature of self or the world; instead, they employ

it as an 'organising principle that explains things' and indicates the 'enigma and dissemblance of phenomena'. See Charles E. Scott, 'The Mask of Nietzsche's Self-Overcoming', in *Nietzsche as Postmodernist: Essays Pro and Contra*, ed. by Clayton Koelb (New York: New York University Press, 1990), pp. 217; 218–29, hereafter *NP*.

16 Both Stuart M. Sperry and Jones note the distancing effect of *The Fall*'s dream framework. See 'Keats, Milton, and *The Fall of Hyperion*', in *PMLA* (1962), pp. 77–84. See also Jones, *KDT*, p. 102.

17 Daniel W. Conway discusses reader responsibility in Nietzsche. See 'Nietzsche contra Nietzsche: The Deconstruction of Zarathustra', in *NP*, pp. 109–10.

# 18

# WORDSWORTH IN THE NURSERY: THE PARODIC SCHOOL OF CRITICISM

## *Nicola Trott*

Source: *The Wordsworth Circle* 32 (2001), 66–77.

This essay traces "simple Wordsworth"—as Byron christened him (*English Bards and Scotch Reviewers*, 125)—back in his infancy, and describes the eighteenth-century tradition of criticism by which he came into being. That tradition was invoked by Wordsworth's adverse reviewers as a stick to beat him with, but my contention is that the "new school of poetry" they belligerently invented actually went hand in hand with their own "new school of criticism." These two, mutually antagonistic "schools" emerged beneath the one roof—that of the recently-founded "Critical Journal," most notably the *Edinburgh Review*. The effect, ironically, was to bring critic and poet into alignment: "Nor know we when to spare, or where to strike,/ Our bards and censors are so much alike" (Byron, *op. cit.*, 91–2). With this correspondence in mind, I notice how, at the turn of the nineteenth century, the language of criticism interacted with the "literary" domain it attempted to legislate. Two examples of such activity interest me here: firstly, the reproduction of periodical representations of the "Lake Poet" in other, parodic forms of writing; secondly, and conversely, the use that the reviews themselves made of parodic devices and techniques. Either way, the contemporary response had a striking purpose in common: it sought to define Wordsworth himself as, unconsciously or otherwise, the parodist of his own poetry. Finally, and taking up the work of a number of recent commentators, I speculate as to why it was *Wordsworth* especially whose writing produced this parodic critical method.

## Infantine Wordsworth

In *Biographia Literaria*, Coleridge recalled that "Mr. Wordsworth's poems" "were for a long time described as being" "silly" and "childish things" (*BL* ii 9). Coleridge encountered this description in Richard Mant's anonymous *Satirico-Didactic Poem, The Simpliciad* (1808), which began by lamenting that the art of poetry had lived "to see the high-soul'd Muse/Condemn'd in leading strings to pipe, and cry,/And lisp the accents of the nursery" (ll. 10–12). Placing the work alongside Gifford's satire of the poetic follies of the 1790s, the *British Critic* recognized *The Simpliciad* as a "new Baviad" (33 [February, 1809], 180)—aware, perhaps, that William Gifford was at this very moment assuming editorship of the new, Tory *Quarterly Review* (whose first number also appeared in February). Mant had signalled his model, first by the form of his title, then by taking up the dialogue between "P" and "F"—Pasquin and Foulder—and yet again by openly citing Gifford's assault on the Della Cruscans (ll. 60–5). However, since current fashions were tending in the opposite direction to the Cruscan, *The Simpliciad* imitated Gifford's imitation of the Satire of Persius to different ends. Mant's argument went as follows: even though genuinely "artless bards" have already provided baby with an ample supply of the "ditty simple," a still "simpler lay/Wrests from their grasp the nursery prize away." For instance, while old-style versifiers sing "Cock Robin," the new go one better and "call Cock Robin brother," a clear step up in silliness (ll. 133, 135). In short, the traditional "brethren of the cradle and the crib" are "Less worthy far of go-cart, pap, and bib" than the most babyish of all bards—the "Bards of the lakes" (ll. 124–7, 128–31).

*The Simpliciad*, for its part, is demonstrably in the leading strings of Francis Jeffrey: the *Edinburgh Review* had used its founding number to open hostilities against what it dubbed the "new school of poetry" (1 [October, 1802], 71), and Mant's sub-title names as its target the very same *Scholars of the New School*. What is more, to the stigma of "simplicity" the *Edinburgh* had recently added the slur of infantilism: Wordsworth's 1807 volumes reminded Jeffrey of the "Childishness" of the *Lyrical Ballads*, while in a review of Crabbe, in early 1808, he castigated the "ambitious fraternity" of "the Wordsworths, and the Southeys, and Coleridges," this time for "labouring to bring back our poetry to the fantastical oddity and puling childishness of Withers, Quarles, or Marvel" (*Edinburgh Review* [hereafter *ER*] 11 [October, 1807], p.214; 12 [April, 1808], p.133). Mant notably refers to modish Simplicity as a "puling, puny child," and singles out the "baby-ish style and phrase fantastical" of Coleridge's poem "To A Young Ass" (*Simpliciad*, 25, 234). His Dedication, meanwhile, addresses itself "To Messrs. W-ll—m W-rdsw-rth, R-b-rt S—th-y, and S.T. C-l—r-dg-" (*Simpliciad*, p.iii); and the couplets that follow present their poetry—which is quoted at the foot of each page in a continuous ironic citation of "Authorities"—as a modern and more juvenile sort of nursery-rhyme.

An Anglican clergyman, Mant objected to the Lakers's open-air nature-worship and déclassé innovations. But it is not irrelevant, perhaps, that he too had recently been receiving an indifferent press—one that had come, curiously enough, from the *Edinburgh Review* itself, which effectively gave Mant warning not to repeat the experiment of publishing his *Poems* (1806) lest he "put himself in the way of more unmerciful critics" (11 [October, 1807], 171, unattributed).[1] The *Edinburgh*'s discouraging treatment had prompted Edward Copleston, Professor of Poetry at Oxford and a tutor at Oriel where Mant had also held a Fellowship, to produce an anonymous pamphlet of *Advice to a Young Reviewer* (1807). There he imagined what a contemporary hack would have made of a poem of Milton's: *L'Allegro*, were it suddenly to appear, would be censured for "trite images of rural scenery, interspersed with vulgarisms in dialect, and traits of vulgar manners [ . . . ] dress[ed] up [ . . . ] in a sing-song jingle" (*Romantic Parodies*, 54; and see Teich, 280–1). The similarities with current responses to Wordsworth, Richard Mant's included, are rather striking. Mant's parodic verse followed hard on the heels of Copleston's parodic review; but *The Simpliciad* occupied much of the same ground in order to satirize the "new school of poetry" and not "the new school of criticism"—as Southey would call it, when deploring *Edinburgh* tactics in the *Quarterly Review* (6 [December, 1811], 412). That Mant should return to the lists with a poem based on *Edinburgh* dicta may seem perverse, given his own treatment; but he might have taken comfort in the thought that Wordsworth was far more culpable even than he: as luck would have it, Jeffrey's assault on Wordsworth's *Poems, in Two Volumes* appeared last of all in the very same number in which his own collection had gained its dubious notice.

This little episode suggests how readily the specific material, and the wider literary culture, of the leading review crossed over into other publishing formats—or, putting it slightly differently, how readily those formats became a way of reviewing by other means. A similar case is met with in Byron, who, like Mant, suffered at the hands of Scotch reviewers: indeed, his *Hours of Idleness* led Jeffrey to "counsel him, that he do forthwith abandon poetry" (*ER* 11 [January, 1808], 286). Like Mant, Byron reacted by turning from personal poetry to a verse satire in which the Lakers were accused of writing "childish verse," fit only to "lull the babe at nurse." Unlike *The Simpliciad*, however, *English Bards and Scotch Reviewers* (1809) directed its animus against the critics as well as the poets (see *BLJ* iii 213), and made a self-conscious attempt to seek out a formal alternative to the Whig Review: "Moved by the great example, I pursue/The selfsame road, but make my own review:/Not seek great Jeffrey's" (ll. 59–61; 48–88, 528–39, 917–18).

*The Simpliciad*, on the other hand, simply versified the formulae of the "new school of criticism." In this respect, it was continuing the work of Peter Bayley's *Poems* (1803) which, much to Wordsworth's dismay, had used the *Edinburgh*'s first salvo against "The followers of simplicity" (1 [October, 1802], 65) to parody "The Idiot Boy"—lest the point be missed, Bayley's note to "The Fisherman's Wife" had compared its "simple" verse with "The simplicity of that most simple of all poets, Mr. W. himself" (see *EY*, 413n; and 455). It was not long before the copy and criteria of the "Scotch Reviewers" were in general circulation. *The Simpliciad* adopted an *Edinburgh* perspective, and, for all its editorial rivalry with the "new school of criticism," the older, Tory *British Critic* responded to *The Simpliciad* in the terms already laid down by Jeffrey: "Of this new school [of poetry] the chief teacher was Mr. W. Wordsworth, who in pursuit of an object laudable in judicious use, went so far into the familiar and even infantine style, as to become frequently ridiculous" (*British Critic* 33 [February, 1809], 180). More inventively, a pseudo-documentary magazine article, "The Bards of the Lake,"[2] picked up a phrase from *The Simpliciad* (1.128) and, using the device of an admiring witness to the Lakers's outdoor pursuits, applied *Edinburgh* charges of sectarianism and sans-culottism to a medley of prose reportage and impromptu song. One by one "the bards arose" and sang, after the spontaneous manner of their primitive Blairite ancestors—a flatulent visionary (Coleridge) "burst[ing] forth" with broad humour in "Breeches. An Ode," a childish "genius" (Wordsworth) versifying a hermit's address to a snail, whose "original simplicity" leaves the reporter at a loss to know "in what class of poetry to place it."

Mant's innovation was to combine the two staples of negative reviewing —simplicity and childishness (on the latter, see Garlitz)—into a single idiolect, of "babyish simpleness in nonsense drest" (*Simpliciad*, 361). This sort of baby-speak soon hardened into the set-piece of a new parodic repertoire. And it too can be dated fairly precisely. Four years on from *The Simpliciad*, and baby was back, in another anonymous production, the *Rejected Addresses: or the New Theatrum Poetarum* (1812), written and published in six weeks by that facetious metropolitan duo, the brothers James and Horace Smith. Their mise-en-scène was provided by a competition to commemorate the re-opening of Drury Lane after a fire; and their imitations of contemporary authors proposed to represent those authors' unavailing efforts to submit the winning entry. In real life, as many as 112 such addresses were turned down by the Committee; but none of these genuine failures, excepting Horace's own, is in the volume (see Beavan, 104–5, 109–10). For the most part, the Smiths burlesque the leading poets of the day, rather than its occasional versifiers: Byron (who in the end agreed to compose the real address), Moore, Scott, Southey, Coleridge, Crabbe—and Wordsworth. The offering "By W.W.," entitled "The Baby's Debut," was immediately seized on by Jeffrey as an opportunity to repeat and reinforce his contempt for the *Poems* of 1807: "We hope it will make him ashamed of his Alice Fell, and the greater part of his last volumes"—the reason for hope being that it "has succeeded perfectly in the imitation of his maukish affectations of childish simplicity and nursery stammering" (*ER* 20 [November, 1812: *Rejected Addresses* came out in October], 438).

"The Baby's Debut" is "*Spoken in the character of Nancy Lake, a girl eight years of age, who is drawn upon the stage in a child's chaise, by Samuel Hughes, her uncle's porter.*" Nancy's vehicle infantilizes the mailcoach in which Alice Fell travelled, even as her surname indicates the geography that Jeffrey had made synonymous with Wordsworth. Her casual talk of "poor brother Bill" puts "We Are Seven" in the picture, and the poem borrows its stanza-form from "Ruth" and makes a passing reference to "The Thorn;" but its larger purpose is to make a Cockney out of a Laker, and, though it plays with the dramatis personae of the lyrical ballads, the Smiths' double-act downplays specific Wordsworthianisms in favour of the theatrical occasion. Having been deprived of a trip to Drury Lane as a punishment for bad behaviour, Nancy is rescued and taken centre-stage by her uncle "Sam," Mr. Lake's porter and shoe-blacker (and suspiciously reminiscent of another Samuel, currently lecturing on the London circuit). Her "Address" rehearses the whole domestic saga, up to the point of her unexpected debut:

> At first I caught hold of the wing,
> And kept away; but Mr. Thing-
>      umbob, the prompter man,
> Gave with his hand my chaise a shove,
> And said, Go on my pretty love,
>      Speak to 'em little Nan.
> You've only got to curtsey, whisp-
> er, hold your chin up, laugh and lisp,
>      And then you're sure to take:
> I've known the day when brats not quite
> Thirteen got fifty pounds a night;
>      Then why not Nancy Lake?

The nonce-name and haplessly run-over line-endings "Mr. Thing-/ umbob," "whisp-/er"—are new departures. So too is the knowing construction of a child-persona by an adult minder: "You've only got to [ . . . ] laugh and lisp,/And then you're sure to take." The prompter-man's image of a childstar derives from "the young Betty mania" of 1803–5, when a boy-actor called Master Betty caused public disorder, an early adjournment of Parliament, and earned vast profits for Drury lane (Macdonald, 79–80; *DNB*). Even Wordsworth had hopes that "the young Roscius," as he was known, would "restore the reign of [ . . . ] Nature" to the stage (*EY*, 518–19). Betty started at the age of twelve; Nancy is making her first appearance at no more than eight, and an archly bashful performance it is: her last act is to "curtsey, like a pretty miss" and "blow a kiss" to her audience. Amidst this slightly sinister bit of theatrical business, a mock-Wordsworthian poetics emerges, involving the dramatizing and marketing of the "artless" and "infantile" to urban theatre-goers hungry for youth and innocence. The poet's "little Actor" (*Ode*, 102) is all set to become a London pro.

Off-stage, Nancy is anything but innocent, however (see Bauer, 556–7). The story of how she came to break a window-pane as she and her "brother Jack" destroyed each other's birthday-presents ensures that a counter-Wordsworthian childishness of temper competes with a "Wordsworthian" childishness of speech (the sight of her family leaving in a hackney coach produces some choice instances of the latter sort of banality and redundancy: "one horse was blind,/The tails of both hung down behind,/Their shoes were on their feet"). Together, Nancy's "two voices" perform the alienating deflection of their model which parody requires in order to do its work. Yet "The Baby's Debut" contrives to be playful; and Simon Dentith has rightly placed the *Rejected Addresses* at the "ludic" end of the "two extremes" of parody, the other, "corrective," pole being occupied by the poetry of the *Anti-Jacobin* (Dentith, 110–11; and see Dyer, 16–17) . When Judge Jeffrey reviewed the *Addresses*, however, he tellingly refused to see these same publications as anything other than "comparable," and fastened upon the "Debut" as a way of bringing Wordsworth before the bench once more (*ER*, 20, 434). His intention, presumably, was to fix the poet back in the anti-jacobin moment, with only its satirico-political hardmen for company; and, indeed, the Address itself furnished some unexpectedly savage material in the shape of an epigraph from the dramatist Richard Cumberland: "The Baby's Debut" was headed by lines declaring "hat[red]" for "Thy lisping prattle and thy mincing gait [ . . . ] Nature's true Ideot I prefer to thee." This baby had teeth.

## Namby-Pamby, Jack-a-Dandy

The *Edinburgh Review* cast Wordsworth's *Poems, in Two Volumes* as "furnishing themselves from vulgar ballads and plebeian nurseries" (*ER* 11 [October, 1807], 218); but the first critic to rock the poet's cradle in 1807 was not Jeffrey but Byron. Still himself a minor, the noble reviewer had taken a dim view of Wordsworth's more "trifling" pieces. Quoting the lines written "at the Foot of Brother's Bridge"—"The cock is crowing,/The stream is flowing,/The small birds twitter,/The lake doth glitter [ . . . ]"—he passed judgment as follows:

> this appears to us neither more nor less than an imitation of such minstrelsy as soothed our cries in the cradle, with the shrill ditty of
>> "Hey de diddle,
>> The cat and the fiddle [ . . . ]"
>> (*Monthly Literary Recreations* 3 [July, 1807], 65–66)

Byron has started what rapidly becomes a classic technique in the critic's sport of Wordsworth-baiting—namely, juxtaposing offending lines from the poet with some genuine "cradle" verses, and thereby equating the two. Typically, it is the "double rhyme"—the rhyme that Dryden had identified with burlesque[3]—that provides the hostile reviewer with an opening (not until Byron himself took it up, to macho-satirico effect, in *Don Juan*, would the feminine ending be rescued from mockery). Once again, what begins in the reviews carries over into the parodies. Take John Hamilton Reynolds, for example, whose pre-emptive strike against *Peter Bell* (1819) sends Peter on a tour of Wordsworth's lowlife characters, all of whom are "rurally related"[4] and all, it turns out, dead in their graves—thus pointing to their author's oblivion in the final stanza. When Reynolds's country-bumpkin of a poet-narrator pauses to echo the same verses as Byron quoted, he mischievously rhymes the moon's "pretty glitter" in a waterfall with the rubbishy "litter" in Lucy Gray's "baby-house" (*Peter Bell*, 13–16). Reynolds had learnt his lesson in nursery Wordsworth from Keats, who in September, 1817, had written to his friend quoting the identical lines of Wordsworth as an instance of how the poet "sometimes, though in a fine way, gives us sentences in the Style of School exercises," before himself turning to do a parody of the whole poem in the form of a comic "description" of Oxford, the seat of grown-up learning where Keats was then staying (*Letters* i 151–2). Or, again, take Peacock's pseudonymous *Sir Proteus: A Satirical Ballad*: by P.M. O'Donovan, Esq. (1814), written in the wake of Wordsworth's accession to the post of Distributor of Stamps, lavishly dedicated to Byron, and printed for the Hookhams, publishers also of Shelley. Although the principal aim is to caricature the new Laureate in a "burlesque of Southey's most elevated style" (Dyer, p.88), the subtitle guys at Wordsworth. "A Satirical Ballad" wears its anti-"lyrical" intentions on its sleeve; and when the garrulous Laker duly appears, he is made to chime his own ballad folk with their siblings (and metrical equals) in the nursery:

> [ . . . ] he chattered, chattered still,
> With meaning none at all,
> Of Jack and Jill, and Harry Gill
> And Alice Fell so small.
> (*Sir Proteus* ii st. 12;
> *Works of Peacock* ii 290)

"The Baby's Debut" had already insinuated a nursery-rhyme element in the shape of Nancy's "brother Jack;" and on his return, as Mr. Paperstamp in *Melincourt* (1817), Peacock's Wordsworth—who is "chiefly remarkable for an affected infantine lisp in his speech, and for always wearing waistcoats of duffil grey"—names himself the greatest genius "since the days of Jack the Giant-killer" (*Melincourt* ch. 28, 39; *Works* ii 301, 398). His nursery connections, who run from "scarlet" Mother Goose to "little Jack Horner," are model con-artists rather than children's entertainers; and, as "Peter Paypaul Paperstamp, Esquire, of Mainchance Villa," the poet leads his cronies in a song celebrating the allegorical meaning of the peculator's rhyme: "Jack Horner's Christmas Pie my learned nurse/Interpreted to mean the *public purse*" (ii 396–8, 418).

The most significant aspect of Byron's review is its exact identification of the critical tradition within which all these different opponents of the infantine Wordsworth are operating. Having adopted an aggressively grown-up line with the senior Laker, his review asks, "what will any reader or auditor, out of the nursery, say to such namby-pamby[?]" (*op. cit.*, p.66). "Such namby-pamby" would have taken Byron's reader straight back to the culture wars of the early eighteenth century. A hundred years earlier, the phrase had been coined to represent a child's efforts to get his tongue round the name of Ambrose Philips. Philips, having been on friendly terms with Pope and Swift, chose to attach himself instead to Addison and the Hanoverian cause, and so became the irresistible butt of his former associates (see Segar, xxiii, xxxviii, xliv–xlv). Scriblerian opportunities for revenge arose with Philips's complimentary verses to the offspring of various patrons, among them these frankly cringing lines "To Miss Margaret Pulteney, daughter of Daniel Pulteney Esq; in the Nursery" (April 27, 1727):

> Dimply damsel, sweetly smiling,
> All caressing, none beguiling,
> But of beauty, fairly blowing,
> Every charm to nature owing [ . . . ]

The name Namby Pamby soon appeared in the following verse, said to have been written in Swift's handwriting—

> Namby Pamby, Jack a Dandy,
> Stole a piece of Sugar-Candy
> From a Grocer's Shoppy-Shop,
> And away did Hoppy-hop.
> (*Works of Addison* vi 696)

—and a version of the same lines also appeared as an epigraph to the first outing of Philips under his new name, in a poem called *Namby-Pamby. A Panegyric on the New Versification, addressed to A——P——, Esq*. This, the most "lethal parody" of Philips, was not by Swift, Pope, or Gay, "but by a writer of musical farces named Henry Carey"—on this occasion presenting himself in the guise of a Captain Gordon (Macdonald, 25; Segar, 182).

To judge from Carey's subtitle, then, there was nothing new in Jeffrey's disdainful proclamation of the "new;" nor, indeed, in the various ironies he and others levelled at the Lake School—such as the call to poetic "reform" ("All ye poets of the age [ ... ] Crop your numbers and conform"), or the satirical allusion to bona fide nursery-verse ("Now he sings of Jacky Horner [ ... ]"), or even the invention of an infantilect:

> Now the venal poet sings
> Baby clouts and baby things [ ... ]
> Little playthings, little toys,
> Little girls and little boys.
> As an actor does his part,
> So the nurses get by heart
> Namby-Pamby's little rhimes,
> Little jingle, little chimes,
> To repeat to missy-miss,
> Piddling ponds of pissy-piss [ ... ]
>    (Carey, in Macdonald, pp.25–7)

A man who was nicknamed Namby Pamby, who wrote poems to children "in the Nursery," and had mock nursery-rhymes circulated in his honour: the inference seems clear enough. The "namby-pamby" tag was intended to cast the contemporary hostility to Wordsworth in something of the same light as the Scriblerian war against Philips. It implied the very continuity of culture which Wordsworth had rejected; and it found grounds for condemnation equally in his violations of political allegiance, linguistic propriety, and poetic dignity. Resurrecting Philips had the effect of placing Wordsworth within an established and hierarchical poetic order, whose codes and criteria—as much social as literary—he had wholly failed to fulfil.

Though Byron hit on the perfect persona for a "simple Wordsworth,"[5] it was Jeffrey who made the negative spin possible. Already, in 1802, he had referred in passing to the new school's predilection for "the *innocence* of Ambrose Philips" (*ER* 1 [October, 1802], 64); and Byron's pointed reference to Wordsworth's "*innocent* odes of the same cast" (*op. cit.*, 66) clinches the connection. Jeffrey's own review of the 1807 *Poems* emerged, three months after Byron's, in October, and with impeccable timing: exactly five years had passed since the *Edinburgh*'s first, founding attack. It noted, with studied casualness, that "By and by, we have a piece of namby-pamby 'to the Small Celandine,' which we should have taken for a professed imitation of one of Mr. Philips's prettyisms." And then again, of "The Kitten and the Falling Leaves," "There is rather too much of Mr. Ambrose Philips here and there in this piece also" (*ER*, 11, 220). Wherever Francis Jeffrey went, the rest were sure to follow: the *British Critic* was soon remarking on the "*namby-pamby* brethren" of the 1807 volumes (33 [March, 1809], 298); and not long after that, the juvenile poetics of the "nursery bards" were turned into nursery-verse: when Mant refers to "numbers

369

shilly-shally, shally-shilly,/So very feeling and so very silly" (*Simpliciad*, 151–2), the ghost of Ambrose is haunting the sound—and rhyming-patterns; and, sure enough, such metrical vulgarities are eventually assigned their proper name, as the poets of the Simpliciad "Trip it in Ambrose Philips's trochaics" (1.279).

The tense of *Biographia Literaria* (Wordsworth's poems "were [ . . . ] described as" "silly" and "childish") suggests that, by the mid-1810s, his infantalization was a thing of the past; but this was far from the case. Even as *Biographia* was being printed, Jeffrey was using a review of *Christabel* to repeat his old attack on "the new school, or, as they may be termed, the wild or lawless poets," whose writings appeared to vie with one another in the production of "the unmeaning or infantine" (*ER* 27 [September, 1816], 59). And, as Reynolds's *Peter Bell* attests, the "infantine" Wordsworth was still going strong in 1819. The poet's latest "Lyrical Ballad" having been advertised but not published, Reynolds was found to find an early model; and in his case it was "The Idiot Boy,"[6] a favourite with parodists, since it tended to make a village idiot of Wordsworth. If anything, the publication of the real *Peter Bell* only settled the matter—thanks partly to its inevitable mediation by Reynolds's "burlesque," and partly to a probable self-review by the parodist himself, in the *Alfred* for May 11, 1819, which argued that his mockery had been limited to the poet's "infantine follies."[7] This pre-publicity seems to have sealed the fate of Wordsworth's poem: classing *Peter Bell* as an "infantine pamphlet," the *Monthly Review* pronounced that

> No lisping was ever more distinctly lisped than the versification of this poem; and no folly was ever more foolishly boasted than that of the writer [ . . . ] The [ . . . ] style [is] of Mr. Newbery's best gilded little volumes for nurseries [ . . . ][8]

John Newbery was a children's writer and bookseller, who incidentally made a habit of assuming juvenile pseudonyms: his "Collection of pretty poems for the amusement of children" (1800), for instance, was issued as "By Tommy Tagg, Esq."

The trick of Ambrose Philips's satirists—to identify the poet with a child-persona—was played and re-played by the reviewers of Wordsworth; and, so familiar was Namby-Pamby in connection with "the Lakeiest Poet" (Reynolds, *Peter Bell*, 196), that the critic for the *Monthly* had merely to utter the double-rhyming exclamation of "unmeaning prittle-prattle" to repeat the association, appealing as he did so from the art of the ballad to life in the nursery: "We can only say that, if a nurse were to talk to any of their children in this manner, a sensible father and mother would be strongly disposed to dismiss her without a character" (*MR*, 422). Thus Wordsworth's poem is dismissed along with the nurse; and, in the following month's review of the *Waggoner* volume, double-rhyme and nursery-verse combine to ridicule "that unrivalled Sonnet, ycleped The *Wild Duck's Nest*:" "Oh 'Goosy-goosy-Gander!' friend of our infancy, resign thine honours! [ . . . ] before an author who wishes (almost) to lay aside *humanity*, at the sight of a wild duck's nest!" (*MR* 90 [September, 1819], 40).

Significant in all these responses is their commitment to the *Lyrical Ballads* phase of Wordsworth's career as an interpretative paradigm for subsequent developments. Significant, too, is the fact that, even though the *Ballads* were the obvious means of attacking Wordsworth, the critical method that made them so emerged only on the publication of *Poems, in Two Volumes*. The first feeding-frenzy came in the reviews of 1807, and produced Mant's *Simpliciad*; the second followed in the wake of the *Rejected Addresses*, which went through sixteen editions in seven years and, by the time of its eighteenth, in 1833, had spanned an entire generation of nursery-rhyme parodists.[9] The Distributor of Stamps episode provided a third occasion for satire; and a fourth and last concentration surrounded the publication of *Peter Bell*. Throughout, the role of Jeffrey was crucial. Launched in late 1802, the *Edinburgh Review* had to hold much of its fire on *Lyrical Ballads* until the *Poems, in Two Volumes* permitted Jeffrey his first direct review of Wordsworth. This delayed reaction to the poet's already well-established reputation for childishness had important consequences for the reception of the later work: Wordsworth, it might be said, was never allowed to grow up. The 1807 volumes were made to seem continuous with the output of an earlier poetic self—a critical assumption which ironically coincides with the poet for whom the child is father to the man. And, as we have seen, another sort of continuity ensured that the 1807 *Poems* were absorbed into a pre-existing critical idiom. In his role as a modern Namby-pamby, Wordsworth found himself the principal, though wholly unintentional, reviver of an entire Augustan satirical tradition. He also, in the process, became the medium through which the "new school of criticism" established its own distinctive procedures and techniques.

## The parodic method of reviewing

Reviewers of Wordsworth pursued their poet not (as did the Scriblerians) in privately printed broadsides, but in publicly circulated journals. Yet their Augustan inheritance was of a kind that led them to make invidious comparisons between lake-poems and nursery-rhymes. The effect was to turn their perception of the "ridiculous" *in* Wordsworth's style into a more active "ridicule" *of* his style. Reviewing, it seems, was drawing on the resources of parody. In this development, as in others, Jeffrey had a critical role to play. And, as it happens, the subject of Wordsworth's reception in the *Edinburgh* later became the occasion for Coleridge to draw an explicit connection between parody and criticism, when a "Selection From [his] Literary Correspondence" published in *Blackwood's* pointedly coupled "the Buffoons of parody, and the Zanies of anonymous criticism" (10 [October, 1821], 259). A similar coupling had emerged a decade earlier. Two years after it was founded in opposition to the *Edinburgh*, the *Quarterly Review* gave Southey an opportunity of settling scores on behalf of the "new school of poetry" (among whose members Jeffrey had repeatedly numbered Southey himself). Southey's review of the poetry of James Montgomery was really a reply to Jeffrey's own, which had "thought proper to crush the rising poet" in "the usual strain." Accordingly, Southey attempted to name and shame the "new school of criticism," first by retorting upon the *Edinburgh* its label for the Lakers, then by exposing its "mischievous" manner of proceeding:

> A burlesque description of the contents of the volume follows, together with a few passages, most easily susceptible of ridicule, as specimens of the poetry; and the critique is thus wound up. "We cannot laugh at this any longer [ . . . ] When every day is bringing forth some new work from the pen of Scott, Campbell, Rogers, Baillie, Sotheby, Wordsworth, or Southey, it is natural to feel some disgust at the undistinguishing voracity which can swallow down three editions of songs to convivial societies, and verses to a pillow."
>
> > (*Quarterly Review* 6 [December, 1811], 412, 413;
> > quoting *ER* 9 [January, 1807], 354)

The method of the *Quarterly*'s great antagonist is explicitly identified as "burlesque." The irony of finding Wordsworth for once in its favour is also drily observed: *Edinburgh* "Critics [ . . . ] will praise one poet in pure malice to another," and "Even Mr. Wordsworth himself is mentioned with praise when the object is to run down Montgomery" (*Quarterly*, 407). In fact, the irony is still sharper, for Jeffrey on Montgomery is almost identical to Jeffrey on Wordsworth (the point being that the former case is subsumed within the latter, "that great sinking fund of bad taste, which is daily wearing down the debt which we have so long owed to the classical writers of antiquity" [*ER*, 347]). Just nine months later, the *Edinburgh*'s review of Wordsworth shows the same closed circle of parodic interpretation: having made themselves "ridiculous," the 1807 volumes are deservedly subject to "ridicule," Jeffrey advising that "the composition in which it is attempted to exhibit" their typically forced "associations"

> will always have the air of parody, or ludicrous and affected singularity. All the world laughs at Elegiac stanzas to a sucking-pig —a Hymn on Washing-day—Sonnets to one's grandmother—or Pindarics on gooseberry-pye; and yet, we are afraid, it will not be quite easy to convince Mr. Wordsworth, that the same ridicule must infallibly attach to most of the pathetic pieces in these volumes.
>
> > (*ER* 11 [October, 1807], 218)

Now it is Wordsworth (rather than Montgomery) who has acquired an "air of parody" by his burlesque proximity to unpoetic subjects, be they pies or pillows. In addition, "Wordsworth" has been made to stand alongside, and thus to represent, a whole class of déclassé and largely "jacobin" poetry: Southey's "Gooseberry-Pie. A Pindaric Ode," and his "colloquial poem," "The Pig;" Lloyd's sonnets "On The Death of Priscilla Farmer, by her grandson," and Barbauld's "Washing-Day" (this last a coded reference also to "The Blind Highland Boy," whose infamous washing-tub provokes outrage later on in Jeffrey's review).

In Jeffrey's words, the effect of the "peculiarities" of the 1807 volumes is "to render them ridiculous" (*ibid.*): the perception that Wordsworth is ridiculous becomes associated with the attempt to render him so—and, with him, the "new school" of which he is declared head. This transition is partly a matter of applying parodic techniques—Jeffrey's satirical italicizing and pointing of Wordsworth quotations, for instance,[10] or his juxtaposition of the "pathetic" and "ludicrous" in poetry. Elsewhere, as we have seen, a similar effect is achieved by placing authentic and nursery verses side-by-side. A variation on this theme finds critics making up spoof rhymes of their own: on its publication in *The Friend*, Coleridge's "Three Graves" attracts a lengthy serial letter in the *Monthly Mirror*, where the piece is identified as Lakeish in its "exquisite simplicity," and pseudo-cradle verses are invented for the occasion. Quoting a stanza of Coleridge's ("These tears will come [ . . . ]"), the correspondent immediately replies with one of his own, a parodic echo of the real thing, complete with accentuated—or namby-pambied—double rhyme: "This tear will come—'tis no use talking—/Indeed I could not stop it;/I dandled her in these old arms,/O! bless it for a poppet" (Jackson, 73, 81–2; Green, 435 n.2, identifies the author as Edward Du Bois, editor of the *Mirror*. Leigh Hunt records his love of in-jokes, *Autobiography*, 181).

These local examples of parodic reviewing practice involve larger critical assumptions. If, as Jeffrey has it, Wordsworth's method of "composition" is such as "will always have the air of parody," then for its part Jeffrey's method of criticism assumes that the new school is *itself* already parodic. Richard Mant, once again in line with *Edinburgh* thinking, makes much the same point in his Dedication to *The Simpliciad*: "I do truly affirm my belief, that in attempting to excite ridicule, I have employed no unfair exaggeration; that the [new] school is incapable of caricature; and that, if a smile be raised by my illustrations, it will be heightened by a perusal of the originals whence they are drawn" (*Simpliciad*, v). The parodic critical method operates a kind of double-bluff: wherever possible, the representation of the poetry under review is referred back to the originals from whence it came. Whatever is parodic in the response is merely a reflection of the text's existing parodic features. The source of parody lies not in the critic, but in the poet himself. Coleridge recognizes just this element of feigned mimesis, and its connection to a disguised or displaced genre of parody, when, in *Biographia*, he names as identical phenomena the "parodies and pretended imitations" of Wordsworth's early poems (ii 9). And, indeed, the technique of pretended imitation is central to the reception of Wordsworth, and to the transition from the review to parodic reviewing and verse parody. The criticism of Wordsworth's "imitation of such minstrelsy as soothed our cries in the cradle" (to quote Byron's review of the 1807 *Poems*) leads over five years to an appreciation of how the Smith brothers had "succeeded perfectly in the imitation of his [ . . . ] nursery stammering" (to quote Jeffrey's review of "The Baby's Debut"). That is, Wordsworth's nursery imitations give rise to parodic imitations of the nursery—Wordsworth that the reviewers themselves invented. This pretended imitation passes from prose review to verse parody, and back again to the reviews: "We hope," says Jeffrey of "The Baby's Debut," "it will make him ashamed of his Alice Fell, and the greater part of his last volumes—of which it is by no means a parody, but a very fair, and indeed we think a flattering imitation" (*ER* 20 [November, 1812], 438). So infectious is the mock-imitation that Coleridge records its persistence among "some affected admirers" of Wordsworth, "with whom he is, forsooth, a *sweet, simple poet*! and *so* natural, that little master Charles, and his younger sister, are *so* charmed with them, that they play at 'Goody Blake,' or at 'Johnny and Betty Foy!'" (*BL* ii 158–9). Even Wordsworth's admirers are unwittingly parodic. Alternatively, of course, Coleridge may be parodying the very method of pretended imitation on which Wordsworth's critics depend. That both possibilities occur shows how close the admiring and ridiculing varieties of the poet's "simplicity" are to one another; and how in either case the assumption of childishness rests upon anecdotal appeals to his adaptation for or by children.

When responding to Wordsworth parody, in "The Baby's Debut," Jeffrey ensures that review and verse are alike joined in an ironic consensus to disclaim any intention to parody: the method of pretended imitation must feign innocence of a genre which of necessity gestures towards and yet deflects, or is deflected away from, an original. When responding to Wordsworth himself, in *Poems, in Two Volumes*, however, Jeffrey transforms an apparently innocuous act of "imitation" into a poetry that is synonymous with a parodic, or namby-pamby, tradition: "the Small Celandine," you recall, is "taken for a professed imitation of one of Mr. Philips's prettyisms." Even more startlingly, the poet becomes an "imitator"—and a *bad* imitator—of his own *Lyrical Ballads* style:

> Even in the worst of these productions, there are, no doubt, occasional little traits of delicate feeling and original fancy; but these are quite lost and obscured in the mass of childishness and insipidity with which they are incorporated; nor can any thing give us a more melancholy view of the debasing effects of this miserable

theory, than that it has given ordinary men a right to wonder at the folly and presumption of a man gifted like Mr. Wordsworth, and made him appear, in his second avowed publication, like a bad imitator of the worst of his former productions.

(ER 11 [October, 1807] 231)

As Coleridge would later concur, it is the theory's fault (BL i 70–1; ii 119–20); but, where he attempts to show a Wordsworth who is instinctively free of his theoretical commitments, Jeffrey insists that they are both inescapable and "debasing." Another passage from this same review, quoted a moment ago, surrounded Wordsworth's "pathetic pieces" with the offensively ludicrous subjects of other poets—sucking-pigs, grandmothers, and gooseberry-pie. Here, similarly, poetic values are "lost and obscured in the mass of childishness and insipidity with which they are incorporated." In either instance, Jeffrey seeks to "attach" to Wordsworth a "ridicule" that has been established through his criticism's parodic relationship to the poetry. What is more, Wordsworth in 1807 is declared to be a pale imitation of Wordsworth in 1800. The throwback to Lyrical Ballads appears to have a function beyond that of tying the Laker to a juvenile poetics and persona: its other point is to make him go from bad to worse—in short, to make him self-parodic.

## The self-parodic school of poetry

In Leigh Hunt's Feast of the Poets, Wordsworth is found "spouting"

> some lines he had made on a straw,
> Shewing how he had found it, and what it was for,
> And how, when 'twas balanc'd, it stood like a spell!—
> And how, when 'twas balanc'd no longer, it fell!
> A wild thing of scorn he describ'd it to be,
> But he said it was patient to heaven's decree:—
> Then he gaz'd upon nothing, and looking forlorn,
> Dropt a *natural* tear for *that wild thing of scorn*!
>
> (Feast of the Poets, 12)

Like other members of his circle, Hunt had mixed views about Wordsworth, and was by no means univocally unappreciative. However, he did share in the wider cultural distaste for the poet's experiments in "childish" ballads (see Swaen, 142)—an antipathy that is signalled by his choice of anapaestic rhyming couplets. In its repetitions, Hunt's verse is itself doubly mischievous, since it performs the parodist's echo of a (fictious) text, even as it parodies the redundancies associated with Wordsworth's own habits of tautology. The final exclamatory emphasis—"*that wild thing of scorn!*"—

corresponds to Jeffrey's manner of drawing attention, by italicized quotation, to whatever seems most self-evidently laughable in the poet's style. For all their differences, the editors of the *Edinburgh* and *Examiner* make common cause here. *The Feast of the Poets* first appeared in the Hunts' *Reflector* (1811). On being lifted out of its magazine format for separate publication, the work gained 110 pages of notes. Directed as much at the poet's fan-club as at the poet himself, the note to the lines just quoted reads: "I am told, on very good authority, that this parody upon Mr. Wordsworth's worse style of writing has been taken for a serious extract from him, and panegyrized accordingly, with much grave wonderment how I could find it ridiculous!" (n.19; *Feast*, 87).

Hunt's disingenuousness could certainly have been learnt from Jeffrey: his *Autobiography* confesses to having been "then unacquainted" with Wordsworth's writings "except through the medium of his deriders" (223). And Jeffrey for his part seems gleefully to have seized upon the possibility, laid out by Hunt, that Wordsworth parody could swap places with Wordsworth poetry,[11] in a review of *The White Doe of Rylstone* which has almost as damning an opening as his infamous article on *The Excursion*:

> This, we think, has the merit of being the very worst poem we ever saw imprinted in a quarto volume [ . . . ] It is just such a work, in short, as some wicked enemy of that [new or Wordsworthian] school might be supposed to have devised, on purpose to make it ridiculous; and when we first took it up, we could not help fancying that some ill-natured critic had taken this harsh method of instructing Mr. Wordsworth, by example, in the nature of those errors, against which our precepts had been so often directed in vain.
>
> (*ER* 25 [October, 1815] 355)

Once again, the anniversary of October—that Glorious Twelfth of the *Edinburgh*'s Lakeland calendar—is observed. The poet's anti-progress has now reached a nadir of debasement. Wordsworth's latest poem is represented as so far gone in self-parody as to be mistaken for the work of a hostile critic: so thoroughly "bad" an imitation could be attributable only to a source outside the "school" itself. That this mock-Wordsworth should have been "devised, on purpose to make it ridiculous," is of course a precise description of the aims and contrivances of the parodic reviewer himself, and of his long-running opposition to the new school. Yet all the while, it is the real Wordsworth who is under review, and whose poem is exposed as the last and "worst" of his *self*-imitations.

The sly jest of "fancying [ . . . ] some ill-natured critic" seems at once to be responding to, and claiming a degree of responsibility for, the "harsh method of instructing Mr. Wordsworth, by example," which emerged in *The Feast of the Poets*, published the previous year. In Hunt's annotation, a parody Wordsworth is said to have been taken by admirers for the genuine article; in Jeffrey's review, the genuine article is purportedly assumed to be the work of "some wicked enemy." Jeffrey capitalized on *Rejected Addresses* by using the imitative model of criticism to pretend that the Smiths's parody or pretended imitation of Wordsworth was a true imitation of the poet. That was sufficiently entangling, perhaps; but the shrewder application of the model comes about when both he and Hunt turn to Wordsworth himself, and play off their own parodic intentions against another, imaginary audience—be it the gormless admirer or the malevolent critic.

Either way, it is the business of parodic reception and reviewing to ensure that parody usurps the place of poetry. Both Hunt and Jeffrey can be seen as giving formal recognition to the requirements of their "method of instructing [ . . . ] by example." The usurpation of Wordsworth's poetry by parody acts out its usurpation by criticism, or by the critical stance that is implicit in its parodic representation. With this in mind, it follows that Reynolds's "ante-natal Peter" (as Shelley christened it [*John Hamilton Reynolds*, 25]) was merely publishing or literalizing a priority of parody to poetry that was already normative in the adverse criticism of Wordsworth. To put it another way, parody had become the original of which the poems were the imitators.

Issued by Keats's publishers, Taylor and Hessey, on April 16, 1819, Reynolds's "skit" upon *Peter Bell* (as Keats called it in his review for *The Examiner* [Swaen, 158]) was the apotheosis of pretended imitation. The poem declared itself to be "a Lyrical Ballad," and ironically vouched for its own authenticity with the words "'I do affirm that I am the real Simon Pure'." Reynolds's epigraph is adapted from Act V of *A Bold Stroke for a Wife* (86), Susanna Centlivre's pro-Hanoverian comedy of 1718: "the real" is his addition to the text. At this point in the play, the male lead, Colonel Fainwell, is speaking to a Quaker preacher called Simon Pure, after he has assumed the latter's identity in order to trick the pious guardian of Miss Lovely into allowing them to marry, and from this situation arose "The compound *simon-pure*, meaning *genuine*" (*Bold Stroke*, xxii–xxiii). Apart from their metrical symmetry, the names "Peter Bell" and "Simon Pure" may well have rung a bell with Reynolds because the two had recently been linked by Peter Pindar, in one of whose Odes "The gossiping Peter telleth a strange Story," where "Truth" features as "a plain Simon Pure, a Quaker preacher,/A moral mender, a disgusting teacher,/That never got a sixpence by her speeches!" (Lyric Odes IX, 1785, reissued in 1816).[12] As well as twitting Wordsworth with its claim to be the genuine article, then, Reynolds's epigraph insinuated the poet's tendency to dogmatism of a sanctimonious or prudish—and impoverishing—kind (something Shelley afterwards developed in *Peter Bell the Third* and which, as it turned out, was curiously apposite to the methodistical aura of the Wordsworth poem).

Reynolds's equation of "Peter Bell" with "Simon Pure" drew attention to the fact that his poem was prompted by Wordsworth's summoning of "those ridiculous associations which vulgar names give rise to."[13] The issue of poetic naming was also one of poetic class, and Reynolds had risen to the bait that the "lyrical ballad" ostentatiously threw in the way of contemporary taste. Later in 1819, Wordsworth doggedly took the idea of a classless poetic to his parodists and critics. Quoting the motto to the *Waggoner* volume—"'What's in a name?/Brutus will start a spirit as soon as Caesar!'"—the *Monthly Review* was quick to reach the logical conclusion: "and, *therefore*, 'the Waggoner' will do as well as Brutus" (90 [September, 1819], 36). While Shakespeare's play casts the shadow of Brutus's overthrow upon Caesar's greatness (see *Julius Caesar* I ii 144–66), Wordsworth implies a challenge to an inherited poetic constitution, or at the very least the equality for poetry of different names. In this context, Reynolds's epigraph has had a further point to make: behind the innocent and successful impostures of Centlivre's Colonel Fainwell lurks the failed attempt of the Stuart Pretender, in the first Jacobite Rebellion of 1715, to overturn the Act of Settlement which secured the throne for a Protestant succession under George I. An active supporter of the Hanoverian Whigs, Centlivre used her play both to defuse and recast this Jacobite plot, and to "Convince our unthinking Britons by what vile arts France lost her liberty."[14] A hundred years later, and the ground of pretence has shifted in the direction of the literary, and the legitimacy (or otherwise) of aspirants to the throne of literature. Significantly enough, when Lamb wrote to Wordsworth about the "mock" *Peter Bell*, he asked "Is there no law against these rascals? I would have this Lambert Simnel whipt at the cart's tail" (Lucas ii 241).[15] Lambert Simnel was one of two pretenders to the throne of England during the reign of Henry VII.

Though Reynolds was clearly a pretender, so too, in his own way, was Wordsworth, since he introduced into poetry claimants to poetic interest who formerly had had no place there. In pretending to be Wordsworth, Reynolds undertook to "feign" as "well" as Centlivre's Colonel. Yet, in selecting his epigraph, he raised the very questions of authorship and authorization which his pseudonymous spoof ostensibly proposed to evade. "Simon Pure" gave a name to the deliberately provoking ways in which his *Peter Bell* simultaneously asserted, and cast doubt on, the poet's validity and identity. A "Preface," signed "W.W.," warned readers to beware of impostors, "As these are the days of counterfeits."[16] A follow-up squib, "Peter Bell v. Peter Bell," launched an authorial suit, but only facetiously, distinguishing "The Burlesque,—by its having a meaning" from "The Real,—by its having an Ass" (ll. 1–2, 13–16).

Coleridge's classification of the period's "pretended imitations" recognized both the pretence, and how the parody might get taken for real. In Reynolds, that threat of displacement was realized: imitation Wordsworth

usurped genuine Wordsworth in a text of the same name. Reynolds provided the impetus—and possibly was himself responsible (Marsh, 274; Jones,
176)—for yet "another fling at Mr. Wordsworth" in *The Dead Asses*, whose
gruesome newspaper-derived tale of two animals left to starve did not deter
one reviewer from feigning to detect the hand of the poet himself, before
ceding priority to his parodist: "The verses [ . . . ] are written so much in
Mr. Wordsworth's style, that we should certainly have taken it for one of
his productions, had not the pseudo Peter Bell convinced us that this lyrical
ballad belonged to the same author" (*New Monthly Magazine* 12 [October,
1819], 332). The trick of putting the parodic cart before the poetic horse (or
ass) has been around in the reviewing of Wordsworth for some time; and it
is interesting, though not surprising, that the reviews reacted to the *Peter
Bell* phenomenon by seizing on it as a confirmation and extension of their
existing parodic methods. The *Eclectic Review* set the tone, archly demanding, "from whom but Mr. Wordsworth could we expect to receive any other
than a burlesque poem under the title of Peter Bell?" (11 [May, 1819], 475).
That does little more than take up the opportunity provided by Reynolds,
of treating "The Real" *Peter Bell* as though it were "The Burlesque." The
intriguing thing, though, is that this review is immediately followed by
a parody—a parody, as it happens, of Hunt (*ibid.*, 475–8). It is as though
the whole frame of Wordsworth's reception has become parodic. And
something like a deliberate journal policy does seem to have been at work: a
few months later, in consecutive numbers of the *Monthly Review*, notices
of Wordsworth poems go hand-in-hand with notices of their parodies. The
August, 1819 issue placed its articles on the two *Peter Bells* side-by-side
(89:421–3); and the September number (90:36–42) did precisely the same
with reviews of *The Waggoner* and the anonymous parody, *Benjamin the
Waggoner*—which, despite its title, was also *Peter Bell*-inspired, and thought
to be by Reynolds (it has since been attributed to J.G. Lockhart: see
Gohn, 69).

The parodic method of reviewing has acquired a formal dimension,
achieving a sort of simultaneous transmission of poem and parody
in which it is the latter that provides the determining context for Wordsworth's reception. Reviewing *The Waggoner*, Wordsworth's half-ironical,
half-indulgent critic "exhort[s] him to cultivate his talent for the ridiculous" on the grounds that "nature has plainly designed him, 'the Prince of
Poetical Burlesque.'" (*MR* 90:39). Having delivered a harsher judgment
on the "infatuated poetaster" of *Peter Bell*, the *Monthly* turns swiftly to the
wider parodic context:

> We really waste *words*, however, on what is scarcely *Word'sworth*
> [ . . . ] Some well-meaning, and, in one case, witty individuals have
> published parodies of Peter Bell, the potter, and of his brother, the
> Waggoner. We shall be required briefly to notice these parodies,

as well as their originals: but in fact the originals themselves are the parodies, or rather the gross burlesques of all that is good in poetry. It is like travestying Cotton's Travesties of Homer and Virgil, to parody Wordsworth's own parodies of other illustrious poets. Nay, he is the buffoon of Nature herself; and [ . . . ] presents to some a *ludicrous*, and to all an *unfaithful* portrait of his pretended original. We say pretended; for in fact it is not Nature, but his own narrow, whimsical, unpoetical idea of Nature, which this strange writer worships.

(MR 89:421)

Wordsworth is parodic twice over: a burlesquer "of all that is good in poetry," he is also "the buffoon of Nature herself;" and in this inferior relation to "his pretended original" becomes himself a pretender of the lowest rank. If Wordsworth is parodic, then his parodists are doubly so. The spectacle of the parody parodied is provided by Charles Cotton, whose seventeenth-century buffooning led to a travesty of Virgil *In English Burlesque*—"I *Sing the Man* (read it who list),/*A Trojan* true as ever pist.)"— which was itself a re-dressing of Paul Scarron's *Virgile Travesti*. Similarly, his *Lucian's Dialogues Newly put into English Fustian* made for a *Burlesque upon Burlesque: or, the Scoffer Scoff'd*. Like Byron and Jeffrey's resurrection of Namby Pamby, the *Monthly*'s citation of the tradition of *Mock-Poem* belittles Wordsworth by putting him low down in a neo-classical hierarchy. This is the parodic school of reviewing as the sprightly guardian of reactionary taste.

Another example of parodic framing arises in a *Blackwood's* number of July, 1819, where among three articles presented under cover of Morgan Odoherty (alias William Maginn) are "an imitation of Wordsworth" and "a mere *jeud'esprit*" comparing "John Gilpin and Mazeppa" (5:433). The verses, titled "Billy Routing, A Lyrical Ballad," are signed "W.W." and tilted at *Peter Bell* through the narrators and characters of the *Ballads.*[17] They are immediately followed by a quizzical prose "analysis" in which Cowper's mock-ballad trades places with Byron's new poem, so that, "in this age of parody," the age's most famous mocker both mocks and is mocked: "Had the poem of John Gilpin appeared immediately after that of Mazeppa, we should have believed, in this age of parody, that Cowper wished to have his joke upon Lord Byron. As it is, we cannot help suspecting that his Lordship has been aiming a sly hit at the bard of Olney; and though his satire is occasionally rather stiff and formal, it cannot be denied that, on the whole, the Hetman of the Cossacks is a very amusing double of the train-band captain of the Cockneys" (434).

The effect on Wordsworth of all this doubling-up is twofold: it ensures that his poetry is ringed round with parody; but, at the same time, it acts to make the parodying *of* his poetry superfluous. The second corollary

380

becomes apparent on turning to the article in the *Monthly Review* which follows its piece on *Peter Bell*. Devoted to the pseudo-*Peter Bell*, it establishes both the priority of Reynolds's text and the redundancy of the enterprise:

> This would be a good burlesque of an author less ridiculous than the original of the present and several similar parodies, were not Wordsworth himself "the great absurd" they draw. Nothing can be added to or taken away from the gross caricature of this author's *simplicity*. "I do affirm that I am the real Simon Pure," says the Parodist, (quoting from the *Bold Stroke for a Wife*"). "I am the man," replies Mr. Wordsworth, in a thousand eloquent stanzas: but we have considered the pretensions of Mr. W. in preceding articles; and we are not to appreciate the merits of his unnecessary mimics.
>
> (*MR* 89:422–3)

Wordsworth is both ersatz and original, at once a mere respondent to "the real Simon Pure" and the paradigm of "the great absurd." Yet, though his mimics may be "unnecessary," the article draws on them just the same: it was *The Simpliciad* which had declared the new school "incapable of caricature" (v).

## The new school of criticism

Parody, which sings alongside another poem, is etymologically disposed to resemble the art of criticism. If, as Marilyn Gaull remarks, the romantic is the period in which parody "comes of age" (43), it is also the period which sees the beginnings of professional criticism. The truism that parody is a form of criticism (see Riewald; and E.V. Knox, quoted, Richardson, 6) was applicable in culturally specific and documentable ways, and a few of these intricate lines of relationship have been traced here. In passing, it has been striking how many of the verse-parodists discussed were themselves, like Gifford and Canning in the 1790s, journalists or journal-editors. Perhaps, then, Romantic verse parody is properly to be regarded as taking up a variety of positions within a "new school of criticism." Not only are parody and criticism intimately related at their rise, but they also interact, each sharing the other's techniques and often copy space. Suggestive in this regard are the multiple crossings-over of form or format within both the reviews themselves—the habitual switches from prose to verse and back again—and the mixed-genre journalism of *The Satirist* or *Blackwood's.*

Reversals are dear to parody; but the parodic reception of Wordsworth appears to have had a specialized interest in those involving his authority, identity and originality—taking genuine Wordsworth for parody, or counterfeit Wordsworth for true coin. These too had formal equivalents, most obviously in the promiscuous blending of real with fake Wordsworth in the

Prefaces and annotations to the *Peter Bell* parodies—such forms being best adapted to mock-solemn declarations of authorial priority and purpose. A blend of this type recurs in "The Nose-Drop: A Physiological Ballad" (1821), which was published under the poet's initials but also, via a "Note, by the Editor," as a posthumous production (a trick picked up from Reynolds, whose Peter Bell comes upon his author in a suicide's grave). In prefacing this, the last of all his literary labours, Wordsworth is found boasting about the juvenility which marked his very first collection of poems:

> I have taken as much pains to avoid what is usually called *poetic diction*, as others ordinarily take to produce it; and, restricting myself from the use of those cut-and-dry figures of speech which have long been regarded as the common inheritance of poets, I have converted their Parnassus into a nursery, and exchanged the winged Pegasus for a hobbyhorse, and the mantle of the Muse for the bib and tucker of a baby.
>
> (Mortenson, 92)

This return to the nursery puts Wordsworth back where he began, and takes me back to where my essay started. I want to end with a reversal of my own, serving partly to turn the tables on the poet's critics. Leigh Hunt observed that the "extreme" to which the "Revolutionists" of the "new" school went was calculated "to make the readers of poetry disgusted with originality and adhere with contempt and resentment to their magazine common-places" (quoted, Dyer 23). Yet there is also a sense in which their contact with the Lake poets provided the occasions on which these common-places were to be refreshed and multifariously redeployed.

Wordsworth's characterization as self-parodic brought his poetry into alignment with the perspective being adopted by his critics; but, with very few exceptions, this parodic criticism insisted that, being staid or simple, the poet was himself unconscious of the parody he displayed: *The Simpliciad* ended by noting his "solemn buffoonery" (47n); the *Eclectic Review* took even his *Waggoner* as proof "that as he is himself devoid of any talent for humour, so he is, through a singular simplicity of mind, insuspectible of the ludicrous" (12 [July 1819]; Smith 300). That Wordsworth lacked a sense of the ridiculous enabled it to be assumed on his behalf, just as his poetry routinely got treated as though it were itself the "doggrel rhime" his critics and parodists supplied (*Simpliciad*, 129). This transference to the parodist's script of the power to amuse has had lasting effects in the criticism of Wordsworth and of "Romanticism" more generally. And yet the possibility of such a transference can ultimately be traced to Wordsworth himself. Steven Jones has noted recently that "the many parodies" of *Peter Bell* "brought out its own latent satiric tendencies," while at the same time "the seeds of absurdity are planted in the text as part of its dialectical potential—then are resisted or displaced" (p.32). Paul D. Sheats has finely observed that "The Thorn" presents both "a trap, baited with a remarkably offensive 'prosaism'," and evidence of "a larger strategy of confrontation that the poet conceived as immediately satiric but ultimately edifying" (pp.93–4). The potential for laughter is excited, but also unaccountably diverted. The peculiarity of the case is connected with its leaning towards the very things which formerly provoked a parodic response: when Carey overheard Namby Pamby, it was, "Now methinks I hear him say,/Boys and girls come out to play!/Moon do's shine as bright as day" (Macdonald, p.27); when Wordsworth quotes Johnny Foy, his "very words" are " 'The cocks did crow to-whoo, to-whoo,/And the sun did shine so cold.' " What was self-evidently ludicrous to the Scriblerian set is transformed into a tale told by an "idiot" signifying, not nothing, but on the contrary the luminous expressiveness that lies in reversing the normal order of things, or in momentary exemptions from the habits that deprive ordinary life of its fullness. And that, apparently, is Wordsworth's way of having his joke and eating it too.

## Notes

1 *Pace* Teich, 280 and *Romantic Parodies*, 54, the *British Critic* was not hostile: on the contrary, its review of Mant's *Poems* expressed "the warmest praise;" and its Preface saw him as a "credit to the Wartonian School" (28 [November, 1806], 559–60, xv).

2 Pub. in *The Satirist*, 1809, and attrib. to its editor, George Manners; see *Romantic Parodies*, 62–7.

3 "A Discourse concerning the Original and Progress of Satire," *Essays* ii 105. Wordsworth's rhymes were a recurrent source of complaint: cf. *Annual Review* 6 (1808), 527: "Forced, imperfect, and double rhymes abounding to an offensive and sometimes ludicrous degree."

4 Reynolds's device produces what Oliver Elton describes as "a mosaic-parody" of *Lyrical Ballads* (i 293).

5 As Byron would be well aware, it was the criticism of Pope's Pastorals for their lack of the "simplicity" associated with "Pastoral Philips" which caused Pope to send an essay to the *Guardian* in which the simple Philips was ridiculed by means of ironic praise.

6 Reynolds's publishers, Taylor and Hessey, named his poem a "burlesque imitation of the 'Idiot Boy' " (quoted, Jones, *Life*, 174; for possible disingenuousness, see Jones, 175).

7 Jones, 176. Reynolds's praise of Wordsworth's "excellencies" (174) is found in his journalism from 1816: *see Selected Prose*, 62, 70–5, 79.

8 *Monthly Review* (hereafter *MR*) 89 (August, 1819), 420; as the reviewer facetiously observes, "This infantine pamphlet is dedicated to Robert Southey, Esq. *P.L.* or Poet Laureate, by William Wordsworth, Esq. *L.P.* or Lake Poet" (419).

9 Bauer's checklist of 47 burlesques and parodies starts in 1801 and ends in 1836 (567–9); of these, "only fifteen [appeared] before 1819" and the increase "parallels the progress of Wordsworth's reputation, which was not firmly established until around 1820. Yet [almost] all [ . . . ] mock poems that Wordsworth had written in 1802 or earlier" (Bauer, 566).

10 Jeffrey's use of typography has been observed by Daniel, 208; see also *The Simpliciad*'s presentation of its "Authorities."

11 However, Hunt's *Autobiography* bemoans his neglect by "the Whig critics," and the *Edinburgh*'s failure to notice *The Feast* in particular (ch. 12; 227–8). Jeffrey did at last recognize Hunt in a review of *Rimini* which, though mixed, took pleasure in it as a product of "the antient school" (*ER* 26 [June, 1816], 477).

12 A Simon Pure also authors a satirical tale called *Hops! Hops!! Hops!!!* (1813).

13 Taylor and Hessey's reply to Coleridge's letter of protest, quoted, Jones, 174. Cf. Keats's professed sorrow "that an appreciator of Wordsworth should show so much temper at this really provoking name of Peter Bell" (1819 journal-letter, quoted, Swaen, 144; his review of Reynolds, which differs slightly, is reprinted Swaen, 158–9).

14 *Bold Stroke*, 4, from the dedication to Philip, Duke and Marquis of Wharton (who had Whig ancestry, but had supported the Pretender); and referring to the 1610 murder of Henry IV of France by a fanatical Catholic, and the loss of Henry's hard-won tolerance for Huguenots under Louis XIV.

15 Yet a usefulness of the "mock" poem for Lamb was that it enabled him to hint at his intense dislike of the real (by report of Crabb Robinson, quoted, Lucas ii 2443–4, he thought it "the worst of Wordsworth's works," objecting to the puerile introduction, the uninteresting ass, the lyric narrative, and the internal audience).

16 The Wordsworth circle duly rose to the bait: Coleridge is said to have pronounced the poem to be the work of Lamb, though as Lucas points out his letter to the publishers about "a base breach of trust" suggests otherwise; Lamb, meanwhile, told Wordsworth he guessed it to be another effort by "one of the sneering brothers—the vile Smiths—but I have heard no name mentioned" (Lucas ii 243, 241).

17 Bauer, after Strout (Bauer, 569, 554n), identifies the author as D.M. ("Delta") Moir, rather than Maginn. "On the other hand," Strout elsewhere notes, "Billy Routing" has Hebrew characters printed after the title. Maginn was an excellent Hebrew scholar" (Strout, 111 n.49). However, Alexander Broadie and Robert Cummings (University of Glasgow) tell me that the Hebrew is "gibberish," containing real words or phrases, but in nonsensical order; in which case, an in-house parody of Maginn's scholarship seems probable.

# Works cited

Addison: *The Works of the Right Honourable Joseph Addison*, Ann R. Hurd, ed. H. G. Bohn, 6 vols. (1854–1856); Bauer, N. Stephen, "Early Burlesques and Parodies of Wordsworth," *JEGP* 74 (1975), 553–69; Beavan, Arthur H., *James and Horace Smith* (1899); *Byron's Letters and Journals (BLJ)*, ed. Leslie A. Marchand, 13 vols. (1973–82); Centlivre, Susanna, *A Bold Stroke for a Wife*, ed. Thalia Stathas (1969); Coleridge: *Biographia Literaria (BL)*, ed. James Engell and W. Jackson Bate (1983); Daniel, Robert, "Jeffrey and Wordsworth: The Shape of Persecution," *Sewanee Review* 50 (1942), 195–213; Dentith, Simon, *Parody* (2000); Dryden: *Essays of John Dryden*, ed. W. P. Ker, 2 vols., 2nd edn. ([1900] 1926); Dyer, Gary, *British Satire and the Politics of Style, 1789–1832* (1997); Elton, Oliver, *A Survey of English Literature, 1780–1830*, 2 vols. (1912); Garlitz, Barbara, "The Baby's Debut: The Contemporary Reaction to Wordsworth's Poetry of Childhood," *Boston University Studies in English* 4 (1960), 85–94; Gaull, Marilyn, "Romantic Humor: The Horse of Knowledge and the Learned Pig," *Mosaic* 9 (1976), 43–64; Gohn, Jack Benoit, "Who Wrote

*Benjamin the Waggoner*? An Inquiry," *TWC* 8 (1977), 69–74; Green, David Bonnell, "Wordsworth and Edward Du Bois," *PQ* 33 (1954), 435–7; Hunt, Leigh, *The Autobiography of Leigh Hunt*, ed. J. E. Morpurgo (London, 1949), and *The Feast of the Poets* (1914), facsimile edn. by Jonathan Wordsworth (1989); Jackson, J. R. de J., ed., *Coleridge: The Critical Heritage* (1970); *John Hamilton Reynolds: Poetry and Prose*, with intro. and notes by George L. Marsh (1928), and *Selected Prose of John Hamilton Reynolds*, ed. Leonidas M. Jones (1966); Jones, Leonidas M., *The Life of John Hamilton Reynolds* (1984); Jones, Steven E., *Satire and Romanticism* (2000); Keats: *The Letters of John Keats*, ed. Hyder Edward Rollins, 2 vols. (1958); Lucas, E. V., ed., *The Letters of Charles Lamb to which are added those of his sister Mary Lamb*, 3 vols. (1935); Macdonald, Dwight, ed., *Parodies: An Anthology from Chaucer to Beerbohm—and After* (1960); Mant, Richard (anon.), *The Simpliciad; A Satirico-Didactic Poem* (1808), facsimile edn. by Jonathan Wordsworth (1991); Marsh, George L., "The *Peter Bell* Parodies of 1819," *MP* 40 (1943), 267–74; Mortenson, Robert, "'The Nose-Drop:' A Parody of Wordsworth," *TWC* 3 (1971), 91–100; Peacock: *The Works of Thomas Love Peacock*, ed. H. F. B. Brett-Smith and C. E. Jones, 10 vols. (1924–34); Richardson, Mrs. Herbert, *Parody*, English Association Pamphlet no. 92 (1935); Riewald, J. G., "Parody as Criticism," *Neophilologus* 50 (1966), 125–48; *Romantic Parodies, 1797–1831*, ed. David A. Kent and D. R. Ewen (1992); Segar, M. G., ed., *The Poems of Ambrose Philips* (1937); Sheats, Paul D., "' 'Tis Three Feet Long and Two Feet Wide:' Wordsworth's 'Thorn' and the Politics of Bathos," *TWC* 22 (1991), 92–100; Smith, Elsie, *An Estimate of William Wordsworth By his Contemporaries 1793–1822* (1932); Strachan, John, ed., *Parodies of the Romantic Age*, vol. 2, *Collected Verse Parody* (1999); Strout, Alan Lang, "Samuel Taylor Coleridge and John Wilson of *Blackwood's Magazine*," *PMLA* 48 (1933), 100–28; Swaen, A. E. H., "Peter Bell," *Anglia* 35 (1923), 136–84; Teich, Nathaniel, "Wordsworth's Reception and Copleston's *Advice* to Romantic Reviewers," *TWC* 6 (1975), 280–2; Wordsworth: *The Letters of William and Dorothy Wordsworth, The Early Years 1787–1805 (EY)*, ed. Ernest de Selincourt, 2nd edn., rev., Chester L. Shaver (1967).